S0-ADB-754

MARRIAGE AND FAMILY

The Quest for Intimacy

MARRIAGE AND FAMILY

The Quest for Intimacy

Robert H. Lauer

U. S. International University at San Diego

Jeannette C. Lauer

U. S. International University at San Diego

 Wm. C. Brown Publishers

Book Team

Editor *Dorian M. Ring*
Developmental Editor *Ann Shaffer*
Production Editor *Kay J. Brimeyer*
Designer *K. Wayne Harms*
Art Editor *Janice M. Roerig*
Photo Editor *Michelle Oberhoffer*
Permissions Editor *Karen L. Storlie*
Visuals Processor *Joyce E. Watters*

Wm. C. Brown Publishers

President *G. Franklin Lewis*
Vice President, Publisher *George Wm. Bergquist*
Vice President, Publisher *Thomas E. Doran*
Vice President, Operations and Production *Beverly Kolz*
National Sales Manager *Virginia S. Moffat*
Advertising Manager *Ann M. Knepper*
Senior Marketing Manager *Kathy Law Laube*
Marketing Manager *Kathleen Nietzke*
Executive Editor *Edgar J. Laube*
Managing Editor, Production *Colleen A. Yonda*
Production Editorial Manager *Julie A. Kennedy*
Production Editorial Manager *Ann Fuerste*
Publishing Services Manager *Karen J. Slaght*
Manager of Visuals and Design *Faye M. Schilling*

Cover and interior design by Elaine Allen
Cover illustration by Robert Phillips
Calligraphy by Joseph Milano

The credits section for this book begins on page 601, and is considered an extension of the copyright page.

Copyright © 1991 by Wm. C. Brown Publishers. All rights reserved

Library of Congress Catalog Card Number: 90–81006

ISBN 0–697–10739–6

No part of this publication may be reproduced, stored in a retrieval system, or transmitted, in any form or by any means, electronic, mechanical, photocopying, recording, or otherwise, without the prior written permission of the publisher.

Printed in the United States of America by Wm. C. Brown Publishers, 2460 Kerper Boulevard, Dubuque, IA 52001

10 9 8 7 6 5 4 3 2 1

To Jeffrey Mathew
Who is embarking on the quest

CONTENTS

PART

1

Seeking Intimate Relationships

PART

2

The Intimate Couple

PART

3

Intimacy in Families

PART 4

Challenges to Intimacy

LIST OF FIGURES

LIST OF TABLES

PREFACE

What do you want out of life? If you are like most Americans, you will probably include happiness in your answer. But where can you find happiness? We have subtitled this book *The Quest for Intimacy* because we believe your personal happiness is crucially tied up with the quality of your intimate relationships. Our purpose is to provide you not only with a basic understanding of marriage and family life, but to show you how you can apply the knowledge you gain and enrich your own life.

In other words, this is not only a text but a practical guide as well. It is both basic and applied social science. The basic part comes in the wealth of information, based on the empirical work of hundreds of researchers. The applied part is found in the principles of intimacy that are specified in each chapter as well as in the "Personal" and "Involvement" inserts (see Special Features on next page). We hope by the time you complete this book, you will have a thorough understanding of marriage and family life today, including the ways in which they bear on our experiences of intimacy; you will also have an understanding of steps you can take to enhance the quality of your own intimate relationships.

Organization of *Marriage and Family: The Quest for Intimacy*

We have organized the book to answer a series of questions. What do Americans believe about marriage and family life and what do they want? What is the meaning of intimate relationships and how do we establish them? What is the nature of intimacy for the married couple? What is the nature of intimacy in the family? What kinds of things threaten our intimate relationships, and how do people cope with those threats?

Chapter 1 addresses the first question of our beliefs and dreams. Part One explores the meaning of intimate relationships and how we establish them. We discuss the process of getting involved with someone and falling in love. We also note the special case of those who remain single, and how they deal with the issue of their intimate relationships.

Part Two looks at the nature of, and problems with, intimacy for the married couple. We discuss such issues as sex roles, sexual relationships, making the transition from singlehood to marriage, communication, conflict, and work. In part Three, we move to intimacy in the family, to the differences that children make in our intimate lives. We also note some of the special characteristics and problems of variant types of families—single-parent, nonwhite, and homosexual families.

Finally, part Four is an examination of various threats to our intimate relationships. Family crises, including alcoholism and violence as well as numerous other stressors, put strains on the family. Separation and divorce are one way of dealing with the strains. Those who do get divorced are most likely to remarry at some point, so the final chapter explores the reconstituted family.

Special Features of *Marriage and Family: The Quest for Intimacy*

A number of pedagogical aids facilitate the usefulness of the book. Each chapter has a brief summary at the beginning and end to provide you with an overview and review of the contents. Glossary terms are set in boldface type and defined and page referenced in the glossary at the end of the book.

Each chapter after the first has three inserts. The "Involvement" section has a project that provides you with some kind of personal involvement in an issue discussed in the chapter. The project is a way of taking the initiative in your own learning; it is a form of self-education. The usefulness of the projects may be enhanced if the entire class participates on a particular project; we give suggestions in most cases on how to do that.

The second type of insert is the "Personal" section. Each of these is an actual experience that has been shared with the authors by someone. We have changed the names, but the people and the circumstances are real. The "Personal" inserts illustrate some principle or principles in the chapters. They should help you grasp the principles better by seeing them at work in a real situation. The "Personal" inserts could also form the basis for some interesting class discussions and analysis.

Finally, each chapter has a "Perspective" section, in which we turn to literature, historical materials, or cross-cultural studies to give an additional perspective on some issue. It is important to see how some aspects of intimate relations are similar and how other aspects vary across space and/or time. Seeing the similarities makes us feel less alone, more a part of all humankind. Seeing the differences helps us become more tolerant and more appreciative of the rich diversity of humans.

Acknowledgments

We are grateful to the personnel at Wm. C. Brown, who have been most helpful and supportive during the writing of this book. We are grateful to each of the reviewers. Their suggestions have, we believe, enhanced the quality of the book.

Finally, we want to give a special note of appreciation to Denny Soinski, our graduate research assistant. Denny did yeoman's service on this project. His research skills and insights have been invaluable.

MARRIAGE AND FAMILY

The Quest for Intimacy

American Myths and Dreams

How many families will you live in by the time you reach middle age? It would not be unusual for you to live in at least five or six (Cherlin 1981:1)! You begin life in your parents' home. If your parents divorce and you live with only one of your parents, you then have a second family. A remarriage by that parent brings you into a third family. If, after leaving home, you cohabit with someone, you have a fourth family. If you later marry and have children, you are in your fifth, and if you divorce and remarry you will be in the sixth family of your life.

Of course, you could live in more or less than six families. Some people spend their lives in only two families—the one into which they were born (their **family of origin**) and the one formed by marriage. Others have experience with more than six. One couple told us that while they were growing up they had had nine different fathers between them. Clearly, different people have differing experiences of family life.

Given a choice, we would all prefer a happy family life. What would that be like? Leo Tolstoy began his famous novel, *Anna Karenina,* with the assertion that all happy families are alike, while unhappy families all differ from each other. Tolstoy was wrong. There are both similarities and differences in each kind of family. In the pursuit of a happy family life, we must understand those similarities and differences. We must gain knowledge of what it takes to *enhance the quality of our intimate relationships,* for **intimacy** is one of our fundamental needs and the source of much of our well-being. Intimacy involves love, affection, caring, and deep attachment to another person. A close, vital relationship with someone—a friend, relative, or spouse—is the basis of personal fulfillment. The major theme of this book, therefore, is understanding and enhancing the quality of our intimate relationships.

In this chapter, we will lay the foundation of our quest for fulfilling, intimate relationships by exploring some of the myths and dreams that exist in society. We will raise the question of whether there can be an ideal form of family. We will observe some of the trends that have been occurring in marriage and family life. And, finally, we will make a few comments about the approach that we will take throughout this book.

Myths about Family Life

How much do you know about American families? And, more importantly, *how* do you know what you know? One way we get information is through experience. We know of our own experience and those of our friends and relatives. Another important source of information is the mass media. Consider, for instance, the family life portrayed on television. If you were a foreigner and the only thing you knew about American families came from television programs, how would you describe a typical family?

The National Institute of Mental Health (1982) sponsored an analysis of television programs, including the way in which 218 family series portrayed life in American homes from 1946 through the 1970s:

> The content analysis showed that television families are much more likely to be in the middle class than in the working class. . . . Many of television's families are glamorous and successful, much more so than in real life. They seldom have problems of making ends meet; most of them seem to be quite successful economically. Many have servants, usually a maid. Unlike real life, there are relatively few working wives (National Institute of Mental Health 1982:68).

The report also noted a tendency to portray the working-class father as "dumb and bumbling" and the middle-class mother as "a giddy fool."

Such programs are likely to generate a certain amount of misunderstanding about the nature of family life. The combination of misleading information in the mass media, misinterpretations of correct information, and inferences made from our own limited experiences creates and leads to the acceptance of various myths, common beliefs about marriage and family life that are incorrect. Because myths help shape our perceptions, expectations, and hopes, they are important and must be considered carefully. Let us look at a few of those concerning marriage and the family.

We've Lost the Extended Family

The **extended family** refers to a group of three or more generations formed as an outgrowth of the parent-child relationship. Grandparents, parents, and children together comprise an extended family. Was that a typical family arrangement earlier in American history? Many people think so. But mounting evidence indicates that three generations gathered around a common hearth is a romanticization of the past. It seems that both in America and elsewhere, the **nuclear family** (husband, wife, and any children) has been the most common arrangement since at least the sixteenth century (Laslett 1977).

There are a number of reasons why the extended family has not been common. First, life expectancy in the past was much lower. Infectious diseases claimed the lives of many individuals before they were old enough to be grand-

We begin life in our family of origin.

parents. Second, children tended to leave home when they married. Like young people today, they preferred to establish their own homes rather than to live with their parents.

People Marry Because They Love Each Other

Why did you, or will you, get married? Your answer probably includes, or will include, the fact of being in love. But love, as we will see in chapter 4, is a complex emotion. It is difficult to define. And the feeling we call "love" might really be something different, or at least involve some other emotions. As Lederer and Jackson (1968:42) point out, we all like to think that we marry for love "but by and large the emotion [we] interpret as love is in reality some other emotion—often a strong sex drive, fear, or a hunger for approval."

Lederer (a writer) and Jackson (a therapist) go on to point out that we generally lose all judgment during courtship. We are driven by an "ecstatic paralysis" to mate with someone and reproduce ourselves. We may also wed because parents and other important people expect us to marry, because we are lonely, because we want economic security, or for various other reasons.

It is not that love is absent when people are considering marriage, but it is a myth to believe that love is the only or even the dominant reason that people marry. Love may be the outgrowth as well as the foundation of a good marriage, but many other factors and feelings are involved when we are wrestling with the decision of whether to marry.

Having Children Increases Marital Satisfaction

"Just Molly and me, and baby makes three," goes an old song. The outcome is a kind of personal "heaven." Most married people plan on having children and most expect that those children will enrich their lives. But whatever the effect of children on people's lives as a whole, they clearly do not always increase satisfaction with the marital relationship.

Most studies show that marital satisfaction decreases for one or both spouses during the child-rearing years (Larson 1988:8). The demands of raising children are such that parents often do not have the time or energy for cultivating their own relationship. Children frequently add financial strains. They require a great deal of energy. They may leave one or both parents exhausted and short-tempered. When children eventually grow up and leave home, the parents may find their marital satisfaction increasing again as they enter into a kind of second honeymoon.

This is not to say that children inevitably detract from the quality of one's life or marriage. As we shall discuss in chapter 14, children have both positive and negative effects. And the effects of children seem to depend on the quality of the marriage in the first place. As Harriman (1986) found, having a good marriage is likely to maximize the benefits and minimize the liabilities of children. Those who have a poor marital relationship, on the other hand, are likely to find that children only add a further strain. Children are generally not the answer to a struggling marriage.

A Good Sex Life Is the Best Predictor of Marital Satisfaction

Tom, a counselor in a university, married when he was twenty-nine. When we talked with him before the wedding, he seemed somewhat ambivalent. He was already having some problems with his fiancée about money and in-laws. He shared very few interests with her. "Why," we asked, "are you marrying her?" "We have a great sex life," he replied. "We're terrific in bed together." One year later Tom divorced his wife. "Great sex" was not enough to save the marriage.

What about marriages that start off better than Tom's, those in which the couples have shared values, interests, and goals? Is sex the best predictor of satisfaction? Again, the answer is no. The way you communicate with your spouse, the way you solve problems, and the way in which you spend your leisure time are all more important than sex (Snyder 1979). Sexual compatibility and sexual fulfillment are important and desirable, but they are not even essential to a meaningful and satisfying marriage. In a survey of 300 couples who had long-term (fifteen years or more), satisfying marriages, we found that agreement about sex was not among the top ten reasons people gave for the quality of their marriages (Lauer and Lauer 1986:179–80). One woman who said she was "extremely happy" with her marriage reported very little sexual activity over the past ten years. This was her second marriage. Her first had been "totally sex and little else." Her second husband's health problems contributed to the decline in sexual activity. "So I suppose a kind of trade-off exists here," she said. "I like absolutely everything else about my current marriage."

In other words, you can have a great sex life and an unhappy marriage. You can even have an unfulfilling sex life and a happy marriage. And, as we shall see in chapter 8, some people have both a fulfilling sex life and a happy marriage. But it isn't the sex that is the most important reason for their marital satisfaction.

Half of All Marriages End in Divorce

We shall discuss divorce rates in detail in chapter 18. Here, we want to put this myth to rest. Interestingly, even professionals sometimes make this claim. Millions of Americans "know" and believe it. It causes a lot of people anxiety as they contemplate marriage. How did this myth arise?

In part, it is due to a misinterpretation of data. You may read, for instance, that there was one divorce for every two marriages in a particular year. Some conclude from those figures that half of marriages are failing. But even a conclusion based on these figures would mean that one-third rather than one-half failed (because three couples, not two, are involved). Furthermore, the figures do not reflect all those marriages that are ongoing in that particular

Will half of all marriages end in divorce?

year. In 1981, for example, the nation reported 2.4 million marriages and 1.2 million divorces, one divorce for every two marriages. But there were also 54 million couples who had been married before 1981 and continued to be married during that year. Consequently, only a little over two percent of married people divorced in that year. Of course, some of those still married in 1981 were divorced in 1982 or subsequent years. Even so, according to pollster Louis Harris, only one of eight marriages ends in divorce at the present time.[1]

Now it is true that the divorce rate varies considerably by generation. That is, those married in recent years are much more likely to divorce than those married in the 1950s or 1960s. It is true that half or more of those married in more recent times will ultimately divorce. Still, the figure of one divorce for every two marriages would have to continue for about thirty years before we could say that half of *all* marriages will end in divorce. And by 1982 the ratio of divorces to marriages had already begun to decline.

The Dangers of Myths

There are more myths than those we have discussed. The important point is to recognize that many of the common beliefs about marriage and family living are wrong. Do not take for granted the truth of something simply because a lot of people agree that it is true. Myths are more than simple mistakes. Accepting myths can detract from the quality of your life.

Consider, for example, the myth that people marry only because they are in love. Americans like to think that arranged marriages and marriages of convenience belong to an earlier era or to a less modernized culture, and that love is the sole reason people wed today. Yet even in contemporary American society, as we shall see in chapter 5, individuals choose a mate for a variety of factors and not just because they are deeply in love. And even when they marry because of feelings of love, they often find that the feelings are fleeting and question whether they were ever "in love" in the first place.

The experience of Bart, a thirty-year-old businessman who married when he was twenty-three, illustrates this point well. At the time of his wedding, he believed he was "madly in love." But four years later, the "feeling of love" no longer existed. Bart had an affair. His wife found out about it and divorced him. Bart was so upset over the divorce that he went into therapy. There he discovered that his feeling of being "madly in love" was a mix of many different emotions and that it really wasn't love at all. And he learned that he had gone into the union with very unrealistic expectations about the nature of love and marriage. Like many people, he was certain that being "madly in love" would last a lifetime and didn't realize that these initial feelings needed to be nourished and eventually replaced by something more substantial. Bart has not remarried. He deeply regrets the mistakes he made, and still fears another relationship. He is somewhat bitter about the myth that led him to this point: "I think I have a better sense of what love means now. I wish someone had drilled that into me ten years ago."

Myths can ruin a good relationship. They blind us to the realities of intimacy. They give us false expectations about the nature of marriage and family life. As such, they are impediments in our quest for well-being.

Changing Patterns of Intimate Relationships

How do you achieve intimacy before you are married? What does it mean to be a husband or wife? What does it mean to be a parent? When are you likely to get married? How many, if any, children will you probably have? The answers to such questions vary, depending on when they are asked. Social life, including patterns of intimacy, is dynamic. Young people in their twenties today, for example, may not have yet contemplated marriage at an age when their parents already had two or three children. In this section, we will look at some of the important changes that have been occurring in intimate relationships in recent years. As you understand the dynamic nature of intimate living, you will develop the realistic grounding necessary to enhance the quality of your own life.

Premarital Sex

There has always been premarital sex. Records indicate that even some of our Puritan forebears were pregnant when they were joined in marriage (Demos 1968). But the approval of, and proportion of those engaging in, premarital sex has increased considerably in recent decades. In a 1982 national survey, 61 percent of never-married women aged fifteen through forty-four said that they had had sexual intercourse.[2] The proportion varied by age and race. For white women, the figures were 17 percent for those at age fifteen, 63 percent at age nineteen, and 80 percent for those between twenty-five and forty-four. For black women, the figures were 28 percent at age fifteen, 81 percent at age nineteen, and 96 percent for those between twenty-five and forty-four.

But there is some evidence that both opinion and behavior currently are changing in a more conservative direction. The level of activity among white teenagers has stayed about the same, but the level among blacks has declined slightly. A 1987 Gallup poll reported that 46 percent of Americans said that premarital sex is wrong.[3] The figure is lower than in 1969 (68 percent), but higher than 1985 (39 percent).

Out-of-Wedlock Births

The number of babies born to unmarried women has also increased significantly over the past few decades (table 1.1). Since 1960, the proportion of all births that occur out of wedlock has increased fourfold. Over 60 percent of all black babies are born out of wedlock, though the rate of increase has not been as high among blacks as it has been among whites.

Table 1.1   Births to Unmarried Women, by Race: 1960–1986

Race	1960	1965	1970	1975	1980	1986
Number (1,000)						
White	82.5	123.7	175.1	186.4	320.1	466.8
Black and other	141.8	167.5	223.6	261.6	345.7	380.3*
Percent						
White	36.8	42.5	43.9	41.6	48.1	55.1
Black and other	63.2	57.5	56.1	58.4	51.9	43.3*
Births as a percent of all births in racial group						
White	2.3	4.0	5.7	7.3	11.0	15.7
Black and other	21.6	26.3	34.9	44.2	48.4	61.2*

*Figures for 1986 are for black only.
Source: U.S. Bureau of the Census 1988:62 and 1989:66.

Teenagers account for about a third of all unmarried mothers. In the past, a pregnant teenager was likely to get married in order to make the child "legitimate." Increasingly, teenaged women have decided against marrying simply to provide the baby with its biological father.

Living Alone

Increasing numbers of people are living alone. By 1986, over 21 million Americans, about 61 percent of them women, were living alone (figure 1.1). This represents a doubling of the number who were living alone in 1970. Some of these people will eventually marry. Others will opt—willingly or unwillingly—to remain single.

Living alone poses serious questions about fulfilling one's intimate needs. Just because a person lives alone does not mean that he or she can exist without intimate relationships. Rather, it means that the individual must find alternative means of fulfilling his or her needs—a topic that we will explore in chapter 6.

Cohabitation

One way that some people fulfill their intimacy needs without getting married is through **cohabitation,** living with someone in an intimate, sexual relationship without being legally married. A little over 4 percent of all couples living together are unmarried. By 1985, approximately two million couples were living together, representing nearly a fourfold increase since 1970.[4] About two-thirds of the couples were under the age of thirty-five.

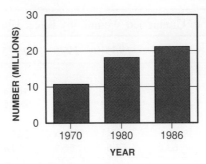

Figure 1.1 *Number of Americans living alone.*
Source: U.S. Bureau of the Census, *Current Population Reports* (Washington, DC: Government Printing Office) March 1986.

Some of those who cohabit will eventually marry. Many of those who opt for cohabitation think it is a way to test their compatibility for marriage, thus beating the odds on the high divorce rate. This is another of the myths that prevail today. We shall see why in chapter 3.

Delayed Marriage

Between 1950 and 1970, half of the females who married did so by the time they were 20.5 years old, and half of males who married did so by the time they were 22.5 years old. In the 1970s, the median age at which people married (that is, the age by which half were married) crept higher. By 1985, it was 23.3 years for women and 25.5 years for men.[5] That represents the highest level for American women ever officially recorded (the statistics have been kept since 1890).

Most people will eventually marry. But they are delaying marriage. The availability of sexual relations among singles, the emphasis on personal growth and freedom, the unwillingness to "settle down" before one has many experiences, and fears about commitment and the high divorce rate are among the factors that may have contributed to the higher age at first marriage.

Birth Rates

An increasing number of women are delaying having their first child until their mid- or even late thirties. This means that they will likely have fewer children. Moreover, because the capacity for getting pregnant tends to decrease with age, some women are involuntarily childless. Others choose to remain childless (see chapter 14). They do not view children as necessary to a fulfilling life.

As a result of later marriages, delayed first births, and an increasing number of childless marriages, the birth rate has declined considerably (figure 1.2). By the mid-1980s, the rate was about half of what it was in 1910. The average number of births to a married woman is now less than two (it was at a post-war high of 3.6 in 1955). Women who tend to have fewer children than the average are likely to be white, employed, and to have thirteen or more years of education.[6]

American Myths and Dreams

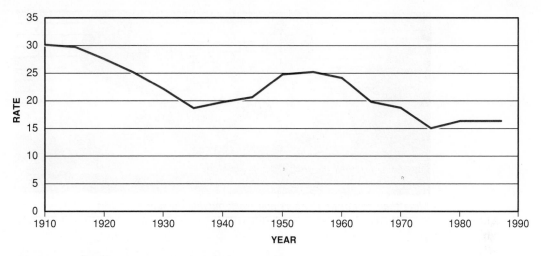

Figure 1.2 *Birth rate per 1000 population: 1910–1987.*
Source: U.S. Bureau of the Census 1989:59.

Household Size

As would be expected from the increasing number of people living alone and the lower birth rates, the average household size in the country has declined. In 1790, the average household contained 5.8 people. The number reflects not only the tendency to have more children, but also the boarders, lodgers, and apprentices who lived with people. By 1960, the average was 3.3 people, and by 1987 the figure was 2.6 (U.S. Bureau of the Census 1988).

The changes in average household size are due to changes in the types of households formed (married couple, single parent, nonfamily) as well as in the size of the specific types. The size of specific types of households varies depending on fertility rates. Both changes in types and in size of types account for the decline (Santi 1987). In the early 1970s, average household size went down mainly because of declining fertility rates. In the second half of the 1970s, fertility rates leveled out, but changes in living arrangements (increasing numbers of nonfamily and single-parent households) kept average household size in a continual decline. In the 1980s, living arrangements continued to be an important factor in declining household size.

Employed Mothers

Women have been participating in the economy in growing numbers since the 1950s. Census Bureau figures show that the proportion of married women (with a husband in the home) who are employed increased from 23.8 percent in 1950 to 56.5 percent in 1988 (U.S. Bureau of the Census 1989:385). The most dramatic increase occurred among women who had children under six years of age. In 1987, for the first time, more than half of the new mothers (those with children under the age of one) stayed in the labor force.[7]

More than half of all mothers now work outside the home.

Some mothers are employed out of necessity; their husbands do not earn enough to support the family. Others work outside the home because they want a better life-style than they could afford with only one income. And still others define their jobs or careers as important to their own fulfillment. Whatever the reasons, a home with an employed father, a stay-at-home mother, and children is now only a small fraction of all American households.

Divorce

Even though the number of people who divorce is exaggerated in popular belief, it is true that the divorce rate has risen dramatically since 1965. By the mid-1970s, the United States had the highest divorce rate in the Western world. After 1981, divorce rates tended to level off and even decline. By 1986, the rate was down to the level it had been in 1975.

A curious thing has happened in divorce rates, however. An analysis of rates from 1975 to 1985 showed differing patterns depending on the age group.[8] For women in their twenties, divorce rates increased from 1975 to 1980, then remained stable through 1985. For women in their thirties, the rates continued to rise throughout the period. As a result, the Census Bureau has projected that more than half of women in their thirties in 1985 will eventually divorce, but that the rates will be lower for women in their twenties. For some reason or reasons yet unknown, women in their thirties in 1985 were more likely to divorce than either older or younger women.

A Concluding Note on Changing Patterns

Clearly, there are both long-term trends and short-term fluctuations in patterns of intimate behavior. Making firm conclusions about the future is therefore hazardous. Some experts, for instance, believe that marriage and family

"It's a Different World"

Patricia is a twenty-five-year-old, black female who has been married three years and has a four-month-old son. She shares with us the aspirations and struggles of a woman caught up in the current trend of new mothers who work:

I work as a counselor at a hospital that provides psychological services and treatment for adolescents with emotional problems. I love my work. I love my baby. And I have a good marriage. We've had our problems, of course. There was friction between my husband, Mike, and me when I was pregnant. I was worried about how I was going to have a baby and keep on working. I didn't want to leave my baby with a stranger. And I knew that Mike wasn't too happy with that idea either. But I didn't want to stop working either. Mike just shrugged it off. "Don't worry about it," was all he would say. I remember getting really angry at him, and telling him that he didn't understand how important the issue was to me. He told me that I was just upset because of the pregnancy, that everything would work out all right, and that I would just have to try to calm myself.

I wanted the baby badly. But I was terrified of having to give up my job. It was more than the fact that I love the work. We need the money. We can't make it on Mike's income alone. I remember one day calling my mother on the telephone. She lives five hundred miles away. I tried to persuade her to come and live with us for awhile and help take care of the baby. She wouldn't do it. She said she needed to stay with dad. I asked her what she would do if she were in my place. Her reply didn't encourage me much: "When I had my babies, I stayed home and took care of them. I don't know what to tell you, Patricia. It's a different world you're living in."

Well, when the baby arrived, Mike really surprised me. He arranged for different hours on his job so that he would be home a lot of the time that I was at work. I helped out by cutting back my work days from five to four. Between us, we're able to be with our son most of the time. It isn't easy, but we're managing. The worst part is that Mike and I don't see each other much except on weekends. That's hard on our marriage, but we think we'll be able to change that in a year or two. It's tough right now, but we have a lot of love in our home and a lot of hope for the future.

patterns will continue to evolve and to diverge from the traditional nuclear family type. They are convinced that we are entering into a new age in which new forms of family are emerging. Others believe that we are on the verge of a conservative trend that will renew the emphasis on traditional patterns. We will make our own position clear when we discuss below what people want. First, however, we want to raise the question of whether there is an ideal pattern.

The Family in Utopia

Is there an ideal form of family life that will satisfy everyone? Through most of recorded history, humans have attempted to portray and, in some cases, establish an ideal human community, one in which all human needs are fulfilled. Edward Bellamy outlined his ideal community in one of the most famous of American utopian novels, *Looking Backward,* which appeared in 1888. According to Bellamy, Utopia was a place where:

> no man any more has any care for the morrow, either for himself or his children, for the nation guarantees the nurture, education, and comfortable maintenance of every citizen from the cradle to the grave (Bellamy, 1960:73).

Utopian writings, like those of Bellamy, give us an author's notion of the ideal way of life and the social arrangements necessary for achieving it. Utopian communities, on the other hand, show us the actual efforts of people to establish their ideal.

In utopia, a number of questions must be answered if all people are to prosper. What is the ideal form of government? What is the ideal way to educate youth? What is the ideal way to provide for the necessities of life—food, clothing, and shelter? And what is the ideal for marriage and family life?

The Family in Utopian Writings

Utopian writers have had varying notions of the ideal form of marriage and the family. Following the views of Plato, some writers have argued that **monogamy** (marriage to one person at a time) and the family should be abolished. Instead, the state regulates childbearing and child-rearing. The rationale for doing away with families is simple—people's first loyalty must be to the state, the source of all benefits. In order to ensure that utopia is not disrupted or destroyed by individualism and selfishness, both private property and the family must be abandoned. A strong indictment of the family is found in Huxley's (1932:25) *Brave New World,* where the family is depicted as the source of virtually all human ills:

> Our Freud had been the first to reveal the appalling dangers of family life. The world was full of fathers—was therefore full of misery; full of mothers—therefore of every kind of perversion from sadism to chastity; full of brothers, sisters, uncles, aunts—full of madness and suicide.

Other utopian writers have not agreed, however. The first book actually to be entitled *Utopia* was written by Sir Thomas More in 1516. More agreed with many of Plato's ideas, but differed strongly with Plato's notions about the family. In fact, he virtually left the family of his day intact. In More's utopia, the government supervises marriages, but does not interfere significantly with family life. Wives obey their husbands, children obey their parents, and the younger serve the older. The nuclear family is maintained. There are communal halls where many families eat together. But, for the most part,

More apparently felt that there was little in marriage and the family life of sixteenth century England that could be improved.

In addition to these two extremes, there are, of course, variations among the utopian writers. For instance, in Bellamy's utopia, the nuclear family continued, but women had a far different position than they had during the Victorian age in which he wrote. Like a man, a woman was employed, and she did not stop when she married:

> Why on earth should she? Married women have no housekeeping
> responsibilities . . . and a husband is not a baby that he should be cared for
> (Bellamy, 1960:172).

Like men, women were provided with occupations for which each was best suited. Bellamy did separate the men's "army of industry" from the women's, on the grounds that women were inferior in strength to men and needed somewhat different kinds of work. But women were encouraged to experience it all—marriage, motherhood, and work. And the highest positions in the "feminine army of industry are entrusted only to women who have been both wives and mothers, as they alone fully represent their sex" (Bellamy 1960:175).

The Family in Utopian Communities

Those who have actually established utopian communities, like their literary counterparts, have also given a variety of answers as to the best form of marriage and family life (Lauer and Lauer 1983:56–89). Some groups believed that monogamous marriage and nuclear families would maintain selfishness and threaten the well-being of the community. They therefore forbade marriage and family. Many of the religious groups that eliminated marriage and the family adopted **celibacy.** The Shakers, the largest and longest-lived of all American utopian groups (1774 to the present), have insisted on strict celibacy. At the high point of their membership in the nineteenth century, the Shakers had communities in various places in the East and Midwest. Each community governed itself, and each was composed only of people who agreed to live the rest of their lives as celibates. Married couples who joined the group were separated; a husband and wife were not allowed to live in the same house for fear they might yield to temptation. The whole community was regarded as the Shaker's family.

The Shakers and other celibate groups argued that sexual relations lead to a host of social ills. One Shaker writer pointed out that sex means gratification of the individual's passions, and the person who indulges in sex will also strive to satisfy all other passions:

> All contentions and wars have their origin in the selfishness of the flesh—for
> land, women, or else. Do away with the spirit of MINE, and the dawn of
> peace begins immediately; happier homes will result, and grinders of the faces
> of the poor need not tremble because of so-called communists, who are only
> attempting to equalize the good things of this life unevenly shared by ungodly,
> unbrotherly monopolists (Anonymous 1878:223–24).

The communal dining hall of the Oneida Colony founded by John Humphrey Nayes.

The individual who lives a life of self-indulgence, then, is contributing to all of the misery of the world, from marital quarrels to political corruption to wars between nations.

Not every utopian who abolished the family opted for celibacy, however. Some have established **group marriage,** a form of marriage in which each member of a group is married to all other opposite-sex persons in that group. One of the more famous communities with group marriage was Oneida, which existed in New York from 1848 to 1881. John Humphrey Noyes, the founder, was a Protestant minister. He believed that his community should be a kingdom of heaven on earth. Jesus had taught that there is no marriage in heaven. Noyes insisted that his earthly utopia follow this same pattern and, as a result, marriage and exclusive arrangements of any sort were not permitted in the Oneida community. However, Noyes claimed that no marriage did not mean no sex. Each member of the Oneida community, therefore, had sexual access to every other member of the opposite sex. In fact, Noyes established a system of record-keeping that prevented any two people from having sexual relations together too frequently. Noyes also instituted a unique system of sexual intercourse and, for some years, conception was closely regulated (Lauer and Lauer 1983:79–82). Children were taken from their mothers when they were infants and reared in the communal nursery. Caretakers taught the children to regard every man in the community as father and every woman as mother. The entire community thus was a single family.

In between the extremes of celibacy and free love, other utopians advocated a more traditional arrangement. Many insisted that sex take place only within monogamous marriage. This is evident even in modern utopian experiments—the communes. Despite a reputation to the contrary, as many as half of contemporary communes have monogamous relationships and nuclear families (Zablocki 1980:339). At The Farm, for example, a modern commune in Tennessee, sex is viewed positively and discussed openly. But the group

The Utopian Quest for Intimacy

In their quest for the ideal society, utopians concerned themselves with creating an intimate community. Through writings, ideologies, values, and shared experiences they sought to bind their members together in close relationship. But what of the celibate communities? Today, we often associate intimacy with sex. If this is the case, how did the celibates satisfy their need for intimacy? Did they deny, ignore, or repress the need? Certainly, this was not the case among the Shakers, who claimed that their groups provided people with a truly close and intimate family unlike those in the larger community. The observations of Fredrika Bremer, a mid-nineteenth century visitor to the Shaker community at Canterbury, New Hampshire, support this claim. Here she describes a game used to teach young girls to love each other and to reinforce the intimacy of the group:

> They placed themselves in a wide circle, each one standing at three or four paces distant from the other. They then began little verses, which, though I can not give literally accurate, were in substance as follows:
>
> > Must I here alone be standing,
> > Having none that I can love;
> > Having none my friend to be,
> > None who will grow fond of me?
>
> On this each little girl approached the one nearest to her, and, taking each other's hands, they laid them upon their hearts and sang

> > Nay, my sister, come thou nearer,
> > And I will to thee be dearer,
> > Be to thee a faithful friend;
> > I will share with thee thy sadness;
> > Thou shalt share with me my gladness!
>
> With this the children all took hold of hands, and slowly moving round in a circle, repeated the while these last words, or something like them; and in so doing approaching nearer and nearer together, wove their arms round each other like a garland of flowers, then sunk upon their knees singing the while a hymn, the first verse of which was
>
> > Heavenly Father, we look down in mercy
> > On this little flock,
> > United in thy name!
> > Give us of thy Holy Spirt, etc.
>
> While singing this hymn, and while still upon their knees, the children all kissed each other, after which they rose up and separated. The beautiful symbolic meaning contained in the whole game, its simplicity, and the beautiful grace with which it was performed; the thought of the difference in the spirit of this game to the bitter reality of many a solitary existence in the great community of the world, affected me deeply; I could not refrain from weeping.

Source: Bremer (1853:575–76).

also claims that any kind of promiscuity is wrong. Premarital sex and adultery are both taboo. The nuclear family is valued and protected.

What Works Best?

The utopian experiments, in contrast to the writings, give us an opportunity to inquire into what really works best for humans. You might decide at the outset that the celibate life could never satisfy people. But the Shakers would disagree. They were often effusive in their praise of the celibate life. They claimed that it increased the length and also the fullness of life. They insisted that celibacy was not a sacrifice of present pleasure for future rewards (heaven). Quite the contrary:

> Shakers do not believe in the propriety of making themselves unhappy and miserable in this world for the sake of being happy in the next. A good Shaker is the most thoroughly happy being in existence. Why not? The world, the flesh, and the devil have no attractions for him; he is at peace with God, himself and his neighbor (Basting 1887:203).

Other Shakers wrote similar praise of the celibate way of life. There are, incidentally, a number of modern communes in which celibacy is practiced for either short terms or as a way of life. Celibacy as an ideal is not confined to past generations.

On the other hand, there were many who could not adapt to the celibate life. They left the communities and searched for utopia elsewhere. What of the traditionalists, those who maintained monogamy and the nuclear family? As with the celibates, most had high praise for the arrangement, but even some of them were not satisfied. And those who experimented with group marriage or free love have had more problems with the arrangement than either the celibates or the traditionalists. For a time group marriage worked well at Oneida, and presently it seems to be working well among the Keristas in San Francisco. In other communities, however, problems abounded. In some cases, individuals who were willing to try, and even ideologically committed to, open relationships found that they could not handle the arrangement. In one rural commune, two teenaged females, one middle-aged man, and two married couples formed a group marriage. The experiment ended abruptly when one of the married men saw his wife with another man, pulled a knife, and dragged her away while shouting "She belongs to me" (Davidson 1970:95).

So what works best? Obviously, no single arrangement fulfills the needs of every individual. Each arrangement works for some people and frustrates others. On balance, the celibates and the traditionalists have had the fewest problems. But every community has had its malcontents. When only one form is defined as ideal, some people are going to be frustrated. People seem to need a diversity of arrangements from which to choose. And diversity is exactly what is available today. As we shall see in detail, some people are opting for a traditional marriage, some for a nontraditional marriage, some for single-hood, some for single parenthood, and so forth. If the lessons of history are worth anything at all, they teach us to cherish our right to diverse arrangements.

What Do We Want?

The utopian experiments suggest that we need a variety of arrangements in marriage and family living in order to satisfy the needs of people. But clearly some of the arrangements will be more attractive than others. Some will meet the needs of more people than will others. What do people want today?

Changes in Traditional Arrangements

If we define a traditional family as one that stays intact except for death, and is composed of an employed father (the breadwinner), a stay-at-home mother (the homemaker), and children, then it is clear it is now the choice of a minority of Americans. Most people no longer regard that arrangement as practical. Moreover, the woman's movement and women's experience in the labor force have sensitized women to the value of employment outside the home. The experience of nonfamily living, which is true for an increasing number of young Americans who leave the parental home before marrying, also contributes to a change in the traditional pattern. Using a national sample of young adults, Waite, Goldscheider, and Witsberger (1986) discovered an erosion of traditional family orientation among those who had spent time in nonfamily living. This period of independent living affects personal plans and goals about marriage and family life. In particular, young women who lived independently were more likely to make plans for employment, expect fewer children, be more accepting of employed mothers, and hold nontraditional views of what it means to be a wife and mother in a family. Young men who lived independently also acquired nontraditional views, but the effects were not as dramatic for them as for the women.

Similarly, Glenn (1987) looked at national polls taken between 1969 and 1986 and found that they generally suggested a lessening of allegiance to the family. In particular, there has been an increasing approval of nontraditional, nonfamily roles for women, a decline in the ideal number of children for a family to have, and an increase in sexual permissiveness. The only "family allegiance" trend that Glenn found was an increase in the proportion of people who think it is a good idea for older people to share a house with their grown children.

Some people who read about the decline in the number of people opting for a traditional family get anxious about the future not only of the family but of society as well. They believe that the family—especially the traditional arrangement—is the heart of society, and if the family disintegrates so will society.

We need to be aware that agonizing words about the death of the family have been with us for centuries:

> The first settlers of New England had sought to create a family unit that would conform strictly to the teachings of the Bible. Within forty years of their arrival in the New World, however, the colonists feared that their families were disintegrating, that parents were growing ever more irresponsible, and that their children were losing respect for authority (Mintz and Kellogg 1988:17).

This does not mean that we should dismiss all warnings about the state of family life today, however. There does seem to be ample reason for concern. We have already noted some of the bases for concern—the high divorce rates, the number of children born out of wedlock, and the number of single-parent homes. There is other evidence that all is not well in the family, whether a traditional or nontraditional family. Hite (1987) published the results of answers from one hundred thousand questionnaires she sent out to various women's groups and organizations. Among her findings:

70 percent of the women married five years or more said they were having extramarital affairs

84 percent of the women were not satisfied emotionally with their relationships with men

95 percent of the women reported some degree of emotional harassment from the men they loved

82 percent of the women married two years or more said they "love" their husbands but are not "in love"

91 percent of the women who were divorced said they, rather than their husbands, were the one who had made the decision to break up the marriage

98 percent of the women said they wanted to make "basic changes" in their love relationships

In considering the implications of these findings, we must note that Hite received only forty-five hundred replies to her letters (a 4.5 percent response rate, which is extremely low). Still, there must be, at a minimum, tens of thousands of women who are clearly unhappy and angry about their relationships with men.

More systematic evidence comes from the national surveys analyzed by Glenn and Weaver (1988). The researchers found that surveys conducted from 1972 to 1986 show a decline in the relationship between marital status and happiness (figure 1.3). The proportion of never-married males who said they were "very happy" increased significantly, as did the proportion of widowed females, while the proportion of married women who said they were "very happy" declined significantly. It appears that marriage is not as central to people's happiness as it was at one time.

In Defense of Marriage and the Family

We have not yet seen the whole picture. Note in figure 1.3 that even though there has been a decline in the relationship between marital status and happiness, married men and women in the 1982 to 1986 period were proportionately happier than were those in any of the other groups. And not every survey yields results that suggest a decline in marital satisfaction. The Roper organization conducted a poll for a woman's magazine and reported that 88 percent of the women would marry the same man again.[9] Only 7 percent said they would not remarry the same man, and the other 5 percent was undecided.

People also continue to put a high value on the family life. Ninety-seven percent of Americans believe that the world is a better place to live when families are happy and healthy, and nearly 90 percent indicate that their own family is one of the most important parts of their lives (Schwartz 1987). Three

Men as well as women say their family is the most important thing they have.

American Myths and Dreams

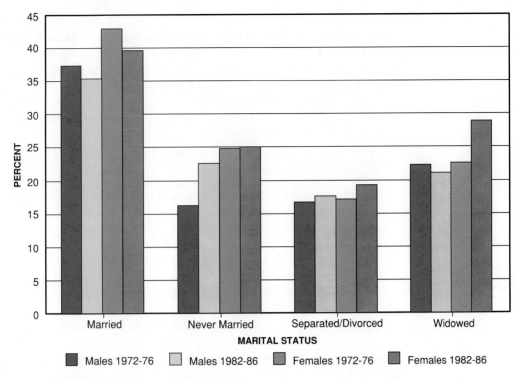

Figure 1.3 *Percent of people who are "very happy."*
Source: Data from Glenn and Weaver 1988:319.

out of four Americans believe that having children is not too limiting on their careers, and nearly as many agree that mothers of young children should work only if it is financially necessary (Schwartz 1987). A Gallup poll reported that as many people in 1986 were very satisfied with their family life as in 1980, and 93 percent were either very satisfied or mostly satisfied.[10]

A nonrandom survey of men reported that 73 percent felt strongly that their family is the most important facet of their lives.[11] Sixty percent of the men rated their marriage as more important than their jobs.

A *Parents Magazine* poll found that parents, adult children, and in-laws have a good deal of close contact with each other (Groller 1987). Over two-thirds of the respondents said they have contact with their parents at least once a week, and over half said they have contact with in-laws at least once a week. When the adult children and parents live in the same area, more than three out of four have weekly contact or more. Forty-four percent said they go to their parents for advice on important matters, and about a fourth said they go to in-laws. Parents also seek advice from their adult children.

Finally, a Canadian survey of adults aged forty and over found that more than half of the respondents reported they had someone in their extended family who could be considered a "kinkeeper," a person who acts to keep family members in touch with each other (Rosenthal 1985). Clearly, family life is alive and well for a great many people.

American Myths and Dreams

Me or We?

How can we make sense out of the conflicting evidence? Are Americans moving away from a family orientation or continuing to affirm that orientation? We have seen evidence that could suggest that either position is correct. Our own position is that Americans are caught up in contradictory feelings. These contradictory feelings derive from contrary values with which we are struggling. On the one hand, there is **familism,** a value on family living. Familism leads us to cherish our families, to subordinate our personal desires if necessary for the good of the family group, and to view marriage as that which demands our commitment and fidelity.

On the other hand, we are a nation that values individualism, the well-being of the individual. American individualism has two strains, one of which emphasizes personal achievement (utilitarian individualism) and the other of which emphasizes personal happiness and fulfillment (expressive individualism) (Bellah, Madsen, Sullivan, Swidler, and Tipton 1985). Utilitarian individualism emphasizes getting ahead for yourself, while expressive individualism emphasizes fulfillment by doing those things that satisfy you.

Expressive individualism has been particularly strong the past few decades, buttressed by a humanistic psychology that has urged people to search for self-fulfillment above all. There is some evidence that we may be retreating from this strong emphasis on expressive individualism. As we heard one therapist put it, "We've been through the *me* generation and now we're trying to go back to a *we* generation." The contradictory attitudes expressed in various polls and surveys, and the discrepancies between some attitudes and behavior, reflect, we believe, the fact that Americans are in the midst of a struggle between "me" and "we." It is a difficult struggle. As Bellah et al. (1985:111) point out, our individualistic ideology makes it hard for us to understand why we should even be concerned about giving to each other:

> Now we are all supposed to be conscious primarily of our assertive selves. To reappropriate a language in which we could all, men and women, see that dependence and independence are deeply related, and that we can be independent persons without denying that we need one another, is a task that has only begun.

In sum, we believe that Americans value marriage and family, but are struggling between familial and individualistic values. We value and need intimacy, but many are not convinced that marriage and family living are the only ways to fulfill those intimacy needs. Indeed, they are not the only arrangements that will satisfy all people. Thus, we are in a process of making a variety of arrangements legitimate. The majority of people will continue to opt for marriage and family living; a substantial minority will find alternative arrangements.

Getting to Know You

Although most Americans agree that the family is a highly important part of their personal lives and well-being, many know little about their extended families. One of the ways we get a better sense of who we are is to know more about the kind of family of which we are a part. In this exercise, therefore, get to know your extended family better. Inquire about members of the family that you both know and don't know—whether grandparents, cousins, or whatever—and try to get pictures of those people. Ask questions of family members to whom you have access: Who is or was the most colorful member of this family in your estimation? What is one of the most interesting stories that you know about our family? What did your parents tell you about their parents or other members of the family?

Summarize your experience by answering the following questions. What have you learned about your family that you didn't know before? How does that make you feel? What difference does it make in the way you think about yourself?

If the entire class engages in this project, share some of the more colorful stories with each other and discuss as a group both the benefits and the pitfalls of discovering more about our families.

'Til Death?

For the majority who opt for marriage and family, what are the prospects? To the extent that our expressive individualistic values prevail, people will enter and remain in a marriage only so long as it is perceived to be personally beneficial to them. They will then divorce and may seek to fulfill their intimacy needs through another marriage. Indeed, some have raised the question of whether any other pattern is realistic if people are to have their needs fulfilled. That is, can two people maintain a long-term relationship that is not only stable but also satisfying to them both?

Over two decades ago, Levinger (1965) argued that relationships can be described in terms of their stability and satisfaction. Some marriages are high on both (a "full-shell" marriage), some are low on both ("no-shell"), and some have one without the other ("half-shell" marriages are those that are happy but for some reason cannot survive; "empty-shell" marriages are those that last but do not bring satisfaction). All four of these types can still be found. For some, the marriage proves to be unsatisfactory almost from the start. Like the young man who married a woman because of the "great sex" they had, the no-shell marriages break up in a short time (half of all marriages that break up do so within the first seven years).

But are there empty-shell marriages, those that are unsatisfactory yet stable? The answer is yes. In our study of 351 long-term marriages (Lauer and Lauer, 1986), the only criterion for being included in the sample was a minimum of fifteen years of marriage. We anticipated that virtually all would have a satisfying union, since people tend not to remain in an unhappy marriage. But in nearly 15 percent (fifty-one) of the couples, one or both of the partners was unhappy to some extent. Why did they stay together? The two major reasons were a sense of duty (religious beliefs or family tradition) and children.

It is the first pattern noted above, of course, the highly stable *and* satisfying marriage that Levinger called full-shell, that has been the ideal in modern American life. But can it happen? Can people live together in a vital, meaningful relationship " 'til death do us part"? Again, the answer is yes. For some people, marriage is still an experience that enhances their physical and mental health and their general sense of well-being:

> Marriage places more demands on people than friendship, but the rewards are enormous for those who are able to work through the differences and annoyances and maintain a growing relationship. For some, the rewards are so immense that marriage is a watershed in their lives (Lauer and Lauer 1988:86).

What are the ingredients of such a marriage? We asked our happy couples to select from thirty-nine factors those that they regarded as most important in their own experience. In order of the frequency with which they were named, the following are the reasons given by husbands and wives:

Husbands	*Wives*
1. My spouse is my best friend.	1. My spouse is my best friend.
2. I like my spouse as a person.	2. I like my spouse as a person.
3. Marriage is a long-term commitment.	3. Marriage is a long-term commitment.
4. Marriage is sacred.	4. Marriage is sacred.
5. We agree on aims and goals.	5. We agree on aims and goals.
6. My spouse has grown more interesting.	6. My spouse has grown more interesting.
7. I want the relationship to succeed.	7. I want the relationship to succeed.
8. An enduring marriage is important to social stability.	8. We laugh together.
9. We laugh together.	9. We agree on a philosophy of life.
10. I am proud of my spouse's achievements.	10. We agree on how and how often to show affection.
11. We agree on a philosophy of life.	11. An enduring marriage is important to social stability.
12. We agree about our sex life.	12. We have a stimulating exchange of ideas.

Even though husbands and wives were interviewed or filled out their questionnaires separately, the first seven items are exactly the same! The order varies somewhat after that, but there are no striking differences between husbands and wives. There seems to be considerable consensus on what it takes to forge a union that is both long-lasting and fulfilling to both partners.

Note that the most important factor is liking your spouse, liking the kind of person to whom you are married, appreciating the kind of person that he or she is. Three of the first six factors relate to the individual's perception of the kind of person the spouse is. It is not only a myth but a dangerous myth that people marry each other purely out of love. As one wife, who rated her marriage as "extremely happy," told us:

> I feel that liking a person in marriage is as important as loving that person. I have to like him so I will love him when things aren't so rosy. Friends enjoy each other's company—enjoy doing things together. . . . That's why friendship really ranks high in my reasons for our happy marriage.

A husband summed up the importance of friendship and liking when he said: "Jen is just the best friend I have. I would rather spend time with her, talk with her, be with her than anyone else." And a wife noted that she liked the kind of person her husband was so much that she would want to be friends with him even if she wasn't married to him.

Next to liking and being friends with one's spouse, people talked about the importance of commitment. Couples in unhappy marriages also ranked commitment high, but there was a difference in their commitment. They were committed primarily to the institution of marriage. Once in a particular union, therefore, they were determined to make it last, regardless of how unhappy they were. In other words, they were committed to maintaining a marriage, but were not really committed to each other. Couples in happy marriages, on the other hand, are committed to marriage and to their spouses. This involves a determination to work through whatever problems might cause dissatisfaction. As expressed by one wife:

> We've remained married because forty years ago our peer group just did. We worked our way through problems that today we might walk away from. Our marriage is firm and filled with respect and love, but it took time and work. In a marriage today, we might have separated. I'm glad we didn't. I can't emphasize this too strongly. I have two children who are divorced. They are still searching for a magical something that isn't obtainable in the real world. Marriage grows through working out problems and going on. Our marriage took forty years and we are still learning.

There are many other factors that are important, such as humor and the ability to handle conflict constructively. The point is that a long-term and satisfying marriage is not merely a matter of finding just the right person who can make you happy. It is a matter of two people who have some positive factors going for them (such as liking each other and sharing similar values) working together in a committed relationship to achieve a mutually satisfying life. Even in an age of rapid change and high divorce rates, the full-shell marriage can be a reality for those who wish it.

American Myths and Dreams   25

APPROACH OF THIS BOOK

We take a multifaceted approach to the study of marriage and family life. First, we believe that the study should be broad-based. Accordingly, we draw on the research of sociologists, historians, social psychologists, family studies experts, psychologists, therapists, and others who have made important contributions to our understanding. Each chapter will also have "Perspective," a boxed insert that draws on historical, anthropological, or literary materials to illuminate some topic.

Second, our approach is personal. We will illustrate points throughout the book with materials from our files on people with whom we have worked (including students). In addition, each chapter will have "Personal," a boxed insert that gives a longer personal account related to some topic in the chapter.

Third, we want the book to be practical. Most of the materials have practical implications. But we have found that readers frequently fail to make application of materials to their own lives. As a student told one of us after a lecture, "I didn't think what you were saying was very useful until you asked us to think about it and write down one or two insights that we could use in our own lives. Then I realized that the lecture had some very practical information." To help with the applications, we are including a number of important principles at the end of each chapter, principles that can be used to enhance the quality of your intimate life.

Finally, we believe that the best learning is participatory. "Involvement," the third boxed insert in each chapter, enables you to participate in some way in learning the materials. We hope some of these will become class projects, and that the results can be pooled and shared. In any case, the more you engage in your own research, the more you participate in the learning process, the more useful will be your educational experience.

SUMMARY

We learn about family life through our own experience and through the mass media. But some of what we know is mythical. Some of the common myths today include: (1) we've lost the extended family; (2) people marry because they love each other; (3) having children increases marital satisfaction; (4) a good sex life is the best predictor of marital satisfaction; and (5) half of all marriages end in divorce. Such myths are dangerous because they can ruin good relationships.

Patterns of intimate relationships change over time. In recent years there has been an increase in premarital sex, out-of-wedlock births, the number of people living alone, the number of people cohabiting, age at first marriage, proportion of mothers who work, and the divorce rate. There has been a decline in birth rates and average household size.

Throughout history, people have thought about the ideal form of family life, one that will satisfy everyone. Utopian writers have advocated everything from retaining existing forms of the family to abolishing the nuclear family altogether. In utopian communities, people have tried celibacy, monogamous marriage, and group marriage. No form seems to work well for everyone; all work well for at least some people, supporting our right to diverse arrangements.

What do Americans want? For various reasons, only a minority still choose the traditional arrangement of employed father, stay-at-home mother, and children. There is some evidence that marriage is not as central to our happiness as it once was. However, Americans still seem largely to affirm monogamous marriage and most indicate satisfaction with their own marriage and family life. One of the problems is that we are caught between our values on familism and individualism. Yet for those who desire a long-term, monogamous relationship, the evidence is that it is still possible and is rewarding to those who achieve it.

1. *Time,* July 13, 1987, p. 21.
2. Cited in *Family Planning Perspectives,* Jan./Feb. 1985, p. 37.
3. *Gallup Report* #263, August, 1987, p. 20.
4. *Family Planning Perspectives,* March/April, 1986, p. 91.
5. Ibid.
6. Ibid., January/February, 1985, p. 36.
7. *New York Times,* June 19, 1988.
8. *Family Planning Perspectives,* May/June, 1986, p. 133.
9. *San Diego Union,* May 11, 1988.
10. *Gallup Report* #255, December, 1986, p. 29.
11. *San Diego Union,* March 24, 1988.

PART ONE

Seeking Intimate Relationships

The Chinese have a word, *jen,* which refers to a quality of humans that leads them to live in society. In other words, humans by nature seek to live with others. Only unnatural and abnormal people, according to Confucian teachings, live outside of human communities, for it is in society that humans are able to fully develop and realize their potential.

We agree with this ancient Chinese view of our need for relationships. Of course, most of us begin life in the context of family relationships. But sooner or later we begin to establish relationships beyond the family. In part I, we shall look at some of the issues, the alternatives, and the problems that arise as we step outside the family and establish additional intimate relationships. Issues, or points of dispute, include such matters as whether cohabitation is a good preparation for marriage, romantic love can last, and singleness is a healthy option. The issues arise, in part, because we do have so many alternatives—singlehood, sex or celibacy, cohabitation, marriage, and the choice of different possible marriage partners. The alternatives and issues mean that some people face problems, times of doubt, and uncertainty about which choices to make.

Getting to Know Someone Else

Why bother? Everyone who has dated as an adolescent knows the anxiety, uncertainty, and even the anguish of building intimate relationships. A middle-aged man recalled his own time of heartache:

> One of the most agonizing times I remember as a young man was the day my steady girl friend told me she was breaking up with me. She and I were of different religious backgrounds, and she decided that it was best for us not to see each other anymore. I sat in my car and cried. Then I drove home, weeping off and on the whole way. I just felt crushed and empty.

Why should you go through all that pain? Why not be a "loner" instead?

In this chapter, we will discuss the problems of the "loner," and the values of intimate relationships. We then will explore the factors involved in establishing relationships, the stages we go through in building intimacy, and the nature of intimacy. Finally, we will offer some principles for enhancing the quality of intimacy that derive from the materials in this chapter.

Getting to know someone can be painful, but it can also be exhilarating.

We Are Social Creatures

Humans, said Aristotle, are social creatures. One of our fundamental needs is to relate to others. John Steinbeck (1962:137–38) noted that, for two successive years, he had spent eight months alone in the Sierra Nevada mountains. After being alone for awhile, he found that he stopped whistling, stopped talking to his dogs, and stopped experiencing some of the emotions he had felt at other times. He realized that such emotions are the result of interacting and talking with others, and when you have no one around you become a different kind of creature. It seems that only in relating to others are we fully human.

Loneliness

Despite the fact that we are social beings, nearly everyone is lonely at one time or another. Some people are lonely a good part of the time. We shall define **loneliness** as a feeling of being isolated from desired relationships. We can distinguish between social and emotional loneliness (Weiss 1973). Social loneliness occurs when you have less interpersonal interaction than you desire. Emotional loneliness occurs when you have fewer intimate relationships than you desire.

Loneliness in Interaction

Loneliness, then, is not the same as aloneness. Most people prefer and benefit from a certain amount of solitude. We "want our space." We also want, and require, relationships that fulfill our intimacy needs. But it isn't enough to interact with people, even a lot of people. That may cure social loneliness, but it doesn't necessarily address emotional loneliness. For example, lonely and nonlonely students who kept diaries of their interaction over a two-day period did not differ in the total number of interactions they had (Jones 1982). But the lonely students did have more of their interaction with strangers and casual acquaintances than did the nonlonely students. As Jones noted:

> Lonely people may have as much contact and hence social opportunities as do nonlonely people, but may be less satisfied with available relationships . . . satisfaction with contacts is more important than the actual frequency (Jones 1982:243).

Emotional loneliness can occur even when you have frequent contact with a particular individual or group of individuals. A young woman who complained of loneliness pointed out that she was a part of a large family, but "everyone is busy." And at her work she had some friends that she saw socially on occasions, but "I can't say that I feel really close to any of them." Being around the same people on a regular basis is not the equivalent of having intimate relationships with those people. There is even loneliness in some marriages (Stapen 1987). A husband or wife may go through periods of feeling distant from the other, depressed and withdrawn, disconnected from any closeness in the relationship. Fulfilling our intimacy needs is not merely a matter of being in another person's presence, even when you are frequently with that person.

Effects of Loneliness

Long-term loneliness can have some serious negative consequences for people. In their nationwide survey of loneliness among Americans, Rubenstein and Shaver (1982:201) listed nineteen symptoms and problems associated with being lonely:

1. Feelings of worthlessness

2. Feeling you just can't go on

3. Constant worry and anxiety

4. Irrational fears

5. Trouble concentrating

6. Feeling irritable and angry

7. Feelings of guilt

8. Crying spells

9. Feeling tired

10. Insomnia

11. Pains in the heart; heart disease

12. Trouble breathing

13. Poor appetite

14. Headaches

15. Digestive problems

16. Loss of interest in sex

17. Being overweight, feeling fat

18. Suffering from a serious disease

19. Having a disabling accident

Jones (1982:239) found that the most prominent characteristic among the lonely that he studied was negativity—"cynical and rejecting attitudes toward other people and life in general, as well as beliefs that imply pessimism and a sense of not being able to control one's destiny." Many of the symptoms listed above are a part of depression. One of the common findings of social scientists is that lonely people tend to be depressed (Levin and Stokes 1986). Of course, it is possible that the depression occurred first, and that depressed people are lonely either because they have isolated themselves from others or that people do not want to associate with them. But while depression no doubt intensifies loneliness, the loneliness occurs first at least among some people (Rich and Scovel 1987).

Clearly, loneliness, which by definition means an inadequate amount of intimacy, leads to an array of other ills. Those ills, in turn, feed back into the loneliness and intensify it. The result is a downward spiral (figure 2.1) that can be difficult to stop.

Sources of Loneliness

Some people are lonely for temporary periods because of such things as the breakup of a relationship, a move to a new location, or an accident or illness that confines them to home. But more persistent loneliness may be hard to break out of when it is rooted in certain social and personal factors.

As far as social factors are concerned, loneliness may reflect a failure of **integration.** That is, the individual may not feel that he or she is a meaningful and significant part of any group, a situation that Emile Durkheim (1933) saw as inherent in modern society. In more primitive societies, according to Durkheim, people are alike in their ideas, values, and aspirations. The entire society is like a close-knit family. As the population grows, as the society becomes more complex, this familial nature of society inevitably breaks down. Differences increase among the people. The society becomes heterogeneous. People are bound together by interdependence, by their need for each other's contributions to the society, rather than by their sense of oneness.

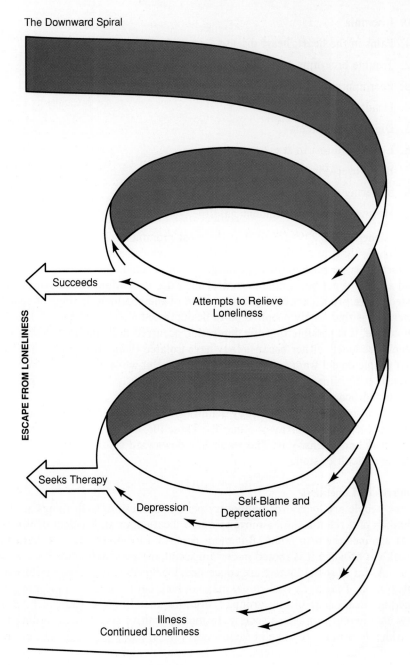

The Downward Spiral

Succeeds

Attempts to Relieve
Loneliness

ESCAPE FROM LONELINESS

Seeks Therapy

Depression

Self-Blame and
Deprecation

Illness
Continued Loneliness

Figure 2.1 *Downward spiral of loneliness.*

But modern society is no longer an integrated whole, rather it is a conglomeration of diverse individuals. However, people need to be integrated into some group. Durkheim felt that neither religion nor the family accomplish this in a modern, industrial society. He predicted that the only source of integration would be occupational organizations.

More recent critics agree that the character of modern society is such that intimate relationships are problematic (and, therefore, loneliness is endemic in the society). Philip Slater (1974:79) wrote about the "simple community" of the past where "everyone has a place, is embedded in nourishing relationships, perceives order and meaning. . . ." In that community, according to Slater, each person sees himself or herself as a part of the whole rather than as an isolated individual.

In contrast to the preindustrial time, when most people were part of an integrated community, Slater (1977:13–14) presented the situation of a modern woman and her struggle to be a part of some whole:

> For a woman today, graduation itself can be exile, a permanent end to community life. If she is married and not working, her community may not extend past the walls of her own house.
>
> Of course, she will have friends, neighbors, and family. She may participate in local activities; she may join clubs and work for causes. But none of these associations are automatic. The relationships are separate and fragmented; the activities are usually diluted by the need to be watching small children or to make arrangements for them. Her various friends may not be part of the same group and may not even know each other.
>
> Furthermore, there is no outside structure supporting these relationships; she must maintain them herself. There is no spot where everyone hangs out; people must be called and invited over. Pregraduation social life may be effortless, but postgraduation social life takes work.

We believe that such criticisms have some merit. It would seem that many Americans are yearning for a sense of community. Over half indicate that they would like to live in a small town of fewer than 10,000 people.

> You know that most of those people couldn't stand to actually live in a town that small, where everyone knows everybody else's business. But they have a hankering, a nostalgia, for a face-to-face community (Winkler 1985:8).

Our mobility as well as the nature of our modern society do make intimate relationships problematic. It seems all too easy to become a lonely nonentity in the midst of a massive, impersonal urban world. But we must temper the criticism with two points. First, we have romanticized the preindustrial community. It did not always provide an integrated and satisfying communal life. Anthropological descriptions of some preindustrial communities show them to be filled with suspicion, distrust, and violence. Second, while there may be more loneliness in modern society, there are also more opportunities and more choices. The city enables one to choose one's intimates. You don't have to be friends with the people next door if you choose not to. There are a great many

Cities offer many groups that can ease loneliness.

 PERSONAL

Searching for Intimacy

Loneliness is a burden from which most people seek to free themselves. But finding satisfying and lasting intimate relationships is not always easy. Ellie is a forty-year-old woman who married her high-school sweetheart at the age of eighteen, then divorced him when she was twenty-one. She is now a high-school counselor. Although she lives alone, this does not mean that she suffers from loneliness. At the same time, she is struggling to establish an ongoing intimate relationship:

> I have been single now for nineteen years. I can foresee being married in five to eight years. So being single is not a dislike of marriage, but a choice. I have used this time to get to know and like myself. And I've gotten to know my parents better as well.
>
> I admit that I was disillusioned after my divorce. I don't remember being against marriage at the time, but I felt an overwhelming lack of trust. And since I had failed at

marriage, I lacked self-confidence and found myself being overly cautious. In the long term, though, I learned to be more independent and self-reliant. As I look back, I find that my choice in relationships after my divorce were bad ones. Although most of them lasted from one to four years, I never wanted to marry any of them. I wanted to live with two of them, and did with one. But I didn't consider marriage, although two of them asked me.

> The first man after my divorce was a tall, good-looking, but uneducated man. I didn't know it at the time, but he was married and had a son. When I found out, I kept going with him because I felt sorry for him. He and his wife had such a bad relationship!
>
> After we had gone together three years, he divorced his wife. I loved the attention he gave me. I thought I was in love. But I wasn't, and I finally told him so. Why did I stay with him so

associations and groups of various kinds in most cities that offer people an opportunity to interact with others who have similar interests. The point is that slipping into loneliness is easier in the modern world, and getting out of it into some intimate relationships may require initiative and effort. But the modern world is not structured in a way to squeeze intimacy totally out of human life.

There are also some individual factors involved in loneliness. Stubborn feelings of loneliness may be rooted in certain childhood experiences. Those who had a parent die when they were children, or who lacked warm and supportive parents while growing up, are more likely to suffer from chronic loneliness as adults (Lobdell and Perlman 1986; Murphy 1986/1987). Lonely adults look back on their childhood and feel that they didn't have enough time with their parents, and that they could not trust their parents to give them the support they needed (Rubenstein and Shaver 1982:39). Feeling abandoned and isolated early in life, they never were able to develop the trust in people necessary to form intimate relationships.

long? I think because it was convenient to have a constant date and satisfying to have a boy friend. But I learned that he lied a lot and couldn't manage money, and that made me lose respect for him. I couldn't be intimate with him after that. We gradually drifted apart.

The next was Ricardo, who I met while I was studying in Mexico. It was a romantic and passionate relationship. He and his family wanted us to marry. But after a year, I realized that he had a drinking problem. I also realized that I couldn't be happy with a man who was overly dominant and that I didn't want to live far away from my parents. That relationship helped me start my list of "things I know I do not want."

Next I met an artist. He was not very good looking. In fact, he was short and ugly. But I enjoyed being admired by an artist. And I thought I was in love again. Then I found out that he too was married. For two volatile years we kept seeing each other, with me playing the role of the understanding "other woman." When I got a teaching job in another city, that relationship ended.

Next on my list was Kevin, a wild engineer. Even now when I think of that jerk I have to smile. He was such a mess of truth and lies. I spent four years with him. He was tall and good-looking and had a real zest for life. This really appealed to me. He was not interested in making a commitment of any kind, though. I wanted to live with him, but he said no. Finally, I realized that I wanted a relationship that was more intimate. Since he wasn't interested, we stopped seeing each other.

Soon after, Bill moved in with me. We lived together about nine months. Bill drank too much beer. He had a job when we met, but he was out of work most of the time we lived together. All of this sounds awful, I know. But I learned something from each one. From Bill, I learned that I do want to be close to and share my life with someone. But I knew that it has to be the right kind of person. My intimacy needs are currently met by relying and depending on friends and my parents. I'm not lonely. I do enjoy my life. I've made some unwise choices in my selection of men, but they've helped me at least know what I don't want in a relationship.

Depending on the source of the loneliness, then, it will be more or less difficult to overcome. In either case, however, people need to work at overcoming loneliness, particularly long-term loneliness, because intimate relationships are an essential part of our well-being.

Fulfillment through Intimacy

A psychotherapist who works with severely mentally disturbed patients in a private hospital told us that she can "mark the beginning of health and recovery in a patient from the time he or she commits to interacting with others." She noted that when patients first come to the hospital they avoid contact with others, refuse to interact in group therapy settings, and resist making friends with other patients. Disturbed people are unable to relate intimately or even casually to others. Lonely people relate casually, but have few or no intimate relationships. Healthy, fulfilled people operate from a base of intimacy.

Our Need for Intimacy

Intimacy is, then, more than merely the icing on the cake of living. It is a fundamental need. We need it from the time we are born. Infants can die if they are deprived of cuddling. As we grow, we tend to expand and alter our sphere of intimacy. Buhrmester and Furman (1987) studied the development of companionship and intimacy among second, fifth, and eighth graders. They had the children rate the importance of companionship and of experiences of intimate disclosure. At all three levels, the children indicated a desire for both companionship and intimacy. But there were some differences in the sources used to fulfill those needs. Parents were more important as a source of companionship for the second and fifth than for the eighth grade students. Same-sex peers were important in all three grades, but they became increasingly important as the children aged. Opposite-sex peers became important as companions for the first time in the eighth grade.

Our need for intimacy continues throughout life. Psychiatrist William Glasser (1984:9–10) argues that the "need to belong" is a part of our genetic makeup:

> As I look inside myself, I find that the need for friends, family, and love—best described as the need to belong—occupies as large a place in my mind as the need to survive. It may not be as immediate as thirst or hunger, but if, over the long pull, I did not have the close, loving family and friends that I almost take for granted, I think that the idea that life is hardly worth living would come occasionally to mind.

Ironically, there is some evidence that intimate relationships have become more important to Americans than they were in the past (Perlman and Fehr 1987:20). We say "ironically" because the trends noted in chapter 1, such as the high rate of divorce and increased number of people living alone, make the fulfillment of intimacy needs more problematic. The struggle of Ellie (see PERSONAL) illustrates the point.

Intimacy and Our Well-being

We feel the need for intimacy. But do intimate relationships have the expected payoff? Do they bring a satisfaction, a sense of fulfillment to our lives that nothing else can do? The answer is yes. And the answer comes from research in a variety of disciplines and from studies of both disturbed and normal populations. One researcher reported that the most common factor named by patients seeking outpatient psychotherapy was the failure to develop an intimate relationship (Horowitz 1979). Other researchers have found that the lack of an intimate relationship in marriage is associated with a number of emotional and physical disorders (Waring and Chelune 1983:183).

Two sociologists who examined the relationship between urbanism and a sense of well-being used data from London, England, Los Angeles, California, and Sydney, Australia (Palisi and Canning 1983). They looked at such things as people's age, education, occupation, location and type of home, marital status, and relationships. In all three cities they found that the best predictor of well-being was the quality of people's social relationships.

Many other studies have shown that our well-being is dependent on "contact with affectively close or intimate partners" (Reiss 1984:34). Two psychologists who used a national sample reported that people high in the desire and ability to engage in intimate relations also tend to have better mental health (McAdams and Bryant 1987). The women who scored high said that they are generally happy and basically satisfied with their work and family roles and their leisure time. Men who scored high reported fewer problems of mental and physical health, less drug and alcohol abuse, and less uncertainty about the future.

If, on the one hand, intimacy enhances our sense of well-being, our satisfaction, and our happiness, on the other hand it acts as a buffer when difficulties come. For example, among women who have suffered serious negative life events (such as divorce or death of a loved one), those without a confidant were ten times more likely to become depressed than those who had an intimate with whom to share their problem (Brown and Harris 1978). Intimate relationships moderate the severity of the impact of negative events.

The Perils of Intimacy

Intimate relationships are two-edged swords. When they go well, they enable a person to achieve a higher level of life satisfaction than otherwise possible. When they go badly, however, they are a bitter and painful experience. Parents, friends, and spouses can enrich us. They can also be a point of agony in our lives.

The extent of possible hurt is illustrated by the numbers of those hospitalized for mental illness who have endured some kind of abuse from an intimate. One study of psychiatric patients discharged over an eighteen-month period reported that 43 percent had a history of abuse, physical or sexual or both (Rieker and Carmen 1986). This does not mean, however, that painful intimate relationships inevitably doom people to mental illness. There are those who take painful relationships, work through them, and emerge as stronger and more mature individuals (Lauer and Lauer 1988:105–16).

The point is that intimate relationships are not a guarantee of well-being. Caution and understanding are necessary tools for establishing helpful relationships. Otherwise, like Ellie, you may make a series of bad choices.

The Nature of Intimacy

We have briefly defined intimacy as a relationship characterized by mutual commitment, affection, and sharing. We need now to look at the meaning of intimacy in more depth. What happens between two people who have an intimate relationship?

The Meaning of Intimacy

Based on his clinical practice, Erik Erikson (1950:255) claimed that a central task of the young adult is to establish intimacy:

> the capacity to commit himself to concrete affiliations and partnerships and to develop the ethical strength to abide by such commitments, even though they may call for significant sacrifices and compromises.

Intimate relations exist prior to adulthood, of course, but different tasks are more central at other ages. The young adult, just emerging from adolescence, faces a decision about with whom to be intimate. The choices that are made are crucial to the continued development of the individual.

Caring and concern for another is an important aspect of intimacy.

In Erikson's view, intimacy includes such things between people as openness, sharing, mutual trust, self-abandon, and commitment. Building on the work of Erikson and others, White, Speisman, Jackson, Bartis, and Costos (1986) developed a measure of intimacy that includes five components. One component is an orientation to the other and to the relationship. This involves the extent to which the individual's thinking, feelings, and behavior are focused on the intimate partner and the relationship rather than his or her self. The second component is caring and concern for the other. The third is sexuality, the degree to which the individual's sexual life emphasizes mutuality rather than personal concerns.

The fourth component is the extent of commitment to the other, and the fifth is the nature or kind of communication with the other. Communication includes such things as how much an individual reveals to the intimate partner, how much he or she listens, and how often he or she initiates communication.

Other researchers find somewhat similar dimensions to intimacy. Two hundred and seventy-seven university students were asked to indicate the difference between an intimate and nonintimate relationship (Roscoe, Kennedy, and Pope 1987). The students defined intimate relations in Erikson's terms of openness, sharing, and trust. But they added physical/sexual interaction to

Erikson's list, and less than 10 percent of them included his notions of self-abandon and commitment. The divergence from Erikson, the researchers speculate, may be due to the fact that the students have just emerged from adolescence and are just beginning the task of establishing their intimate lives. They may still be uncertain as to whether it is possible to give so much to someone else and still retain their own individuality. Or it may be due to the fact that changes have occurred since Erikson's formulation, and that people are less willing to include commitment and self-abandon in their intimate relationships.

In our view, intimacy has somewhat different meanings for various people. But there is a core meaning that is applicable to all people. And we would include affection, sharing (including communication), and commitment as part of the core of a satisfying intimate relationship.

Intimacy and Equity

Equity is fairness, in the sense that people are rewarded in proportion to their contributions to something or someone. Equity theory states that people strive to maintain a system of fairness such that each person in the system receives rewards that reflect his or her contribution (Walster, Walster, and Berscheid 1978). In relationships, this means that people must perceive, in the long run at least, that they are receiving about as much from the relationship as they are giving to it. An intimate relationship that is one-sided in terms of giving *or* receiving will probably not last.

For example, Elaine Walster and her associates interviewed more than five hundred college students about various aspects of their dating relationships (Walster, Walster, and Traupmann 1978). Those who perceived their relationships to be equitable, or who felt they were *slightly* overbenefited, were happier and more contented than those who did not (figure 2.2). Those who felt they were giving more than they were receiving from the relationships tended to be angry. Those who believed they were receiving a good deal more than they were giving, on the other hand, tended to feel guilty. People in relatively equitable relationships also felt more confident about them and were more likely to view them as stable and potentially long-term.

A sense of equity, then, is an important part of a fulfilling intimate relationship. This is true throughout our lives. Karen Rook (1987) used a sample of 120 elderly widowed women to investigate equity in relationships. She also found that women who felt either overbenefitted or underbenefitted had less satisfactory relationships. In fact, they were more likely to feel lonely than were those who perceived equity.

Intimacy as Self-Sustaining

Just as loneliness tends to generate a downward, self-sustaining cycle (figure 2.1), intimacy tends to generate an upward, self-sustaining cycle. That is, an intimate relationship tends to create certain kinds of behavior, attitudes, and

What Does Intimacy Mean?

As noted in the text, there are some variations in the meaning of intimacy to people. Conduct your own research into the matter by first taking the following test and then asking six or more other people to also take it:

What qualities or characteristics make a relationship an intimate one? Check each one that applies:

caring
sharing
physical/sexual
  interaction
trust/faith
openness
honesty/sincerity
acceptance
respect
mutuality/reciprocity

understanding
communication
friendship/
  companionship
commitment
self-abandon
similar interests
security
love

Which characteristics are chosen most often? Are any of them omitted altogether? Roscoe, Kennedy, and Pope (1987) found that the five most frequently mentioned characteristics, in order of mention, were: sharing, physical/sexual interaction, trust/faith, openness, and love.

If the entire class does this project, you can assign people to survey different groups: males, females, adolescents, young adults, older adults, and so on. Tabulate the results from the entire class and see if there are any group differences. Roscoe, Kennedy, and Pope (1987) did find some slight differences between the male and female adolescents they surveyed. What do your results suggest about the quality of intimate relationships today?

feelings that tend to maintain and even intensify the sense of intimacy. Surveying some of the research done on intimacy, Perlman and Fehr (1987:31–32) point out nine changes that occur as intimacy develops:

1. The amount of interaction between the intimates increases. They are likely to meet more often, for longer periods of time, and in a greater number of locations.

2. The intimates gain an increasing amount of personal knowledge about each other. They disclose more and more about themselves (see the following section on self-disclosure). They develop a private language that contains meanings only they understand. For example, a couple may have a code word that means "let's leave" when they are in a group situation, or special terms of affection that communicate feelings of love.

3. People in an intimate relationship become increasingly knowledgeable about each other's attitudes and behavior. They are able, to some extent, to anticipate what the other will do or think.

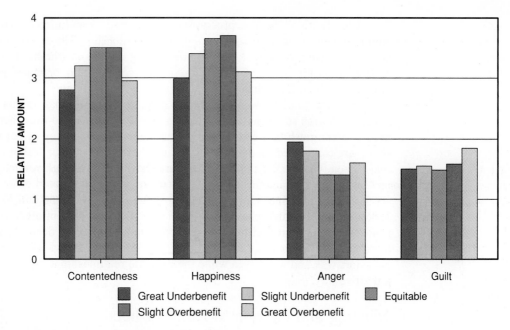

Figure 2.2 *Equity and satisfaction in relationships.*
Source: Data from Walster, Walster, and Traupman 1978:87.

4. Commitment to the relationship tends to grow, along with a sense of greater investment of both persons.

5. There is an increasing sense of "we-ness," a sense that the intimates form a unit bound together by certain shared interests.

6. Increasingly, the intimates feel that their own well-being is tied up with that of the relationship. If the relationship fails, it will not be something that can be easily shrugged off. If the relationship succeeds, it means that each of them will benefit personally.

7. Various positive emotions, such as love, trust, and caring, tend to become stronger.

8. There is a desire to remain physically close and accessible to each other. The intimates prefer to avoid long-term separation.

9. The relationship tends to be viewed as a special one, such that each sees the other as to some extent irreplaceable. It isn't a matter of "I'll die without you," but a sense that the relationship is unique and rewarding. As a man in a long-term marriage put it: "I know that I could probably find someone else that I would love, but the chances of another relationship like the one I have are pretty slim. We really have something special going for us."

Clearly, all of the nine processes not only result from intimacy but also tend to enhance and perpetuate an intimate relationship. The nine processes occur to varying degrees of intensity depending in part on whether the intimate relationship is one of friendship, dating, cohabitation, or marriage. In any case, intimacy, like loneliness, tends to be self-sustaining.

We need to add a word of caution here, however. Intimacy is not self-sustaining in the sense that you will always feel a closeness to the other. We need to distinguish between intimacy as a feeling and intimacy as behavior. If you are committed to another person and share some of your feelings with that person, you are engaging in intimate behavior even though you may not feel intimate at the moment (perhaps you are angry or agitated or anxious about something). Intimacy as a feeling is "episodic" (Wynne and Wynne 1986). Some intimate behaviors are also episodic. Intimacy, in other words, is not something that is either always increasing and there, or decreasing and leaving us. In the normal course of life, our intimate feelings and intimate behaviors wax and wane even while the intimate relationship is developing in a positive way.

Meeting and Getting to Know Others

How does the intimate relationship begin? Obviously, it is something that develops over time. There is no instant intimacy. In this section, we will look at some of the factors involved in the process, including factors that we use to select and choose from among those available for an intimate relationship.

First Impressions

First impressions are important, because they may determine whether we shall pursue a relationship. You may decide after the first few moments that another person is, or is not, the kind of person you want to know better. And, of course, others make similar judgments about you based on their first impressions. It is important to realize that first impressions are not necessarily accurate. Sometimes our first impressions are based on the similarity of a person to someone else we know. Or they grow out of some **stereotype.** For example, you may see a fat man laughing. Is he one of those typical "jolly fat" types? Or does he just happen to be laughing at the time when you see him?

General Appearance

We all tend to make snap judgments about others based on such things as physical appearance and demeanor. A woman wrote to an advice columnist because she was concerned about the impression she was making on others. She was a natural blonde, she pointed out, and for much of her life she felt that people hadn't taken her seriously because of the "dumb blonde" stereotype. But then she started wearing glasses, and people began to treat her differently. Glasses are associated with intelligence. She wondered, however, if she would make an even better impression by dyeing her hair, since the blonde hair might cancel out some of the impact of the glasses. The columnist replied that intelligent people do not operate on the assumption that blondes are dumb and people with glasses are intelligent. But the columnist was not totally correct. Many people—even intelligent, informed ones—make judgments about others that are based on such myths. While this does not mean that we should obediently shape our behavior according to the prevailing myths, we do need to be aware that people do react to us on the basis of our appearance.

If we have even a brief interaction with someone, we are likely to form a number of impressions about him or her. In an early, unpublished experiment, an instructor invited a friend, who was unknown to the students, to come into his classroom (Allport 1961:501). The friend was only in the room for about a minute, during which the instructor asked him what he thought of the weather. The man made a few neutral comments, then left. The instructor asked the students to "list your first impressions" of the man. On the average, students listed between five and six different impressions, ranging from such things as quiet and cultivated, to "trying to please," to "nice guy, congenial." Their first impressions included such things as personal traits, physical characteristics, judgments about the man's motivations, ethnic characteristics, speculations about the man's status and role, and the effect he had on them. Obviously, first impressions are often not very reliable, but they are a factor in whether or not we pursue a relationship.

Appearance is an important element in first impressions.

Nonverbal Cues

Experts assert that anywhere between 50 and 80 percent of meaning is communicated without words. We communicate meaning not only by what we say, but also by a variety of **nonverbal cues**—facial expressions, body positions, gestures, and paralanguage (inflection, rate of speech, loudness of speaking). Given a contradiction between someone's verbal and nonverbal statements, we will tend to believe the latter. For example, if someone says "I love you," but has a hesitancy or lack of emotion in the words, we will tend to disbelieve or at least question the statement.

Nonverbal cues are an important source of our first impressions. We define the man who slouches as lacking in self-confidence or assertiveness. We define the woman who smiles broadly as a happy person. We use a variety of nonverbal cues rather than a single cue to make judgments about others, of course. In an experiment carried out in a bar, two female associates of the experimenter established eye contact with males (Walsh and Hewitt 1985). In some cases, they made eye contact once and, in other cases, a number of times during a five-minute period. Once eye contact was made, the woman smiled in some cases but not in others. When the woman made repeated eye contact and smiled, the man approached her in 60 percent of the cases. When eye contact was made only once, or when the woman did not smile, approach occurred in less than 20 percent of the cases.

Nonverbal cues are not always interpreted correctly. In particular, there is a tendency for males to read more sexual content into nonverbal cues (Abbey

1982). A man may define a woman's friendliness as sexual interest. He may hear more sexual innuendos in conversation than are intended. He may see a woman as being seductive or flirtatious when she is just trying to be sociable. Generally, women are more accurate in interpreting nonverbal cues than are men. But whether we interpret them accurately or not, we all attend to them, and we behave on the basis of the way we have defined them.

Opening Lines

Verbal cues are also important. Favorable impressions depend on *what* is said as well as *how* it is said. As with the women in the bar, nonverbal gestures may gain the attention of another person. They may indicate that you are interested in establishing a relationship. But what then? What do you say to someone you have never met before? What do you use as an opening line?

Three psychologists who asked that question conducted research on male and female preference for opening lines (Kleinke, Meeker, and Staneski 1986). In one of their studies, university students and employees evaluated a number of opening lines used by men to meet women. In another study, university students and employees evaluated opening lines women used to meet men. The researchers compiled their list of opening lines by asking students to record all the ones they could think of.

They grouped the opening lines into three categories. The "direct approach" consisted of such openings as "You look like a warm person" and "Hi. I like you." The "innocuous approach" is illustrated by such lines as "Are you a student?" and "Where are you from?" The "cute-flippant" approach consisted of opening lines like "I'm easy. Are you?" and "Do you fool around?" The subjects agreed that the cute-flippant lines were the least desirable, though the women disliked them more than the men. Women preferred the innocuous approach, while men leaned more toward a direct approach.

What Attracts?

Are you now, or have you been, in an intimate relationship with someone? If so, think about what it was that first attracted you to that person. Was there some kind of "chemistry" that occurred? Was the attraction instantaneous? What were the qualities of the person that appealed to you? Social scientists have been interested in such questions, and have found a number of factors involved in interpersonal attraction.

Physical Attractiveness

Beauty may be only skin-deep, but it is an important factor in attraction. It is particularly important in first impressions, when there is little other available information about someone. It diminishes in importance, though it doesn't completely lose its importance, in longer-term relationships or where other

Getting Acquainted Victorian Style

The ease or difficulty of establishing a heterosexual relationship varies from time to time and society to society. Such relationships have been more problematic in other times and places than they are in our society today. Samuel Butler's *The Way of All Flesh* is a portrait of Victorian England. Although Theobald, one of the characters in the novel, eventually fell in love and married, the problem of meeting and getting to know women was agonizing for him. This is how Butler describes Theobald's problems:

Theobald knew nothing about women. The only women he had been thrown in contact with were his sisters, two of whom were always correcting him, and a few school friends whom these had got their father to ask to Elmhurst. These young ladies had either been so shy that they and Theobald had never amalgamated, or they had been supposed to be clever and had said smart things to him. He did not say smart things himself and did not want other people to say them. Besides, they talked about music—and he hated music—or pictures—and he hated pictures—or books and, except the classics, he hated books. And then sometimes he wanted to dance with them, and he did not know how to dance, and did not want to know.

At Mrs. Cowey's parties again he had seen some young ladies and had been introduced to them. He had tried to make himself agreeable, but was always left with the impression that he had not been successful. . . . The result of his experience was that women had never done him any good and he was not accustomed to associate them with any pleasure. . . . As for kissing, he had never kissed a woman in his life except his sister—and my own sisters when we were all small children together. Over and above these kisses, he had until quite lately been required to imprint a solemn, flabby night kiss night and morning upon his father's cheek, and this, to the best of my belief, was the extent of Theobald's knowledge in the matter of kissing, at the time of which I am now writing. The result of the foregoing was that he had come to dislike women, as mysterious beings whose ways were not as his ways, nor their thoughts as his thoughts.

Source: Samuel Butler, *The Way of All Flesh* (New York: Signet Classic, 1960), pp. 41–42.

information is available. The importance of physical attractiveness is illustrated by an account that Nancy, a female student, shared with us:

Until I was sixteen, I was very unattractive. Actually, I was pretty ugly. I was overweight, wore nurdy glasses, had very bad skin, and my hair was always messy looking. I didn't date anybody until I was sixteen, and even then it was for only a few days. I had been madly in love with a guy that I pursued since I was fourteen. But I wasn't successful. He was the hunk of our class.

Everybody liked him and he could have chosen among several girls in my class. So I didn't expect him to go out with me, although I wanted it very much. His rejection reinforced my belief that I was terribly unattractive. And that hurt my self-esteem. It was a vicious cycle. The more my self-esteem went down, the more unattractive I became.

Everything suddenly changed when I was sixteen and a half. I lost weight. I got contact lenses. And I got a haircut that looked good on me. I became a different person. My self-esteem went up just by looking into the mirror. It didn't change my status at school much, but when I went away on vacation I realized that I had become attractive. Suddenly a number of guys asked me to go out with them, and people seemed generally friendlier than they were before. Just by changing my looks, I changed that whole vicious cycle that had been so painful.

Nancy's experience illustrates some of the findings of research. Attractive persons are more self-accepting, and self-acceptance enhances attractiveness. The more we see ourselves as attractive, the more self-esteem we have at all ages—as children, adolescents, and adults. We also tend to believe that physically attractive people possess socially desirable personality traits, and we expect them to be more successful than those who are less attractive (Berscheid and Walster 1978). When we see someone who is physically attractive to us, we are likely to define that person as more likable, friendly, confident, sensitive, and flexible than someone who is less attractive. Obviously, then, we perceive physically attractive people as more desirable dating partners.

In essence, we tend to operate on the principle that what is beautiful is good. When we perceive someone to be physically attractive, we are likely to also attribute a host of other positive qualities to that person. Of course, that initial judgment may change as we get to know the person. But the physically attractive person has an advantage in the quest for intimacy, because more people will desire and seek to know him or her.

Similarity

Do opposites attract? That may work for magnets, but for people, it is similarity rather than differences that attract us to each other. At later stages, some differences may enhance an intimate relationship, as we shall discuss in subsequent chapters. Initially, however, we are attracted to people who are like us in their attitudes and values, and put off by those who are different from us. As Berscheid and Walster (1978:88) summarize the research:

> The answer to the question, "Does attitudinal similarity generate liking?" is a resounding "yes." When we discover that others share our beliefs and attitudes, it is satisfying: we like them. When we discover that others disagree with us, it is unsettling; it's hard to like such persons.

In fact, when we perceive someone to be different we may communicate with that person in a way that says "I am not available." This was one of the findings of two researchers who wanted to see if couples who developed an intimate relationship behaved differently with each from the start than those who only have a casual relationship.[1] The researchers used thirty couples who were dating steadily and paired together sixty people who were strangers to each other. They told some of the pairs of strangers that they were like each other and told others that they were dissimilar. Each pair talked together for ten minutes on a number of selected topics.

After observing all of the couples' discussions, the researchers concluded that the pairs of strangers who believed themselves similar to each other communicated very much like steadily dating couples. On the other hand, those who believed themselves to be dissimilar communicated with each other in a way that said that they were unavailable for an intimate relationship.

Sometimes, it may be nonverbal cues that enable us to decide that the other is similar or dissimilar. Eisenman (1985) raised the question of whether students who were marijuana users would be more attracted to other users even if they didn't know about the drug use. He paired fifty marijuana users with fifty other users on one occasion and then fifty nonusers on another occasion. The students talked with each other for about ten minutes on each occasion, ostensibly to choose a partner for an experiment. The discussion was held in the presence of the experimenter; there was no mention of drug usage. Nevertheless, users tended to choose other users for partners and nonusers tended to choose nonusers. Eisenman noted that this supports the notion that similarity leads to attraction, but that we need to investigate the kinds of cues that lead people to choose others who are similar to them.

Incidentally, similarity may be difficult to simulate. An experiment with college students (DePaulo, Stone, and Lassiter 1985) reported that those who tried to feign agreement with an attractive person were not adept at the attempt. If you try to appear to be similar with someone in order to be attractive to that person, your efforts may be obvious.

Why does similarity lead to attraction? Isn't dissimilarity more interesting and exciting? Actually there are a number of reasons why we tend to like those who are similar to us. First, we feel more confident with someone who is like us. That person, we believe, is more likely to reciprocate our feelings than is someone who is very different. Second, those who are similar to us build our self-esteem, because they agree with our attitudes and values, which helps to validate us. All of us need social validation for our attitudes and values. Think, for example, of one of your beliefs about marriage. Do you believe that marriage should be confined to one man and one woman? What if you were the only person in the world to hold such a belief? What if everyone else argued that marriage should involve a man and a number of women or a woman and a number of men. How long would you be able to hold on to your belief?

Third, similarity facilitates the development of intimacy. Sharing thoughts and feelings and ideas is much easier with those who are similar to us, and the sharing is likely to be rewarded (approved) and reciprocated. Those who are very different from us may not understand why we feel the way we do about certain matters or why we believe what we do. Intimacy is more difficult under such circumstances.

Other Factors in Attraction

As in all human behavior, there are multiple factors involved in attraction. **Propinquity,** nearness in place, is important. We tend to like people who live near us or who are close to us in some setting (classrooms, workplaces, etc.). A classic study by Festinger, Schachter, and Back (1950) looked at the development of friendships among married students in a new housing project. The researchers asked the subjects to name their three closest friends. They found that next-door neighbors were most frequently named as best friends, followed by those who were only two doors away. Propinquity was the most important factor in determining friendship patterns.

Propinquity may be important because it leads to greater familiarity with those people who are near us. And familiarity is also a factor in attraction. We tend to like people who are familiar to us. Repeated exposure to something or someone can increase our liking, especially if we are neutral or positive initially (Zajonc 1968).

As Nancy's story suggested, self-esteem is also a factor in attraction. We tend to prefer others who have about the same level of self-esteem as we have (Abloff and Hewitt 1985). We particularly find those with lower self-esteem to be less attractive to us. A different aspect of self-esteem and attraction is that we tend to like people who enhance our own self-esteem. Others enhance our self-esteem when they agree with our ideas, when they compliment us, and when they treat us as special in some sense. For example, you are treated as special and, accordingly, you will tend to be attracted to someone whose expressions of affection are exclusively for you (Kimble and Kardes 1987). A young woman who brushed off the flirtatious behavior of a handsome man as of no consequence explained: "He does that with every woman he meets. It's nothing special for him to flirt with me. I don't intend to be just another one of his long line of conquests."

In sum, there are many factors other than "chemistry" that draw people together and make them attractive to each other. At this point, it would be interesting for you to rethink your own intimate relationship and the reasons you gave earlier for what attracted you to him or her.

Developing a Relationship

Once attracted to someone as a friend or potential lover, the relationship develops over time. Again, thinking of an intimate relationship with which you have been involved, can you identify different stages or phases in it? That is, did the relationship at a certain point enter a new stage or phase and become a different kind of relationship than it had been earlier? Social scientists who are interested in the development of relationships have tried to identify such stages or phases. We will use the four-stage model proposed by Carl Backman (1981:239–67).

First Stage: Initial Meeting and Awareness

If we begin at the point when the two intimates have not yet met, we can raise the question of what factors go into any two people getting together. We have already suggested that propinquity is important. But we can go beyond that and raise the question of what determines propinquity. That is, the people who live near you are not there by pure chance. Propinquity and similarity tend to work together. People who are alike tend to live in the same area, have similar leisure interests, and belong to similar kinds of organizations. The probability is, in other words, that those who are around are also similar to you in many ways. In particular, we are likely to grow up in neighborhoods and go to school with people from the same social class. A **social class** is a group of people with similar income, education, and occupational prestige. People in the same class also tend to have similar values and attitudes. Middle-class people tend not to interact much with upper- or lower-class people, at least not in a setting that lends itself to the initiation and development of an intimate relationship.

Thus, there are social factors that lead to clusterings of relatively similar people. Of course, the more mobile you are, the more likely you are to sense dissimilarities with others. Moving from a rural area to the city or from one part of the country to another part can make you more aware of the differences among people. A Midwestern student who moved to California to go to school said: "I lived in California for three years before I felt like I was no longer in a foreign country." Gradually, the student got involved in some organizations and found people who shared his interests. As he got to know like-minded people, he no longer felt he was in a foreign country.

Second Stage: The Selection Process

Once we are aware of the choices we have, of the variety of relatively similar and dissimilar people with whom we interact, we select out those with whom we would like to develop a relationship. We have noted above the important factors in the selection process—first impressions and the various bases for attraction.

But there are two additional considerations that need to be mentioned in the selection process. First, we all operate within the context of the **norms** of our groups. A norm is simply an expected pattern of behavior. Families tend to have norms about the kind of people with whom it is desirable to interact. In fact, many stories and movies, like Shakespeare's classic tale, *Romeo and Juliet,* or the movie, *Guess Who's Coming to Dinner* (which focused on an interracial marriage), have been based on the problems that arise when people decide to have an intimate relationship with someone who breaks family norms.

There are many reasons why we select someone for a relationship.

For any particular family, the norm may dictate against intimate relationships (either friendship or love relationships) with people of other religions, other races, a different social class, or simply with those who have a personality that the family finds offensive.

For example, a male student reported that his father had once asked him not to spend time with a certain neighborhood friend. At first, the father was rather vague about the reasons. But eventually, the student came to understand:

> My friend was different from other kids in our neighborhood. It's hard to say just how he was different. He just didn't like to do the kinds of things other kids did. Actually, he was a little effeminate. I knew he wasn't a homosexual. But my father was afraid he might be. And he was afraid that he would somehow contaminate me if I spent much time with him.

One of Nancy's problems, in addition to her self-acknowledged lack of attractiveness, was that her father didn't want her to date anyone outside of her religion. Nancy said that this increased her difficulties in finding a boyfriend; there just weren't many available Jewish boys around. She was embarrassed to admit that her first date didn't occur until she was sixteen, but she abided by her family's norm.

A second consideration in the selection process is the compromises that we make. We are drawn to others that we consider physically attractive, but we may not try to establish a relationship with the person we regard as the most attractive. Why not? We tend to befriend those who are near us, but we may not want to have a friendship with the lonely person who lives next door. Why not? We are attracted to those who are like us, but we may avoid a certain individual even though that person shares our same political and religious philosophy. Why?

There is no single answer to such questions, but one factor that operates in the selection process is compromise. We compromise with our inclinations or ideals because of other factors. For example, we may not try to establish a relationship with a person, who is much more attractive than we are, because we assume that the relationship will not endure; that person will find someone equally attractive and abandon us. To be safe, we generally try to establish an intimate relationship with someone we regard as roughly equal to our own attractiveness (Kalick and Hamilton 1986). Or we may not establish an intimate relationship with the person next door because we already have as many such relationships as we can handle. Or we may avoid the person who shares our political and religious philosophy because that person is somewhat obnoxious. Ideals and inclinations frequently have to be compromised in accord with such practical considerations.

Third Stage: Developing Intimacy

Once a relationship begins, certain mechanisms come into play to lead the participants into intimacy. These mechanisms begin almost immediately, but they take on a new intensity and depth in the third stage.

Self-Disclosure

One of the most important mechanisms in the development of intimacy is **self-disclosure,** the honest revealing of oneself to another person. At first, people reveal things about themselves that are relatively safe. As intimacy develops, an increasing amount of private information may be shared. In the early part of the relationship, there tends to be equity in self-disclosure; each person reveals about the same amount of information as he or she is receiving from the other.

What kinds of things are revealed? We can classify self-disclosed materials into four kinds (Waring and Chelune 1983). First, there is a sharing of emotions. Intimates tell each other how they feel about things. Second, there is a sharing of needs. Intimates reveal what they see as their personal needs in the relationship as well as more general needs. Third, there is a sharing of thoughts, beliefs, attitudes, and even fantasies. "I'm never sure what you're thinking" is as damaging a statement about intimacy as "I'm never sure what you're feeling." Finally, there is a sharing of self-awareness, the way each feels and thinks about himself or herself as a person.

Sharing our feelings, needs, thoughts, and self-awareness with someone else is both a result of intimacy and a creator of greater intimacy. In a study of 231 dating couples, researchers found that the more the partners engaged in self-disclosure to the other, the more they reported love feelings for each other and the closer they regarded themselves to each other (Rubin, Hill, Peplau, Dunkel-Schetter 1980). Another study, of forty-four nursing students, reported the kind of upward spiral we discussed above: intimacy leads to further self-disclosure, which, in turn, enhances the sense of intimacy (Falk and Wagner 1985). Finally, a study of thirty-eight dating couples over a four-month period revealed that those who were still together had a greater amount of self-disclosure in the initial phases of the relationship than did those who broke up during the period (Berg and McQuinn 1986).

Because self-disclosure is tied up so closely with the development of intimacy, we tend to disclose ourselves only to a few (we cannot have intimate relations with a great many people), and only to those with whom we expect to have intimacy. Self-disclosure is, after all, a risky process. The more you disclose, the more vulnerable you are to being manipulated, controlled, scorned, and embarrassed. One of the hallmarks of an intimate relationship, therefore, is trust. We trust the other *not* to react negatively, to support us, and to hold what we say in confidence.

As we disclose ourselves in an intimate relationship, trust tends to grow, enhancing the sense of intimacy. There are a number of other benefits of self-disclosure for intimacy. The more the self-disclosure, the greater the level of satisfaction with the relationship (Jorgensen and Gaudy 1980). Self-disclosure can increase the attraction of people toward each other (Archer and Cook 1986). It can enhance the sense of compatibility as partners become increasingly aware of their similarities and at ease with the views of each other. In general, self-disclosure is not all there is to intimacy, but it is a large and essential part of any intimate relationship.

We should note that there are some sex differences in self-disclosure. Among children, girls seem to seek intimate disclosures in their friendships at an earlier age than boys do (Buhrmester and Furman 1987). Among adults, both men and women tend to disclose more to females than to males. Women generally, however, tend to be willing to disclose more than do men. Women, for example, are more willing to talk about their feelings of depression, anxiety, anger, and fear than are men (Snell, Miller, and Belk 1988). We shall see some reasons for this in chapter 7 when we discuss sex roles.

Interdependence and Commitment

An increasing sense of interdependence develops during the third stage of intimacy. Each partner is dependent on the other to fulfill some of his or her needs. Each has some power in the relationship, therefore, because of the dependence of the other. But the power may not be equal because of differing amounts of commitment to the relationship. An intimate relationship may be more important to one partner than the other. The one with the most interest in maintaining the relationship is likely to be the most committed to it. And the person who is the most committed can be exploited because that person has the most to lose if the relationship breaks up (Backman 1981:261).

In an ideal situation, issues of power and inequity would not arise. But human life is not ideal. People bring varying amounts of commitment to a relationship. Interdependence seldom if ever means an equal amount of dependence of each partner. And power issues, as we shall see in chapter 11, come into most of our intimate relationships.

In essence, then, interdependence and commitment are both essential elements of a developing intimacy. But they are also problem areas that can lead to the dissolution as well as the maintenance of the relationship.

Fourth Stage: Maintaining or Dissolving the Relationship

In this final stage, processes will be operating that will tend either to maintain or dissolve an intimate relationship. As Backman (1981:262) notes, commitment "is rarely complete, nor is it unchanging." Rather, the extent of commitment tends to reflect the perceived rewards and costs. Whether a friendship, date, or marriage, most of us will reflect at some point on the rewards and costs of the relationship. We will evaluate the relationship in terms of what we think we deserve out of it and the costs in time, money, and energy that are required to maintain it.

Evaluations of costs and rewards can and do change over time, of course. Individuals develop, altering their sense of what they need and what they want. A woman may begin a relationship with a man, for example, with the idea that she only wants some companionship and fun. She may eventually cohabit with him. And she may later decide that she wants to marry this person. Our needs and wants are never static. One of the ironies of an intimate relationship is the fact that those things that fulfill needs at one point in time may become a problem at a later point. For example, the woman who marries a man because he is very careful about spending money may later resent his frugality when they have become financially successful.

Our evaluation of the rewards and costs change also because we observe and compare our relationships with those of other people. Such an evaluation can work in two ways. We may decide that our relationship is costing too much, or we may decide that we are fortunate for having a uniquely rewarding relationship. Observing others may deepen as well as lessen our commitment.

Once a relationship begins to dissolve, many of the processes that built the intimacy work in reverse. For example, intimacy develops as people reward each other in an equitable fashion. A kind of "tit-for-tat" process occurs as rewards are reciprocated in an ongoing fashion. A reverse process, in which there is an "eye for an eye and a tooth for a tooth" on a continuing basis may occur as a relationship dissolves. People begin to punish each other in various ways. And each injury, each slight, each hurt is reciprocated.

Similarly, intimacy grows as people support each other's self-esteem. In dissolution, they may attack each other's self-esteem in various ways. Self-disclosure, the heart of intimacy, may also reverse. The partners may even fear to disclose anything because of the possibility of its being used against them. Trust, interdependence, and commitment all decline as a relationship deteriorates.

"It is sad," a man remarked to us as we watched a joyous and expensive wedding, "to think that they put so much into this and in a few years the marriage might crumble." Intimate relationships do dissolve. Some should. But many continue. People maintain friendships and marriages for the duration of their lives. In either case, such factors as self-disclosure, trust, and commitment are crucial ingredients.

PRINCIPLES FOR ENHANCING INTIMACY

Beginning with this chapter, we will briefly note some of the principles that can be derived from materials in the chapter and used to enhance the quality of your own intimate relationships. A major premise of the chapter, of course, is the point that intimate relationships are a necessary part of our well-being. Some of the important principles are:

1. Like it or not, people often initially decide on the social desirability of another person by how he or she looks or behaves. The clothes worn, the words spoken, the attitudes assumed become a shorthand method for determining whether you want to get to know someone better or whether that person wants to pursue a relationship with you. Since first impressions are important, therefore, pay attention to your dress, your demeanor, your speech. Make them consistent with the kind of person you are.

2. You are most likely to have an intimate relationship with someone who is similar to you in attitudes and values. Thus, it is important to learn as much as possible about the other person's attitudes and values. Do not think that simply because you have an initial, strong attraction to someone, your feelings of "love" will overcome any differences that exist.

3. Self-esteem is crucial to fulfilling intimate relationships. Anything you do to increase your self-esteem will enhance your relationships and, thereby, your well-being. There are books to help you build self-esteem. Your self-esteem will also grow to the extent that you associate with people who value you and compliment you on your traits and abilities. Finally, find something that you're good at and pursue that interest; achievement is an integral part of self-esteem.

4. Equity is important to intimacy. You can't build an intimate relationship by giving so much to the other that the other feels overbenefitted. You must both give and receive, so that each of you feels that the relationship is equitable.

5. Self-disclosure is the heart of intimacy. Many people believe they disclose more than they actually do (Stevens, Rice, and Johnson 1986). It is helpful to check with your partner to see if you are disclosing enough about your feelings and thoughts.

6. Intimacy is cyclic. You won't always feel close to your intimate partner. Work through the difficult times, realizing that they are normal and not a sign that the relationship is about to dissolve. In fact, persistence and hard work are essential ingredients in a thriving relationship.

SUMMARY

As social creatures, we need intimate relationships. Without them, we feel lonely. Social loneliness means less interaction than you desire; emotional loneliness is less intimacy than you desire. Long-term loneliness has serious physical and emotional consequences for people. Loneliness results from both social (modern, urban society) and personal (certain childhood experiences) factors.

Intimacy is a fundamental human need. Intimate relationships enhance our well-being, though they can also be a source of deep distress when they do not work out well. Intimacy includes such things as affection, sharing, and commitment. Intimate relationships must be equitable if they are to endure. Intimate relations, like loneliness, tend to be self-sustaining, though feelings of intimacy are episodic.

Intimate relationships develop over time. Initially, first impressions make a difference in whether we will be attracted to someone else. General appearance, nonverbal cues, and opening lines are important in forming first impressions. Those most likely to attract us are people who are physically attractive, who are similar to us in attitudes and values, who are near and familiar to us, and who have about the same level of self-esteem as we have.

There are four stages in the development of an intimate relationship. The first stage is the initial meeting and awareness of someone else. Social factors mean that this is likely to occur with people who are similar to us. The second stage involves the selection process, which involves our group norms and a certain amount of compromise. The third stage is the development of intimacy, a process crucially dependent on self-disclosure and marked by an increasing sense of interdependence and commitment. In the fourth stage, processes are at work to either maintain or dissolve the relationship. Evaluations of costs and rewards are important in the fourth stage.

1. Reported in *Psychology Today,* February, 1988, p. 13.

3

Getting Involved

How would you feel if one of your parents went with you on a date? Or what if it was absolutely necessary to convince your girlfriend's father that you were a suitable mate if you were to have any hope of marrying her? Such things happened earlier in American history. Then, as now, getting involved with someone was a social process. There are norms in every era that govern dating and courtship. The social nature of these practices is underscored by the fact that today we do not date merely in accord with biological needs but also according to social imperatives. That is, it is not sexual maturation alone that determines when we shall start dating. Rather, there are also social pressures and norms that tell us when it is appropriate to enter the world of dating (Dornbusch, Carlsmith, Gross, Martin, Jennings, Rosenberg, and Duke 1981).

In this chapter, we will examine the processes of dating and courtship. We will discuss some facts about premarital sex as an aspect of dating. We will study cohabitation, which some social scientists view as a part of the courtship process (because many who cohabit eventually marry). Finally, we will note what happens when a relationship doesn't work out and people go through the painful process of breaking up.

Holding hands is part of the normative behavior of dating.

Dating

Getting involved with someone else frequently begins with a date. At least, dating plays a part in the development of a serious relationship, though, as we shall see below, dating has more functions than simply that of finding a potential spouse.

Finding People to Date

Where do you meet people to date? In the past, adults would frequently help to arrange meetings between young people. Before World War I, young people dated regularly only if they planned on getting married. But patterns of dating have changed over time, even over the past few decades (Strouse 1987). For example, in the 1950s and 1960s young people commonly got together in planned, formal dates. In the 1970s, however, the emphasis began to shift to more casual and spontaneous forms of getting together. Young people gathered at parties, parking lots, and bars. Some even paired off for the evening. But despite the informality and spontaneity, finding dates continues to be one of the problematic aspects of life. For those in school, a classmate is a likely prospect. The workplace is another common source, as are various clubs and organizations, mutual friends, and singles bars.

Once out of school, however, many single adults discover that it is harder to find dates. Some try and ultimately tire of the singles bars. That does not mean that the desire to meet someone diminishes. Both the difficulty and the desire is evident in the phenomenon of dating services and the use of the "personal ads" that have arisen to help people get together. Dating services use computer analysis to match people, or video tapes to let people choose someone who appeals to them. The services are available in most urban areas.

Many newspapers now feature large numbers of personal ads in their classified section. The advertisers normally give information on their sex, race, marital status (single or divorced), and interests. People of all ages use the ads, and some become creative in their efforts as the following two examples from a Southwestern newspaper illustrate:

> Catholic widow, 57, 5'5", 128 lbs., healthy, employed, lonely, honest, sincere, would like to meet 58–65 year old gentleman, healthy, honest, sincere for friend/companion.

> Couch potatoes pass this ad! Attractive, single white female, 5'5", 122 lbs., brown/brown, seeking a go-getter, 22 to 31. Must be tender, fun-loving, like dancing, dining out, football and much more. No drugs or diseases, please.

How many people use the ads or services? We do not know, but a Canadian study reported that 5 percent of single adults surveyed had placed ads (Austrom and Hanel 1985). Studies of the ads show certain patterns. In terms of what people want, an analysis of eight hundred ads from newspapers on both the east and the west coast reported that men generally seem more concerned with physical characteristics, while women emphasize psychological factors (Deaux and Hanna 1984). In terms of both what people want and offer, another study (Koestner and Wheeler 1988) found three patterns:

1. Women were more likely to note their "male-valued" traits (such as enjoying sports and the outdoors) while men were more likely to point out their "female-valued" traits (such as sensitivity).

2. Women were more likely to offer weight and seek a desirable height, while men tended to offer height and seek a desirable weight.

3. Women were more likely to talk about their attractiveness and to ask for professional status in a man, while men were more likely to offer professional status and seek attractiveness in a woman.

We do not know how effective such ads are, but their use seems to be increasing. The increase, however, may reflect the fact that such ads are considered more socially acceptable now rather than their high success rate.

Selecting a Dating Partner

As the personal ads indicate, people are selective about whom they date. No matter how anxious an individual is to form a relationship, he or she is not likely to accept just anyone for the sake of having someone. What determines who will be acceptable?

Basically, we use the same criteria noted in the last chapter for what makes people attractive to us. The personal ads well illustrate the fact that one important criterion is that a dating partner should be physically attractive. In fact, one study found that physical attractiveness is a major factor in the decision to date a person (Jones and Adams 1982). Males who are thin, and those of both sexes who are overweight, tend to have a more difficult time in forming a relationship (Kallen and Doughty 1984). Other aspects of physical appearance also affect the ease or difficulty of getting a date.

Physical attractiveness is not the only criterion for selecting a dating partner. Indeed, one's purpose for dating and one's age both make a difference in the criteria one uses for selecting dates. Nevid (1984) asked 545 undergraduate students to rate various factors in terms of their importance for a purely sexual or a meaningful (long-term) relationship. Males rated physical characteristics more highly than did females for both kinds of relationships. However, attractiveness was rated highly by both males and females for a purely sexual relationship. And for a meaningful relationship, both males and females gave the highest ratings to such qualities as personality, honesty, fidelity, warmth, and sensitivity.

Ironically, then, the things we value for the long-term are not necessarily the criteria used to initiate a relationship with someone. This is particularly true at younger ages. Early adolescents (sixth graders) are more likely to place a higher value on a person's superficial appearance. Late adolescents (college students) are more likely to be concerned about a long-term relationship and are, consequently, more likely to try to find dates who have desirable interpersonal skills and not merely physical appeal (Roscoe, Diana, and Brooks 1987).

Functions of Dating

We have already indicated that people date for differing reasons. We will examine the various functions of dating separately, but keep in mind that a particular date may serve more than one of the following functions and that we date for different reasons at different ages.

Recreation

We all have a need for recreation, for a time when we can relax and have fun. One way to do this is to date. Dating takes us out of the world of work or study and into a world of relating and enjoying. Early and middle adolescents (sixth and eleventh graders) are likely to see dating primarily in terms of recreation. For them, the major purpose of dating is to secure some degree of personal gratification (Roscoe, Diana, and Brooks 1987). For the older individual, however, dating is likely to serve additional purposes.

Intimacy/Companionship

College students recognize recreation as one function of dating, but they emphasize the importance of companionship and intimacy as purposes of dating (Roscoe, Diana, and Brooks 1987). There is some difference between males and females, with males looking for sexual intimacy and females hoping for interpersonal intimacy as a primary objective in dating.

Dating, we should note, is not confined to the young. People date after a divorce or after the death of a spouse. Two researchers who studied dating patterns among those over sixty reported that companionship and intimacy were primary purposes of dating (Bulcroft and O'Connor 1986). Older people date in order to have an emotional and sexual outlet not otherwise available to them. And they do some of the same things on dates as younger people. They go to the movies, go out for pizza, attend dances, and even camp and travel together. Clearly, dating enhances the quality of life for older people.

Mate Selection

Mate selection is the most obvious function of dating. We date others in the hope of eventually finding someone to marry. In fact, one of the predictors of stability in a dating relationship is whether the two people believe that there is a chance of marriage (Lloyd, Cate, and Henton 1984).

Status Attainment

One of the findings of the study of older dating couples was that dating enhances the **status,** or prestige, of the female. Dating serves the same purpose for younger people. Those who date during early and middle adolescence are likely to gain prestige. They enhance their status with their peers because they show themselves to be not only more grown up but also desirable individuals. That this is important is illustrated by the young woman who told us of her severe embarrassment in high school because no boy asked her out on a date when most of the other girls her age were already dating.

It is not just dating per se, but dating particular people that can enhance status. Among adolescents, for example, the young man who dates a cheerleader or a very popular classmate, or the young woman who dates an athlete or prominent classmate, gains even more status.

Changing Patterns of Dating

As noted in the text, patterns of dating have changed over time. To get a better sense of the changes that have occurred recently, interview three men or three women about their dating experiences. Select one who is under twenty years of age, another between thirty-five and forty, and a third over sixty. In each case, explore the dating experiences of the individual during adolescence. Ask such questions as: Who initiated dates, males or females? What did you typically do on a date? What influence did your parents have over your dates? What did you feel were the purposes of dating? What was one of your most memorable dates?

Compare the results from the three different generations. What did you find that was similar and what was different? If the entire class participates in this project, see if there are gender differences as well as age differences. Did those who interviewed men find different answers to the questions from those who interviewed women?

Socialization

Socialization refers to the process of learning to function effectively in a group. We are not born with the knowledge of how to be a student, an employee, a member of a church, or a member of a family. We learn how to function in the various groups in which we participate. One of the things we have to learn is how to get along with people of the opposite sex, and dating is a way of doing this. The lack of socialization into heterosexual relationships early in life (we interact mostly with same-sex others before puberty) is one of the reasons for the awkwardness of first dating situations. In dating, we begin to learn how to relate more meaningfully to someone of the opposite sex. That means we are learning the skills necessary for a future long-term relationship.

Patterns of Dating

As a social phenomenon, dating differs not only across generations, but across societies and among different groups within a particular society as well. In any society, of course, there are norms about dating that are supposed to apply to all groups. Individuals and groups may break these norms, but those who do will probably pay a price. For example, take the issue of who initiates a date in our society. For the most part, men are expected to take the initiative and ask the female for a date. Even though the woman's movement has rectified some of the inequalities in relationships, it has not eliminated this expectation.

Shared-cost dating has become more common.

To be sure, many people reject the idea that a woman must wait for a man to ask her out. And many women, including feminists, also insist on sharing the expenses of a date (Korman 1983). Part of the rationale for this behavior is the belief that the woman who allows a man to assume all of the costs of a date may be under some obligation to provide him with sexual favors in return. In a shared-cost date, the two people are equal and may each decide whether the relationship should include sexual activity. The egalitarian nature of the shared-expense date gives a woman more discretion about her behavior. She does not have to feel that she "owes" her date anything sexually. She can ask a man out, share the costs of the evening, and feel free to engage or not engage in sexual activity.

Nevertheless, when male undergraduates were asked about their impressions of women who ask men out, they rated such women as more sexually active and more flexible and agreeable (Muehlenhard and Scardino 1985). Ironically, the woman who believes in equality, who breaks a traditional norm and initiates a date, may have to face the fact that the man regards her as more sexually interested and available than if he had asked her out in the first place.

Although, according to the prevailing social norms, a woman does not generally initiate a date, it is acceptable for her to indicate interest in a man. There are a variety of verbal and nonverbal cues that let a man know of her interest (Muehlenhard, Koralewski, Andrews, and Burdick 1986). Among some of the more effective verbal cues are compliments, continuation rather than termination of a conversation, giving her telephone number, listening to a man without interrupting him, giving extended rather than terse answers to questions of the man, and responding to what a man says (laughing at his jokes and commenting on things he says). Nonverbal cues that indicate interest include maintaining eye contact, smiling a lot, leaning toward him, touching him, catching his eye while laughing at someone else's joke, and speaking in an animated way. All of these cues suggest an interest in dating the man. A woman can use all of them with impunity, but if she decides to initiate the date she faces the possibility of a misinterpretation of her character.

People not only differ in dating patterns because of ideological commitments (such as those of feminists), but also because of differing family backgrounds. For example, how does something like the death of a parent or the divorce of parents affect dating patterns? Three researchers who investigated these questions compared undergraduates from intact homes with those from homes where one parent had died and those from homes where the parents were divorced or permanently separated (Booth, Brinkerhoff, and White 1984). There were 2,538 students in the sample. The researchers discovered a number of differences among the three groups (figure 3.1). In essence, they found that parental divorce increases dating and sexual activity somewhat. The researchers noted that dating activity increased even more if there was a good deal of conflict during and after the divorce, and if the parent who kept the child remained single. In other words, students who had suffered the most with parental problems had the highest level of dating activity. They also reported less satisfaction with their relationships.

Why are the children of divorced parents likely to have higher levels of dating activity? One possible reason is that they are modeling the activity of their parents, who tend to have high levels of sexual activity and cohabitation. Also those who suffered more through their parents' divorce and report lower satisfaction with their own relationships may be determined not to repeat their parents' mistakes; consequently, they may be more critical about their own relationships. In any case, the point is that our dating patterns reflect not merely personal preference but our experiences in varying kinds of families.

Dating patterns also differ among various racial and ethnic groups. Black parents, for example, tend to exert more control over dating, particularly over their female children (Dornbusch, Carlsmith, Leiderman, Hastorf, Gross, and Ritter 1984). Black females tend to enter the dating world at a somewhat later age than their white counterparts because of this control. Another way in which black patterns differ is the expense-sharing noted above. Staples (1981:60–61) reported that it is not the women themselves, but black men who frequently expect and ask women to share the costs. Black women who expect a more traditional pattern label such men as stingy. Black women also complained to Staples about the passiveness of men, many of whom expect women not only to share costs but to initiate the date as well.

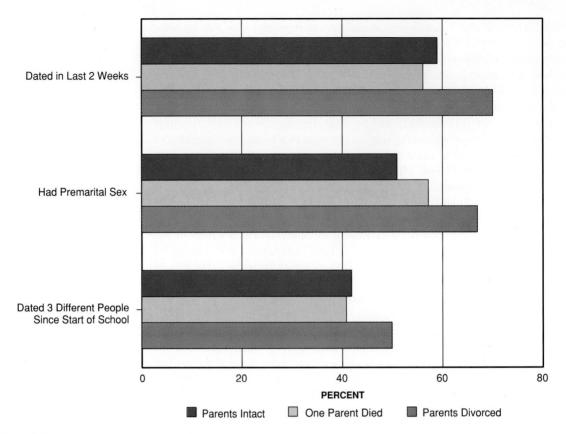

Figure 3.1 *Dating activity and parents' marriage.*
Source: Data from Booth, Brinkerhoff, and White 1984:88.

Dating Problems

Dating always has its problematic aspects. At the least, there is usually some anxiety about how well things will go and whether one's date will have a good time. But there are also serious problems that arise in dating. Unfortunately, dating can, and too frequently does, involve violence between the partners.

Violence in Dating

Violence is the use of force to injure or abuse someone. Violent behavior that occurs in dating situations includes pushing, grabbing, shoving, slapping, kicking, biting, hitting with the fist, and date rape (which we will discuss shortly). How much violence is there? Different studies report varying amounts (because local rather than national samples are usually involved). In one sample of 644 high school students, 12 percent said they had been involved in abusive behavior (Henton, Cate, Koval, Lloyd, and Christopher 1983). Another study reported that 35.5 percent of 256 high school students had experienced violence in a dating situation (O'Keefe, Brockopp, and Chew 1986). And more

Seeking Intimate Relationships

than 60 percent of the single people in still another sample said they had been either abused or abusive or aggressive when dating (Laner and Thompson 1982). Even if we use the lowest figure, we are talking about an enormous amount of violent behavior in dating throughout the nation.

Not everyone is equally likely to be a perpetrator or a victim. The rates for use of violence seem to be about the same for males and females, but females are recipients of more severe violent acts (Makepeace 1986). Females report more instances of sexual assaults, and physical and emotional injury than do males.

One study reported that those from high-income, white families and those who cohabit report higher levels of violence in their relationships than do others (Lane and Gwartney-Gibbs 1985). Researchers have also found that males who engage in violence in dating relationships are more likely to be in a longer-term relationship, and to have been punished harshly as a child; females who engage in violence are more likely than others to feel jealousy and to believe that they should have control over the relationship (DeMaris 1987; Stets and Pirog-Good 1987). Finally, those who experience violence in dating relationships tend to have more problems generally than others, including school, work, and drug abuse problems (Makepeace 1987).

What this all boils down to is that your likelihood of getting into a violent situation increases when you go out with a troubled individual or when your relationship gets more serious. Why should the likelihood increase in a more serious relationship? Perhaps because issues of power and control become more central, or because the intensity of the more intimate relationship enhances the intensity of reactions to frustrations and betrayals (Stets and Pirog-Good 1987:245).

Date Rape
Sexual aggression occurs frequently in dating. Sexual aggression refers to any kind of unwanted sexual activity, from kissing to sexual intercourse. In one survey of 635 college students, the researchers found that 77.6 percent of the women and 57.3 percent of the men admitted to having experienced some kind of sexual aggression in the dating situation (Muehlenhard and Linton, 1987). More than one out of four of the women reported a date touching her genitals under her clothes against her will, and more than one out of five said that she had been involved in unwanted sexual intercourse. Unwanted intercourse is rape, whatever the justification may have been for the act.

Forcible **rape** is attempted, or actual, sexual intercourse by the threat or use of force. Rape is one of the most severe forms of violence that occurs in dating. One of the myths of rape is that it occurs between strangers. But only about half of rapes are committed by a stranger; the rest are by acquaintances, friends, or relatives.

Muehlenhard (1988) asked a sample of undergraduates under what circumstances they would justify a man having sex with a woman against her wishes. The students were most likely to justify the act when the woman initiated the date, when they went to the man's apartment, and when the man paid the expenses. The male students were more likely to justify the rape than were the female students and were also more likely to misinterpret certain acts (like going to a man's apartment) as an indication of sexual interest on the part of the woman.

Clearly, one of the problems women encounter in dating situations is the tendency for men to justify violent behavior, including rape, under certain conditions. Attitudes that justify rape begin early in life, as illustrated by a survey of seventeen hundred sixth- to ninth-graders in Rhode Island.[1] Nearly a fourth of the boys and a sixth of the girls agreed that it was acceptable for a man to force a woman to have sex with him if he has spent money on her (clearly, feminists are correct in claiming that there is frequently an assumption that the woman owes the man who pays for a date). In addition, 51 percent of the boys and 41 percent of the girls said that a man has the right to force a woman to kiss him if he has spent a lot of money on her. And 65 percent of the boys and 57 percent of the girls in seventh through ninth grades said it is acceptable for a man to force a woman to have sex if they have been dating for more than six months!

As long as such attitudes continue, women will face a problem of sexual violence in dating situations. Many people's attitudes need to change in order to make violence unacceptable and maintain dating as an experience of recreation and romance.

Premarital Sex

We will discuss premarital sex again in chapter 6, when we talk about some of the problems and issues of teenage sex. Here we want to look at attitudes and behavior regarding premarital sex, which occurs largely in dating situations. What are the social expectations? What are our attitudes about premarital sex? And how much premarital sex is there?

The Double Standard

The double standard has long been a fixture of American society. That is, we do not expect the same behavior of females as of males. In terms of premarital sex, this means that boys traditionally were expected to have some experience while girls were expected to remain virgins until marriage. In his classic study of a small Missouri town, James West (1945:194) captured the essence of the double standard:

> It is expected . . . that most boys will acquire a limited amount of sexual experience before marriage, as they are expected to experiment with drinking and "running around." All these "outlaw traits" are associated with a young man's "sowing his wild oats." It is better if he sows his wild oats outside the community, if possible. . . . A girl who sows any wild oats, at home or abroad, is disgraced, and her parents are disgraced.

Has the double standard changed? To some extent it has. Premarital sexual activity is nearly as acceptable for females as for males. However, in an experimental study, three researchers reported that students asked to evaluate sexual activity rated a female, but not a male, more negatively if she had intercourse in a casual rather than a steady dating relationship or as a teenager rather than as a young woman of twenty-one (Sprecher, McKinney, and Orbuch 1987). The researchers believe that this means we have a "transitional" double standard. We are moving toward equality of expectations, but haven't quite gotten there yet.

Changing Attitudes

Although the double standard accepted the fact that most boys would have premarital sexual experience, it did not mean that such behavior was considered ideal. Surveys conducted in 1937 and 1959 reported that only 30 percent of the respondents agreed that premarital sex was "all right" for a man, and 22 percent agreed that it was "all right" for a woman (Hyde 1986:312). Such attitudes have changed rapidly in the last few decades, however. In Gallup polls, the percentage of respondents who agreed that premarital sex is "not wrong" rose from 21 percent in 1969 to 43 percent in 1973, 52 percent in 1985, then down again to 48 percent in 1987 (*Gallup Report* #263, August, 1987). The proportion believing that premarital sex is not wrong varies by a number of factors, including sex, age, education, and religion (figure 3.2).

The more religious people are, the less likely they are to approve of premarital sex.

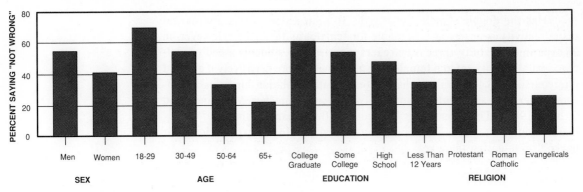

Figure 3.2 *Proportion agreeing that premarital sex is not wrong.*
Source: Data from *Gallup Report* #263, August 1987:21.

It is interesting that a majority of Catholics agreed that premarital sex is "not wrong" in the 1987 poll. Officially, the Catholic Church continues to teach that premarital relationships are a sin. A 1976 declaration from the Congregation for the Doctrine of the Faith noted that many people now justify premarital sex in cases where people intend to marry and where they have an affection for each other that is like that in the marital state. But even in those cases, sex "is contrary to Christian doctrine which states that every genital act must be within the framework of marriage" (quoted in Hyde 1986:609).

Evangelical Christians, the elderly, and those who live in the South are the least likely to affirm that premarital sex is all right. The young are particularly accepting. A survey of over 1,000 adolescent girls, aged twelve to eighteen years, reported that most did not consider premarital sex a sin even if they did not want to engage in it themselves (Konopka 1983). College students have reported that they prefer partners for dating who are moderately experienced sexually (Jacoby and Williams 1985).

Attitudes about sex also differ depending on the stage of the dating (Roche 1986). In the earlier stages of dating, males expect sexual intimacy sooner than do females. Females tend to link sexual relations with commitment in the relationship. So early on, males and females have different attitudes about what is appropriate. In later stages, when dating involves an exclusive relationship with one person with whom one is in love, there are no differences between males and females; both tend to approve of sexual relations under such circumstances.

Changing Behavior

Attitudes do not necessarily reflect behavior. That is, because people approve of premarital sex does not mean that they are actually engaging in it. How much premarital sexual behavior actually occurs, and how does the amount now compare with the past?

Seeking Intimate Relationships

Table 3.1	Premarital Sexual Activity among Women Aged 15–19: 1971–1982

	Proportion Sexually Active
1971	30.4
1976	43.4
1979	49.8
1982	44.9

Sandra L. Hofferth, et al., "Premarital Sexual Activity Among U.S. Teenage Women Over the Past Three Decades," *Family Planning Perspectives*, Vol. 19: No. 2, pp. 46–53, March/April 1987. © The Alan Guttmacher Institute.

Extent of Premarital Sex

We pointed out in chapter 1 that the amount of premarital sex has increased considerably in recent decades. In the famous Kinsey studies of the 1940s, the data showed that about a third of all females and 71 percent of all males had premarital sexual relations by the age of 25 (Hyde 1986:306). By the 1970s, the proportions had risen dramatically. Table 3.1 shows the incidence among teenaged women living in metropolitan areas (the first three are from the National Surveys of Young Women; the 1982 figure is from the National Survey of Family Growth). Like attitudes, premarital behavior may be in a somewhat more conservative pattern in the 1980s. Some people may be choosing to abstain from sex until after marriage for fear of contracting a sexually transmitted disease or because they are convinced that this is a better course for them to follow personally. Of course, the important point is that whether to engage or not engage in premarital sex is a personal decision. A student who decided to wait until marriage for sex told us how she handled it:

> I'm up front with the guys I date. I tell them that I don't have hangups. I really look forward to sex. But I just believe that it should wait until marriage. That turns some guys off. At first, I was troubled by some guys that I liked who didn't want to date me anymore because of my attitude. But I decided that if a guy didn't respect me for my stand on sex, we probably shouldn't be together anyway.

Although some young women, and young men as well, opt for abstinence, the amount of premarital sexual activity is quite high. About two-thirds of American women have sexual intercourse before marriage.[2] Nearly half of women married in the early 1960s were virgins at the time of marriage; only 21 percent of those married between 1975 and 1979 were virgins.

Premarital Sex and Equity

Whether sex occurs when dating depends on a number of factors. In the last chapter, we noted the importance of equity in relationships. The relationships that are most likely to be defined as satisfying happen when the partners perceive equity or a slight amount of under- or overbenefit. We would expect that the more the partners define a relationship as satisfying, the more likely they are to engage in sexual relations. In fact, this is what happens.

Those who are in fairly equitable relationships have the most sexual intercourse (Walster, Walster, and Traupmann 1978). Those who feel either greatly underbenefitted or greatly overbenefited are more likely to stop before "going all the way." And if they do have sex, they are less likely to do so because both of them want it. The equity of the relationship, then, is an important factor in whether sexual intercourse occurs.

Premarital Sex and Social Background

As in the case of dating patterns, premarital sexual patterns vary depending on different social background factors. *Race* is one of those factors. Data from the 1982 National Survey of Family Growth show that 45 percent of Hispanic women, 35 percent of white women, and 9 percent of black women waited until marriage to have sexual intercourse.[3] The survey also found that black women tend to have a longer period of sexual activity before marriage than do white women. Twenty-six percent of black women and 11 percent of white women became sexually active five or more years before marrying.

Family background is another factor that causes variation in premarital sexual activity. Styles of parenting as well as the parents' marital status affect the likelihood of engaging in premarital sex. Although young people have more permissive sexual attitudes and behavioral patterns than their parents, children tend to reflect the attitudes of their parents. Thus, mothers with more permissive attitudes are likely to have children who are more sexually active (Thornton and Camburn 1987:323–40).

In addition to their attitudes, the way that parents discipline their children is important. A study of 2,423 adolescents aged fifteen to eighteen reported that sexual activity was highest among those young people who perceived their parents as having few or no rules or as not being at all strict (Miller, McCoy, Olson, and Wallace 1986). Sexual activity was lowest among those who perceived their parents as moderately strict. Those who reported very strict parents with many rules indicated a level of sexual activity between the other two groups. These results are in accord with others that show that both severe and permissive discipline are likely to lead to more deviant behavior than a moderately strict home environment.

Clearly, both the attitudes of parents and their manner of relating to the child are important factors. This is underscored by the results of a national survey of fifteen– and sixteen–year olds (Moore, Peterson, and Furstenberg 1986). The researchers found that the daughters of parents with traditional attitudes, who talked to them about sex, are less likely than others to be sexually active. This study defined parents with more traditional attitudes as those who tended to agree that marriages are better when the husband works and the wife takes care of the home and children, that children are better off if their mothers do not work, and that children develop permanent emotional problems when their parents divorce.

One other important factor related to family background is the marital status of the parents. We saw that dating patterns differed somewhat among the children of the divorced as compared with children from intact homes or homes where a parent had died. Sexual activity also varies. Women from divorced families (including those where the custodial parent has remarried) report significantly more sexual activity than those from intact families (Kinnaird and Gerrard 1986).

Courtship

Courtship is the process whereby two people agree to commit themselves to marriage. While finding a mate is only one of the functions of dating (and not all dating), dating is obviously a part of courtship. In this section we will look at factors that make it likely that a relationship will move into courtship, the importance of courtship, and some differing patterns of courtship.

Moving into Courtship

What makes it likely that dating will turn into courtship? Actually the same factors discussed in chapter 2 that sustain and enhance an intimate relationship are operative among those couples who move into courtship. For example, equity, the growth of trust, an increasing amount of self-disclosure, and the development of shared attitudes and values characterize courtship. In a longitudinal study, Stephen (1985) reported that as couples move into and through courtship they become more alike in a variety of attitudes, beliefs, and values. They seem to be constructing a shared and unique world of their own. Couples who fail to do this are more likely to break up.

Thus, courtship means that the process of building an intimate relationship is continuing. The couple that moves from casual dating into courtship is constructing a more intense intimacy than is otherwise possible.

The Length of Courtship

To say that courtship is a process means that it takes place over a period of time. How much time? And does it make any difference? The authors personally know of couples who met and were married in as few as twenty-eight days and had satisfying marriages for the rest of their lives. We know of others who courted for years before marriage, and eventually divorced, but they are the exceptions. Generally, a marriage is less likely to succeed if there is a very short courtship.

A study of fifty-one middle-aged, married women investigated marital satisfaction and length of courtship (Grover, Russell, Schumm, and Paff-Bergen 1985). All of the women were in their first marriage. Their ages ranged from thirty-two to seventy-one, and they had been married an average of twenty-three years. The researchers divided the women into four groups according to the amount of time spent in courtship (dating prior to engagement or marriage): five months or less, six to eleven months, one to two years, and more than two years. The amount of satisfaction with the marriage went up in each group; those who courted more than two years were the happiest with their marriages.

Of course, some of those who had dated for less than six months were also happy in their marriages. But they also were more likely to admit regret over having married, to say that their spouses got on their nerves, and to acknowledge some degree of dissatisfaction with the marriage. It seems then that the longer a couple goes together, the less likely they are to discover hidden incompatibilities after marriage.

Patterns of Courtship

Although people may move through courtship in very different ways, there are a number of typical steps associated with the process (King and Christensen 1983):

1. Mutual attraction leads to an increase in interaction and communication.

2. The two partners are defined as a couple by themselves and by relatives, friends, and acquaintances.

3. The partners declare their love to each other and agree to an exclusive relationship.

4. The couple discuss the future of their relationship and joke or dream about the possibility of marriage.

5. The two people coordinate their activities, financial resources, and schedules so that they can function as a couple in important matters.

6. The two people make a final commitment to each other, and may begin to cohabit and/or plan a wedding.

Courtship moves through a number of stages before people finally make a commitment to each other.

Even among those who go through this typical pattern, there may be differences. Surra (1985) examined the courtship patterns of thirty couples who had been married ten months or less. She asked about their perceptions of the likelihood of marriage and their activities at various stages of their relationships. She found four patterns of courtship: the accelerated, the accelerated-arrested, the intermediate, and the prolonged type.

In the accelerated type, the couple moved quickly and smoothly to marriage. Such couples tended increasingly to share tasks (shopping, housework, etc.) and leisure activities and to isolate themselves to some extent from other people. The accelerated-arrested pattern also involved sharing of tasks and leisure activities, but couples in this pattern had some doubts at the point of engagement. At that point, they tended to revert back somewhat to more individual activities. As a result, the engagement period was longer, amounting to nearly 60 percent of the overall courtship process.

In the intermediate courtship pattern, the partners tended to stay more involved with their individual activities and shared fewer tasks. Their courtship lasted a bit longer than the first two types. Finally, the prolonged pattern involved a very long courtship, as much as six to seven years. About 65 percent of that time was spent in serious dating, however, and 22 percent in engagement. Those in the prolonged pattern increased their sharing of tasks, though not as much as those in the first two groups. Those in the prolonged pattern also maintained more of their individual activities than did the others.

Bundling

In eighteenth century, colonial America, **bundling**—two people sleeping without undressing on the same bed—was a common practice. Bundling provided a place to sleep for travelers (for whom there was a scarcity of available beds) and for young people who were courting. For example, a young man who visited a young woman during a severe New England winter needed a place to sleep for the night. It would hardly be possible for him, if he traveled any distance at all, to return over the rough, snow-covered roads at night. He would, therefore, bundle with the young woman. This would also give the couple the opportunity to talk and get to know each other better.

Any sexual activity, of course, was forbidden. The couple was not even supposed to embrace. The records of premarital pregnancy and the tirades of preachers testify to the fact that the rules were frequently broken. Eventually, moral opposition led to the demise of the practice. The following is a commentary by an early historian (Stiles 1871:50–53) on the practice and its consequences for the Connecticut colonists, who, pointed out the historian, had multiplied to an "incredible" degree:

> This amazing increase may, indeed, be partly ascribed to a singular custom prevalent among them, commonly known by the name of bundling—a superstitious rite observed by the young people of both sexes, with which they usually terminated their festivities, and which was kept up with religious strictness by the more bigoted and vulgar part of the community. This ceremony was likewise, in those primitive times, considered as an indispensable preliminary to matrimony. . . . To this sagacious custom do I chiefly attribute the unparalleled increase of the Yankee tribe; for it is a certain fact, well authenticated by court records and parish registers, that wherever the practice of bundling prevailed, there was an

Engagement

The final phase of courtship is generally the engagement period. At one time, we could have considered engagement as a postcourtship period, because once people were engaged the commitment to marriage was nearly irreversible. But by the time of Burgess and Wallin's (1953) study of one thousand engaged couples, the researchers found that between a third and a half of the couples had more than one engagement before they were married. Engagement, in other words, is a kind of last testing period before the commitment to marry is finalized.

During the engagement period, a couple has an opportunity to closely examine their relationship. They can get a better picture of how each behaves in a variety of situations, including the somewhat stressful task of planning and executing a wedding. They have an opportunity to interact more closely with future in-laws, and to get a sense of the expectations of the fiancé(e) about relationships with future in-laws.

amazing number of sturdy brats annually born unto the state.

Hear also that learned divine, the Rev. Samuel Peters, who thus discourseth at length upon the custom of bundling:

Notwithstanding the modesty of the females is such that it would be accounted the greatest rudeness for a gentleman to speak before a lady of a garter, knee, or leg, yet it is thought but a piece of civility to ask her to bundle, a custom as old as the first settlement in 1634. It is certainly innocent, virtuous and prudent, or the puritans would not have permitted it to prevail among their offspring. . . . People who are influenced more by lust, than a serious faith in God, ought never to bundle. . . . I am no advocate for temptation; yet must say, that bundling has prevailed 160 years in New England, and, I verily believe, with ten times more chastity than the sitting on a sofa.

Clearly, the historian was appalled by the practice and by the minister's defense of it. Most ministers, however, did not defend the practice. In fact, they took steps to eliminate it. A Massachusetts minister, the Rev. Jason Haven, pastored a church in which bundling and, consequently, premarital pregnancy, was very common. He finally acted:

Mr. Haven, in a long and memorable discourse, sought out the cause of the growing sin, and suggested the proper remedy. He attributed the frequent recurrence of the fault to the custom then prevalent, of females admitting young men to their beds, who sought their company with intentions of marriage. And he exhorted all to abandon that custom, and no longer expose themselves to temptations which so many were found unable to resist. . . . The females blushed and hung down their heads. The men, too, hung down their heads, and now and then looked out from under their fallen eyebrows, to observe how others supported the attack. If the outward appearance of the assembly was somewhat composed, there was a violent internal agitation in many minds. . . . The custom was abandoned. The sexes learned to cultivate the proper degree of delicacy in their intercourse, and instances of unlawful cohabitation in this town since that time have been extremely rare (Stiles 1871:78–79).

In a sense, then, an engagement is a final countdown period in which potential problem areas can be detected before the union is finalized. This is not to say that every couple uses the engagement period in such a productive way. But judging from the number of people who have more than one engagement, a considerable number of couples use the time for a more intensive examination of their potential for a happy union.

Cohabitation

Technically, cohabitation is also a part of courtship for many couples. We will examine it separately because it has become a common method of establishing an intimate relationship, increasing rapidly since 1970 (table 3.2). In fact, cohabitation may now be the most typical path to marriage. (However, we

Table 3.2 Number of Unmarried Couples Living Together: 1970–1987 (in thousands)

	1970	1980	1985	1987
Number of couples	523	1589	1983	2334
Number with children under 15	196	431	603	720

Source: U.S. Bureau of the Census 1988:42 and 1989:44.

should note that for some people cohabitation has become an alternative to marriage.) Examination of marriages in an Oregon county found an increase from 13 percent in 1970 to 53 percent of cohabitation prior to marriage (Gwartney-Gibbs 1986). And a 1987 national survey reported that 44 percent of those married between 1980 and 1984, and 58 percent of those who had remarried, had cohabited.[4]

Who Cohabits?

Not everyone is equally likely to cohabit. Those who are very religious are less likely than others. Compared with noncohabitors, those who cohabit are likely to have earlier and more sexual experience (Newcomb 1986). The most systematic and large-scale comparison is provided by Tanfer (1987). Using data from a 1983 national survey of twenty- to twenty-nine-year-old never-married women, she found that cohabitors, compared to noncohabitors, tend to:

Have less education (45.9 percent of those with less than twelve years and 22.2 percent of those with more than twelve years of education cohabited)

Have no religion (48 percent, compared with a little over 28 percent of Protestants and Catholics who cohabited)

Tend not to be working (48.4 percent; 27.1 percent worked and 25.3 percent were in school)

Live in large, urban areas (38 percent live in cities of 100,000 or more)

She also noted that rates of cohabitation are much higher in the West (43.6 percent) than other regions of the country (between 25 and 29 percent).

Tanfer also looked for any attitudinal differences between cohabitors and noncohabitors. She found very few. Cohabitors, as we would expect, have less conventional attitudes about marriage. Interestingly enough, however, 31.7 percent of those who had ever cohabited, 34.7 percent of those currently cohabiting, but only 26.9 percent of those who had never cohabited said that they wish they were married.

Patterns of Cohabitation

We have noted that while some people cohabit as a kind of trial marriage, others do not. There are varying reasons for cohabiting and various kinds of arrangements that people make. In terms of the purpose of cohabitation, Ridley, Peterman, and Avery (1978) identify four types. The "*Linus blanket*" type (based on the popular *Peanuts* cartoon) is a relationship in which one of the partners is highly dependent and/or insecure. Such a person may prefer any kind of relationship to being alone. This relationship is unlikely to endure, because the nondependent partner will probably weary of the endless needs of the other.

In a relationship of *emancipation,* one or both partners use the cohabitation to gain independence from parental values and influence. They may, for instance, come from a sexually repressive home and use cohabitation in order to establish their own sexual values. In any case, the focus tends to be on the relationship with the parents rather than with the partner. The partner tends to be an instrument used for other purposes. A genuine intimate relationship is difficult to develop under such circumstances.

A relationship of *convenience* is the third type. The man generally wants a sexual relationship and someone to care for his home. The woman acquires a sexual relationship, a place to live, and financial care—the same things she would get in a traditional marriage, but without as much security. In this kind of relationship, it is usually the man who is opposed to the idea of marriage.

Finally, there is the *testing* relationship, cohabitation that is a trial marriage. The two partners are committed to each other and may be contemplating marriage. They decide to cohabit as a final testing of their relationship. If it works, they will marry.

These four types are a useful way to categorize cohabiting relationships. But they do not capture the full variety of patterns. They focus on motives, purposes, and styles of relating. We could also categorize relationships according to whether they include children or not. As table 3.2 shows, there were 720,000 couples cohabiting in 1987 who had children under the age of fifteen in their home. What difference does having children make in the cohabiting relationship? The question has not yet been addressed by research.

Finally, we could discuss differing patterns of relationships among heterosexual and homosexual partners. Some research has been conducted that examines the differences between cohabiting heterosexual, **gay** (male homosexual), and **lesbian** (female homosexual) couples. In terms of the quality of the relationship, as measured by a scale of marital satisfaction, there is little overall difference among the three types of couples (Kurdick and Schmitt 1986). Rather, all three types of couples seem to go through similar stages of their relationship. In the first year, the *blending stage,* the partners tend to be "head over heels" in love and there is a good deal of sexual activity. In the *nesting stage,* the second and third years, there is a decline in the intensity of their passion, the emergence of some doubts about the relationship, and an emphasis on homemaking and finding compatibility in the relationship. Finally, the *maintaining stage* occurs during the fourth and fifth years. The couple now establishes certain traditions and typical patterns (such as ways of dealing with conflict).

In the research by Kurdick and Schmitt (1986), the stage was more important than the type of couple in determining relationship quality. This does not mean, however, that there were no differences among the couples. In their large-scale study of American couples, Blumstein and Schwartz (1983) looked at the areas of money, work, and sex. They found numerous differences between cohabiting heterosexual, gay, and lesbian couples (as well as married couples). We will give a few examples. With respect to money, they asked couples how often they fought over money management. Lesbians fought less than either gay or heterosexual couples. When asked about the extent to which the couples were relationship-centered or work-centered, 30 percent of the heterosexuals, 27 percent of the gays, and 41 percent of the lesbians said that both partners were relationship-centered. Finally, regarding the frequency of sexual relations, results varied depending on the number of years the couple had been together. But the lesbians had far less sex than gays or heterosexuals. In fact, 47 percent of lesbians who had been together for ten years or more reported having sex once a month or less (compared to 33 percent of gay couples; data were not available for cohabiting heterosexuals who were together more than ten years).

In sum, cohabitation is not the same experience for everyone. The nature of any individual's experience depends on such things as the motives and purposes of the two partners, the length of time the two have been together, and whether the relationship is heterosexual or homosexual.

Cohabitation Compared with Marriage

For many couples, cohabitation is a testing ground for marriage. How accurate is the test? How much is marriage like cohabitation? Married and cohabiting couples face the same kinds of problems—money, sex, division of labor in the home, and so forth. Nevertheless, just as there are differences among varying kinds of cohabitors, there are differences between the experiences of marriage and cohabitation.

Interestingly, Kurdek and Schmitt (1986) found that the married couples in their sample reported less tension than any of the three kinds of cohabiting couples. A study of communication patterns in married and in cohabiting couples reported that the younger married couples were more communicative and more satisfied than the younger cohabiting couples (Yelsma 1986).

On the other hand, Rotkin (1983) studied twenty married and twenty cohabiting graduate student couples and found that the married couples tended to give higher priority than the cohabiting couples to the male's career. This involved the woman's willingness to make her own aspirations and plans secondary in the case of any decisions that affected the male's career. Cohabiting couples who were not planning to marry were more egalitarian, giving equal weight to the career aspirations of both the male and the female.

Finally, the experience of marriage differs in some ways from that of cohabitation in the areas of money, work, and sex. Once again, we can illustrate the differences by reference to the three questions noted above from the research of Blumstein and Schwartz (1983). With regard to conflict over money management, the researchers found that married couples fight more than the cohabiting couples. Only 23 percent said that they never fight about money management, compared with 31 percent of heterosexual cohabitors, 26 percent of gays, and 31 percent of lesbians. On the question about work, the married couples tended to be more work-centered (rather than relationship-centered) than any of the cohabiting groups. And in the matter of frequency of sex, married couples reported a lower frequency than the heterosexual cohabitors and gays, but higher than the lesbians.

The differences noted above are not generally dramatic ones. One could argue, therefore, that cohabitation provides a reasonably good testing ground for marriage. People face up to the same kinds of problems. They have many of the same kinds of experiences, though with differing degrees of intensity. How well, then, has cohabitation prepared those couples who eventually marry?

Cohabitation as a Preparation for Marriage

One way to test the extent to which cohabitation helps people to have a more satisfying marriage is to look at the rate of marital breakup between those who cohabited and those who did not. James White (1987, 1989) did this for a sample of 10,472 Canadians. Among those who had cohabited, about 40 percent eventually married. He found a negative effect on marital stability for those who cohabited with only one person and subsequently married that person. For others, cohabitation had no effect on marital stability. A study of Swedish women, on the other hand, reported that those who cohabited have an almost 80 percent higher marital breakup rate than those who did not cohabit (Bennett, Blanc, and Bloom 1988). The higher rate only applied to the first seven years of marriage, however. Those married eight years or more had similar breakup rates whether or not they had cohabited.

And what of Americans? First, available studies are not consistent. Some have found little or no difference between those who cohabit and those who don't (Watson and DeMeo 1987). But DeMaris and Leslie (1984) reported that those who cohabited among their survey of 309 recently married couples had a lower degree of marital satisfaction. In addition, two researchers who interviewed a random sample of thirteen thousand Americans in 1987 found that, after ten years of marriage, 53 percent of those who had cohabited but only 28 percent of those who had never cohabited, were divorced.[5]

At best, then, according to the American studies, cohabitation brings no advantage to those who desire a stable and satisfying marriage. At worst, cohabitors may be at a disadvantage according to an increasing amount of research. It isn't clear why there should be a disadvantage. It may be that those who opt for cohabitation are less committed to the idea of marriage in the first place (DeMaris and Leslie 1984) found that women who had cohabited perceived the quality of commitment in their marriage as lower than did those who had not cohabited). At any rate, in spite of growing numbers, and in spite of the logic of cohabitation as a testing and training ground for marriage, the research suggests that noncohabitors are more likely than cohabitors to have a satisfying and stable marriage.

Breaking Up

As noted earlier, a good many of those who eventually marry will have been engaged more than once prior to marriage. And most people are in more than one serious relationship before marriage. That means that most people have the painful experience of breaking up.

Most people have the painful experience of breaking an intimate relationship.

Who Breaks Up?

On the basis of factors we have discussed that keep a relationship going, we could make some reasonable inferences about when a relationship is likely to break up. If, for instance, there is perceived inequity, or the lack of self-disclosure, or the absence of other factors that enhance intimacy, we would expect a relationship not to last.

But there may be other factors as well. Simpson (1987) surveyed 222 undergraduate students about people they were dating. He gathered data about such things as satisfaction with the relationship, closeness, sexual relationships, and perceived ease of finding a different partner. Three months later, he again surveyed the students to see if they were still dating the same person. Those who were still together differed from those who had broken up on five measures. At the time of the first survey, those who stayed together indicated greater satisfaction with the relationship. They had been dating their partner a longer period of time. They had sexual relations with the partner. They had a more difficult time conceiving of a desirable alternative partner. Finally, they tended to have an exclusive relationship. Clearly, those who stayed together had a lot of positive factors at work in their relationship at the time of the first survey.

Responding to Deterioration

There are a variety of ways that people can react when the quality of a relationship deteriorates. Rusbult (1987) has identified four kinds of responses: exit, voice, loyalty, and neglect. *Exit* refers to a response of withdrawal or threatened withdrawal from the relationship. Those who decide to stop going or living together, to try being "just friends" instead of lovers, or to stop seeing each other altogether have chosen the response of exit.

Voice is the response of facing up to, and trying to talk through, the problems. Discussion, compromise, counseling, and efforts to change oneself or one's partner are ways of dealing with the problems by voice. *Loyalty* is the response of staying with the partner in spite of the problems. Those who opt for loyalty do not try to resolve the problems; they simply try to endure them. They may believe that the situation will improve in time. They may insist that they must have faith in the relationship and the partner.

Finally, *neglect* is a refusal to face the problems and a willingness to let the relationship die. Some examples of behavior that fit the category of neglect are

> ignoring the partner or spending less time together, refusing to discuss problems, treating the partner badly emotionally or physically, criticizing the partner for things unrelated to the real problem, "just letting things fall apart," chronically complaining without offering solutions to problems . . . (Rusbult 1987:213).

As Rusbult notes, the terms used may be a little misleading. Voice does not refer only to talking. Rather, voice represents active and constructive reactions. Exit refers to active and destructive behavior. Loyalty is passive, constructive behavior. And neglect is passive, destructive behavior.

The Birth, Life, and Death of a Relationship

Frank is a graduate student whose account of a relationship illustrates many of the points we made in this chapter and chapter 2. When Frank came face to face with a problem that he believed too great for the relationship to continue, he used the response of exit:

> I enjoy working out at a local health spa. One day while running around the track I saw a very physically attractive female. She had an excellent build, a tan, and blond hair. I decided to talk to her as we ran. After chatting a bit, I took a risk and asked her if she would be interested in getting some yogurt. She responded with an enthusiastic "yes."
>
> I was dating a few other women at the time. But I wasn't really interested in developing an intimate relationship with any of them. But I wanted to get more involved. I was ready for an intimate relationship. I thought this beautiful blond woman might be the one.
>
> We hit it off really well from the beginning. I found it easy to talk to her. I felt very comfortable being with her. We both shared things about our families, values, school, work, and other interests. We sat at the table in the yogurt shop for an hour. As we were leaving, I asked her if she would like to go out some night for dinner. Again, she said "yes" enthusiastically. And she gave me a hug. That hug, along with her facial expressions and the way she looked at me told me that she was interested in getting to know me better.
>
> For the next month, we dated three or four times a week. We went to the beach, the mountains, parks, movies, dinner, and sometimes we just went to her place or mine and talked

Differing personalities will prefer different responses, but there are also other reasons for selecting a response (Rusbult 1987:227–28). Research has shown that people exit when they believe that they have nothing to lose by doing so and that the relationship is not worth saving. A combination of dissatisfaction with the relationship, a sense of minimal investment in the relationship, and a belief that there are good alternatives will make exit a likely response. Exit tends to be used more by younger people in relationships that have been going on for only a short time.

Voice is a response that is appropriate when the relationship is valued but in danger. People who have been satisfied with the relationship and invested themselves in it are more likely to try the response of voice. Females are more likely than males to use voice.

Loyalty is an effort to maintain the status quo. People who have been satisfied with the relationship, feel invested in it, perceive few or no better about our lives and our aspirations. I fell head-over-heels in love with her. I bought her clothes, flowers, cards—all kinds of things to let her know how I felt. Being in love with her made me feel more satisfied, more secure, and more peaceful.

It turned out that we had similar political, religious, and social perspectives. And we were in the same graduate program, though at different universities. We had a lot to talk about, and the more we talked the more we realized how much alike we were. The relationship soon became sexual, and that deepened our love for each other. I had truly found the intimate relationship that I had wanted.

After a month, we agreed to date each other exclusively. I felt a growing commitment to her. We only lived about a mile apart, so we began to spend most of our evenings together. It was a natural thing to make the decision to live together. I felt that we had the "chemistry" necessary to make the thing go. And I believed that living together would deepen our commitment and our intimacy.

I moved into her apartment. We then had to figure out the finances. We agreed on a plan for paying specific items like rent and food. Everything seemed to be going well. Then, about a month after I had moved in with her, I found out that she had problems with cocaine. She had somehow kept that part of her life separate from me. I asked her to stop snorting the stuff and to get treatment. She refused. I felt betrayed. I asked her what or who was first in her life. I was stunned when she said it was the cocaine.

I was in agony. I had a lot of beautiful memories already, and we had only known each other for a few months. But as she became more irresponsible with her money and failed to pay specific bills, our relationship deteriorated. Finally, I decided to simply walk away from the relationship. That was tough, because I had really committed myself to her and I expected this to be a long-term relationship. But she had made it clear that I was not her first commitment in life. Maybe I should have tried to stay and help her. But I thought I knew her, and I guess I never really did.

alternatives, and believe the problems are relatively minor may opt for loyalty. Loyalty tends to be used more by older people who have been in a relationship for a longer period of time. Females are also more likely than males to use loyalty.

Neglect is a destructive response that is used by those who don't know how to mend the relationship and are probably not motivated to do so in any case. Neglect is more common when both satisfaction and investment in the relationship have been low. Males are more likely than females to use neglect.

In using the terms *constructive* and *destructive,* we should beware of a tendency to think that it is always bad for relationships to break up. It is generally always painful, but it is not always bad. There are relationships that are destructive to the individuals involved. They *should* break up. Each case must be judged on its own merits in order to determine whether staying together or breaking up is best for the individuals involved.

PRINCIPLES FOR ENHANCING INTIMACY

1. If you are dating for purposes of potential mate selection, do not make the mistake of looking for perfection. As Sills (1984) points out, we sometimes sabotage ourselves by limiting our choices. From a field of ten, we only will date the top two. Even if two of the ten are totally unacceptable to us, this still leaves six remaining possibilities whom we also reject. Sills suggests that a mate could probably be found among the six, while a status symbol will be found in those top two.

2. If you are female, support equality in relationships, and are attracted to a certain male, ask him for a date. This is one way to overcome his shyness or to find out quickly whether or not he is interested in you. However, do recognize that some people may label your actions as aggressive, unfeminine, or even as a sexual come-on.

3. Because violence is an all too frequent occurrence in dating, avoid relationships with troubled individuals. And if violence should occur, don't persist in the relationship and do seek the aid and advice of a parent, friend, or counselor.

4. Premarital sex should be a matter of personal choice. Never allow yourself to be pressured or threatened into engaging in sex. It is a serious decision that demands responsible and mature behavior. One approach is to think through the decision before the occasion arises. Read as much on the topic as you can. Talk to your parents, another family member, trusted counselor, or friend. Determine what your personal values, inclinations, and concerns are. Then you are ready to decide.

5. Longer courtships generally result in more satisfying marriages. Get to know the person you plan to marry; that is, find out about his or her values, interests, goals, patterns of behavior, and familial relationships. Every indicator suggests that this will improve your chances for a successful and lasting marriage.

6. Although the breaking up of a relationship is often a painful process, it is also often a necessary and, in the long run, a beneficial one.

Seeking Intimate Relationships

Getting involved begins with the dating process. People find dates at school, work, in singles bars, and through friends, newspaper ads, and dating services. We select dating partners because we find them attractive in one way or another.

Dating has numerous functions, including recreation, companionship, gaining status, socialization, and mate selection. Every society has norms about dating that regulates such things as who initiates the date. Patterns of dating will differ, however, among various groups in the society. Violence occurs in many dating situations. Three-fourths of women and over half of men say they have experienced some kind of sexual aggression during a date.

Sexual activity on dates is now nearly as acceptable for females as it is for males. About half of the people polled believe premarital sex is not wrong, though the proportion varies by such things as sex, age, family background, education, and religion. By the 1980s, about two-thirds of American women reported having sexual intercourse before marriage.

Courtship is the process in which two people agree to commit themselves to marriage. The factors that enhance an intimate relationship, such as self-disclosure, are also likely to move a relationship into courtship. Generally, a longer courtship is associated with a more stable marriage. The final phase of courtship is the engagement, which is a final testing period of the relationship. Somewhere between a third and a half of people have more than one engagement before marrying.

Cohabitation is a part of the courtship process for some people and an alternative to marriage for others. About half of those who marry have cohabited before marriage. Cohabitors tend to be less religious, less well educated, and living in large, urban areas. Women who cohabit tend not to be employed. There are various types of cohabitation, including the "Linus blanket," emancipation, convenience, and testing relationships. The kind of experience one has in cohabiting depends on such things as the motives involved, the length of time the partners have been together, and whether the relationship is heterosexual or homosexual. Contrary to popular thought, there is no evidence that cohabitation is a good preparation for marriage.

The breakup of a relationship is a common experience. Four ways that people respond to a deteriorating relationship are exit (leaving), voice (confronting and attempting to work through problems), loyalty (sticking it out), and neglect (refusal to admit problems, allowing the relationship to die).

---

1. Reported in *San Diego Union,* May 3, 1988.

2. *Family Planning Perspectives* 17 (September/October, 1985):222.

3. Ibid.

4. *San Diego Union,* April 23, 1988.

5. Ibid.

4

Falling in Love

When *Psychology Today* sought readers' views on love and romance, one of the questions asked was, "What do you look for in your relationship with your partner?" (Rubenstein 1983). The most popular response was love (figure 4.1), followed by companionship, and then other things. But if you look for love, what exactly is it you're really seeking? What does it mean to love? We use the term in many different ways, obviously. We say that we love pizza, love our new car, love to ski, love our parents, love our spouses, and so forth.

In this chapter, we will try to bring some clarity to this "love" that people agree is so important in their lives. We will discuss the multifaceted nature of loving another person. We will look at the different ways of loving. And we will examine one of the barriers to a loving relationship—jealousy.

The Meaning of Love

When we use the same word to express our feelings for food, activities, possessions, and people, it is little wonder that it is difficult to define what we mean by love. When applied to a lover or spouse, the term means, among other things, a deep and passionate affection. But there is more to love than passion. In fact, there is more to love than feelings.

We all need and look for love.

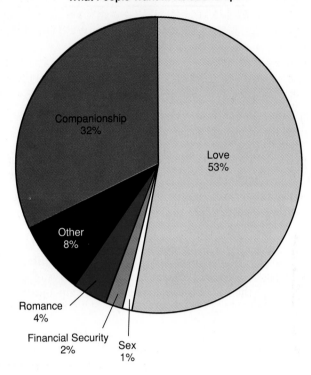

What People Want in Relationships

Love
53%

Companionship
32%

Other
8%

Romance
4%

Financial Security
2%

Sex
1%

Figure 4.1 *What people want in relationships.*
Source: Data from Rubenstein 1983:46.

The richness of the term *love* is illustrated by four ancient Greek words that are all translated as love (Lewis 1960). *Storge* (pronounced store-gay) is the kind of love found in the affection between parents and their children. It is, Lewis (1960:54) pointed out, the least discriminating kind of love, because "almost anyone can become an object of affection: the ugly, the stupid, even the exasperating." As such, it is to be cherished, because it is love in spite of the lack of those qualities we discussed earlier as the main factors in attraction.

The second word is *philia* (fill-ee-ah). It is the kind of love that exists between friends. To the Greeks, this was the highest form of love, for philia referred to a warm and close relationship with the characteristics of intimacy we have discussed—sharing, affection, and commitment. It is an intense sharing between two people who have similar perspectives on life.

Eros (air-os) is the third love. Eros, from which we get "erotic," is love between men and women. It includes sexual love. Aristotle said that eros makes people long to be in each other's presence. In other words, eros is more than lust. It is more than a desire for sex. It is desire for sex with a particular person.

Seeking Intimate Relationships

In eros, one is preoccupied with thoughts about the person and the longing to be with the person. As Lewis (1960:150) put it, "it is the very mark of Eros that . . . we had rather share unhappiness with the Beloved than be happy on any other terms."

Finally, there is *agape* (a-gah-pay), a love that is independent of one's feelings for another. To practice agape is to act in behalf of the well-being of someone else, whether you like that person or not. Like storge, agape does not depend on the attractiveness of the other. Rather, it is a love in which we *will* to act beneficially toward another.

As we discuss recent studies of love, we will meet these types again. Modern research underscores the wisdom in the ancient distinctions. Love, as an old song puts it, is a "many-splendored" rather than a simple thing.

When You Fall in Love

When you fall in love, exactly what is it into which you are falling? In terms of the above discussion, most people no doubt have eros in mind. But how do we fall in love? How do we get to the point with someone where we feel intensely and are preoccupied with that person? And how can we tell if it is really love or something else that we feel?

The Process of Falling

How to Make a Man Fall in Love with You is the title of a popular book (Cabot 1984). The author promises that if a woman follows what she calls *The Love Plan,* she will never again have to experience that desperate and helpless waiting for some kind of chemistry to occur with a man. The Love Plan shows the way to make a man, to whom the woman is strongly attracted, fall in love with her.

Whether the book's plan works, we cannot say. It does illustrate, however, the desire of people to have the experience of falling in love. Moreover, the book has an interesting thesis: falling in love is something more than just a chance event that occurs when two people suddenly realize that there is "chemistry" between them. Indeed, falling in love is, for most of us, a complex process.

The Love-Prone

In the *Psychology Today* survey referred to earlier, Rubenstein (1983:44) reported that there is a small proportion of people (about 4 percent) who say they fall in love over and over again, often "at first sight," and sometimes are in love with several individuals at the same time. These "love-prone" people tend to fall in love for the first time at a comparatively young age (14.5 years, on the average). They believe that sex and chemistry, rather than qualities like trust, are important to an enduring romance. Although they tend to have sex more frequently than others, they report less satisfaction with their love lives. If married, they are more likely to have extramarital affairs and are more apt to believe that their chances of divorce are high.

The Rest of Us

Although some people do experience "love at first sight," including some who are not "love-prone," falling in love is a process for most of us. Ira Reiss (1960) has characterized the development of love in terms of four separate but interrelated processes: rapport, self-revelation, mutual dependency, and intimacy need fulfillment. When two people first meet, they will assess the extent to which they feel comfortable and attracted to each other. Is the other person easy to talk with? Do you like being around that person? Do you seem to have certain attitudes, values, and interests in common? If so, you may quickly develop a **rapport** between you, a harmonious and comfortable relationship.

Once rapport is established, you feel relaxed with the other person and the two of you are likely to engage in self-revelation (or, in terms we have used, self-disclosure). We have pointed out that increasing self-disclosure is a characteristic of a developing intimacy. Except for those rare cases of love at first sight, it is difficult for us to feel love for another until there is some mutual knowledge about each other. You may feel strongly attracted to someone. You may have sexual desire for someone. But falling in love is more than attraction and sexual desire. It is attraction to and desire for a person with certain qualities, attitudes, and mannerisms.

Self-disclosure not only provides two people with the knowledge about each other that is an essential ingredient to falling in love. It also leads to the next process—mutual dependency. You become mutually dependent because you do things that require the other person to be present:

> One needs the other person as an audience for one's jokes, as a confidant(e) for the expression of one's fears and wishes, as a partner for one's sexual experiences, and so on. Thus, habits of behaving develop that cannot be fulfilled alone, and in this way one becomes dependent on the other person (Reiss and Lee 1988:101).

Finally, then, mutual dependency leads to the fulfillment of our intimacy needs. We all need someone to love, someone in whom we can confide, someone with whom we can share experiences, someone who loves and appreciates us. As such intimacy needs are fulfilled, we are falling in love.

Reiss points out that the four processes are interdependent. If something happens to any one of them, it will adversely affect the development or maintenance of a love relationship. For example, if problems of some sort lead to conflict and a reduction in self-disclosure, mutual dependency and the fulfillment of intimacy needs tend to be reduced also. That leads to a breakdown of rapport, which may in turn depress the amount of self-disclosure. The relationship could go into a downward spiral to break up if something doesn't happen to reverse the process.

His Falling and Her Falling

Although the process described by Reiss applies to both males and females, there are also some gender differences in experiences of falling in love. Men and women have somewhat different expectations about love. Typically, women have been more concerned with relationships and men more concerned with work. Thus, women come to a relationship with concerns about emotional closeness and communication, while men are more concerned with practical help and sex (Cancian 1985).

Perhaps because of their greater concern with relationships, college-age women fall in love more frequently than do college-age men (Dion and Dion 1975). But because of concern about the quality of the relationship, women are more cautious. They are likely to compare any potential relationship with alternatives. As a result, men tend to fall in love more quickly than women and women tend to fall out of love more quickly than men (Rubin, Peplau, and Hill 1981). Men try to hang on longer to a deteriorating love relationship (Walster and Walster 1978), and have a harder time adjusting to a broken relationship than do women. Finally, women are more likely than men to break up a romantic relationship.

How Can You Tell If It's Love?

When a student told us that she was "madly in love" with a young man, we asked her how she knew what she felt was really love. She looked startled for a moment, then replied, "You just *know*. You *know* when you're in love." Actually, it isn't as easy as it might seem to know when we are feeling love or something else. Read Laura's account (PERSONAL) carefully. Was it really love into which she fell when she met Kent?

Misattribution of Arousal

Two social psychologists, Ellen Berscheid and Elaine Walster (1974), have set forth a "two-component" theory of love. The theory is based on the fact that differing emotions can produce similar kinds of physical arousal (such as a pounding heart or sweating). In a classic experiment, Schachter and Singer (1962) injected volunteer subjects with adrenalin. Among other things, the drug increases heart and breathing rates. The subjects were told that they were testing a new vitamin. Some were told that they would have physical symptoms. Others were told nothing or were led to expect symptoms (such as numbness) that they would not experience. Each group was sent to a waiting room for a twenty-minute period. While there, a confederate of the experimenter acted extremely happy in some cases and angry in others. The confederate's behavior did not affect those who had been correctly informed of what symptoms to expect. But those who had been misinformed or not informed tended to feel the same kind of emotion displayed by the confederate. In other words, exactly the same kind of physical symptoms were defined as happiness by some and anger by others.

Building on the work of Schachter and Singer, Berscheid and Walster (1974) suggested that at least in some cases the feeling of love may be a case of **misattribution of arousal,** attributing the wrong emotion to physical arousal.

Falling in Love—Twice

Laura is a vibrant woman in her late thirties. She talks about falling in and out of love and then back in love again. She also tells about the ways in which her parents influenced her love relationships and her need for intimacy:

My first experience with falling in love came in college. I married my first real love. Prior to that I don't recall having had serious feelings about anyone. Except, of course, for a few infatuations.

My initial attraction to Brian was his understanding and ability to listen and respond to me. I missed this kind of intimacy with my parents. I was never close to either of them. I don't think they know, or ever did know, much about me. Mother was not a good listener, and I didn't talk much with my father. They were close with each other, but I wasn't included. I grew up without learning how to be intimate with another person.

So I was immediately hooked by Brian because he paid attention to me. He looked like a hippie, with his beard and worn jeans. My parents didn't like him, and mother told me I would get bored with him. We were just good friends for several years. Then he went away for a year. He kept in touch through his letters. I lost twenty pounds while he was gone. I really missed him. But I guess the weight loss was good. When he returned, he obviously found me even more attractive than before and started pursuing a love relationship.

Our romance was an adventure. My parents had never been interested in cultural activities. Brian took me to poetry readings, classical concerts, and dinners with fascinating people. We stayed up some nights talking and discussing ideas until dawn. He wrote stories and poetry and shared them with me. We dreamed of him as an English professor in a university some day.

Brian eventually proposed and I accepted. But there was a price to pay. Brian put his dream of being a professor on hold and went into business. We were married soon after. It was wonderful at first. I felt like we were little

In other words, there may be times when we believe we feel passionate love because we are aroused and the conditions are such that the conclusion is reasonable. Additional research supports this theory.

In one experiment, men were put into a condition of either high or low arousal by running in place for either two minutes or fifteen seconds (White, Fishbein, and Rutstein 1981). After the exercise, each man watched a videotape of an attractive or unattractive woman he was supposed to meet. After seeing the tape, each man rated the woman's traits and her attractiveness. Those in the high-arousal condition rated the attractive woman more physically attractive, more sexy, and more desirable to date and kiss than those in the low-arousal condition. The unattractive woman received lower ratings from those in the high-arousal than those in the low-arousal condition.

kids playing house. It was fun to cook, to have friends over, to be together. It was the first time in my life that I could share my thoughts and feelings with someone.

After some years, however, I got restless. There were times that I felt too close to Brian. I shared so much of myself with him that I began to feel the need for space and distance. The intimacy I had longed for was now suffocating me. I didn't share my feelings with Brian, though. I didn't understand what was happening to me, only that I felt closed in. I felt trapped and knew that I had to get out. The intimacy of our relationship seemed more painful to me than the estrangement with which I had grown up. Brian was shocked when I told him. But he finally agreed to a separation and, before the year was over, to a divorce.

I adjusted to being single, I guess. But within a year, a new man entered my life. Kent was divorced. He was sophisticated, traveled to France once a year to buy wine, and owned horses. I truly believed I had found my white knight. This time I fell in love with a beautifully decorated, intriguing package. The only thing missing was the closeness that I had experienced with Brian. My intimacy level with Kent was more like that with my parents. I had all the space I needed. Kent had a family much like mine, so he was also comfortable with less intimacy.

Kent and I lived together for two years, and the experience caused me to re-evaluate myself as well as my marriage and relationship with Brian. Frankly, I was confused. I missed him and the intimacy we had shared. Yet I still remembered my feelings of suffocation and of being too close. My confusion led me to several months of counseling, a good deal of soul-searching, and finally to a better understanding of myself. I also began to realize that I still loved Brian and wanted to share my life with him. Fortunately, Brian and I had maintained our friendship, despite the divorce, and gradually our relationship once again became an intimate one. We were remarried two years later—that was over ten years ago. At times it hasn't been easy. I have had to work at keeping the barriers down, and Brian has had to work at allowing me enough space. But this time, it's for keeps!

In another experiment, some of the male subjects were aroused by being told that blood would be drawn from them (Gold, Ryckman, and Mosley 1984). Both the aroused and nonaroused subjects were introduced to a woman. In each case, the woman, who was a confederate of the experimenters, displayed dissimilar attitudes from the man. In spite of the fact that attraction is higher toward those with similar attitudes, the aroused males scored higher on measures of liking and love for the woman. They also perceived the woman to be more similar to themselves than did the nonaroused males.

Clearly, then, in some situations we may mistakenly attribute arousal to a feeling of love. It may not be wise to define your feelings as love when you meet someone after just being aroused in some way. Arousal can occur through exercise, drinking, caffeine, stimulating movies, and so forth. Perhaps some of the cases of love at first sight are the result of just such circumstances.

When aroused, we may define our feelings as attraction to someone.

Some Tests of Love

So how can you tell if it's love? Peele and Brodsky (1976) offer some interesting questions to consider. These questions will help you decide if what you are feeling is a loving and healthy relationship or what they call a form of addiction. They point out that some people get into a relationship in order to deal with problems. Such relationships are not really love. Rather, a healthy love should be able to respond positively to most of the following six questions (Peele and Brodsky 1976:83–84):

1. Do you and your lover each believe in your own personal value? That is, do you think well of yourself as a person? Do you have high self-esteem?

2. Has your relationship improved each of you? Are you in some way a better, stronger, more attractive individual? Do you value the relationship because of that improvement?

3. Do you each maintain some separate interests? Do you have meaningful relationships apart from your lover?

4. Is your relationship an integral part of your total life rather than a kind of side interest?

Table 4.1 Responses to Question of Marrying Someone You Do Not Love: 1967–1984

	1967		1976		1984	
	Male	**Female**	**Male**	**Female**	**Male**	**Female**
	Percent					
Yes	11.7	4.0	1.7	4.6	1.7	3.6
No	64.6	24.3	86.2	80.0	85.6	84.9
Undecided	23.7	71.7	12.1	15.4	12.7	11.5

Sources: William M. Kephart, "Some Correlates of Romantic Love" in *Journal of Marriage and the Family*, 29:470–74, 1967; and Jeffrey A. Simpson, et al., "The Association Between Romantic Love and Marriage: Kephart (1967) Twice Revisited" in *Personality and Social Psychology Bulletin*, 12:363–72, 1986.

5. Are you each capable of respecting the other's growth and interests without being possessive or jealous?

6. Are you friends? Would you still want to relate to each other even if you weren't lovers?

Such questions take us beyond eros, the passionate kind of love we have been discussing so far. And it may not be possible to answer all of the questions early in a relationship. But neither can you answer the question of whether it's love you feel for someone very early in a relationship. The ultimate test of a loving relationship is time. If it is possible to respond positively to the above questions over a period of time, you will be able to look back and say, "I fell in love."

Passionate Versus Companionate Love

If someone had all of the qualities that you desired in another person, would you marry that person if you were not in love with him or her? The question was posed to over 1,000 college students in the mid-1960s, to 246 students in 1976, and to 339 students in 1984. As table 4.1 shows, there were some striking differences between the first (1967) and the other two (1976, 1984) time periods. If the students' attitudes were representative of Americans as a whole, then we can say that in the 1960s men, but not women, believed that love is necessary for marriage. By the next decade, however, both men and women agreed that love is a precondition of marriage. The researchers speculate that the change could have occurred because women are no longer as economically dependent on men as they once were. Before women had the educational, legal, and economic means for self-sufficiency, they had to be more pragmatic about marriage. They needed, above all, a man who would be a good provider. Now, both men and women can and do take a romantic approach. Love, not security, is viewed as the foundation for marriage.

What kind of love? The love that most people have in mind when they think of the precondition for an exclusive relationship, living together, or marriage is eros. Such love is sometimes called romantic love, or passionate love. We will use the term **passionate love** and define it as a preoccupation and intense longing for union with a particular other. In contrast, **companionate love** is affection for, and commitment to, someone with whom one is deeply involved. Thus, companionate love is similar to philia.

But does everyone agree that passionate love is necessary for marriage or some other kind of exclusive commitment? And how long can passionate love last? In this section, we will address these questions. Then, we will look a little more closely at the experience of passionate love.

The Emergence of Passionate Love

People have always experienced passionate love, but the notion that passionate love is a precondition for a relationship like marriage is a relatively new idea in human history. In fact, in Greek and Roman mythology love and marriage were not connected with each other. The goddess of marriage was different from the goddess of love. In the past, writers extolled sexual love, and some extolled nonsexual kinds of love, but in neither case was marriage the context. Marriages, throughout most of human history, were contracted for various purposes such as security, help, and procreation, but not for love.

Then something happened during the twelfth century in Europe. A new ideal about the relationship between men and women emerged, the idea of "courtly love." At first, the idea was confined mainly to the aristocracy, and spread by troubadors, knights who composed poems and sang them. The love they wrote and sang about was something new: it involved a preoccupation with the beloved, a longing for union with the beloved, a proclamation of the lover's undying commitment and loyalty.

There is no single explanation for the sudden appearance and spread of the idea of passionate love. It may have been due, in part, to the rediscovery of ancient Greek and Roman writings, to a reaction against the brutality of the era, to the shortage of noble women compared to the number of knights, and to antichurch feelings (Reiss and Lee 1988:98). At any rate, sex was placed in a new context, a new kind of relationship between men and women. And while originally the relationship was one that was cultivated outside of marriage, the idea gradually spread to the premarital state. Romantic liaisons eventually became romantic courtship. The ideals expressed by the twelfth century troubadors ultimately became the experience expected by young people as the route to marriage.

Romantic, or passionate, love as a precondition of marriage is still not universal, however. In a study of ideas about romantic love among Japanese, American, and West German students, researchers found that the Japanese had significantly lower approval scores than the West Germans (Simmons, Vom Kolke, and Shimizu 1986). The Americans' score fell in between the other two. While conditions are changing, family considerations are still an important factor in the choice of a mate in Japan.

Seeking Intimate Relationships

Those passionately in love may have trouble concentrating on other matters.

We should also note that many American observers bemoan rather than applaud our emphasis on passionate love. Some consider it to be an enemy of a lasting marital love, for passionate love cannot be maintained over an indefinite period of time (Lederer and Jackson 1968; Liebowitz 1983). It is frequently an exhilirating experience while it lasts, but the point is that it does not and cannot last indefinitely. And those who believe that something has gone wrong with their marriage because of the passing of passionate love are living in a fantasy world that will lead inevitably to marital troubles.

The Experience of Passionate Love

How often have you had the experience of passionate love? Not everyone has had such an experience. And among those who do, some experience it only once, while others experience it many times in their lifetime. Often it is a bittersweet experience—the individual may have trouble concentrating on other matters or may be frustrated because of separation from the loved one. Adolescents, those from about twelve or thirteen to twenty-one or twenty-two years of age, are particularly prone to falling into a state of passionate love.

Measuring Passionate Love

Passionate love has been compared with the "high" of certain drugs (amphetamines). But there are more than feelings involved. We also think in certain ways and behave in certain ways when we have passionate love for someone. Hatfield and Sprecher (1986) have developed a scale for measuring these various facets. The scale helps us better understand the nature of passionate love.

In brief, if you are passionately in love with someone, according to the scale, you would tend to:

Think in certain ways, such as
—Persistently reflect about the other person
—Idealize his or her qualities (such as kindness and beauty)
—Desire to know, and be known by, him or her
Feel in certain ways, such as
—Have sexual desires for him or her
—Feel bad when things are not going well between the two of you
—Desire a close and permanent relationship
—Feel physically aroused by him or her
Behave in certain ways, such as
—Try to find out how the person feels about you
—Study the other person
—Serve and help him or her

To see the extent to which you are now passionately in love with someone, or the extent to which you felt such love for someone in the past, take the short form of the test shown in figure 4.2. Does the scale seem to adequately capture your own experience? Keep in mind that no two people's experience of something is ever precisely the same. Let us look at some research that underscores the point.

Different Kinds of Lovers

When you were an infant, you became emotionally attached to your mother or other primary caregiver, and you were distressed if you were separated. Depending on your experiences, you may have developed one of three kinds of attachment styles with your mother, and there is a tendency to carry the same style into adult relationships. Thus, Cindy Hazan and Phillip Shaver (1987) investigated attachment styles among 574 adults who responded to a newspaper advertisement. They found the same three styles identified among infants: the secure, avoidant, and anxious/ambivalent.

With regard to romantic lovers, secure lovers are those who find it fairly easy to get close to others. Secure lovers are comfortable depending on others and having others depend on them. They don't worry frequently about a relationship either getting too close or being terminated.

Please think of the person whom you love most passionately right now. If you are not in love right now, please think of the last person you loved passionately. If you have never been in love, think of the person whom you came closest to caring for in that way. Keep this person in mind as you complete this section of the questionnaire. (The person you choose should be of the opposite sex if you are heterosexual or of the same sex if you are homosexual.) Try to tell us how you felt at the time when your feelings were the most intense.

Mark a number beside each question in accord with the following:

1	2	3	4	5	6	7	8	9

Not at all   Moderately   Definitely
true   true   true

___ 1. I would feel despair if ___ left me.
___ 2. Sometimes I feel I can't control my thoughts; they are obsessively on ___ .
___ 3. I feel happy when I am doing something to make ___ happy.
___ 4. I would rather be with ___ than anyone else.
___ 5. I'd get jealous if I thought ___ were falling in love with someone else.
___ 6. I yearn to know all about ___ .
___ 7. I want ___ — physically, emotionally, mentally.
___ 8. I have an endless appetite for affection from ___ .
___ 9. For me, ___ is the perfect romantic partner.
___ 10. I sense my body responding when ___ touches me.
___ 11. ___ always seems to be on my mind.
___ 12. I want ___ to know me—my thoughts, my fears, and my hopes.
___ 13. I eagerly look for signs indicating ___ ' s desire for me.
___ 14. I possess a powerful attraction for ___ .
___ 15. I get extremely depressed when things don't go right in my relationship with ___ .

Figure 4.2 *Passionate love scale.*

Avoidant lovers are somewhat uncomfortable about a close relationship with others. They don't trust other people, and therefore are unwilling to depend on others. They may get nervous when someone gets too close to them. They feel that others often want more intimacy than they are willing to provide.

Finally, anxious/ambivalent lovers perceive a reluctance on the part of others to get close to them. They worry about a partner not staying with them or not loving them. They desire to "merge completely" with someone else, a desire that may frighten rather than attract the other person.

How many people fall into each of these styles? In Hazen and Shaver's sample, a little over half were secure (figure 4.3). Twenty-four percent were avoidant and 20 percent were anxious/ambivalent. Secure lovers, of course, are most likely to have relationships that are happy, trusting, supportive, and lasting. The other two types will have more problems of jealousy, frustration, and other negative emotions connected with their relationships.

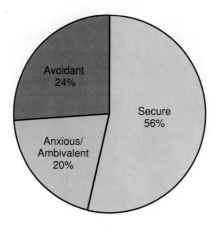

Figure 4.3 *Types of lovers.*
Source: Data from Hazen and Shaver 1987:337.

From Passionate Love to Companionate Love

As we noted, passionate love cannot last indefinitely. This is fortunate, because the passionate lover might accomplish very little else in his or her life. Gradually, passionate love yields to companionate love as the dominant form of a relationship. The change tends to occur when a relationship has lasted between six and thirty months (Hyde 1986:354).

As the flush of passion fades, the lovers stop idealizing each other. They notice imperfections. They find things that are annoying. They experience periods of boredom and irritation. They may begin to question whether they want to remain in the relationship. They may wonder whether the relationship will ultimately be the satisfying experience they had expected and hoped for. In other words, the realities of life set in. The lovers come down from the mountaintop of romantic fantasy and start coping with the vexations of two imperfect humans trying to establish a long-term, meaningful relationship.

We have known students who lament the inevitability of the process. "I would like to live forever in a state of passionate love," one declared with fervor. But such a statement overlooks a number of things. For one, the state of passionate love has its own vexations as we have noted. Second, passionate love is time and energy consuming. It may divert us from other things that are important to our growth. And third, the passing of passionate love is not the same as the death of passion. As we shall note below, people in long-term marriages frequently report a passion for each other (including strong sexual desire) that lasts for forty years or more. But the passion in a long-term relationship is episodic rather than continuing. As such, it allows people to engage in other matters with their full attention and faculties.

Companionate love, then, does not mean that a relationship has lost its fire. Rather, it means that two people have found a firm basis for a lasting relationship. And that relationship is likely to have times of passion as well as times of friendship. In a real sense, the transition to companionate love is not

Love: A Nineteenth Century View

Dr. John Cowan, M.D., was the author of a popular marriage manual in the nineteenth century. His views, common during this time, reflect a backing away during the Victorian era from the romantic love ideal. After providing a list of bases for choosing a mate, such as similarities in age, temper, intelligence, and habits, he lectured his readers about love:

> If this mode of mate-choosing is physiologically and psychologically right, as all clear-minded and right-thinking persons will allow, then it must, as a result, dispense with the attribute of love as a preliminary requirement. And so it does. Love, in the popular sense of the term, as applied to the union of the sexes, is a fallacy, and is not only not required, but is an impossibility in the initial requisites to the choice of a wife or husband.
>
> Perfect sexual love comes only of a perfect union—a union of resemblance in mind, soul and body, and this is one reason for my so earnestly advising the employment of the reason in selection; for in and through the intellect you only can choose one who approximates to your standard of character in all its details. The union being consummated, perfect love results as naturally and harmoniously as do all the workings of all other of Nature's laws, and this love, guided by the moral sentiments, through

the similarity of [the two people], grows strong, more lasting, pure and holy through the days and months of life's pilgrimage. . . .

> A woman marries a man because, as she says (and perhaps believes), she loves him. How? Because her self-esteem prompts her to avoid being an "old maid," and inhabitiveness or love of home, and acquisitiveness or love of money, prompts her to marry the man of her choice. It matters not what may be the man's acquirements as compared with hers, provided he possess money and a home for her. This woman marries through love; but it is a selfish, animal love, and is widely different from the pure and holy love that comes of a perfect union of soul with soul.
>
> A man marries a woman because, as he says (and probably believes) he loves her. How? Because, through his ideality or love for the beautiful, and through his perverted amativeness or love for the gross and sensual, ambition prompts him to marry her. This man marries for love; but it is a love that is as evanescent as the wind, and a miserable help to happiness.

Source: John Cowan, M.D., *The Science of a New Life* (New York: J. S. Olgivie, 1869), pp. 45–47.

---

a loss but a gain. If the relationship survives the scrutiny and questioning, it may anchor the individuals in a rewarding and lasting union. This is illustrated in the following excerpt from an account shared with us by a fifty-year-old woman who has been married for over twenty years:

> We couldn't get enough of each other during courtship and for the first year of our marriage. But increasingly after that other responsibilities—our professional commitments and then the kids—seemed to intrude on our lovemaking. We often joked about having to make a date for sex. We warned

each other about using it or losing it. At times our hit-or-miss love life was a source of real anxiety. But I am happy to report that we have come to terms with the problem. We are more deeply commited to each other than ever before. True, we find ourselves having sex less frequently than we want, but now we don't worry about it. We know each other well, and we are about as intimate as any couple could be.

Loving and Liking

Can you like someone without loving that person? You probably would answer yes. And can you love someone without liking that person? A lot of people answer "no" to that question. But recall that agape love is independent of feelings for the other, which means that it is possible to love without liking.

Such thoughts raise the question of the relationship between loving and liking. Both the passionate and companionate love styles we have discussed imply that you like as well as love the other. But exactly what does it mean to like someone? Is liking merely a milder form of loving? Are loving and liking similar in some ways? Or are they completely different?

Rubin's Love Scale

One useful way to understanding the relationship between liking and loving is Zick Rubin's (1970) Love Scale. Rubin developed a series of questions that measure both love and liking. The love questions tap into three dimensions of loving: attachment, caring, and intimacy. Attachment refers to the desire to be with and approved by the loved one. Caring is the desire to give to the loved one, and intimacy is close and confidential communication. Two examples of the kind of questions that measure love are: "I would do almost anything for _____ " and "If I could never be with _____ , I would feel miserable." Clearly, such statements reflect intense emotion.

The measures of liking are less emotional in tone. They reflect the attitudes and feelings we are likely to have for friends. Two examples are: "In my opinion, _____ is an exceptionally mature person" and "I have great confidence in _____'s good judgment." To like someone, then, means to respect, admire, and enjoy being with that person.

In research using the Rubin scales, there is some overlap between loving and liking (Sternberg 1987:338). That is, subjects who rate someone are likely to score that person relatively high on both scales, or low on both scales. But there is a difference in the scores for friends and those for lovers. Both the love and liking scores tend to be higher for dating partners than for same-sex friends. But whereas the liking score for partners is only slightly higher than that for friends, the love score is considerably higher. In other words, when we love someone, we tend to like that person as well, and to like that person even more than we like our friends.

Friends enjoy being with each other most of the time.

Love and Friendship

Keith Davis (1985) has also addressed the question of loving and liking. He put it in terms of the characteristics of love versus those of friendship. There are, he says, eight qualities in friendship. Friends

1. enjoy being with each other most of the time

2. accept each other as they are

3. trust each other to act out of concern for the other's best interest

4. respect the judgments of each other

5. help and support each other

6. share experiences and feelings

7. understand each other's feelings and thoughts

8. feel at ease with each other, so that the relationship is based on openness and honesty rather than pretence

The preceding list adds a few dimensions to the respect, admiration, and enjoyment in the Rubin scale. Liking also means a desire to help and a willingness to share. Love includes all of the eight plus two more. Lovers are characterized by a passion cluster and a caring cluster. The passion cluster includes those qualities of passionate love that we have already discussed. The caring cluster includes a willingness to give "to the point of extreme self-sacrifice" and a "championing of each other's interests" to ensure the success of each (Davis 1985:24–25).

In Davis's research, spouses and lovers tended to score higher than friends on all the characteristics. However, friends got slightly higher scores on trust and feeling at ease, and substantially higher scores on acceptance. Apparently lovers and spouses make more efforts to change each other than do friends. And they are more likely to be critical of each other than are friends.

Both friends and lovers enhance our well-being. And they do so in some similar and different ways. To be liked by a friend provides us with some experiences that are desirable. We may or may not like our friends quite as strongly as we like our lovers, but liking and being liked by a friend adds to the quality of our lives.

A Triangular Theory of Love

Liking and loving. Passionate love and companionate love. How are they all related? Or are they? Robert J. Sternberg (1987) believes they are. He has developed what he calls a triangular theory of love that shows how various kinds of love are related. His theory asserts that we can understand love best by viewing it in terms of three components. These components can be thought of as the vertices of a triangle. At the top is intimacy. On the left is passion. And on the right is decision/commitment.

Intimacy is a feeling of being connected or bonded to another. Passion is the passionate love we have discussed. The decision/commitment component has two factors. In the short run, there is the factor of deciding that you love someone. In the long run, there is the factor of committing yourself to maintain the love over time. As Sternberg noted, these two factors are separable. That is, you can decide you love someone without committing yourself to maintain that love over an extended period of time. And there are people who are committed who have never consciously decided or admitted their love.

Using these three components, we have a number of different types of love, ranging from the lack of all three (nonlove) to the "consummate love" that involves the presence of all three (table 4.2). Sternberg defined liking as intimacy without either passion or decision/commitment. There is a closeness, a bonding in the experience of liking someone, but there is no passion or long-term commitment.

Table 4.2 Types of Love

Type of Love	Intimacy	Presence of Passion	Decision/ Commitment
Nonlove	No	No	No
Liking	Yes	No	No
Infatuation	No	Yes	No
Empty	No	No	Yes
Romantic	Yes	Yes	No
Companionate	Yes	No	Yes
Fatuous	No	Yes	Yes
Consummate	Yes	Yes	Yes

From Robert J. Sternberg, "Liking Versus Loving: A Comparative Evaluation of Theories" in *Psychological Bulletin*, 102:340. Copyright 1987 by the American Psychological Association. Reprinted by permission.

When you feel highly aroused by someone that you don't know and for whom you have no commitment, you experience *infatuation*. If you for some reason commit yourself to a person without knowing or feeling passion for him or her, your love is an *empty* one. This may occur in some long-term relationships that have become stagnant. The two partners no longer feel much for each other and no longer share a great deal, but for religious reasons, convenience, or reasons of economic and family pressure they stay in the relationship.

In *romantic* love, you feel intimate and passionate but have not yet committed yourself to the other. *Companionate* love has intimacy and commitment but not passion. It is the kind of love that characterizes long-term friendships and some marriages in which the passion has died.

An interesting type that emerges from Sternberg's scheme is *fatuous* love, in which there is passion and commitment but no intimacy. Sternberg (1987:340) said that this is the kind of love that is "sometimes associated with Hollywood and with whirlwind courtships." He called it fatuous because the people make a commitment in the midst of the dizzying experience of passion rather than in the context of a stabilizing experience of intimacy.

Finally, there is *consummate* love, in which all three components exist. This is the complete love, the love that most of us desire and strive for. The fact that you attain consummate love with someone, unfortunately, does not mean that you will maintain it. But it is attainable, and it is the most rewarding of all love experiences.

Sternberg's typology is very useful for understanding differing kinds of experiences of love. He showed us the complexity of love. For example, we have noted that the idea that there is a transition from passionate to companionate love in long-term relationships is misleading if it is taken to mean that all passion dies. Sternberg's findings agree as reflected in the idea of consummate love in which passion and long-term commitment can coexist. Indeed, we found such love in our study of long-term marriages. Companionate love was the dominant form for some of the couples who had been married fifteen or more years. But others spoke of continuing passion in the relationship. As one woman put it: "We knew that if the passion died we would still have a friendly relationship. Thank God, the passion hasn't died. In fact, it has gotten more intense" (Lauer and Lauer 1986:71).

Applying Sternberg's typology to your own experience can help you better understand the nature of your relationships and why a particular relationship is either rewarding or is in some way falling short of your expectations. Which of the various types of love have you experienced? Which are you experiencing at the present time?

Styles of Loving

Another useful way to understand love is found in the typology of John Alan Lee (1973). Lee used three of the Greek terms we discussed at the beginning of the chapter—eros, storge, and agape. He added three more—ludus, mania, and pragma—to get six different styles of loving. Ludus is playful love. Mania is a possessive, dependent love. And pragma is a logical kind of love.

Six Types of Lovers

The *erotic lover* tends to focus on the physical, and particularly the sexual, aspects of the relationship. Erotic lovers may have ideal partners in mind, and may fall immediately in love when meeting someone who fits the ideal image.

The *ludic lover* views love as a pleasant pastime, but not something in which to get deeply involved. Ludic lovers have little or no commitment to the other. They may be involved in several love affairs simultaneously.

Storgic lovers have a kind of quiet affection for the other. A storgic relationship tends to develop slowly but to be stable. There is no overwhelming passion, no points of exhiliration. Rather, a storgic love is a slow, perhaps unwitting, process of development.

The *manic lover* combines something of eros and ludus. The manic lover is intensely preoccupied with the beloved, feels intense jealousy, and alternates between ecstasy and despair in the relationship. The manic lover feels the passion of eros but plays the games of ludus as he or she tries to cope with swinging feelings and fear of loss.

A *pragmatic lover* is also a combination to some extent, of ludus and storge. The pragmatic lover may take careful stock of the other, including consciously assessing the characteristics of the other. The pragmatic lover tries to find a partner who has a particular set of characteristics that he or she desires in another. To that extent, the pragmatic lover is playing a game. But pragma can also be a stable and growing kind of love.

Finally, the *agapic lover* acts in behalf of the well-being of the other without demanding or perhaps even expecting any benefits in return. Agape is other-focused, patient, kind. It makes no demands for itself. It seeks only to serve the other. It is the kind of love that psychoanalyst Erich Fromm (1956:22) wrote about: "Love is the active concern for the life and the growth of that which we love."

While we can talk about the six different styles, and the corresponding six different types of lovers, in practice we use at least some of each of the styles. But there can be a dominant style. And that can change over time or from one relationship to another. In addition, there is a general tendency for males to be more ludic and more erotic than females in their love styles, while females tend to be somewhat more manic, storgic, and pragmatic (Dion and Dion 1985:229). Styles also vary by religious commitment (Hendrick and Hendrick 1987). Those who define themselves as very religious score higher than others on storge, pragma, and agape, and lower on ludus. Those neutral about religion had the highest scores on eros and ludus. There were no differences between the groups on mania scores.

The extent to which you use each of the styles is important. You form your own unique style out of a mixture of the six. But the result is not merely a matter of personal preference. There are serious implications for your well-being and for your relationships.

Implications of Differing Styles of Loving

If you are now in love, to what extent do each of the styles characterize your relationship? And if you are not in love at the present, to what extent have you used each of the styles in past relationships? Clyde Hendrick and Susan Hendrick (1988) raised these questions with more than nine hundred undergraduate students. They measured love styles by the extent of agreement to such statements as "I enjoy playing the 'game of love' with a number of different partners" (ludus) and "It is hard to say exactly where friendship ends and love begins" (storge). They found differences between those who said they were in love and those who said they were not. As figure 4.4 shows, people in love report higher scores on eros and agape and lower scores on ludus than those not in love. There were no significant differences between the two groups on storge, mania, or pragma.

Thus, people in love differ from those not in love. In another study using the six styles, the researchers found that satisfaction with the relationship varied by love style (Hendrick, Hendrick, and Adler 1988). Fifty-seven heterosexual couples participated in the study. For both men and women, higher levels of satisfaction with the relationship were associated with eros and lower levels were associated with ludus. People apparently like passion but dislike games. Indeed, "it may be fully as important not to be game-playing or manipulative as it is to be passionate, disclosing, and committed" (Hendrick, Hendrick, and Adler 1988:986).

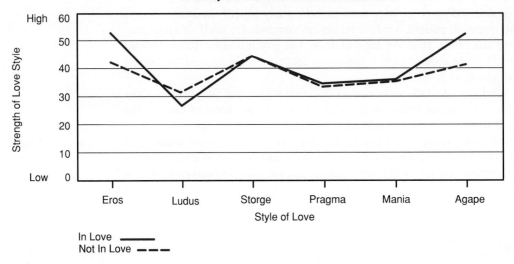

Figure 4.4 *Love styles of those in love and not in love.*
Source: Data from Hendrick and Hendrick 1988:175.

There were some sex differences in the styles related to satisfaction. For women, higher levels of satisfaction were associated with storge, and mania was associated with lower levels of satisfaction. For men, high levels of satisfaction were found among those whose female partner perceived agape as a part of her love style.

Finally, the partners tended to be alike in their scores on the various love scales. It seems that we tend to gravitate toward those who are not only similar to us in background, values, and attitudes, but also in styles of loving.

Love Threatened—Jealousy

A male graduate student told us that one of the more unsettling experiences of his life occurred when he took his girlfriend to a party: "She spent most of the evening talking to and laughing with some guy she met there. I was so mad I could feel myself shaking. It literally made me sick to my stomach." What the student experienced was an intense case of **jealousy,** which is a negative emotional reaction to a real or imagined threat to a love relationship. In the case of the student, the threat was imagined. His girlfriend had met someone who shared her esoteric interest in French literature. But she was not romantically attracted to the man. The fact that the threat was imagined, however, did not lessen the intensity of the reaction.

It is interesting to note that prior to the 1970s, popular writers frequently considered a certain amount of jealousy to be normal and even good. Among married people, for example, jealousy could be thought to be evidence

Love and the Soaps

Millions of American men and women of all ages watch soap operas on television. What is shown is important, because such shows help shape people's expectations and values about love relationships. Watch one of the programs such as "Days of Our Lives," "Santa Barbara," or "As the World Turns." Look at each of the love relationships shown and write up an analysis by addressing the following questions. Use Sternberg's and Lee's typologies of love in your analysis.

1. What kinds of love do family members show each other? How does that square with your ideals?

2. What kinds of heterosexual love relationships exist? To what extent do they agree or disagree with materials in this chapter? How would you evaluate the relationships in terms of your own values?

3. What, if any, kinds of love relationships are missing? Why do you think they are not a part of the program?

4. If the love relationships shown were typical of real life, how would you summarize the nature of love today?

If the entire class participates in this project, have different members watch different programs. Compare the results. Are soap operas giving a consistent portrait of love? If so, why? If not, what are the implications?

Jealousy is likely when someone defines a love relationship as threatened.

of love. A moderate amount of jealousy could cause an individual to examine and realize the value of a relationship, thereby strengthening the bonds (Clanton and Smith 1977). But as the emphasis on personal growth and well-being increased, more and more writers began to see jealousy as evidence of some deficiency in relationships. If jealousy is a deficiency, then perhaps *all* relationships are deficient. Sexual jealousy seems to be universal. It is a signal that the individual wants to protect his or her relationship. In their study of 103 individuals who ranged in age from twenty-one to sixty-four, Pines and Aronson (1983) reported that all had experienced jealousy at some point in their lives. The frequency and intensity of the experience differed among the subjects. But all had felt jealous and the nature of the experience was quite similar for all of the subjects.

Who Is Most Jealous?

If the frequency and intensity of jealousy varies, what kind of people get most jealous? Some believe that women are more likely than men to be jealous. But there seem to be few sex differences in the experience of jealousy. There are some people, both men and women, who have what might be called a jealous personality. Pines and Aronson (1983:124) pointed out that those who were more jealous at the time of their research also tended to report a greater amount of jealousy throughout their lives. This suggests a jealousy component in the personality of some individuals. Unfortunately, their research did not investigate any possible causes. Psychologists would no doubt look for a problematic relationship with the mother. Freud suggested that jealousy begins early in life when the infant strives for the exclusive love of the mother. The infant who, for whatever reason, feels threatened or thwarted in securing the mother's love may develop problems with jealousy throughout life.

As we might expect, people who are insecure in their love relationships are more likely to feel jealous. Those who feel that they have few alternatives will also tend to be more jealous. Hansen (1985b) studied 220 married people and reported that, regardless of the quality of the marriage, those who saw themselves as having few alternatives to the marriage were more likely to experience jealousy.

People with lower self-esteem have more problems with jealousy. In a *Psychology Today* survey of nearly twenty-five thousand readers, those who reported the most jealousy also had problems with self-esteem (Salovey and Rodin 1985:28). They tended to have a lower opinion of themselves and to see a larger gap than others did between what they are and what they would ideally like to be.

Another interesting finding that emerged from the *Psychology Today* survey was the relationship between marital status and jealousy. Separated and divorced people reported the highest rates of jealousy, followed by cohabiting people. Separated and divorced people were the most likely to look through a lover's personal belongings and listen in on a lover's telephone conversation with someone else. Perhaps the traumatic experience of the disruption of the previous relationship intensified problems with jealousy among the separated and divorced. Cohabiting couples may have problems of jealousy because of the lower levels of commitment to the relationship (compared with that of married people). At any rate, married people seem to have less problem with jealousy than cohabiting, separated, or divorced individuals. And the longer the marriage, the less is jealousy likely to be a problem.

Situations That Provoke Jealousy

What can rouse jealousy in a partner? Virtually anything for the person who is intensely jealous. But certain situations seem to arouse jealous feelings in nearly everyone. The party situation noted at the beginning of this section is one that is likely to provoke most people. In fact, when readers in the *Psychology Today* survey rated their reactions to different situations, the one that provoked the most intense feelings of jealousy was a party attended by a couple in which one of the partners spends a lot of time with someone else. Basically, any situation in which one partner feels that something is happening that threatens the relationship will provoke jealousy.

One way to think about jealousy-provoking situations is that they violate our expectations for our relationships. Marriage is for most people an exclusive relationship. So is cohabitation. Even dating partners may develop such expectations early in the relationship. Hansen (1985a) studied dating jealousy among more than three hundred students. He found that a significant proportion expected their partners to give up close personal friendships with people of the opposite sex. And most expected sexual exclusiveness from the earliest stages of their relationships. When our expectations are violated, we feel threatened. Jealousy is a sign that we want to protect the relationship.

Consequences of Jealousy

While jealousy may be a normal reaction, it can be a destructive one when it becomes too intense and too frequent. There are, for instance, consequences for our personal well-being:

> For most subjects, extreme jealousy was associated with feeling hot, nervous, and shaky; and experiencing fast heartbeat, and emptiness in the stomach. The emotional reactions felt most strongly were anxiety, fear of loss, pain, anger, vulnerability, and hopelessness (Pines and Aronson 1983:131).

In addition, jealousy may lead to a loss of self-esteem (Buunk and Bringle 1987:129). When the threat is real, when there is a particular third person involved, the jealous individual is likely to compare himself or herself with the rival. Is the rival inferior or superior? If superior, the rival is an assault on the jealous person's self-esteem. And the assault on self-esteem is particularly strong if the rival is seen as superior in sexual abilities (Buunk and Bringle 1987:130).

Finally, jealousy may lead to the loss of the partner. Ironically, it is the fear of loss that creates jealousy in the first place. When jealousy is too intense and too frequent (and perhaps too frequently imagined rather than real), it becomes a self-fulfilling prophecy. The individual creates the very loss that he or she had feared by distrusting and accusing the partner. In the Pines and Aronson (1983:124) study, the more jealousy the subjects reported at the time, the more relationships they had experienced that had ended because of their jealousy.

PRINCIPLES FOR ENHANCING INTIMACY

1. Although "love at first sight" seems romantic, enduring love needs time to develop. Shared interests, shared confidences, and shared experiences take time to evolve. But the intimacy and love they produce are worth the wait.

2. Don't confuse arousal with love. Remember that such things as vigorous exercise, heavy drinking, or sexy movies can arouse and trick our emotions into thinking that we are in love.

3. To verify your own feelings, use the six indicators of a healthy love found in this chapter to examine your relationships. Remember, however, that a love relationship takes time to develop and that initially it may not measure up to all the indicators.

4. Don't expect passionate love to be unending. It may be the storybook ideal, but it tends to give way to something even better—companionate love. Companionate love maintains the passion but moves beyond the obsessions and irritations of passionate love. Companionate love not only provides you with the intimacy and security that each of us needs; it also frees you to deal with other areas of your life.

5. Because love relationships that are built on friendship seem to be the most satisfying and enduring, it is important to like as well as love a person before you make a commitment. If you feel a strong passion for someone but like nothing about that person, recognize that the relationship is going to have problems and will likely not last.

6. Work at overcoming jealousy; if jealousy is a serious problem, there are books on it and books on self-change that can help you overcome it. Jealousy can wreck a relationship. The "green-eyed monster," even if it is a response to a real threat, can cause you to react irrationally and excessively. And, in the process, you may lose the love relationship you are trying to protect.

SUMMARY

The multifaceted meaning of love is illustrated by four ancient Greek words that are all translated "love." *Storge* is love between parents and children. *Philia* is love between friends. *Eros* involves sexual and romantic love between men and women. *Agape* is a love that is independent of feelings, working in behalf of the well-being of the other.

Falling in love is a complex process. A few people are love-prone, falling in love over and over again and often at first sight. Most people go through a series of phases when falling in love: rapport, self-revelation, mutual dependency, and the fulfillment of intimacy needs. Men fall in love more frequently and quickly than women. Women fall out of love more quickly and are more likely than men to break up a relationship.

It is not easy to know when we are in love. In some cases, we may mistakenly attribute physiological arousal to feelings of love. There are tests of love that are more useful than one's own feelings.

We may distinguish between passionate love, a preoccupation and intense longing for someone, and companionate love, affection and commitment to someone with whom one is deeply involved. Passionate love is relatively new in human history. It affects our feelings, thoughts, and behavior. Companionate love is a gain rather than a loss in the relationship. It can anchor two people in a lasting and meaningful union.

When we love someone, we tend to like that person as well. In the most meaningful love relationships, the liking is stronger than the liking we have for friends.

Intimacy, passion, and decision/commitment are the three components of Sternberg's triangular theory of love. The most rewarding love has all three. Various other kinds of love have one or two of the three.

John Alan Lee identified six styles of love. Erotic lovers focus on the physical and sexual. Ludic lovers view love as a game. Storgic lovers have a quiet affection for another. Manic lovers have the passion of eros but play the games of ludus. Pragmatic lovers take a rational approach, assessing the other for desirable traits. Agapic lovers act in behalf of the well-being of the other, expecting nothing in return.

Jealousy seems to afflict men and women equally. It may be the result of personality problems and/or may be provoked by certain situations that are defined as threatening to the relationship. Jealousy is destructive when it is too intense and too frequent.

5

Mate Selection

I s there a "one and only" for you? Is there a perfect soul mate out there, waiting to be discovered by you? If you believe such things, you have very romantic notions about love and marriage. Rather than there being just one perfect mate for you, you probably could have a satisfying marriage with a number of others. This is not to say that you could be happily married to just anyone, however. In this chapter, we will look briefly at some notions of how mate selection should proceed. Then we will discuss people's expectations for a mate. We will examine various factors that can narrow the field for you, many of which you might be unaware. Finally, we will look at how you can hedge your bets by being sensitive to the factors that predict marital satisfaction.

Is there a "one and only" for you?

Is There a Best Way to Select a Mate?

Would you be better off selecting your own mate or having the selection made for you? You may be horrified at the very thought of having a mate chosen for you, but the practice has been very common throughout human history. Parents or so-called matchmakers may arrange the marriage between two young people who have had little or no contact with each other. In some cases, the matches are arranged while the partners are still children.

For example, matchmakers were the rule in Japan prior to World War II (Murstein 1974:490–92). Young men and women had little contact with each other in school or play. Moreover, the Japanese felt that marriage was too important to be left to the whims of the immature. Parents had to be involved in the process. But families did not deal directly with each other in order to avoid the embarrassment of rejection. Instead, the matchmaker (*nakodo*) acted as a go-between. Sometimes the nakodo would be a friend or relative, and sometimes a paid professional. In any case, the nakodo had the job of introducing the families to each other, negotiating the conditions of the marriage, and participating in the wedding ceremony if the match was finalized. The only contact between the two young people, before a formal introduction at which both families would be present, might be a time when the young woman would walk with her mother so that the prospective groom could see what she looked like (from a distance, of course).

In societies with arranged marriages, political and economic considerations are considered far more important than love. Lee and Stone (1980:323) reported that 80 percent of seventy-six nonindustrial societies with arranged marriages have little or no emphasis on romantic love. This is not to say that arranged marriages are loveless; no doubt many couples grow to love each other over the course of the marriage.

While arranged marriages are more common in nonindustrial societies, some of those societies also allow people to choose their own mates. Lee and Stone (1980) had 114 societies in their total sample. They found that a third allowed people to select their own mates, and love was generally considered to be an important criterion in the selection.

The ideal in most modern societies is for people to select their own mates. Presumably, this results in a love match that will bring greater satisfaction to both partners. But, to return to the original question, which method is best? If we use stability of the marriage as a criterion, arranged marriages are best. If we use satisfaction with the relationship as a criterion, we do not have enough evidence to make a judgment. It is interesting to note that the writers of utopian novels, who have tried to depict their ideal for a society, most frequently have made mate selection a matter of state control (Weiss 1969:142–47). Although some of the utopian writers suggested either individual or parental choice, most either allowed the state to choose or had the state lay down the rules of selection. The purpose of taking the choice out of individual hands, of course, was to ensure the well-being of the total group. For example, people

Shirishana-Yanomama Mate Selection

The Shirishana-Yanomama are a fierce group of Indians who live in northwest Brazil. John Peters, who worked as a missionary among these Indians, is now a sociologist in Canada. He has written about their four types of mate selection. Each involves individual choice, but only by the male:

The selection of the Yanomama heterosexual partner is done by the male while the female is still quite young. Most betrothals are made when the girl is an infant, or at least before age three. In one case the yet unborn child of a pregnant woman was requested, in the event the baby would be a female. Possibly the unnatural sex ratio of three males for every two females in 1958 contributed to this early selection process among the 120 Shirishana. The sex ratio imbalance practice continued until the mid-seventies, when the sex ratio was much more balanced. By that time some females were betrothed as late as age seven or eight years of age.

Men initiate the betrothal at the time they become hunters of the game in the forest: some time after 15 years of age. . . . The ideal match is a bilateral cross-cousin union. In other words, a male chooses his father's sister's daughter or his mother's brother's daughter. . . .

A second and preferred means of mate selection is sister exchange. Two non-kin single men wish to acquire wives, and have sisters who have not been promised to anyone. They exchange sisters.

As in all other types of mate selection, women in sister exchange betrothals have no influence in the decision. For instance, after about six years of marriage I asked As- why she married Te-. She spontaneously glanced at her brother and said, "Because he wanted his (pointing to her husband) sister." . . .

[The third method is to choose someone in the "wanima relationship," which includes only every second generation of unrelated females. The females chosen may be from one's own or another group of the Yanomama.]

In each of the three ways of mate selection mentioned above, bride payment and service is made.

The fourth and more brutal method to acquire a wife is by means of a raid. A village is attacked, often in revenge for death from a previous surprise attack or a presumed act of witchcraft, or for the single reason to acquire women. Reasons for raiding are not always consistent. Several men might be killed or wounded and available young women between the ages of 6 and 30 are kidnapped. Should the victim have children she usually is forced to flee without them.

From John F. Peters, "Yanomama Mate Selection and Marriage" in *Journal of Comparative Family Studies,* 18 (Spring, 1987):80–81. *Journal of Comparative Family Studies:* Department of Sociology, University of Calgary, Calgary, Alberta T2N 1N4, Canada. Reprinted by permission.

likely to pass on inheritable diseases might not be allowed to marry. The writers believed that such measures would not only enhance the well-being of the society, but also maximize happiness within marriage as well.

Few of us are likely to be persuaded that arranged marriages are better than those secured through individual choice. Both kinds have their advantages and their disadvantages. There probably is no best way. But, if in our society mate selection is going to be a matter of individual determination, we should at least be aware of the problems and processes involved in the choices we make.

What We Expect in a Mate

What do you regard as the qualities in an ideal mate? More importantly, what qualities do you want in your own mate? A male undergraduate student offered his list of qualities of an ideal wife (Bales 1929):

1. *Intelligence* is easily the most important virtue. . . . I could never be happy and married to a dumbbell.

2. *Character.* I use this term in a general way and subdivide it to make my meaning clear.

    a. *Unselfishness,* in my opinion, is the first requisite to married happiness. I don't mean that I expect a wife to forget herself in bovine devotion to me but I am certain that I have no sympathy for the woman whose first thought is of herself.
    b. *Loyalty* can be the most beautiful of traits. The trials of a man's life can be met with greater courage and left with fewer scars because of the staunch comradeship of a loyal wife.
    c. *Honesty* is of self-evident importance. I refer to absence of deceit and to frankness.
    d. *Sympathy* . . . I know that I can be more successful if my wife has some understanding of me and the difficulties of my work.
    e. *Energy.* Personal laziness is unforgivable.
    f. *Sex purity.*

3. *Disposition.* I refer to buoyancy of nature.

4. *Health.*

5. *Appearance.* My humble wish is that my wife be sufficiently handsome so that no one will pity me. Neatness and taste are far more important than natural beauty.

6. *Education,* in itself, is not especially admirable but it does lead to similarity of taste.

7. *Business ability.* I have seen too many men driven to grayness and imminent insanity by their wives' faulty financial cooperation.

8. *Domesticity.* I still believe in the tradition that a woman's chief function is that of a homemaker if she chooses to marry.

The preceding was written in 1929. Clearly, at least some of our ideals have changed. A list given us by a female student in 1988 had the following qualities for her ideal mate:

1. Have a strong religious commitment.
2. Be career-oriented with hopes and plans for the future.
3. Be physically attractive, have a healthy body.
4. Come from an emotionally healthy family.
5. Be sexually satisfying.
6. Enjoy being physically active.
7. Be independent.
8. Be committed to the relationship, and want security and trust within the marriage.
9. Be romantic. Bring me flowers and cards. Take me out to dinner. Dance alone with me at home.
10. Be exciting and enjoy change.

How do the two lists square with your own ideals? What do most Americans want?

Qualities Desired in a Mate

The question of what most Americans look for in a mate has been addressed in both popular and professional sources. Nearly fifty thousand women responded to a poll conducted by *Family Circle* magazine on various aspects of family life (Jacoby 1987). One of the questions asked what things most pleased and displeased them about their husbands. The two qualities that pleased women the most were expressing love and functioning as a good provider. The qualities that most displeased the respondents were sulking when hurt or angry, easy loss of temper, and lack of communication.

In a survey of 332 undergraduates, researchers had the students rank fifteen characteristics according to their importance in a heterosexual relationship (Daniel, O'Brien, McCabe, and Quinter 1985). The five most important qualities were intelligence, sensitivity, physical attractiveness, a sense of humor, and ambition. The list is consistent with the *Family Circle* survey. Sensitive people should be more likely to openly express their love and avoid being noncommunicative. And intelligent and ambitious people have the qualities that should make for good providers.

Finally, Buss and Barnes (1986) surveyed ninety-two married couples and one hundred unmarried undergraduate students to identify the characteristics that people desire in a mate. The ten most frequently named qualities are shown in table 5.1. While there were some similarities between the two groups, there were also some differences. The differences suggest that once

Table 5.1 Most Valued Qualities in a Mate

92 married couples	100 unmarried students
1. Good companion	1. Kind and understanding
2. Considerate	2. Exciting personality
3. Honest	3. Intelligent
4. Affectionate	4. Physically attractive
5. Dependable	5. Healthy
6. Intelligent	6. Easygoing
7. Kind	7. Creative
8. Understanding	8. Wants children
9. Interesting to talk to	9. College graduate
10. Loyal	10. Good earning capacity

From David M. Buss and Michael Barnes, "Preferences in Human Mate Selection" in *Journal of Personality and Social Psychology*, 50:562, 568. Copyright 1986 by the American Psychological Association. Reprinted by permission.

A sense of humor is one of the qualities we value in others.

people are married, they may value other qualities in their mate than when they were dating. In other words, some of the qualities you are looking for in a mate may not be the kinds of things that will be important in a good marital relationship. And some of the qualities you overlook may prove to be quite important for the relationship.

There were also some sex differences in the results. Among the married couples, women gave greater emphasis than men to such qualities as considerate, dependable, and kind. They also appreciated such qualities as being fond of children, well-liked by others, and having a good earning capacity. The husbands gave greater emphasis to such things as being physically attractive and a good cook. Among the unmarried students, males also rated physical

Dates and Mates: What Do People Want?

Have you ever thought about the kind of person you want to marry? What kinds of qualities do you want him or her to possess? How does this compare with the kind of person you prefer to date? Are there differences? Do you think that these findings are typical of your peers as well?

Interview six students. Ask three of them to make a list of the qualities they prefer in someone they date. Ask three others to list the qualities they want in someone they marry. Compare the two sets of lists. What similarities and differences are there? What do you see as the implications of your findings for the quality of relationships? Do people look for qualities in dates that are likely to lead to satisfying marriages? How do your lists compare with those given in table 5.1?

If the entire class participates in this project, have half the class interview males only and the other half females only. Then compare the results along the lines suggested above, but noting gender differences in preferences for both dating and mating.

attractiveness more important than did females. The females had greater interest than the males in a partner being a college graduate and having good earning capacity.

Thus, while males and females value a lot of the same things in a partner, there are some differences. Women are still concerned about men fulfilling their traditional role as a breadwinner. Men are concerned that their partners present a good appearance. Such concerns reflect a society that remains male-dominated. Females worry about financial security. Males want to display their prizes before others. Fortunately, people are concerned about other matters in their mates as well.

Exchange and Equity

If you asked people what they expect in a mate, they will name the kind of qualities just discussed. They are not likely to say that they also expect someone who will strike up a good bargain with them in the relationship. Yet there is a sense in which we can talk about mate selection as a process of exchange in which people seek equity.

In an exchange relationship, people seek to maximize their rewards and minimize their costs. This does not mean that people seek to take advantage of others, for most of us also believe in equity and are most comfortable in relationships where there is relative equity. But two different relationships could offer equity while also offering differing rewards. For example, a man may propose a traditional marriage to a woman. He offers to be the breadwinner. In return for giving her economic security, he expects her to take care of the home and the children. They will also, of course, provide each other with emotional support and a sexual relationship. The two people might both see this as an equitable arrangement, and be willing to engage in the exchange. Another man might offer the same woman an egalitarian marriage. They will both be employed outside the home and share in the responsibilities around the house. This, too, is an equitable arrangement. But depending on the woman's values and aspirations, the rewards are very different. If she values a career for herself, she will define the second proposal as one that is much more rewarding.

Even though we don't consciously think in terms of bargaining and exchange, there are always assumptions about what each mate will give and what each will receive. There are likely to be assumptions about who will handle which tasks in the home. In an era of changing roles, the assumptions of the two partners may be different. The result will be bargaining and negotiation after marriage. As one student told us:

> When I was married, I thought he would do all the repairs around the house and he thought I would do all the cleaning and washing. I had no intention of doing all the housework and he didn't have the faintest idea about how to repair things. But I not only know how, I also love to do this kind of work. We had some arguments about it all. But now we share the housework and cooking. And I do a lot of the repair work.

It is interesting to ponder how many marriages begin with differing expectations on the part of the partners. When those expectations confront reality, the bargaining process begins. The partners must try to clarify the nature of the exchange and bring about consensual equity in the marriage.

Narrowing the Field: Assortative Mating

Theoretically, there are millions of people you might marry. Realistically, there are relatively few. The choices for women are even fewer than those for men, because of the sex composition of the population. As table 5.2 shows, after age twenty-four there is fewer than one male for each female in the United States. That is largely due to the smaller proportion of black males age twenty-five and above. After age forty-four, however, there is fewer than one man per woman for both blacks and whites. The proportion of men to women changes over time because of such things as war (thus the lower proportion in 1950 than in 1986 for those fourteen to forty-four years of age). Over time, the gap between life expectancy for men and women has also widened (thus the lower proportion of males to females in the older groups in 1986 than earlier).

Table 5.2 Ratio Of Males to Females: 1950–1987
(Number of Males Per 100 Females)

Age	1950	1960	1970	1980	1987 Total	White	Black
Under 14	103.7	103.4	103.9	104.6	104.9	105.4	103.1
14–24 years	98.2	98.7	98.7	101.9	102.4	102.9	97.9
25–44 years	96.4	95.7	95.5	97.4	98.8	100.8	86.9
45–64 years	100.1	95.7	91.6	90.7	91.8	93.2	81.8
65 and over	89.6	82.8	72.1	67.6	68.4	68.3	67.1

Source: U.S. Bureau of the Census 1989:16.

Mate Selection as a Filtering Process

It would, then, be impossible for everyone of marriageable age in the nation to be married at the same time. But even if there were equal numbers of men and women, not everyone would be equally desirable. We are selective about choosing a mate. In particular, we tend to select someone who is like us in various ways. This is the principle of **homogamy,** which refers to marriage between two people who are similar in social and demographic characteristics such as age, race, ethnicity, and religion. Some social scientists use the term **assortative mating,** which is a broader concept that refers to marriage between two people who are similar on one or more characteristics. In addition to social and demographic characteristics, assortative mating may be based on personality traits, values, attitudes, and various other factors that we shall discuss below. Sometimes the term homogamy is used to include these other characteristics, but we prefer to restrict it to social and demographic factors.

Assortative mating stresses the fact that mate selection is nonrandom. That is, if we used no such criteria as age or race or any of the others to select a mate, then married partners should have a lot of differences between them. But the similarities are far greater than the differences. Mate selection is clearly not a random affair.

There are, of course, some people who do marry others who are unlike themselves. **Heterogamy** is marriage between two people who are dissimilar in some social and demographic characteristics. The difference may be along one dimension, such as a fifty-year-old woman who marries a twenty-five-year-old man who is like her in most respects except age. Or the dissimilarities may be more pronounced, such as a black Baptist man who marries a white Jewish woman who is ten years younger than he is. Sometimes a person will "marry up." **Hypergamy** is marriage with someone who is from a higher socioeconomic background. In other words, hypergamy is a particular kind of heterogamy.

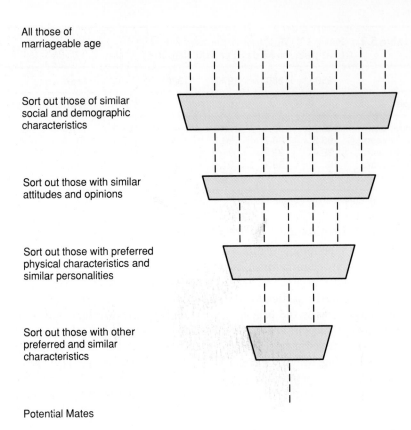

All those of
marriageable age

Sort out those of similar
social and demographic
characteristics

Sort out those with similar
attitudes and opinions

Sort out those with preferred
physical characteristics and
similar personalities

Sort out those with other
preferred and similar
characteristics

Potential Mates

Figure 5.1 *Mate selection as a filtering process.*

To get a sense of your own perspectives on these ideas, make a list of the qualities of the person you would prefer to marry. Write down the person's race, ethnic background, age, nationality, religion, and educational level. Also list any preferences you have in terms of height, weight, other physical characteristics, any personality characteristics, and any particular attitudes and values. Then make a second list of what you feel you would *accept* (as opposed to prefer) on each of the characteristics. To what extent are you similar to the person you have in mind? To what extent would you accept heterogamy?

Basically, what you have done is put people through a filtering system. In fact, we can think of mate selection as a kind of filtering process in which we sort out people according to various characteristics (figure 5.1). In the following sections, we will look at some of the more common characteristics that are used.

Age

Age is the most prominent factor along which we sort people out in mate selection. Men's age, on the average, is about two years older than that of women at the time of marriage. The similarity in age is especially common among

Seeking Intimate Relationships

Those who are dissimilar in age have marriages as good as those who are homogamous.

younger couples. Those who marry at older ages, or those going into a second marriage, are more likely to have a larger age gap between the two partners (Buss 1985).

Age homogamy has been increasing since the beginning of the century (Atkinson and Glass 1985). Women have tended more and more to marry men who are within four years of their own age. There has also been a decline in the number of older women who marry younger men.

An examination of age heterogamy in marriage reported that it is more common among people in lower socioeconomic classes (Vera, Berardo, and Berardo 1985). The research also reported that those who are dissimilar in age have no poorer quality marriages than those who are homogamous. The popular idea that a large age difference is likely to lead to more problems was not supported by the data. The researchers suggested two possible reasons. First, there tends to be lower marital satisfaction in the lower socioeconomic strata, so that the age-heterogamous effects observed in the past were really the effects of socioeconomic status. Alternatively, the results might reflect the fact that age has become, as some researchers have suggested, a less important determinant of our attitudes and behavior.

Ethnic Background

Does it matter if your ancestry is Irish or German or Chinese when it comes to getting married? It does to some people. In a small Illinois agricultural community over a fifty-year period, twenty-one out of twenty-three Germans married other Germans and sixteen out of twenty-five Irish married other Irish (Davis-Brown, Salamon, and Surra 1987). Ethnic background is becoming less of a criterion of selection, however. Since World War II the rate of intermarriage among many ethnic groups has risen considerably. Alba and Golden (1986) examined 27,597 marriages among couples with differing ethnic backgrounds. The couples were not people who had immigrated from other countries, but those who had been Americans for at least one or more generations. While the rates were not as high as they were before World War II, there is still a considerable amount of marriage within ethnic groups.

More Europeans intermarried with other groups than married within their own group. Still, a third of those of British background married other Britishers, and the rates of marriage within the ethnic group were around 25 percent for Irish, Germans, French, and Scandinavians. Among non-Europeans, the rates of marriage within ethnic groups were generally higher. Over 72 percent of Mexicans and 74.4 percent of Asians married within their own groups.

Table 5.3	Interracial Marriages: 1987 (Numbers in Thousands)			
			Race of wife	
		White	*Black*	*Other*
Race of husband	**White**	46,597	56	358
	Black	121	3,674	33
	Other	223	8	1,216

Source: U.S. Bureau of the Census, *Current Population Reports,* Series P-20, No. 424, "Household and Family Characteristics: March 1987" (Washington, DC: Government Printing Office) 1988:94.

Race

Race imposes more constraints than ethnic background on our marital choices. As table 5.3 shows, the white-black line is seldom crossed. The number of black-white marriages has nearly tripled since 1970, but they still represent far less than one percent of all marriages. More than 98 percent of Americans marry within their own racial group.

Religion

In their study of one thousand engaged couples in the 1940s, Burgess and Wallin (1943) found that religious affiliation was one of the strongest homogamous factors. And it was religious affiliation, rather than religious activity or degree of religious commitment, that was important in mate selection. Indeed, up through at least the 1950s popular magazines carried articles on the perils of interfaith marriages and/or the ways to cope with an interfaith union.

Unfortunately, the Census Bureau has not collected information about interreligious marriages since the late 1950s. However, Glenn (1982) used data from national surveys conducted during the 1970s to identify patterns and trends. He found that religion has become somewhat less important as a factor in marriage since the 1950s. However, it is still strong (figure 5.2). Nearly 90 percent of Americans married within their faith in the 1970s. This represented only a small drop from the 93.6 percent figure of 1957. And not only do people tend to marry within the broad religious categories, but also within specific denominations. Among Protestants, over three-fourths married within their denomination.

Glenn also looked at data on the reported happiness of the marriages. He found that men with religiously homogamous marriages were more likely than those in heterogamous marriages to report being "very happy" with the marriage. There was little difference between homogamous and heterogamous

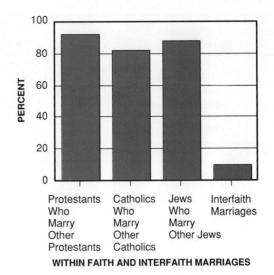

Figure 5.2 *Religious affiliation and marriage: 1973–1978.*
Source: Data from Glenn 1982:557.

women. Those least likely to report being very happy with the marriage were religious men and women married to a spouse with no religion (although more than half of those said they were very happy).

Education

Men tend to marry women who are either at their own educational level or somewhat below them in education. As figure 5.3 shows, educational homogamy is fairly strong, though not as strong as religion, race, or age. Still, in two-thirds of American marriages the two partners are at roughly the same educational level. In 18.2 percent of the cases, the husband has a higher educational level, and in the remaining 14.7 percent the wife has a higher educational level. Less than 1 percent of the marriages involve a large gap, with one partner being a college graduate and the other having failed to complete high school.

Personality

Some scholars have argued that people marry those who will complement their own personality. That is, we marry people who are different from us, but who mesh well with us. Thus, an individual who tends to be volatile might marry someone who is even-keeled, helping the volatile person to maintain more control. But as reasonable as that sounds, the evidence shows that we tend to marry people who are more like than unlike us in personality.

Seeking Intimate Relationships

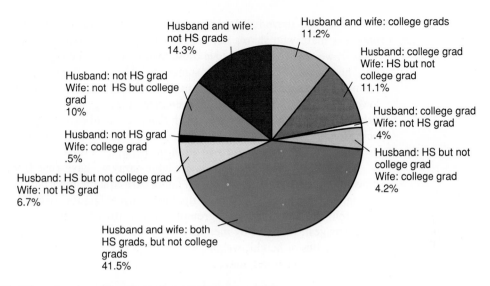

Figure 5.3 *Educational combinations of married couples: 1985.*
Source: U.S. Bureau of the Census, *Current Population Reports,* Series P-23, No. 150, "Population Profile of the United States: 1984–85" (Washington, DC: Government Printing Office) 1987:28.

Buss (1985), for example, examined married couples along sixteen personality traits. The traits included such things as tendencies to dominance, extraversion, and quarrelsomeness. He had used self-ratings, and ratings by the spouse and an independent observer to minimize the possibility of erroneous results. He found a small, but positive correlation between spouses on the personality traits. That is, spouses tend to be more like than unlike each other in their personalities.

As in the case of other variables, those with similar personalities seem to more likely to have satisfying relationships. An older study by Pickford, Signori, and Rempel (1966) used three groups of thirty-five married couples. One group was composed of those happily married. A second group consisted of those having troubles in their marriage. Couples on the verge of separation comprised the third group. They found that the happily married couples were more likely than the others to be similar in their personality traits.

And So Forth

Our list goes on and on. As Buss (1985:47) points out, the tendency to select a mate that is similar to you is so strong that one person suggested we use the term *assortative narcissism.* Or as Buss and Barnes (1986) put it:

> The range of characteristics that show positive assortment can only be described as staggering. Couples show assortment for age, race, religion, social status, cognitive abilities, values, interests, attitudes, personality dispositions, drinking, smoking, classes of acts, physical attractiveness, and a host of other physical variables such as height, weight, lung volume, and ear lobe length.

Even the above list does not exhaust all of the factors. We are likely to choose a mate who shares our sense of humor (Murstein and Brust 1985). That is, we tend to like and love those who find the same things funny as we do. Those whose first language is something other than English tend to marry within their language group (Stevens and Schoen 1988), particularly those at lower educational levels. There are even more marriages between people whose first name begins with the same letter than we would expect by chance (Kopelman and Lang 1985). Such alliterative homogamy, like some of the others we noted, is less pronounced now than formerly.

In going from age to alliterative homogamy we have gone from the significant to the trivial. Clearly, not all factors are equally important nor equally strong. As Buss (1985:49) sums it up, the strongest factors are age, education, race, religion, and ethnic background. Similar attitudes and opinions are the next strongest, followed by mental ability, socioeconomic status; the physical characteristics of height, weight, eye color; personality traits; number of siblings; and various other characteristics.

Why Assortative Mating?

What factors are at work in assortative mating? Why do we tend to select someone who is like us along so many dimensions? Is it indeed a case of narcissism, or is something else operating in the decision-making process?

Propinquity

As someone has said, even if there is a "one and only" for you, he or she is likely to live within driving distance. Most of us marry someone who is located nearby. The "nearby" may be a neighborhood, a city, a college campus, or a workplace. Thus, we are likely to marry someone of the same age and educational level because many people meet a future mate in school. We are likely to marry someone of the same religion because many meet at a church or synagogue. Racial and ethnic housing patterns make it more likely that we will interact with, be attracted to, and eventually marry someone within our own racial and ethnic group.

In other words, the various social and demographic factors are powerful because they tend to cluster us with others who are similar to us. And we search for our mates among those who are near at hand. Thus, in the study of the small Illinois agricultural community, the researchers found that recent shifts toward more heterogamy were the result of a breakdown in ethnic and religious segregation in the community (Davis-Brown, Salamon, and Surra 1987:52). As the everyday contact of diverse people increased, rates of intermarriage also increased.

Attraction

As noted in chapter 2, we tend to be attracted to those who are like us. This is not necessarily the same as narcissism, however. Rather, it may be a case of feeling more comfortable with the familiar. We know how to relate to people who are like us. We have more experience with them, both in the family and among those nearby in neighborhoods, schools, and churches. Many stories and movies have pointed out the discomfort and difficulties people face who try to function in a foreign land or even among people of a different social class in their own country. Terms like *snobbish, common, uppity, cliquish,* and *rude* sometimes may be rooted in the uncomfortable person's feelings as much as in the behavior of the group. A young woman whose brother acquired great wealth in business told about her own problem with his new set of friends:

> He wanted to fix me up with one of his single friends. I said I'd rather meet this fellow in a group setting. So I went to one of their parties. I thought they were all really snooty. My brother said they liked me a lot. I couldn't believe that at first. But I guess he was right. I just didn't feel comfortable with them. They didn't talk about things that I knew anything about. I still haven't let my brother fix me up. I don't know if I ever will.

Some people cross such social boundaries as class, race, nationality, and ethnicity with relative ease. Others find that they can relate to people who are different, but they are not sufficiently comfortable with them to form an intimate relationship. In other words, the principle of attraction means that we reject those who are dissimilar as much as it means that we choose those who are similar to us. This is not necessarily a judgment about the worth of other people. It may be simply a matter of sorting out people according to how much we feel at ease with them.

Family Traditions and Pressures

While we like to think that mate selection is purely a matter of personal choice, there is still the factor of the family's reaction to the selection. Your parents may no longer choose your mate, but it is unlikely that you will completely ignore their views. Indeed, you may reject some possible mates before the relationship gets started because you know that your parents would strongly disapprove.

Family traditions and pressures are one reason why matters such as race, religion, and ethnicity are still important. It is in the family that we first learn about the importance of religion, for example. And we also learn about the problems that will attend an interreligious, interracial, or interethnic marriage.

Family traditions and pressures can work in the opposite direction as well. That is, you may be pressured to marry someone about whom you have doubts because all of your family members like and approve of that person.

Parents don't choose our mates for us, but they influence our decision.

The authors once counseled with a couple who had virtually no interests in common. They came from the same town, had the same socioeconomic background, and were members of the same church. But he had a college degree and she was only a high-school graduate. And they were dramatically different in the kinds of things they enjoyed doing, in their beliefs about family finances, in their child-rearing philosophies, and in a variety of attitudes about life. We asked them why they had married in the first place. The man reflected a moment, then said: "I guess because everybody expected us to get married. Both our families thought it was a good match, so we just went along with them." They are now divorced.

When you marry, you do not just marry an individual. You marry into a family. That family, therefore, will have some voice in deciding whether you are an appropriate choice.

Should I Marry My Baby's Father?

Patti is a twenty-six-year-old single mother. The father of the child wanted to marry Patti, but she refused. Her story shows how some of the things that might initially attract us to another person are not sufficient for a long-term relationship. Patti's marriage would have been a heterogamous one. She decided that it wouldn't work:

> I guess I am an idealistic person, but I always pictured myself in a wonderful life with a loving spouse with whom I would share things. I was attracted to Paul, my daughter's father, because he was so good looking. I thought that anyone that good looking would have a lot of other good qualities. So I didn't pay attention to some of the warning signs, like the fact that he dressed carelessly and didn't take care of himself very well.
>
> Anyway, we had a whirlwind relationship that quickly involved sex. And I got pregnant. He suggested that we should get married. We weren't even living together yet. I guess the idea of getting married and living with Paul made me think about the kind of relationship we had. I had felt, but hadn't even admitted to myself, that there were some serious problems. We were so different in so many ways. Paul has no interest in reading or learning anything. He can sit for hours and just watch television. He is also not very good at just sitting and talking about things. When I thought about the things we had

> in common, they didn't seem as important as the things we didn't have in common.
>
> During my pregnancy, I felt physically and emotionally unable to break up with him. I tried a couple of times. But each time, he would talk pleadingly with me, send me flowers and cards, and promise to become more like the person I wanted him to be. I was so afraid of being alone that I agreed to continue the relationship. But I kept putting him off about the marriage. Besides, I needed his help and wanted to share parenthood with him.
>
> For awhile, because he didn't want our relationship to end, I thought that being a father might change him. But he wasn't as involved or as enthusiastic as I was about the baby. Finally, I guess I realized that he wouldn't change. It hit me one day that the worst part of each day was the time I spent with Paul. I got tense as soon as I saw him. He had little to say to me; I had to carry on the conversation. One day I just told him that it was over. He tried to persuade me again, and sent the usual flowers and cards. But I wouldn't see him again.
>
> I certainly don't regret breaking up with him. He's never tried to see his daughter. She's three now, and I love her dearly. I guess my major problem with her now is trying to decide what I'm going to tell her about her father some day when she asks.

Hedging Your Bets: Predictors of Marital Satisfaction

Even if you select someone who is similar to you, it doesn't guarantee that the marriage will be a happy or lasting one. The nineteenth-century philosopher John Stuart Mill was so impressed with the problems of finding a suitable mate that he called marriage a lottery. He said that those who calculate the odds of winding up in a happy union would probably not even take the risk of trying (Rose 1983:108–9). We do not believe that the odds are that great. But we do agree that there is always a risk and that people should make the effort to minimize the risk of a bad match. One way to do that is to attend to the principle of similarity. That is, the more alike you are on social, demographic, and various other factors, the more likely will the marriage succeed. But there are other ways, for we know about many of the factors that are associated with marital satisfaction.

Timing

By timing we refer to such things as the length of the courtship and the age at marriage. There are people who have whirlwind courtships that result in marriage in a matter of days or weeks. Some of them last and are satisfying unions. But the odds are against it. You are more likely to have a rewarding marriage if you have a longer courtship. Grover, Russell, Schumm, and Paff-Bergen (1985) looked at the marital satisfaction of fifty-one middle-aged wives and found a strong correlation between satisfaction and the length of time the women had dated their husbands.

Similarly, one of the strong predictors of stability and satisfaction is age at marriage. Again, there are some who marry as teenagers and wind up in long-term, happy unions. But it is a great risk. There is also, however, a popular notion that later marriages may be problematic because people get "set in their ways." Robert Bitter (1986) used a national sample of married people to investigate the question of whether late marriages are less stable. His conclusions are fascinating. He found that there is a marriage "squeeze" as people delay getting married until their thirties or forties. That is, there are fewer homogeneous choices available. People who marry later, therefore, are more likely to have a heterogamous union. And it is the heterogamy rather than the later age that results in a higher level of instability. If you marry later and have a homogamous union, your chances of breaking up are less than if you married at an earlier age.

Equity

We have frequently mentioned the importance of perceived equity in a relationship. It is important for marriage as well as other intimate relationships. A study of 162 couples reported that the greater the perceived equity in the relationship, the more that both spouses were satisfied (Davidson 1984). The point we want to make here is that if you don't feel equity in your relationship now, it is unlikely that you will do so after marriage. In fact, problems of equity may come up after marriage even when they didn't exist before the marriage.

Home responsibilities are one area in which the question of equity may arise. Some couples never discuss matters before marriage that are likely to be sources of conflict afterward: who will take care of the laundry, the cooking, the housecleaning, the finances, and all of the multitude of other things that must be done? Problems of equity may also arise in such areas as emotional support. If one of the partners is always giving and the other always receiving the major part of the support, the giver is likely to grow weary of the inequity. In most cases, the germs of such problems are already evident in the intimate relationship that exists before the marriage. It is wise, therefore, for those contemplating marriage to ask to what extent they feel equity in the relationship.

Communication

One of the most important factors in marriage is the pattern of communication. The ability to talk over problems effectively is particularly important. We shall discuss communication in depth in chapter 10. Here we want to underscore its importance as a help in predicting whether a potential marriage might succeed. The way you communicate before marriage is the best indicator of how you are likely to communicate afterward. Indeed, some research has shown that communication patterns prior to marriage are one of the best predictors of how well the marriage will succeed (Goleman 1985).

Good communication involves not only the ability to discuss problems, but also self-disclosure, a sharing of daily events, interesting "small talk," and positive conversation about the spouse (words that convey respect, affection, love, etc.). Again, the point is to examine the relationship prior to marriage to see to what extent it is characterized by good communication patterns. As Patti (PERSONAL) said, one of the reasons she decided not to marry Paul was his inability to sustain meaningful conversation with her. Paul seemed to become articulate only when he saw that the relationship was in jeopardy. It is unlikely that he would have easily altered his style after marriage.

Effective communication and similarity, incidentally, tend to go together. For instance, if you have different religious, family, or work values than a potential spouse, you will be handicapped when you try to solve problems in which those values are pertinent (Craddock 1980). Similarity enhances the ease of communicating effectively and of resolving the various kinds of problems that inevitably confront married couples.

PREPARE: A Multifactor Approach

As in the case of assortative mating, there are a good many other factors that go into a satisfying marriage. Problems can arise from a great many things, ranging from such things as dissimilar attitudes to incompatible body clocks

Marital satisfaction is enhanced when a couple agrees on how to have fun.

(one spouse may be a morning and the other an evening person). Predicting marital satisfaction requires a variety of factors.

But not all factors are equally important. One effort to determine which are the most crucial is PREPARE, an instrument devised by Dr. David Olson and his colleagues to predict marital success among those contemplating marriage. PREPARE was developed in 1977 and validated by David Fournier in 1978 on the basis of one thousand premarital couples and two hundred clergy who had used the instrument. Following this validation, some revisions were made and a second version appeared in 1979. Results from subsequent research are impressive. For example, Fowers and Olson (1986) tested 164 engaged couples, then studied them again three years later. They found that satisfied couples had scored considerably higher on the instrument than those who canceled their engagement or who married and were dissatisfied or who had divorced. They point out that PREPARE scores predicted with 80 to 90 percent accuracy which couples were separated and divorced and which were happily married!

PREPARE measures eleven different areas: the extent to which the couple has realistic expectations; personality issues; communication; conflict resolution; management of finances; leisure activities; the sexual relationship; children and marriage; family and friends; equalitarian roles; and religious orientation. For example, the sexual relationship is evaluated by such measures as the extent to which you would be willing to try almost any sexual activity your partner wanted and the extent to which you believe the two of you talk freely about sexual expectations and interests. The religious orientation is evaluated by such measures as the extent to which you feel it is important to pray with your partner and believe that you and your partner find the same meaning in religion.

The researchers not only measured each partner's score, but also looked at the extent to which the partners agreed in each area. The eleven areas are all important in predicting marital satisfaction. In many cases, the important thing is not that you believe a particular way about something, but that you and your partner believe the same thing (religious orientation, for example). In other cases, you may believe the same thing but it can be dysfunctional for a stable, satisfying marriage (for example, both may believe that good marriages are free of conflict).

It is important to keep in mind that no instrument is perfect. You may have serious differences with someone on one or more of the eleven areas prior to marriage. You may continue to have those differences afterward, yet have a meaningful and stable relationship. But the odds are not with you. The more agreement you have in these eleven areas, the more likely you are to have a satisfying marriage.

A Final Caveat

Even with an instrument like PREPARE, it is difficult to predict long-term satisfaction. After all, the researchers only did a three-year follow-up. We don't know if the instrument will also predict much longer relationships. There are a number of reasons why long-term satisfaction is difficult to predict prior to marriage. One is that our knowledge of another person is always limited. Even though a good deal of self-disclosure goes on in a relationship, there is usually also a good deal of "putting your best foot forward" during courtship. People may not reveal some of the more problematic aspects of their lives until after the marriage.

Second, everyone changes over time. You may seem to be perfectly compatible with a partner now. But both of you will be different people in ten years. What if you change in ways that make you less compatible? One couple shared with us problems they were having in the tenth year of their marriage that they couldn't have anticipated. The wife had decided to go to college to pursue a degree and a career. Their two children were both in school, and she was not satisfied staying at home. Her husband had not attended college and felt threatened by her plans. Moreover, he could not understand her excitement about her classes, her interest in a variety of subjects that meant nothing to him. Eventually he began to ridicule the things she would tell him. She, in turn, stopped talking to him about her interests. Soon, they fell into a pattern of living separate lives while sharing a house and two children. They were different people than when they were first married. And the differences led to less rather than more compatibility.

Our needs as well as our interests change over time. In some cases, something that attracted two people initially becomes a problem as time passes. For example, Janice is a data processor who married Frank because he was strong and assertive. He seemed like the kind of person who would not be defeated by life, and who would always be able to support his family. But after a few years, Frank's strength began to look more like domination to her. He wanted complete control of their finances. Even though she worked, he insisted on giving her an allowance and managing the rest of the budget himself. At the time of their marriage, Janice felt she needed a strong and assertive husband. Some years later, she felt able to care for herself if necessary. Frank's aggressive nature had become a liability because of her changing needs.

Such changes cannot be predicted. We can never be certain, therefore, that a relationship will be lasting and satisfying. But we can increase our odds by attending to the things that we know are part of long-term, satisfying marriages.

PRINCIPLES FOR ENHANCING INTIMACY

1. Although most Americans reject the notion of arranged marriages, it is a good idea to talk over your choice of a prospective mate with a trusted older or more experienced person. This person should be someone who knows you well and who has your best interests at heart. If he or she has major reservations about your choice, listen and consider the comments carefully.

2. If you haven't selected a mate as yet or even if you already have someone in mind, take the time to seriously consider what kind of person you want him or her to be. Make a list of those characteristics that you really feel are essential in someone with whom you plan to spend your life, and refer to it often.

3. If you are contemplating marriage in the near future, it is vital to know what your prospective mate expects from you and from your relationship. Talk about your shared and individual goals, about your respective roles in the marriage, about if and when you are going to have children, and so forth.

4. The old adage says that opposites attract, but it doesn't acknowledge that opposites often produce an unsatisfactory union. The evidence shows that the greater the similiarity between you and your spouse, the greater your chances for a happy and enduring marriage.

5. Take time before you marry to get to know your future mate. A longer courtship gives you a greater opportunity to know more fully your spouse-to-be and to establish the patterns of communication that are so essential to a successful marriage.

In many societies, marriages have been arranged by parents rather than through the choice of the individuals getting married. Political and economic considerations in those societies are more important than love. In most modern societies, the ideal is for people to select their own mates.

Most of us know the kinds of things we prefer and those we dislike in a mate. The unmarried prefer such qualities as kindness, understanding, an exciting personality, intelligence, attractiveness, and good health. Married people have some of the same and some different preferences. There are also some gender differences in preferences. In addition, people will be more satisfied when they are in a relationship of equity.

While the number of eligible mates is theoretically enormous, practically there are only a few for each of us. Because of the sex ratio, women have fewer choices than men. Mate selection is a filtering process. We engage in assortative mating, which means that most people have homogamous rather than heterogamous marriages. Assortative mating takes place along the lines of age, ethnic background, race, religion, education, personality, and a variety of other factors. Assortative mating occurs because of a number of factors, including propinquity, attraction, and family traditions and pressures.

A homogamous marriage doesn't guarantee stability or satisfaction. Homogamous marriages are more likely than heterogamous to last and to be happy, but there are a number of additional factors that enhance your chances. A longer courtship and later age at marriage both increase the probability of a lasting and satisfying union. Other factors include perceived equity, good communication patterns, and the various areas covered in the PREPARE instrument.

Long-term satisfaction is difficult to predict for two reasons. First, our knowledge of someone is always limited. People may not reveal problematic aspects of their lives until after the marriage. Second, our needs and interests change over time. They may change in a way that makes a couple more compatible, but they can also change in a way that makes the couple diverge from each other.

The Single Option

One well-known producer of frozen foods now has over eighty different offerings that are designed to feed just one person. The food industry, like American business generally, is aware of the growing number of people who are single. Traditionally, our society has operated on the premise that most people will marry. But today an increasing number of people are choosing the single life. Many are delaying marriage, others are choosing not to engage in it at all, and still others, who had been married, have once again returned to the single life.

Thirty years ago, the majority of Americans believed that there was something wrong with the person who opted for the single life. Even today, people tend to judge the single more severely. Over four hundred college students evaluated the personality traits of married men and women higher than those of the unmarried (Etaugh and Stern 1984). A survey of three thousand singles in various parts of the country reported that over half felt some pressure to marry (Simenauer and Carroll 1982:332). The pressure came from parents, co-workers, dates, and personal feelings. Still, about 45 percent said they never felt any pressure, and the majority of Americans now agree that there is nothing wrong with choosing to be single. In this chapter, we shall look at the extent of singleness and why people opt for it. We will discuss some of the aspects of the single life. And we will see how single people manage to fulfill their needs for intimacy. It should be noted that this is a relatively new and underdeveloped area of study. There are not a great many studies, and those that exist tend to have small samples and focus disproportionately on women. Many of our conclusions, therefore, are tentative.

Increasing numbers of Americans are single, though not always by choice.

How Many Singles?

As figure 6.1 shows, the proportion of Americans who are unmarried has risen steadily. Moreover, the rise in the unmarried ranks has not been due merely to an increase in divorce. Greater numbers of both males and females are choosing to remain single for longer periods of time and, in some cases, for life (table 6.1). By 1987, only about 63 percent of the population was married. Over 65.1 million Americans, eighteen years and older, were unmarried. Of these, 38.2 million had never been married; the others were either widowed or divorced. The figures are particularly pronounced for the younger age groups. Among those between twenty-five and thirty-four years of age, the proportion who remain unmarried has more than doubled since 1970.

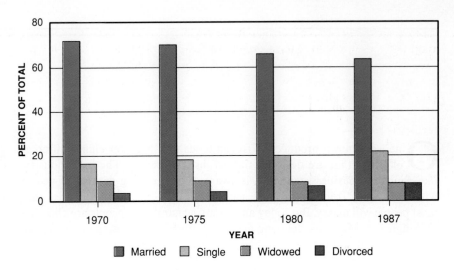

Figure 6.1 *Marital status of the population: 1970–1987.*
Source: U.S. Bureau of the Census 1989:42.

Table 6.1	Single (Never-Married) Persons as Percent of Total Population: 1970–1987							
	Male				Female			
Age	*1970*	*1975*	*1980*	*1987*	*1970*	*1975*	*1980*	*1987*
Total	18.9	20.8	23.8	25.3	13.7	14.6	17.1	18.6
18–19 years	92.8	93.1	94.3	96.8	75.6	77.7	82.8	89.8
20–24 years	54.7	59.9	68.8	77.7	35.8	40.3	50.2	60.8
25–29 years	19.1	22.3	33.1	42.2	10.5	13.8	20.9	28.8
30–34 years	9.4	11.1	15.9	23.1	6.2	7.5	9.5	14.6
35–39 years	7.2	8.6	7.8	12.4	5.4	5.0	6.2	8.4
40–44 years	6.3	7.2	7.1	6.9	4.9	4.8	4.8	6.4
45–54 years	7.5	6.3	6.1	5.9	4.9	4.6	4.7	4.5
55–64 years	7.8	6.5	5.3	5.8	6.8	5.1	4.5	4.2
65 and over	7.5	4.7	4.9	4.5	7.7	5.8	5.9	5.5

Source: U.S. Bureau of the Census 1989:43.

We need to keep these figures in perspective however. Note that overall 25.3 percent of males and 18.6 percent of females were unmarried in 1987. These figures are still lower than those around the beginning of the century. For example, census figures show that for those eighteen years and older in 1910, 33.3 percent of males and 23.3 percent of females were unmarried. In other words, we have not yet reached as high a proportion of singles in the society as existed in the first years of the century. Many factors, as we shall discuss, contribute to the decision to remain single. It also may be that marriage patterns follow long-term cycles and that at some point in the future the proportion of the unmarried will drop again. For the foreseeable future, however, it seems that singles will comprise a large and probably increasing proportion of the population.

Myths about Singles

Who are the people who are single? As noted in figure 6.1, the unmarried category includes the divorced, the widowed, and the never-married. There is a popular stereotype of the never-married as being either *"swingers—the beautiful people who are constantly going to parties, who have uncommitted lives and a lot of uncommitted sex"* or *"lonely losers,"* who are depressed a good deal of the time (Stein 1976:2–3). But most singles fall into neither of those categories. Like other groups who have been subjected to something of a social stigma, singles have had to battle stereotypes and myths.

Cargan and Melko (1982) surveyed four hundred people in Dayton, Ohio, including some married, never-married, divorced, and remarried individuals. They used their data to counter seven myths about the never-married (Cargan and Melko 1982:193–202):

1. They are still tied to their mothers' apron strings. In fact, the researchers found little difference between the never-married and others in their perceptions of parents and other relatives.

2. They are selfish. Some people believe that singles do not get married simply because they are too centered on themselves, leading lives of self-indulgence and pursuing self-interests. But Cargan and Melko found that they value friends more highly than do the married and contribute more to community service.

3. They are financially well-off. The married people in the researchers' sample were better off economically than the never-married. Indeed, in the society as a whole, married people are likely to be better off than singles. There are a sufficient number of affluent, single professionals to lend credibility to the myth. But comparing singles to families, a far greater proportion are in poverty.

4. They are happier. This is a myth held by singles themselves, many of whom tend to think that they are happier than married people. Married people think otherwise. The evidence, as we shall discuss, suggests that marrieds have an advantage in the area of well-being.

5. There are more singles now than ever. As we pointed out, there are far more singles than there were in 1970. But the proportion in 1987 was not as high as it was in the first four decades of the century.

The Awfulness of Being Unmarried

In Puritan New England, there was a stigma attached to the single state. The Puritans asserted that God had ordained humans to live in societies, "first, of Family, Secondly Church, Thirdly, Commonwealth" (John Cotton, quoted in Morgan 1944:18). The consequences of this belief for those who were unmarried are illustrated by a nineteenth-century historian (Earle 1893:36–37):

> In the early days of the New England colonies no more embarrassing or hampering condition, no greater temporal ill could befall any adult Puritan than to be unmarried. What could he do, how could he live in that new land without a wife? There were no housekeepers—and he would scarcely have been allowed to have one if there were. What could a woman do in that new settlement among unbroken forests, uncultivated lands, without a husband? The colonists married early, and they married often. Widowers and widows hastened to join their fortunes and sorrows. The father and mother of Governor Winslow had been widow and widower seven and twelve weeks, respectively, when they joined their families and themselves in mutual benefit, if not in mutual love. At a later day the impatient Governor of New Hampshire married a lady but ten days widowed. Bachelors were rare indeed, and were regarded askance and with intense disfavor by the entire community, were almost in the position of suspected criminals. They were seldom permitted to live alone, or even to choose their residence, but had to find a domicile wherever and with whomsoever the Court assigned. In Hartford [bachelors] had to pay twenty shillings a week to the town for the selfish luxury of solitary living. No colonial law seems to me more arbitrary or more comic than this order issued in the town of Eastham, Mass., in 1695, namely:
>
> > Every unmarried man in the township shall kill six blackbirds or three crows while he remains single; as a penalty for not doing it, shall not be married until he obey this order.

6. Being and staying single is an acceptable way of life. This is another myth of singles themselves, who like to assert it but don't practice it for the most part. Most singles plan on getting married at some point. In the Cargan and Melko study, most believed that they would be married within about five years.

7. Something is wrong with those who never marry. Evidence also belies this myth. An individual who postpones or even decides against marriage is not suffering from some disorder. Singles have greater problems with loneliness and with maintaining their happiness. But there are advantages as well as disadvantages to their status, and they may decide that the former outweigh the latter.

Table 6.2   Types of Singles

	Voluntary	*Involuntary*
Marital experience	The widowed and divorced who do not want to remarry	The widowed and divorced who want to remarry
No marital experience	The never-married who are postponing or forgoing marriage	The never-married who want to marry

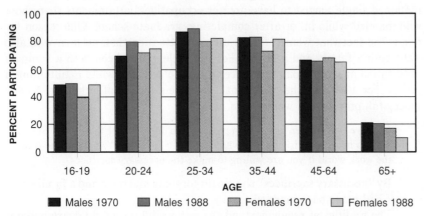

Figure 6.2 *Labor force participation rates of the never-married: 1970–1988.*
Source: U.S. Bureau of the Census 1989:385.

Why People Are Single

There is both a voluntary and an involuntary singlehood, and there are a number of reasons why individuals fall into one or the other of those categories (table 6.2). We do not know how many are voluntarily single. A Canadian study reported that 46 percent of 482 unmarried adults (mean age 33.9 years) said they were single by choice. The study of three thousand Americans found that only a third of men and a fifth of women are single because they prefer the life-style or do not want to be married (Simenauer and Carroll 1982:322). Clearly, millions of Americans choose to be single, some for life and others following a divorce or death of a spouse. Millions of others prefer to marry, but for various reasons have not or cannot. Let us look at some of the factors involved in people remaining single.

Career

Increasing proportions of both males and females in the age categories where marriage is most likely are participating in the labor force (figure 6.2). More importantly, an increasing number of males and females define marriage as

Some people choose to delay or forego marriage in order to establish a career.

an impediment to a career, and have opted to delay or forgo marriage in order to establish themselves in a career. When asked about their plans for the future, women who anticipate being housewives at age thirty-five are likely to marry in their twenties, but those who foresee a career are likely to delay marriage (Cherlin 1980).

Most single women believe that remaining unmarried will help them in their careers (Rollins 1986). And, in fact, they may be correct. A study of 663 professional women found that length of singlehood is related to career advancement (Houseknecht, Vaughan, and Statham 1987). Those women who remained single tended to have greater occupational attainments than those who married while in, or after completing, graduate school. One reason for this is the fact that women face a different situation than do men who also want both a family and a career. For the male, it has been both a common expectation and common experience to pursue a career while maintaining a family. For a woman, the choice may be more a matter of either/or. As one successful, professional woman told us:

> I believe that women have the opportunity to do whatever they want. But you have to make a decision about what you really do want. You can make it in the work world if you are willing to make the necessary sacrifices.

By "necessary sacrifices" she meant forgoing marriage and a family. She herself had never been married.

The realities of pregnancy and the responsibilities of childcare make it difficult for a woman to combine career and family. In addition, she may be expected to make her own career subservient to that of her husband. If he has an opportunity to advance by moving to a different locale, she may be counted on to follow him even if the move is detrimental to her own career. These and other problems of the employed, married woman will be discussed more fully in chapter 12.

It is not surprising, therefore, that the more educated (and, thus, probably the more career-minded) a woman is, the less likely she is to be married at an early age. Glick (1984) reported some statistics from the 1980 census. Among women twenty-five to twenty-nine years of age, 82 percent of those with eleven or less years of school were married; in comparison, 62 percent of those with seventeen or more years were married. Moreover, he estimated that about 90 percent of those with a high-school education or less would eventually marry, compared to 83 percent of those with seventeen years or more of schooling.

Men as well as women are delaying marriage in order to establish themselves firmly in a career. The following statements illustrate the perspectives of two men who have delayed marriage:

> Since I completed college, achieving success in my profession has been my primary goal. As a result, I've consciously put more effort into my career than I have my social life. I have worked long hours and traveled a lot—both of which, I felt, would be detrimental to a wife and family. Recently, I have

begun to think that the time is right. My practice is going extremely well. I have my own home. I honestly think that now I can have both a successful career and a good marriage (thirty-eight-year-old, male lawyer).

I definitely would like to get married. I feel part of me is ready emotionally. The only hindrance is that I haven't carved out my niche professionally. Personal development and finding myself has been my priority as opposed to putting my attention on material things and a career. Now I'm in a transition state, trying to establish myself in a new business. I don't want marriage and a family to take priority over finding the ultimate career for myself. Maybe in six months I'll have it together. And then I'll be ready (thirty-three-year-old, male businessman).

In sum, while marriage, a family, and meaningful work are all important to most Americans, many believe that they cannot pursue them simultaneously. They have opted to establish themselves in their career first, before beginning the pursuit of marriage and a family.

Availability of Sex

Sir Thomas More wrote in his *Utopia* that no one would want marriage if sex were available outside marriage. While that overstates the case, it is true that the ready availability of sex is a factor in remaining single. Many people now wait to marry until after the years of their strongest sex drive. For the single person there is the possibility of sex with a variety of partners. There is no single person to whom one is pledged to be faithful. Some singles regard the freedom and opportunity to have multiple sexual partners as one of the more important attractions of singlehood.

Personal Freedom

What does it mean to be free? We all cherish freedom, but what precisely does it mean? One single, a thirty-four-year-old professor at a state university, defined it this way for us:

I'm a free man. I can go where I want and do what I want when I want. I don't have to answer to anyone else. I don't have to worry about coming home late or explain to someone why I'm late. I don't have to forgo a trip because I can't afford to take a family. I can pursue new interests without worrying about whether a wife would want to pursue them with me. Frankly, I don't want to have all of my decisions shackled by considerations of other people.

To the extent that you agree with the professor's definition of freedom, you will find more of it in singlehood than in marriage. His statement is probably extreme for the tastes of most people. But he does capture something of what many single people find appealing—the freedom to be spontaneous, to travel, to pursue interests, and to change careers without having to worry about the consequences of his actions for a family. Simenauer and Carroll (1982:347) reported that nearly half of the three thousand singles they studied named mobility and freedom as one of the greatest advantages of their status.

Men seem more concerned than women about retaining their personal freedom. Although the sample was quite small (fifty never-married people), Greenglass (1985) found that nearly three-fourths of the men, but only 8 percent of the women, regarded marriage as a threat to their freedom.

There is, however, another aspect to freedom that seems to be of concern to women. In her study of fifty single women between the ages of 60 and 101, Simon (1987) reported that most of them had turned down marriage proposals. The most common reason for refusing marriage was a fear of becoming a subordinate creature. "You see, dear," one woman explained, "it's *marriage* I avoid, not men. Why would I ever want to be a wife? . . . A wife is someone's servant. A woman is someone's friend" (Simon 1987:31–32). Another woman compared marriage to a state that is "dangerously close to slavery."

Desire for Personal Growth

The thirty-three-year-old businessman previously quoted pointed out that his first priority had been personal growth. Once he felt he had achieved this, he could establish himself in a career and then think about marriage. His is not an isolated case. Other singles, both men and women, express similar sentiments, emphasizing the need for personal growth before establishing a long-term relationship. In the Simenauer and Carroll study (1982:347), the second most frequently named advantage of singleness was having the time to pursue personal interests (named by 17 percent of the men and 21 percent of the women). One of the differences that Gigy (1980) found between sixty-six never-married and thirty-seven married women was that the former placed a higher value on personal growth and achievement while the latter placed a higher value on relationships. Thus, the never-married were more likely to place high value on such things as competence, economic success, self-improvement, learning new things, and mastering fresh challenges. The married were more likely to place highest value on such things as love and affection, friends, and a happy marriage.

Social Conditions

Social circumstances can also affect your chances of getting married. Both wars and economic depressions tend to result in lower marriage rates and later age at marriage (Trovato 1988). For the generation born around 1910, the Great Depression that began in 1929 left a number of people single who would otherwise have preferred to get married. In some cases, women of marriageable age felt that they had to stay unmarried and go to work both to contribute to their own support and to the survival of their parents and siblings (Allen and Pickett 1987:522). And even if the woman could not find work, she might not find a man who could afford to get married.

In addition to major upheavals like wars and depressions, there are changing sex ratios that affect the likelihood of marriage. If the number of men and women were equal, there would be the potential for every person in

Table 6.3 Sex Ratios: 1920–1987
(Number of males per 100 females)

	1920	1930	1940	1950	1960	1970	1980	1987		
								Total	White	Black
All ages	104.1	102.5	100.7	98.6	97.1	94.8	94.5	94.9	95.6	90.2
25–44 years	105.1	101.8	98.5	96.4	95.7	95.5	97.4	98.8	100.8	86.9

Source: U.S. Bureau of the Census 1989:16.

The marriage squeeze occurs when the number of men and women are unequal.

the society to have a heterosexual, monogamous relationship. But partly because of wars and partly because of differing birth and death rates, the numbers are never quite equal. The **sex ratio,** the number of males per one hundred females, varies from decade to decade (table 6.3).

When the number of males per one hundred females, or the number of females per one hundred males gets low, there is a "marriage squeeze." As the table shows, before 1940 there were more males than females. Now, there are millions more females than males (over 7 million more in 1987, aged eighteen and above). The marriage squeeze affected men who wanted to marry prior to 1940. Since then, it has affected females.

The marriage squeeze occurs in many societies and it tends to have the same kind of consequences. In his examination of 111 different countries, South (1988) found that when there is an undersupply of women, there is an increase in the marriage and fertility rates for women. There is also a decline in women's average age at marriage, their literacy rate, and the divorce rate. These tendencies are highest in those countries where women tend not to participate in the labor force.

Note in table 6.3 that the marriage squeeze in the United States is particularly severe for black women. Young black men have higher mortality rates than white men. They are more likely than white men to be imprisoned or in the military. There is also a higher proportion of homosexuals among black men. Some black men marry white women. Finally, middle-class black women are further hampered by the fact that more of them graduate from college than do black men. The result is that black women at all socioeconomic levels have fewer choices, and are more likely than whites to find themselves in a state of involuntary singlehood (Staples 1981).

Family Background

A professional woman who is in her mid-thirties and single said that one of the factors in her decision not to get married before she had established herself in a career was the experience of her parents:

> I've known most of my life that I didn't want to have the same kind of relationship that my parents have. My mother got married because she wanted to get away from her parents, and she needed someone to support her financially. When things didn't work out well, she felt trapped. She felt she couldn't manage economically on her own, especially with the responsibility of her kids. So she just stayed in a bad marriage.

Coming from a home where there has been discord or a disruption may make an individual hesitant to repeat the same kind of mistake. Thus, a study of 134 college females found that those who came from homes where there was discord or where the parents had separated had more negative feelings about marriage (Long 1987).

Personal Characteristics

There are a number of characteristics such as personality traits and personal attitudes that can contribute to whether or not one will remain single. In their study of Canadian singles, Austrom and Hanel (1985) reported that one of the most common reasons given by males for being single was shyness. Another common reason was the desire to be involved in multiple relationships.

Some people, for various reasons, have a fear of making a commitment to someone else. Eleven percent of the men and 7 percent of the women in

Simenauer and Carroll's (1982:321) sample said that they were single because marriage involves too much commitment and responsibility. One therapist who has worked with men who fear commitment wrote:

> These men view personal commitment as being boxed in, being put in a position where they are exposed and vulnerable to their partners. Making plans for the future in such uncertain relationships seems frightening. In contrast, having a sense of future in their careers seems imperative, an integral part of their lives (Freudenberger 1987:46).

Another common reason people give for being single is that they simply haven't found the right person. In most cases, they have been through a series of relationships, but none of them has worked out. No one has quite met the expectations and the standards set by the individual for a suitable mate. It may be a case of setting standards that are too high. It may be an excuse for avoiding commitment. Or it may be that the individual is a victim of the marriage squeeze or circumstances that have prevented him or her from meeting an appropriate partner.

Finally, although they represent a minority of those who are single, we should keep in mind that some people simply prefer the single life. They view singlehood as an opportunity to pursue things that they value more than marriage and a family.

Single Life-Styles

If singles are not the swingers or the losers as suggested by popular stereotypes, what kind of life-styles do they have? Work and career are predominant for many singles. What goes on in the rest of their lives?

Living Arrangements

To be single is not necessarily to live alone. Some live with parents. In 1984, 45 percent of young adults aged twenty to twenty-four and 14 percent of those aged twenty-five to twenty-nine lived with their parents (Glick and Lin 1986:108). Interestingly, for both age groups a greater proportion of males than females lived with parents. In his study of 47 older men, Rubinstein (1986) interviewed eleven who had never been married. Nine of them lived with one or both parents until the parents died. Their age at the time of the death of the last parent ranged from thirty-seven to sixty-one.

In addition, there are a variety of other living arrangements. Some singles live alone, some share apartments with friends, some cohabit, and an increasing number are buying their own homes. In some cases, singles band together in nonsexual pairs or triads to purchase a home. Such an arrangement may be purely a business one, though it is more likely to occur between those who are friends.

The choice of living arrangement has obvious affects on other aspects of life-style. The single person who lives with his or her parents will have restrictions that the home owner does not have. The single who shares an apartment with a friend will have constraints that the single who lives alone in an apartment does not have. But for financial reasons or personal needs or both, most singles prefer to live with someone.

Sex

The popular image of the single is a young person "on the loose" who is free to engage in numerous sexual relationships. The reality is different, both in terms of amount and satisfaction.

Masters, Johnson, and Kolodny (1988:251) identify a number of common patterns of sexual behavior among single young adults. The *experimenter* seeks to experience the full variety of sexual behavior with as many partners as possible, viewing the world as a "sexual smorgasbord" to be enjoyed fully until he or she settles down. The *seeker* engages in sexual intercourse in order to find an ideal mate. Living with someone is one way to test out sexual compatibility and, presumably, marital possibilities. The *traditionalist* believes in sexual intercourse only in serious relationships. The traditionalist may have a number of sexual partners before marrying, but is likely to have only one partner at a time and rarely or never in a purely casual situation.

In popular myth, the experimenter is one of the most common types of single. In actuality, experimenters are a minority of the singles. Moreover, there seems to be an increasing amount of disillusionment with casual sex. Those who experience so-called one-night stands find them less than satisfying in the long run. As a thirty-year-old woman put it:

> You just can't compare the quality of sex with someone you hardly know and feel nothing for with the quality of sex in a caring relationship. Casual sex is just mechanical, one-dimensional release. Sex with someone I care about is warmer and psychologically far more satisfying (in Masters, Johnson, and Kolodny 1988:252).

Cargan and Melko (1982:241) found that singles have less sex than marrieds. Sixty-seven percent of the never-married in their sample had sex once a week or less, compared to only 36 percent of the marrieds. Twelve percent of the never-married and 28 percent of the married had sex three or more times a week. They also reported that the marrieds were more satisfied with their sex lives. Four-fifths of the married, but only about half of the singles, said they were sexually satisfied.

Leisure

Without family responsibilities, singles should have more opportunities for leisure activities. And those activities can be matters of personal choice rather than ones that will please a spouse or other family member. Singles do in fact tend to go out more than married people. Cargan and Melko (1982:232) found

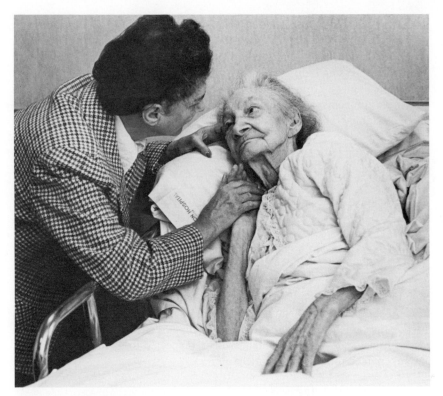

Single women frequently assume the care of aging parents.

that 31 percent of the never-married, 22 percent of the divorced, but only 8 percent of the married had three or more social outings per week.

There are some differences between marrieds and singles not only in frequency but also in the kind of activities preferred. Singles prefer movies, nightclubs, and theater more than marrieds. Married people prefer restaurants, visiting relatives, and social clubs somewhat more than singles (Cargan and Melko 1982:85). Interestingly, singles and marrieds watched about the same amount of television. But singles tend to spend more time visiting friends, engaging in hobbies and sports, and getting involved in community service.

Family Relations

In a comparison of singles and marrieds on family relations, the marrieds were much more likely to have warm and stable relationships with their parents (Cargan and Melko 1982:76). Singles are more likely to fight with their parents. It isn't clear why this is so. The proportion of singles who recall growing up with loving and warm parents is close to that of marrieds (60 percent of singles and 64 percent of marrieds). Perhaps the conflict reflects the parents' desire for the single child to marry and some ongoing tension surrounding that issue. It is also possible that at least some singles who recall warm and loving parents actually came from families that had what family therapists call "enmeshed" relationships. That is, they stressed togetherness and solidarity to the point of suppressing individuality on the part of family members. The tension that some singles have with their parents may reflect their ongoing struggle to achieve autonomy. Unfortunately, in an enmeshed family the individual who tries to establish his or her independence will be defined as engaging in betrayal rather than in the quest for personal growth. There is one aspect of the single's relation with parents that seems to particularly affect single women, namely, being entrusted with the care of aging parents. In a study of women born around 1910, Allen and Pickett (1987) found that some felt they had to remain single, live at home, and contribute to the financial care of the family. A common situation was for the last daughter left at home to remain there and care for her widowed mother. As one woman said, "I had to take my mother into consideration. No, I couldn't do anything. She had to be my prime concern" (Allen and Pickett 1987:522). Similarly, in her study of fifty never-married women, Simon (1987:60) noted that all but two had partly or totally supported aging parents. The two exceptions came from affluent homes. Women who remain single and whose siblings are married are likely, therefore, to assume the responsibility for the care of aging parents. This is consistent with the traditional sex role for women, who are expected to be the nurturers and caretakers (see the discussion in chapter 7).

Singles and Old Age

When married people retire, they have the option of focusing time and energy on children and grandchildren. What do singles do at this point in their lives? What happens when parents have died or when the individual no longer has the work that may have dominated his or her life?

An analysis of data collected by the U.S. Bureau of the Census showed that retirement tends not to pose such a crisis for the never-married (Keith 1985). The never-married actually adjusted better to retirement than the divorced. On the other hand, there is some degree of isolation among older singles. The data from the Census Bureau showed that about a third of older singles never see neighbors, about 30 percent never see friends, and 21 percent of the men and 14 percent of the women never see relatives (Keith 1986:392). Even larger proportions never talk to neighbors, friends, or relatives on the telephone. To keep the data in perspective, more than half of older singles *do* see friends, relatives, and neighbors.

A prime reason for isolation among the men is health problems. Isolated women tend to have less education and to have worked in lower-level occupations. Those who are not isolated engage in a range of activities. The activities vary by gender. Older single men tend to get involved in physical activities such as home maintenance and repairs, walking, exercise, and sports. Older

Observing Singles

Most communities now have regular activities for single people. Check your newspaper or call local churches to find out what kind of activities are available in your area. Attend one or more group activities. Carefully listen to and observe the people and their activities. Attend to nonverbal as well as verbal behavior. That is, watch the expressions on people's faces. Note if they seem truly involved. Watch for signs of satisfaction or dissatisfaction. If possible, discuss with some of the singles about what is their interest in the group, and what the group means to them.

Write up an account of your visit or visits. What conclusions would you draw about the life-styles of singles in your area? What functions does the group seem to serve in the lives of the participants (recall, for instance, the functions of dating discussed in chapter 3)? To what extent are singles participating in groups in order to find a possible mate? To what extent do singles seem to get their intimacy needs fulfilled by the group? How would you compare the singles' groups with family activities and with groups of marrieds you have observed?

If the entire class participates in this exercise, have students visit differing kinds of groups. You can include singles' bars or other places where singles tend to hang out. Compare the various groups. Do they have diverse or similar functions for singles? Do different kinds of people attend the differing groups? Why? If all you knew about singleness came from the observations about these groups, to what extent would you find lifelong singlehood appealing?

single women tend to be engaged in hobbies, volunteer work, church activities, and affiliation with relatives (Keith and Nauta 1988).

Older singles also continue to be involved in heterosexual relationships, including dating and sex (Bulcroft and O'Conner-Roden 1986). To older singles, dating means a committed and long-term relationship. It is analogous to going steady at a younger age. Some of the same feelings also recur. Older people who date report having the symptoms of romantic love, including sweaty palms, the inability to concentrate, and an intense desire for union. What do older people do on dates? Some of the same things that younger people do—get a pizza, go to the movies, and go to dances. They also may go camping together, attend an opera, or fly to another city for a weekend.

As with any other group, older singles are a diverse lot. Some are quite active and satisfied. Others are neither. The older single has a different lifestyle from the older married person, but he or she is not devoid of satisfaction because of the loss of work.

Singles and Loneliness

We have seen that singles engage in numerous and diverse activities. But involvement in activities does not mean that an individual is no longer lonely and that his or her intimacy needs are being met. Simenauer and Carroll (1982:347) found that over 40 percent of their respondents considered loneliness the greatest disadvantage of singlehood. However, those most likely to feel lonely are in the lower income brackets, which suggests that they may be less able to engage in a variety of stimulating activities. Still, national surveys show that single people report more feelings of loneliness than the married. In one survey, people were asked if they had felt very lonely or remote from other people during the past week (Weiss 1981:161). Twenty-seven percent of single women and 23 percent of single men said that they had experienced severe loneliness the preceding week. The comparable figures for the married were 10 percent for women and 6 percent for men.

Although all singles are not lonely, your chances of being lonely are much greater if you are single than if you are married. Singles also are more likely than marrieds to define some activities as lonely experiences. For example, Cargan and Melko (1982:246) found that 46 percent of singles and 34 percent of marrieds thought dining alone to be a lonely activity. And 23 percent of singles but only 15 percent of marrieds said that they were depressed when they were alone. In addition, singles were more likely to indicate that they often have no one with whom to share and discuss things.

Loneliness is more than an uncomfortable feeling. Chronic, intense loneliness may lead to a variety of physical and emotional ills. That is one reason why there is a higher incidence of such ills among singles.

Singles and Health

In general, married people are healthier than single people. Kobrin and Hendershot (1977) used mortality rates in the United States to test the thesis that marriage contributes to a long life. They examined twenty thousand deaths of people aged thirty-five to eighty-four. They found that death rates were lower for married people than the nonmarried in all age brackets. They concluded that the ties of marriage and family somehow protect people, probably by providing them with the intimate relationships that are vital to human well-being.

There are also lower rates of emotional problems among the married. Singles are more likely to suffer from such things as depression and various personality disorders. For instance, in a sample representative of the Chicago area, 12 percent of the married and 20 percent of the never-married scored highest on a measure of depression (Pearlin and Johnson 1981:168). Cargan and Melko (1982:141) reported a number of differences between marrieds and singles:

> More singles suffer from behavioral symptoms, such as nightmares or crying spells, than marrieds, but the difference is negligible. On the other hand, the responses on the direct symptoms are decisive: More singles worry, more are likely to feel guilty, despondent, worthless, or lonely.

There are some gender differences we should note. While the married are healthier than the unmarried, single women are much healthier than single men. In fact, single men are the unhealthiest of all groups. In part, this may be due to the fact that there is a higher proportion of professionals among single women than among single men. Professional men tend to marry and stay married longer than others. Professional women are more likely than other women to marry late, divorce, or remain single. Professionals also tend to have better health than those in low-paying, blue-collar jobs.

But the gender differences also reflect what Jessie Bernard (1972) called "his" marriage and "her" marriage. Men seem to benefit, in terms of health, more from marriage than do women. The poor health of single men may reflect not only a lack of intimate relations but also the stress of trying to maintain a household by someone who has never been trained in domestic skills (Davis and Strong 1977). Married men have the best health of all. Married women are better off than singles, but they do not benefit healthwise from marriage as much as men do. In particular, women who are in a traditional role in the home (wife and homemaker) are especially prone to higher rates of illness (Lauer 1989:149). In other words, it is the restrictive nature of the traditional role that is stressful for women and leads to higher rates of both mental and physical illness among married women than among married men. Nevertheless, married women still have an edge over single women.

Intimacy and Life Satisfaction

Much of the preceding indicates that, despite the growing number opting for temporary or permanent singlehood, singles are at a disadvantage in some of the things we highly value. In this section, we will focus on the bottom line: How do singles compare with marrieds in intimacy and life satisfaction?

Intimacy

Recall that while our needs for intimacy differ, all of us require some intimate relationships. How do singles handle their own needs?

Intimate Relationships

Singles may fulfill some of their intimacy needs by living with their parents, a friend, or acquaintance, or by cohabiting. Those who live alone have a greater challenge. Whatever the living arrangements, however, singles employ a variety of means to establish relationships with others. There are the more traditional means of meeting people through family, friends, school, and religious groups. And there are the relatively newer methods of singles bars, groups, ads, and dating services. The popularity of such methods shows that singles are aware of their needs for intimacy and are anxious to establish and maintain intimate relationships.

By establishing a number of relationships, singles in effect may create their own family. A **network family** is a support group of non-kin. One does

Singles use various methods to fulfill their intimacy needs.

not live with the network family, but the members are always available to help and support each other in the same way as a family related by blood or marriage.

In her study of single women, Simon (1987:91f) noted the crucial importance of friendships. The women had pictures of their friends on display in their homes or apartments. They would talk about their friends when discussing such things as work, travel, recreation, and retirement. A common pattern involved a close, daily, long-term friendship with another person (usually another woman) while also joining a circle of two to five additional friends. The circle might meet once or twice a week, either as a group or in pairs.

The women tended to develop their bonds during their thirties, when it began to appear that they would not marry. They found other women who had made the same choice (or who had the choice forced on them by circumstances) and cemented what would be a long-term relationship. As the friendships developed, the women made long-term plans, including plans about what they would do after retirement. For example, one woman talked about her friend, Maureen, whom she had met in nursing school. They wound up employed in the same hospital, and decided to buy a house together:

> Since then we've been like hand and glove. We took all our vacations together and used them to travel all over the world. Her friends were mine and vice versa. When I reached fifty-five, I began to think about retirement. I tried to convince Maureen to enroll in the same retirement community as me for whenever we got too old to be in our house. . . . She took a year to think about it and then agreed (Simon 1987:97).

Thus, the women have a number of close companions, at least some of whom have shared a series of experiences with them. They have established effective network families that provide them with many of the intimate needs of a marriage.

Sexual Intimacy

One thing the network family does not provide is the fulfillment of one's sexual needs. Yet sex is an important need. In fact, one study of sixty single women in the thirty-five to sixty-five age group noted that half of the women mentioned the meeting of their sexual needs as a necessary part of a satisfying life (Loewenstein, Freud, Bloch, Campion, Epstein, Gale, and Salvatore 1981). Some had found fulfillment, and others had not.

We have already pointed out that singles have sex less often than marrieds and report less sexual satisfaction than marrieds. It seems that, at least in terms of the sexual aspect of intimacy, singles are less likely than marrieds to find fulfillment. Even those who choose to be single may find themselves struggling with their sexual needs. According to Laurel Richardson (1986), an increasing number of women who are single by choice or by circumstance are opting for affairs with married men in order to deal with their sexual needs. She found that professional women, those who have opted to give priority to careers, are especially prone to getting involved with married men. Such women have delayed marriage in order to establish themselves in their careers. But when they decide that they are ready to consider marrying, they find a shortage of available men. In order to deal with their need for an intimate, heterosexual relationship, they resorted to an affair.

Unfortunately, the affairs tend to grow difficult and counterproductive over time. As one woman said, her affair drained her energy and ultimately led to her being hurt: "It ended up being very costly to me, to my career and my life in general" (Richardson 1986:27).

Sexual intimacy does not necessarily involve sexual intercourse. In fact, Richardson pointed out that sexual intercourse is not the major activity in the affairs she studied. The subjects did have intercourse, but they also had a good deal of heterosexual closeness, including the sharing and affection that go into intimate relationships. Touching, caressing, admiring, supporting, and caring by someone of the opposite sex is an important part of fulfilling our needs for sexual intimacy. Singles are faced with less likelihood of experiencing such sexual intimacy.

The Question of Children

We will explore the role of children in our intimate needs in chapter 14. Clearly, some people regard children as an important part of their fulfillment. Some people desire the parent-child intimacy whether or not they are married. And at least some women who are childless regret the fact when they are past the childbearing years (Loewenstein et al. 1981).

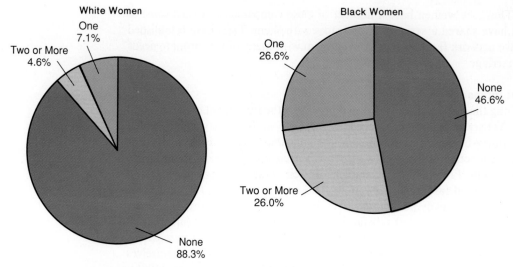

Figure 6.3 *Children ever born to single women, 18–44 years of age, by race: 1987.*
Source: U.S. Bureau of the Census 1989:68.

Victor Callan (1986b) studied forty-two single women who said they wanted to remain childless and sixty who wanted one or more children. He found that those who preferred to be childless tended to be more pessimistic and less loving than the others. Those who preferred either no children or only one child were more concerned about their financial and social independence than those who desired two children. Thus, various factors enter into our desire to have or not have children. As in the case of getting married, one factor is the concern about one's independence and freedom. Interestingly, even some of those women who were more concerned about independence still wanted to have one child.

A good many single women are having children. Not every case represents one in which the child was wanted, of course, but by 1987 about 36 percent of single women between the ages of eighteen and forty-four had given birth to at least one child (see figure 6.3). Black single women are much more likely than whites to have children. But they are also more likely to have children when they are younger (in their teens and twenties).

Single women who have children are more likely to be in the lower socioeconomic levels. As such, they are doubly handicapped in their efforts at parenting. Not only do they lack the help of a husband and father, but they also must deal with the problems of a paucity of financial resources. Single mothers are the most impoverished group in the nation. They may fulfill some of their intimacy needs through their children, but the costs in terms of financial and emotional stress are high.

Life Satisfaction

If the pursuit of happiness is one of the fundamental rights of all Americans, how do singles fare? How can we sum it all up in terms of life satisfaction?

Factors in Life Satisfaction

When singles are asked about the factors that go into their life satisfaction, their answers are similar to those of other Americans (Simenauer and Carroll 1982:334–37). Good health is one of the most important factors. Ironically, as just noted singles are less likely than marrieds to enjoy good health. Other things mentioned by singles include career, personal growth, financial security, love, and social and family life. A good sex life is also important to most singles. The list, of course, comes from all types of singles, including some who hope to marry at some point.

Some research asks singles about their satisfaction with life and then relates that with various factors in their lives. Many of the same factors noted above turn out to be significant. For instance, in their study of sixty single women, Loewenstein et al. (1981) found that life satisfaction was higher among those women who had good health, were not lonely, lived with a female housemate, had many casual friends, and were deeply involved in their work.

A study of male and female never-marrieds focused on the role of social support and loneliness in life satisfaction (Cockrum and White 1985). The researchers found that friends were important to both males and females. Visiting friends enabled them to deal with loneliness. There were gender differences, however. For men, life satisfaction depended on having a network of individuals with whom they could share their interests and their values. For women, life satisfaction was higher when they had people with whom they could establish close, emotional bonds. These differences are consistent with the gender patterns we shall discuss in the next chapter.

How Satisfied Are Singles?

The life satisfaction of singles, like that of marrieds, varies over the course of their lives. For singles, the thirties seem to be one of the more difficult times. Developmental psychologists point out that the thirties are a time of reevaluation of people's lives. "A restless vitality wells up as we approach 30. Almost everyone wants to make some alteration" (Sheehy 1976:198). We look at the decisions we have made in our twenties and question whether they are correct and whether we want to stick with them for the rest of our lives. For singles, the reevaluation includes the single state, the possibility that they may never marry and/or have children, the problem of intimate relationships, and the question of whether a career will be ultimately satisfying. In her study of thirty-six single men and sixty-three single women, Rollins (1986:123) noted that the only ones who had significantly contemplated suicide were women between the ages of thirty and thirty-nine. After the thirties, however, life satisfaction may improve. Individuals who accept their single status and establish a network family may express high satisfaction with their lives.

Researchers have tried to get at the life satisfaction of people by phrasing questions in a variety of ways. Simenauer and Carroll (1982:351) asked singles whether, on the whole, being single had been a pleasant or unpleasant experience. Twenty-three percent of the men and 12 percent of the women said "it's been wonderful." But overall, about 60 percent of men and slightly more than 50 percent of women indicated that they enjoyed aspects of being single, while the others said that they did not enjoy the single life.

Simenauer and Carroll have no sample of marrieds, of course, with which to compare the results. Cargan and Melko (1982:173f) reported the results from both married and singles when people were asked whether they were happy. More than two-thirds of their sample indicated that they were at least moderately happy. But in every age group, including those under thirty, a greater proportion of marrieds than of singles said that they were happy. Interestingly, a greater proportion of marrieds (83 percent) than of singles (75 percent) also agreed that they were getting "a lot of fun out of life."

The same pattern appeared in national surveys reported by Ward (1981:347). A greater proportion of twenty-five- to forty-nine-year-old married people reported themselves as "very happy" (39.4 percent) than did the widowed (20.5 percent), the divorced/separated (16.5 percent) or the never-married (15.5 percent). In the fifty and above age category, the married still led the others (43.2 percent), but the never-married were the next most likely to say they were very happy (26.1 percent), followed by the widowed (23.8 percent) and the divorced/separated (20.3 percent). Clearly, married people

Singles are less likely than the married to define themselves as having happy, exciting lives.

Seeking Intimate Relationships

PERSONAL

Struggling with Singlehood

Kim is a computer specialist who has been struggling with her need for intimacy and her aspirations for a career. She talks about some of the advantages and disadvantages of her singlehood, and how she has tried to fulfill her intimacy needs while remaining single. Like many singles in their thirties, she is now re-evaluating her life, and she has made an important decision about her future:

I will celebrate my thirty-first birthday in a few days, and I have never been married. In my mother's day, I would have been labeled a "spinster." Today, I am referred to as a "professional woman."

As a single woman, I have fulfilled my need for intimacy in much the same way as married people do. My relationships with men have been what is termed serial monogamy. I have been romantically involved with only a handful of men. The relationships have lasted anywhere from six months to five years. Two men asked me to marry them. I asked two others to marry me. The result is that I am still single, although marriage remains as one of my personal goals.

Friendships, family ties, and professional relationships have fulfilled my other needs for intimacy. Having relocated numerous times over the past twenty years, I have developed the capacity to meet and get to know people. Moving can be a lonely experience, and becoming acquainted with new places and people is a difficult task. Being single has both hurt and helped me to adjust to the moves. It's hurt because I've been lonely. It's helped, because I've been free to meet people at my own discretion, without having to consider someone else's needs. When I've not had access to family members, I've cultivated my own family of friends.

For the last ten years, I've lived alone. I've known both the delight of privacy and the gloom of loneliness. I no longer choose to live by myself. I have concluded that I prefer, and need, to share my life and my living quarters with a man. One of my goals now is to find someone and get married. That has finally become as important to me as my career.

are more likely to say they are happy than any of the types of single people. Moreover, they are also more likely to define their lives as exciting. In response to the question of whether people found life exciting, pretty routine, or dull, a larger proportion of the never-married (54.4 percent), in the twenty-five to forty-nine age group, said exciting. About 48 percent of the married and 40 percent of the widowed and divorced said that they found life exciting. In the fifty and above age group, the married again came out ahead. A little over 41 percent of the married and about a third of the other groups agreed that their lives were exciting.

To sum up, some singles, whether never-married, divorced, or widowed, prefer their life-style and find it satisfying. Yet singles are less likely than the married to perceive themselves as having happy, exciting lives. It may be that

The Single Option   165

the differences are accounted for by those who are involuntarily single, and who are therefore less satisfied with their status. But we have no research to answer the question of whether the involuntary differ from the voluntary singles. If there are no differences, then millions of Americans are making a deliberate choice that will somewhat lower their chances of a happy and fulfilling life.

PRINCIPLES FOR ENHANCING INTIMACY

1. If your highest goal as a woman is professional advancement, you are more likely to reach that goal if you remain single. Unfortunately, the demands of pregnancy, children, and maintaining a home generally place a far greater burden on the employed woman than on her husband.

2. Although sex is more readily available and is an attractive prospect for many singles, the freedom of the "one-night stand" has its risks—disease, physical abuse from a less than well-known lover, lack of intimacy, and even feelings of heightened loneliness when it is over. Your physical and emotional well-being demands that you acknowledge and seek to minimize these risks.

3. If you want to marry, and frequently turn potential spouses down because they are just not "the right person," you need to ask yourself whether your expectations are too high or whether there is some factor in your personal or familial past that is keeping you from making a commitment.

4. A single life can be a happy, fulfilled one. An essential ingredient generally is a network of friends with whom you can find satisfactory living arrangements, share social activities and common interests, and most importantly, develop intimate relations.

5. Marriage can involve giving up some freedom and independence, but the benefits outweigh the possible losses. Every indicator suggests that more married than single people are happy and physically and emotionally healthy.

The proportion of Americans who are single has risen steadily. By 1987, only about 63 percent were married. The proportion of single people is still lower, however, than it was in the first decades of the century. Singles include the never-married, the divorced, and the widowed. There are a number of beliefs about singles that are myths, such as the idea that singles are selfish, financially well-to-do, happier, and others.

There is both voluntary and involuntary singlehood. There are a number of factors involved in people remaining single. Some singles give priority to their careers. Sex is readily available. Some singles believe that marriage would be a threat to their personal freedom. The desire for personal growth may take priority over relationships. Social conditions, such as the sex ratio, may prevent some from marrying. Certain family experiences may lead some people to be hesitant about, or even reject, marriage. And a number of personality characteristics, such as shyness and fear of commitment, keep some single.

The single life-style includes a diversity of living arrangements, from living with parents to sharing an apartment to living alone. Singles on the whole have less sex than married people. They are likely to engage in more and somewhat different leisure activities than the married. Singles are less likely than marrieds to have warm and stable relationships with their parents. Single women, however, may find themselves caring for their aging parents. A minority of older singles face a problem of isolation, which tends to impair their health. Many older singles continue to be involved in heterosexual relationships, including dating and sexual relations.

Single people have more problems with loneliness and more physical and mental health problems than the married. There are various ways to establish and maintain intimate relationships; healthy singles tend to have network families. Sex and children are also a problem for singles, who tend to be more deprived than married people of these sources of intimacy.

Life satisfaction tends to vary through the individual's life, whether married or single. For singles, the thirties seem to be one of the more difficult ages. Many singles prefer their life-style and find it satisfying. But overall, singles are less likely than the married to perceive themselves as having happy and exciting lives.

PART TWO

The Intimate Couple

When a group of undergraduates was asked to define an intimate relationship, a number of the students asked whether the instructor meant intimacy between a male and a female, between friends, or between parents and children. The students were correct in realizing that the nature of intimacy changes somewhat from one type of relationship to another.

In this section, we will look at intimacy in heterosexual couples. We begin with some questions about developing intimate heterosexual relationships. What does it mean to be a male or a female? What part does sexuality play in the life of an intimate couple? What is involved in making the transition from singlehood to marriage?

Then we examine the challenges people face as they seek to deepen their intimacy in marriage. What is the role of communication? What is the meaning of conflict, and how and why do couples fight? How will the couple deal with the division of labor both in and outside of the home? These are some of the questions that young adults face when they begin their quest for mature intimacy.

7

Sex Roles

According to a Harvard physician, Dr. Dudley Sargent, the physique of women has changed. He observed: "Twenty years ago women were the very antithesis of men in physical proportions." But now women have begun looking more like men. "It is to be hoped," said Dr. Sargent, "that women do not grow to be more like men than they are today. . . . The danger of women becoming too mannish is imminent."[1] The doctor also pointed out that men have changed and are in danger of becoming too "effeminate."

Dr. Sargent's remarks were made in 1910. They illustrate the ongoing concern that people have about men being men and women being women. But what does it mean to be a man? What does it mean to be a woman? In this chapter, we will explore this complex issue. We will look at similarities and differences between the sexes. We will explore the meaning of sex roles and the way in which we develop those roles. Finally, we will examine the consequences of sex roles, including the implications of those roles for intimate relationships.

What does it mean to be a man?

Men and Women: How Do They Differ?

As an interesting exercise, write down five ways you believe that men and women are alike and five ways in which they differ. When you have finished this chapter, look at your list again and see if you want to make any changes in it. Keep in mind that even social scientists do not completely agree on how the two sexes differ and in what ways they are similar.

Some Commonalities of Men and Women

While we will focus more on differences than similarities, we want to underscore the fact that there are some similarities. Both men and women have some of the same fundamental needs: survival, self-esteem, intimacy, and growth. Both need the sense of having some control over their lives. Both need to achieve. Both need recreation. When we talk about the basic needs of humans, neither sex is exempt, even though they may fulfill those needs in somewhat different ways.

In addition, some recent research shows that men and women are similar in areas in which we formerly thought they were different. For example, women have typically been viewed as more emotional than men. But that may only be partly true. Psychologist Anthony Greenwald found that women are no better than men in recalling emotion-laden words.[2] But he also found that women give the words higher ratings on emotional intensity than did men. It may be, therefore, that men and women react to events with similar emotions, but that women are prone to describe their reactions in more emotional terms.

Many people also believe that men and women differ in their responses to erotic stimuli. Presumably, men are more aroused than women by such stimuli. However, when researchers measured arousal by physiological changes (rather than self-reports), women and men showed very similar kinds of response (Rubinsky, Eckerman, Rubinsky, and Hoover 1987). A third example of supposed difference is in the tendency to cooperate. Women are said to be more cooperative than men in group tasks. But the differences appear to be very small, and gender is not as important as other factors in determining whether someone will be cooperative (Stockard, Van de Kragt, and Dodge 1988).

Finally, women are thought to conform more than men. Even many social scientists have asserted that women are easier to persuade and more prone to comply with group pressures than are men. Indeed, some experimental evidence supported such a position. Yet in a review of all the available evidence, Alice Eagly (1978) argued that the case is not closed on gender differences in conformity. In most settings, Eagly found that women are not more easily influenced than men. In group settings where pressure is exerted on each member to conform, the findings are somewhat mixed. Although most studies do not show any gender differences, about a third did report women to be more conforming in group settings than men. We are not certain about the reasons for these findings. One explanation is that men generally have higher status in our society, and higher-status individuals have more latitude for nonconformity than do lower-status individuals.

The point is that there are similarities, including some that go against the conventional wisdom. Men and women are different, but not as different as some people think (figure 7.1).

Gender Differences

Men and women differ in numerous ways, including everything from women's longer average life span to their differing attitudes on social issues. We will not discuss the obvious physical differences. Instead, we will focus on some of the diverse social and psychological characteristics.

Ability

If you read a poem, a story, or an article, do you think your evaluation of it would be influenced by the name of the author? You probably think not. But studies have shown that when people are led to believe that something is the work of a male, they are likely to rate it higher than others who believe the work was produced by a female. Among other things, people have rated males higher on essays, paintings, and applications for a job or for study abroad (Kahn 1984:360). Studies have also shown that people believe that males will perform better in virtually all occupations.

In other words, males are believed to be superior to females in their abilities. However, although there are differences in abilities, males are not generally superior to females. On intelligence tests, girls evidence superior verbal ability. They score higher than boys on tests that demand an understanding of complex language, creative writing, analogies, fluency, and spelling. Boys, on the other hand, have better spatial and quantitative ability. They score higher on math tests and do better on tasks that require visual and spatial perception.

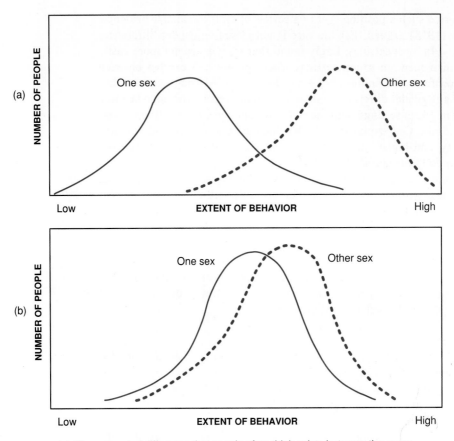

(a) The amount of difference that people often think exists between the sexes
(b) The extent of sex differences actually found for social behaviors

Figure 7.1 *Perceived versus actual sex differences.*

The reasons for these differences are still debated; some people believe that they are rooted in the brain, while others believe they are a product of socialization.

The notion that men can perform better than women in all occupations is also untrue. One reason some people give for the presumed difference is that women are less involved with the workplace than are men. Some businessmen have been reluctant to promote women into the upper ranks of management because they assume that women are not as committed to their careers as are men. Yet given equivalent kinds of work, women may be more involved than men, and their involvement may increase over time while men's may decline (Lorence 1987). When women are given the same opportunities as men, both their competence and their motivation are equal to men's for most tasks. Again, where superior spatial and visual skills are required, men may be more competent. And where superior verbal skills are required, women may be more

Table 7.1 Percent of Females Employed in Selected Occupations: 1987

Occupation	Percent Female
All occupations	44.8
Managerial and professional	44.3
Managers, Medicine and Health	59.9
Purchasing Managers	27.8
Architects	12.6
Engineers	6.9
Math and Computer Scientists	34.1
Physicians	19.5
Elementary Schoolteachers	85.3
Lawyers and Judges	19.7
Librarians	85.6
Technical, sales, and administrative support	64.7
Licensed Practical Nurses	97.0
Electronic Technicians	14.3
Insurance Sales	27.4
Cashiers	83.0
Secretaries	99.1
Service occupations	60.6
Childcare Workers	96.9
Firefighting and fire prevention	2.0
Police and Detectives	11.4
Waiters and Waitresses	85.1
Precision production, craft, repair	8.5
Mechanics and Repairers	3.4
Carpenters	1.2
Operators, fabricators, laborers	25.8
Pressing Machine Operators	64.3
Motor Vehicle Operators	10.1
Farming, forestry, fishing	15.8
Farm Workers	21.7
Fishers, Hunters, Trappers	9.1

Source: U.S. Bureau of the Census 1989:388–89.

competent. Still either sex can perform well in nearly all kinds of work. The fact that people have not fully accepted this notion, however, may be seen in the extent to which many occupations are still dominated by one sex or the other (table 7.1).

Aggression

It appears universally true that men are more aggressive than women. Anthropologists have reported that violence typically occurs at the hands of men in all societies. The difference appears even in people's dreams. Men in tribal societies are more likely to dream of sexual intercourse, wives, weapons, and animals, while women are more likely to dream of husbands and children, mothers and fathers, and of crying (Konner 1982:56).

Men are more aggressive by almost any measure. Men commit more violent crimes than women. They are more likely to assault someone. In social psychological experiments, males are typically more aggressive than women in their responses.

However, we need to note that there are different kinds of situations and different kinds of aggression. In a situation where people are provoked or angered, men are more likely than women to use physical aggression while women are more likely to use verbal aggression. In situations where there is no provocation, men seem to be consistently more aggressive than women (Kahn 1984:384).

Interaction: Quantity and Quality

In a study of ninety-six college students, Reis (1986:95–96) found that females have more interactions with other people per day than do males. He also reported on the quality of the interaction. Interestingly, the quality varied by the gender of the participants. The least meaningful interaction reported was that between two males. Heterosexual and all-female interaction was rated higher in terms of quality and satisfaction than all-male interaction. Even when males interacted with best friends, they did not find the interaction as satisfying as when they interacted with a female.

Why is the quality of interaction rated as better when there is at least one female involved? Females appear to be more skilled than males in maintaining quality interaction because of certain aspects of their conversational style. Women do much of the work in starting and maintaining conversations. Women have a questioning style that includes a number of characteristics (Kohn 1988:66):

Women ask more questions than men. One analysis of conversations between professional couples reported that the women asked three times as many questions as the men.

Women have a questioning tone to their statements. The tone asks for confirmation from the listener that the speaker is correct.

Women use more tag questions. Tag questions occur at the end of sentences and encourage the listener to respond. For instance: "This is a beautiful day, isn't it?" and "School gets to be a drag sometimes, don't you think?"

Women are more likely to begin with a question. "Guess what?" and other leading questions are meant to capture the listener's attention.

Women use more qualifiers ("sort of," "maybe," etc.) and intensifiers ("really") than men. The qualifiers and intensifiers give hints to the listener about how to react.

Adolescent girls report higher levels of intimacy than do boys, and girls tend to have their highest level with their girl friends.

The interpersonal skills of females emerge early in their lives. A survey of over two thousand seventh- through tenth-grade adolescents found that the girls reported higher levels of intimacy than the boys (Blyth and Foster-Clark 1987). The students were asked to rate their relationships with various people who were important to them (friends, parents, siblings, or others). Then they indicated to what extent they had an intimate relationship with each of those people. Intimacy was measured by the students' responses to four questions: How much do you go to this person for advice? How much does this person accept you no matter what you do? How much does this person understand what you're really like? How much do you share your inner feelings with this person?

Girls reported higher levels of intimacy overall. In addition, they reported the highest level of intimacy with their same-sex friend (figure 7.2). Boys, in contrast, reported higher levels of intimacy with their parents than with their same-sex friends.

Note that one of the ways that the researchers measured intimacy was the question about self-disclosure of inner feelings. Females continue the pattern of greater self-disclosure into adulthood (Snell, Belk, Flowers, and Warren 1988). We have noted in earlier chapters that self-disclosure is an essential part of an intimate relationship, and that the amount of self-disclosure increases as the relationship intensifies. The greater ease of the female to engage in self-disclosure means that she is more skilled than the male in creating intimacy.

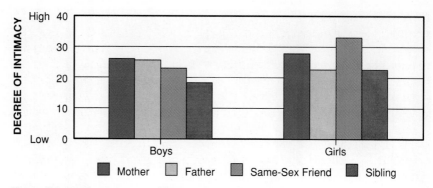

Figure 7.2 *Intimacy scores of boys versus girls.*
Source: Data from Blyth and Foster-Clark 1987:711.

Nonverbal Behavior

It has been estimated that anywhere between 50 and 80 percent of the meaning in a conversation is communicated nonverbally. The same words can take on quite different meanings depending on one's facial expression, gestures, voice tone, and inflection. For example, depending on the nonverbal cues, the three words "I love you" could mean sarcasm, indifference (suggesting that the speaker said them only to try to placate the other), disbelief (I love *you*?), true devotion, or a variety of things in between. Nonverbal behavior, then, is a crucial part of intimate relationships.

There are gender differences in nonverbal behavior. Women are more skilled at interpreting nonverbal behavior. They also tend to use somewhat different kinds of nonverbal behavior. Both of these differences enhance the ability of women to form and maintain intimate relationships. For example, eye contact is an important nonverbal component of intimacy. Researchers who have watched videotapes of people conversing note that pairs of women have more eye contact than do pairs of men (Kahn 1984:366). And women are more likely to maintain eye contact when they are sitting close to each other, while men are more likely to maintain eye contact when farther apart from each other.

From an early age, females seem to use eye contact to communicate intimacy more than do males. And from an early age, females are superior in communicating nonverbal emotional messages. In fact, boys seem to get poorer at sending nonverbal emotional messages as they get older. Overall, then, women's nonverbal behavior suggests that they are warm, friendly, and attentive to others. Men's nonverbal behavior suggests that they have high status, and are important and somewhat distant.

The Intimate Couple

Keeping Differences in Perspective

Clearly, not every woman is warm, friendly, and attentive to others. Nor does every man act superior and distant. Similarly, every man is not more aggressive than any woman. There are differences, but the differences refer to averages in whole groups (recall figure 7.1). Thus, it is more accurate to say that more men than women are highly aggressive, rather than to say that men are more aggressive than women. And it is more accurate to say that more women than men are warm, friendly, and attentive to others rather than to say that women are warmer, more friendly, and more attentive than men.

The difference in language may seem subtle, but it is an important difference. It helps us keep in mind that there are numerous similarities between the sexes, and that at least some of the differences are relatively small.

Sex, Sex Role, and Sex-Role Orientation

Are you male or female? How much does the answer tell us about your behavior? As the above discussion indicates, it tells us some things, but not a great deal. We need to ask some additional questions of you. What kinds of behavior do you see as appropriate for someone of your sex? And to what extent do you see yourself having both masculine and feminine traits?

The questions refer to the fact that we need to distinguish between sex, sex role, and sex-role orientation. We use sex interchangeably with **gender,** whether you are male or female. **Sex role** refers to the behavior associated with being either male or female. And **sex-role orientation** refers to the conception of yourself as having some combination of masculine and feminine traits.

Many people think that being male or female is a major factor in determining behavior. Indeed, we all do tend to treat people differently by gender. But for many kinds of behavior, sex roles and sex-role orientations are even more important than gender.

Sex Roles

Are men and women equal in American society? One way to answer the question is to ask about sex roles. What kind of behavior do we expect from the two sexes? Traditionally, the differences have been well defined.

Traditional Sex Roles

For the last few decades, researchers have inquired into the stereotypes that people have of men and women. Both men and women tend to agree on the attributes that they believe are typical of each sex. In essence, men are generally held to be strong, independent, successful, courageous, aggressive, and logical. Women are viewed as more gentle, dependent on men for support and protection, nurturing, emotional, and submissive. Traditional roles—men as breadwinners and women as homemakers—reflected these qualities.

Men, then, are expected to be achievement-oriented, dominant, strong, and self-controlled. Or as one researcher put it, there are four distinct norms that are the basis for the male sex role (Brannon 1976):

1. "No sissy stuff." Men must not do anything that might appear to be feminine. A man who engages in an activity that people define as feminine, such as appearing to be too emotional, is something less than a true man.

2. "The Big Wheel." Men need to act in such a way that they are respected and admired. This means that they must be successful in something. Ideally, they should be successful in everything they do, especially in functioning as the breadwinner in the family.

3. "The Sturdy Oak." Men are strong, silent types of humans. They stay calm in the midst of turmoil and difficulty. They face up to crises without showing any weakness and without giving way to emotions. They keep intimate feelings to themselves.

4. "Give 'Em Hell." Men love adventure, risk, danger, violence. A man who refuses to take risks is a dull man.

In contrast, two reseachers who developed a measure of traditional versus nontraditional behaviors for women, used questions such as the following (Robinson and Follingstad 1985):

"If trying to get your own way, how likely are you to use tears with a person of the opposite sex within the next year at least once?"

"How frequently have you pretended to know less than you really knew to protect the ego of a person of the opposite sex during the past year?"

"How likely are you to wait in the car for a person of the opposite sex to open the door for you during the next year?"

According to their study, the more likely their respondents were to engage in these behaviors, the more traditional they were.

Clearly, the traditional male is someone who is in control of his life, who acts with reason and determination to achieve goals and complete tasks. The traditional female is someone who is dependent on that male, who tries to protect the male from any threats to his ego, and who must resort to emotions rather than reason when she tries to influence him.

Consequences of the Traditional Roles

To some extent the traditional roles are stereotypes. That is, few if any people have followed them precisely. But to the extent that people have approximated those roles, certain consequences for a wide range of behavior follow, one of which is illustrated in table 7.1—the tendency to consider certain occupations as more appropriate for one sex than the other.

There are numerous additional consequences. For instance, three sociologists found a number of correlates among those men who agree more with the traditional male sex role (Thompson, Grisanti, and Pleck 1985). The more traditional men expressed more anxiety about being perceived as a homosexual. They were more favorable toward Type A behavior, such as rapid speaking, preoccupation with one's work, impatience, and a generally aggressive, competitive approach. Type A behavior has been identified as increasing one's risk of coronary heart disease. The more traditional males were also less inclined to disclose intimate matters to females, and more desirable of being in control (including making the decisions) in intimate relationships.

Even though our ideas about sex roles have been changing (see PERSPECTIVE), many people still react to others on the basis of those traditional roles. For instance, a man who acts passive and dependent or a woman who insists on pursuing a career in a male-dominated occupation may be defined as maladjusted. Males who behave in a dominant fashion may be rated as more attractive by females (Sadalla, Kenrick, and Vershure 1987). Men who engage in nurturing behavior may be defined as less masculine, less strong, and less likely to be achievers than other men (Draper and Gordon 1986).

In an interesting experiment with undergraduates, students were divided into heterosexual pairs and watched a horror movie (Zillmann, Weaver, Mundorf, and Aust 1986). Men enjoyed the movie most when they were with a woman who acted distressed, and least when they were with a woman who appeared in control. Women enjoyed the movie most when they were with a man who was in control and least when they were with a man who acted distressed. In other words, enjoyment was enhanced by being with someone who acted in accord with the traditional sex roles.

One final example involves housework. Traditionally, the woman was the homemaker and the man was the breadwinner. While the majority of women now work, most of them retain major responsibility for doing the housework. In a survey of its readers, *Working Mother* magazine reported that most of the women do the largest part of the cooking and cleaning when they get home from work (Schoonmaker 1988). For example, 92 percent said they do the laundry regularly, 67 percent regularly vacuum, and 77 percent regularly cook. Whatever people may say about their ideals, traditional sex roles continue to influence their behavior.

Woman's Work

Some people have argued that the traditional roles do not contradict the notion of equality. The struggle of women to gain rights such as voting and equal opportunities in the workplace has proceeded in the face of such arguments as the one below, offered by a nineteenth-century physician in his book on the ethics of marriage:

> Nature clearly indicates that woman was intended to be man's companion and coworker. Nature arranged that woman should be man's equal—not that she should be his equivalent nor that she should do a man's work—that she should bear her fair share of the burdens [of] life, and should have her full share of the compensation.
>
> Broadly considered, Nature arranged that man should be the provider of means of subsistence, and that woman should be the dispenser of these means. [It is true that a woman can do the kind of work that men do.] But without going into the details of man's work and his superiority over woman in it, let us consider woman's work. In the first place, it certainly *is* woman's work, for it cannot be done by a man, however willing a man might be to do it; and, in the second place, it is absolutely necessary, for the world would soon come to an end without it; in the third place, it is a more honorable and important work than man's; and, finally, if woman does her work well and thoroughly, it requires all her time and vitality. So woman is debarred from doing a man's work not because she *cannot* do it, but because her own work is all she can possibly attend to. The key to the question, What is woman's work? is the fact that Nature has imposed on her the most of the burden of reproduction. The rest of woman's work follows naturally, for as she is brought into peculiarly close relations with the human individual at its tenderest age . . . the Creator has endowed woman with a special store of the gentler and finer qualities of mind and heart, and has given her a peculiar adaptability for planning and executing little details connected with the distribution of means of subsistence to the ends of the comfort and happiness of those about her. But in doing this, woman is the homemaker and housekeeper, and this is just what God meant her to be—just this and nothing more.

Source: Pomeroy (1888:125–28).

Sex-Role Orientation

As we pointed out, few if any people have conformed precisely to the traditional roles. Most people have some combination of the qualities or traits of each role. Social scientists call those traits associated with the traditional male role **instrumental,** and those associated with the traditional female role **expressive.** Instrumental traits, such as aggressiveness, competitiveness, self-confidence, and logic, enable people to achieve goals. Expressive traits, such as warmth, caring, sensitivity, and nurturance, enable people to establish good interpersonal relationships.

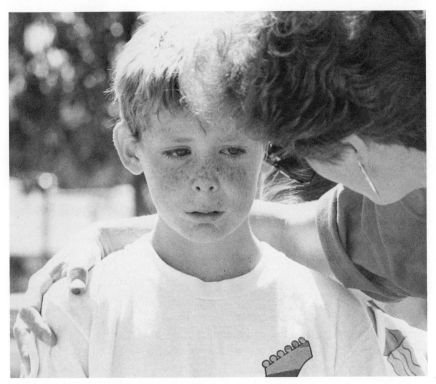

Many parents have told their sons, "Boys don't cry." But we all need to develop both expressive and instrumental traits.

The way to find someone's sex-role orientation is to ask them to describe themselves in terms of the various traits. Those who select predominantly instrumental traits are masculine, while those who select predominantly expressive traits are feminine in their orientation. For example, the Personal Attributes Questionnaire, developed by Spence and Helmreich (1978), asks respondents to rate themselves on a number of traits such as the following:

Not at all aggressive A. . .B. . .C. . .D. . .E Very aggressive
Not at all emotional   A. . .B. . .C. . .D. . .E Very emotional
Very rough   A. . .B. . .C. . .D. . .E Very gentle

A strong masculine response would be E on the aggressive scale and A on the emotional and rough/gentle scales. A strong feminine response would be the opposite.

At first, it seems reasonable to assume that masculine and feminine are the two extremes of one dimension. That is, the more masculine you are, the less feminine and vice versa. But social scientists agree that masculinity and

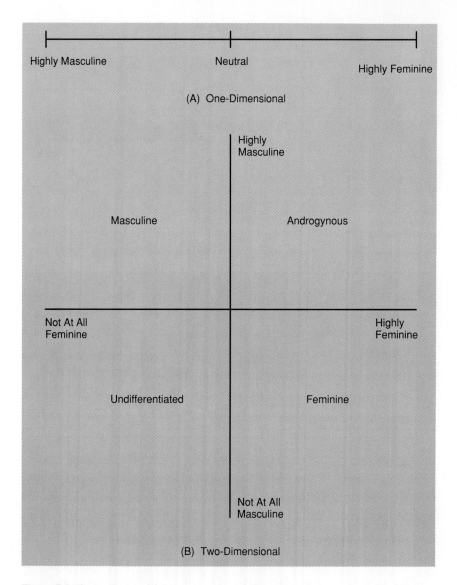

Figure 7.3 *Sex-role orientation as one or two dimensional.*

femininity are not opposites that exclude each other. Instead of a continuum, with masculine at one end and feminine at the other, sex-role orientation must be understood as two-dimensional (figure 7.3). Thus, an individual can be high on both, low on both, or high on one and low on the other dimension. The smallest category, in terms of numbers of people, is the undifferentiated, in which an individual sees himself or herself as low on both masculine and feminine traits. You would be undifferentiated if you saw yourself as moderately aggressive (in between "very" and "not at all"), moderately independent, moderately emotional, and so on.

The Intimate Couple

As figure 7.3 indicates, an individual can be aggressive and competitive and independent and also gentle and sensitive. Such people, as figure 7.3 indicates, are called androgynous. **Androgyny** is a term coined by Sandra Bem (1974) to describe those people who possess both masculine, or instrumental, and feminine, or expressive, traits. Bem has argued that androgynous individuals are healthier and more adaptable than others. This makes sense, because they should have a greater range of behaviors available to them to meet diverse demands of differing situations. We shall see to what extent androgyny does facilitate people's functioning.

Sex Roles: Nature or Nurture?

One of the controversies surrounding sex roles is whether they reflect human nature. Are more women than men expressive because there is something in their biological makeup that leads them to behave in that way? Or do sex roles reflect socialization, the way in which children are nurtured? Those who stress nurture over nature may prefer to use the term *gender role* rather than *sex role,* arguing that the former emphasizes the social and the latter the biological aspects. We shall stay with the term *sex role* because it is the more common.

In addressing the nature versus nurture controversy, we should note that differences between males and females develop quite early in life. There are certain differences even in infants (girl babies, for example, tend to smile more than boy babies). By the time they are three years old, children show definite preferences for toys that are stereotypically appropriate for their own gender (dolls for girls, trucks for boys) (O'Brien and Huston 1985). And by the time children are five and in kindergarten, children clearly assign certain activities and tasks as more appropriate for one gender than another (Bardwell, Cochran, and Walker 1986). They believe, for instance, that women put up drapes and men build houses. How can we account for the differences?

How Much Is Biological?

Sigmund Freud (1949) set forth an influential case for the biological basis of sex roles. Freud's arguments were summed up in his famous idea that *anatomy is destiny.* He argued that girls reach the point in their development when they realize that they are anatomically different from boys. They lack a penis, and therefore they feel severely deprived. This leads to "penis envy." According to Freud, only in the act of conceiving and giving birth to a child can a woman find fulfillment. But she never fully overcomes her penis envy, so that jealousy and envy are more prominent in women than in men. Without going into the details of his theory, we should note that Freud also concluded that women are naturally more passive, submissive, and neurotic than men. All of this results from women's psychological reaction to their physiology.

Those who draw on research about the brain and hormones also stress innate biological differences (Kolata 1983). The differences are used to explain such things as the higher levels of aggression among males, the greater verbal abilities of females, and the greater mathematical, visual, and spatial skills of males. For example, some researchers believe that the higher levels of the hormone testosterone are present during the development of the brain in the male fetus. The higher levels seem to alter the anatomy of the brain, making the right hemisphere dominant. This, in turn, results in the tendency for males to have superior mathematical ability.

The amount of research is too voluminous to examine here. Fortunately, a biologist, Anne Fausto-Sterling (1985), has examined the full range of research, looking in detail at the research on the brain and on sex hormones and its implications for sex differences. She concluded that there are definite limitations in the extent to which we are shaped by biological factors. With respect to brain structure, she noted that genetic factors are important but "extensive development of nervous connections occurs after birth, influenced profoundly by individual experience" (Fausto-Sterling 1985:77). Rather than a simple casual relationship between biological factors and human behavior, then, she argued that the mind, body, and culture all interact with each other. No human behavior can be explained solely and completely in either biological or social terms. Behavior is always a function of multiple factors, she asserted, and we cannot say how much of any particular behavior is biological and how much is social.

The Importance of Nurture

Fausto-Sterling, then, convincingly made a case that nurture is an important part of sex-role behavior. What additional evidence exists to support this view? Some of the evidence comes from history and from the observation of other cultures. Historically, American men and women have not always behaved in strict accord with what we have called the traditional sex roles. In the American colonies, women functioned as innkeepers, printers, and the head of dame schools. Further, they were actively involved in the economics of their family and social affairs of their community. In the mid-nineteenth century, as the nation industrialized and the middle classes grew, new ideas about proper sex roles developed. Indeed, women's roles narrrowed significantly. Women were to be freed from hard work so that they could engage in the more feminine pursuits of music, art, and embroidery. Greater emphasis was placed on the proper dress, appearance, and decorative function of women. Increasingly, as men's work took them away from the home, women's place became the home. They were to create and maintain the home as a refuge for their husband and children in the face of an increasingly impersonal and hostile environment.

Looking at other cultures, we also find deviations from traditional roles in America. In her study of three primitive cultures in New Guinea, Margaret Mead (1969) concluded that the meaning of being male or female is largely a matter of cultural conditioning. Many of the traits we think of as masculine or feminine are "as lightly linked to sex as are the clothing, the manners, and the form of headdress that a society at a given period assigns to either sex" (Mead 1969:260). Among the Tchambuli, for example, the women were in command and were concerned with the practical matters of tribal life such as fishing and trading. They also took the initiative in mating. The men, in contrast, concerned themselves with their personal appearance, their jewelry, and their rivalries and jealousies in their efforts to get the attention of women.

Finally, there is some evidence from research in developmental psychology that underscores the importance of socialization in sex roles. According to the stereotype, females are more nurturing than males. But there is evidence that girls are not *naturally* more nurturing than boys (Melson and Fogel 1988). Until about the age of four or five, boys tend to be equally as interested as girls in babies and their care. As they get older and become more aware of their gender identity, boys become less involved and less interested in babies. They *learn* to engage in the traditional less nurturing male role.

In sum, the evidence we have supports the earlier conclusions of Chafetz (1974:27–28) who drew a number of conclusions about the relative influence of biological and social factors:

1. Most of the traits and behaviors identified as masculine or feminine in a society are not innate. Those defined as masculine in one society may be feminine in another, and vice versa.

2. There are a few *tendencies* that are innately linked to gender, such as the male tendency to greater aggression. But social factors can virtually eliminate the effects of the tendencies.

3. Whatever innate differences exist, they are quantitative rather than qualitative. That is, we cannot say that men are aggressive while women are passive. But, as we stated earlier, more men than women are highly aggressive.

Socialization and Sex-Role Orientation

Since socialization is important in sex-role development, we need to identify the major sources of that socialization. Reflect back on your own experience. How did you learn what it means to be masculine and feminine? Probably, the three most important sources were family, school, and the media.

The Family

Our earliest exposure to what it means to be masculine and feminine comes from our parents. We learn from them and tend to model ourselves after them. We learn not only from listening to them, but also by observing their attitudes and behavior. This means that differing family experiences should result in differing orientations.

One way that families differ is in terms of parents' notions about appropriate sex roles. Some parents are more egalitarian than others. Some are more insistent on particular kinds of behavior than others. There are various reasons, no doubt, why parents try to impose particular kinds of behavior on us. One of our female students, who scored masculine on a measure of sex-role orientation, told us that her brother died when she was a child. Thereafter, her father treated her "in ways that are usually reserved for bringing up a son. He taught me to do yard work, play baseball, to be achievement-oriented, and to keep my emotions to myself." Her masculine orientation is understandable. Unfortunately, it has caused her some problems in intimate relationships, since she is "often at a loss as how to communicate and behave with a guy."

Families also differ in their economic resources. In his study of the effects of economic depression during the 1930s, Elder (1974) found that the extent of deprivation had an impact on the roles adopted by children. Girls from more deprived families were likely to have mothers who had to work to help support the family. The girls had to assume responsiblity for housework, and as they matured they tended to marry early and continue the homemaker role. Boys from more deprived families tended to choose careers earlier in life and to have a more orderly career. Girls from more affluent families were able to obtain more education. By the time they were adults in the 1950s, they tended to be working and to continue working even after marriage. Their education enabled them to depart from the traditional homemaker role assumed by their mothers.

Still another way in which families differ is their structure. Will it make a difference if you have one parent rather than two during part or most of your early years? The answer is yes, though the effects may not be as striking as you would expect. Actually, results of studies have been somewhat contradictory. In an effort to make sense of them all, Stevenson and Black (1988) examined all available studies (sixty-seven total) that compared effects on sex-role development when fathers were present and when fathers were absent. They found no impact on females. Among males, they found that preschool boys with fathers absent make less stereotypical choices of toys and activities than those boys with fathers present. Older father-absent boys were found to be more stereotypically masculine in their behavior than father-present boys, however, particularly in aggressive behavior.

School

In one sense, the schools teach equality between the sexes, because they group boys and girls together and apply the same standards to both. But when one looks at the books used and the way in which teachers interact with pupils, it is clear that there are different expectations for the sexes. For example, a survey of 134 reading books used in elementary schools in New Jersey showed five boy-centered for every two girl-centered stories, three times as many adult male characters as female adult characters in major roles, six times as many male as female biographies, and even more male than female animal stories (Deckard 1975:32). More recently, there have been some efforts to change the situation. But children are still likely to learn that they live in a male-dominated world where men are engaged in demanding, exciting activities and women are keepers of the home and family.

Young children are likely to learn from books that they live in a male-dominated world.

Similarly, there are differences, sometimes subtle, in the ways that teachers relate to boys and girls (Association of American Colleges 1982). Teachers tend to ask boys more difficult questions. They are more likely to urge boys to try harder if the boys are wrong or unsuccessful at first, implying that the boys have the ability to succeed. They tend to give boys instructions on how to do the work for themselves, but take the girls through the work process step by step or even do it for them. Teachers may not intend it, but their behavior can communicate quite different messages to boys and girls about expectations and potential.

The Media
The media generally are influential in shaping our notions of appropriate sex roles. However, we will concentrate on what is perhaps the most influential—television. The National Institute of Mental Health (1982:54–56) has summed up some of the facts about television programming that can affect sex-role development:

1. In male-female interaction, men are usually more dominant.

2. Men on television are rational, ambitious, smart, competitive, powerful, stable, violent, and tolerant, while the women are sensitive, romantic, attractive, happy, warm, sociable, peaceful, fair, submissive, and timid.

3. For men, the emphasis is on strength, performance, and skill; for women, it is on attractiveness and desirability.

4. Marriage and family are not important to television's men. One study found that for nearly half of the men, it wasn't possible to tell if they were married, a fact that was true for only 11 percent of the women.

It seems that television is more likely than not to support aspects of the traditional roles for men and women. There are, of course, pressures to change, and some evidence of change. A study of commercials from 1971 to 1985 found some improvement (Bretl and Cantol 1988). Men and women appeared equally often as central characters in prime-time commercials by 1985. There was still a lower percentage of females than of males who were employed, but males were increasingly shown as spouses and parents. Women were still more likely to be seen in domestic settings, advertising products used around the home. The greatest inequality in 1985 occurred in the narrators. About 90 percent of all narrators of commercials were still men.

Women may have come a long way. But there is a long way to go if equality is the goal. And television, along with school and family practices, continues to reinforce to some extent the traditional roles.

Changing Sex Roles and Orientations

As noted, what we have called the traditional roles emerged in the mid-nineteenth century. Sex roles vary over time and between societies. Sex orientations also change over time and may even vary over an individual's life span.

Changing Patterns

There is evidence that people are becoming less traditional in their attitudes about sex roles. In a study involving 239 adults and their beliefs about the age at which infants could first perform various skills, some rated boys, some rated girls, and some rated "babies" (no gender specified) (Paludi and Gullo 1986). Contrary to past research, the sex label of the infant did not affect the ratings. Another study reported that female college freshmen from 1969 to 1984 placed increasing emphasis on achievement goals (Fiorentine 1988). Over that period of time an increasing proportion of the women indicated that they had one or more of the following goals: to become an authority in their field; to be well-off financially; to obtain recognition from colleagues; and to have administrative responsibility. Moreover, studies using national samples of adults show that women's sex-role attitudes became increasingly nontraditional from the early 1960s to the late 1970s (Cherlin and Walters 1981).

In essence, those who reject the traditional model tend to affirm more egalitarian roles. They believe that women should have the same opportunities as men, and that men can and should engage in some of the traditional female

Sex-Role Development: My Personal Journey

Write your autobiography, focusing on sex-role development. You can organize your autobiography along the lines of answers to the following questions:

1. What does it mean to you to be someone of your gender? That is, what kinds of traits and qualities do you have as a male or female?

2. To what extent are you like and different from your same-sex parent? Describe that parent. If you didn't grow up with a same-sex parent, describe the person who you believe was most influential in shaping your ideas.

3. What messages did you get from your parents about appropriate traits? What kinds of things did they encourage? Discourage?

4. What school experiences do you recall that shaped your development?

5. Who are some of the same-sex people you admire, and some that you dislike, on television? How do you think they influenced you?

6. What is your ideal for someone of your sex? To what extent are you like your ideal?

7. How do you think you will continue to develop? What can you do to further your development along the lines you desire?

If the entire class does this project, it would be useful to have a few males and a few females share their autobiographies. Compare and contrast the male with the female accounts.

pursuits (such as the nurturing of children). William McBroom (1987), for example, measured traditionalism by the extent of agreement with ideas such as women are too independent now, a woman's place is in the home, and a husband should help with housework. He found that both male and female students became less traditional over the period between 1975 and 1980, but women changed more than men.

With such changes in attitudes, we would expect some changes in sex-role orientations. There is evidence that orientations are changing, and the change seems to be in the direction of increasing androgeny (Pedersen and Bond 1985). In the study of female freshmen noted earlier, although an increasing proportion affirmed achievement goals, there was no decrease in the value placed on domestic and nurturing goals (Fiorentine 1988). The more we value egalitarianism in sex roles, the more people are likely to become androgynous in their orientations.

Lingering Traditionalism

Traditional roles are not dead. Recall the occupational sex ratios (table 7.1), the reactions of people at horror movies, and the fact that women who work still bear the brunt of the responsibility for housework and child-rearing. Women tend to be more egalitarian than men in their views (King and King 1985). But both men and women show some evidence of lingering traditionalism. One study reported that both men and women continue to believe that men are more forceful, independent, stubborn, and reckless than women, and that women are more mannerly, giving, emotional, and submissive than men (Werner and LaRussa 1985). A study of adolescents found that boys in 1982, like those in 1956, continued to believe in male dominance and female subordination more than did girls (Lewin and Tragos 1987). The girls in 1982, however, revealed significantly less dissatisfaction with being female than the girls in 1956.

The importance of such findings is in their impact on the quality of our life and intimate relationships. The traditional female is feminine in orientation, not androgynous or masculine. The traditional male is masculine, not androgynous or feminine. Is that the best arrangement? Let us look at the impact of orientations on our behavior and our well-being.

Sex-Role Orientation: What Difference Does It Make?

What difference do you think it would make in your life if you were the opposite sex? Clearly, it would make some significant differences. There are also important differences that depend on your sex-role orientation.

Communication

We have seen that women tend to have a different conversational style than men. There are also differences, however, depending on your sex-role orientation. Individuals of both sexes who have a masculine orientation are likely to talk more in small groups (Jose and McCarthy 1988). Those with a masculine orientation are also more likely to overlap or interrupt the speech of someone else (Drass 1986).

More importantly, sex-role orientation affects such things as our ability to handle conflict and the way in which we will try to influence someone. With regard to conflict, Yelsma and Brown (1985) found sex-role orientation to be more important than sex. They studied ninety-one married couples and found that androgynous and masculine spouses tended to handle conflict more constructively than feminine spouses.

With regard to influence, there is a variety of tactics that can be used. *Manipulation* involves such things as dropping hints, flattering someone, and behaving seductively. *Supplication* includes pleading, crying, and acting helpless. *Bullying* is the use of threats, insults, ridicule. *Autocracy* refers to such things as insisting and asserting one's authority. *Bargaining* involves reasoning and the willingness to compromise. Finally, *disengagement* is withdrawing in some way (sulking, leaving the scene).

In a study of 235 intimate couples, researchers found that more feminine spouses are more likely to use supplication, while more masculine spouses tend to avoid both supplication and bargaining (Howard, Blumstein, and Schwartz 1986). Supplication is a relatively weak tactic. Thus, those with a feminine orientation are less likely to be influential and more likely to be influenced by a partner.

Self-Concept

Your **self-concept** is the totality of the beliefs and attitudes you have about yourself. Your self-concept is important because the way you think about yourself is an integral part of your psychological health. You can't be a healthy individual if you don't think well of yourself, and if you don't have a high degree of self-esteem.

Who is likely to have the higher self-esteem? The research consistently indicates that both males and females who are high in masculine traits have higher self-esteem than others. Adolescents who score high on masculinity see themselves as more socially and physically competent, and have higher self-esteem scores, than those low on masculinity (Cate and Sugawara 1986). Among adult women, masculinity is a better predictor of self-esteem than a woman's educational or occupational achievements (Long 1986).

Two things are important to keep in mind here. First, androgynous as well as masculine people score high on masculinity. The point is that it is the masculinity rather than the androgyny per se that makes the difference. And second, masculinity refers to the perception of traits that are associated with the traditional male role, that is, to instrumental traits. Masculinity and femininity are unfortunate choices for terms, because we are not saying that a masculine sex-orientation in a woman means that she is any less of a woman or that she is "mannish." Rather, a masculine orientation for either males or females simply means the possession of such traits as independence, being active rather than passive, competitiveness, and the ability to make decisions. It is understandable that people who perceive themselves to have such traits would also have high self-esteem. And it is clear that having such traits does not mean that the individual lacks kindness or sensitivity or a willingness to be helpful.

Mental Health

Earlier, some researchers expected psychological health to be highest when there was congruence between gender and sex-role orientation (males would be masculine and females would be feminine in their orientation). Research shows that is not true. On the other hand, Sandra Bem and some others expected psychological health to be highest among androgynous people. While the results of the research are still somewhat inconsistent, it appears that the androgynous model is questionable. Furthermore, after looking at thirty-two studies of the relationship between sex-role orientation and depression and adjustment, Whitley (1984) found that masculinity among both males and females is associated with higher self-esteem, higher adjustment, and less depression.

Again, keep in mind the meaning of masculinity here as discussed. It is the instrumental traits that are important. For instance, two psychologists who studied stress and coping reactions among 211 undergraduates also found that a high masculine orientation is an advantage (Nezu and Nezu 1987). The high-masculine subjects had significantly lower levels of depression and anxiety. And compared to low-masculine subjects, they rated their problem-solving ability as more effective; engaged in more active and fewer avoidance methods of coping with stress; and engaged in more problem-focused and less emotion-focused coping styles.

Are, then, the feminine traits a handicap? The answer is no, because androgynous individuals have both the masculine and feminine traits and the same advantages as masculine types in terms of self-concept and mental health. Is there, then, any advantage at all to androgyny? We would say there is. The expressive traits can help with social adjustment by increasing interpersonal skills (Payne 1987). Some researchers continue to find that expressive traits, though to a lesser degree than the instrumental, make some contribution to our mental health (Stoppard and Paisley 1987). Also a study of the adjustment of women to the death of a spouse reported that androgynous widows had a more positive adjustment than the feminine, masculine, or undifferentiated (Solie and Fielder 1987/1988). Androgyny does not have as many benefits as some researchers anticipated, but it seems clear that there are at least some advantages to an androgynous orientation.

Sex-Role Orientation and Intimacy

We have seen that males and females differ somewhat in their attitudes toward love and sexuality. People also differ by sex-role orientation. In fact, sex-role orientation may be more important than gender in explaining differences. Three researchers who surveyed 286 undergraduates found males to be more ludic and females to be more pragmatic and manic in their love styles (Bailey, Hendrick, and Hendrick 1987). They also found males to be more sexually permissive. Yet they found more and stronger effects for sex-role orientation. Androgynous subjects endorsed eros the most, and undifferentiated subjects endorsed it the least. Ludic love was endorsed most by masculine and least by feminine subjects. Those who were feminine gave strongest support to manic love, and, along with androgynous subjects, to agape. Masculine and undifferentiated subjects were the most, and feminine subjects the least, permissive in their sexual attitudes. Finally, undifferentiated subjects scored significantly

Androgynous people tend to be more aware and expressive of love-feelings.

Can Marriage Survive a Modern Woman?

Denny is a thirty-six-year-old man who says that he isn't sure if marriages today can "survive a modern woman." He bases this on his own experience, in which he and his former wife struggled unsuccessfully to establish consensual roles:

My views were influenced by my parents. My father was the breadwinner, while my mother was responsible for caring for the children and taking care of the home. I don't recall ever seeing my father iron clothes or do any kind of housework. He was a good provider, and my mother was a good homemaker. I have noticed, however, that as they have grown older, there is a merging into more shared tasks.

I was married at twenty-two. My wife had just graduated, so she worked while I finished my degree. We didn't have much in the way of possessions, but we loved each other and expected our marriage to last. After I graduated and went to work, we had children. Within three years, we had two children and a home in suburbia. I was working two jobs in order to pay the mortgage. My wife, by mutual agreement, stayed home with the kids in their early years.

After our youngest began kindergarten, my wife went back to work. At first it was a period of liberation. We now shared the financial responsibility. But she wanted me to share the work around the home. I did some cooking, washed clothes, and vacuumed as needed. But I grew increasingly resentful. And her job got more and more demanding, which meant that we had less and less time together. I felt like I was being both mother and father in the home.

Instead of talking about our growing apart, we tried to ignore it. I thought maybe it would all take care of itself. When it became clear that things weren't going to get better, I asked her to quit her job. She got very angry and refused. I told her I would rather go back to working two jobs than have things the way they had become. She said I was being very unreasonable.

Anyway, the upshot of it is that we finally settled the issue by getting divorced. That really hurt. I still don't understand why she had to work so many hours. I really wonder if working women and good families are both possible.

lower than others on scales that measured responsible sexuality (e.g., using birth control), a tolerance for varied sexual practices, and a belief in sexual relations as the ultimate form of human communication.

Other research also underscores the importance of sex-role orientation for love relationships. One study found that androgynous subjects were more aware of love feelings and more expressive in their love feelings (Ganong and Coleman 1987). Of the four types, the androgynous scored highest on verbal expression of love, self-disclosure, willingness to tolerate faults in the loved one, and tendency to express love emotions.

With such differences, we would expect people to have varying degrees of satisfaction in their relationships depending on their sex-role orientations and the combination of orientations in the couple. Indeed, in a study of 331 couples Bowen (1987) found that those with the lowest levels of marital adjustment were couples in which the husband was traditional and the wife more modern in sex-role orientation. Various other combinations could produce satisfaction. However, those who tend to report the greatest levels of satisfaction are men and women who are androgynous (Cooper, Chassin, and Zeiss 1985).

PRINCIPLES FOR ENHANCING INTIMACY

1. Although traditionally many vocations and professions have been closed to them, women should no longer be deterred from pursuing what they most want to do. When women are given the same opportunities as men, they perform as well as men at most tasks.

2. The skills of effective communication and interaction with others can be learned. And because they are more proficient in these skills, women provide appropriate models of behavior for men.

3. If you should choose a behavior or way of life that goes beyond the traditional norms of how a male or female should act, realize that you may encounter criticism. Even though our ideas about sex roles have expanded, many people still react to others on the basis of traditional expectations.

4. An important way to gain self-esteem is to cultivate the traits—such as independence, decisiveness, and competitiveness—that are typically labeled masculine.

5. Those traits—warmth, caring, sensitivity, and nurturance—that are traditionally labeled as female are as appropriate for men as they are for women. These traits help people meet their needs for intimacy. Remember that most of the traits that we generally label as masculine or feminine are not innate, but learned.

There are both similarities and differences between men and women. Both have some of the same fundamental needs, and both respond to some situations in similar ways. The differences include superior verbal ability of females and superior spatial and quantitative ability of males; a greater proportion of men who are highly aggressive; more interpersonal skills among females; and better ability by females to interpret nonverbal cues.

We need to distinguish between gender (male or female), sex role (behavior associated with being male or female), and sex-role orientation (conception of the self as having some combination of male and female traits). The traditional sex roles suggest that men are strong, independent, aggressive, and logical, while women are gentle, dependent, nurturing, and emotional. Your sex-role orientation may be masculine (primarily instrumental traits), feminine (primarily expressive traits), androgynous (high on both masculine and feminine traits), or undifferentiated (low on both kinds of traits).

Whether sex roles reflect nature or nurture is a matter of controversy. Evidence from biologists and psychologists as well as cross-cultural studies indicate that most of the traits and behaviors identified as masculine or feminine are not innate, but reflect social factors such as socialization. We have gender-related tendencies, but these can be modified by social factors. Our sex-role orientation is also social, the result of socialization by the family, school, and media.

Sex roles and sex-role orientations change over time. People are becoming less traditional in their attitudes about sex roles. There is some lingering traditionalism, however, that affects both attitudes and behavior.

Sex-role orientations make a difference in various areas of our lives, including the way we communicate, our self-concepts, and our mental health. Androgynous people have a number of advantages over others, although for some things such as mental health it is the masculine component that leads to the advantage. Sex-role orientations also affect intimacy, with androgynous people reporting the greatest levels of satisfaction.

1. Reported in the *St. Louis Post-Dispatch,* November 28, 1910.
2. Reported in *Psychology Today,* June, 1986, p. 12.

8

Sexuality

What is the most intense form of human intimacy? Some people would answer "sex." But sex can be alienating as well as bonding, meaningless as well as exhilarating. Even when it is highly gratifying, sex may not hold a relationship together. Hank got married when he was in his early thirties. When we discussed his impending marriage with him, he told us that he knew it would require a lot of work because he and his future wife had a lot of differences. "What do you have in common?" we asked. The only thing Hank could think of was: "We have great sex together." Hank's marriage was built on little else. Within a year after the marriage, Hank and his wife were divorced. "Great sex" didn't make a lasting marriage.

In this chapter we will look at the meaning of sex and how it affects our relationships. We will examine some of the problems involved with teenage sex, including unwanted pregnancies. We will discuss such issues as contraception, abortion, sexual diseases and dysfunctions, and extramarital sex. And we will see the role of sex in marriage, including long-term marriage.

Sex is an important part of intimacy.

The Meaning of Sex

In our discussion of sex roles, we pointed out that humans are social as well as biological creatures. For many kinds of behavior, being born a male or female is not as important as the society in which you live and the way in which you think of yourself. Similarly, we shall see that sex, one of the strong drives in humans, is not merely a biological phenomenon. Sexually, we are social as well as biological creatures. We need to examine both aspects of sexuality.

Sex as Physical: The Response Cycle

In the 1960s, William Masters and Virginia Johnson pioneered the investigation of the responses of the body to sexual intercourse. The researchers identified four stages of human sexual response: excitement, plateau, orgasm, and resolution (Masters, Johnson, and Kolodny 1988:80–95). During the response, there are two basic physiological reactions. One involves an increased concentration of blood in bodily tissues in the genitals and the female breasts. The other is increased energy in the nerves and muscles throughout the body.

Excitement, the first stage of arousal, is the result of some kind of physical or psychological stimulation. You can become excited by someone stroking your body, by kissing, by reading erotic literature, by having someone look at you seductively, by remembering a previous sexual experience, by fantasizing about sex, and so on. In the woman, along with various other physiological changes, excitement leads to **vaginal** lubrication, usually within ten to thirty seconds. In the man, similar physiological reactions result in erection of the **penis,** usually within three to eight seconds in young males.

The excitement stage may or may not lead to the next phase. Something may interfere with continued response, such as a telephone ringing, something that the partner says or does, or a thought that suddenly comes into one's mind. But if the process continues, you move into the second stage, the *plateau.* As figure 8.1 shows, in the plateau stage there is a continuing high level of arousal, preparing the way for orgasm. The actual length of the plateau varies from individual to individual. For men who have trouble controlling **ejaculation,** the plateau may be extremely short. For women, a brief plateau sometimes precedes an intense orgasm. Others find a longer plateau to be a kind of sexual high that is very satisfying.

Both men and women continue to experience physiological changes during the plateau. The woman's vagina becomes increasingly moist and the tissues swell with blood. The portion of the vagina nearest the opening becomes so congested that the penis tends to be gripped because of the reduced size of the vaginal opening. The back part of the vagina opens up and out to accommodate the erect penis. In the male, the penis is fully erect, the **testes** are fluid-swollen, enlarged, and pulled up closer to the body. During the plateau stage, both males and females have increased heart rates, faster breathing, and increased blood pressure.

The Intimate Couple

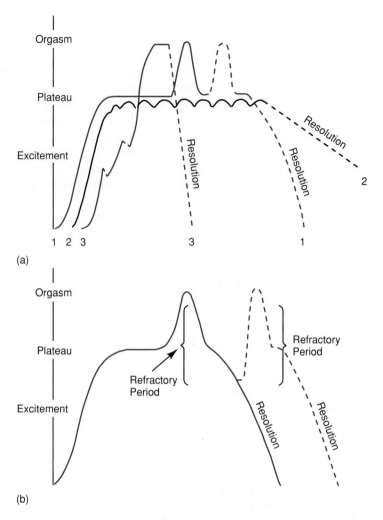

(a) Three types of female response. Pattern 1 is multiple orgasm. Pattern 2 is arousal without orgasm. Pattern 3 involves a number of small declines in excitement and a very rapid resolution.

(b) The typical male pattern of response. The dotted line indicates the possibility of a second orgasm and ejaculation after the refractory period.

Figure 8.1 *The sexual response cycle.*

Orgasm, the third stage, is a discharge of the sexual tension that has been built up and maintained during the plateau. The orgasm takes the least time of any of the stages. Usually it involves muscular contractions and intense physical feelings that occur in the matter of a few seconds and are followed by rapid relaxation. Again, there are physiological changes that occur in both men and women. In both, there is a good deal of involuntary muscular contraction throughout the body. Sometimes the contractions happen in the facial muscles, making the face appear to be frowning or in pain. But normally such an expression reflects a high level of arousal rather than any pain or displeasure.

Women may have anywhere from three to fifteen muscular contractions during orgasm. These contractions occur in various muscles throughout their bodies. They also have changes in their brain wave patterns. Women may have multiple orgasms if they have continuing stimulation and interest (pattern 1 in figure 8.1). For men, orgasm occurs in two distinct phases. In the first phase, muscular contractions force **semen** through the penis. The man experiences a sense of having gotten to the point where he can no longer control himself; ejaculation is inevitable. In the second phase, additional muscular contractions lead to ejaculation.

Following orgasm, there is a **refractory period** for the male, a time following orgasm in which the individual needs to recover and is incapable of having an additional orgasm or ejaculation. The refractory period may last anywhere from minutes to hours. As the male ages, the refractory period gets longer. For the male, the refractory period is part of the fourth stage, *resolution*. Resolution is a return to a state of being sexually unaroused. In both males and females, the various physiological changes reverse and the individual becomes like he or she was prior to arousal. If the individual has been highly aroused without orgasm having occurred, the resolution will take longer.

Sex as Social

Although sex is one of the basic drives in humans, the expression of sex is still a social phenomenon. That is, we learn how to behave as sexual beings. Despite the notion that sex involves "doing what comes naturally," there is more learned than unlearned sexual activity.

Both sex roles and sex-role orientations affect sexual activity. For instance, in the traditional female sex role, the woman does not take the initiative in sex. She also must not appear to be too eager. Under those circumstances, a woman might sometimes say "no" when she really desires sex and means "yes." A study of female undergraduates found that nearly 40 percent had engaged in such token resistance at least once (Muehlenhard and Hollabaugh 1988). The women gave three types of reasons for their token resistance. Some reasons were practical—not wanting to appear to be promiscuous or the fear of disease. Others were related to inhibition—having religious or moral concerns or fearing physical discomfort (for virgins). The third category was manipulative—playing games with the man or being angry with him. The most common response was the first, however, the fear of appearing promiscuous. Women who are influenced by the traditional roles, or who are in a relationship with males who are so influenced, may be reluctant to appear too eager for sex.

Sex-role orientations may also influence sexual behavior. Although there has not been much research, one study reported that the masculine sex-role orientation for both men and women was associated with more frequent sexual intercourse (Leary and Snell 1988). Those scoring high on instrumental traits also tended to have more oral sex and more relaxed feelings about sex.

Thus, there is a variety of factors that affect our sexual behavior. There are variations in behavior both within and between societies. Differences in arousal, techniques, and the experience of unwanted sex further underscore the social nature of our sexual behavior.

Sexual Arousal

There is enormous variation in the extent to which people in differing societies and within a particular society are aroused. Levels of sexual activity between societies vary from the extremely low level of the Grand Valley Dani to the unusually high level of the people of Mangaia (both groups are in the South Pacific) (Lauer and Lauer 1983:5–6). The Dani do not begin to have sexual relations until about two years after marriage. Weddings are held only about once each four to six years. The frequency of sexual relations is so low that the population is barely maintained. A couple will abstain from sex for four to six years after the birth of a child. Moreover, there is little extramarital sex, and no evidence of homosexuality or masturbation. The Dani simply seem to have little interest.

By contrast, sex is a principal interest among the Mangaians. Nearly all, both male and female, have considerable premarital experience with a variety of partners. The Mangaians claim that a typical eighteen-year-old male will have, on the average, three orgasms per night each night of the week. A twenty-eight-year-old male will have about two orgasms per night, five to six times each week. In their late forties, males have an orgasm two to three times a week.

Sexual Techniques

You probably regard mouth-to-mouth kissing as erotic. The Mangaians did not regard it as such until Westerners influenced them. Most Americans regard foreplay as essential to satisfying sex. In other societies, however, foreplay varies from being virtually absent to consuming even more time than it does among Americans (Ford and Beach 1951:41).

The preferred position for intercourse also varies from one society to another. Among the Trobriand Islanders, the man squats and draws the woman toward him until her legs rest on his hips or his elbows. Islanders maintain that this position gives the man considerable freedom of movement and that it does not inhibit the woman in her movements of response (Malinowski 1932:285).

The point is that the diversity in techniques underscores the fact that sexual behavior is learned. What is defined as erotic by some people may be defined as disgusting by others. What is defined as good and pleasurable by some will be defined as evil by others. Social factors are powerful, and they may modify, facilitate, or suppress the expression of the sex drive.

Nearly everyone experiences some unwanted sexual activity.

Unwanted Sex

In an ideal world, there would be reciprocal desire between two people. People in love would desire sexual relations with each other at the same time. In the real world, there is a good deal of unwanted sex, sex that occurs when the individual is not aroused and does not want to engage in the activity. It is not always our sex drive that is at work when we have sexual relations.

How many people engage in unwanted sex? A survey of 275 undergraduate women reported that more than half had been pressured into kissing, breast and genital manipulation, and oral contact with their partner's genitals (Christopher 1988). They were likely to be pressured into kissing and some fondling even on casual dates. Pressures to engage in oral-genital contact and sexual intercourse were more likely to occur in serious dating.

Interestingly, men also report unwanted sexual activity. In their study of 507 men and 486 women in introductory psychology classes, Muehlenhard and Cook (1988) found that 97.5 percent of the women and 93.5 percent of the men had experienced unwanted sexual activity (kissing, petting, intercourse). More men (62.7 percent) than women (46.3 percent) said that they had experienced unwanted intercourse. What were the reasons they gave for

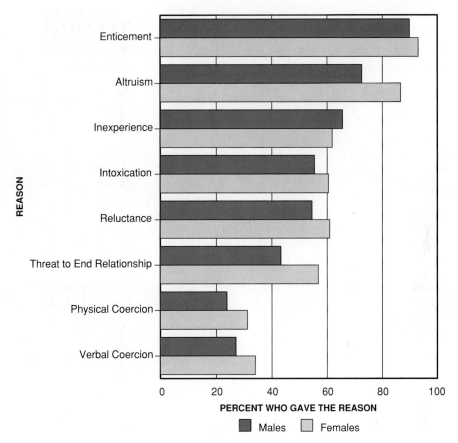

Figure 8.2 *Reasons for agreeing to unwanted sexual activity.*
Source: Data from Muehlenhard and Cook 1988:65.

yielding to the pressures? There were many, but the most common was enticement (figure 8.2), some kind of seductive behavior on the part of the other person. The other person may have started taking off his or her clothes, for example, or aroused the enticed person by touching him or her. "Altruism," another common reason, includes such things as knowing the partner wants the activity and engaging in it in order to satisfy the partner's needs even though you are not in the mood. "Inexperience" means agreeing to the activity not from desire but from a sense that you need to have the experience. "Reluctance" refers to being with someone and not knowing anything else to do, or wanting to make the other feel attractive, or feeling obligated because the person has spent time and money on you. According to their self-reports, both males and females engage in a certain amount of kissing, petting, and even intercourse for such reasons.

Sex and Society

As we look at sexual beliefs and practices throughout the world we find both similarities with, and differences from, our own society. Investigate some kinds of sexual beliefs and/or practices in another society that differ from those in your society (e.g., frequency and/or positions of intercourse, the meaning of sex, attitudes about premarital and/or extramarital sex, what techniques and practices are considered erotic, etc.). Compare them with your society and with your personal values. How do you feel about the beliefs and/or practices of the other society? Do you think that they are more or less preferable to those of your own? Why?

One way to carry on your investigation is through the library. You can check journals such as *The Journal of Sex Research*. Or you can use the *Social Science Index* or *Psychological Abstracts* to locate appropriate articles. Studies by anthropologists are also excellent sources.

Another way to carry on the investigation is to interview someone from another country. If that person is willing to discuss the topic with you, ask him or her to describe sexual attitudes and/or behavior in some area such as premarital sex or sexual techniques.

If the entire class engages in this project, each student could be responsible for a different society. Discuss the findings in terms of the questions given in the first column.

Sex and Intimate Relationships

Human love, according to Erich Fromm (1956), does not reflect a Freudian sexual instinct. Rather, Fromm argued, sexual desire reflects the human need for love and union. In other words, the need for intimacy has primacy over sex. We agree that intimacy is a more fundamental need than the need for sex. The sex drive is strong, and we need to find some outlet for sexual tension. But that tension can be dealt with in ways other than sexual intercourse, if necessary. There are, after all, healthy celibates. You can be celibate and be fulfilled. But you cannot be fulfilled without intimacy.

Sexual relations, then, may be seen as one way to fulfill intimacy needs. Sometimes we want sexual relations because we need to love someone. Indeed, our attitudes about sex reflect our styles of love. Recall the six styles of loving that we discussed in chapter 4—eros, ludus, storge, pragma, mania, and agape. The different styles are related to diverse sexual attitudes and practices (Hendrick and Hendrick 1987). Those who score high on ludic love are more likely to be sexually permissive in their attitudes. They tend to agree, for example, that casual sex is acceptable and they prefer to have sex with many partners. Ludic lovers are also prone, along with pragmatic lovers, to view sex as essentially a physical phenomenon, the main purpose of which is to enjoy oneself. Consequently, they believe sex is best when they focus on their own pleasure.

People who score high on agapic love, in contrast, tend to be less permissive and also to believe in sex as a form of intense communion. That is, they believe that sex gets better as the relationship develops, that sex between people in love is the ultimate form of human interaction, and that intercourse is an "almost overwhelming experience." People who score high in erotic love, and to some extent those who score high in manic love, also see sex as intense communion.

Despite the preferences of ludic lovers, a number of experts have argued that sex without intimacy—the casual sex of the one-night stand, for example—is of little use to humans (Fromm 1956). At best, casual sex fails to fulfill our intimacy needs. At worst, it leaves us feeling more empty and lonely than we were before the experience. Instead of enhancing the quality of our intimate lives, sex without intimacy can become an impediment to the development of relationships that add to our well-being (Cobliner 1988). The ludic lover is likely to find that his or her quest for fulfillment is frustratingly elusive in spite of many sexual encounters (see PERSONAL).

Actually, most people seem to sense the fact that sex needs to be an expression of an intimate relationship. Most Americans, for example, do not approve of **promiscuity,** frequent and indiscriminate sexual relations with many partners as preferred by ludic lovers. Nor do they want to establish a relationship with someone who has been promiscuous. Most men prefer sexual intercourse within a caring relationship. Women tend to enjoy intercourse only in the context of a committed as well as a caring relationship (McCabe 1987).

Sexual activity is a natural expression of feelings of intimacy. In fact, as someone has put it, sex never ages. In most societies, people continue to have sexual relations throughout life. A study of 202 men and women aged 80 to 102 reported a variety of sexual activity (Bretschneider and McCoy 1988). Although only 14 percent of the women and 29 percent of the men were married, 62 percent of the men and 30 percent of the women were having sexual intercourse, ranging from once a year to once a day. The most common activity for both men and women was touching and caressing; 83 percent of the men and 64 percent of the women engaged in this behavior. The subjects also reported engaging in masturbation. Many did not answer the question about masturbation, but among those who did 72 percent of the men and 40 percent of the women still masturbated at times.

Sex and the Search for Intimacy

Charles, a young single man, was a ludic lover. He went through the effort to find a fulfilling intimacy through sex. He shares with us the conclusions he has reached in his twenty-eighth year:

While I was in college, I lived on campus for two years. I was really promiscuous. I had sex relations with many women. I thoroughly enjoyed it. I thought of myself as a real stud, and I enjoyed the envy of some of my male friends. In time, my sexual experiences had an unexpected and interesting effect on me. I discovered that my so-called manhood, though sexually fulfilled, lacked a quality of intimacy that became more profound as my need for emotional closeness increased. I had thought that what I—and any real man—needed was a lot of good sex. But the more sex I had, the more I came to realize that something was missing. I would never have believed it a few years earlier, but one day I admitted to myself that sex wasn't enough. I wanted to have something more with a woman than her body.

Unfortunately, I had gotten the label of being a "player." So it became more and more difficult to develop closeness in a relationship. The women I wanted to go out with had the idea that I was a shallow person only looking for a good time. My reputation was established and it was keeping me from developing the intimacy that I now yearned for. The only women who were interested were the ones just like me. Or just like I used to be. They didn't even appeal to me anymore.

I couldn't do anything until I moved away. After graduation, I went to work in another city. I knew I had to change my life-style. I decided to play it cool with women. I was still hot to trot. I really missed having sex. But I finally realized that it wasn't going to help me to keep on the way I had been in college. I wanted to make love and please myself and my lover. But more than that, I wanted to emotionally caress a woman and understand her and relate to her. And I wanted her to do that to me as well.

I'm in a kind of limbo right now. I have dated some women and I am starting to develop a relationship with one that I think may lead to what I need. In any case, I know that I can't let sex be a deterrent to intimacy anymore. I know what I need. And I know that I can't get it in a one-night stand.

Teenage Sex

As noted in chapter 3, about two-thirds of American women have sex prior to marriage. Here, however, we want to focus on the teenager, because there are problems of sexually transmitted diseases, pregnancies, and abortions among teenagers. How many teenagers have sex, and at what age do they start? And what are some of the consequences of being sexually active?

Table 8.1 Unwanted Births of Ever-Married Women, 15–24 Years Old: 1973, 1982

	Percent Unwanted at Conception	
	1973	**1982**
All races	8.1	6.4
White	6.3	4.9
Black	18.6	18.0

Source: U.S. Bureau of the Census 1988:68.

Extent of Sex among Teenagers

There are numerous surveys with somewhat differing results, but in general national surveys show that the majority of teenagers become sexually active between the ages of sixteen and nineteen (Kahn, Kalsbeek, and Hofferth 1988:201). A small proportion (0.2 percent) become sexually active as early as the age of twelve. By the time they are nineteen, more than half of white and about three-fourths of black teenagers have had sex relations (Kahn, Kalsbeek, and Hofferth 1988:191).

The probability of being sexually active varies by a number of factors. Among fifteen- to seventeen-year-olds, for example, it has been found that males were more likely than females to have had sexual intercourse (Miller and Olson 1988). The same study reported that adolescents who rarely attended church, who did not live with both parents, and whose parents had lower levels of education were more likely than others to have had sexual intercourse.

Unwanted Pregnancy and Early Childbearing

One of the consequences of teenage sex is a high rate of unwanted pregnancies and giving birth at an early age. Some researchers believe that the United States has the highest rate of unwanted pregnancies in the West. About one out of ten sexually active adolescent women will become pregnant each year. Many will bear children. In 1986, 12.6 percent of all births were to teenage mothers (U.S. Bureau of the Census 1989:66). Many teenage mothers give birth to children who are unwanted at the time of conception, in part because of the mother being unmarried. But only in part. Married people also bear children who are unwanted at the time of conception (see table 8.1). The fact that a child was not wanted at the time of conception does not mean that the child was still unwanted at birth, of course. But we can justly wonder about the well-being of those children who were unwanted. In 1982, including women of all ages, between 6 and 7 million babies were born who were unwanted at the time of conception.

Many sexually active teenagers do not use birth control measures.

Why Pregnancy?

Birth control measures are readily available in most communities. Why, then, do so many teenagers get pregnant? First, even with the use of birth control measures, some pregnancies occur among sexually active women. But many do not use birth control (see the discussion on contraceptives). Teenage sex occurs at a time in life when the sex drive is the strongest among males, and impulsiveness and the inability to defer gratification is strong among both males and females. The first experience of sexual intercourse may be an unplanned response to strong emotions, making it unlikely that any plans for birth control have been made. Fewer than one out of six females use some method of birth control the first time they have sexual intercourse (Stark 1986b:28).

Second, we need to realize that not all teenagers find the prospect of pregnancy to be unsettling. A survey of over thirteen thousand female high school sophomores reported that 41 percent of the blacks, 29 percent of the Hispanics, and 23 percent of whites indicated that they would, or at least would consider, having a child out of wedlock (Abrahamse, Morrison, and Waite 1988).

Why would a teenager want to get pregnant out of wedlock? There are a variety of reasons (Stark 1986b:30). Some may feel isolated and alone, and feel that a baby is the one way to find someone to love. Others may use pregnancy to get attention, to assert their independence from their parents, or, particularly for those in the lower socioeconomic strata, to do something creative in a world of very limited opportunities. As the latter suggests, pregnancy is more likely among those in the lower socioeconomic strata.

Third, there are certain parental attitudes and behaviors that can significantly reduce the likelihood of out-of-wedlock pregnancy (Hanson, Myers, and Ginsburg 1987). Among white girls, the likelihood of pregnancy is less if they feel that they have control over their lives, they have high educational aspirations, and they have concerned parents who teach them to be responsible and talk with them. Among black girls, the likelihood of pregnancy is less if the parents are concerned about them and have high expectations for their educational achievements.

Finally, among both whites and blacks, the chances of pregnancy are much higher if the girl is going steady and if she has had discipline problems in school. In essence, then, girls who feel good about themselves, have high expectations and aspirations for their lives, and have good relationships with concerned parents are much less likely to get pregnant than others. This is only partly due to a lower amount of sexual activity. It is also due to a greater probability of using birth control.

Some Consequences of Teenage Births

Whether wanted or not, the children of teenagers differ in important ways from other children. And the parents of those children differ from parents who wait at least until their twenties to have children.

Teenagers who give birth during their high school years are far less likely to complete their high school education than are others. A national study pointed out that teenage families with children are more likely to be poor and fatherless. Teenage parents are more likely to suffer from chronic unemployment, to become dependent on public welfare, and to remain dependent longer than those who delay childbearing.[1] When they do get jobs, they are more likely to get low-paying ones. And it is the female who bears the brunt of these negative consequences. Only a minority marry the father. A third or more of the mothers never see the fathers again. Others see the father some, but do not marry him and may get little or no support from him.

The news is not all bad. A study of 1590 inner-city female adolescents by Stiffman, Earls, Robins, Jung, and Kulbok (1987) shows both the negative and the more hopeful findings. The researchers divided the young women into three groups: those who had ever been pregnant, those who were sexually active but never pregnant, and those who were sexually inactive. The girls ranged in age from thirteen to eighteen. The proportion who were sexually inactive declined and the proportion of those who had ever been pregnant increased with age. Those who lived with both biological parents were more likely than others to be sexually inactive and less likely to have ever been pregnant. The three groups did not differ on measures of physical health. On mental health, however, there were a number of differences. The sexually active who had never been pregnant had the highest rates of conduct disorder and of anxiety. Those who had ever been pregnant were nearly twice as likely as the sexually inactive to have three or more symptoms of conduct disorder. Finally, the sexually active groups had higher rates of alcohol and drug abuse and depressive symptoms than those who were sexually inactive.

On the more hopeful side, in addition to equally good physical health, the females who had ever been pregnant had no greater number of current relationship problems or stressful life events than the never-pregnant group. In other words, while those who are sexually inactive had a higher level of well-being than the others, the never-pregnant sexually active group was not manifestly better off in terms of their current life situation than those who had been pregnant.

But will those who had ever been pregnant acquire additional disadvantages as they grow older? A study over a seventeen-year period of three hundred Baltimore women who had been teenage mothers sheds some light on the question (Furstenberg, Brooks-Gunn, and Morgan 1987). The women did have some long-term negative consequences of their early childbearing, including diminished economic mobility and less likelihood of marriage. When they did marry, they had higher rates of breakup. They were more likely than others to become the heads of households, which meant a greater probability of living in poverty. At the same time, the researchers point out that the situation of some of the mothers improved over time. Some had returned to school, and nearly all had at least part-time work. Two-thirds were not on public assistance. And many had fewer children than they had desired or expected in their earlier years. Thus, women are not doomed to poverty and deprivation if they bear children in their teenage years, but the risks are much higher. And those risks involve the children as well as the parents. The consequences for the children are mostly negative. Those consequences begin early, because among teenage mothers there are higher rates of infant mortality, a greater probability of birth defects, higher rates of mental retardation, and a greater risk of head and spinal injuries to the infant (Bolton 1980:31). Children born to teenage mothers, particularly those who were unplanned, are at greater risk of abuse and neglect. And the children have a greater probability of spending their childhood in poverty, and of doing poorly in school.

Clearly, there is little that is positive to be said for teenage pregnancy and childbearing. Both parents and children are likely to suffer a wide variety of negative consequences. Your chances for maximizing your well-being and the quality of your intimate relationships are much less if you bear children in your teens.

Contraception

Contraception, a method of birth control, is the use of devices or techniques to prevent fertilization. When a couple wants to avoid pregnancy, knowledge and use of effective contraception can enhance sexual pleasure and intensify sexual intimacy by removing the fear of conception. Table 8.2 shows common methods, how they work, and some of their benefits and limitations. In addition to the devices, there are techniques that people have used, some of which are of little or no use. For example, some people believe that a woman cannot get pregnant the first time she has intercourse and, therefore, no device need be used. That belief has resulted in many pregnancies. Others use the rhythm method, in which a woman tries to determine (usually by charting her body temperature) when she is fertile. She must avoid intercourse during her fertile period. Again, as many couples have discovered, the rhythm method is imprecise. Still others try withdrawal (removing the penis from the vagina before ejaculation) or a vaginal douche immediately after intercourse. These were the two most popular methods in the nineteenth century. Neither is reliable. Even if withdrawal occurs before ejaculation, many men have a leakage of seminal fluid prior to ejaculation that can result in pregnancy. And the vaginal douche, ironically, may actually facilitate pregnancy. Rather than flushing out, the douche may force sperm up into the cervix. Moreover, some of the sperm may have already traveled into the cervix, making the douche useless.

Thus, there are both effective and ineffective methods of contraception. Some of the modern methods may not be quite as ineffective or hazardous as the ancient Egyptian mixture that contained crocodile dung, but people continue to use methods that are not effective. In part, this is due to a lack of education. National surveys have shown that 30 percent of adolescents have no sex education in high school, and 38 percent never study birth control methods.[2] In other words, a substantial proportion of adolescents get no formal sexual education in the years when most are becoming sexually active. Of course, not all who receive the information make use of it. An unwanted pregnancy is a painful experience. Today, there is ample information available; no one need get pregnant out of ignorance.

Table 8.2 Methods of Birth Control

Popular name	Description	Effectiveness (pregnancies per 100 women using method for 1 year)	Advantages	Disadvantages
The pill (oral contraceptive; consultation with physician required)	Contains synthetic hormones (estrogens and progestin) to inhibit ovulation. The body reacts as if pregnancy has occurred and so does not release an egg. No egg—no conception. The pills are usually taken for 20 or 21 consecutive days; menstruation begins shortly thereafter.	Combined pills, 2*	Simple to take, removed from sexual act, highly reliable, reversible. Useful side effects: relief of premenstrual tension, reduction in menstrual flow, regularization of menstruation, relief of acne.	Weight gain (5–50 percent of users), breast enlargement and sensitivity; some users have increased headaches, nausea, and spotting. Increased possibility of vein thrombosis (blood clotting) and slight increase in blood pressure. Must be taken regularly. A causal relationship to cancer can neither be established nor refuted.
IUD (intrauterine device; consultation with physician required)	Metal or plastic object that comes in various shapes and is placed within the uterus and left there. Exactly how it works is not known. Hypotheses are that endocrine changes occur, that the fertilized egg cannot implant in the uterine wall because of irritation, that spontaneous abortion is caused.	3–6	Once inserted, user need do nothing more about birth control. High reliability, reversible, relatively inexpensive. Must be checked periodically to see if still in place.	Insertion procedure requires specialist and may be uncomfortable and painful. Uterine cramping, increased menstrual bleeding. Between 4 and 30 percent are expelled in first year after insertion. Occasional perforation of the uterine wall. Occasional pregnancy that is complicated by the presence of the IUD. Associated with pelvic inflammatory disease.
Diaphragm and jelly (consultation with physician required)	Flexible hemispherical rubber dome inserted into the vagina to block entrance to the cervix, thus providing a barrier to sperm. Usually used with spermicidal cream or jelly.	10–16	Can be left in place up to 24 hours. Reliable, harmless, reversible. Can be inserted up to 2 hours before intercourse.	Disliked by many women because it requires self-manipulation of genitals to insert and is messy because of cream. If improperly fitted, it will fail. Must be refitted periodically, especially after pregnancy. Psychological aversion may make its use inconsistent.

Source: U.S. Department of Health and Human Services, *Contraceptive Efficacy among Married Women Aged 15–44 Years,* Publication No. (PHS) 80–1981 (Hyattsville, MD: U.S. National Center for Health Statistics) 1980 and pamphlets published by Planned Parenthood Federation.

Table 8.2 Continued

Popular name	Description	Effectiveness (pregnancies per 100 women using method for 1 year)	Advantages	Disadvantages
Condom	Thin, strong sheath or cover, usually of latex, worn over the penis to prevent sperm from entering the vagina.	7–14	Simple to obtain and use; free of objectionable side effects. Quality control has improved with government regulation. Protection against various sexually transmitted diseases.	Must be applied just before intercourse. Can slip off, especially after ejaculation when penis returns to flaccid state. Occasional rupture. Interferes with sensation and spontaneity.
Chemical methods	Numerous products to be inserted into the vagina to block sperm from the uterus and/or to act as a spermicide. Vaginal foams are creams packed under pressure (like foam shaving cream) and inserted with an applicator. Vaginal suppositories are small cone-shaped objects that melt in the vagina; vaginal tablets also melt in the vagina.	13–17 (More effective when used in conjunction with another method, such as the diaphragm.)	Foams appear to be most effective, followed by creams, jellies, suppositories, tablets. Harmless, simple, reversible, easily available.	Minor irritations and temporary burning sensations. Messy. Must be used just before intercourse and reapplied for each act of intercourse.
Sponge	Small sponge that fits over the cervix, blocking and killing sperm.	9–11	Simple to purchase and use. Can be inserted hours before intercourse and left in place up to 24 hours.	Possible health problems, including toxic shock syndrome and vaginitis. Difficult to remove. May make intercourse dry.
Sterilization	Surgical procedure to make an individual sterile	Less than 1	Safest method. Does not affect sexual drive. No planning or additional steps before intercourse necessary.	May be irreversible. Possibility of postoperative infections for women.
Withdrawal (coitus interruptus)	Man withdraws penis from vagina before ejaculation of semen.	16–18	Simple, costless, requires no other devices.	Requires great control by the male. Possible semen leakage before ejaculation. Possible psychological reaction against necessary control and ejaculation outside the vagina. May severely limit sexual gratification of both partners.

Table 8.2   Continued

Popular name	Description	Effectiveness (pregnancies per 100 women using method for 1 year)	Advantages	Disadvantages
Rhythm	Abstinence from intercourse during fertile period each month.	10–29	Approved by the Roman Catholic church. Costless, requires no other devices.	Woman's menstrual period must be regular. Demands accurate date keeping and strong self-control. Difficult to determine fertile period exactly.

Note: Individuals vary in their reaction to contraceptive devices. Advantages and disadvantages listed are general ones.

*If taken regularly pregnancy will not occur. If one or more pills are missed, there is a chance of pregnancy. Combination pills contain both estrogen and progesterone.

Amount and Kinds of Contraceptive Use

Although few women desire to get pregnant when they first become sexually active, only a minority use a contraceptive method (figure 8.3). Among those who do use a contraceptive method at the time of first intercourse, 39 percent use a condom, 28 percent use the pill, and 19 percent try withdrawal (U.S. Department of Health and Human Services 1986:6). The majority of people, however, do not take contraceptive measures until six to twelve months after sexual intercourse begins. And even then the use of contraceptives is not always regular.

Although its use has declined somewhat, the pill is still the most commonly used device, particularly among younger couples. The next most commonly used methods are the condom and the diaphragm. Among married women, there has been a dramatic increase since 1965 in **sterilization** as a method of birth control (table 8.3). By 1982, a fourth of married women (24.7 percent of whites and 34.4 percent of blacks) were surgically sterile. The majority of women in the country are either sterile (including the nonsurgically sterile) or using contraceptives. A little over a fourth of women are nonusers, about 5 percent are in the recovery period after the birth of a child, and 4.2 percent are trying to get pregnant (U.S. Bureau of the Census 1989:69).

Who Uses Contraceptives

Who is most likely and least likely to use some form of contraception? We can distinguish the groups on the basis of age and other characteristics.

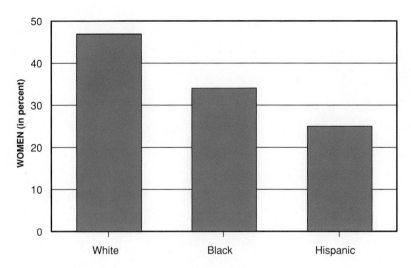

Figure 8.3 *Percent of women 15–44 years of age who used a contraceptive method at first sexual intercourse: 1982.*
Source: U.S. Department of Health and Human Services 1986:5.

Table 8.3 Percent Distribution of Married Women 15–44 Years of Age Using Contraception Methods: 1965–1982

Year	Total	Sterilization		Pill	IUD	Diaphragm	Condom	Other
		Female	Male					
		Percent						
1965	100.0	7.2	5.2	23.9	1.2	9.9	22.0	30.6
1973	100.0	12.3	11.2	36.1	9.6	3.4	13.5	13.9
1976	100.0	14.1	13.3	33.2	9.3	4.2	10.8	15.1
1982	100.0	25.6	15.4	19.8	7.1	6.7	14.4	11.1

Source: U.S. Department of Health and Human Services 1986:15.

Age Differences

As the discussion so far indicates, contraceptive use is less likely among younger people who are sexually active. Part of the reason is what Burger and Burns (1988) call the "illusion of unique invulnerability." They found that under-graduate women who were sexually active tended to view themselves as less likely than other students or other women to become pregnant. This sense of invulnerability is the same thing that leads people into various kinds of self-destructive behavior. For example, many people who smoke or have an unhealthy diet feel that they will escape the negative consequences of their behavior even though others do not. Similarly, the young woman who adopts the

Contraceptives are readily available in most communities.

stance of "I just don't think that I will get pregnant" is less likely to use birth control methods . . . and quite likely to get pregnant.

Some younger people, of course, do use contraceptives. Those who have good communication with their parents about sexual matters generally and contraception in particular are more likely to use contraceptives (Burger and Burns 1988). Peer influence is also important. Those who perceive their peers as using contraceptives are more likely to use them for themselves.

One other important related factor is the age at which the individual first has sexual intercourse. Those who have intercourse early (age sixteen or younger) are less likely than those who begin sexual relations later to know about and use effective methods of contraception (Faulkenberry, Vincent, James, and Johnson 1987). The early experimenters are also less likely to use effective contraception at the time of first intercourse.

Other Factors

Would a very religious person be more or less likely to use contraception? The answer depends on the person's age and marital status. Religion is one of the background factors that affects contraceptive use, but it doesn't affect it in the way you might expect. Some religions teach that contraception is wrong. They also teach that sexual relations outside of marriage are wrong. Married people in those religions may refrain from using contraceptives (although many do use them), with the result that they have large families. Some younger, unmarried people, however, may refrain from the use of contraception but not from sexual relations (Studer and Thornton 1987). Not as many of the very religious young people are sexually active. But among those who are, they are less likely than others to use effective contraception. It is as though they are willing to violate one but not two of their religion's precepts.

Various other factors also affect people's likelihood of using contraception, and of using effective versus ineffective contraception (Sack, Billingham, and Howard 1985). Those who use effective contraceptive methods are likely to have friends who are also users, to be more sexually active than those who do not use effective methods, and to know their sexual partners for a longer period of time.

Abortion

Abortion, the expulsion of the fetus from the uterus, is a highly controversial subject. Abortion may be either spontaneous (so-called natural abortion) or induced by some medical or surgical procedure. We include the topic here because induced abortion is used as a method of birth control.

Abortion has been used throughout history to deal with unwanted pregnancies. In the United States, abortion was illegal in most states until the Supreme Court's famous 1973 decision in the *Roe v. Wade* case. That case allowed abortion on demand in the first trimester of the pregnancy. The case was the result of increasing pressures from various groups to give legitimacy to the procedure and protect women from the pain and risks of back-alley abortions. Some women died and many others nearly died from illegal abortions, which could be performed by people who were anything from bookies to midwives.

How many pregnancies end in abortion? It is estimated that about 40 percent of teenage pregnancies are aborted. Among all women, the proportion of abortions has risen dramatically since 1973. In 1973, 744,600 legal abortions were performed, representing 193 abortions for every 1,000 live births. By 1985, the number was nearly 1.6 million abortions, representing 425 abortions for every 1,000 live births (U.S. Bureau of the Census 1989:70). Nearly 3 percent of women aged fifteen to forty-four have an abortion in any given year.

Table 8.4 Legal Abortions, by Selected Characteristics: 1973–1983

Characteristic	Number (1,000)							Percent Distribution			Abortion Ratio[1]		
	1973	1975	1979	1980	1981	1982	1983	1973	1980	1983	1973	1980	1983
Total legal abortions	**745**	**1,034**	**1,498**	**1,554**	**1,577**	**1,574**	**1,575**	**100.0**	**100.0**	**100.0**	**193**	**300**	**304**
Age of woman:													
Less than 15 years old	12	15	16	15	15	15	16	1.6	1.0	1.0	476	607	626
15–19 years old	232	325	445	445	433	419	411	31.2	28.6	26.1	280	451	464
20–24 years old	241	332	526	549	555	552	548	32.3	35.4	34.8	181	310	325
25–29 years old	130	189	284	304	316	326	328	17.4	19.6	20.8	128	213	223
30–34 years old	73	100	142	153	167	168	172	9.7	9.8	10.9	165	213	213
35–39 years old	41	53	65	67	70	73	78	5.5	4.3	5.0	246	317	296
40 years old and over	17	21	20	21	21	21	21	2.3	1.3	1.4	334	461	439
Race of woman:													
White	549	701	1,062	1,094	1,108	1,095	1,084	73.7	70.4	68.8	178	274	274
Black and other	196	333	435	460	470	479	491	26.3	29.6	31.2	252	392	401
Marital status of woman:													
Married	216	272	322	320	299	300	295	29.0	20.6	18.7	74	98	93
Unmarried	528	762	1,176	1,234	1,279	1,274	1,280	71.0	79.4	81.3	564	649	632
Number of prior live births:													
None	411	543	868	900	912	903	890	55.2	57.9	56.5	242	365	369
1	115	194	287	305	312	321	329	15.4	19.6	20.9	108	208	217
2	104	156	207	216	220	222	228	13.9	13.9	14.4	190	283	291
3	61	78	82	83	85	82	83	8.1	5.3	5.3	228	288	287
4 or more	55	64	53	51	49	46	45	7.4	3.3	2.9	196	251	241
Number of prior induced abortions:													
None	(NA)	822	1,025	1,043	1,023	994	964	(NA)	67.1	61.2	(NA)	(NA)	(NA)
1	(NA)	170	352	373	390	398	406	(NA)	24.0	25.8	(NA)	(NA)	(NA)
2 or more	(NA)	42	121	138	165	182	205	(NA)	8.9	13.0	(NA)	(NA)	(NA)
Weeks of gestation:													
Less than 9 weeks	284	481	749	800	810	806	792	38.2	51.5	50.3	(NA)	(NA)	(NA)
9–10 weeks	222	290	413	417	424	420	424	29.7	26.8	26.9	(NA)	(NA)	(NA)
11–12 weeks	131	151	204	202	204	205	210	17.5	13.0	13.3	(NA)	(NA)	(NA)
13 weeks or more	108	112	133	136	139	143	149	14.6	8.7	9.5	(NA)	(NA)	(NA)

NA Not Available. [1]Number of abortions per 1,000 abortions and live births. Live births are those that occurred from July 1 of year shown through June 30 of the following year (to match time of conception with abortions).

Source: U.S. Bureau of the Census 1989:70.

A slight majority of Americans favor a woman's right to choose whether or not to have an abortion. Pro-choice people, however, do not necessarily opt for an abortion for themselves, but they feel that the matter of continuing or terminating a pregnancy is a personal decision. Young women who perceive friends and relatives to have positive attitudes toward abortion and who are more career-oriented are likely to have more positive attitudes about abortion for themselves (Brazzell and Acock 1988).

Whether a woman opts for abortion depends on a number of additional factors as shown in table 8.4. Note that abortions are more common among younger women, blacks, and the unmarried.

The Intimate Couple

There are psychological risks in abortion for at least some women. Women who abort may feel a certain amount of guilt, sadness, and loss. Many clinics have both pre- and postprocedure counseling in order to help with such problems. One young woman who had two abortions told us that she is now ready to bear a child: "But I'm having trouble getting pregnant. I'm beginning to feel like I had my children and they died." She was clearly grieving over losses that had occurred some years earlier. Only in a few cases, however, are the problems severe enough to warrant psychiatric care. For the most part, the emotional gains outweigh the negative consequences (Osofsky and Osofsky 1972).

Sex in Marriage

Among the things necessary for a successful marriage, how would you rate a good sex life? Is it very important, or not very important? Three out of four Americans say that it is "very important."[3] A good sex life can greatly enhance the quality of a couple's intimacy. But what does it mean to have a "good" sex life? Is that measured by frequency of sex? By the number of orgasms? By variety? The relationship between sex and marriage is not a simple one.

Sexual Practices in Marriage

The sex life of married couples has changed considerably over the last few decades. As the famed Kinsey studies reported (Kinsey, Pomeroy, and Martin 1948; Kinsey, Pomeroy, Martin, and Gebhard 1953), in the 1940s only a minority of married people engaged in oral sex, either **fellatio** or **cunnilingus.** Now, a majority of married people engage in oral sex at least some of the time (Hunt 1974). In addition, married couples now, compared with earlier decades, engage in much more foreplay and try or use a greater number of positions in intercourse (Hunt 1974). These latter changes may reflect an increased concern with the woman's enjoyment and orgasm, both of which tend to be enhanced if more time is given to sexual activity.

How frequently do married people have sexual relations? The answer depends on how many years they have been married. In their survey of American couples, Blumstein and Schwartz (1983:196) found that 45 percent of those married up to two years, 27 percent of those married two to ten years, and 18 percent of those married more than ten years engaged in sex three times a week or more. The most common practice among those married two years or more was one to three times a week.

On the average, then, couples in their twenties and thirties have intercourse two or three times per week while for those past fifty the frequency is once a week or less (Masters, Johnson, and Kolodny 1988:396). Averages should not obscure the fact that the range is considerable. Some couples never have sex relations while others may have them every day or a number of times each day. It is also important to realize that average does not mean "normal." People sometimes read such statistics and believe that something is wrong with them if they do not follow the average practice. But sexual needs and desires vary widely. There is no "normal" frequency.

Sexual Satisfaction and Marital Satisfaction

How correct are the three out of four who say that a good sex life is very important to a successful marriage? It depends on how we define "good." First, there is no relationship between frequency of sexual activity and the stability of the relationship (Blumstein and Schwartz 1983:312). People who have relatively infrequent sex stay together as long as those who have sex frequently.

Second, a good sex life must include something more than intercourse (including the foreplay). A *Ladies' Home Journal* poll of its readers reported that 57 percent agree that intercourse is a basic part of marriage, but that various forms of affection such as hugging and kissing are more important.[4] A man married twenty-five years told us that he "remembers little about sexual intercourse" in the early years of his marriage. But he does remember "laying at night in my wife's arms. In that way, she was telling me that I was all right. That was very important." Sex, he noted, was not as important as caring and affection. In fact, it is precisely such caring and affection that enables couples to have a satisfying sex life. Once again, we can have intimacy without sex, but we cannot have satisfying sex without intimacy. In other words, sexual satisfaction is likely to be the result of, rather than the cause of, marital satisfaction.

Third, although sexual satisfaction is important, it is less important than other things in the quality of an intimate relationship. A study of 250 couples reported that sexuality is only weakly related to people's perception of the quality of their intimacy (Patton and Waring 1985). More important than sex in intimacy are such things as the ease with which differences are handled, the extent to which the partners express affection, the degree of commitment to the marriage, and the amount of self-disclosure.

Finally, in our study of long-term married couples, we came to three conclusions about the role of sex (Lauer and Lauer 1986:73):

1. A couple can have a meaningful sexual relationship for the duration of their marriage; neither age nor amount of years together necessarily diminish the quality of sex.

2. Some couples have long-term, satisfying marriages even though one or both has a less-than-ideal sex life.

Sexual activity remains strong and important to many people as they age.

3. The most important thing in a couple's sexual relationship is agreement about the arrangement.

The last point stresses something we mentioned earlier—there is no such thing as a normal or ideal sex life for all couples. It isn't the kind or frequency of sexual activities that is most important, but the extent to which the couple agrees on whatever arrangement they make.

Changes in Marital Sex over the Life Span

Perhaps the most obvious change in sexual activity over the course of a marriage is the decline in frequency. That decline is a function of a number of factors. As people age, their sexual needs and desires change. For most, sex becomes somewhat less urgent. In addition, people come to recognize that other things are as important or more important in their relationships.

Still, sexual activity remains strong and important to many people as they age. For a variety of reasons, however, the preferred form of activity may change. A study of ninety-nine men and women aged sixty to eighty-five investigated changes in preferred sexual activity over the course of the adult years (Turner and Adams 1988). The researchers found that for forty-seven of their subjects, there was no change. They still preferred the same activity as they did in their earlier years (for forty of the forty-seven, intercourse; for the others, such things as petting and masturbation). Some who had preferred petting in earlier years, now preferred intercourse. And some who had preferred intercourse, now preferred petting, masturbation, or fantasies.

Health can also alter a couple's sexual pattern. People who must take pain-killing drugs or medication for high blood pressure may find their sexual functioning impaired. Chronic health problems like arthritis and diabetes can diminish sexual desire and activity. A hysterectomy may make intercourse more painful for a woman.

A third factor in changing sexual relations is work. Someone has coined the term *DINS* to refer to those couples who have double income and no sex. Two-career couples may find that they have little energy for sex after work and household chores. Some professionals work weekends as well as long hours during the week. Such schedules do not lend themselves to either intimacy or passionate sexual encounters.

Fourth, the arrival of children may drastically alter a couple's sex life. A survey of nearly six thousand parents reported a marked decline in sexual relations among the couples after the birth of children (Rubenstein 1988). More than a fifth of the couples said they have sexual relations once a month or less, and another third said they have sex between once a week and twice a month. Many new mothers indicated a decline in sexual enjoyment. The most common reasons for the decline in frequency were being tired and lack of desire. Importantly, the same survey found that 40 percent of the new mothers and 55 percent of new fathers said they were more in love than ever with their spouses.

Finally, our study of long-term marrieds identified three patterns in sexual functioning. In one pattern, the level and satisfaction with the couple's sex life remained fairly stable over time. A second pattern involved a decline in sexual frequency. Sometimes that was associated with less sexual satisfaction, but in other cases it was not. Third, the sex life of some couples improved over time. In some cases, even the frequency increased. Independently of frequency, however, some couples perceived the quality of their sex life as improving over time. As a woman married forty years told us: "It's better than ever."

Extramarital Sex

What do you think about someone who is married having sex with a partner other than his or her spouse? How does that affect marital intimacy? In a national survey, 90 percent of the respondents said that such behavior is always or almost always wrong.[5] Most feel that extramarital sex damages the marital relationship. In spite of that opinion, a substantial proportion of Americans engage in extramarital sexual relations. A number of popular magazines have taken polls of their readers. Of course, the results vary widely depending on the particular readership. For example, 20 percent of the respondents to a *Ladies' Home Journal* poll said that they had engaged in extramarital sex, while well over half of those responding to a poll in *Cosmopolitan* said that they had been involved in an affair outside of their marriage. The true proportion is probably somewhere in between those figures. Many social scientists put the figure at around half of all married people by the age of forty. However, Blumstein and Schwartz (1983:276) found that only 26 percent of husbands and 21 percent of wives acknowledged any extramarital sexual relations. And many of those involved a single instance.

Even if we use the lowest figure, it is clear that many people engage in extramarital sex who say they do not approve of it. And because only one of the partners in some marriages have the extramarital relationship, a great many couples are affected. Tens of millions of Americans face the problem of a spouse who has been unfaithful. The extent of the unfaithfulness varies, of course. Extramarital sex may involve either an affair or a one-night stand. Affairs may continue on for weeks or even years, with regular or periodic sexual relations. The one-night stand involves a single encounter. Clearly, an affair is much more difficult to maintain than the single encounter.

Why Extramarital Sex?

Many married people fantasize about what it would be like to have sex with someone other than their spouse. But fantasies are not usually enough to motivate someone to have extramarital sex. Those who have such liaisons indicate a variety of reasons. For women, the main motivator seems to be a sense of emotional need. That is, the woman does not feel that all of her emotional needs are being met by her husband. In one survey of married women, 72 percent said that their affair was the result of emotional dissatisfaction with the husband (Grosskopf 1983:195). For men, the motivation is more likely to be a purely sexual one—the desire for variety or for more frequent sex. More than three out of four males attribute their extramarital activity to the strength of their sex drive (Pestrak, Martin, and Martin 1985:110). These gender differences in motivation are reinforced by the reasons that people give for *not* having extramarital sex: a concern about straining the marriage by men and a lack of desire or interest by women (Pestrak, Martin, and Martin 1985:109).

There are other reasons that people give. They may be sexually frustrated (a substantial proportion of women indicate sexual dissatisfaction with their husbands). They may believe that they were seduced. They may use an affair or one-night stand to get revenge against a mate who has cheated or who has angered them. In general, the lower an individual evaluates his or her marriage and the quality of his or her sex life, the more likely that individual is to have extramarital activity (Thompson 1983). In other words, the rate of extramarital sex in the nation is an indicator of marital problems. Extramarital sex causes problems, but it also reflects a troubled relationship.

Some Consequences of Extramarital Sex

On the positive side, some people report that the extramarital experience provided them with a brief but meaningful thrill. But for the most part, extramarital sex doesn't solve people's problems; it only intensifies them.

For one thing, most people find the extramarital experience to be less satisfying than their overall sexual pleasure with their spouses (Hunt 1974). The thrill of engaging in the forbidden turns out to be a disappointment instead.

In addition, there is the crisis in the marriage if the extramarital activity is discovered. The betrayed spouse is likely to undergo a time of great trauma. He or she may have trouble concentrating, sleeping, and eating. There may be a preoccupation with the betrayal and an agonizing effort to try to understand it. There may be a feeling of having been victimized to the extent that marital trust is no longer possible. A wife who discovered her husband's extramarital activity told an interviewer that in the week following her discovery she found herself standing in a department store with no idea why she had come there. She said that she felt "as if the very floor I stood on were moving, waving and buckling underneath me. It was as if I myself, and the world around me, were completely unreal" (Scarf 1987:138).

In some cases, the discovery of infidelity leads to a rupture that cannot be healed. The couple ultimately divorces. But many marriages survive extramarital sex, even when it is discovered. The main problems that the couple must work through are the factors in their relationship that might have contributed to the infidelity and the problem of a spouse who was emotionally involved with someone else (having your spouse emotionally involved seems harder to cope with than the purely sexual involvement).

At times, both spouses may be having extramarital activity, sometimes knowingly and sometimes not. Even in those cases, the marriage might survive. A professional woman shared the following account with us:

> We have a two-career marriage. We seemed to have less and less time for each other. I got involved in an affair with a man at work. Then one day I discovered that my husband was also having an affair. That made me furious! Suddenly we had to confront the fact that our marriage was on the rocks. We both agreed that we didn't want it to end. We were both hurt, but we got counseling and worked through the pain. That was three years ago. So far, it's working well. And I intend for that to continue.

Sexual Diseases and Dysfunctions

Our examination of sexual diseases and dysfunctions is necessarily brief. But it is important that you at least be familiar with them. Getting, or the fear of getting, a disease can lower or even eliminate the intimacy of sexual relations. You should also be aware of some of the rules of safe sex, our final topic in this chapter.

How to Choose a Mistress

Some Americans believe that our forefathers uniformly condemned sex outside of marriage. But there have always been diverse viewpoints about sexual activity. Benjamin Franklin, revered founding father, was a man who believed in the sublime pleasure of sexual activity and also in the strength of the sexual drive. In a letter written in 1745, he advised a young friend to get married in order to fulfill his sexual needs. But he also realized that the young man was not ready for marriage, so he advised him on the proper way to choose a sexual partner. In particular, he urged him to select old women rather than young ones. Following are the reasons he offers:

1. Because as they have more Knowledge of the World and their Minds are better stor'd with Observations, their Conversation is more improving and more lastingly agreeable.

2. Because when Women cease to be handsome, they study to be good . . . there is hardly such a thing to be found as an old Woman who is not a good Woman.

3. Because there is no hazard of Children, which irregularly produc'd may be attended with much Inconvenience.

4. Because thro' more Experience, they are more prudent and discreet in conducting an Intrigue to prevent Suspicion. The Commerce with them is therefore safer with regard to your Reputation. And with regard to theirs, if the Affair should happen to be known, considerate People might be rather inclin'd to excuse an old Woman who would kindly take care of a young Man, form his Manners by her good Counsels, and prevent his ruining his Health and Fortune among mercenary Prostitutes.

5. Because . . . covering all above with a Basket, and regarding only what is below the Girdle, it is impossible of two Women to know an old from a young one. And as in the dark all Cats are grey, the Pleasure of corporal Enjoyment with an old Woman is at least equal, and frequently superior, every Knack being by Practice capable of Improvement.

6. Because the Sin is less. The debauching a Virgin may be her Ruin, and make her for Life unhappy.

7. Because the Compunction is less. The having made a young Girl miserable may give you frequent bitter Reflections, none of which can attend the making an old Woman happy.

8. They are so *grateful*!!

From Benjamin Franklin, "Advice to a Young Man on the Choice of a Mistress." Copyright © The Rosenbach Foundation, Philadelphia, PA.

Sexual Diseases

Sexually transmitted diseases (a term now preferred rather than *venereal diseases*) have plagued humankind throughout history. Some believe that with the advent of AIDS, the risk is greater than ever, but many people died of sexual diseases before the advent of modern medicines that can cure or control most of those diseases.

Table 8.5 Reported Cases of Sexually Transmitted Diseases: 1960–1987

Disease	1960	1970	Year 1980	1981	1983	1987
Gonorrhea (1,000)	259	600	1004	991	900	781
Syphilis (1,000)	122	91	69	73	75	87
AIDS	199			199	2117	21070
Others (1,000)	2.8	2.2	1.0	1.2	1.2	5.3

Source: U.S. Bureau of the Census 1989:111.

Incidence

A substantial number of Americans suffer from one or more sexually transmitted diseases. As table 8.5 shows, nearly a million Americans acquire one of the diseases each year. The most common disease is gonorrhea, though its incidence has declined. Keep in mind that the numbers in table 8.4 refer to the new cases reported each year. There are undoubtedly many that are not reported. Clearly, a considerable number of Americans suffer from a sexually transmitted disease at one time or another in their lives. "Suffer" is the appropriate word, because, depending on the particular disease acquired, people may experience fear, anger, guilt, and a damaged self-esteem in addition to the physical consequences.

Major Types of Sexually Transmitted Diseases

Gonorrhea is one of the oldest forms of sexual disease. The incidence today is much higher than it was prior to 1980. It can be transmitted by any kind of sexual contact, including kissing. In men, gonorrhea causes a thick discharge from the penis and burning while urinating. In women, it has no visible symptoms but it can damage their fallopian tubes, causing them to become infertile, suffer lower abdominal pain, nausea, and pain during intercourse. Gonorrhea is treated with penicillin.

Syphilis appeared in Europe in the fifteenth century (Masters, Johnson, and Kolodny 1988:563), killing hundreds of thousands of people. It is transmitted by sexual contact, but can also be transmitted in a blood transfusion or, if a pregnant woman acquires it, to the fetus. The first symptom of syphilis is a sore on some part of the body. The sore usually heals and goes away, but untreated syphilis will go into a second stage involving rash, fever, and pains. If still untreated, it can result in brain damage, heart problems, and, ultimately, death. It also is treated with penicillin.

Genital herpes is caused by viruses. It is transmitted by sexual intercourse and shows up in the form of painful blisters on or in the area of the genitals. The blisters eventually disappear, but they may reappear periodically because the virus continues to live in the human body. Some people suffer repeated seven- to fourteen-day periods of the sores. At the present, there is no cure for genital herpes.

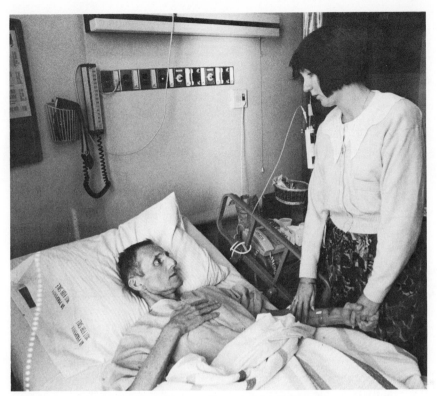

AIDS is now the deadliest of the sexually transmitted diseases.

AIDS, or acquired immunodeficiency syndrome, is caused by a virus that attacks certain white blood cells, eventually causing the individual's immune system to stop functioning. The individual then falls prey to one infection after another. Even normally mild diseases can prove fatal. Many AIDS patients develop rare cancers or suffer serious brain damage. AIDS spreads in a number of ways, including anal or vaginal intercourse with an infected person, blood transfusions, accidental exchange of blood from a contaminated hypodermic needle, and from infected mothers to their infants before or during birth. Up to this point, those most likely to get AIDS have been homosexual and bisexual men (figure 8.4), but the incidence among heterosexuals has been increasing. There is no known cure, though some drugs may mitigate the disease or possibly control it.

Finally, *chlamydial infections* are caused by a bacterium. Although little attention has been paid to them in the past, they are the most common bacterial sexually transmitted disease, with perhaps 3 to 4 million cases arising annually (Sanders, Dosser, Mullis, and Bidon 1986). Among adolescents, chlamydia occurs in anywhere from 8 to 25 percent of sexually active girls

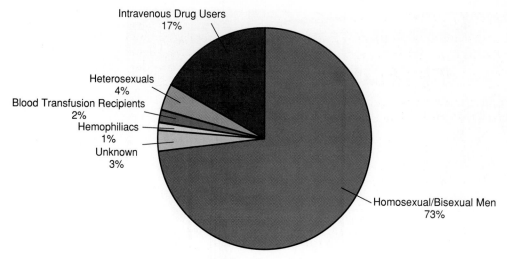

Figure 8.4 *Who are the victims of AIDS?*
Source: Data from *The New York Times*, September 25, 1988.

and 9 percent of sexually active boys.[6] It is not included in table 8.5 because chlamydial infections are not reportable nationally. Chlamydia results in a variety of symptoms, such as infection of the urethra in males and infections in the reproductive system of females. It can even lead to infertility in females. It is readily treatable by drugs.

Sexually Transmitted Diseases and Sexual Behavior

The possibility of acquiring a sexually transmitted disease has done little in the past to change sexual behavior. An individual's sexual behavior may change once he or she has contracted the disease, of course. But few people have abstained from sexual relations or from a variety of sexual partners out of the fear of disease. AIDS may be changing that.

There is evidence that many people are sufficiently concerned about AIDS to change or at least consider a change in their sexual behavior (Carroll 1988). *Glamour* magazine polled single women in 1987 about how AIDS had changed their lives. Sixty-seven percent said they had become more selective, 22 percent said they had become monogamous, and 11 percent said they had become celibate.[7] It is too early to know, however, whether there will be long-term changes in American's sexual behavior because of the fear of contracting AIDS.

The Intimate Couple

Sexual Dysfunctions

Famed English author and reformer, John Ruskin, courted a young woman to whom he wrote flowery phrases like: "You are like the bright—soft—swelling—lovely fields of a high glacier covered with fresh morning snow" (Rose 1983:54). Ruskin won her heart, and they were married. A few years later they were divorced, because Ruskin could never consummate the union. He was one of many people for whom sex is more of a problem than an experience of intimacy.

Types of Sexual Dysfunctions

A **sexual dysfunction** is any impairment of the physical responses in sexual activity. For males, the major sexual dysfunctions have to do with penile *erection* and *ejaculation* (Masters, Johnson, and Kolodny 1988:500). The man may be unable to have or maintain an erection that is firm enough for intercourse. Or he may ejaculate before the woman is sufficiently aroused for orgasm or even before inserting his penis into her vagina. In a few cases, the man's problem may be the opposite: difficulty, or even an inability to ejaculate within the vagina.

For women, the main kinds of sexual dysfunction include *vaginismus* (involuntary spasms of the muscles around the vagina, preventing penetration by the penis or making it painful), *anorgasmia* (difficulty, or an inability to reach orgasm), and *painful intercourse.*

From 10 to 20 percent of sexual dysfunctions have organic causes such as diabetes, drug abuse, and infections. A variety of psychological and social factors are involved in most cases. The individual may have developed negative sexual attitudes, suffer from anxiety or guilt, feel hostile or alienated from the sexual partner, and so forth. Such factors generally require some kind of therapy so that the individual can develop a satisfying sex life.

Prevalence of Sexual Dysfunctions

The number of people with sexual dysfunctions is high. A survey of nearly five hundred students found that 13 percent reported some sexual performance dysfunctions (Spencer and Zeiss 1987). A study of happily married couples reported that half of the wives said they had some difficulty becoming sexually aroused and 15 percent said they were unable to have an orgasm (Scarf 1987:280). The husbands had fewer problems, but 10 percent had difficulties with erections and over one third were troubled with premature ejaculation.

Inhibited Sexual Desire

Inhibited sexual desire is a problem but not, strictly speaking, a dysfunction. It does not necessarily involve any physical impairment. It can, however, cause considerable stress. Like sexual dysfunctions, inhibited desire can be rooted in such things as hostility, fear, and anxiety. It may also be the result of the kind of fatigue that two-career couples experience.

In an effort to sort out some of the causes of inhibited desire, a group of social workers studied ninety married women who had come to a sex and marital therapy clinic for help with various sexual problems (Stuart, Hammond, and Pett 1987). Fifty-nine of the women had problems with inhibited desire, while the rest had various dysfunctions though normal desire. Those with inhibited desire, in contrast with the others, perceived their parents to have less affectionate interaction and more negative attitudes toward sex. They were more likely than those with normal desire to have had premarital intercourse. And, most importantly, those with inhibited desire reported far greater dissatisfaction with the quality of the marital relationship, including such factors as trust, commitment, emotional closeness, love, and attractiveness of the spouse. For these women, inhibited desire grew out of poor marital interaction, a conclusion underscored by the fact that most of the women developed the problem gradually after they were married.

We do not know how many people have inhibited sexual desire. Probably anywhere from 20 to 50 percent of people experience it at some point in their lives, some more severely than others. The problem may go away if the couple can outlast it and build or maintain a generally good marital relationship. For some, however, the problem will require therapy.

Safe Sex

The only truly safe sex is no sex. Few people are so concerned about safety that they will opt for celibacy; however, it is helpful to consider some guidelines for maximizing safety:

1. Be careful about whom you allow to be a sexual partner. How well do you know the person and his or her sexual history? Does the person have any signs of infection?

2. Minimize the number of sexual partners you have. A 1988 survey indicated that hundreds of thousands of young Americans have at least ten sexual partners a year.[8] This greatly enhances their risk of acquiring a sexually transmitted disease, including AIDS. The safest sex is between two people who have an exclusive relationship.

3. Discuss health and sexual concerns with the partner before you have sexual relations. It isn't an invasion of privacy to question someone about their sexual history when the issue is one of your health and even your life.

4. Use available protection during sexual relations. In particular, experts recommend that males always use a condom, even if the woman is using another birth control device. Condoms do not give absolute

protection, but they maximize the safety of sexual intercourse. Experts also recommend that you wash your genitals carefully and thoroughly both before and after sexual relations.

5. Have regular medical checkups. You should be specifically checked for sexually transmitted diseases if you or your partner have sexual relations with more than one person.

6. Know the symptoms of the various diseases. We have briefly noted many of them. But you should be familiar with all the symptoms. Some of the diseases are insidious in that they may appear to go away, only to return in a more advanced and damaging phase.

7. Consult a physician immediately if you have contracted, or been exposed to, a sexually transmitted disease. You may be embarrassed, but keep in mind that you are dealing with your health, your reproductive capacity, and perhaps even your life.

PRINCIPLES FOR ENHANCING INTIMACY

1. Sex is a vital and human function, but it is a very complex one as well. If you want to experience the fullness of your sexual potential, it is important to develop an understanding about the physical and emotional factors that are involved in sex.

2. Sex is not a substitute for intimacy. To be most satisfying, sex needs to be the expression of an intimate relationship rather than an effort to create intimacy.

3. An unwanted pregnancy is a difficult and painful experience. Knowledge about sexuality and the use of effective contraceptives are the best ways to avoid unwanted pregnancies.

4. Extramarital affairs generally create more problems than they solve for people. In fact, they often cause great personal trauma for the people involved. It is more satisfying to work through the problems in your marriage than to seek escape in an affair.

5. Sexually transmitted diseases pose a significant danger for the sexually active. It is important that you know about the symptoms and consequences of these various diseases as well as the ways you can avoid them.

6. Although sexual dysfunctions are fairly common, they are treatable and need not detract from the quality of an intimate relationship.

7. Sex can be one of the more gratifying of human experiences. But satisfying sex is ultimately responsible sex. Learn the seven guidelines to safe sex and make them a part of your intimate interactions with others.

SUMMARY

Sex is both a physical and a social phenomenon. Physically, sex may be described in terms of the response cycle of excitement, plateau, orgasm, and resolution. As a social phenomenon, sex is a function of learning, and of our sex roles and sex-role orientations. The social nature of sex is illustrated by variations in sexual arousal and techniques, and by the amount of unwanted sex in which people engage.

Sex is an important part of intimate relationships. The need for intimacy has primacy over the need for sex. Sexual activity is a natural expression of the feeling of intimacy with someone.

The majority of teenagers become sexually active between the ages of sixteen and nineteen. One consequence of teenage sex is a high rate of unwanted pregnancies at an early age. Teenagers get pregnant for a variety of reasons, including a lack of responsible use of birth-control measures. Some teenagers may want to get pregnant because of loneliness, alienation from parents, or the need to assert their independence or to do something creative. Concerned parents who talk with their children are less likely to have teenagers who get pregnant.

The consequences of teenage childbearing are mostly negative. The parents are less likely to complete their education, and more likely to remain poor. Only a minority of women marry the father, so that the woman assumes the child-rearing responsibilities. Some of the mothers will escape poverty, but the risks of a poorer quality of life for them and their children are much higher than they are for those who bear children after their teen years.

Contraception refers to methods of preventing fertilization. Some, such as the rhythm method and withdrawal, are of little use. Others are fairly effective. Only a minority of women use a contraceptive method when they first become sexually active. The pill, condoms, and the diaphragm are common devices. Among married women, there has been a dramatic increase in sterilization since 1965. Contraceptive use is more likely among those who perceive their peers as being users, those who have good communication with their parents, and those who are less religious.

Abortion is a form of birth control for some people. The proportion of legal abortions has risen dramatically since 1973. There is nearly one abortion for every two live births now. A slight majority of Americans favor the woman's right to choose whether to have an abortion. There are some psychological risks; many clinics have both pre- and postabortion counseling.

The sex life of the married has changed over the past few decades, with an increasing amount of foreplay and variations in technique. Couples in their twenties and thirties have intercourse two to three times a week on the average, though the range is considerable. Sexual satisfaction is not essential to marital satisfaction, though most happy couples do have meaningful sex lives. Frequency tends to decline for various reasons, but quality can remain high or even increase as the couple ages.

Although the great majority of Americans disapprove of extramarital sex, a fourth or more have at least one extramarital experience. Emotional need tends to motivate women, while men are more likely to have a purely sexual motivation. For the most part, extramarital activity intensifies marital problems.

A substantial number of Americans suffer from one or more sexually transmitted diseases. Gonorrhea, syphilis, genital herpes, chlamydial infections, and AIDS are the most common diseases. Sexual dysfunctions are also common. Men's dysfunctions primarily involve problems of erection and ejaculation. Among women, the main problems are vaginismus, anorgasmia, and painful intercourse. Both men and women may have inhibited sexual desire at some point in their lives.

Widespread concern about disease, particularly AIDS, raises the question of safe sex. There are no guarantees, but there are a number of steps that each person can take to minimize the chances of acquiring a sexually transmitted disease. The safest sex is between two people who have an exclusive relationship.

---

1. *Family Planning Perspectives* 19 (1987):119.

2. *Public Opinion,* September/October 1986, p. 38.

3. *Public Opinion,* December/January 1986, p. 25.

4. *Ladies' Home Journal,* October 1988, p. 119.

5. *Public Opinion,* November/December 1987, p. 39.

6. *Los Angeles Times,* October 24, 1988.

7. *Glamour,* July 1988, p. 152.

8. *New York Times,* September 25, 1988.

Getting Married

In his description of an ideal society, Sir Thomas More wrote that the Utopians severely punished anyone engaging in premarital sex. The reason, as we pointed out in chapter 6, was that his Utopians believed that if you could have sex outside of marriage no one would ever get married. Apart from the availability of sexual relations, why, he asked, would one put up with all the inconveniences of being married?

There are some people, like the young man we discussed at the beginning of the last chapter, who marry primarily for sexual reasons. But, as we shall see, there are many other reasons for getting married. In spite of Sir Thomas's dire warning, the bulk of Americans marry in the face of readily available sexual relations outside marriage.

In this chapter, in addition to looking at reasons that people marry, we shall look at some different types of marriages and explore our various expectations when we marry. We will see some of the common adjustments that people have to make when they marry, along with changes in the first year of marriage. Finally, we will discuss the meaning of commitment and the way in which it affects the quality of married life.

Marriage is a time of celebration and high expectations.

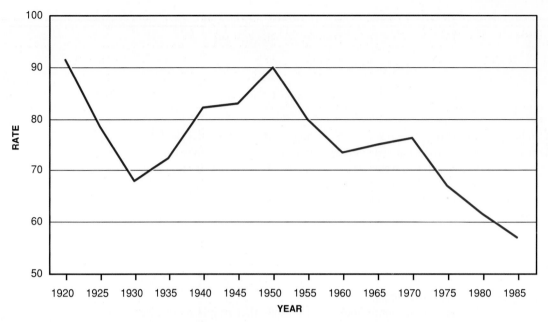

Figure 9.1 *Marriage rates, 1920–1985 (rate per 1000 women, age 15 and over).*
Source: U.S. Bureau of the Census, *Historical Statistics of the United States.* Washington, DC: Government Printing Office.

What Are Your Chances of Getting Married?

Most Americans want to marry, and most—90 percent or more—will. However, your chances vary depending on a number of factors.

Marital Status of the Population

The **marriage rate,** the proportion of unmarried women aged fifteen and over who get married in a year, fluctuates considerably over time (figure 9.1). The lowest figure recorded in this century was 56.0 in 1932. Only the rates during the depression years of the 1930s were lower than those of the 1980s. The lower rates reflect such things as delayed age at first marriage and increasing numbers who remain single for one reason or another.

When the marriage rate is combined with divorce and widowhood, we find that the proportion of the population that is married during any year has declined over the past few decades. In 1970, 71.7 percent of Americans were married; by 1987, the proportion had declined to 62.9 percent (U.S. Bureau of the Census 1989:42). People's marital status varies, of course, by such things

The Intimate Couple

Table 9.1 Marital Status of the Population, by Sex and Age: 1987

Sex and Age	Number of persons (1,000)					Percent Distribution				
	Total	Single	Married	Widowed	Divorced	Total	Single	Married	Widowed	Divorced
Male	83,706	21,145	54,854	2,120	5,586	100.0	25.3	65.5	2.5	6.7
18–19 years old	3,530	3,418	111	—	1	100.0	96.8	3.1	—	—
20–24 years old	9,499	7,380	1,965	11	144	100.0	77.7	20.7	.1	1.5
25–29 years old	10,694	4,513	5,597	3	581	100.0	42.2	52.3	—	5.4
30–34 years old	10,448	2,414	7,186	13	835	100.0	23.1	68.8	.1	8.0
35–39 years old	9,163	1,137	7,018	14	995	100.0	12.4	76.6	.2	10.9
40–44 years old	7,365	509	6,025	35	797	100.0	6.9	81.8	.5	10.8
45–54 years old	11,151	658	9,379	129	985	100.0	5.9	84.1	1.2	8.8
55–64 years old	10,277	591	8,641	293	752	100.0	5.8	84.1	2.9	7.3
65–74 years old	7,608	354	6,200	685	368	100.0	4.7	81.5	9.0	4.8
75 years old and over	3,970	172	2,731	937	129	100.0	4.3	68.8	23.6	3.2
Female	91,901	17,097	55,639	11,123	8,041	100.0	18.6	60.5	12.1	8.7
18–19 years old	3,574	3,208	355	—	12	100.0	89.8	9.9	—	.3
20–24 years old	9,859	5,990	3,546	8	315	100.0	60.8	36.0	.1	3.2
25–29 years old	10,942	3,152	6,926	35	830	100.0	28.8	63.3	.3	7.6
30–34 years old	10,552	1,545	7,744	84	1,178	100.0	14.6	73.4	.8	11.2
35–39 years old	9,423	796	7,229	118	1,280	100.0	8.4	76.7	1.3	13.6
40–44 years old	7,680	493	5,892	184	1,111	100.0	6.4	76.7	2.4	14.5
45–54 years old	11,866	528	9,095	689	1,554	100.0	4.5	76.6	5.8	13.1
55–64 years old	11,606	485	8,138	1,935	1,048	100.0	4.2	70.1	16.7	9.0
65–74 years old	9,624	463	5,100	3,529	531	100.0	4.8	53.0	36.7	5.5
75 years old and over	6,773	435	1,615	4,541	182	100.0	6.4	23.8	67.0	2.7

— Represents zero or rounds to zero.
Source: U.S. Bureau of the Census 1989:41.

as sex and age (table 9.1). Those least likely to be married are men twenty-four and younger, and women younger than twenty and older than seventy-five.

Who Does, and Doesn't, Marry?

The question of who will and will not marry is not merely one of preference. We noted in chapter 6 that some people are involuntarily single because of the marriage squeeze. Census Bureau projections indicate a reversal of the squeeze occurring throughout the 1990s for people in their twenties. That is, there will be an excess of men to women. It will be men, not women, who will face the greater chance of involuntary singlehood.

Under some conditions, the marriage squeeze can be exacerbated by the norm that the man should be older than the woman he marries. There is some evidence that this norm has been changing, with an increasing proportion of men marrying women older than they are (Wheeler and Gunter 1987). The proportion, however, is still quite small. Those who continue to hold to the traditional norm will find their choices more severely limited.

Age enters into your chances of getting married in another way. There is an increasing probability of marriage with each year after the age of fifteen until the age of twenty-four. Then the probability begins to decline (Exter 1987). How rapidly does it decline? The question stirred up quite a debate in 1986 when a Harvard-Yale study indicated that women with four or more years of college had virtually no chance of getting married if they had not already done so by the age of forty-five (Exter 1987). The Census Bureau countered with its own statistics, asserting that such women had a 10 percent chance of getting married by age sixty-five. In either case, it is clear that the chances of getting married are fairly slim for college-educated women who are still single in their forties. They are only slightly better for women with four years of high school—about 21 percent for those aged forty and 12 percent for those aged forty-five according to the Census Bureau, and virtually no chance according to the Harvard-Yale study.

Perhaps the major reason for the discrepancy between the two reports is the differing assumptions they made. Unlike the Harvard-Yale study, the Census Bureau assumed that college-educated women were simply postponing marriage. Thus, for women in their forties:

> If you are unmarried but still want to marry, your chances are probably closer to the Census Bureau figures. If you are not sure you want to marry, then your chances are probably closer to those of the Harvard-Yale study (Exter 1987:51–52).

Why Do People Marry?

If someone says to you, "I'm going to get married," you are not likely to ask why. You no doubt assume that the two people are in love and want to live together and perhaps have children together. But as we noted in chapter 1, people marry for reasons other than love. In fact, some social scientists believe that the full meaning of love only emerges during the course of a marriage, not prior to marriage. This isn't to say that the two people do not feel that they are in love. However, there are other reasons for getting married.

Social Expectations

The expectation is that you will get married, as illustrated by the fact that there are still some negative attitudes toward people who opt to remain single. All societies have the **institution** of marriage, which is a societal way of regulating heterosexual relationships. Even the most primitive people, such as the Dobu (see PERSPECTIVE), have well-defined rules about people getting married and generally expect that most will marry.

In other words, to say that marriage is a social institution is to point out that there are norms and expectations that govern it. These vary from one society to another, but they serve the same basic functions. Among other things, the institution of marriage prevents heterosexual relationships from deteriorating into chaos (a married person is, at least theoretically, off-limits to others

Dobu Marriage

Marriage customs, including wedding ceremonies, vary considerably. Anthropologist Ruth Benedict studied a number of preindustrial peoples, including the Dobu of the South Pacific. In the passage below, she describes some of the things that happen when the Dobu marry. She found that the Dobuans generally were lawless and treacherous. Four to twenty villages form a unit that is hostile to other such units. But marriage must take place between people from differing units, which means that it may bring together two villages between which there is a great deal of enmity:

> Marriage brings with it no amelioration of hostility. From its begining the institutions that surround it make for conflict and hard feelings between the two groups. Marriage is set in motion by a hostile act of the mother-in-law. She blocks with her own person the door of her house within which the youth is sleeping with her daughter, and he is trapped for the public ceremony of betrothal. Before this, since the time of puberty, the boy has slept each night in the houses of unmarried girls. By custom his own house is closed to him. He avoids entanglements for several years by spreading his favours widely and leaving the house well before daylight. When he is trapped at last, it is usually because he has tired of his roaming and has settled upon a more constant companion. He ceases to be so careful about early rising. Nevertheless, he is never thought of as being ready to undertake the indignities of marriage, and the event is forced upon him by the old witch in the doorway, his future mother-in-law. When the villagers, the maternal kin of the girl, see the old woman immobile in her doorway, they gather, and under the stare of the public the two descend and sit on a mat upon the ground. The villagers stare at them for half an hour and gradually disperse, nothing more; the couple are formally betrothed.
>
> [The betrothal lasts about a year, during which time the boy has to work for his parents-in-law as well as tend to his own garden. There is an exchange of gifts between relatives of the young couple, but no friendly mingling.]
>
> The marriage ceremony itself consists in the groom's receiving from his mother-in-law in her village a mouthful of food of her cooking, and the bride's similarly receiving food from her mother-in-law in the village of her husband. . . . From marriage until death the couple live in alternate years in the village of the husband and the village of the wife.

Excerpts from *PATTERNS OF CULTURE* by Ruth Benedict. Copyright 1914 by Ruth Benedict. Copyright © renewed 1962 by Ruth Valentine. Reprinted by permission of Houghton Mifflin Company.

who might be sexually attracted to that person). It provides a normative way of perpetuating the group, by specifying a context in which sexual relations and the bearing and care of children will occur.

Thus, marriage as an institution is important to the well-being of the total group. Individuals who scorn such an institution are a threat to the group and to its survival. It is understandable, then, that we are raised with the expectation that we will marry. That expectation is communicated to us through

An important reason for marriage is to have someone with whom to share your life.

family and friends. In a survey of men, *Playboy* magazine reported that nearly one of five said that one of the "very important" reasons for their marriage was that their families and friends expected them to marry (the men could give more than one reason).[1]

If quiet expectations do not motivate an individual, a family may resort to more overt expectations in the form of pressures of various kinds. Parents may pressure their children into marriage because they are embarrassed if the children remain single or because they feel that the children will be happier if married. Unfortunately, sometimes the pressures lead to a marriage that is premature and doomed to failure.

Social Ideals and Personal Fulfillment

We have seen that most Americans still value a monogamous union that results in children and that lasts a lifetime. To grow up in a society with that kind of ideal means that you are likely to accept it for your own. It becomes not merely the ideal of most people, as portrayed in stories, television, and family conversations, but your own ideal as well. In other words, through socialization you develop the sense that marriage is the way to fulfill some of your basic needs and to attain the highest reaches of happiness.

In the *Playboy* survey we noted, about three-fourths of the men said that a very important reason for their marriage was their desire to have another person with whom to share their lives. Forty percent said they married in order to be self-fulfilled and about a third said they married to have stability and order in their lives.

Similarly, Gail Sheehy (1976:145–54) interviewed 115 men who had married in their twenties, asking among other things why they had gotten married. One reason was to "fill some vacancy in themselves." That is, they recognized some quality in which they were deficient and married someone who had that quality. They expected to find fulfillment by a relationship with someone who had the quality (such as vitality or caring) that they lacked. Others married for "safety." They wanted someone on whom they could depend for support.

Desire for Children

Over 40 percent of the men in the *Playboy* survey said that the desire to have children was a very important reason for their marriage. As we have seen, some people have children outside of marriage. However, there are many difficulties for those who take that option. If you want to have and raise children, it is a far easier task if you are married.

Marriage as a Practical Solution

Some people view marriage as a practical solution to various problems and challenges. Sheehy noted that some of the men she interviewed admitted that they married in order to get away from home. Some married because they believed a wife would help them realize their ambitions, like the physician who needed a helpmate through medical school. Some marry in order to have a steady sex life (nearly 30 percent of the men in the *Playboy* survey gave this as one of their reasons). Some recognize that singlehood is too lonely and/or difficult for them. Marriage is a practical and acceptable way to deal with these problems.

Types of Marriage

Because people get married for a variety of reasons, and because their experiences of marriage are quite diverse, we would expect to find different types of marriage. However, there is no single way to classify marriage by differing types. We could divide them up on the basis of communication styles, amount of conflict, degree of homogamy, or any other basis we choose. Some of the more useful classification schemes, we believe, use alternative life-styles, or the nature of the relationship.

Classified by Alternative Life-Styles

Which is most appealing to you, a traditional marriage or some other lifestyle (figure 9.2)? The traditional marriage is one in which the husband is the breadwinner and major decision maker, the wife is a homemaker, there are children, the spouses have sexual relations only with each other, and the union

Would you prefer a more traditional or nontraditional kind of marriage? Circle your anwer to the statements below, then read the directions beneath the statements on how to score yourself.

1. A wife should respond to her husband's sexual overtures even when she is not interested.

    1. Agree strongly　　2. Agree mildly　　3. Disagree mildly　　4. Disagree strongly

2. In general, the father should have greater authority than the mother in the bringing up of children.

    1. Agree strongly　　2. Agree mildly　　3. Disagree mildly　　4. Disagree strongly

3. Only when the wife works should the husband help with housework.

    1. Agree strongly　　2. Agree mildly　　3. Disagree mildly　　4. Disagree strongly

4. Husbands and wives should be equal partners in planning the family budget.

    4. Agree strongly　　3. Agree mildly　　2. Disagree mildly　　1. Disagree strongly

5. In marriage, the husband should make the major decisions.

    1. Agree strongly　　2. Agree mildly　　3. Disagree mildly　　4. Disagree strongly

6. If both husband and wife agree that sexually fidelity isn't important, there's no reason why both shouldn't have extramarital affairs if they want to.

    4. Agree strongly　　3. Agree mildly　　2. Disagree mildly　　1. Disagree strongly

7. If a child gets sick and his wife works, the husband should be just as willing as she to stay home from work and take care of that child.

    4. Agree strongly　　3. Agree mildly　　2. Disagree mildly　　1. Disagree strongly

8. In general, men should leave the housework to women.

    1. Agree strongly　　2. Agree mildly　　3. Disagree mildly　　4. Disagree strongly

9. Married women should keep their money and spend it as they please.

    4. Agree strongly　　3. Agree mildly　　2. Disagree mildly　　1. Disagree strongly

10. In the family, both of the spouses ought to have as much say on important matters.

    4. Agree strongly　　3. Agree mildly　　2. Disagree mildly　　1. Disagree strongly

Add your total. Note that "agree strongly" is sometimes worth one and sometimes worth four. It is your total score that is important, not whether you agreed or diasgreed more often. Your score may vary from 10 to 40. If you score 30 to 40, you are nontraditional. A score of 20 to 30 means you take a middle-of-the-road position. A score of 10 to 20 puts you into the traditional category.

Figure 9.2 *Rate your marital preference.*
Source: Karen Oppenheim Mason, *Sex-Role Attitude Items and Scales from U.S. Sample Surveys* (Rockville, MD: National Institute of Mental Health) 1975:16–19.

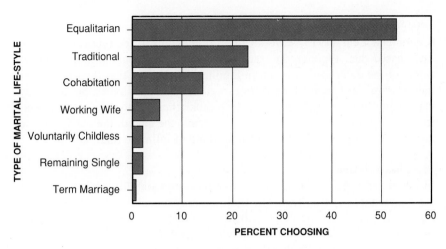

Figure 9.3 *First choices of marital life-styles of 181 high-school students.*
Source: Data from Violet, Garland, and Pendleton 1986:1060.

lasts a lifetime. Three researchers who asked high-school students to rate their preferences gave the students a range of alternative life-styles to the traditional marriage just described (Violet, Garland, and Pendleton 1986). The students overwhelmingly gave an equalitarian marriage (one in which husband and wife both are employed and have an equal voice in decisions that are made) as their first choice (figure 9.3).

They defined a working-wife marriage as one where the husband is still the major decision maker even though the wife is employed full or part-time. Term marriage refers to an arrangement that is like a renewable contract. The couple contract to get married for a particular period of time, such as five years. If they do not renew the contract, the marriage automatically ends.

The researchers offered the students a number of other life-styles, such as group marriage (in which a number of males and females are all married to each other), swinging (marriage in which both spouses agree that sex with other partners is acceptable), and homosexual marriage. None of the students selected these other life-styles, however.

Other studies have reported the same result. The first choice of both high-school and college students is an equalitarian marriage. Whether they will maintain that preference when they are married and begin to live out some of the implications is another matter. We know the meaning of one partner being dominant, but how do you know when there is equity (see Adjusting to Marriage)?

Classified by Structure of the Relationships

Kantor and Lehr (1975) have divided families into three types of systems. They based their types on the results of thousands of hours of intense observation of the daily lives of nineteen families. We believe that their classification is useful for types of marriages as well as types of families, because they focused on the ways that people relate to each other and to their environment. In essence, they posited three kinds of systems: the closed, the open, and the random. Each type involves a distinctive kind of intimate relationship.

The Closed System

In the closed-type family, there is an emphasis on stability, obligations, and the maintenance of tradition. The tradition may be ethnic, religious, or ideological. Whatever its source, it embodies the ideal of what is right and good and is therefore the ultimate authority for family life.

Intimacy in a closed-type family is likely to be stable but more earnest and sincere than passionate:

> It is expected and natural that members share good feelings with one another. Loyalties based on blood ties are usually honored above those to friends. Affections are deeply rooted in each member's strong and enduring sense of belonging. Feelings of tenderness predominate. Even in times of conflict or separation, fidelity is maintained (Kantor and Lehr 1975:145).

In other words, closed-type family members care deeply about each other, but they are muted in their expression of that caring. They experience intimacy in the context of stable, caring, highly structured relationships.

The Open System

Open-type families strive for consensus in ideas and feelings. They are sensitive to the needs of each individual as well as to the well-being of the family unit. They express their emotions more openly and more intensely than do those in the closed system. They encourage each other to be open and honest in their opinions and their feelings. What a person feels is not as important as honesty in expressing the feeling. In other words, it is all right to be angry. It is not all right to be angry and to hide it by pretending not to be angry.

In contrast to the closed system, where people rely on stable affections, those in the open system may search for new emotional experiences. The "emotional mandate is to *share and not withhold* whatever is being felt" (Kantor and Lehr 1975:145). Thus, intimacy in an open system involves an open, experimental, fluid pattern of relationships; intimacy occurs in the context of deeply felt and shared emotional experiences.

The Random System

Random-type families focus on the needs of individual members. Individual members are free to pursue their own interests without being concerned about either the tradition in the closed-type or the consent in the open-type family.

Who Prefers a Traditional Marriage?

How do you think other people would score on the self-assessment test you took in figure 9.2? Do you think you are typical or different from other people in your attitudes? Make copies of the test and conduct your own research to see how other people feel. One way to do such research is to ask a number of questions about who is most likely to prefer the traditional and who is most likely to prefer the nontraditional union.

For example, do you think that males or females will be more traditional? Will there be differences between older and younger people? Will the more or less educated people prefer a traditional union? Will there be any differences by race?

Decide on which of the questions you would like to try to answer. Of course, you will not have a large enough sample to make a firm conclusion, but if the entire class participates in the project you could have a sufficient number of responses to be comfortable with your results.

It is important to research only one of the questions. For example, if you are interested primarily in gender differences, try to have an equal number of males and females. Select people who are all of the same race. And select those who are as close as possible in age and education. Otherwise, you can't be sure if any differences you find are due to gender or one of the other factors.

After you score the questionnaires, answer the following questions. Were there any differences between the two groups you studied? If so, which group was the most traditional? How can you account for your results? Did your results turn out differently from what you anticipated? What conclusions would you draw or what are the implications of your findings (assuming that a larger survey of the population would produce similar results)?

There is likely to be a certain amount of caprice, novelty, and humor in the family as the members strive to "raise experience to levels of originality and inspiration" (Kantor and Lehr 1975:146). Members are likely to experience the full range of emotions, and to do so with more intensity than those in either the closed- or open-type system. Spontaneity, intensity, and freedom are cherished by family members.

Like those in the open system, random-type members seek new emotional experiences. Unlike those in open systems, however, they do not constrain the search by the consent of other family members. Intimacy occurs at the random intersection of individual explorations rather than in the context of stability or consent, for those in a random system "have faith in the efficacy of creative anarchy" (Kantor and Lehr 1975:147). They abhor coercion. The appropriate way to influence another family member is to inspire him or her to a different pattern of behavior.

Diversity in Relationships

As you read the three kinds of systems, you probably have different reactions to each. Which is most appealing to you? The point is that there are diverse ways of relating to others in the intimacy of marriage and family life, including some that would be modifications of one of the above types. None of these ways is inherently better than others. Different people function better in one or the other system of relationships. Obviously, you are likely to have a more satisfying marriage to the extent that you join with someone who shares your preference.

Expectations

When people marry, they have certain expectations about what their marriage will involve. Among other things, they tend to expect that marriage will make them happy and fulfilled, that it will last, and that their spouse will be faithful. Some of these expectations may be unrealistic. If, for instance, you expect that your spouse is always going to make you happy, or that your relationship will be invulnerable to infidelity, your expectations are unrealistic.

Yet even if your expectations are all realistic, it doesn't mean that your marriage will be free of problems. You may or may not have the same expectations as the person you marry. You each may have realistic expectations, but they may be incompatible with each other. Unfortunately, sometimes we don't communicate what we expect until after we are married.

Our Private Contracts

Marriage is a contract between two people. It is a legal contract in the sense that the partners can bring each other to court to require performance or to dissolve the relationship. It is a social contract in the sense that family and friends feel that they have a stake in the relationship and the right to intervene or at least to bring pressure to bear on the couple. It is an interpersonal contract in the sense that the partners agree to commit themselves to each other for the duration of their lives. All of these contracts may result in anguish because the spouses also bring to the marriage their private contracts, which basically involve assumptions that each make about the nature of the relationship and their mutual obligations. Each partner has a private contract, then, in the sense that each *assumes* that there is agreement about various matters that were never discussed.

An example of how private contracts result in problems is illustrated in the case of a couple called Bill and Lucille (Sager and Hunt 1979:49–54). Each was involved in a career. They had a two-bedroom apartment. Bill used the second bedroom for a home office, though each knew that eventually it would be a nursery. Lucille intended to have children, but she wanted to wait. She had helped raise some of her younger siblings and was in no hurry to get back into the routine. However, Bill had been an only child, and a lonely child.

Although few couples have prenuptial contracts, every marriage is a private contract in which each spouse assumes there is agreement on various matters.

He had envied his peers who had brothers and sisters. He was anxious to have children while he was young enough to do things with them.

Unfortunately, Bill had not talked to Lucille about his feelings. When he suggested they begin their family, she tried to avoid the matter. Eventually, she realized how important it was to him, so she agreed. They had a girl. A year later, Bill wanted to try again. He badly wanted a son. Again, Lucille resisted. They were having financial problems, and she wanted to go back to work. In time, she gave in again. They had a son. Bill got a better job, and they bought a home in the suburbs. They seemed to have it all, but they weren't happy. In fact, their marriage was in serious trouble. They needed marriage counseling. And it was all unnecessary. They could have saved "a good bit of time, money, and suffering if they had known right away that each was furious with the other for not living up to the terms of *an agreement they never made*" (Sager and Hunt 1979:51).

Bill and Lucille each felt that the other had not lived up to the terms of their agreement. But they never had an agreement. They had two private contracts. They entered marriage with different expectations about children. Lucille had originally expected to keep her job, which was very gratifying to her, and delay having a family. She changed the terms of her contract to allow Bill to fulfill his. She had a daughter and son and became a homemaker. However, with a large mortgage and other debts, Bill became increasingly anxious about money and eventually wanted Lucille to go back to work. He expected her to carry a share of the financial load. Because she gave up her hopes to please

Table 9.2 Comparison of Spouses' Expectations about Who Should Perform Marital Roles

Expectations for wife's traditional roles:	Childcare	Housework
Agree job should be shared	84%	38%
Agree it is wife's job	2	30
Husband: wife's job/Wife: should share	7	13
Husband: should share/Wife: wife's job	8	20
Total	101%	101%
(N)	(483)	(488)

Expectations for husband's traditional roles:	Money management	Income earning
Agree job should be shared	69%	24%
Agree it is husband's job	9	43
Wife: husband's job/Husband: should share	5	9
Wife: should share/Husband: husband's job	17	25
Total	100%	101%
(N)	(487)	(484)

© 1986 by the Society for the Study of Social Problems. Reprinted from Hiller, Dana V. and William W. Philliber, *Social Problems*, Vol. 33, No. 3, February 1986, pp. 191–201, by permission.

her husband, she now expects him to be the breadwinner and support the lifestyle they have achieved. They both feel that their own expectations are reasonable. Yet they continue to clash because the terms of their private contracts, while changing, are not compatible with each other.

Role Expectations

When private contracts clash, it is frequently over role expectations. Bill originally assumed he would have a more traditional wife, who would willingly sacrifice her career to bear and care for their children. However, he came to a point where he felt he needed an employed wife. Lucille originally assumed they would have an egalitarian marriage, with each of them working outside of the home. She came to a point where she decided that he could be the family breadwinner.

Bill and Lucille are not unique in their problem. The question of the husband role and the wife role is a vexing one in many marriages. What are people's expectations about those roles? And do husbands and wives agree? In an effort to answer the questions, Hiller and Philliber (1986) surveyed 489 married couples, inquiring about their expectations with regard to childcare, housework, money management, and earning income. With regard to expectations, the researchers found that the couples tended to agree that childcare, housework, and money management should be shared (table 9.2). Interestingly, there was a tendency for spouses to believe that the husband should bear primary responsibility for earning the family income. Note that 68 percent of the husbands and and 52 percent of the wives agreed that earning income is the husband's job.

Hiller and Philliber investigated various other aspects of expectations about marital roles and drew a number of conclusions. First, spouses do not want to give up their own traditional roles, though they appear to be quite willing to participate in the traditional roles of the opposite sex. Second, spouses correctly perceive their partners' expectations about half the time. Husbands are more accurate than wives. Third, each spouse tends to think that he or she carries more of the burden of household duties than the partner thinks he or she carries. Finally, the researchers note that

> despite the fact that 69 percent of the wives in our sample were working outside the home, the traditional division of labor and dominant role of the male "head-of-household" were still very much in evidence in these marriages (Hiller and Philliber 1986:200).

Clearly, there are a sufficient number of discrepancies between the expectations of husbands and wives to account for a good deal of discontent and conflict in marriages. Couples who want to avoid problems will find themselves engaging in a process of negotiation about marital roles.

Negotiation: Changing Personal Contracts

Bill and Lucille had problems because neither was aware of the other's private contract, neither discussed the fact that the original contracts had been broken, and neither tried to initiate a process of negotiation to try to clarify and rework expectations. They desperately needed to understand and work with each other's private contract.

Negotiation is a process of working through clashing expectations. In negotiation, the expectations of each partner are brought out into the open. That is, the private contracts must become joint knowledge. Sometimes the individuals are not even aware of their own private contracts. They only recognize that something the partner has done has frustrated, angered, or disappointed them. Once the differing expectations are acknowledged, then the process of "give-and-take" can begin as the couple examines their various options and comes to a satisfactory compromise.

Consider the following example of clashing expectations and successful negotiation. A married student told us that she was appalled when she found that her new husband threw his clothes on the floor at night. "I thought that any civilized man would either hang his clothes up or put them in the wash." At first, she picked them up herself. Then she grew angry with him. When she became somewhat cold and distant, he asked her what was bothering her. He was surprised at her response. He expected her, as his wife, to pick up his clothes. His mother had done that. She curtly informed him that she would not be a mother to him.

They soon were able to negotiate a settlement. He agreed that he could change a lifelong habit, and she agreed to remind him and to be patient until he had established a new habit. She became aware of the fact that her private contract included a provision about her husband's neatness and help in keeping the house clean. She was unaware of that until she saw the clothes on the floor. His private contract included the expectation that his wife would behave like his mother in some ways. He, too, was unaware of that until his wife confronted him with her anger.

Not all clashing expectations are negotiated that easily. It is important for couples to recognize the existence of private contracts, the probability of differences in expectations, and the importance of negotiation for working through the differences.

The Marriage Contract: Clarifying Expectations

Instead of waiting until problems arise to clarify and negotiate private contracts, a couple can avoid at least some of the problems of marriage by formulating a marriage contract prior to the wedding. This can be a formal, legal document such as a prenuptial agreement that is drawn up by a lawyer. A legal contract, however, may signify a certain lack of trust at the outset of a marriage. Many people are not comfortable with such an arrangement. Moreover, the legal contract will not cover some of the matters in our private contracts that generate problems.

Instead of a legal contract, some couples write informal marriage contracts in order to clarify their expectations (Garrett 1982). These contracts are not legally binding, but they do help the couple to begin their married life with a better understanding of what each expects and, consequently, with less likelihood of friction and conflict over some common issues in marriage. Among other things, Garrett (1982) suggests that you discuss and include the following in your marriage contract:

1. Will the wife use the husband's last name, her own name, or a hyphenated name?

2. What will be the division of labor in the home? Who will do the cooking, cleaning, washing, repairs, and so on?

3. Will you have children? If so, how many and when?

4. Will you use contraception? What kind?

5. If you have children, how will you divide up the childcare responsibilities? What kind of discipline will you use?

6. What will you do about housing? Will housing decisions be made in the light of the husband's career, the wife's career, or both?

7. Who will be the breadwinner? How will financial decisions be made and who will be responsible for paying bills?

8. What will be your relationships with in-laws? Will you spend part or all of your vacation time with parents or relatives?

9. How much of your leisure will you spend together and how much separately?

10. What are your sexual expectations?

11. How will you change the terms of this contract over the course of your marriage?

The last point is important because no contract should be unalterable. A marriage contract reflects the way you feel at a certain point in time. One or both partners may want to change the terms. The points should always be open to negotiation. Informal contracts are meant to facilitate the ongoing development of intimacy, not bind partners to an inflexible pattern.

Adjusting to Marriage

To get married is to enter a new social world. Even those who have cohabited for a number of years frequently say that their relationship changes when they get married. There are adjustments to be made, whether or not you have lived together prior to marriage. In part, adjustments reflect the differing expectations we discussed above. In part, they reflect the nature of the new social world into which people enter—a world of new responsibilities, new options such as childbearing, and new relationships such as in-laws.

His Marriage and Her Marriage

Jessie Bernard (1972) argued that every marriage is really two marriages, his and hers. That is, men and women have substantially different experiences in marriage. Traditionally, women have had less power, and that means that they have had to make more adjustments than men. An old study of over five hundred marriages reported that the wife made more adjustments than the husband (Burgess and Cottrell 1939). That finding still seems to hold true.

Why must women make more adjustments? Consider some of the typical things that happen in marriage. A man is less likely than a woman to change his vocation or to drop out of the labor force. He is unlikely to move his residence to accommodate his wife's career, while she may move frequently to accommodate him. In spite of egalitarian attitudes, women still bear the brunt of housekeeping chores in most homes. When children come, women tend to assume the major responsibility for childcare.

Furthermore, women are more likely than men to have their private contracts violated. For women, talking things over is an important part of an intimate relationship, and men tend to talk to them in an intimacy-building fashion during courtship (Goleman 1986). But after marriage, the husband may spend less and less time talking with his wife about their relationship.

Marital adjustment is more difficult for those who begin with a disadvantage, such as very young age.

She finds herself deprived of an important facet of her intimacy needs. Worse, she had been led to believe by her husband's behavior that the intimate communication would be a part of their marriage.

Starting with Two Strikes

Adjustment in some marriages is more difficult because they begin at a disadvantage. We have discussed the problems with teenage marriages, for instance. Teenage couples truly begin their married life with two strikes already against them. They frequently face the problem of low income and perhaps of thwarted educational and career hopes at a time in life when they lack the maturity to cope effectively with such things.

Student marriages also begin with some disadvantages, whether the student is married to an employed spouse or another student. There are likely to be problems about the use of time and other strains associated with student marriages (Dyk 1987). The time problems become acute if the student is also employed part- or full-time. School schedules are relatively inflexible. An employed spouse may get weary of always having to accommodate to the demands of professors on his or her partner. When the employed spouse is the husband, and he has more traditional sex-role attitudes, the probability of conflict increases even more (Dyk 1987:330). The strains associated with student marriages arise from the student being so stressed or preoccupied with school work that the marital relationship suffers. Students can get emotionally, intellectually, and physically weary. If the spouse does not understand and fully support the student, marital problems are more likely.

There are various other marriages that begin at a disadvantage. If the woman is pregnant at the time of marriage, there is the additional adjustment of becoming parents. If the couple is not homogamous, there will be many adjustments to make. The point is that even under the best of circumstances, learning to live intimately with another person requires adjustments. It is unfortunate if the couple begins with disadvantages as well as challenges.

Establishing Equity and Consensus

If you have not worked out a marriage contract, you will have to work on the problems of equity and consensus in such areas as the division of labor around the home, your sex life, your social life, and other matters. We have underscored the importance of equity in relationships. A certain amount of consensus is also important. That is, the spouses must agree, or at least perceive that they agree, on various attitudes and behaviors. Couples in long-term, satisfying marriages do not agree on everything, but in our research 84.4 percent felt that they always or almost always agreed on aims, goals, and things they believed important (Lauer and Lauer 1986:97). A husband put it this way:

> I think the success of our marriage is due in large part to having many common values and that we agree on basically most things that are important in our lives together. This is particularly true for issues related to careers, money, and family life-style.

A relationship based on equity and consensus seems to come rather easily to some couples. Others have a more difficult time. One way to establish equity and consensus, for those who are struggling, is for each spouse to make a list of preferences. For example, in considering the division of labor in the home, the couple can first make a list of the various chores. Then each spouse ranks the chores from most to least desirable. The rankings are compared and the final division of labor negotiated.

Adjustment and In-Law Relationships

A marriage and family therapist told us that he believes as many as 60 percent of all marriages have some tension because of the relationship between the mother-in-law and daughter-in-law. A 1981 Gallup poll reported that 48 percent of Americans believe that living away from in-laws is "very important" to a successful marriage. Popular magazines carry articles regularly that tell people how to deal with in-law problems. In other words, in-laws are important factors in many marriages. You don't marry an individual. You marry into a family.

In spite of their importance, there has been little research on in-law relationships. In some unpublished research, we asked 233 people, with a mean age of 38.3 years and married a mean of 11.4 years, to discuss their in-law relationships. Specifically, we asked which in-law relationship had been the most significant for them, in either a positive or negative sense and how the in-law relationships had affected their marriage. Only seven said that they didn't regard any of their in-laws as significant (because they lived at too great a distance from them). All of the others acknowledged that an in-law had been significant in some way in their lives.

We found the mother-in-law most likely to be named as the significant in-law relationship (table 9.3). Significant in what sense? Evelyn Duvall (1954:187), in the most recent large-scale study of in-law relationships, reported that 36.8 percent of her respondents named mothers-in-law as the most difficult in-law relationship. We found that about half of those who said their mother-in-law was most significant indicated the relationship was a negative one and half said it was a positive one. Similarly, Arnstein (1985) reported that 48 percent of mother-in-law/daughter-in-law relationships are "good" and 52 percent are "poor." In our research, people defined positive relationships with in-laws as supportive, caring, accepting, warm, and friendly. They described negative relationships as intrusive, domineering, cool, or aloof.

In terms of adjustment, it is important to note that the in-law relationship is more likely to be a positive than a negative one. Overall, 58 percent of our subjects said their significant relationship was a positive one, while 32 percent defined it as negative. The other 10 percent said that it was mixed, including both positive and negative aspects (such as a mother-in-law who was initially supportive but who became intrusive when the couple had children).

Table 9.3 Most Significant In-Law Relationship

	Sex of respondent		
	Male *(N = 88)*	*Female* *(N = 138)*	*Total* *(N = 226)*
	Percent		
Mother-in-law	39.8	52.2	47.3
Father-in-law	26.1	14.5	19.0
Both mother- and father-in-law	13.6	12.3	12.8
Brother- or sister-in-law	20.5	15.9	17.8
Other	0	5.1	3.1
Total	100.0	100.0	100.0

Copyright © 1986 Robert H. Lauer and Jeanette C. Lauer. Reprinted by permission.

In-laws, then, can help couples in their adjustment. Some in-laws are problems, and make adjustment more difficult. However, in-laws are more likely to be resources than problems. As a young husband told us:

> When I got married, I got, in my father-in-law, the father to whom I could finally talk. He has been invaluable to me over the years. I could never go to my own father with some of the problems I've faced. I can always go to my father-in-law. He's been a security net.

First-Year Changes

When a young couple returned from their honeymoon, a friend said to them, "Well, it's all downhill from here on." The friend was disillusioned with her marriage, and her disillusionment was rooted in her unrealistic expectations. She had thought of marriage as a kind of endless honeymoon. It isn't. Changes in a couple's relationship begin in the first year of marriage (Huston, McHale, and Crouter 1986). These changes reflect the realities of intimate living in a complex society.

For one thing, the feelings of the spouses change. By the end of the first year, you are likely to feel somewhat less satisfied with the amount of interaction you have with your spouse. You will probably feel less satisfied with the extent to which your spouse initiates activity that pleases you and the frequency with which you have physical intimacy. Wives tend to report less satisfaction in these areas than husbands, both at the beginning of the marriage and at the end of the first year (Huston, McHale, and Crouter 1986:121). It is important to keep in mind that we are *not* saying that people are dissatisfied with their marriages after a year. Most couples still feel positively about their

The Intimate Couple

In-Laws: The Good and the Bad

Henry is sixty-one years old. He has been married for thirty-five years. He has experienced both the good and the bad in in-law relationships. Both his father- and mother-in-law have had an impact on his life and his marriage. He had great admiration for his father-in-law. His mother-in-law is another matter:

My father-in-law is dead now, but he was the most significant in-law I had. He was seventy-three when I met him. His wife was fifty-eight and she supported the family until she retired at sixty-five. He adapted well to the role of taking care of the house. He did the cooking and cleaning, never complained about anything to anyone, and was always there to talk with me about my problems.

He lived for the first ten years of my marriage. He encouraged me to pursue my goals, and taught me to be compassionate. Every night, he massaged his wife's feet. He had lived through a great deal of poverty and stress, but I never heard him gripe about it and I never heard him curse. He was a kind and gentle man who made me feel welcome into the family and supported me when I was getting my own career going.

My mother-in-law, on the other hand, is still alive and still a problem. She is selfish and thoughtless. Never in the thirty-five years of our marriage has she offered to help us or anyone that I know of. I can count the number of dinners I have had in her house on one hand. Because of her self-centered behavior and her constant demands on my wife, I have gotten—I still get—very depressed and angry. In the early years of our marriage, we argued a lot about her mother. If it hadn't been for my father-in-law, we would have had a much more difficult time. For about the last five years, we have learned to ignore her self-centered ways. We try to remember that she is very old and we reach out to her even though she will not reciprocate.

interaction, but they are not as euphoric as they were at the time of their wedding. The positive feelings are still there, but they have moderated.

Behavior and activities also tend to change. Spouses report a diminished amount of joint household and leisure activities. There tends to be an increase in household and other kinds of work activity, and a decrease of about 20 percent in joint leisure activity. The decline in leisure and increase in work activity is particularly strong if the couple has a baby during the first year.

There is a slight decline in the amount of time spouses spend talking with each other. More importantly, there is a significant decline in behavior that reflects affection. Married people report that by the end of the first year their spouses less frequently engaged in such things as

Approving and complimenting the partner

Doing or saying something to make the partner laugh

The marital relationship becomes increasingly task-oriented during the first year after the wedding.

Telling the partner "I love you"

Taking the initiative in sex

Doing something nice for the partner

Showing physical affection and having sexual relations

Discussing their feelings and problems

Talking over things that happened during the day

The number of such activities declined by about 40 percent from their level at the beginning of the marriage (Huston, McHale, and Crouter 1986:123). Again, it is important to underscore the fact that this does not mean that such things were absent, only that they were less frequent after a year. The overall amount of companionship does not change much, but it becomes more instrumental, more task-oriented, and less focused on romance and affection.

In other words, by the end of the first year couples are well on their way to a realistic mode of living together. Their time and energy are devoted not only to each other but to building careers and perhaps to beginning a family.

Our intimacy needs are fundamental, but we also have needs for achievement and for security. Human life is not a honeymoon. Marriage is not a honeymoon. On the other hand, it is important to keep in mind that the exhiliration of the honeymoon can be periodically recaptured in a long-term relationship.

Commitment

Why commitment at the end of the chapter on getting married? Doesn't commitment come during courtship? Isn't it a prerequisite of marriage? Yes and no. Commitment is a part of the courtship process. However, commitment is not invulnerable to change. Even during the courtship, people frequently waver in their commitment to the other. In marriage, there is a reciprocal relationship between commitment and the satisfaction and stability of the union. That is, commitment facilitates satisfaction and stability and, in turn, satisfaction and stability breed commitment. Commitment is a living part of the marriage, not an insurance policy that is irrevocable.

The Meaning of Commitment

For Americans, commitment in marriage seems to mean three things: promise, dedication, and attachment (Quinn 1982). There is a promise or pledge to engage in something that will include some difficult times (for better or worse, says the traditional marriage vow). There is a dedication to the joint goal of staying together and forming a meaningful family unit. This means there is an attachment between the two people, an emotional attachment that results from joint dedication to their goal.

In essence, then, commitment means "a promise of dedication to a relationship in which there is an emotional attachment to another person who has made the same promise" (Lauer and Lauer 1986:50). It is important to note that the commitment is to the person, and not simply to the institution of marriage. One difference between those with long-term satisfying marriages and those with long-term but unsatisfying unions is that the former are committed more to the spouse while the latter are committed more to the institution (Lauer and Lauer 1986). Commitment to the institution means that there are family pressures or religious beliefs that make the person unwilling to break the union even though he or she is unhappy with it.

The Role of Commitment

Commitment is a valuable resource in marriage. Those who are committed to their spouses as persons have significantly fewer marriage problems (Swensen and Trahaug 1985). Commitment to the person means that you are determined to work through troubled times. In contrast, commitment to the institution means a willingness to simply endure troubles rather than to work through them. Those who work through, rather than endure or wait them out, problems find the quality of their relationship greatly enhanced.

Commitment also gives the partners a sense of security. A wife told us that she occasionally experienced a "flash of emotion" that could turn into jealousy. Nevertheless, she views that as her own problem and not the fault of her husband, because she knows that they are committed to each other. Neither of them, she said with confidence, would put the marriage into jeopardy. Each has a sense of security with the other.

Commitment has benefits that go beyond enriching the marital relationship. A happy marriage in which there is a firm sense of commitment becomes a strong resource for dealing with the stresses of life. For instance, two researchers studied thousands of Israeli men over a five-year period to try to determine how a particular heart problem, angina pectoris, develops.[2] They found that one of the better predictors of those men who were at high risk was the answer to the question: "Does your wife show you her love?" Those who answered "no" were more likely to develop the heart disorder. Or as a husband told us: "To know that you have someone that loves you, and on whom you can depend no matter what problems may arise, is really important. It's like having a crutch under a broken leg that you can rely on to support you."

Building Commitment

As we have noted, commitment can change. Married people can act in a way that intensifies the commitment of each to the union or in ways that erode that commitment. One way to build commitment is to make sure that each partner feels a sense of equity in the relationship (Sabatelli and Cecil-Pigo 1985). It is very difficult to maintain commitment to a person if you feel that you are seriously underrewarded, that you are giving far more to the relationship than the other. There are times in any relationship, of course, when one person has to give more, perhaps far more, than the other. But that should balance out over time. Few, if any, people can maintain commitment in the face of inequity.

Commitment also grows as people's satisfaction with their relationship increases. While some decline in the affectional behavior noted is both normal and necessary after the honeymoon period, it is important for the couple to guard romance. The expression of affection is important throughout the marriage. It isn't enough to merely *feel* affectionate. That affection must be *expressed*. There is an old story about a reticent New Englander who said that he loved his wife so much it was all he could do to keep from telling her about it. Men generally have a more difficult time than women in openly expressing affection. But it is the expression, not merely the presence, of affectionate feelings that is necessary for building commitment.

Finally, commitment can be built by planning shared activities that are gratifying to both partners (Lauer and Lauer 1986:62). Sharing fun times, times of achievement, or times of adventure intensifies people's commitment as well as providing them with intimate experiences. The more you have a history of shared, gratifying experiences, the deeper your commitment is likely to become.

1. When, why, and who you marry should be your personal decision. But you need to be aware of the risks involved in marrying too early. Teenage and student marriages face unique difficulties that can place an intolerable burden on the relationship. There are also risks, however, in waiting too long. If you are a female, the chances of marriage after age forty are slim. It is important to be aware of these risks, but do not let them dictate your decision in this important matter.

2. It is important, before your wedding, to talk about the kind of marriage you and your future mate want. Do you both agree that you want a relationship based on traditional roles or one with equalitarian roles? Do you have "private contracts," assumptions, and expectations which you have not shared with each other? A thorough discussion of these can minimize difficulties after you are married.

3. The first year of marriage generally seems to challenge the popular expection of "happily ever after." All too frequently, the demands of building a life together change the patterns of interaction and intimacy that characterized your courtship. It is vital, first of all, to understand and prepare to deal with these changes. Then, it is important to begin a lifelong process of working to maintain the romance and to deepen the intimacy in your relationship.

4. Remember that when you marry you not only gain a spouse but also another family. Learn as much as you can about your future mate's relationship with his or her family before your wedding. This will not only tell you much about your spouse but also about the kinds of problems you are likely to encounter when you become a member of the family. Recognize potential problem areas, and plan to deal with them in a constructive manner. But keep yourself open to the benefits of an additional family; the benefits will likely outweigh the difficulties.

5. Commitment—the "Big C"—frightens many people today. Yet it is an essential ingredient in a successful marriage. Commitment to the institution of marriage provides you with the time to work out and grow through the problems that inevitably assault any relationship. Even more important is commitment to your spouse. The goal of this kind of commitment is both the happiness and well-being of your mate and also a growing and dynamic relationship.

SUMMARY

Although most Americans marry, your chances vary depending on a number of factors. The marriage rate fluctuates over time; only the rates during the 1930s were lower than those in the 1980s. The rates reflect more than preference. Sex ratios and age are factors as well. The longer you wait, the less your chances are of being married.

People marry for various reasons in addition to being in love. One reason is conformity to social expectations. Another reason is the idea that marriage and children are the ideal and most fulfilling state for humans. The desire to have children is a third reason. Finally, some define marriage as a practical solution to various problems and challenges.

We may classify marriages by alternative life-styles or by the nature of the relationship. Among the alternative life-styles are the traditional marriage, the equalitarian marriage, the employed-wife marriage, term marriage, group marriage, swinging, and the homosexual marriage. Marriages classified by the nature of the relationship include the closed-, open-, and random-type systems.

We all have expectations when we marry. Even if we marry with all realistic expectations, we will not have a problem-free relationship. Each partner tends to bring a private contract to the marriage, a set of assumptions about various matters that have not been discussed. When private contracts clash, it is frequently a clash over role expectations. Even in egalitarian marriages, spouses tend not to want to give up their own traditional roles; they are willing, however, to participate in the traditional role of the other.

Negotiation is necessary to work through clashing expectations. In negotiation, private contracts must become joint knowledge. Negotiations can also occur before marriage, as the couple formulates a marriage contract to avoid some problems after they are married.

When you marry you enter a new social world. There are many adjustments to make, even if you have lived together. The adjustments are not the same for both sexes. There is "his" marriage and "her" marriage. Women generally have to make more adjustments than men. Adjustment is more difficult when the marriage begins with disadvantages. Student, teenage, and heterogamous marriages all begin with some disadvantages. One important facet of adjustment is establishing equity and consensus in the relationship. In-laws also require adjustment, though overall they are more likely to be resources than problems.

During the first year of marriage, feelings and patterns of behavior change. Satisfaction tends to decline somewhat. Interaction tends to become more instrumental, more task-oriented, and less focused on romance and affection.

Commitment is not only the basis for marriage but the outcome of a satisfying relationship. Commitment means promise, dedication, and attachment. In stable and satisfying marriages, there is commitment to the spouse as an individual as well as commitment to marriage as an institution. Commitment can be built up by attending to the kinds of things that enhance the quality of the relationship.

---

1. "The Playboy Report on American Men," *Playboy Magazine*, March, 1979, pp. 232–35.
2. *New York Times*, June 5, 1988.

10

The Challenge of Communication

"When I use a word," said Humpty Dumpty in Lewis Carroll's *Through the Looking-Glass*, "it means just what I choose it to mean— neither more nor less." He was wrong. We would all like for our words to mean exactly what we choose for them to mean, in the sense that those who hear us understand us perfectly. However, communication is a complicated process. The meaning we convey to others depends on more than our intention.

It is important to understand the complexities of communication. Much of the satisfaction and dissatisfaction of marriage and family life is rooted in the way that people communicate. In this chapter, therefore, we will look at communication as an intricate process that has manifold possibilities for miscommunication. We will discuss the importance of listening as a part of effective communication. We will look at impediments to good communication and the kinds of communication that are satisfying to people. Communication is integrally tied up with marital intimacy and satisfaction, another topic that we will explore. Finally, we will suggest some ways to improve communication between partners.

Communication is crucial for intimate relationships.

The Nature of Communication

At the outset, we must underscore the point that it is impossible *not* to communicate. Some people use what they call the "silent treatment" as a method of dealing with conflict. The victim of the silent treatment may complain that his or her spouse "won't communicate with me." Still the silent treatment itself is a powerful form of communication, telling the partner that the silent one is angry and unwilling to discuss the problem. We are always communicating to each other, in the sense that our words, our lack of words, and our expressions are interpreted by others to say something about our mood, our feelings, and perhaps about our relationships.

Verbal Communication

When most people use the term *communication* they probably are thinking of verbal communication, the use of words to convey our ideas to others. All animals engage in communication of some kind. But humans are symbolic creatures; we create, manipulate, and employ symbols to direct our own behavior and to influence the behavior of others (Lauer and Handel 1983:80). Symbols are shared meanings. Language is a system of these symbols. When we use a particular symbol, such as "love," we engage in a certain amount of shared meaning with others.

Of course, our symbols do not have a standardized and single meaning that is the same for everyone. For instance, if you say "I love you" to someone, you may mean that you feel a deep attachment, or that you are sexually attracted to the person, or that you find being with the other person a delightful experience, or some combination of these or other meanings. Also the meaning that the other person imputes to your statement may be different from what you intended. As we shall see below, there are multiple opportunities for us to miscommunicate with each other, no matter how precise we try to be with our words.

Nonverbal Communication

"I love you" may not only mean something positive, but something negative as well. Depending on the inflection you put on the words, you could give quite contrary meanings to them. They could be put in the form of a question, a surprised reaction to someone's inquiry. They could be stated with sarcasm, indicating not only a lack of love but a degree of contempt for the other. They could be said with an air of indifference, suggesting a failed effort to appease an anxious and unloved inquirer. They could be stated with passion, conveying an intensity of feeling for the other.

Thus, words are only a part of the meaning in communication. Equally important as the words we use is the way in which we express them—the numerous nonverbal cues we use while communicating. It is estimated that anywhere from 50 to 80 percent of the meaning we convey is through the nonverbal part of our communication.

Kinds of Nonverbal Communication

There are many different kinds of nonverbal cues that you offer to others when communicating. One cue is the clothing you wear. If you go out on a date, what you wear may tell the other person something about how you feel or about the kind of person you are. The message is not necessarily what you intend to give. For example, a student told us that she broke up with her boy friend because he was always so sloppily dressed when they dated. She said that he tried to reconcile with her, insisting that he thought he was being "cool" and casual rather than sloppy. She interpreted his dress as a lack of interest in himself and a lack of respect for her. In spite of his protests, she refused to date him any more.

Facial expressions and eye behavior are important aspects of nonverbal communication. They are difficult to control, though some people learn to control their facial expressions. They exercise such control in order to mask some kind of emotion they are feeling (Malandro and Barker 1983:21). Eye behavior is even more difficult to control. Our eyes tell others about how we are feeling, how interested we are, how much self-confidence we have, and how trustworthy we are (no one wants to be known as "shifty-eyed").

Touching is still another important kind of nonverbal behavior. Between lovers, a decline in touching is an important message about feelings. Touching someone while talking to them may indicate affection or remorse. Gripping someone may indicate anger or frustration. It is important to keep in mind that these meanings may be independent of any words that are being said. For example, a man may proclaim "I love you" to a woman while holding her arm in a viselike grip. The woman is likely to define that as threatening rather than an expression of affection.

Finally, all of the cues we give in oral speech apart from the content of the words themselves are one of the most important kinds of nonverbal communication. As illustrated above by the diverse and contrary meanings that can be given to the phrase "I love you," the tone of voice and the emphasis given to words radically affect the meaning that is communicated. For instance, a woman says to her husband, "How about a movie tonight?" Think of the different meanings he can give to her by responding with the same word. "Uh, okay" (interpreted by her as willingness but no enthusiasm). "Oh *kay*" (interpreted by her as an idea he loves). "*Oh* kay" (interpreted by her to mean "we're doing what *you* want to do again"). "*Ohhh* kay" (hesitation in his voice, interpreted by her to mean "I'll do it, but I had something else in mind that I prefer doing").

Functions of Nonverbal Behavior

Nonverbal cues have at least six different functions in communication (Malandro and Barker 1983:14–15). First, they *complement* our words. If you say "I love you" and touch or embrace the other, you are reinforcing the meaning of your words. Sometimes people may not really believe what we say, or at least may have doubts, unless we reinforce the words with some kind of nonverbal behavior.

Nonverbal cues may also *contradict* our words. A student told us how happy he was to be married, but the pained look on his face contradicted what he was saying. Eventually, he admitted to some serious problems that he and his new wife were having. At times, the nonverbal rather than the verbal message is more reliable.

Third, nonverbal cues *repeat* the message. Repeating differs from complementing because the latter cannot stand alone. To touch or hug someone may have diverse meanings with the words "I love you." But if two lovers have developed their own special language, such as touching the fingers to the lips as a way of saying "I love you," then they are using a nonverbal cue to repeat the message of love. The message is given without the words. They may be at a party, catch each other's eye, and give the nonverbal signal of love. No words need be spoken.

Fourth, nonverbal cues *regulate* communication. People develop signals to let each other know when they approve of what the other says (such as nodding the head), when they disapprove (a frown), and when they want to interrupt and speak themselves (such as lifting a finger). Such nonverbal cues help to regulate the verbal interaction between them.

Fifth, nonverbal cues may *substitute* for words. A man may ask his wife if she still loves him, and she may respond by smiling and kissing him. Thereby she responds affirmatively though wordlessly. Finally, nonverbal cues may *accent* the verbal message. A pause, an emphasis on a particular word, a touch—all can be used to emphasize a particular point that is being made verbally. "I love you," spoken slowly and with a slight pause between each word may be a way of reassuring a lover who has had doubts about the relationship.

Communication as an Interaction Process

What you communicate to someone depends not only on what you say and how you say it, but on how the other person interprets what you say and how you say it. Figure 10.1 shows a model of communication as a process of interaction. The sender has certain ideas and feelings that he or she must encode into language. The encoded message is transmitted through the media, the verbal and nonverbal channels we use. The dotted line indicates that part of the process is the sender hearing his or her own words and evaluating them.

The receiver decodes, or interprets, the message and filters it through his or her ideas and feelings before encoding a reply. At that point the receiver becomes a sender and the process continues. Let us take a concrete example to underscore the fact that at each phase of the process there can be **static,** interference of some kind with accurate communication.

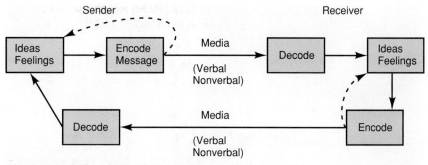

Figure 10.1 *The communication process.*

A Discussion about Sex

Chuck and Linda are a fictitious married couple who are having a discussion about their sexual relationship. Our commentary on their dialogue is enclosed in brackets:

> **Chuck:** I think that women don't have as strong a sexual drive as men. [Chuck desires to have sex more often than Linda. He is upset, but isn't sure if he feels anger, frustration, or both. He also wants to avoid offending Linda. He knows she is frequently stressed from dealing with both her career and their family. He encodes his desire into a statement that is a "feeler." He wants to know how she will respond to the idea. Yet when he hears his words, he thinks he might have chosen a better way to start the conversation. He prepares himself to back off if she reacts badly.]
>
> **Linda:** I don't know why you would say that. [She notices a slight edge to Chuck's voice. She decodes what he has said as a personal complaint. She knows he has wanted sex more often than she has. She isn't sure if that's why he made the statement. If he has, it will open the way to a larger discussion. She feels that he doesn't understand the strain of being both a mother and a career woman. Perhaps if he helped around the house more, she would have more energy. But she, too, doesn't want to offend. Basically, they have a satisfying marriage. She makes her response as terse and neutral as possible.]
>
> **Chuck:** I just think it's true. [He saw her mouth tighten when she replied. He interprets that as a warning signal that pursuing the topic could lead to an argument. Even though her words suggest that she would not agree that she has a weaker sex drive, her nonverbal cues warn him that this is an emotional topic. He decides to be neutral in his response.]
>
> **Linda:** Well, I've got too much to do to talk about something silly like that. [Hearing a softening in his voice, she defines him as unwilling to confront the issue directly. This angers her. She decides to force him to cut off the discussion or get to the point. In case he wants to pursue it, she has opened the door to what she regards as the real problem—an inequity in household responsibilities.]

Nonverbal cues are an important part of communication. What would you think if this person said to you, "I'm not angry"?

Such conversations can go on endlessly without the couple ever directly discussing the real issue. They communicated, but Linda was never certain what Chuck really wanted to say. And he felt that she was unaware of his feelings about their sex life. Merely because people are talking together does not mean that they are communicating accurately with each other.

Communication Static

Chuck and Linda illustrate some of the manifold ways in which static gets into the communication process. The sender, the media of transmission, and the receiver are all sources of static (Pneuman and Bruehl 1982). Senders may transmit with static because they aren't certain of their own feelings or ideas. Because Chuck was unsure of his own feelings, it was difficult for him to open the conversation in a helpful way. As a result, he sent ambiguous information to Linda. Ambiguous or insufficient information can also result from poor communication habits, such as assuming that one's thoughts or feelings can be inferred accurately without careful communication.

The Intimate Couple

Sender static can also result from certain mannerisms. For instance, a sender who uses "you know" or "uh" repeatedly, or who uses exaggerated nonverbal gestures while speaking may so distract the listener that accurate communication is very difficult.

Static occurs in the media when there is a discrepancy between the nonverbal and verbal communication. Chuck and Linda each noticed nonverbal signs that feelings were more intense than the words would indicate. Discrepancies between the verbal and nonverbal leave the hearer somewhat bewildered as to which medium of communication to accept. The man who insists he is not angry when his face is distorted with emotion is sending an ambiguous message. His wife knows that his words do not tell all, but she is not sure if the emotion expressed on his face is anger or something else. Media static may also occur if there are too many distractions in the environment (noisy children, for example, who keep grabbing the attention of one or both parents who are trying to discuss an interpersonal issue).

Receiver static occurs when the listener filters the message through his or her own ideas and feelings—selecting, expanding, and interpreting the words and nonverbal cues to make sense of the message. Chuck interpreted Linda's frequent lack of sexual desire as insufficient passion for him. Linda interpreted Chuck's ambiguity as an unwillingness to confront the issue directly. He never knew that she resented having a disproportionate share of responsiblity for the home. She never knew he was sufficiently sensitive to her needs to recognize that she felt stressed over her workload. Each assumed things about the other, because it was important for each to make sense of the situation. Lacking sufficient and accurate information from the other, each interpreted the other in a way that made sense, even though neither reached a satisfying conclusion.

Communicating Feelings

As Chuck and Linda illustrate, when we talk with others we inevitably communicate feelings as well as ideas. Feelings are very important in the marital relationship. The way you think your spouse feels about things may be more crucial to your relationship than what your spouse says. Research has shown that the accurate communication of feelings is as complicated and as subject to distortion as the communication of ideas (Gaelick, Bodenhausen, and Wyer 1985). As figure 10.2 shows, there is a circular process involved in the communication of feelings. The feelings you intend to communicate are interpreted by the other, and may or may not be perceived correctly. The other person has an affective reaction to his or her perception of your feelings, and communicates that to you. You interpret the other's feelings, compare that with what you expected, and have your own affective reaction. You then communicate additional feelings, and the cycle continues.

Because of the interpretation that always occurs, the cycle has both intended and unintended communication. Thus, in their study of twenty-nine couples, psychologists Gaelick, Bodenhausen, and Wyer (1985) found that people believe they reciprocate both positive and negative feelings that they

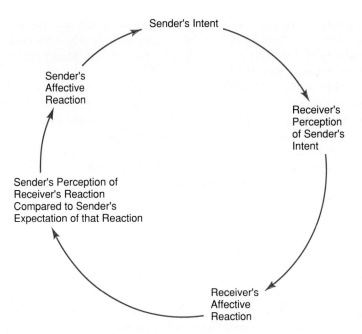

Figure 10.2 *Intended and unintended communication of feelings.*
Source: Data from Gaelick, Bodenhausen, and Wyer 1985:1248.

perceive from their partners. They had the couples engage in three conversations. One dealt with the events of the day, the second with a conflict they were having, and the third with what they liked best about living together. Although the subjects believed that they generally reciprocated the feeling they perceived their partners to convey, and also believed their partners reciprocated their own expression of emotion, the researchers concluded that, in actuality, they only reciprocated hostility. Among these twenty-nine couples, at least, there was not much accuracy in perceiving the expression of positive emotions.

The researchers also found two interesting gender differences in the communication of feelings. The men tended to distort the messages of their female partners in a negative direction, interpreting the lack of positive feelings as an indication of hostility. The women tended to distort the messages of their male partners in a positive direction, interpreting the lack of hostility as an indication of positive feelings. Clearly, neither feelings nor ideas are easily and accurately communicated to those we love. Effective communication is a complex and difficult task. One thing that is essential is effective listening.

Listening

Psychiatrist Karl Menninger (1942:275) once wrote that listening may be even more important than talking: "I believe listening to be one of the most powerful and influential techniques of human intercourse." However, there are various ways we can listen to others, not all of which are helpful to effective communication.

Styles of Poor Listening

There are a number of styles of listening that impede effective communication (Burley-Allen 1982:48–51). Some people habitually listen in one or more of these ways, while others may fall into them on occasion.

The Faker

Fakers only pretend to be listening. They may smile while you talk to them. They may nod their heads. They may appear to be intent, but they are either thinking about something else or are so intent on appearing to be listening that they do not hear what you are saying.

Ellen, an undergraduate, broke her engagement because she found that her fiancé consistently faked his listening:

> I realized how little he paid attention to me when I told him one day my doctor wanted me to have another test. He had found some suspicious cells in my cervix. Mike just looked at me and smiled. I really exploded. I was scared to death. He apologized. Said he was worried about an exam. I began probing into some other things I thought we had talked about. He couldn't remember half the things I had told him!

The Dependent Listener

Some people primarily want to please the speaker. They are so concerned about whether the speaker has a good impression of them, that they are unable to listen and respond appropriately. Dependent listeners may agree excessively with what the speaker says, not because they really agree but because they want to maintain the good will of the speaker.

A woman, for example, who is overly dependent on her husband may not listen to what he is saying because she is concerned primarily to please him rather than to understand and help him. Unfortunately, she does not realize that the relationship she is so desperate to maintain may be jeopardized rather than strengthened by her behavior. By striving to please, dependent listeners are frustrating at best. They may be valued by the individual who only wants someone to support whatever he or she says and does, but they are unable to build fulfilling relationships.

The Interrupter

Interrupters never allow the other to finish. They may be afraid that they will forget something important they want to say. Or they may feel that it is necessary to respond to a point as soon as it is made. Or they may simply be more concerned with their own thoughts and feelings than with those of others. In any case, they barrage the other with words rather than offering the other an understanding ear.

Here is how an interrupter might function:

Wife: I really had a rough day today. I thought my boss was going to. . . .
Husband: I bet your day wasn't any worse than mine. I couldn't believe the way my clerks were fouling up today. I think I'm going to have to bring them in one by one for some additional training.
Wife: Yeah, those people can drive you up a wall at times. Well, my boss just about went through the ceiling. . . .
Husband: You've got to stop letting him get to you. Just tell him you'll quit if he keeps on.
Wife: I can understand why he got upset. I didn't have the report ready. But he doesn't realize that. . . .
Husband: He gets upset at anything. I don't know how you stand working for him.

Note that the interrupting husband never lets his wife completely finish. The wife has no opportunity to talk out her feelings and frustrations. The husband simply breaks in with his own problems, or tries to give her a quick-fix solution. He isn't listening, because he is making no effort to fully understand her and the experience of her day.

The Self-Conscious Listener

Some people are concerned primarily with their own status in the eyes of the other rather than with the ideas and feelings of the other. Trying to impress the other person, they don't listen with understanding.

A woman who wants her husband to think of her as intelligent, for example, might be so concerned with that image that she doesn't really listen to him. Instead of trying to understand what he is saying, she will be thinking about how to respond in order to impress him with the quality of her mind. Or, she may want to impress him with the fact that she is indispensable to him, that she can help him with any of his problems. Again, instead of listening carefully and trying to understand him, she may be constantly framing her replies in order to appear helpful.

The Intellectual Listener

Intellectual listeners attend only to the words of the other. They make a rational appraisal of what the other has said verbally, but they ignore the nonverbal cues (including the feelings that are communicated nonverbally).

The intellectual listener may develop this style because of the type of work in which he or she engages. Consider the case of Frank, a computer programmer, who had learned to be thoroughly logical and systematic in order to succeed in his work. He tried to apply the same procedure to his marriage, however, and found himself in trouble:

> He was so busy analyzing what was communicated to him, he didn't have time to just be there with the other person. His wife often told him he was a nitpicker. She felt he was overly critical of her and the children because he seldom accepted what she said. He would challenge her thought processes. He spent most of their communication time analyzing what she said as if he had to turn it into a program (Burley-Allen 1982:51).

Frank was a highly intelligent person, but he had to learn how to listen.

Improving Listening Skills

How do you learn to listen? How can you learn to listen so that you understand the other person and the other knows you understand? One thing is to avoid the styles we have described above. Beyond that, Madelyn Burley-Allen (1982:96–98) suggests a number of things you can do to improve your listening skills generally. Some of those particularly appropriate for intimate relationships are:

1. Take the initiative in communication. Unfortunately, we tend to think of listening as a passive activity. But effective listening has to be active. You have to look at your partner and concentrate on what he or she is saying. You need to watch the nonverbal cues and listen to the words carefully and strive to understand exactly what he or she is trying to communicate. It is also helpful to respond to various things with noncommital remarks such as "I see," "That's interesting," and so on.

2. Resist distractions. The distractions may be in the environment, such as noise in the home, or they may be in your mind, such as preoccupation with some problem or concern. In either case, you must consciously decide to put aside the distractions for awhile and focus on what your partner is saying.

3. Control your emotions and your tendency to respond before your partner is finished. We all have certain "hot buttons," words or ideas that create an emotional reaction in us. At that point we are likely to stop listening and start formulating a reply. Your emotions, in other words, can turn you into an interrupter. It is important to resist that tendency. Hear your partner out completely.

4. Ask questions and rephrase to clarify your partner's meaning. In effective listening, questions are used not to cast suspicion on motives (such as "Are you saying that just to annoy me?"), but to get clarification (such as "Are you saying then that you are really hurt because I was late?"). Effective listeners are particularly aware of the

Good listening skills can be practiced everywhere.

value of rephrasing what the other has said. Rephrasing is done to clarify, to check for accuracy, to check for feelings, or simply to show interest and understanding.

For example, a husband says to his wife: "We have blown our budget to bits this month. You've got to stop spending so much money." She could respond angrily: "What about the money you spend? It's not all my fault." That is likely to start an argument. An effective listening response would rephrase the husband's statement. She might say: "You feel that our budget problems are due mainly to my spending habits?" (clarification); or "You're angry because of the way I spend money" (check for feelings). This provides her husband with the opportunity to respond in a constructive way to their budget difficulties.

5. Make use of the speed of your thoughts by summarizing. We think faster than we can speak. You can make use of this by periodically summarizing what your partner has said. It is important that you not only use your thinking to formulate responses, but also to summarize in an effort to understand exactly what your partner is getting at.

6. Practice. You can enhance your listening skills by practicing with everyone, not merely your intimate partner. The more you try to be an effective listener with people, the more skill you will gain. And, we might add, the more you will enhance the quality of your relationships.

Impediments to Communication

"If people would only learn to communicate." The complaint has been uttered numberless times. The implication is that many of our problems could be solved. Why, then, don't people communicate? As we have seen, it isn't just a matter of not talking. Not many relationships fall into the silent pattern of Ethan and Zeena's (see PERSPECTIVE). But the misunderstandings and speculations

The Silent Marriage

Edith Wharton's classic story, *Ethan Frome,* relates the unhappy life of a man who lost first his mother and then his wife to silence. The story illustrates the problems of communication and the sterile nature of relationships that lack good communication. Frome's father had died accidentally, and Ethan was left to care for his mother who had become ill after the loss of her husband. She had been a "talker" until his death, but from then on "the sound of her voice was seldom heard." A cousin, Zeena, came to stay with them and help nurse his mother. After the mother's death, Zeena prepared to return home, but Ethan, dreading the idea of being alone, asked her to stay. They were married. Within a year, Zeena also became sickly. Note in the following excerpt the role that both Ethan and Zeena played in the deteriorating communication:

> Then she too fell silent. Perhaps it was the inevitable effect of life on the farm, or perhaps, as she sometimes said, it was because Ethan "never listened." The charge was not wholly unfounded. When she spoke it was only to complain, and to complain of things not in his power to remedy: and to check a tendency to

impatient retort he had first formed the habit of not answering her, and finally of thinking of other things while she talked. Of late, however, since he had had reasons for observing her more closely, her silence had begun to trouble him. He recalled his mother's growing taciturnity, and wondered if Zeena were also turning "queer." Women did, he knew. Zeena, who had at her fingers' ends the pathological chart of the whole region, had cited many cases of the kind while she was nursing his mother; and he himself knew of certain lonely farmhouses in the neighborhood where stricken creatures pined, and of others where sudden tragedy had come of their presence. At times, looking at Zeena's shut face, he felt the chill of such forebodings. At other times her silence seemed deliberately assumed to conceal far-reaching intentions, mysterious conclusions drawn from suspicions and resentments impossible to guess.

Source: Edith Wharton, *Ethan Frome* (New York: Charles Scribners' Sons, 1911), pp. 77–79.

that characterized Ethan and Zeena plague even many of those who *are* talking to each other. What happens?

The failure to listen is one obvious impediment to effective communication. In addition, we need to be aware of certain kinds of destructive messages and of important gender differences in communication patterns.

Destructive Messages

When people communicate effectively, they are able to build intimacy, to share meaningful times together, and to understand each other more fully. Ineffective communication, on the other hand, impedes intimacy and facilitates misunderstanding, feelings of rejection, and conflict. There are a number of common destructive messages that characterize ineffective communication (Liberman, Wheeler, de Visser, Kuehnel, and Kuehnel 1980:90). It is important to note that there may be times when some of these messages are appropriate and even necessary. But if they become part of an individual's style of communicating, or if they are used too frequently or at inappropriate times, they impede effective communication.

Ordering may be occasionally necessary with children, but it is likely to generate such things as fear, anger, resistance, or resentment in an intimate partner. "Stop doing that," "You have to . . . ," and "You must . . ." are the kinds of phrases used in ordering. Ironically, the partner may be quite willing to do what you want, but will resist and perhaps refuse simply because you ordered rather than requested. Ordering turns the interaction into a power struggle rather than an opportunity for effective communication between equals.

Threatening tends to generate the same emotions as ordering. It can also lead to passivity or despair. Again, to threaten the other is to engage in a power struggle rather than effective communication.

Moralizing sends a message that the partner should feel guilty, or morally inferior, or that the partner needs guidance and direction from others. "You ought not . . ." and "You should . . ." are moralizing phrases. Moralizing also can be accomplished nonverbally by a look of disgust or disapproval.

Providing solutions is a parental approach to a relationship. The words may sound like a suggestion, but the nonverbal cues can indicate a kind of parental guidance and even the superiority of the questioner: "Why don't you clean off the table during the commercial?" or "Why don't you balance your checkbook each time you write a check?"

Lecturing is a more forceful way of providing guidance and solutions to problems. "You will have to learn how to keep the house clean if you want to be a good wife." "You will have to be more forceful at work and demand a raise if you are going to be a good father and husband." Lecturing also tends to diminish the self-esteem of the partner and underscore the superiority of the one giving the lecture.

Criticizing can lead to conflict-habituated marriage. Or it can lead to a lowered self-esteem and dependency in the criticized partner. "You're always so messy," "You never do anything properly," and "You're so dumb when it comes to money matters" are examples of criticizing that can mar a relationship.

Ridiculing is sometimes used with good intentions (in the mistaken belief that the other person will see how ridiculous his or her behavior or ideas are and change). Sometimes the intentions are not so good (the person who uses ridicule may be demonstrating his or her own superiority over the other). In either case, ridicule will generate more resistance and resentment than change and intimacy. "You're talking like an idiot" and "You're a slob" are examples of ridicule. You can't engage in effective communication with someone who hurls such biting phrases.

Analyzing is the attribution of motives to someone. The world is full of amateur psychoanalysts who tell others why they behave the way they do and why they think and feel as they do. "You're only doing that to hurt me" and "You're only smiling to cover up your hostility" are examples of analyzing. This angers us, because the analyst invades our privacy and suggests motivations that we believe to be wrong. If the analyst is a very powerful and admired person in our lives, we may believe the analysis and lose self-esteem. In either case, effective communication breaks down.

Interrogating is another power tactic that conveys a sense of distrust of the other. "Can you give me one good reason why you won't go to the party?" and "You're not telling the truth, are you?" are examples of interrogation. Interrogation is used to coerce information rather than to engage in dialogue.

Finally, *withdrawing* is a way of saying "I refuse to discuss this any more." Withdrawal is an overt end to verbal interaction. "I'm tired; I'm going to bed" and the "silent treatment" are examples of withdrawal. Note that we did not say that withdrawal is an end to communication. The withdrawer is still communicating, but the communication is no longer effective in the sense that it is an ongoing process of interaction in which both people increase their understanding of the other.

Gender Differences as an Impediment

In the play *My Fair Lady,* Henry Higgins sings a song of bewilderment in which he asks why a woman can't be more like a man. Higgins doesn't understand women and particularly doesn't understand why they react differently from his male friends. His perplexity symbolizes that of many who run into problems of communication because they do not understand basic gender differences.

Psychiatrist Aaron Beck (1988) has noted some of the important differences in male-male versus female-female communication, such as men rarely talk about personal matters. Beck wrote that he only learned that one of his close male friends was going to be a grandfather when the man's wife told Beck's wife about it.

In addition to the differences in subject matter that tend to characterize men's and women's conversations, there are fundamental differences in style. We noted these in chapter 7 (e.g., women tend to raise more questions than men).

It is important to recognize these gender differences in order to minimize misunderstandings in communication. As Beck pointed out, women tend to believe that the marriage is working as long as they and their husbands can keep talking about it. Men may think that it is not working if they have to keep talking about it.

Why Husbands and Wives Don't Talk to Each Other

"He doesn't talk to me." It's one of the most common complaints. Why does communication sometimes lapse into a kind of silent tolerance? Why do some couples become like Ethan and Zeena (see PERSPECTIVE)? Any of the previously discussed factors may come into play in a marriage. One or both partners may develop a style of sending out destructive messages. There may be a lack of understanding of gender differences. The result of such things is that conversations become a form of punishment rather than reward. And few of us are willing to engage consistently in behavior that we define as punishing.

For instance, Faye is a housewife with two preschool children. Her husband, Tom, is an architect. They have a stable marriage of ten years, though they do not converse as readily as they once did. In particular, Faye complains about Tom's reluctance to talk:

> I'm hungry for adult conversation and companionship by the time Tom comes home from work. But sometimes it's like I have to yank every word out of him. I feel like he could spend the rest of his life with me without ever initiating a conversation.

Tom is educated, knowledgeable, and interested in a variety of topics from sports to politics. Why doesn't he talk with Faye? Tom told the marriage enrichment group that he and Faye were attending one night: "Sometimes people don't talk to each other because of the way one of them responds." When pressed about what he meant, he said:

> Suppose I come home and tell Faye that I'm thinking of starting my own firm, or even of getting out of architecture all together and trying a different career that will be more satisfying to me. Then she tells me that's a dumb idea because I have a wife and two kids to support and a good job and I ought to be thinking about more productive things.

Faye admitted that it sounded like something she would say. She got frightened when he talked about such things. So she would cut him off and ridicule the idea. As a result, Tom had unwittingly fallen into the habit of initiating very little conversation. Tom and Faye are working on improving their communication. They have a basically sound relationship, but effective communication had deteriorated because neither had understood the other, and Tom had chosen the typical male response of lapsing into relative silence.

Satisfying Communication

If you have a satisfying pattern of communication, will that guarantee a satisfying marriage? The answer is no. Satisfying communication is not sufficient. On the other hand, it *is* necessary. You can't have a satisfying marriage without satisfying communication, even though the latter won't guarantee a

All the Talk Was Useless

One of the important points in this chapter is that talking together doesn't necessarily mean that effective communication is occurring. Jenny is a nurse who was married for fifteen years to Phil, a psychologist. She was twenty-two and he was thirty when they married. They talked a lot, but it didn't save their marriage. Jenny recalls the relationship with a tinge of sadness in her words:

> We were both introspective kinds of people. When I was a child I was lonely and I rarely, if ever, confided totally in another person. Phil also had a difficult childhood. So we were both insecure. The result was that, though we talked a lot, we didn't talk about anything that would threaten our security.
>
> Before we were married, we talked about where we would live and how our careers would go and how our marriage would be a good one. But we didn't discuss things like potential problems, or things we liked and didn't like about each other. And we certainly didn't talk about how we would make decisions and who would control the finances. That was unfortunate, because a lot of the troubles we had later on really were the result of a power struggle between us.
>
> While we were married, we argued, we discussed, and we hit impasses on many things. We disagreed about our in-laws. I thought he should be more accepting of my parents, and he thought I should feel more warmly toward his parents. We argued about money constantly. We fought about each other's spending habits. We also talked a lot about things we agreed on. We both loved movies, and we discussed them. We told each other about our work and the things that happened on the job. Phil was supportive when I was stressed at work, and I think I helped him when he was worn down by some of his patients. But the arguments consumed an increasing amount of our conversation as the years went by.
>
> So in the end, all the talk was useless. Because we didn't talk about the really crucial things. We never discussed our own fears and vulnerabilities with each other. We never talked about our differences for what they were—a struggle for control in the relationship. We just fought more and more. The final breakup came within two months of our fifteenth anniversary. We never even discussed the breakup. We didn't talk about the reasons for it. We never talked about how we each felt. We just slipped quietly apart. And the marriage ended.

happy union. We should note that what is "satisfying" will differ somewhat for various couples. Nevertheless, people who come to therapists with marital problems report a variety of communication problems, including too little conversation, too few things to talk about, too much criticism, and general dissatisfaction with conversations.

What kind of things go into satisfying communication? What makes people happy with the communication pattern of their relationship? Communication is more satisfying to us when we feel understood and when we

Pleasant mealtime conversations help make marital communication more satisfying.

have agreement with the other (Allen and Thompson 1984). We can even go beyond "satisfying" and talk about "peak communication experiences," which are

> our 'greatest moments' in interpersonal communication, our moments of highest mutual understanding, happiness and fulfillment deriving from the process of communication (Gordon 1985:824).

Such experiences occur when we perceive that the communication is with someone for whom we have a loving acceptance and from whom we gain new insights. It is marked by a spontaneous playfulness, absorption in the process, and a certain amount of self-forgetfulness.

There are numerous other things that can be said about satisfying communication. Perhaps it can best be summed up by noting that the most frequently used measure of marital communication is one developed by Bienvenu (1978). His Marital Communication Inventory is used by researchers and therapists to study and improve communication. A sampling of items shows that marital communication is more satisfying and effective the more often the spouses:

Discuss the way they will spend their income

Discuss their work and interests with each other

Express their feelings to each other

Avoid saying things that irritate each other

Have pleasant mealtime conversations

Listen to each other

Perceive that they are understood by the other

Support each other

Communicate affection and regard

Avoid the silent treatment

Confide in each other

Communication, Marital Satisfaction, and Intimacy

Satisfying communication facilitates the growth of both marital satisfaction and intimacy. Couples that are satisfied with their relationship, who define their marriage as a happy one, and who indicate high levels of intimacy also report satisfying patterns of communication.

Everyday Conversations

We saw that the marriage of Jenny and Phil (see PERSONAL) ended because they never talked about the serious issues in their relationship. We should not conclude that *only* the serious issues are an important part of the communication pattern of a couple, however. Everyday conversations and discussing the events of the day are significant for marital satisfaction.

In fact, research with thirty-one married couples suggests that everyday conversations may be one of the more important ingredients in a satisfying marriage (Holman and Brock 1986). The researchers tested the couples using the Marital Communication Inventory and a measure of marital satisfaction. They found that marital satisfaction was closely related to empathy in communication, everyday discussions, and the lack of negative kinds of communication (fault-finding, nagging, the silent treatment, etc.). But the strongest of the relationships was that between everyday discussions and overall satisfaction. The researchers concluded that effective listening and speaking skills are important but that

> proficiency in these skills does not make up for easy conversation with a spouse about the events of the day (Holman and Brock 1986:92).

Self-Disclosure

We have seen that self-disclosure comes up repeatedly as an essential factor in an intimate relationship. In marriage, self-disclosure enhances both satisfaction and intimacy. The more that a spouse engages in self-disclosure, the more that both partners are likely to be highly satisfied with the relationship (Hansen and Schuldt 1984). And self-disclosure accounts for more than half the variation in intimacy among couples (Waring and Chelune 1983).

We never outgrow our need to engage in self-disclosure and to have our partner disclose to us. A study of 120 older couples (average age, 68.9 years; average years married, 42) examined the relationship between self-disclosure of feelings and life satisfaction (Sanders et al. 1987). Husbands were more satisfied with their lives to the extent that they disclosed feelings of pleasure and love to their wives, and received love disclosure from their wives. Wives were more satisfied with their lives to the extent that they disclosed feelings of pleasure to their husbands and received disclosure of love and sadness from their husbands. The researchers also investigated disclosure of anger, but it was not related to life satisfaction.

The fact that disclosing love, pleasure, and sadness enhanced satisfaction, while disclosing anger was unrelated to satisfaction, raises the question of what kinds of disclosure contribute to intimacy and marital satisfaction. As Fitzpatrick (1988:179) points out:

> No relationship is able to sustain total openness and intimacy over long periods of time. . . . From the beginning, there is a tension between the need to self-disclose and the need to protect the partner from the consequences of such disclosure.

Thus, keeping the lines of communication open in a marriage does not mean that there is an indiscriminate and continuous flow of words and feelings between the partners.

For one thing, self-disclosure should be equitable. A study of troubled versus satisfied marriages reported that there was a relatively equal amount of self-disclosure among the satisfied couples (Chelune, Rosenfeld, and Waring 1985). In the troubled marriages, the wives tended to disclose more than the husbands. Second, self-disclosure should always be done with discretion. A general rule of thumb is that in a satisfying marriage you can disclose any-

Table 10.1 Marital Happiness and Stimulating Exchange of Ideas

Frequency of exchange	Degree of happiness		
	Both happy	One unhappy	Both unhappy
	Percent		
At least daily	28.3	21.9	18.4
Once or twice a week	47.3	29.7	26.3
Once or twice a month	17.8	28.1	18.4
Less than once a month	6.5	20.3	36.8
	99.9	100.0	99.9
	(N = 505)	(N = 64)	(N = 38)

Copyright © 1986 Robert H. Lauer and Jeanette C. Lauer. Reprinted by permission.

thing to your spouse, but you never disclose everything. Exactly what should and should not be disclosed may vary from one couple to another. It is always appropriate to disclose such things as feelings of pleasure and love. (Perhaps we should say it is imperative to express those feelings. It isn't enough to feel them internally.) Marital satisfaction is enhanced by the *disclosure*, not just the experience, of pleasure and love. It is appropriate to disclose things that are troubling to you, or matters of serious concern. Yet as long as they can be handled by you in other ways, it is usually better not to disclose those things that you know will hurt or anger your spouse.

Other Aspects of Communication

There are certain other aspects of communication that are also related to marital satisfaction and intimacy. In their study of 111 married couples, Boyd and Roach (1977) reported a relationship between satisfaction and characteristics of communication. One characteristic of the more satisfied couples was clear and direct messages. That is, they had honest and open communication: "I say what I really think." Second, the satisfied couples reported good listening skills: "I check out and try to clarify what my spouse says so that I am sure that I understand him." Third, the satisfied couples openly expressed respect and esteem for each other.

Finally, in our study of long-term marriages, we found three differences between those in happy, unhappy, and mixed (one partner happy and one unhappy) marriages (tables 10.1, 10.2, and 10.3). Couples in happy marriages tend more frequently to have a stimulating exchange of ideas, to laugh together, and to calmly discuss something. In other words, in happy marriages there are more—and also more stimulating and fun-filled—conversations.

Table 10.2 Marital Happiness and Laughing Together

Frequency of discussions	Degree of happiness		
	Both happy	One unhappy	Both unhappy
	Percent		
At least daily	72.8	32.8	34.2
Once or twice a week	23.7	37.5	23.7
Once or twice a month	1.8	25.0	26.3
Less than once a month	1.8	4.7	15.8
	100.1	100.0	100.0
	(N = 506)	(N = 64)	(N = 38)

Copyright © 1986 Robert H. Lauer and Jeanette C. Lauer. Reprinted by permission.

Table 10.3 Marital Happiness and Calm Discussions

Frequency of discussions	Degree of happiness		
	Both happy	One unhappy	Both unhappy
	Percent		
At least daily	61.7	35.9	21.1
Once or twice a week	29.6	28.1	28.9
Once or twice a month	7.3	28.1	18.4
Less than once a month	1.4	7.8	31.6
	100.0	99.9	100.0
	(N = 506)	(N = 64)	(N = 38)

Copyright © 1986 Robert H. Lauer and Jeanette C. Lauer. Reprinted by permission.

Improving Communication Skills

There are numerous books, workshops, and courses designed to help people improve their communication skills. Marriage and family therapists spend a good deal of their time helping troubled clients with their communication patterns. In addition, you also can improve your own skills by attending to some basic rules and practicing them at every opportunity.

Rules

All rules for improving communication skills revolve about the goals of making us more effective senders and more effective receivers. Effective senders are those who transmit clear messages, and who do so in a nonthreatening way. To transmit a clear message, you need to listen to your own words carefully (figure 10.1) and continue to modify what you say until the message accurately reflects your feelings and ideas. At the same time, the message should

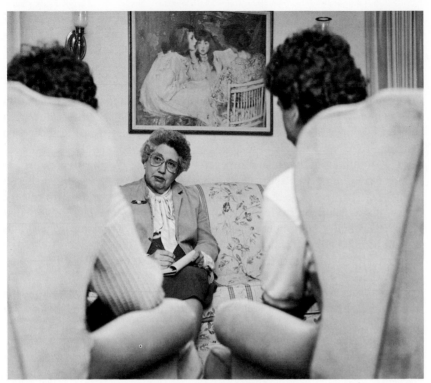

Some couples must go through counseling in order to learn to communicate in a nonthreatening way.

be an invitation to dialogue and not an attack. Those who send their messages using some of the destructive styles discussed will threaten their partners in one way or another.

Unfortunately, a clear message sent in a nonthreatening manner does not guarantee accurate communication. When you communicate with someone, you are engaging in a process of interaction in which each of you is interpreting the verbal and nonverbal cues of the other. That interpretation may or may not be accurate. It can only be accurate when each of you has learned to be an effective receiver as well as an effective sender. To be an effective receiver means, above all, to be a good listener. Family therapist Virginia Satir (1972:70) pointed out that one of the common communication types she observed was the *distractor*. A distractor is someone who never responds directly to what is said by the other. The distractor tries to avoid the issue by ignoring it and bringing up something more pleasant. For example, a wife may say to her husband, "I was really hurt when you didn't tell me you would be so late." He might respond: "How about taking in a movie tonight?" In doing so, he is not actively listening to her. He has played the role of distractor. You only actively listen when your response indicates that you understand and follow through in the direction suggested by the sender.

Practice

You can improve your own communication skills by attending to the ideas in this chapter when you talk with others. Even when you listen to a lecture, you can hone your skills by using some of the ideas discussed in the section on listening (e.g., summarizing the speaker's points in your mind).

In addition, there are certain exercises that are specifically designed to improve communication skills. Lederer and Jackson (1968:277–84) suggest a number of exercises, one of which requires intimate partners to acknowledge everything the other says for a two-week period. In fact, they suggest that each acknowledge and in turn have the acknowledgment acknowledged. This should be done no matter how trivial the original statement seems to be. For instance, one of the partners may say, "It is cold today." The other should acknowledge the observation in some way, such as: "Yes, I noticed that it is cold also," or "You're right. It's colder than yesterday." The one who made the original statement could then acknowledge the acknowledgment: "So you noticed it too."

The exercise may seem silly at times. But two points are important. First, it will be done for more serious as well as trivial matters. And second, it is good practice in developing "confirmation" in communication (Montgomery 1981). Confirmation is a way of letting the other know that you are listening and that you understand and accept the feelings of the other.

One further example of a helpful exercise is the communication game suggested by Satir (1972:80–95). In addition to the distractor, Satir identified three other types of communication that she found common in her work as a therapist: the *placator* is always agreeable, always trying to please; the *blamer* is always finding fault and acts superior to others; and the *computer* is the ultrarational individual who logically analyzes everything. Most people play one or more of those roles at some time.

Satir suggests playing the game with three people (to represent a family of mother, father, and child), but it also can be played with two as well. Play the game with someone with whom you are intimate. Let us say that it is a spouse or an intimate partner. Decide on a topic of conversation, perhaps a problem you are currently having or plans for a date or vacation. Then each select a way of communicating. For example, you might begin as the blamer and your partner could be the distractor. Discuss the topic for about five minutes or so. Then talk about how each of you felt when you were playing that role.

After the discussion, each partner assumes a second way of communicating, and so on until each has played all four roles. An interesting aspect of this game, Satir noted, is the ease with which people construct an appropriate dialogue. That is because most of us have had practice already at each of the

Improving Your Communication

One way to improve your communication skills is to engage in the exercises suggested in this section. For example, you can use the four ways of communicating offered by Satir and play the game with two other members of your family. After you have each had a chance to play all of the four roles, write down some of your conclusions. What did you learn about communication patterns in your family? With which of the roles did you feel most comfortable? Most uncomfortable? How did the other family members react to the differing roles? What changes would you like to make in your family's pattern of communications on the basis of this experience?

An alternative way to improve communication skills is to observe others and critique their communication pattern on the basis of the materials presented in this chapter. Because it is difficult to observe an actual situation, you can watch a number of episodes of some TV series that deals with marriage and/or family life. Look for such things as effective sending and receiving of messages, static, nonverbal cues, destructive messages, styles of poor listening, and so forth. How would you rate the communication patterns portrayed? What principles of effective communication do they uphold and which ones do they violate?

dialogue. That is because most of us have had practice already at each of the ways of communicating. In the course of playing the game, however, people learn a great deal about themselves and their relationships. You will probably find some of the ways of communicating very repugnant or very difficult for you. Some men react strongly to being a placator and some women find it very difficult to be a blamer.

The major point is that communication skills are like any other. They can be improved by practice. For those who wish to enhance the quality of their intimate relationships, good communication skills are an imperative.

PRINCIPLES FOR ENHANCING INTIMACY

1. Effective communication is essential to a successful relationship, but it doesn't seem to come naturally or easily. It takes determination and effort. Effective communication requires commitment and hard work for the duration of the relationship.

2. Many people complain that it is the lack of communication that is hurting or even destroying their relationship. It is important to remember, however, that you are always communicating something.

Even when you refuse to talk to your partner and give him or her the "silent treatment," you are communicating a powerful message. Unfortunately, what you seem to be saying is that this relationship is not worth talking about. And, not surprisingly, the relationship will be worthless if the silence persists.

3. There is some truth to the old adage "your actions speak louder than your words." For example, your facial expressions, body language, tone of voice, and physical appearance convey a message. At times, it is not the message you intend. Yet to the recipient of the message, nonverbal communication is often a more forceful indicator of your feelings than the words you use. Be open to your partner's readings of your nonverbal cues; you can both learn something about your true feelings.

4. Cultivate the capacity of effective listening. Generally, we master easily the technique of ineffective listening—partial attention, premature conclusions, misunderstood intentions, and so forth. Effective listening, however, involves the need to understand what the other person is really saying and to respond in a way that demonstrates this understanding.

5. Effective communication is not a cure-all for every troubled relationship. At times, effective communication convincingly reveals that the relationship cannot or should not be salvaged. As a necessary ingredient of a vital intimate relationship, however, effective communication is worth the risk.

SUMMARY

It is impossible not to communicate. We communicate nonverbally as well as verbally. Clothing, facial expressions, eye behavior, touching, and various oral cues such as inflection are a part of nonverbal communication. Nonverbal cues may complement, contradict, repeat, regulate, substitute for, or accent our verbal messages.

Communication is an interaction process in which the sender encodes feelings and ideas and transmits them to the receiver who must decode them in the context of his or her own feelings and ideas. Communication static can occur in any part of this process. Feelings as well as ideas are subject to the process of interpretation by each party in the communication.

Listening is a crucial part of communication. Some listening styles impede effective communication, including the faker, the dependent listener, the interrupter, the self-conscious listener, and the intellectual listener. There are various techniques that anyone can use to improve his or her listening skills.

There are a number of destructive messages that are impediments to effective communication. Ordering, threatening, moralizing, providing solutions, lecturing, criticizing, ridiculing, analyzing, interrogating, and withdrawing are forms of destructive messages. These messages may be appropriate and useful at times, but they are destructive when used regularly or at inappropriate times.

It is important to recognize gender differences in communication in order to minimize problems. Women tend to believe the marriage is working as long as they can keep discussing it with their husbands. Men tend to believe the marriage is not working if they have to keep discussing it.

Satisfying communication is crucial to a satisfying marriage, though the former will not guarantee the latter. Communication is satisfying when we feel that we are understood and that the other agrees with us. Marital communication is more satisfying to the extent that the couple discusses both trivial and important matters, avoids irritating each other, and listens to each other.

Satisfying communication facilitates the development of both marital satisfaction and intimacy. Everyday conversations and self-disclosure are particularly important to satisfaction and a deepening intimacy. People in happy marriages have, more frequently than others, a stimulating exchange of ideas, calm discussions, and times of laughing together.

Communication skills can improve by attending to some basic rules and practicing. A good communicator must be both an effective sender and an effective receiver. Various exercises can help make you a more effective communicator.

11

Marriage as Struggle

In our fantasies, marriage is a romantic adventure. In reality, marriage is a struggle as well as an adventure. It is a struggle in a number of ways. Consider the explanation of John Ruskin, famed nineteenth century author and reformer, for the unhappy state of his own union:

> I married her thinking her so young and affectionate that I might influence her as I chose, and make of her just such a wife as I wanted. It appeared that *she* married *me* thinking she could make of me just the *husband she* wanted. I was grieved and disappointed at finding I could not change her, and she was humiliated and irritated at finding she could not change me (quoted in Rose 1983:61).

As Ruskin found to his chagrin, marriage can involve conflict and a struggle for power within the relationship. Power and conflict are a normal part of intimate relationships. They can wreck a relationship. But they need not lead to dissatisfaction in marriage and can, in fact, enhance the quality of the relationship if the partners handle them well.

In this chapter, we will examine the issues of power and conflict. We will look at power in terms of its meaning, importance, sources, and role in the struggles of marriage. We will also discuss the meaning and role of conflict. We will see the kinds of things that people fight about, the way in which they fight, and some methods of "good" fighting.

Marriage is a struggle as well as an adventure.

Power in Marriage

Who is the head of the house? Who is in control in the marriage? Americans like to think of marriage as a relationship of equals. Yet how equal are marriages? We can only answer the question after we look at power in relationships and at the way in which marriage can become a struggle over power.

The Meaning of Power

What do you actually do when you exert power in a relationship? That is, what does it mean to have interpersonal power? And how can you tell who has the power in a relationship?

Defining Power

A dictionary definition equates power with the possession of such things as authority, influence, and control. Social psychologists like to make a finer distinction:

> Interpersonal power is the ability to get another person to think, feel, or do something they would not have ordinarily done spontaneously. If one possesses the means to affect another, one has *power* vis-à-vis that person. If one uses one's power, it is called *influence*. If one's influence is successful, it is called *control* (Frieze, Parsons, Johnson, Ruble, and Zellman 1978:302).

We will use **power** as defined above, that is, as the ability to get someone to think or feel or act in a way that he or she would not have done spontaneously. It is important to note that this does not imply that the person didn't want to think, feel, or act in that way. Power doesn't necessarily involve coercion. It doesn't necessarily mean that you influence your partner in a way that is contrary to his or her inclination. In other words, we should not think of the use of power as something inherently negative or wrong. Of course, power can be abused and misused. However, it can also be used to enhance the well-being of others, as illustrated by the work of therapists and the influence of physical fitness experts.

Measuring Power

Think about any marital relationship you know fairly well. Which spouse has the most power? How do you know? Researchers have struggled with these questions, but have generally measured marital power on the basis of who makes the major decisions. For example, who has the final say on such matters as buying a house, the kind of car to purchase, the vacation, and the choice

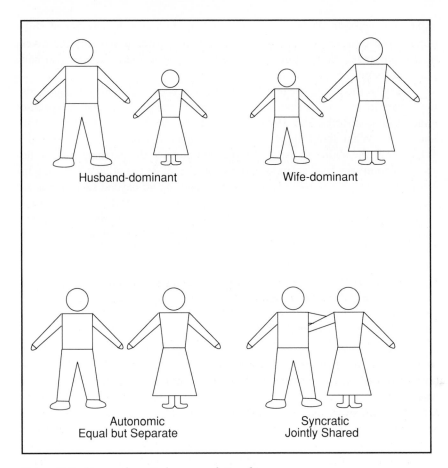

Husband-dominant

Wife-dominant

Autonomic
Equal but Separate

Syncratic
Jointly Shared

Figure 11.1 *Types of marital power relationships.*

of work for either spouse? In a classic study, Blood and Wolfe (1960) used the responses to such questions to identify patterns of power in marriages. They found four different patterns (figure 11.1). The wife-dominant was the least frequent pattern, comprising about 3 percent of the couples. About a fourth were husband-dominant. The rest, the great majority, were relatively equalitarian in their decision making. There were two types of equalitarian marriages, however. In the "autonomic" the decision making was equal but separate. That is, each spouse had authority over certain areas. In the "syncratic" the spouses shared authority over all decisions.

The methodology of Blood and Wolfe has been criticized on a number of grounds. For one thing, they gave equal weight to all kinds of decisions. But we may question whether the decision about the weekly food budget is as significant as the question of whether and where each spouse works. Another criticism is that they didn't include many important decisions (they used only eight), for example, decisions about sexual matters and the number of children, if any, to have. A third criticism is that they interviewed only the wives in the marriages. What differences might they have found if they also had asked husbands about who made the decisions?

Finally, Blood and Wolfe (and others) have been criticized on the grounds that power involves more than simply who makes the final decisions on specific issues (Safilios-Rothschild 1970). What about the division of labor in the household? What about the way in which conflicts are handled and resolved? What about the ability to use techniques to influence the partner, such as the spouse who makes good sexual relations contingent on the other's behaving in a particular way? The point is that power issues do go beyond such things as who decides which car to buy. Power, whether in a marriage or any other social situation, is difficult to measure. For the sake of clarity, therefore, it is preferable to specify the kind of power we are measuring. In the Blood and Wolfe study, for instance, we could classify the marriages as husband-dominant in eight decision-making areas, wife-dominant in eight decision-making areas, and so forth. Their research may not have measured the full scope of power, but their findings are not trivial.

Why Is Power Important?

A student told us that he didn't believe in power in a marriage. "I wouldn't want to have any power over my wife, and I wouldn't want her to have any power over me. Power contradicts the very meaning of marriage." His ideal was of a totally equal relationship in which power is banished by mutual consent. But that overlooks the point that power is an integral part of human relationships. It also overlooks the point that to be equal does not mean to be powerless.

In fact, we need power. At a more general level, to have power, to have some sense of control over our lives is important to our mental health. People who feel helpless are likely to become depressed and be vulnerable to various kinds of physical and mental ills (McLeod 1986). Those who define themselves as having some degree of control over the circumstances of their lives, on the other hand, are better able to not only cope but to master the various crises of life (Lauer and Lauer 1988).

We also need power in marriage. As Frieze et al. (1978:318) pointed out, there are many situations in marriage where the spouses may want to influence each other:

> one partner might want the other to clean or repair something; to change a personal habit; to see a doctor; to go somewhere on an outing; to change the television channel.

There are both trivial and important areas in which husbands and wives seek to influence each other. In some cases, the influence is used for one's own benefit, in some cases for the benefit of the partner, and in some cases for the smooth functioning of the household and/or the relationship.

Thus, the use of power is inevitable in an intimate relationship. The way the power is used and the perceived balance of power in the relationship are important to marital satisfaction. Madden (1987) measured power in thirty-seven couples in two ways: according to who made final decisions and according to the extent to which each spouse had control over which tasks he or she did. She found that for both the husbands and the wives, marital satisfaction was related to perceived control over tasks. Who performed which chores around the home was not as important as having a choice. In the most satisfying relationships, the partners believed that each had relatively equal and moderately high control over tasks.

Madden raised the question of why control over decision making was not a factor in satisfaction among her couples. She suggested the possibility that equality in decision making has become the norm so that it is no longer an issue. Mashal's (1985) study is consistent with this line of reasoning. Mashal measured power in terms of decision making, but she also asked the twenty couples in her study about their ideal (that is, who *ideally* should make the decision or who the individual would *prefer* to make the decision). She found that marital satisfaction was positively related to the perception of joint authority and also to congruence between ideal and perceived actual control.

Both studies used samples too small to conclude that couples now are more likely to equally share the authority for making decisions. Still it does seem clear that how you handle power is important to your marital satisfaction. You are more likely to be satisfied with your relationship if you feel that you have some control over it, if there is equity in the use of power, and if the pattern of power accords with your ideals or preferences.

Sources of Power

Where do we get power? What would give you more power than your mate, or your mate more power than you?

Resource Theory

Resource theory was formulated by Blood and Wolfe (1960), who argued that the balance of power in a marriage will reflect the relative resources that each partner has. The power over the decision-making process, they said,

> stems primarily from the resources which the individual can provide to meet the needs of his marriage partner and to upgrade his decision-making skills (Blood and Wolfe 1960:44).

Whoever has the most resources will have the most power. For example, one important resource is money. The spouse with the highest income (which normally means the one with the most education and highest-status occupation as well) will probably have the most power in the relationship.

Because money is one of the more important resources, it is understandable that the male generally has had the most power in American family life. To the extent that the husband has been the breadwinner, or has been the main

Women's marital power tends to increase when they earn part of the family income.

contributor to the family's financial resources, he has also assumed the authority to decide how the income will be spent. Thus, Blumstein and Schwartz (1983:54) found that in a third of those marriages in which the husband earned $8,000 more than the wife, the husband was the more powerful spouse. When the spouses' income was about equal, the husband had more power in only 18 percent of the marriages. Power here refers to the authority to decide how the money shall be spent. Generally, however, the husband's power in money matters spills over into other areas as well.

The relationship between contribution to resources and power does not occur everywhere, but it may be seen in a variety of societies other than the United States. Lee and Petersen (1983) examined the power of wives and the extent to which the wives contributed to food production in 113 nonindustrial societies. They found that the greater the role of wives in food production, the more they tended to have power in the marriage.

There are, of course, important resources other than the material ones. It has been suggested, for instance, that women have often used sex to achieve a balance of power with the economically dominant men in their lives (Blumstein and Schwartz 1983:219–21). Historically, sex has been the main commodity that women could withhold or bestow in order to achieve their desires, which often went far beyond personal sexual gratification.

In addition, emotional support, budgeting skills, the ability to organize and maintain an efficient home, and parenting skills may be important resources. In other words, whatever you have that can help meet the needs of your partner is a resource in your marriage. For example, a female executive told us that she accorded her husband equal authority to make decisions in their marriage because, among other things, "he is such a good father." Although she contributed much more income than he did to the family, she valued his ability to be a good father to her children (he was the stepfather to her children from a previous marriage). His parenting skills were a resource that balanced out her greater financial contribution.

An important nonmaterial resource is a person's interest in maintaining the relationship. Waller (1951) formulated the "principle of least interest," which states that the partner who is least interested in maintaining the relationship has the most power. Consider the situation from the point of view of the one with the most interest. If you are more concerned than your spouse in keeping a marriage going, you are likely to defer to your spouse in various decisions and to strive to please your spouse in diverse matters. In other words, your spouse will have more power in the relationship than you. Even if your spouse does not intentionally exploit the situation, your behavior will be that of a less powerful person interacting with a more powerful person.

It is vital to keep in mind that resources are only resources if they meet the needs of the other. That is, to bring a large income to a marriage may or may not be an important resource. If the partner has a large income of his or her own, money may not be as important as other things. Or if the spouse who

The Intimate Couple

Table 11.1 Types of Power in Marriage

Type	Reason for compliance	Example
Coercive	Avoid punishment by spouse	Tired wife agrees to sex to avoid husband's verbal abuse
Reward	Obtain rewards from spouse	Husband becomes less messy as wife praises him for helping keep a clean house
Legitimate	Spouse has the right to ask and you have duty to comply	Husband agrees to share household tasks with working wife because he is committed to equality
Expert	Spouse has special knowledge or expertise	Wife trusts husband's judgment about cars and lets him decide which one to buy
Referent	Identify with, and admire, spouse and want to please him or her	Husband goes to opera and tries to learn more about, and enjoy, operatic music that wife loves
Informational	Persuaded by spouse that what spouse wants is in your own best interests	Wife votes Democratic even though she is a Republican because husband convinces her that women will benefit more under Democrats

From Bertram H. Raven, et al, "The Bases of Conjugal Power" in *Power in Families,* pp. 217–32. Copyright © 1975 Halstead Press, New York, NY.

earns the income, or most of the income, is abusive or lacks good communication skills or has difficulty expressing affection, the money may be insufficient to hold the marriage together. In other words, we must look at all of the resources each individual has. It is your resource profile, not a particular resource, that will determine your potential power. And it is your resource profile in the context of the needs of your partner that will determine your actual power in the relationship.

Types of Power
Raven, Centers, and Rodrigues (1975) identified six different kinds of power that people can exert in a marriage (table 11.1). Note that the six types represent differing kinds of resources that people have. In their study of 746 subjects, Raven, Centers, and Rodrigues (1975) found that the most common types of power that people perceive their spouses to exert are referent, expert, and legitimate. Women most frequently ascribed referent and expert power to their husbands. Men most frequently ascribed referent power to their wives, with legitimate power coming in a distant second. Of course, the type of power used depends on the situation. A decision about whether to visit a friend or relative is likely to be settled on the basis of legitimate or referent power. A decision about cleaning or repairing something in the home is likely to be settled by legitimate or expert power.

The type of power also varies by how satisfied the individual is with the marriage. Those in less satisfactory marriages are far more likely to ascribe coercive power to their mates than those in satisfying unions.

Marriage as a Power Struggle

A wife says to her husband, "We're going to the movies tonight." He likes to go to the movies, and is not even averse to going that night. Still he doesn't like the way she has put it. She didn't ask whether he wanted to go. She simply informed him that they were going. He responds, therefore: "Not me. You can go if you want, but I'm staying home."

What has happened in this situation illustrates **reactance theory,** which states that when someone tries to force us to engage in a behavior, even though the behavior is consistent with our attitudes, we are likely to resist and may even change our attitudes (Brehm 1966). As stated earlier, we all need to have some control over our lives. At any time, there is a limited number of areas in which we feel we have a choice. We will not take lightly to someone trying to take one of those areas of choice away from us.

Thus, this couple had the beginnings of a power struggle over the choice of how to spend a free evening. It was an unnecessary struggle in that particular case, being spurred on by an unfortunate way of stating a desire. In other cases, the struggle can be more intense. Every marriage has some power struggles. Yet some marriages are an ongoing struggle for power as long as the marriage lasts.

Types of Power Interaction

There are various ways that spouses can attempt to either exert or avoid power when communicating with each other (Fitzpatrick 1988:116–17). First, a conversation can be either *symmetrical* or *complementary*. In a symmetrical discussion, the two spouses send similar messages, messages designed to control how the relationship is defined. There are, in turn, three types of symmetrical discussions. In *competitive symmetry,* the couple is engaged in a situation of escalating conflict. For example, the husband may say: "I don't want to go out tonight. I've worked hard today." The wife responds: "You never want to go anywhere. I've worked hard, too, but you don't care how I feel about it." Each is trying to control the definition of the situation, and each is doing it in a way that escalates the conflict.

In *neutralized symmetry,* the spouses have respect for each other and each tries to avoid exerting control. The wife says: "It looks like snow tonight." The husband responds: "If we go out, we better leave early and drive slowly." Each has left the way open for the other to express feelings about going out on a snowy night before they come to a final decision.

In *submissive symmetry,* both spouses try to give control to the other. A husband may say: "How are we going to pay all of our bills this month?" The wife may respond: "Please don't get upset. What do you think we should do?" Neither wants to take control of the situation.

Unequal before the Law

Inequities in marital power may be based not only on unequal resources, but also on custom and even law. In the nineteenth century, American women had much less power than men in all realms of life, including marriage. Elizabeth Cady Stanton, a prominent feminist, wrote a letter to the *New York Tribune* in 1855 in which she pointed out some of the legal constraints faced by women:

> Now, it must strike every careful thinker that an immense difference rests in the fact that man has made the laws, cunningly and selfishly, for his own purpose. From Coke down to Kent, who can cite one clause of the marriage contract where woman has the advantage?
>
> In entering this compact, the man gives up nothing that he before possessed—he is a man still; while the legal existence of the woman is suspended during marriage, and henceforth she is known but in and through the husband. She is nameless, purseless, childless—though a woman, an heiress, and a mother.
>
> Blackstone says: "The husband and wife are one, and that one is the husband." Kent says:
>
> The legal effects of marriage are generally deducible from the principle of common law, by which the husband and wife are regarded as one person, and her legal existence and authority lost or suspended during the continuance of the matrimonial union.

> An unmarried woman can make contracts, sue and be sued, enjoy the rights or property, to her inheritance—to her wages—to her person—to her children; but in marriage, she is robbed by law of all and every natural civil right.
>
> The disability of the wife to contract, so as to bind herself, arises not from want of discretion, but because she has entered into an indissoluble connection by which she is placed under the power and protection of her husband.—Kent, vol. 2, p. 127.
>
> If the contract be equal, whence come the terms "marital power"—"marital rights"—"obedience and restraint"—"dominion and control"—"power and protection"—etc., etc.? Many cases are stated, showing the exercise of a most questionable power over the wife, sustained by the courts.
>
> The laws on Divorce are quite as unequal as those of Marriage; yes, far more so. The advantages seem to be all on one side, and the penalties on the other. In case of divorce, if the husband be the guilty party, he still retains the greater part of the property. If the wife be the guilty party, she goes out of the partnership penniless.

Source: Excerpted from Stanton's letter to the *New York Tribune*, May 30, 1855.

In *complementary interaction*, the two spouses indicate agreement that one is dominant and the other submissive. For example, a husband may say: "Why don't you return this spotted shirt? You're better at that than I am." The wife responds: "Yes, I am. I'll do it." Or a husband may say: "Let's go to the ball game tonight. I don't feel like staying home." The wife responds, "Okay," even though baseball is not her favorite sport.

As the above illustrate, people do not always try to exert power. Sometimes they deliberately refrain from it, trying to relate to the spouse as an equal. Sometimes they try to give the power to the spouse, or submit to a spouse who is exercising power. But sometimes both spouses try to take control. And in some marriages the struggle goes on more or less continuously as every issue becomes a battleground on which to test the relative power of each.

Conflict in Marriage

If a couple is engaged in a power struggle, they are, by definition, having conflict. However, even if they are not in an ongoing power struggle, they will likely have conflict. The lack of conflict is not necessarily the sign of a good marriage. In fact, marriage counselors note that many of the couples who come to them have not been fighting. Some marriages die because the partners no longer care enough about each other to even fight. A healthy marriage, then, has some degree of conflict. "Some degree" can mean anything from very seldom to frequently. Fitzpatrick (1988:76) found that couples whom she called *separates* had less companionship and sharing than others and also tried to avoid open conflict. These couples indicated less satisfaction with the marriage than more traditional couples (those with a high degree of sharing and companionship), but they were not dissatisfied. Some traditional couples also have minimal conflict. Still, "happily ever after" should not be taken to mean "we'll never fight."

The Functions of Conflict

Conflict can have both positive and negative consequences for a marriage. Few people enjoy interpersonal conflict, so it is easier for most of us to think of the negative rather than the positive consequences. The most negative, assuming that one or both partners wants to maintain the marriage, is dissolution. If the marriage is maintained, and the conflict continues at a high intensity, spouses might find their self-esteem lowered, their enthusiasm for the marriage dissipating, their differences magnified, and their energy consumed. If there are children in the home, the conflict may lead to a lowering of the children's self-esteem (Amato 1986) and to a lower quality of intimate relationships when they mature (Albers, Doane, and Mintz 1986).

Yet conflict need not have such deleterious consequences. In fact, it can have some very positive consequences. People with good conflict management skills tend to have a higher level of marital adjustment (Yelsma 1984). By handling conflict appropriately, they enhance the quality of their relationship and create a more intense sense of intimacy. Their marriage is strengthened rather than threatened by the conflict. Well-managed conflict also has a number of other positive functions:

1. Conflict brings issues out into the open. The couple that engages in good fighting (see the example in #2) will avoid an interpersonal cold war and the resentments that tend to build and corrode the relationship.

High levels of conflict can harm children.

2. Conflict helps clarify issues. Jack, a twenty-nine-year-old chemical engineer, is married to Donna, a teacher. He told us about a conflict that helped clarify an issue for them:

> We were on our way back from a ski trip. We've found that our car trips are often ideal times for marital communication. On this trip, Donna brought up the issue of cleaning up the dog's mess in the back yard. Before we got the dog, she had promised she would clean up after it. It was a job I didn't want. But now she was apparently tired of it. I told her I would only consider a change if she would offer me something in return. "Let's negotiate," I said. "If I clean it up, what will you do for me in return?" At that she got really angry. And we argued for most of the way home.
>
> Well, it turned out that she was really upset because she thought I wasn't carrying my share of the work around the house. The dog's mess allowed us to get to the heart of the matter, and we spent the last part of our trip working out an arrangement that made both of us feel better.

3. We can grow through conflict. We grow by striving, not by easing along. Handled properly, conflict will increase your awareness of the kind of person you are and can become (Coser 1956:33).

4. Small conflicts help to defuse more serious conflict. Molehills can become mountains. Ignoring small problems can lead to a buildup of resentment that will eventually explode in a more serious fight.

5. Conflict can create and maintain an equitable balance of power (Coser 1956:133). Two spouses who carry on conflict as equals, each affirming his or her own position and striving to understand the position of the other, demonstrate that each has power in the relationship. In other words, while conflict can be a manifestation of a power struggle, it can also be a means of establishing a power balance. Balanced power means a more satisfying relationship.

What People Fight About

Have you ever had an argument with someone knowing that what you supposedly were fighting about was not the real issue? For instance, we noted previously that, although Jack and Donna started arguing over who was going to clean up after the dog, they were really fighting about a larger issue: the division of labor in the home. We need to be careful in conflict, therefore, to distinguish between overt and underlying issues. Sometimes what people initially argue about is the real issue, and sometimes it isn't. Conflict can only be constructive if you learn to focus on the real issue.

What are the issues over which people fight? Blood and Wolfe (1960) found that money issues (both producing and spending income) were the major area of conflict in about a fourth of the marriages they studied. Scanzoni (1970) reported that money issues were the major focus of conflict in 38 percent of marriages. The next most frequently named area of major conflict in both studies was children (discipline, how many to have, and so forth).

Money, children, and other issues like sex continue to be major issues over which people have conflict (Scarf 1987:11). But there are countless topics that enter into marital conflict. In an effort to classify the things that people say they fight about into a small number of categories, three researchers asked fifty married and fifty cohabiting couples to describe four problems that occurred in their relationships (Cunningham, Braiker, and Kelley 1982). The spouses ranked the problems in order of their importance to their marriage and their happiness. The researchers were able to put the problems into twelve categories (figure 11.2). *Decision conflicts,* the most frequent of the categories, involves disagreement over such things as what to do, where to live, and allocation of time. *Failure to give attention/reward* includes lack of affection, too little sex, and inadequate appreciation and support. *Division and fulfillment of responsibility* refers to such matters as finances and who does which chores. *Sloppy, impulsive, or careless behavior* involves contrary standards about neatness, spending money, being punctual, and so forth. These four categories accounted for about half of the problems.

For the most part, men and women—both married and cohabiting individuals—were similar in terms of how frequently they mentioned problems in each category. However, there were a few differences. Males reported *dependence on partner, passivity* (partner is too dependent, passive, indecisive, or lacking in motivation and self-confidence) four times as frequently as females and *sloppy, impulsive or careless behavior* twice as often as females.

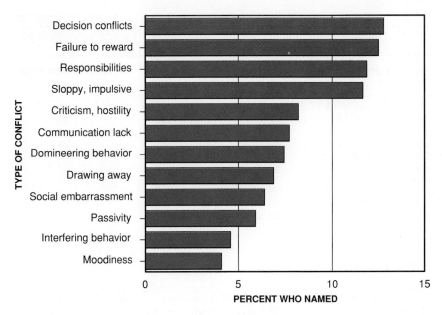

Figure 11.2 *Areas of conflict in intimate relations.*
Source: Data from Cunningham, Braiker, and Kelly 1982:421–22.

The most frequent complaint by wives was *failure to give attention/reward.*
Three times as many females (half of all the wives) as males reported such
failure as a problem.

Finally, what about couples who are in serious trouble, serious enough
to be seeing a therapist? What kinds of conflict do therapists see in marriages
they counsel? Geiss and O'Leary (1981) have answered the question on the
basis of responses from 116 professional therapists. They asked the therapists
to estimate the proportion of couples they had seen during the past year who
had complaints in each of twenty-nine areas. The results are shown in table
11.2. Communication was a problem for the bulk of the clients. The therapists
also rated communication problems as those that have the most damaging
effect on the marital relationship. After communication, the therapists said
that the ten most damaging problems are, in order of importance, unrealistic
expectations of marriage or the spouse, power struggles, serious individual
problems, role conflict, lack of loving feelings, demonstration of affection, alcoholism, extramarital affairs, and sex (Geiss and O'Leary 1981:516).

What, then, do people fight about? In general, everything and anything.
But some problems are clearly more common than others, and some are more
damaging to the relationship than others. The one problem that stands out as
of overriding importance if the marriage is to survive and be healthy is communication. Both spouses must have, or learn, good communication skills or
the conflict is likely to be destructive to the marriage.

Table 11.2	Mean Percentage of Couples Who Identified Problems in 29 Areas of Marriage (Based on Therapists' Estimates)		
Problem area	**Mean percentage of couples**	**Problem area**	**Mean percentage of couples**
Communication	84	In-laws/relatives	29
Unrealistic expectations of marriage or spouse	56	Conventionality	27
		Jealousy	26
		Employment/job	24
Demonstration of affection	55	Recreation/leisure time	24
Lack of loving feelings	55	Alcoholism	21
Sex	52	Problems related to previous marriage	20
Power struggles	52	Psychosomatic problems	20
Decision making/ problem solving	49	Friends	19
Money management/ finances	39	Addictive behavior other than alcoholism	14
Value conflicts	38	Personal habits/ appearance	14
Role conflict	38	Physical abuse	12
Children	37	Religious differences	10
Serious individual problems	35	Health problems/ physical handicap	9
Extramarital affairs	29	Incest	5
Household management	29		

Reprinted from Volume 7 Number 4 of *Journal of Marital and Family Therapy.* Copyright 1981 American Association for Marriage and Family Therapy. Reprinted by permission.

Sources of Tension

To know what people fight about is not necessarily to know why they fight. As we have pointed out, few people fight because they enjoy conflict. Rather, there are a number of sources of tension in our lives that make conflict inevitable. These sources are at various levels of social life. We are affected not only by our relationships, but also by the organizations and the social institutions in which we necessarily function (Garbarino 1982). Accordingly, we will look at social, interpersonal, and personal sources of tension.

Social Sources

Issues about money are a common battleground in marriages. Those issues become more widespread and more acute in times of economic depression. In the years following the Great Depression of 1929, economic problems led to a serious decline in marital quality among working-class and middle-class couples (Liker and Elder 1983). Men who were no longer able to find work to support their families became tense, irritable, and even explosive. In general, tension and conflict increased in families as couples tried to adjust to diminished income. We should note that the effects were not nearly so pronounced

External events, like a national depression, increase marital problems.

among those who had a strong marriage before the economic hard times. A strong marriage is a buffer against the stress of social adversity, though even in those marriages the difficult times increased the tension.

Thus, changes in the national economy can have a severe impact on marriage and family life. Financial stress increases the amount of both personal and interpersonal problems. Unemployment, for instance, can lead to mental illness, problems of physical health, depression, and violent behavior in the family, including child abuse (Ulrichson and Hira 1985). Unemployment, unfortunately, is something over which many people have little control. National recessions, depressed local economies, and such things as plant closings confront many people with short- or long-term unemployment. This is likely to mean tension and increased conflict in the marriage.

The economy also brings about adverse consequences in other ways. A high rate of inflation can add to our financial distress. Buying a first home, which is depicted in the media as a joyous event, can actually be extremely stressful (Meyer 1987). Moving to a new home is often disruptive and may create more financial stress than the couple anticipated. In some areas of the country, the price of new housing is so high that young couples despair of ever owning their own home, and some obtain a home only by going into an indebtedness that strains their relationship as well as their pocketbook.

Another social factor that creates tension in marriage is the illusions that prevail in our society. One such illusion is the notion that a marriage can be conflict-free. Whoever first coined that unfortunate phrase "happily ever after" has done a disservice to countless couples who are startled to find out that it can't be done. Starry-eyed young people who have such unrealistic expectations about marriage may find it difficult to cope with even minor disagreements with their spouses.

A second illusion is the belief that whatever problems there are, they will improve with time (Lasswell 1985). "Time heals all wounds" is another poor choice for a principle of life. In point of fact, a significant number of problems do not get better merely because of the passage of time. In a marriage, unless the spouses attend to them, minor problems can escalate into major problems rather than dissipating with time. Half of all serious marital problems arise in the first two years of marriage, but couples who come to marriage counselors have, on the average, been married for seven years.

Other illusions are the various unrealistic expectations we hold about marriage or the meaning of being a husband and a wife. The point here is that these illusions are rooted in our social context. The culture itself gives birth to these expectations through folklore, movies, books, and magazines. In that sense, our culture has not adequately prepared us for the realities of marriage.

Finally, various kinds of change in the society can combine to create tensions in the family. For example, many couples assume that their children will get a college education. Indeed, the job market seems to demand such an education. Yet the cost has soared in recent years. Yearly tuition and living expenses for a student at some private universities equals the total annual family income of a large number of Americans.

Or consider the following combination of changes. Young people are delaying marriage, and when they marry, often wind up divorced. In addition, the cost of housing has increased dramatically, and has made it difficult for young people to obtain a home of their own. The combination of these factors means that a good many adult children are living with their parents, often in less than harmonious circumstances. Also there is a tendency for marital conflict to increase between mother and father as parent-child conflict increases in such homes (Suitor and Pillemer 1987).

Thus, there are a number of sources of tension in the society that come to bear on marriages. The tensions increase the frequency of marital conflict. Sometimes we fight because we are strained by factors that are beyond our control.

Interpersonal and Personal Sources
Of course, conflict also arises from tensions within the relationship and within the individual spouses. Psychiatrist Martin Goldberg (1987) points out six areas of marital interaction that underlie much of the conflict in a marriage.

These include the areas of power and control, nurturance, intimacy and privacy, trust, fidelity, and differences in style. Goldberg says that while money, sex, child-rearing, in-laws, decisions about whether to have children, and substance abuse are the most common topics of disagreement, frequently we can understand arguments over such matters better by looking at the possible underlying causes.

First, then, there is the area of *power and control,* which is a matter of "who tells whom what to do and when." This is the area of interaction in which power struggles occur, though they are often disguised. For instance, arguments about discipline of children may reflect the struggle of two competing philosophies of child-rearing for control of the situation. It becomes more than a matter of disagreement over the appropriate way to discipline; it becomes a matter of who will have the final say in how the children are reared.

Second, there is the area of *nurturance,* which is a matter of "who takes care of whom and how." Ideally, of course, each spouse takes care of the other's needs. When that happens, there is not likely to be conflict arising from this area. But if one of the partners feels neglected, conflict is likely. Goldberg (1987) gives the example of a couple, Ron and Jill, who had a harmonious marriage for the first five years. Ron was an insurance salesman. His job was sufficiently stressful and uncertain so that he needed, and received, Jill's continuing reassurance and emotional support. Then they had a baby. Their relationship began to steadily deteriorate. Jill increasingly focused her nurturing on the baby, and Ron became increasingly hostile and discontented. He began staying out late and drinking to excess. When Jill and Ron fought about his drinking and absence from the home, what was the real issue? Clearly, it was his need for nurturance, which was no longer being fulfilled.

Third, there is the area of *intimacy and privacy,* which involves the amount of interaction versus the amount of aloneness that each partner desires. People who complain that their spouses won't give them "their space," or that their spouses tend to "smother" them, or that their spouses are detached and distant all have problems in this area of intimate interaction. If both partners have roughly the same needs for intimacy and privacy, their relationship will be harmonious in this area. If their needs are widely different, they are likely to have serious conflict. A divorced woman told us that she finally left her husband of seven years because she had to have her space:

> Phil is a loving, caring man. But I grew up in a home where we just didn't do a lot of touching and feeling. I was the only child, and I spent a lot of time by myself. I still prefer to spend hours alone. Phil couldn't handle that. And I couldn't handle his wanting to be around me all the time. Even when we were fighting about other things, like going somewhere or whether to have friends over, the real problem was the difference in how much we wanted to be together and with other people.

Trust is the fourth area of interaction that can give rise to problems. Trust is basic to a marriage. Couples can argue about many things and still have a satisfying marriage if there is a basic foundation of trust. When trust declines or is lacking, the relationship is likely to deteriorate and may sink into a series of severe arguments. If you don't trust your spouse, if you don't have a firm sense that your spouse is honest, supportive, and loyal, you will probably find yourself continually challenging your spouse on a variety of issues. When a spouse isn't trusted, then all sorts of behavior become suspect—being late, going somewhere alone, being with a friend of the opposite sex, mild criticism of your behavior, and so on. The real issue is not the behavior of the spouse, but the lack of trust. Thus, a husband says to his wife, "That color of red doesn't look very good on you." In a situation of little trust, she may translate his statement into something like: "He is criticizing me. He finds other women more attractive than he finds me. He doesn't really like me anymore."

The fifth area of interaction involves *fidelity,* which means more than sexual faithfulness: "it can be more precisely defined as general adherence to one's marital vows" (Goldberg 1987:48–49). In other words, it is faithfulness to the expectations that the spouses had for each other when they were married. That means that you can commit infidelity without ever having a sexual relationship with someone else. Goldberg provides the example of Rita and Jeff, who have been married for three turbulent years. When they were married, they wrote their wedding vows and pledged to put each other first above all other people. Each claims that the other has broken the vows. Jeff insists that Rita is spending an inordinate amount of time with her parents, who live a short distance from them. He says that she has given them priority over him. Rita, on the other hand, says that Jeff gives priorities to three of his old friends, with whom he spends a good deal of time at local bars. Neither has been sexually unfaithful to the other, but their marriage is in serious trouble in the area of fidelity.

Finally, there are *differences in style* that underlie many conflicts. Differences in style include diverse preferences for recreation and for order versus clutter. Differences in style also involve diverse ways of thinking and dealing with problems. Some people are more emotional than others. Some are more rational. Some people confront anxiety-provoking situations head on; some shrink from them and try to deny their existence. There are numerous ways in which people differ from each other that can result in conflicts (recall our earlier discussion about the importance of homogamy for a satisfying marriage). The important point for couples is to recognize when these differences in style are the actual issue rather than something else about which they are fighting.

For example, Vern and Sally, two young professionals, fought continually about leisure time. He preferred to stay home and read the paper, plan his investments, and watch television. She preferred to have dinner out and then go dancing or attend a movie. Each thought the other was being obstinate

Fighting: From "I Do" 'Til Death

We have listed the major areas of marital conflict in this section. We should point out, however, that the amount of conflict and the things that people fight about vary over the course of a marriage. A man married thirty years told us: "We have arguments from time to time. But we fought more in the first six months of our marriage than we did over the next thirty years."

How much difference is there over time in the frequency of conflict and the kinds of things that people fight about? In this project, you will attempt to answer the question. Interview six people who have been married five years or less, six who have been married fifteen to twenty years, and six who have been married thirty or more years. (You may want to work with two others, and each of you can interview six people in one of the categories.)

Prepare a questionnaire for your subjects (your instructor can help with this). Tell them that you are researching the amount and kinds of conflict in marriages. Point out that their names will not be on the questionnaire, and that you would appreciate a frank response. On the questionnaire, have them record their age, sex, and number of years married. Have them circle their response to the following:

How frequently do you and your spouse have arguments?

1. Never
2. Less than once a month
3. Once or twice a month
4. Once or twice a week
5. Daily

Then let them respond to an open-ended question: What are the issues or topics about which you and your spouse argue?

Tabulate the responses by number of years married. Are there any differences in frequency or in the kinds of things that people say they argue about? What are they? How would you explain the differences or lack of differences? Also note if there are any differences in the responses given by men and women.

If the entire class participates in this project, group all of the responses for each of the three categories (number of years married). The larger number of responses will give you more confidence in answering the above questions.

and dull. Neither thought of the problem in terms of differences in style, neither of which was inherently bad or wrong. Neither thought in terms of some compromise that would accord the other a measure of leisure satisfaction until they worked through their problem with a marriage counselor.

These six areas of interaction can be sources of tension in a marriage. When the tension erupts into conflict, the fighting will be most productive if the couple recognizes the underlying issue.

In school, we learn to be competitors, but competition between spouses can be destructive.

Styles of Conflict

How do you handle conflict? That is, do you see yourself as basically a "no-holds-barred" type of person, a conflict-avoider, a reasonable individual who will fight only if necessary, or something else? You probably have a dominant style, and you will use that style consistently in various situations of interpersonal conflict (Sternberg and Dobson 1987). Whether the conflict is with a lover, a spouse, a relative, a boss, a co-worker, or a neighbor, we tend to be consistent in our style of fighting.

Social scientists who specialize in interpersonal conflict have identified five different styles (Wilmot and Wilmot 1978). Each of us tends primarily to use one or two of them with which we feel most comfortable. The styles differ in terms of how concerned we are with our own interests versus how concerned we are about the interests of the people with whom we are fighting.

One style is *competition,* which involves a high concern for oneself and a low concern for the other. If this is your dominant style, you view conflict as a kind of war. The object is to win the fight, not to be concerned about the other person. A competitive spouse is a dominant spouse, one who has to always be ahead in the struggle for power in the marriage. If both spouses are competitive in their conflict style, the fighting may become vicious and protracted.

It is easy for Americans to enter a marriage as competitors, of course, because our culture teaches us to be competitive. We are socialized through the schools and the media to approach life as competitors. Unfortunately, it isn't the best preparation for a marriage.

Avoidance is the second style. If you are an avoider, you have little concern either for your own interests or for the interests of the other. You are mainly concerned about maintaining peace, even if the peace is a hollow or destructive one because differences are never resolved. Such peace will be hollow or destructive because the interests of the partners may be thwarted by the lack of conflict. For example, a woman who resents her husband's lack of affection may say nothing because she doesn't want to engage in an argument. She values peace highly. But she is serving neither her own interests nor those of her husband well. Instead, she is putting her marriage into jeopardy.

Third, *accommodation* is the opposite of competition. It is a neglect of one's own interests in order to pursue the interests of the other. If you are an accommodator, you may engage in the conflict, but you will always give in to your partner. Unlike the avoider, you do not shrink away from all conflict. But neither can you assert your own interests in the face of those of your partner. Ultimately, you give in because you do not want to offend or deny your partner.

Compromise involves some concern about both one's own interests and the interests of the other. "Some" concern means a moderate amount, enough to seek a solution that is satisfactory to both people but not enough to struggle for an optimal solution. If you are a compromiser, you will assert yourself in conflict, but you will moderate your position when necessary in order to reach an outcome that is acceptable to both yourself and your partner.

Finally, *collaboration* is the opposite of avoidance. It is a high degree of concern both for one's own interests and for the interests of the partner. If you are a collaborator, you will pursue your own interests vigorously while still maintaining a high degree of concern for the interests of your partner. You will not allow your partner to accommodate himself or herself to you. You will not want him or her even to compromise. You want to continue the struggle until you have an optimal solution, one that is in the best interests of each of you. As may be evident, collaboration is time- and energy-consuming. In some cases, it may not even be possible to collaborate (when one of the spouses strongly prefers to keep things as they are, so that any new arrangement will be a compromise for that spouse). Still, when it is possible, collaboration is the best way to work out conflict in marriage.

We will illustrate the styles with an example. A husband and wife both work. They have two children. For years, the husband has allowed the wife to do the cooking and to assume the major burden of responsibility for the home. He believes that this is appropriate. She resents it. How might she react? If she is an avoider, she will say nothing. She will continue to agonize inwardly and battle with her growing resentment. If she is a competitor, she probably confronted her husband early in their marriage, and insisted that he do his share of work. She may even have tried to get him to do more than would have satisfied her. If she is an accommodator, she might have stood up to him initially, but backed down when he insisted that the home was her responsibility. If she is a compromiser, she would have battled with him until they had worked out a division of labor that was acceptable to each. If she is a collaborator, she would have persisted until they not only had an acceptable division of labor, but each was convinced that the solution enhanced their individual and their interpersonal well-being.

Of course, the outcome would depend on the husband's style as well as the wife's. Some combinations, such as two competitors or two avoiders, can be disastrous for a marriage. Some combinations, such as a competitor and an accommodator, may be efficient but not necessarily conducive to maximizing the well-being of both partners. Other combinations, such as two collaborators or a collaborator and a compromiser or two compromisers, are more conducive to a stable and satisfying relationship.

We should note two things here. First, you can change your style. It is important to know what your dominant style is, how you tend to approach interpersonal conflict. But if that style does not help your relationships, you can change it. Second, each of the styles is appropriate at some time or other. There are times when a spouse who is typically, say, a compromiser, should be an accommodator (if the issue is more important to the partner). There are times when it is best to avoid certain conflicts (when one or both spouses are tired or too agitated to be reasonable). No single style is appropriate for every situation, but some are better than others as a dominant style.

Good Fighting

Androgynous and masculine spouses tend to have a more constructive approach to interpersonal conflict than do feminine or undifferentiated spouses (Yelsma and Brown 1985). However, neither your sex role nor your dominant style can prevent you from learning the principles of good fighting. In our study of long-term marriages, we discovered eight principles that couples in happy marriages use to engage in constructive conflict. Each principle is not necessarily appropriate for every conflict, but the principles comprise a set of tools that can be used to ensure that marital conflict is "good fighting" rather than destructive.

Maintain Your Perspective

There are some things not worth fighting about. "We don't treat everything as a disaster," as one husband put it. People who fight over trivial matters are probably engaging in a power struggle. Couples who have a strong relationship save their energies for the issues that are really important. This means that sometimes one spouse simply accommodates the other, or that both spouses recognize that the issue is trivial and decide to avoid it.

Learning How to Fight

Joshua was married three years ago while he was still in graduate school. He and his wife, Kay, each began their marriage with a dominant style of conflict. Both found that they had to change their style if their marriage was to survive and be mutually satisfying. Joshua talks about the way in which they discussed their styles and agreed to change:

> Kay and I had a rough way to go for awhile. She came from a large family where she learned to handle conflict primarily by avoiding it. I, on the other hand, preferred the "bull-in-the-china-shop" approach. I tended to try to control other people by rational argument, by persuasive charm, or by open hostility. I did whatever it took to win.
>
> It didn't take long for us to realize that our approaches to our differences were very destructive. But it wasn't easy to give them up. We had used them for too many years. We talked about our ways of fighting. I told her that she made me furious by not confronting our differences. I resented it when she would clam up or shut down if she felt threatened. She said that I intimidated and frustrated her by my aggressiveness. She said that sometimes she even felt rage because I was willing to "hit below the belt" if necessary to control things.
>
> We got some books and read what the experts had to say.
>
> Then we talked about whether we could change and learn how to solve our differences by listening, caring, and negotiation. That's what the books told us to do, but neither of us had tried those methods before. We started working on our differing approaches about a year ago. For me it has mainly been a matter of learning to shut up and listen, *really* listen with compassion and acceptance. I have to learn not to come at our differences like a prize fighter. For her, it has been a matter of becoming more assertive, open, and confident about verbalizing her feelings and her thoughts.
>
> It hasn't been easy. We still break the rules at times. But we're getting better at it. We are learning to fight effectively. Actually, we don't even fight as much anymore. Some of our fights were about the ways we were fighting and not about other things. Now that we're better at handling conflict, we feel a much more intense intimacy. That's something new for me. I always felt good about winning fights before. It's been a kind of a thrill to feel more intimate when we've handled an argument well together. I still feel like a winner, even if I don't get what I wanted.

Develop Tension Outlets

We noted above that there are tensions in life that can lead to marital conflict. Whether you are a student, a business person, or a homemaker, you probably have a sufficient amount of tension in your life so that you need some kind of outlet for it. Humor, exercise, meditation, and sports are some of the tension outlets that people use. You need to find something that works for you, and use it to get rid of some of the tension that otherwise can erupt into conflict in your intimate relationships.

Avoid Festering Resentment

If accommodating your partner means you have maintained your perspective on an issue that is trivial to you, the accommodation is useful. If it means that you are denying your own interests and building resentment, the accommodation is destructive. It is vital to openly confront those things that are important to you, and to resolve them. People in long-term, happy marriages do not allow their conflict to continue indefinitely on a hot- or cold-war basis.

Avoiding the buildup of resentment means that each partner must be open and honest about his or her feelings. Spouses should not have to speculate or guess about the feelings of each other. That can lead to misinterpretation and more serious conflict. For example, a man may have a grim look on his face. He has had some serious problems at work and is concerned about job security. But he says nothing. His wife tries to interpret his grimness and decides that he is angry at her for some reason. That makes her angry. He senses this and becomes even moodier, wondering why he can't have some warmth and security at home when his work is so problematic. They speak curtly and coldly with each other. Each resents what the other is doing, but neither has any understanding of what has happened.

Be Sensitive to Timing

Many conflicts that could otherwise have been handled constructively work out badly for a couple simply because they occurred at the wrong time:

> Openly confronting conflict does not necessarily mean immediate attention to an issue. Some people are receptive to problem-solving in the morning and some in the evening. Few if any people can handle conflict well when they are exhausted. In addition, there are times when it is simply inappropriate to raise an issue. The wife who criticizes her husband's appearance just as they are walking into a party, or the husband who angrily tells his wife in front of friends that she neglects his needs both illustrate insensitivity to timing (Lauer and Lauer 1986:125).

Another time at which it is usually best to avoid conflict is when one of the spouses is extremely angry. Conflict can only be constructive to the relationship when both people can function rationally as well as emotionally.

Communicate without Ceasing

While communication is not a cure-all, it is important not to handle conflict with the silent treatment or by simply hoping that everything will turn out well with the passage of time. It is, however, the quality of communication that occurs and not simply the fact of communication. Recall from the last chapter that listening is a crucial part of effective communication. In conflict, we are particularly prone to want to make our own point rather than to listen carefully to what the other is saying.

In addition, the communication must have a certain calmness to it. Again, the spouse who is extremely angry is not likely to function well in conflict.

Extreme anger can result in verbal aggression, in saying things that one will later regret and that reflect the anger of the moment rather than fundamental feelings. Nearly every one of the three hundred happily married couples in our long-term marriage project advised against arguing when one or both of the spouses is very angry. As one wife of thirty-three years said: "Find something to do until you are both calm, and then talk things out."

Be Flexible, Willing to Compromise

People who are happily married for many years believe in the importance of both accommodation and compromise in conflict. Give in when the issue does not matter that much to you and prepare to compromise when the issue is important to you. Collaboration is desirable, but not always practical. Compromise, therefore, is not a surrender and not an acceptance of an inferior solution. Rather, compromise may frequently be the only realistic way to handle differences between two people, each of whom understands both his or her own needs and interests and those of the spouse.

Use Conflict to Attack Problems, Not Your Spouse

This is one of the most important principles. It stresses the fact that a couple needs to approach conflict as a problem-solving rather than a spouse-bashing exercise. If you are very angry or frustrated, you may tend to attack your spouse as the cause of your agony. Your energies will better serve your relationship if they are directed toward the problem. Define the conflict as a disagreement, as a problem that must be solved together, rather than as a battle of personalities. As a husband put it: "We always have good outcomes from our arguments if we remember one simple rule. Namely, that we each must approach our disagreement by saying to the other, 'We have a problem,' rather than 'You are a problem.' "

Keep Loving While You Are Fighting

Marital therapists point out that at times spouses are going to fight unfairly. Exaggerated positions, extreme statements, and some "low blows" are likely to occur at times in any relationship. Nevertheless, the couples in our study insisted that the goal is to keep loving while you are fighting. Loving and fighting may sound like incompatible activities. But two things should be kept in mind. First, in line with the last principle, good fighting involves an attack on a problem rather than on the spouse. And second, the love we are talking about here is agapic love, acting out of concern for the well-being of the other independently of our feelings at the moment. Thus, when you refuse to hurt your partner during conflict (by, e.g., not throwing out cutting remarks that you know will injure him or her), you are continuing to love. To keep the conflict within the bounds of reason, to avoid attacking the spouse, to, as one wife put it, keep in mind the things you like about your spouse even while you are fighting, are some of the ways that you can continue to love during conflict.

PRINCIPLES FOR ENHANCING INTIMACY

1. Individuals need power; that is, each of us needs some degree of control over our lives. Moreover, this need for power extends into our marriages. There are situations—some critical, others less so—when we need to influence or wield power over our spouse. Power, of course, can be abused. We unfortunately may attempt to dominate or totally control our mate. In a satisfying marriage, however, each spouse has power and shares it on a generally equal basis.

2. Power struggles and conflict in a marriage are not necessarily destructive. In fact, they can be an indication of a healthy and vital relationship and should be treated as such. When a conflict arises, it should be viewed as a shared problem that needs a solution, and not as a sign that the relationship is doomed.

3. In order to deal positively with a conflict in marriage, it is essential to identify the true source of the difficulty. If, for example, the problem concerns financial arrangements, then you need to focus on money matters not on extraneous factors, like blaming your in-laws for overindulging your spouse or complaining about the tax policies of the federal government. Instead, examine your spending patterns: Are you overextending yourselves financially? Are you trying to buy too large of a house or too expensive of a car too quickly? Are you buying too much on credit? Concentrating on the real nature of your conflict takes insight, determination, and courage. But it is essential to a meaningful resolution of your problems.

4. Effective handling of conflict takes patience and persistence. However, you can build your skills by consulting the experts—books and articles written by professionals in marriage and the family, marriage enrichment seminars, as well as mature and successful couples. Learn the secrets of "good fighting" from them and then consistently apply them in your marriage.

5. People deal with conflict in different ways. In order to deal constructively with problems and power struggles, it is important for you to understand your own as well as your mate's style of handling conflict. You may find that it is essential for you to accommodate, to some extent, your style to that of your mate if solutions are to be found.

Power is the ability to get someone to think or feel or act in a way that he or she would not have done spontaneously. The use of power is not inherently negative or wrong. It can be used to help as well as to control others. Marital power has typically been measured on the basis of which spouse makes the final decisions. Power is important to both our personal and our marital well-being.

Resource theory asserts that we get power from the resources we bring to a relationship, including income, emotional support, sexual availability, and parenting skills. The principle of least interest says that the partner with the least interest in maintaining the relationship has the most power. Six types of power can be used in marriage: coercive, reward, legitimate, expert, referent, and informational.

Marriage may be analyzed as a power struggle. Spouses attempt to exert or avoid power when communicating with each other. In a symmetrical discussion, the two spouses send similar messages that are designed to control how the relationship is defined. In complementary discussion, the two spouses indicate agreement that one is dominant and the other is submissive.

Like power, conflict can have both positive and negative consequences for a marriage. Among the positive results are issues are brought into the open and clarified, people may grow through conflict, small conflicts diffuse more serious conflict, and conflict can create and maintain an equitable balance of power.

Money, children, and other issues like sex continue to be major issues over which people have conflict. Therapists report that troubled couples who come to them are most likely to have problems in the areas of communication, unrealistic expectations, showing and feeling love and affection, sex, and power struggles.

There are a number of sources of tension that make marital conflict inevitable. Social sources include the vagaries of the economy, cultural illusions about marriage, and various kinds of social change. Interpersonal and personal sources include such things as issues of power and control, nurturance, intimacy and privacy, trust, fidelity, and differences in style.

Common styles of conflict include competition, avoidance, accommodation, compromise, and collaboration. "Good" fighting occurs when a couple follows certain principles, such as maintaining perspective, developing tension outlets, avoiding festering resentment, being sensitive to timing, continuing to communicate, being willing to compromise, using conflict to attack problems rather than the spouse, and continuing to love the spouse even while fighting.

12

Work and Home

In the 1950s, "I Love Lucy" was one of the most popular television shows. A mother who grew up watching and enjoying the show told us: "I won't let my children watch the reruns. I was stunned when I realized how sexist the show was." One of the sexist aspects that angered the woman was the fact that Lucy always wanted to work outside the home, but her husband wouldn't allow it. A decade or so later, the "Bob Newhart Show" was one of the most popular. He was a psychologist and his wife, Emily, was a teacher. They had a two-career marriage. By this time, increasing numbers of women, including wives on television, were working outside the home.

These two shows dramatize the change in attitudes and behavior about work that have occurred in American society. In this chapter, we will look at those changes. We will discuss why women have entered the labor force in large numbers and the impact that employed wives and mothers have on individual and family well-being.

Increasingly, women plan for careers as well as marriage.

His Work and Her Work

Throughout most of human history the great majority of people lived on farms or in peasant villages. As historian Carl Degler (1980:5) has pointed out, for nearly everyone

> the family was a cooperative economic unit, with children and mother working along with husband, even though usually there was a division of labor by gender. . . . Even those relatively few families which lived and worked in towns acted as cooperative enterprises in their shops, inns, and other businesses. Home and work were close together, and wife and husband participated in both.

This situation changed rapidly and dramatically with the rise of industrialization.

Industrialization meant that some of the things women did in the home, such as making clothes, would increasingly take place in the factory or shop. Women did continue, of course, to cook and clean and nurture their families. But in the emerging industrial economy, paid labor became a primary source of income and the essence of the meaning of *work*. What women did in the home was no longer defined as *work*.

The role of housewife developed in this context. It is a role that can be described in terms of four characteristics (Oakley 1974). First, it is allocated almost exclusively to women. Second, it is associated with economic dependence, because the housewife must lean on her husband for support. Third, it is defined generally as *nonwork*, or at least as not *real* work. This is illustrated by the response often given by housewives to the question, "Do you work?" The answer is, "No, I'm just a housewife." Finally, the role is given priority by women over other roles. Housework and childcare is considered the primary responsibility of the housewife, a responsibility that must take priority over anything else that a woman might wish to do (such as outside employment or a career). Around 1900, if a married woman was employed people thought that something was wrong. "Her husband was absent, crippled, or incompetent" (Degler 1980:386).

Since the rise of industrialization, then, there has been a tendency for "his" work to be paid labor outside the home and "her" work to be that of the housewife. "Her" work has a number of drawbacks that "his" work may not have. The housewife is relatively isolated in her work, and frequently has to cope with the problem of loneliness. If she has children, she may not be lonely, but she feels keenly the need for adult interaction. Housework also tends to be repetitive, boring, and endless.

This is not to say that housewives all loathe what they do. Many women who have spent the bulk of their lives as housewives indicate great satisfaction. But clearly a great number of women have not found the role to be adequate to their needs. As we shall see in the next section, over the past few decades women have been opting for employment or career roles in great numbers.

Table 12.1   The Female Labor Force: 1940–1988
(Persons 14 years old and over through 1965; 16 years old
and older thereafter)

Year	Number (per 1,000)	Percent of female population
1940	13,840	27.4
1944	18,449	35.0
1950	17,795	31.4
1955	20,154	33.5
1960	22,516	34.8
1965	25,952	36.7
1970	31,233	42.6
1975	36,981	46.0
1980	44,934	51.1
1985	50,891	54.5
1988	53,987	55.9

Source: U.S. Bureau of the Census 1989:385.

Changing Patterns of Working

Earlier in our history, some people argued that "his" work and "her" work reflected human nature. That is, they believed that men are programmed for work outside the home and women are programmed for being housewives. Yet the forces that kept most women in the home in the past were social and cultural, not biological. In recent decades, the situation has changed dramatically.

Women in the Labor Force

At the turn of the century, only about one out of five adult women were in the labor force. By 1940, the rate was still less than a third of the female population. The rate increased during World War II, then fell again after the war was over. In the 1960s and 1970s, however, the proportion of women going into the labor force increased rapidly (table 12.1). Over half of women aged sixteen and above are now in the labor force. We should note that working- and lower-class women have always been more likely than middle-class women to be in the labor force. For example, the famous "Middletown" study found that almost half of working-class wives were employed full-time during the early 1920s (Caplow, Bahr, Chadwick, Hill, and Williamson 1982:97).

It is important to keep in mind that the labor force includes part-time and full-time workers and also those who are unemployed but looking for work. Interestingly, while the participation of women has been steadily going up, that of men has been steadily going down (figure 12.1). We are not sure of the reasons for this, but the figure suggests a trend toward convergence of rates. At some point in the future, the labor force may be equally divided between men and women.

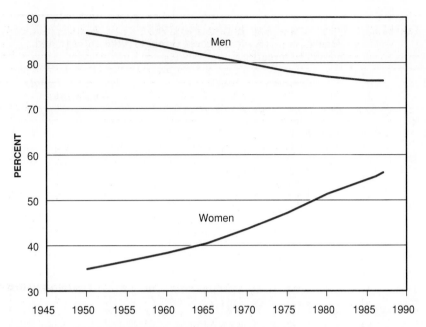

Figure 12.1 *Civilian labor force participation rates, by sex.*
Source: U.S. Bureau of the Census 1989:376.

Married Women and Employment

The figures in table 12.1 are for all women, whether single, married, sepa-rated, divorced, or widowed. Moreover, some of the women are in jobs and some are pursuing careers. These are important distinctions that need to be addressed.

Marital and Family Status of Employed Women

Table 12.2 shows the labor-force participation rates for women with varying marital and family statuses. Note that the most dramatic increase in partic-ipation rates has occurred among married women with children under the age of six. There are well over 10 million children, less than six years old, whose mothers work. In fact, over half of mothers with children under one year of age are now in the labor force.

Clearly, women are opting for worker as well as housewife roles. Again, we need to keep in mind that there are substantial numbers of married women who are not in the labor force. While a slight majority of women with infants prefer to work, a considerable number prefer to stay home and care for their children themselves. The important point is that women have options, and many of them are opting for different roles than those of their mothers and grand-mothers.

The Intimate Couple

Table 12.2 Marital and Family Status and Labor Force Participation of Women: 1960–1988 (For women 14 years and older in 1960; thereafter, 16 years and older)

Item	Total			No children under 18			Children 6–17 only			Children under 6		
	Married[1]	Separated	Divorced	Married[1]	Separated	Divorced	Married[1]	Separated	Divorced	Married[1]	Separated	Divorced
In labor force (mil.)												
1960	12.3	(NA)	(NA)	5.7	(NA)	(NA)	4.1	(NA)	(NA)	2.5	(NA)	(NA)
1970	18.4	1.4	1.9	8.2	.7	1.1	6.3	.4	.6	3.9	.3	.3
1980	24.9	1.9	4.4	11.2	.9	2.3	8.4	.6	1.6	5.2	.4	.5
1982	25.8	2.1	5.2	11.8	1.0	2.7	8.3	.7	1.8	5.7	.5	.6
1983	26.2	1.9	5.2	12.1	.8	2.8	8.3	.6	1.8	5.9	.5	.6
1984	26.9	2.0	5.5	12.3	.9	3.0	8.3	.7	1.9	6.2	.4	.6
1985	27.7	2.0	5.9	12.8	1.0	3.3	8.5	.7	2.0	6.4	.4	.6
1986	28.2	2.1	6.2	12.9	1.0	3.5	8.8	.6	2.0	6.6	.5	.7
1987	29.2	2.1	6.1	13.2	1.0	3.4	9.0	.7	2.0	7.0	.4	.7
1988	29.8	2.2	6.2	13.5	1.1	3.7	9.3	.7	1.9	7.0	.4	.6
Participation rate[2]												
1960	30.5	(NA)	(NA)	34.7	(NA)	(NA)	39.0	(NA)	(NA)	18.6	(NA)	(NA)
1970	40.8	52.1	71.5	42.2	52.3	67.7	49.2	60.6	82.4	30.3	45.4	63.3
1980	50.1	59.4	74.5	46.0	58.9	71.4	61.7	66.3	82.3	45.1	52.2	68.3
1982	51.2	60.0	74.9	46.2	57.5	71.6	63.2	68.4	83.6	48.7	55.2	67.2
1983	51.8	58.7	74.6	46.6	55.6	71.7	63.8	68.7	82.2	49.9	53.8	66.7
1984	52.8	60.9	74.3	47.2	59.1	70.5	65.4	70.1	84.1	51.8	53.9	67.7
1985	54.2	61.3	75.0	48.2	60.0	72.1	67.8	70.9	83.4	53.4	53.2	67.5
1986	54.6	62.2	76.0	48.2	60.4	72.1	68.4	70.6	84.7	53.8	57.4	73.8
1987	55.8	61.4	75.4	48.4	57.9	71.9	70.6	72.6	84.5	56.8	55.1	70.5
1988	56.5	60.9	75.7	48.9	60.1	73.0	72.5	69.3	83.9	57.1	53.0	70.1

NA Not available [1]Husband present [2]Percent of women in each specific category in the labor force
Source: U.S. Bureau of the Census 1989:386.

Jobs and Careers

Some women who work have a job. Others are in a career. We can distinguish between jobs and careers in a number of ways. Careers normally require extensive training—a college education or even graduate school. Careers tend to be more structured in that there is a pattern of mobility people tend to follow. In the university, for instance, you may begin as an instructor and gradually move up to the position of full professor. Moving up through the ranks is a common pattern in education, business, government, and social service agencies. Careers may also be pursued by individuals such as therapists. In that case, mobility may involve moving from being an assistant, to another therapist, to one's own practice, to the head of one's own clinic. Finally, a career involves commitment. You can frequently take or leave a particular job, but if you are in a career you probably have a commitment to go as far as you can. You want to get to the top of your field, or as close to the top as possible.

The distinction between job and career leads to the important distinction between a **dual-earner** and **dual-career** family. The dual-earner family is one in which both spouses are involved in paid work, and one or both view the work only as a job. In other words, one of the spouses in the dual-earner family may be pursuing a career, while the other is merely holding down a job. In the dual-career family, on the other hand, both spouses are engaged in careers, which means that both are committed to employment that has a long-term pattern of mobility.

The dual-career family is a type of dual-earner family. In the dual-career family, there is no assumption that either spouse will subordinate his or her career to the interests of the other, and both are committed to combining professional and family roles. As may be clear already, such a family places a lot of demands on the spouses and has a great deal of potential for conflict and stress (see "Problems of Dual-Career Families" later in this chapter). Unfortunately, we do not know how many of the women who work outside the home are holding jobs and how many are involved in a career. In either case, however, there is a problem over who will do the "family work," the housekeeping and childcare that formerly was the work of the housewife.

Who's Minding the House?

With a declining proportion of men in the labor force, a growing emphasis on egalitarian marriages, and an increasing number of women working outside the home and contributing to the support of the family, you might expect that there is a greater sharing by men and women of the family work. Yet the evidence suggests that progress in sharing has been less than many hoped for.

The evidence is based on national surveys of how people use their time. The surveys show change toward sharing, but nothing like equality (Robinson 1988). According to the surveys, in 1985 women spent about two hours working at home for every hour spent by men. In 1975 women reported spending three hours for every hour spent by men and in 1965 they reported six hours for every hour spent by men.

In terms of total hours, in 1985 men averaged 9.8 hours of housework weekly and women averaged 19.5 hours. Moreover, there was still a tendency for men and women to engage in traditional kinds of tasks. Women were most likely to do the cooking, washing of dishes, housecleaning, laundry, and ironing. Men were most likely to do household repairs and outdoor chores. Pet care, gardening, and bill paying tended to be shared. The net result is that employed women come home to a "second shift" (Hochschild 1989). Over a year's time, an employed woman may work the equivalent of a month of twenty-four-hour days more than her employed husband.

What change has occurred is not all due to people's commitment to equality. One reason for the change is the decline in the number of children in households, and in the number of households that have children. Children result in more cooking and cleaning chores, and most of those chores are still done by the mother.

There are a number of factors that affect the extent to which the husband will share in family work. Catherine Ross (1987) used data from a national sample to investigate the division of labor in homes. She found that when the wife is employed, the husband tends to increase his share of household work. The more educated the husband, and the more nontraditional his sex-role beliefs, the more likely he is to increase his share. Husbands also share if the difference between their income and that of their wives is small. Nevertheless, overall, three-fourths of wives who work full-time still do the most of the housework.

Why Do Women Want to Work Outside the Home?

The woman who opts for an outside job or career faces the prospect of a good deal less leisure time. She is likely to get some additional help from her husband, but not enough to make their total work load equitable. What, then, is the motivation for women to work?

To begin with, we should note that there are many women that work outside of the home who would prefer not to and many who are not employed who would prefer to do so. Blumstein and Schwartz (1983:118) found that 39 percent of wives and 31 percent of husbands believed that both spouses should work outside the home. Among couples who disagreed, there were more wives who wanted to work than husbands who were willing for them to work. On the other hand, a women's magazine surveyed fifty thousand of its readers and reported that 45.1 percent of women who were employed thirty-five to forty hours a week and 67.6 percent of all the respondents said that they would quit their jobs and stay home with their children if that were possible (Jacoby 1987:14). "If that were possible" suggests that at least some employed women feel financially constrained to continue working outside the home. A national survey by the Roper Organization reported that 57 percent of employed women said that they would have a hard time economically if they did not work.[1]

One motivation, then, is economic. Many women are employed in order to maintain a standard of living that they believe is otherwise not possible for them and their families. Whether the woman has a job or a career, she is likely to be more committed to the work to the extent that she perceives her income as necessary for her family's financial security (Steffy and Jones 1988).

However women, like men, work for a variety of reasons. College-educated women, as well as women who are getting a college education, are likely to desire high-status, professional careers because they define such careers as fulfilling (Regan and Roland 1985). But even those who do not opt for careers may define employment as essential to their personal fulfillment. Some women do not like housework and/or feel that they have abilities that can only be fully used in some kind of work outside the home. Others desire social contacts and stimulation that they can find in employment outside the home. With the likelihood of having fewer children, more education, and a wider range of opportunities than existed in the past, wives will increasingly look to the labor force as a source of their satisfaction.

Still another reason to work is the power gained. We have noted before that power is an important resource to all of us. We each need to feel that we have some control over the circumstances of our lives. Women may work in order to get their own income and thus increase their sense of power. That increased power may make their marriage a more equitable one. It may give a woman a sense of security in case her marriage fails or her husband dies.

Finally, what about the effects of employment on marital and family relations? We will explore these in more detail, but here we want to note that employed women generally do not believe that their marriages or families suffer. In the Roper survey previously mentioned, 49 percent of the women said that they believed they are more interesting persons to their husbands because of their work. Forty-one percent said that they feel they give as much to their children as nonemployed mothers because of the way they spend time with them. Only 15 percent said they would be a better mother and 10 percent said they would be a better wife if they did not work.

Dual-Career Families

There are more dual-earner families in America than single-earner families. We do not know how many of the dual-earner families are dual-career, but the number is undoubtedly substantial and growing. If you complete your college degree, or go on for graduate work, you have a good chance of being a part of a dual-career family. It is important to know the nature of such a family, the problems peculiar to it, and some of the satisfactions that can be gained through it.

More or Less Equal?

We have seen repeatedly that equity is a crucial part of a satisfying, intimate relationship. By definition, it would seem that the dual-career family is an equitable relationship. The assumption underlying such an arrangement is that each spouse will be committed both to a career and to the family. Neither spouse will subordinate his or her career to that of the partner. The implication is that because the spouses are equal in their dual commitments, they must take equal responsibility for family work in order for the arrangement to be viable.

In practice, dual-career families tend to fall somewhat short of equality. Hertz (1986) argued that they are at least more equal than other kinds of families. She pointed out two areas in which there is greater equality. First, they tend to be equal partners in the marriage, sharing decision-making power to a greater extent than do couples in more traditional marriages. Second, the wives are more equal because they have the option to pursue a career as well as bear and rear children.

Still, there tends to be something less than full equality in dual-career marriages. Data from a national sample showed that while dual-career wives engage in significantly fewer hours of housework than do full-time housewives,

Woman's Commitment to Work

Dr. John Cowan, whose views on love we quoted in chapter 4, said many things about male-female relationships that people today would consider archaic and even outrageous. But he was ahead of his time in advocating women's rights to vote, to own, possess, and manage property, and to work. He quotes from a letter by Florence Nightingale, the famous nineteenth-century nurse, who advised women to commit themselves fully to whatever work they undertook:

1. But I would also say to all young ladies who are called to any particular vocation, qualify yourselves for it as a man does for his work. Don't think you can undertake it otherwise. No one should attempt to teach the Greek language until he is master of the language; and this he can become only by hard study. And,

2. If you are called to man's work, do not exact a woman's privileges—the privilege of inaccuracy, of weakness, ye muddleheads. Submit yourselves to the rules of business as men do, by which alone you can make God's business succeed; for He has never said that He will give His success and His blessing to inefficiency—to sketching and unfinished work.

3. It has happened to me more than once to be told by women: 'Yes, but you had personal freedom.' Nothing can well be further from the truth. I question whether God has ever brought any one through more difficulties and contradictions than I have had.

4. But to women I would say, look upon your work, whether it be an accustomed or an unaccustomed work, as upon a trust confided to you. This will keep you alike from discouragement and from presumption, from idleness and from overtaxing yourself.

Dr. Cowan then gives his opinion about the effects on women who follow Nightingale's advice to dedicate themselves to their work:

As far as women become self-supporting, they will be emancipated from the bondage of dependence, and be more free in respect to marriage. This relation will not be entered upon to secure a support, as is so often done now, but more from the promptings of affection. The home will not be less sacred and hallowed, but will rest on a more secure basis.

Source: John Cowan, M.D., *The Science of a New Life* (New York: J. S. Ogilvie Publishers, 1869), pp. 384–85.

they do not differ from wives who have jobs rather than careers (Berardo, Shehan, and Leslie 1987). Moreover, the dual-career husbands do not spend more hours each week in housework than do career men who are married to housewives. In terms of family work, then, the evidence suggests that the dual-career family still places the greatest burden on the woman.

There may also be something less than equality in terms of whose career takes priority. Theoretically, neither career has priority over the other. In the past, the wife generally subordinated her work to that of her husband. If he had an offer in another city, or had to move to another location to advance his career, she would move with him even if it meant losing her job or retarding her career. In the dual-career marriage, any move should be by consensus, and ideally should not impede either career.

While they did not ask only those in dual-career marriages, two national public opinion polls raised questions about equality in the area of career priorities.[2] In one poll, people were asked to respond to the idea that it is more important for a wife to support her husband's career than to have a career herself. About a third of all respondents agreed, and even a fourth of college graduates agreed. In the second poll, people were asked about a situation in which both husband and wife work and the husband is offered a job in another city. Assuming that the couple has no children, what should they do? Seventy-two percent of the women and 62 percent of the men said that the wife should quit her job, relocate, and try to find a job in the new place. When the question was turned around, with the wife being offered the job in another city, however, 55 percent of the women and 58 percent of the men said that the wife should turn down the offer so that the husband could continue with his job.

Types of Dual-Career Families

While all dual-career families by definition involve a twofold commitment, there are variations in the way that the spouses handle their work and family roles. Moreover, there are differing structural arrangements, perhaps the most radical of which is the commuter marriage.

Three Types of Marital Roles

In her study of men in dual-career families, Gilbert (1985) identified three different types of arrangements: the traditional, the participant, and the role-sharing. In the *traditional* dual-career family, the wife simply adds a new role—that of a career woman. She continues to be responsible for the family work. The problems of coordination and time that emerge are problems that she must resolve. This arrangement, of course, violates the principle of equity that underlies the idea of two careers. Nevertheless, it is one pattern that some couples have adopted.

In the *participant* dual-career family, the husband assumes some of the responsibilities of childcare. Husband and wife may even share equally the parenting of the children. But the wife still retains the responsibility for housework. As suggested by the studies on time use, this type is fairly common.

Finally, in the *role-sharing* dual-career family, both spouses are actively involved in family work, both childcare and household tasks. The role-sharing family implements the principle of equity. The spouses share family power and responsibilities equally as each pursues a meaningful career.

Which of the three patterns is adopted by any particular couple depends on a variety of personal, interpersonal, and social factors. For example, a personal factor may be the attitudes and values of the spouses. If their values are

are still somewhat traditional, the couple may feel most comfortable with a participant family. An interpersonal factor could be the balance of power in the relationship. If the male has been dominant, he may insist on something less than role-sharing in order to accept his wife's career. She may accede because she has become habituated to his dominance in important decisions. Finally, such things as occupational demands and structures as well as social support systems are examples of social factors. One of the partners may have less flexibility than the other. The wife may be a lawyer and be unable to pursue her career fully without role-sharing. Or the parents of the couple may exert pressure one way or another.

In other words, the type of family arrangement that the couple works out reflects more than their preference. A host of factors come to bear on them as they seek to cope with the difficult task of maintaining two careers and a family. The roles they finally work out may or may not be in accord with their preference, but they may perceive the arrangement as the only one that is viable for them. For example, a university professor who is married to an attorney told us:

> My husband spends many more hours at his office than I do at mine. We didn't have our degrees when we were first married. I knew that he would have long hours as an attorney, but I didn't realize that I would wind up doing more than my share of housework. But I have come to terms with that. I know that if he was the professor and I was the attorney, he would do most of the housework. That's just the way it is.

Commuter Marriages

The **commuter marriage** is a dual-career marriage in which the spouses live in different locations. In spite of the distance between them, they still maintain their dual commitment to work and to family. And they may not consider this just a temporary arrangement. Rather, they willingly spend thousands of dollars a year commuting back and forth to be together on weekends and holidays. They may also telephone each other every day or every other day (Gerstel and Gross 1984:56).

In other words, the spouses in a commuter marriage retain their commitment to each other and to their individual careers in spite of the immense difficulties and inconvenience. They do not prefer to live apart, but they don't want to give up either their careers or each other.

Commuter marriages work better when there are no children involved. However, even without children, the couple faces some unique problems. One is the problem of intimacy. How do you fulfill your need for intimacy when you are with your spouse less than half the time? Moreover, according to Gerstel and Gross, some wives in commuter marriages report that each time they are together again with their husbands they need some time in order to reestablish the sense of intimacy.

Spouses in a commuter marriage invest a great deal of time and money in travel in order to keep the marriage going.

The daily or every-other-day telephoning is one way that some couples try to deal with the intimacy problem. Others note that the time spent together is better because of the separation. There may be less arguing because the spouses feel that they must make the best of their shared time. There may also be more effort put into the quality of the relationship. As one woman said, the periods of separation enhance the romance in her marriage (Gerstel and Gross 1984:76). Although she is exhausted when she arrives home (and there are tears when they part), her husband greets her with wine or flowers or perfume and he draws her bath. He makes her feel special.

For some people, then, the commuter marriage appears to work. We don't have evidence about the long-term consequences of such marriages. Can they survive decades of separation? If they do, what kind of relationship will the couple have when one or both retire? How will they adjust to living together all the time?

Problems of Dual-Career Families

We have already seen some of the problems of the dual-career family—equity, working out the marital roles, and the special problems of those in a commuter marriage. We will note a variety of other troublesome areas below when we discuss the problems of the dual-earner family generally. Here we want to look at a number of specific difficulties that are somewhat unusual because of the commitment of both spouses to a career.

Time Management

One of the common complaints of those in dual-career marriages is the lack of time. There is insufficient time for each spouse to be alone and also insufficient time for them to be together as a couple. The problem is intensified if the couple has children and if one or both have high need for achievement in their career (Rice 1979:55).

Careful planning and cooperation by all family members is important in order to minimize conflicts over time. Some couples resolve the problem by following detailed schedules. Others try to depend on the good will and good sense of each member of the family, hoping that all of the demands of work and home will be met without the rigid structuring of time. The latter may not succeed. Rice (1979:58) told of one couple that tried to operate without a schedule. The wife said, "We just see what needs doing and do it." But increasingly things were not being done around the home. Finally, the couple was forced to sit down and write up a schedule, including such details as a half-hour a day for them to be together without the children.

Children

An initial issue is whether to have children because the "presence of children in a dual-career family vastly affects the complexity and viability of this lifestyle" (Gilbert and Rachlin 1987:19). If the couple opts for children, then they face the question of who will care for them. They probably have the resources to hire outsiders. But because of their own values and attitudes, and those of their parents and siblings, they may feel pressure to care for the children themselves and even to revert back to more traditional roles. Couples who have worked out an acceptable arrangement before children face new difficulties once a baby enters the home.

Which parent will be the primary caregiver? Traditionally, that is the responsibility of the mother, and she is still largely responsible even among dual-career families. Maternity leaves and more flexible schedules for mothers tend to reinforce that traditional responsibility. Indeed, if a couple decided to share equally in the task, they would encounter difficulties and even resistance from others. For example, if a father decided to take time off in order to stay home and care for his infant, it would be "like he has lace on his jockey shorts. You don't do that in America" (Gilbert and Rachlin 1987:20). In addition, such a practice is made more difficult by the fact that paternity leave is not generally a fringe benefit.

Social pressures and practices thus work against an equal sharing of child-rearing. This may be one reason that there are fewer children on the average in dual-career than in more traditional marriages. There is also a tendency in dual-career families for the spouses to postpone childbearing until they have established themselves in their careers.

When the children reach school age, problems of childcare are lessened somewhat but not eliminated. Who will stay at home on the days when there is no school? Who will respond if the school calls and says that the child is sick? Again, the burden is likely to fall on the mother. The woman, therefore, is likely to make more career adjustments and sacrifices than the man.

Relationships with Other People

Dual-career couples may deal with time constraints by limiting their activity with other people. They are likely to engage in leisure and social activities primarily or exclusively with other dual-career people, particularly with those with whom they work. Interacting with colleagues, however, means that the couple runs the risk of overinvestment in career and too little investment in the marital relationship. David Rice (1979:61), a psychiatrist, pointed out that "the greatest problem encountered in the social relationship area relates to the natural forming of close relationships with one's colleagues and resultant spouse jealousy."

Rice (1979:62–63) related the case of Alice and Jeff, who had married while both were in graduate school. They came to a therapist when they were in their late thirties. They were both active in their careers at that time and had two children. Jeff had formed a close relationship with a female colleague who was having problems in her marriage. Jeff and the colleague acknowledged their feelings for each other, but decided to just be friends. Jeff, however, felt guilty and talked about the matter with Alice. She seemed to accept the situation easily, particularly because it had not become a sexual relationship. But because her intimacy needs were not being met by Jeff, Alice also became involved in a close friendship with a colleague, a man with whom she worked on several projects. Jeff, like Alice, was able to accept her feelings.

Unfortunately, Jeff and Alice had lost their sense of intimacy with each other. Each had entered an intimate, though nonsexual, relationship at work. With the demands of their careers being heavy, and some basic intimacy needs being met by colleagues, their own relationship deteriorated. Dual-career couples have a more severe challenge than others in the area of maintaining their intimate relationship with each other.

The Dual-Career Wife

The wife in a dual-career family, as we have noted, has more problems than the husband. She is more likely than he to bear the brunt of the conflicts between work, spouse, and children. She may try to cope with the conflicts in a number of ways that are not healthy for her. For one, she may engage in role expansion, agreeing to a traditional dual-career arrangement. That is, she tries to become the "superwoman," the woman who is the perfect mother, the best homemaker, the ideal wife, and the high-achieving career woman.

Whether employed outside the home or not, women still assume the major responsibility for housework.

The woman who tries to "have it all" may be driven in part by guilt or by a sense of responsibility for the welfare of her family. In any case, she is likely to fall victim to various consequences of stress: depression, anxiety, irritability, and problems with eating and sleeping. One such woman, Margaret, has an administrative position in health services. She seems to have it all—the career and the family. But one day she told us: "I never thought I'd be saying this. But I'd like to chuck it all—my work, my kids, even my husband. I'm tired. My most prevalent fantasy is to have my own apartment with only myself to take care of." Margaret has reached a point of exhaustion.

Unfortunately, in many cases, husbands expect wives to be "superwomen." Men may support equality in principle, but in practice they still tend to operate from a position of entitlement (Gilbert and Rachlin 1987:15–16). That is, men in our society are socialized to regard themselves as entitled to do whatever is necessary in order to be successful in their work and provide for their family. For many men, success means that they do not have to do housework. A man is entitled to pursue his career without the constraints of time and energy given to family work.

Even in a dual-career family, then, there is a tendency for the husband to decide what is an equitable division of labor in the home, to assume whatever share he has decided is fair, and to expect that everything is all right. He may even expect to receive gratitude from his wife for his willingness to share the household responsibilities. She, on the other hand, even though she is as fully engaged in a career as he is, will get no expressions of gratitude for doing her share because it is her responsibility in the first place.

Satisfactions of a Dual-Career Family

In spite of the gloomy picture painted previously, there are a number of satisfactions in the dual-career family that make the arrangement worth all the potential problems. Some of these satisfactions are the same as those of the dual-earner family, involving the benefits that accrue to women through work (see Work and Well-being). But some are unique or more intense for those in the dual-career family.

For a woman, the satisfactions

> include the opportunity to develop professionally and to establish a sense of self separate from a man and children, economic independence, greater intellectual companionship and contentment, and higher self-esteem (Gilbert and Rachlin 1987:27).

Thus, some of the benefits relate to the need for a sense of control over our lives. A woman who has a sense of her own separate identity and a feeling of being independent will be healthier and more satisfied than one who cannot separate herself from her family and who is economically and emotionally dependent on her husband. The other benefits relate to our intimacy needs. The woman who has higher self-esteem, who is emotionally healthy and satisfied, and who is able to be an intellectual companion rather than a servile mate to her husband, will likely have a far more meaningful marriage.

But what are the benefits for the husband? Traditionally, he used his career, at least in part, to fulfill the "good provider role" (Bernard 1981). He had little involvement in the home, but he gave his wife and children a solid financial base. What has a man gained by having his wife also engage in a career? As Gilbert and Rachlin (1987:27) noted,

> the foremost potential benefits of dual-career marriage for the male spouse are freedom from the mantle of total economic responsibility and family dependency and opportunities to involve himself in parenting and to express his inherent needs to nurture and bond.

The husband may also gain a more meaningful marital relationship. If his wife is happier or more fulfilled with a career outside of the home, then this will have a positive impact on their marriage.

There are benefits to the family generally as well. The higher income level will give all family members many options that they would not otherwise have. To the extent that they approach the role-sharing dual-career family, they will have the opportunity to share in an experience of equality that many Americans value but miss. They will also have the opportunity to experience a life-style in which the constraints of traditional sex roles are no longer operative. Also the children may find that they develop a sense of responsibility, independence, and competence earlier in life and more completely because they too must assume a certain share of family work.

Exploring the Dual-Career Family

If you have grown up in a dual-career family, reflect on the materials in this section and write up an account of your experiences. How do your experiences square with the materials presented? Based on your experience, what are the major problems and the greatest rewards and satisfactions in a dual-career family, and particularly for the children? What changes in our society would you suggest in order to help dual-career families cope with their challenges?

If you have not grown up in a dual-career family, look through six or so issues of a women's magazine, such as *Working Woman*. Find a number of articles that address the issue of the dual-career family. What are the problems identified in the articles? What are the rewards and satisfactions? How do they compare with the materials in this chapter? Interview a woman who is in a dual-career family. Ask her what she believes to be the most serious problems and the greatest benefits from such an arrangement. Then tell her about the kinds of problems and satisfactions discussed in this chapter. Ask her to comment on them in terms of her own experiences. What kinds of things did she identify as problems and satisfactions? How does her experience square with the materials in the chapter? If a number of students do this project, let each one choose a different magazine and a different person to interview. Then compare all the results. What are your overall conclusions?

In sum, the potential satisfactions and rewards of the dual-career family are great. So are the potential problems. Some dual-career families, therefore, are going to break apart from stress and conflict; however, others are going to be an exciting adventure in growth. We hope as societal norms and arrangements change, those in dual-career families will get increasing support in their efforts.

Problems of Dual-Earner Couples

For the dual-earner couple generally, as with the dual-career couple in particular, the decision to have both spouses work is a trade-off. That is, there are satisfactions to be gained and certain problems and challenges to be faced. In this section, we will look at the problems and challenges, including the effects on marital satisfaction. In the final section, we will see the payoffs for the individual well-being of the spouses.

Dual-earner spouses who differ in their standards of housecare may have conflict over their division of labor.

Family Work

We have seen that although there is evidence of a greater amount of sharing in the family work by the husbands of employed women, the husband's share is far less than equal. Using a large sample of 3,649 couples, Kamo (1988) found that husbands are likely to assume a more equitable share to the extent that the spouses' incomes, work status (whether part-time or full-time workers), and power in the relationship are relatively equal, and to the extent that they have nontraditional sex-role orientations.

The way that a couple comes to terms with the division of labor in the home is important for their marital satisfaction. As we would expect, satisfaction is highest when there is perceived equity. But what is equity? Husbands and wives both want an equitable arrangement; yet husbands do not want to spend many hours on housework, which suggests that they would prefer equity in the context of lower standards of housecare than that preferred by their wives (Benin and Agostinelli 1988). Wives, on the other hand, prefer equality or even something less than an equal share of household work. They are not as satisfied if the husband's share of family work is consumed by child-care and traditional male chores as they are if he participates in some traditional female chores (Benin and Agostinelli 1988).

Thus, husbands and wives tend to approach the notion of an equitable division of family work somewhat differently. Because there are no norms to guide them, each couple will have to negotiate the division of labor in the home with a view toward achieving mutual satisfaction.

Table 12.3 Frequency of Work-Family Conflict

Group *In percent*	*Not at all*	*Not too much*	*Somewhat*	*A lot*
Total sample	24.3	41.3	24.0	10.4
Employed husbands	25.9	40.4	23.6	10.1
Wife employed	26.7	41.8	21.0	10.5
No children	35.1	37.1	20.3	7.4
Youngest 0–5 years	22.9	41.3	22.9	12.8
Youngest 6–17 years	20.0	46.8	20.7	12.3
Wife not employed	25.0	38.7	26.6	9.7
No children	35.0	38.7	20.0	6.3
Youngest 0–5 years	20.4	32.8	37.1	9.7
Youngest 6–17 years	20.3	45.6	20.9	13.3
Employed wives	22.5	40.5	26.5	10.5
Husband employed	22.9	39.1	27.7	10.4
No children	37.1	33.7	18.5	10.7
Youngest 0–5 years	11.8	40.3	36.1	11.8
Youngest 6–17 years	16.3	43.5	31.0	9.2
Husband not employed	18.6	55.8	14.0	11.6
Employed women in one-parent families	17.0	58.0	13.6	11.4
Youngest 0–5 years	18.6	55.8	9.3	16.3
Youngest 6–17 years	15.6	60.0	17.8	6.7

Source: U.S. Bureau of Labor Statistics, "Conflicts Between Work and Family Life" in *Monthly Labor Review*, 103.

Stress, Intimacy, and Family Life

In the dual-career family, we noted, women have more adjustments to make than do men. They tend to carry a larger share of the load of family work. Women who are employed have more "hassles" of every kind than women who do not work outside the home (Alpert and Culbertson 1987). Unfortunately, these facts may not be fully recognized by their husbands. In a study of the kinds of stress experienced by thirty-four dual-career couples, the researchers found that husbands perceived their wives to experience less stress than that reported by the wives (White, Mascalo, Thomas, and Shoun 1986). The wives also reported somewhat more stress with family roles than with work roles. The wives also were less satisfied than the husbands with the quality of the emotional intimacy in their marriages.

Home Versus the Workplace

Stress with family roles occurs in part because of the tension between the demands of the workplace and the demands of home. And men as well as women experience these conflicting demands. As table 12.3 shows, employed husbands and employed wives report about the same amount of conflict overall, though employed husbands with nonemployed wives have somewhat less conflict than those whose wives work outside the home.

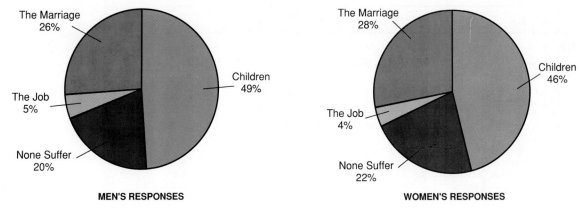

Figure 12.2 *What suffers when women work?*
Source: Data from *Public Opinion,* December/January 1986:31.

Using data from a national survey, Patricia Voydanoff (1988) explored people's perceptions of work/family conflict, which was defined as the extent that job and family life interfere with each other. She pointed out that such conflict can be due either to the incompatible time demands or to a spillover of strains from one domain to the other. She found that both employment and home factors contribute to people's conflict. Employment factors associated with higher degrees of conflict are long working hours and workload pressure (being required to work too hard or too fast). The only family factor related to conflict, however, was the presence of more than one child in the home. These factors contributed to conflict for both husbands and wives, though the work factors were somewhat more important for the husbands and the family factor somewhat more important for the wives.

The Costs of Women Working Outside the Home

Stress arises if people perceive that their families are suffering in some way from their employment. Many believe that a woman who works outside the home cannot give as good care to her children as the woman who is a housewife. A substantial number of both men and women believe that either the children or the marriage get slighted if the woman is employed (figure 12.2). However, how do the children feel? According to surveys, fewer children than parents believe the effects are negative (Roper and Keller 1988). Sixty-two percent of parents, but only 39 percent of children, agreed that both parents working outside the home has a bad effect on preteen children. Forty-eight percent of parents and only 18 percent of teenagers felt that there are bad effects for teenaged children. On the other hand, about 10 percent of parents and a fourth of children believe that there are good effects whatever the age of the children, and the rest say that there are no effects. In general, children of employed parents believe that they have a positive life-style, and that their families are strong in caring and support (Knaub 1986). The major problems they see are with time constraints.

Time constraints mean that the dual-earner family may have to work a little harder and plan a little more carefully in order to maintain a high level of intimacy and to keep stress at a minimum for all members of the family. Another factor that will affect the quality of life in a dual-earner family is the attitude that various family members hold toward the woman working outside the home. If every member of the family agrees that it is a good thing for the woman to be employed, any negative consequences will be minimized. But disagreements can create problems.

Finally, we should look not simply at people's perceptions, but at whatever concrete data we have on the effects of women's employment on family life. In a survey of research over a ten-year period, Claire Etaugh (1974) concluded that the relationship between a mother and her children depended on the quality and intensity of interaction and not on whether the mother was employed. Etaugh found no negative effects on children of any age. More recent research, however, raises some questions about that conclusion (Meredith 1986). At least for infants younger than two years, the research is contradictory. Some of it shows that the infants frequently receive inadequate care and that there may be problems in the mother-child bonding. It may be that babies who are cared for by others are less securely attached to their mothers. Such infants may have problems with insecurity later in life.

Role Negotiation

As late as the 1950s, few people had problems about roles in their marriage. The husband was the "good provider" and the wife cared for the home and children. However, with the increasing numbers of dual-earner families since that time, problems have developed about roles. Who does what? How can a couple achieve an equitable division of labor? As we might expect, there is little, if any, agreement on the answers. Each couple must negotiate its own compromise about family roles.

Not only is there no social consensus, but specific couples also are likely to disagree. The problems are illustrated by research of eighty-three dual-earner couples who each had at least one preschool child (Chassin, Zeiss, Cooper, and Reaven 1985). The researchers investigated the perceptions of spousal, parental, and worker roles held by the partners.

They found general agreement on perceptions of worker and husband roles but a considerable amount of disagreement on wife and parental roles. Compared to their husbands, women saw the wife's role as more powerless, more dependent, more child-oriented, and less glamorous. Men viewed the father role as more dependent, more tied-down, and more child-oriented than did the women. Women viewed the mother role as more sensitive, warmer, and less glamorous than did the men.

Generally, the partners saw a lot of overlap between the wife and mother roles. But women rated the employed-woman role as more unfeeling, more independent, more sophisticated and glamorous, and more interesting and tense than the roles of wife and mother. Men rated the employed-woman role as meaner, less good, more independent, more sophisticated, more serious, and colder than the roles of wife and mother.

The researchers also found that women perceived the wife role as less desirable than did the men, suggesting that "the men in this dual-worker sample may underestimate their wives' discontent with the wife role" (Chassin et al. 1985:308). That difference is a potential source of conflict. Another possible source of conflict is the women's lower evaluation than the men's of the father role, suggesting that the wives may undervalue their husbands' contribution to child-rearing. Finally, the overlap between wife and mother and the gap between those roles and the employed woman role indicate conflict between the home and work roles. In particular, women in dual-earner families may see themselves as involved in a " 'trade-off' between the independence, freedom and glamour of the worker role and the sensitivity, warmth and relaxation of the wife and mother roles" (Chassin et al. 1985:308). The wife and mother roles, of course, are more consistent with traditional notions of femininity.

"Whatever works for you" is probably a good rule to follow as partners negotiate such differences. What you settle on as acceptable roles for you and your spouse is not as important as the fact that you settle on something. Agreement about roles is crucial to your marital satisfaction.

Marital Satisfaction

If you are in a dual-earner family, you are at greater risk of separation and divorce (Booth, Johnson, White, and Edwards 1984). The risk may be even greater in a dual-career family, because women who are highly committed to a career tend to have lower marital adjustment and satisfaction (Ladewig and McGee 1986). Still if you successfully negotiate family roles and come to an equitable division of labor in the home, you have resolved some of the major problems of the dual-earner family.

In point of fact, in spite of the difficulties, many couples successfully deal with the problems of the dual-earner family and achieve marital satisfaction. In fact, Smith (1985) examined twenty-seven studies that involved 4,602 subjects and compared those in dual-earner and single-earner families. The studies looked at overall marital adjustment and four specific areas of adjustment: physical (love, affection, sexual relations), companionship (sharing interests, tasks, and activities), communication (self-disclosure, small talk, listening), and tensions and regrets (conflict, willingness to marry same person again).

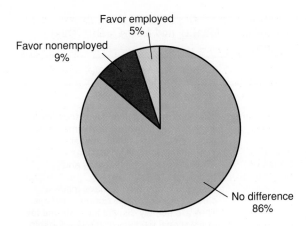

Figure 12.3 *Studies of wife employment and marital adjustment.*
Source: Data from Smith 1985:485.

As figure 12.3 shows, the bulk of studies show no differences in overall adjustment between dual-earner families and those where the woman is a housewife. In fact, the majority of studies show no difference in any of the specific areas. Where a substantial proportion of studies found differences, in the areas of physical relations and companionship, the results tend to favor families with housewives over the dual-earner families. But it is clear that the majority of couples seem to be working out the problems faced by the dual-earner family.

The dual-career family, which poses somewhat greater challenges than that of the dual-earner, can also have a high degree of marital satisfaction. Thomas, Albrecht, and White (1984) studied thirty-four dual-career couples and were able to classify fourteen of them as "high quality" and twenty as "low quality." The factors differentiating the two groups are shown in table 12.4. Clearly, those in the high-quality marriages have successfully worked through issues of equity and role, and have forged good patterns of communication and companionship.

Work and Well-Being

What would you do if you won a lottery? Would you retire and live happily ever after in glorious leisure? Probably not. Many people who have won lotteries have continued to work. Others have quit their jobs, but they have gone into other kinds of work or have found some way to spend their time. Humans do not generally function well without some kind of meaningful activity to occupy them.

Table 12.4	Characteristics of High-Quality and Low-Quality Dual-Career Marriages

High-quality marriages	Low-quality marriages
Wives	**Wives**
They report little or no difficulty discussing work-related activities, problems, and achievements with their husbands. They perceive husbands as supportive with child-rearing and household tasks. They are satisfied with their work situations.	They report much difficulty discussing work-related activities, problems, and achievements with their husbands. They perceive husbands as less supportive with child-rearing and household tasks. They are more likely to have made a career shift or change during marriage. They are acutely dissatisfied with the level of emotional intimacy in the relationship.
Husbands	**Husbands**
Their support for wives' careers has increased since marriage. Their perceptions of wives' role overload and stress levels are similar to what wives report.	Their support for wives' careers has decreased since marriage. Their perceptions of wives' role overload and stress levels are lower than wives report.
Marital Dyad	**Marital Dyad**
They agree husband's career is preeminent. They are more likely to be involved in similar career pursuits (similar professions). They have older children and more jointly share childcare responsibilities. They are satisfied with levels of emotional, sexual, intellectual, recreational, and social intimacy within the relationship.	There is less agreement regarding whose career is preeminent. They are less likely to be involved in similar career pursuits (similar professions). They have younger children and report much stress due to conflict with children's schedules and/or childcare arrangements. They are dissatisfied with levels of emotional, sexual, intellectual, recreational, and social intimacy within the relationship.

From Sandra Thomas, et al., "Determinants of Marital Quality in Dual-Career Couples" in *Family Relations*, 33:521. Copyright © 1984 National Council on Family Relations, St. Paul, MN. Reprinted by permission.

Meaningful work, as Freud once observed, is one of the crucial bases of our well-being. Of course, not everyone who has a job has "meaningful" work. Yet one of the characteristics of Americans in recent decades is the increasing

> concern for work as a source of self-respect and nonmaterial reward—challenge, growth, personal fulfillment, interesting and meaningful work, the opportunity to advance and to accumulate, and the chance to lead a safe, healthy life (Kanter 1978:53).

In other words, more and more Americans are expecting their employment to be fulfilling to them. To what extent can people find such personal fulfillment in a dual-earner family?

Career-oriented women are happier when they can combine full-time work with marriage and family.

The Intimate Couple

Employed and Married, and Loving Both

Phyllis is a high-school counselor in her forties. She and Roger have four children. They have had their share of difficult times, but overall she sees the marriage as a very good one, and believes that working outside the home has enhanced the quality of their family life:

During our twenty-one years of marriage, being happily employed has probably contributed as much to our happiness as anything else. I taught for two years before we married. It was very fulfilling, and the idea of my quitting to be a "good wife" was neither discussed nor considered. Because of my job, I felt a sense of accomplishment, competence, pride, and independence, all of which contributed to my being a very happy person. Roger was just as fortunate in his career choice. He found excitement and challenge in being an architect.

In our twenties, life was amazingly wonderful. Everything was new and thrilling— our jobs, our marriage, our friends, and the babies. We both worked hard and were very conscientious about our jobs. Roger was willing from the beginning to help out a great deal with the children, everything from changing diapers to getting up for middle-of-the-night feedings. We shared chores around the house, but with no particular division of labor. Having his help with the mundane, routine aspects of home life endeared him to me greatly and helped me to continue working.

Our jobs were important to both of us, because they gave us a sense of our individuality. We have never been suffocated or stifled by each other. Most of the time, we have worked at having enough togetherness to know that we were married. Our careers help us to view each other as competent people and this creates a mutual respect for each other as spouses and as professional people.

During our thirties, however, our professions brought about some frustrations and tensions. Roger had become a licensed architect and opened his own office. I had gone back to college to get my master's degree so that I could change from teaching to counseling. We had two more children, but Roger's work week had gone from fifty to what seemed like ninety hours a week. Time together became scarce. Our relationship became strained. I felt neglected. I was so busy that it took awhile, but I gradually realized that I was terribly frustrated and angry. It all came out when we took a vacation. We spent most of the time talking about our situation. We both felt like we needed a vacation after the vacation. But it did help us to make some adjustments. We hired a cleaning lady, planned to spend a number of weekends away from home with just the two of us, and tried to do more things together. We realized that intimacy didn't just happen for us as it did in the first years of our marriage. We now had to put energy and effort into maintaining our intimate relationship.

In our forties, life has quieted down a bit. Roger is somewhat burned out with his work. He's looking for new challenges. I think I am too. So we're talking about what we can do to make our lives more exciting. We've got some ideas, and are looking forward to the future.

There's no doubt about it. In spite of the frustrations we've had, the net effect of both of us being employed is that we have been able to maintain a high quality of intimacy during most of our years of marriage.

Life Satisfaction

The effects of one or both spouses working outside the home on life satisfaction are somewhat different for men and women. Overall, when women are asked about how happy they are, employed women and housewives report about the same amount of happiness (Benin and Nienstedt 1985). However, for women who are career-oriented, happiness is greater when they are employed full-time than when they are unemployed or employed only part-time (Pietromonaco, Manis, and Markus 1987). For married women who are not career-oriented, being employed or unemployed seems to make no difference in happiness.

The evidence with regard to men is somewhat contradictory. Using national surveys from 1978 to 1983, Benin and Nienstedt (1985) found that husbands of housewives and husbands of employed wives reported no differences in their happiness. Their overall happiness was greater to the extent that they were happily married and satisfied with their jobs. Also using data from a national survey, however, Stanley, Hunt, and Hunt (1986) reported that men in dual-earner families are less satisfied with their work, their marriages, and their personal lives than are the husbands of housewives. They also found that the lower satisfaction occurred mainly among younger, highly educated, successful men without children.

The authors speculate that the reason for this may be that the men in the dual-earner families feel deprived when they compare themselves to men who have the full-time services of a housewife. They may also feel some slight to their manhood for not being the sole support of the family, the good provider. Other research supports the notion that when husbands of employed wives feel deprived or less adequate as family breadwinners, they may have lower levels of job and life satisfaction (Staines, Pottick, and Fudge 1986).

We may conclude, then, that on the whole men and women in dual-earner families do not differ from those in single-earner families in overall life satisfaction. But women who are career-oriented will have lower satisfaction if they are not employed full-time. And men in dual-earner families who feel that they are deprived or whose self-esteem is threatened by not being the good provider, will also have lower satisfaction.

Mental and Physical Health

In a sense, work presents us with one of the dilemmas of human life. On the one hand, work-induced stress is associated with such physical health problems as coronary heart disease, migraines, peptic ulcers, and hypertension (Lauer 1989:390). On the other hand, the stress of being forcibly unemployed can be as serious as the stress of working in undesirable conditions or an unfulfilling job. Unemployment leads to higher rates of suicide, mental illness, and various physical problems (Lauer 1989:392). The way to deal with the dilemma, of course, is to find work that is meaningful and fulfilling.

Having the option to work outside the home is important for wives. Women have higher rates of both physical and mental ailments than do men. For many women, it is the restrictive nature of the traditional role of wife and mother that creates stress and leads to high rates of illness (Lauer 1989:149). Thus, women who are dissatisfied with the housewife role and not employed have more problems with depression than do other women (Shehan, Burg, and Rexroat 1986). A national survey of women and their physical health reported that the healthiest women are those who are employed and married, followed by those employed and not married, those married but not in the labor force, and finally those unmarried and not in the labor force (Verbrugge and Madans 1985).

On the whole, then, wives who work outside the home are mentally and physically healthier than those who do not. However, there are other factors that bear on the outcome of a wife's employment. One is her preference. As we noted above, some women prefer not to be employed. Using data from a national sample, Ross, Mirowsky, and Huber (1983) found that both spouses are less depressed when the wife's employment status is consistent with their preferences. The researchers also found, incidentally, that employed wives are less depressed when their husbands help with the housework.

Coping Strategies

Given an equitable relationship and agreement about work status, the partners in a dual-earner family will still benefit from using certain coping strategies to deal with various problems. Women in particular must deal with the additional workload that they typically assume. Even if a woman is in an egalitarian marriage, the two spouses will have to deal with the problems that arise from time constraints.

A study of sixty-nine women in dual-earner families with children reported a number of ways that women handle the problems of time management and self-care (McLaughlin, Cormier, and Cormier 1988). Time-management strategies are those that enable a woman to control her personal and professional time. Self-care strategies are those that enable a woman to care for her physical and emotional well-being. The more women used the strategies, the better their marital adjustment and the lower their levels of distress.

For *time-management,* the coping strategies used, in order of frequency, were:

Do more than one task at a time

Have contingency plans

Say "no" to additional time demands

Break large jobs down into smaller subtasks

Budget your time so that you are not overwhelmed

Make a priority list of your tasks

Ask the family to help

Leave outside work in the workplace; don't bring it home

Make "to-do" lists

Utilize outside help

Fifty-five percent of the women said that they never use the last strategy—utilizing outside help. Every other strategy was used at least to some extent by the great bulk of the women.

For *self-care,* the coping strategies used, in order of frequency, were:

Give self permission to be a less-than-perfect housekeeper

Allow special time for each child

Eat nutritionally balanced meals

Engage in family activities

Give self permission to be a less-than-perfect mother

Give self permission to be a less-than-perfect wife

Stress quality rather than quantity time

Interact with spouse

Lower standards for housework

Take time for yourself to do something you enjoy

Engage in hobby

Attend social or community group meetings

Exercise

Twenty-eight percent of the women said that they never exercised. Every other strategy was used at least to some extent by the great majority of the women.

It is interesting to note that the self-care strategies include giving oneself permission to be less-than-perfect as a housekeeper, wife, and mother. In other words, the women who are coping well have learned to avoid trying to be superwomen. They know that they cannot be all things to all people. As a result, they are able to work outside the home, enjoy a family, and still maintain their personal well-being.

1. Women today have numerous role options available to them. Women can choose among career, marriage, and motherhood—or any combination of these. They can decide to stay at home or continue to work outside the home after they have children. Increased confusion, however, often accompanies enlarged options as individuals struggle to decide what is the best pattern for their lives. When faced with such choices, it is vital for you to gain an understanding of your needs as well as those of your spouse and to consider carefully your personal and your shared goals.

2. It is very important to negotiate role expectations before marriage. Each person needs to define clearly what role he or she expects to play in the marriage and what the role of the other will be. Then, compromises need to be negotiated. Be aware that the roles you decide on are not etched in concrete. The process of negotiation and compromise will be repeated throughout your marriage as circumstances change.

3. Women who decide to combine the responsibilities of job, children, and home must recognize and come to terms with the enormity of their tasks and their own limitations. They can't do everything equally well all of the time. If you choose to assume these roles, you need to make a list of priorities, reduce your expectations, eliminate the less valuable tasks, and seek help when necessary.

4. Research indicates that husbands in dual-earner marriages do not share equally in family work. It is important that housework—including childcare—be viewed as "our" work and not just "her" work. Otherwise, there may be a sense of inequity on the part of the wife.

5. Often because she is not a wage-earner, the work of the housewife is not highly valued by society nor, for that matter, by her husband. If your wife chooses to stop work and stay at home after you have children, you need to support her in this choice and acknowledge the valuable task she is performing. You also need to encourage your wife to see friends, find ways of retaining career ties, and generally maintain interests outside the home. In this way, she will avoid the feelings of isolation that often plague housewives.

SUMMARY

Since industrialization, "his" work has mainly been to function as a provider and "her" work has been to care for the home. But in the industrial economy, only paid labor has been defined as work. The housewife has an isolated role that tends to be devalued.

Since the 1960s, women have gone into the labor force in increasing numbers. Most married as well as single women now work outside the home; the most dramatic increase in labor force participation has occured among married women with children under the age of six. Women may take jobs or enter careers. Those who are employed become part of either a dual-earner or dual-career family. With women employed, men have assumed a larger proportion of family work, but women still do the bulk of that work.

Some women prefer not to work outside the home. Those who do may work for economic reasons, for the fulfillment that work brings, or for the power gained. Employed women generally do not believe that their marriages or families suffer because they work.

In some ways, dual-career families are more egalitarian than others. The wife is still likely to do more family work than the husband, and his career is still likely to take priority over hers. Dual-career families may be traditional, participant, or role-sharing. The commuter marriage is a special form of the dual-career family, and poses a serious challenge to the maintenance of intimacy for the couple. Some of the other serious problems of dual-career families are time management; whether to have, and how to raise, children; maintaining relationships with others without jeopardizing the marital relation; and the special problems of the dual-career wife, who may be tempted to try to become a superwoman. There are also satisfactions in the dual-career family, enough to make the arrangement worth all the potential problems.

Dual-earner couples face a number of challenges and problems in the areas of family work (who does what in the home?), balancing home and work demands, maintaining intimacy, and satisfactorily negotiating roles. Dual-earner families are at a greater risk of disruption. Yet many couples deal with the difficulties and achieve marital satisfaction.

While the life satisfaction of those in single-earner is as high as those in dual-earner families, women who are career-oriented will have lower satisfaction if they are not employed and men who feel deprived or whose self-esteem is threatened will have lower satisfaction if their wives are employed. Women who work outside the home are physically and mentally healthier than those who do not, particularly when the employment is in accord with their preference. An employed woman's adjustment is facilitated when she uses various coping strategies to deal with such problems as time constraints and her need to care for her physical and emotional well-being.

---

1. *Public Opinion,* December/January 1986, p. 30.

2. Ibid., p. 26.

PART THREE

Intimacy in Families

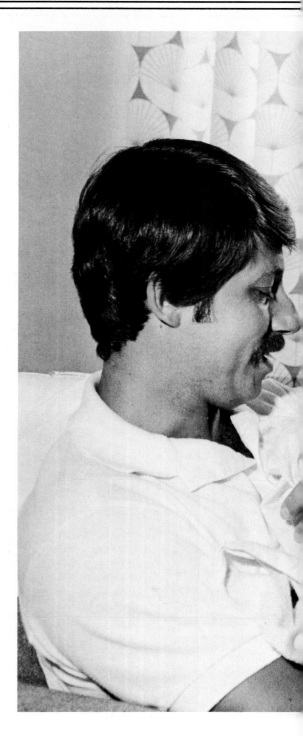

At some point or other in our lives, we all face the problem of establishing meaningful intimate relationships with more than a partner. As children, we strive to maintain intimacy with our parents. Once married, most of us will have one or more children. Bringing children into the home poses new challenges and new tasks in our quest for intimacy.

As with the marital relationship, meaningful intimate relationships are not guaranteed simply because a group of people live together in the same house. In some ways, in fact, the challenge of intimacy is more difficult as the family grows.

In this third part, then, we will examine family life over the life cycle, including the child-rearing years. We will discuss some of the issues that arise by virtue of enlarging the family beyond two people. And we will examine the special problems of those who struggle to establish a family that is different from the two-parent, white household.

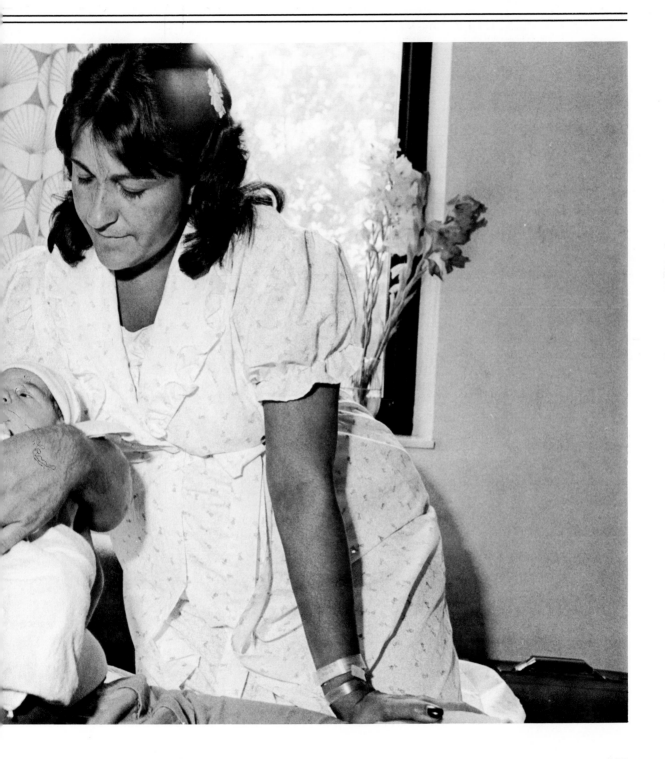

13

Becoming a Parent

Someone has said that a new baby is total demand at one end and total irresponsibility at the other. If so, who would want one of those creatures around the house? Actually, most married people do, though most people also want fewer children than did past generations of parents. In this chapter, we shall look at changing patterns of childbearing, why most people want children, and why some do not. We will examine the problem of infertility. We will see how people cope with involuntary childlessness or loss of a child through death or spontaneous abortion. We will briefly discuss some of the relatively new technologies to help people who would have remained childless in the past.

Children have significant consequences for the quality of our lives. We will discuss those consequences, along with the somewhat different parenting experiences of men and women. Finally, we will explore the consequences of differing parenting styles for the well-being of children.

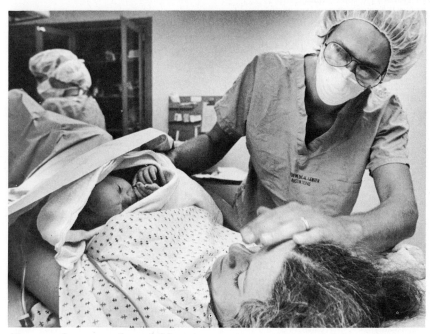

Most couples want to have children.

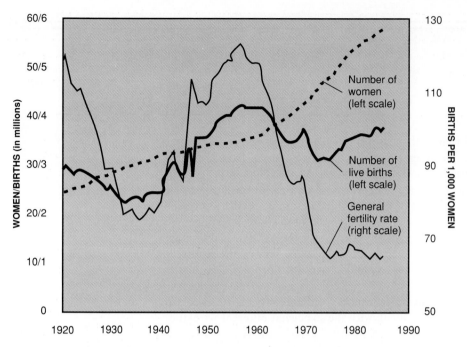

Figure 13.1 *Number of women, number of live births, and births per 1000 women.*
Source: U.S. Bureau of the Census, *Current Population Reports,* Series P-23, No. 159, "Population Profile of the United States: 1989" (Washington, DC: Government Printing Office) 1989:5.

Changing Patterns of Childbearing

We saw in chapter 1 that the **birth rate** in the United States has declined considerably during this century. In fact, since the early 1970s, the birth rate has been below the replacement level. That is, if the birth rate continues at this level for an extended period of time, the population will decline unless we have a lowered death rate and/or a sufficient number of immigrants to make up the difference.

Birth Rates

As figure 13.1 shows, the number of live births has gone up since 1975, but that is because of the rise in the number of women of childbearing age (women born during the "baby-boom" years of 1946 to 1964). Eventually, the number of women in their childbearing years will decline. And if the birth rate remains low, the population may either stabilize or decline. This has happened in some other countries, particularly in some of the European nations.

Some people believe that the declining birth rate is due only to fewer middle- and upper-class white babies, and that the poor and minorities are continuing to bear children in great numbers. It is true that birth rates tend to be higher among the poor and minorities, but they, too, have declined. In 1960, for example, the birth rate for whites was 113.2 per 1,000 women, and

Intimacy in Families

Table 13.1 Families, by Number of Own Children under 18 Years Old: 1970–1987

Race, hispanic origin, and year	Number of families (1,000)	Percent distribution by number of own children under 18 years old						Average size of family
		All families	None	1	2	3	4 or more	
All families[1]								
1970	51,586	100.0	44.1	18.2	17.4	10.6	9.8	3.58
1975	55,712	100.0	46.0	19.7	18.0	9.3	6.9	3.42
1980	59,550	100.0	47.9	20.9	19.3	7.8	4.1	3.29
1985	62,706	100.0	50.4	20.9	18.6	7.2	3.0	3.23
1987	64,491	100.0	50.5	21.3	18.5	6.9	2.8	3.19
White families								
1970	46,261	100.0	44.8	18.2	17.7	10.5	8.8	3.52
1975	49,451	100.0	47.2	19.4	18.0	9.2	6.2	3.36
1980	52,243	100.0	49.3	20.5	19.1	7.5	3.6	3.23
1985	54,400	100.0	51.8	20.5	18.3	6.8	2.6	3.16
1987	55,676	100.0	52.0	20.7	18.3	6.6	2.4	3.13
Black families								
1970	4,887	100.0	38.9	17.6	14.8	10.1	18.5	4.13
1975	5,498	100.0	36.8	22.0	17.0	10.6	13.6	3.90
1980	6,184	100.0	38.2	23.4	20.0	10.2	8.2	3.67
1985	6,778	100.0	42.6	23.3	19.6	9.0	5.5	3.60
1987	7,096	100.0	41.0	25.1	19.5	8.8	5.6	3.52
Hispanic families[2]								
1970	2,004	100.0	29.8	19.5	19.4	13.3	18.1	(NA)
1975	2,447	100.0	29.4	23.1	19.7	13.4	14.5	(NA)
1980	3,029	100.0	31.2	22.4	23.0	13.4	9.9	3.90
1985	3,939	100.0	33.9	22.9	22.0	12.2	8.9	3.88
1987	4,403	100.0	35.1	22.3	23.2	12.9	6.5	3.83

NA Not available.

[1]Includes other races, not shown separately.

[2]Hispanic persons may be of any race. 1970 data as of April. Based on Census of Population.

Source: U.S. Bureau of the Census 1989:51.

for blacks it was 153.5 per 1,000 women. By 1985, the rates had declined to 63.0 for whites and 82.2 for blacks (U.S. Bureau of the Census 1988:60).

Thus, while the rates for minorities are higher than those of whites, all groups have lower birth rates than they did in the past. This is reflected also in the declining proportion of families of all races with three or more children and the increasing proportion of families of all races with no children (table 13.1). Uniformly, Americans are having fewer children.

Overall, table 13.2 shows a profile of the women who had children in 1986. Note that the birth rate is highest among Hispanics, those who are married with spouse present, and those who are in the lower socioeconomic strata (as indicated by level of education and income). The one, interesting exception to this pattern is the relatively high rate among women who have five or more years of college education. Unfortunately, we have no research to answer the question of why their rate is higher than that of some other women.

Table 13.2 Social and Economic Characteristics of Women, 18–44 Years Old, Who Gave Birth in 1987

Characteristic	Total, 18 to 44 years old			18 to 29 years old		
	Number of women (1,000)	Women who have had a child in the last year		Number of women (1,000)	Women who have had a child in the last year	
		Total births per 1,000 women	First births per 1,000 women		Total births per 1,000 women	First births per 1,000 women
Total[1]	52,139	71.0	27.4	24,265	103.9	48.0
White	43,634	68.5	27.5	20,091	100.3	48.4
Black	6,734	83.2	24.8	3,402	123.0	44.6
Hispanic[2]	4,296	95.8	24.4	2,239	126.7	40.2
Married, spouse present	29,413	97.4	37.7	9,962	183.1	87.0
Married, spouse absent[3]	2,087	60.8	20.7	847	123.9	50.0
Widowed or divorced	5,337	23.5	4.7	1,194	57.3	15.2
Single	15,302	38.1	16.5	12,262	42.7	19.5
Years of school completed:						
Not a high school graduate	7,868	92.7	27.2	4,001	149.4	50.5
High School, 4 years	22,202	71.6	27.9	10,517	114.7	52.7
College: 1–3 years	12,050	61.6	25.4	6,149	71.3	38.1
4 or more years	10,019	63.9	28.8	3,598	77.4	48.8
4 years	6,668	66.7	30.4	2,859	76.1	48.2
5 or more years	3,350	58.4	25.6	739	82.3	50.8
Labor force status: In labor force	37,925	49.6	23.1	17,703	71.1	39.4
Employed	35,351	47.1	22.4	16,095	68.0	38.7
Unemployed	2,574	84.1	32.7	1,608	102.3	46.5
Not in labor force	14,214	128.0	38.8	6,562	192.4	71.3
Occupation of employed women:						
Managerial-professional	8,779	48.1	24.4	3,035	67.3	44.2
Technical, sales, and admin. support	16,135	47.6	23.9	7,907	70.1	40.2
Service workers	6,129	46.2	20.2	3,297	62.4	33.8
Precision prod., craft, and repair	853	26.7	13.8	318	33.2	16.0
Operators, fabricators, and laborers	3,047	47.7	17.6	1,336	75.9	37.8
Farming, forestry, and fishing	408	56.6	9.6	202	83.8	19.5
Family income: Under $10,000	8,140	95.1	27.7	4,679	136.1	46.4
$10,000–$14,999	5,472	83.1	34.0	3,076	114.8	55.3
$15,000–$19,999	5,044	76.5	32.5	2,547	117.6	58.7
$20,000–$24,999	5,170	71.6	25.2	2,436	102.7	44.8
$25,000–$29,999	4,635	80.3	33.6	2,041	124.9	64.5
$30,000–$34,999	4,861	63.4	26.5	2,044	106.1	51.0
$35,000 and over	17,081	54.7	24.0	6,701	66.4	38.4

—Represents or rounds to zero.

[1]Includes women of other races and women with family income not reported, not shown separately.

[2]Hispanic persons may be of any race.

[3]Includes separated women.

Source: U.S. Bureau of the Census 1989:67.

Table 13.2 Continued

30 to 44 years old

| Number of women (1,000) | Women who have had a child in the last year | |
	Total births per 1,000 women	First births per 1,000 women
27,874	42.3	9.4
23,543	41.3	9.6
3,331	42.5	4.6
2,057	62.1	7.3
19,451	53.5	12.4
1,240	17.6	.8
4,143	13.8	1.6
3,040	19.7	4.3
3,868	34.1	3.1
11,685	32.8	5.5
5,901	51.4	12.2
6,421	56.4	17.6
3,809	59.7	17.0
2,612	51.6	18.5
20,222	30.8	8.9
19,256	29.7	8.8
966	53.7	9.8
7,653	72.8	10.9
5,744	37.9	14.0
8,227	26.0	8.2
2,832	27.3	4.3
535	22.8	12.6
1,710	25.6	1.9
206	29.9	—
3,462	39.8	2.3
2,396	42.5	6.6
2,496	34.4	5.8
2,735	44.0	7.8
2,594	45.1	9.3
2,817	32.4	8.7
10,380	47.1	14.7

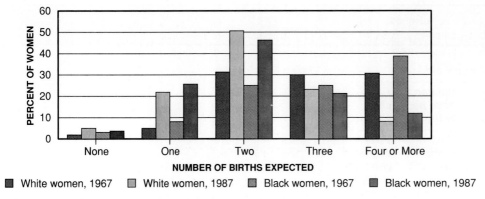

Figure 13.2 *Lifetime births expected by wives, 18–34 years old: 1967–1987.*
Source: U.S. Bureau of the Census 1980:65 and 1989:69.

Preferences for Size and Sex

One thing that affects the birth rate is the preferred size of one's family, the ideal number of children. That ideal has changed over time. Since the 1930s, the Gallup Organization has periodically asked people about the ideal size of a family.[1] In 1936, 30 percent said four or more children, 29 percent said three children, and 29 percent said two children was ideal. By 1985, only 11 percent said four or more children and another 21 percent said three children was ideal. The majority of the respondents, 56 percent, named two children as the ideal.

The same decline is reflected in the responses of married women to the Census Bureau's question as to how many children they expect to have. The proportion expecting to have no children has increased, while the proportion expecting to have three or more has declined over time (figure 13.2).

These changing preferences and expectations are reflected in actual birth rates. Another factor that can affect birth rates is sex preference. A survey of 1,169 college students who were not yet parents reported that they had definite preferences for the sex of first- and second-born children (Goldfarb 1988). The preferences were: 51.7 percent of the men and 42.6 percent of the women preferred boy-girl; 14.8 percent of the men and 29.2 percent of the women preferred girl-boy; 21.4 percent of the men and 12.7 percent of the women preferred boy-boy; and 5.0 percent of the men and 9.2 percent of the women preferred girl-girl.

Most people who want two children prefer to have one girl and one boy, whatever the order. If a couple has two children of the same sex, they may have a third child in the hope of having an opposite-sex offspring even though their ideal was two children.

Intimacy in Families

To Bear or Not to Bear

Do you want to have children? Why or why not? Think about the matter a bit before you read the following materials. Reflect on how your own thoughts compare with those of others.

Why People Want to Have Children

As we pointed out in chapter 8, some people who have children do not want them, at least not at the time of conception. Millions of children, perhaps as many as one out of ten, are born each year who were unwanted when they were conceived. These children may be the result of an "accident" (birth control measures that didn't work), pressure by a spouse or family, or some other factor. But the majority of women who have children wanted them at the time they conceived. Why? The reasons are many (Berelson 1979; Gerson 1986), and there may be one or more of the following reasons that motivate a particular couple.

Experience of Happiness in a Family

If you grew up in a family that provided you with meaningful experiences, you are likely to want to have your own family. For example, women who perceive their fathers as being warm, affectionate, and helpful, and who recall their family life as a happy one, are more highly motivated than others to have children (Gerson 1986:58).

We all tend to try to recreate the situations that made us happy in the past. If you associate happiness with family life, therefore, you are likely to want your own family.

Personal Fulfillment

Having children may be perceived as not only adding to our happiness, but to our fulfillment as humans. Some people believe that the experience of having a child is unique, that it adds a dimension to life that is unparalleled by any other. Children enable us to express "life values" (Gerson 1986:59). Friends who have children may convey that impression to you. The mass media may reinforce it through stories of parents who find ultimate joy in the experience of childbirth.

The fulfillment, of course, comes not only at the time of birth, but through the child-rearing years. To love and be loved, to share in the growing child's delights of discovery and learning, to shape the life of another, are unique experiences that many people find personally fulfilling. A professional man, deeply involved in his career, said to us: "I can't conceive of my life without my children." Although he is very successful, he finds his children to be an indispensable part of his growth.

Personal and Family Legacy

There is within many if not most of us a desire to leave our imprint on the world in some way. In addition, there is a desire to carry on the family line. Frequently these desires only awaken as you get older, but at some point you are likely to experience them. Children are the means of satisfying those desires. They are your personal legacy to humanity. And they are the extension of your family line (Berelson 1979).

The importance of this is illustrated by the woman attorney who told us that she insisted on retaining her maiden name and wanted to have children with that name. "My parents had three girls," she said. "If I don't keep my maiden name and have children by that name, it will die out. And that would deeply hurt my father."

Personal Status

In some cultures, having children is a means of achieving high status in the community. Among the ancient Jews, for example, a woman was not considered fully human until she bore a son. In some contemporary societies, women still gain status by bearing children and men gain status (demonstrating their manhood) by fathering children.

For some Americans, having children is also an avenue to higher status. The enhanced status may come from family members, friends, or colleagues. After all, to both achieve in your work and fulfill the responsibilities of parenthood means that you are a very competent person.

Religious Beliefs

Those who identify with an organized religion are more likely to want children than those who do not (Gerson 1986:58). Most religions are strongly pro-family. Some religions, such as Roman Catholicism and Mormonism, stress theological reasons for people having large families. A couple strongly committed to such a religious faith may feel that they are fulfilling the will of God by having not merely one but many children.

Social Expectations

When we ask why people "want" children, we need to recognize that there are some who have children without necessarily either wanting or not wanting them. That is, they do not think much about the matter in such terms. They believe that everyone who is married should have children as a matter of course because that is normal and typical. In our society, there are in fact many pressures, some subtle and some not-so-subtle, for married people to have children.

While the expectations are changing somewhat, it is still true that married people are expected to have children. No couple, after all, has to explain why they decided to have a baby. But explanations are usually in order if a couple decides not to have children. Moreover, a couple that announces a forthcoming child is likely to be greeted with smiles and congratulations. A couple that declares their intention to remain child-free is likely to be greeted with quizzical looks and perhaps frowns. Clearly, we still expect married people to have children if they can.

The Child-Free Option

In spite of all the reasons for having children, increasing numbers of couples have opted to be child-free. For many, in fact, it is not just a matter of preference but of determination. In the early 1980s, nearly 39 percent of couples could not have children because either the husband or wife was surgically sterile (U.S. Bureau of the Census 1988:66). About a fourth of those couples had no children. In other words, about one of every ten couples in which the wife was in the childbearing years was sterile by choice.

The choice is not an easy one for most people. One woman told us: "I have agonized more and cried more about this decision than any I have ever made." But just as there are many reasons why people want to have children, there are also many reasons why they decide to remain child-free (Bernard 1975). For any particular couple, the reasons are likely to include one or more of the following.

Personal Fulfillment

Not everyone believes that fulfillment comes best through children. Some people feel that children impede rather than facilitate personal fulfillment (Ramu and Tavuchis 1986). They opt to remain child-free, therefore, in order that they may find fulfillment through their work, their interests, and/or their adult relationships. Children require time and energy that they prefer to put into other pursuits, those they believe more likely to yield them personal satisfaction and growth.

Focus on Career

People strongly committed to a career, and particularly the dual-career couple, may prefer to remain child-free. As we noted in the last chapter, dual-career couples face some difficult questions when they decide to have children. For some, the questions themselves are reason enough not to have children. Neither the husband nor the wife may be willing to use work time and energy for child-rearing tasks.

As this suggests, women who are not career-oriented, and those who tend to agree that women should take care of the home and men should be breadwinners, are more likely to become mothers and to have more than one child. One researcher found that 38 percent of such traditional women, compared to 14 percent of nontraditional women, have three or more children (Nock 1987). Additionally, nontraditional women are twice as likely as traditional women to have no children.

A search for harmony
A quest for balance
A hope for the future

ZPG
An Idea with a Future

For various reasons, some couples decide to remain child-free.

Economic Costs of Children

In addition to time and energy, children cost a great deal of money. Some people feel that the costs are not worth the benefits, that it will cost them more than whatever satisfactions they gain from becoming parents (Callan 1986a). The financial costs vary over time, but the proportion of family income required has not varied for the past few decades (Espenshade 1984). A family with two children in the middle-income range will spend about 40 to 45 percent of its after-tax income on the children.

There are indirect as well as direct costs. Consider the fact that children may narrow the range of economic opportunities parents will have. Women in particular may have to make career compromises if they have children. Men, too, may be constrained in their careers if, for example, a move that would mean career advancement must be deferred because of children's school needs. For example, a child may be one year away from graduating from a primary or secondary school. Or a child may be in a program that is unavailable in the new area. Such opportunity costs are economic as well as personal; the family may lose a considerable amount of potential income.

Focus on the Marriage

Some people feel that children will detract from the marital relationship, and they prefer to focus their energies on that relationship (Ramu and Tavuchis 1986). Those in child-free marriages talk about the freedom they have, and the continuing romance and sex in their relationships. They feel that they are able to spend more time together and develop a more intimate relationship than would be possible with children. Joan, an artist in her forties, expresses her feelings this way:

> My husband and I have talked about having children many times. But we realized that we were talking about this because other people expected us to have children as much as from our own desires. I guess I would like to have children eventually, but we both have careers and we cherish our marriage. I don't want to sacrifice my marriage to the children. I've seen other people do that. We won't. Our relationship means too much to us.

Doubts about Parenting Skills

Clearly, not everyone makes a good parent. Good parenting requires certain skills, and some people question whether they have those skills. They feel that they do not want to be parents unless they can do a good job, and they're not sure they can cope with the demands of parenting. As a graduate student put it: "I would love to be a mother, but I don't think I have the patience to deal with children. I just don't think I would be a good enough mother." Her desire to mother was not stronger than her doubts about her skills, so she opted to remain child-free.

To Be a Parent?
The Agonies of the Decision

Lori and Ben are in their late twenties. She is a graduate student in biology and he is a practicing engineer. Lori talks about their struggle with the question of whether or not to have children. Like many couples, it has not been a settled question for them. Through their years together they have both changed in their attitudes. And although they seem to be in agreement now, the issue continues to trouble them:

I think that both of us would like to have children once I'm finished with school and have gotten my career started. We've made a decision to wait until then. And we think we might have two children. It is interesting that our attitudes have changed over the years. Ben absolutely did *not* want children when we were first married. But I assumed that we would have them anyway after three or four years. I thought he would probably change his mind.

But as I progressed in college and became more career-oriented, my attitude changed and became like his. I decided that I preferred to pursue my career and not get involved with the hassles of a family. However, by then Ben had changed. He had gotten much more warm-hearted and affectionate with children. When we were first married, he had a kind of dread of them. He felt they were too much responsibility

and too much of a burden. I always had a more tender feeling about children, but now I've gotten to feel somewhat more fearful of the vast responsibility that's involved. Maybe that's because we've both finally come to a point where we agree that we will have children. But I'm not sure how it's going to work out with both of us pursuing careers.

Anyway, something really interesting happened this past week. I've always religiously taken my birth-control pills. We've been very responsible. We didn't want any unplanned pregnancy. But a few days ago I accidentally dropped my pill between the kitchen counter and the stove. I got Ben to move the stove away from the wall so I could retrieve it. But we couldn't find it. I would have joyfully popped that peach-colored pill into my mouth even though it had fallen into a thick layer of dust. But it was lost.

I realized that my panic over losing the pill showed that I'm not ready yet for motherhood. I expect to feel differently in a few years. I really do want to have children. And Ben says he is now definitely ready. Life is sure complicated, isn't it?

Involuntary Childlessness

If this were a perfect world, those who wanted children would have them, and those who didn't would not. But just as there are a substantial number of unwanted pregnancies, there are a substantial number of people who want children but who cannot bear their own.

Table 13.3 Ability to Bear Children of Currently Married Couples, By Age of Wife, Number of Prior Births, and Race: 1982

Race and fertility status	All women, 15–44 years	Age of wife			Number of prior births			
		15–24 years	25–34 years	35–44 years	0	1	2	3 or more
All races[1] (1,000)	**28,231**	**4,741**	**12,924**	**10,566**	**5,098**	**5,891**	**9,042**	**8,201**
Percent distribution:								
Surgically sterile[2]	38.9	7.2	31.6	62.0	9.9	17.7	46.9	63.3
Infertile[3]	8.5	8.7	7.3	9.7	19.6	10.8	5.0	[4]3.8
Fecund[5]	52.6	84.1	61.0	28.3	70.5	71.5	48.1	32.9
White (1,000)	**25,195**	**4,323**	**11,457**	**9,414**	**4,678**	**5,254**	**8,107**	**7,156**
Percent distribution:								
Surgically sterile[2]	38.9	7.3	31.5	62.3	9.8	18.5	47.2	63.4
Infertile[3]	8.1	8.0	7.0	9.6	19.1	10.1	4.7	[4]3.4
Fecund[5]	53.0	84.7	61.4	28.1	71.1	71.4	48.0	33.2
Black (1,000)	**2,130**	**328**	**1,025**	**778**	**252**	**410**	**678**	**790**
Percent distribution:								
Surgically sterile[2]	36.2	7.4	31.8	54.1	10.1	8.5	34.9	60.0
Infertile[3]	13.1	11.9	11.5	15.7	30.6	18.5	8.9	[4]8.3
Fecund[5]	50.7	80.7	56.7	30.2	59.4	73.0	56.2	31.8

[1]Includes other races not shown separately.
[2]Includes sterilization of the husband or the wife.
[3]Continuously married, had not used cntraception, and had not become pregnant for at least 12 months before the date of interview.
[4]Figure does not meet standards of reliability or precision.
[5]Neither surgically sterile nor infertile.
Source: U.S. Bureau of the Census 1988:66.

Infertility

Infertility is usually defined as the inability to conceive after a year of unprotected sexual intercourse. Infertility does not mean that a couple has no children. As table 13.3 shows, about the same proportion of those who have one or more children are infertile as those without any children. Those with children who are infertile desire more children, but are unable to conceive.

Infertility affects women in all age groups to about the same extent (table 13.3). It may occur before a couple has children, or after they have one or more children. In any case, the result is that between two to three million couples, or about one-fifth of all couples, desire but cannot have more children. Some will be able to bear with medical assistance. Others will remain infertile.

What causes infertility? There are numerous factors involved. Sustained exposure to environmental factors such as toxic chemicals can render an individual sterile. Sexually transmitted diseases can damage a woman's Fallopian tubes. Infections from intrauterine contraceptive devices have made some women infertile. Both men and women can suffer from infertility. Let us look briefly at the more common types.[2]

Female infertility can be due to **endometriosis,** a disease in which the tissue that lines the inside of the uterus begins to grow outside as well. The growth may prevent the sperm from meeting the egg in the Fallopian tubes. The causes of endometriosis are unknown. It tends to affect women in their twenties and thirties who have not had children. It can frequently be corrected by drugs or surgery.

Various other conditions can also cause blockage of the Fallopian tubes, thus preventing conception. Scar tissue from inflammations is a common cause of blocked tubes. The blockage can sometimes be resolved through surgery.

A third reason that a woman may be infertile is that she doesn't **ovulate** properly; that is, her body does not release the egg as it should. Drugs may correct this situation.

Finally, a woman's body may, for various reasons, hinder the sperm or even kill it. Again, drug therapy may be effective in resolving the problem. Or the couple may be able to make use of some of the new technologies available.

Male infertility is somewhat less common than female, but may also arise from a number of different factors. Males are infertile generally because they have a low sperm count, or because their sperm do not swim as fast as they should. Low sperm counts may result from injury, from infection (particularly from having mumps after childhood), exposure to radiation, birth defects, or a variety of other disorders (Masters, Johnson, and Kolodny 1988:144). Sperm production also may be decreased by alcohol and drug use, including some prescription drugs. Male infertility can sometimes be treated through drugs or surgery.

In spite of our knowledge of the sources of infertility, there are some cases in which the tests yield nothing. That is, some people seem to have no detectable problem that prevents conception, yet they continue to be unable to conceive. In such cases, they may try some of the technologies described below in the section "Options," though for some couples the expense of such procedures makes them unattainable.

Coping with Infertility

If you strongly desire to have a child, but are unable to conceive after a year or more of unprotected sexual relations, you may find yourself struggling to cope with this unexpected situation. Most of us believe that if we want to have children, we can. When we want to and find that we cannot, we are likely to be quite distressed.

A study that compared infertile women with mothers and voluntarily childless wives found that the infertile women reported lower general levels of well-being, and rated their lives as less interesting, emptier, and less rewarding than did other women (Callan 1987). Infertility is not simply a biological condition. It deeply affects people. In fact, as Menning's (1977) analysis of infertility shows, the discovery that you or your spouse is infertile may lead to a process similar to that endured by people who become aware that they are dying.

Technology has opened up many new options for those who are infertile.

The first stage of the process is *surprise*. People simply do not expect to be infertile, particularly those who are achievement-oriented and think of themselves as capable of dealing adequately with the obstacles of life. Surprise is followed by *denial,* a sense that "this can't happen to me." Then there is *anger,* anger because of the pain and inconvenience of the tests, anger at the pressures from family and friends, anger at the inappropriate comments of people, and perhaps anger at those who seem to have children easily or those who have them but don't want them.

Guilt is the fourth stage. Some people may feel that God is punishing them for their sins. Some find other ways to blame themselves for the condition. *Depression* is a typical fifth part of the process. There is a sense of loss, a sadness, perhaps even a sense of despair. Associated with the sense of loss is *grief.* Those who are infertile grieve because they cannot produce another living being, similar to those who grieve because they have lost a living being. Unfortunately, while those who lose someone through death are expected to grieve openly, that may be more difficult for the infertile. After all, their loss is not of an actual but only a potential person. As such, it may not be viewed as a real and significant loss by many people.

In addition to, and perhaps partly because of, the various negative emotions experienced, the couple is likely to have some problems in their relationship. Sometimes a crisis draws a couple together and enhances their intimacy. The crisis of infertility, at least initially, sometimes strains rather than strengthens the intimate relationship. In a study of eighty-one men and women affected by infertility, the researchers found that both men and women tended to report a decrease in the frequency of sexual relations (Sabatelli, Meth, and Gavazzi 1988). The majority of the women and 42 percent of the men also reported decreased satisfaction with their sexual relationships. Four of ten of the women reported increased conflict with their husbands, though nearly two-thirds said that the emotional support of their husbands had increased since they learned of their infertility. Thus, both bonding and straining forces are at work in the period following the discovery of infertility.

Infertility, then, is a challenge to the marital relationship. It

> can result in a questioning of the meaning and purposes of marriage and requires that the couple reconstruct the purposes and goals of marriage . . . , a process that can place a considerable strain on relationships (Sabatelli, Meth, and Gavazzi 1988:338).

The final stage of the process is *resolution*. A couple may resolve their situation in a number of ways. Some may accept the fact that they will not have children and get on with their lives. Most will probably first attempt various other ways to have a child. As we shall see below, however, using new technologies or going the route of adoption can be very expensive and frustrating experiences. Many couples do not fully resolve their infertility for years. Those with a strong relationship will ultimately be strengthened for having worked through the crisis; those with weak bonds may break up.

Options for the Infertile

Those who are infertile and who want children, or more children than they already have, can choose from a variety of options. Hundreds of thousands of couples explore these options every year, and they may spend a billion dollars or more on doctors and treatments in their efforts to have a baby (Office of Technology Assessment 1988). An individual couple may spend anywhere from hundreds of dollars to $20,000 or more on infertility diagnosis and treatment.

Artificial Insemination

Artificial insemination is the injection of sperm into a woman's vagina. To result in conception, of course, the procedure must be carried out at the time the woman is ovulating (releasing an egg). Artificial insemination uses either the husband's semen (abbreviated AIH) or that of an anonymous donor (abbreviated AID).

AIH is useful when the husband's sperm count is low. The physician can take a larger amount of sperm from several ejaculations. AIH can also be done using fresh semen and inserting it into the vagina at the mouth of the uterus. Only a small portion of the sperm get to that location during intercourse, so the chances of conception are enhanced by the AIH procedure.

If the husband is sterile, or his sperm count is exceptionally low, AID may be used (this is also an option for single women who want a child). The couple will normally select a donor from an anonymous list that gives information about health, intelligence, and various physical characteristics. If fresh semen is used, the pregnancy rate with AID is about 75 percent; the rate is around 60 percent when frozen semen from a sperm bank is used (Masters, Johnson, and Kolodny 1988:146).

AID is less acceptable to people than AIH. Some religions view the procedure as morally wrong. Even the courts have occasionally defined it as adultery. Some men feel humiliated; some women are reluctant to have another man be the biological father of their children. One way that a couple can minimize potential problems is to have the physician mix the sperm of the husband with that of a donor so that the couple can't be sure who the natural father is. Generally, however, men whose wives conceive by AID assume the father's role with enthusiasm.

In Vitro Fertilization

If the infertility is due to damaged or blocked Fallopian tubes and the condition cannot be corrected, the couple may opt for **in vitro fertilization.** In this procedure, the eggs are removed from the woman's body. They are fertilized with sperm in a laboratory. The resulting embryo is then implanted in the woman's uterus.

The first case of in vitro fertilization leading to pregnancy and birth of a child occurred in England. In 1978, Louise Brown was born as a result of the work of Doctors Patrick Steptoe and Robert Edwards. The Brown baby was the first success after more than a decade of research and more than thirty failed attempts.

Since 1978, fertility clinics have opened up around the world. In 1987, there were fourteen thousand attempts at in vitro fertilization in the United States alone (Office of Technology Assessment 1988). An attempt, unfortunately, still does not mean success. Clinics have differing success rates, but the average is somewhere around 15 to 20 percent.[3]

Some people are opposed to in vitro fertilization on the grounds that it violates God's way or the "natural" way. Some people also are disturbed by the fact that clinics normally fertilize a number of eggs. The first step in the procedure is to give the woman daily hormone injections to stimulate egg production. Thus, the woman produces a number of eggs, and each is fertilized.

Intimacy in Families

Extra fertilized eggs may be discarded (in some the cells are not dividing normally anyway). To some people, this is the same as abortion—in other words, it is a form of murder because they regard the fertilized egg as a human.

For other people, however, procedures such as in vitro fertilization mean that they have the opportunity to become parents. Without the procedure, they would not have children of their own. To deny them the use of the procedure is to deny them the opportunity to have children.

Surrogate Mothers

When the wife is infertile, or when she is incapable of carrying a child, a couple may opt for a surrogate mother. The surrogate mother is a woman who volunteers to carry the baby of the couple and give it to them at the time of birth. Typically, she signs a contract with them and is paid a fee for her services. The woman may receive anywhere from a few to tens of thousands of dollars. Lawyer's fees may also amount to thousands of dollars.

The surrogate mother may be inseminated with the husband's sperm or, if the husband is also infertile, she may be inseminated with the sperm of a donor. If the wife still has functioning ovaries, she can provide an egg, use in vitro fertilization, and have the resulting embryo implanted in the surrogate mother.

As with all the possibilities discussed in this section, the option of a surrogate mother is controversial. In part, each option may present problems because technology has become available before legal and ethical guidelines have been developed to deal with various complications. For instance, two cases during the 1980s illustrate some of the complex and painful problems involved with surrogate motherhood.

The first case occurred in 1983. A Michigan woman gave birth to a deformed baby. A New York man had contracted with her to have a child by AID, but rejected it when he discovered it was deformed. He believed that he had firm legal grounds for the rejection because he was not the child's biological father. The surrogate mother didn't want the child, either. Newspaper headlines pointed out that the nation now had an "unclaimed" infant. Eventually, the surrogate mother agreed to keep the child. Future cases may be more difficult if both parties are adamant in their refusal to accept such a child.

The second case occurred in 1986 when Mary Beth Whitehead of New Jersey gave birth to "Baby M." She had contracted with a couple to act as a surrogate mother and had been inseminated with the sperm of the husband. After the girl was born, she didn't want to give it up. She felt she had a right to keep the child because she was the biological mother. She and her husband fled with the girl to Florida. Ultimately, a New Jersey court awarded the girl to the couple who had contracted for her, arguing that Mrs. Whitehead must honor the contract she had signed.

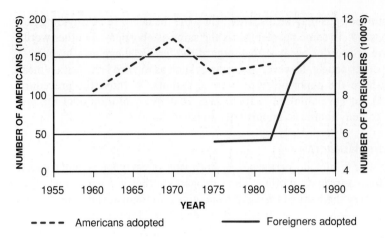

Figure 13.3 *Number of adoptions: 1960–1987.*
Source: U.S. Bureau of the Census 1989:370.

Adoption

If the above methods fail, or if a couple has some kind of objection to using them, adoption is a final option. Between 100 and 150 thousand children are adopted each year (figure 13.3). Unfortunately, however, there are probably at least thirty-five couples who want to adopt a child for every child available. Women who adopt are likely to be white, in their thirties and forties, financially well-off, and have at least some college education (Bachrach 1986). That means that adopted children generally have the benefits of being in a home that has a relatively high socioeconomic status.

There are various ways to adopt a child, and various sources of children available for adoption. In the past, a common source was the children of unwed mothers. But the combination of the high rate of abortion and the increasing number of unwed women who opt to keep a child has made this a declining source. Another source are orphans. But the number of orphans in the nation has also declined significantly over the past few decades. Some Americans are adopting children from other countries. In recent years, thousands of children have been adopted from places such as Korea, Colombia, the Philippines, and India (U.S. Bureau of the Census 1989:366).

Children may be adopted either through an agency or through a private transaction. Governmental agencies are the least expensive way to adopt a child, because the adoptive parents only pay the legal fees involved. But their requirements are very strict, the time involved is long (usually a minimum of nine months, and it may stretch into years), and the number of children available is small. Private agencies can handle the matter in less time, but they are more expensive.

Intimacy in Families

Couples can adopt a child through an agency or a private transaction.

Instead of going through an agency, some people attempt a private transaction, either through a physician or a lawyer who specializes in private adoptions. Those who use the services of a lawyer may engage in what is called an *open adoption,* which became fairly common in the 1980s. Open adoptions are in sharp contrast to the secretive processes of the past. If you adopted a child through an agency in past years, you would not know the biological parents and they would not know you. The secrecy would, in theory, protect the child, the adoptive parents, and the biological parents. The mother, who was frequently unwed, would not have to bear the stigma of having a child without a husband, and she could get on with her life. The adoptive parents would not have to worry about the mother wanting to have a close relationship with her child at some point in the future. And the child would not be caught between the two sets of parents.

But adopted children want to know about their biological parents. They may insist on their right to have information about their genetic heritage. In many cases, they have won the right to such information and have helped to change the laws. In an open adoption, the child faces an opposite kind of situation. The nature of an open adoption is well illustrated by a case known to the authors. We shall use fictitious names, but the facts are all accurate.

Sandra is a young woman who became pregnant while unmarried. She did not want to have an abortion, but she was financially and emotionally unable to care for a baby. She contacted a lawyer who specialized in open adoptions.

Problems and Possibilities with Options

What is your initial reaction to the various options mentioned in this chapter—artificial insemination (do you feel differently about AIH and AID?), in vitro fertilization, surrogate mothers, and adoption? Which would be acceptable to you and which would be unacceptable? Why?

Select one of the options and make some notes about your feelings. Then research it in the popular literature. Use the *Readers' Guide To Periodical Literature* to find articles. Begin with the latest issue available and work back in time until you have found at least ten articles that deal with your option.

How is the option treated in the popular literature? What kinds of legal and ethical problems are posed by that option? What are the effects of the option on people's well-being? What arguments pro and con are offered? How do the popular articles compare with your own feelings? Did anything you read change any of your feelings? If so, how?

If the class participates in this project, set up a debate using the information gathered in the text and the popular sources. Assign some students to take a strong pro position and others to take a strong con position. Discuss such things as the ethical, legal, interpersonal (quality of the couple's intimacy) and personal consequences of the option. Let the class then respond and vote on which option they prefer.

The Smiths, a couple in their late thirties, were unable to have children, but badly wanted them. They had contacted the same lawyer. The lawyer gave Sandra eight biographies of couples who wanted to adopt; the Smiths were one of the eight.

Sandra was three months pregnant at the time. She selected the Smiths. The lawyer then arranged for a meeting between Sandra and the Smiths. Sandra felt that she had made the right choice. Thereafter, the Smiths and Sandra met on a weekly basis. They went with her to her Lamaze classes, and were present at the birth. The boy is now about six months old. Sandra and the Smiths are friends. The Smiths will tell their son about his mother when he is older. He will have the opportunity to meet her and interact with her. At this point, they are negotiating about the amount of time that Sandra will spend with the boy.

The cost of the adoption was about the same as that of a private agency. Both Sandra and the Smiths are quite happy with the arrangement. This is not to say that there will be no problems in the future, but open adoptions seem to work well for many people.

Children and the Quality of Life

The reasons given above for why people want to have children imply that the children will enhance the quality of life. What does the evidence say?

The Stresses of Raising Children

Clearly, raising children is a demanding and sometimes agonizing task. Stress, in the form of emotional and physical strain and tension, will be experienced by all parents at some time and by a few a good deal of the time. Evidence of this may be seen in the numerous support groups that have been developed to help parents. Support groups are needed because there is very little formal training available for the task, even though most people agree that raising a child is one of the most important and challenging jobs that one ever undertakes.

Support groups are available to help at virtually every stage of parenting. There are both national and local groups. For example, the following groups are among those available to parents in Los Angeles (the same or similar groups are available throughout the nation):[4] The La Leche League offers women an opportunity to meet together to learn about breast feeding and to share practical mothering tips. Children are viewed as assets, and the purpose is to enhance the quality of mothering. The Straight Talk Clinic Parenting Group helps parents learn positive methods of discipline. Toughlove is a support group that provides support to those who have problems with difficult adolescents. Parent education classes also are available in local school districts. They furnish aid in such matters as sex education, communication skills, and helping the child in school. Parents without Partners is a support group for single parents. Parents Anonymous offers help to those who abuse or who fear they are about to abuse their children. Various other groups offer specialized help and support to those suffering from depression after delivery, to mothers of twins, to parents of hyperactive children, and to parents of children with learning disabilities.

The stresses of child-rearing may begin as soon as the infant is brought home. Most people respond to a baby with tenderness, but babies can evoke frustration as well. A study of over one hundred mothers and fathers of infants three to five months old found a number of sources of stress (Ventura 1987).

About a third of the mothers and two-thirds of the fathers described stresses that resulted from their multiple role demands (the typical problems of the dual-earner family). The effort to meet adequately the demands of work, marriage, and children can be exhausting.

The care of the infant is also stressful.

> The infant's fussy behavior in relation to feeding or soothing techniques was the major stress reported by 35% of mothers and 20% of fathers (Ventura 1987:27).

Mothers said they often felt guilty, helpless, or angry when trying to care for a fussy infant. Fathers felt stress because they didn't know what to do when the infant would not sleep or respond to their attempts to soothe it. Some of the subjects (14 percent of mothers and 11 percent of fathers) also reported being stressed with each other. They had increased marital conflict, less frequent sexual relations, and felt a lack of support from each other since the arrival of their baby. Finally, they had to cope with these stresses while also dealing with problems outside the nuclear family—18 percent of mothers and 5 percent of fathers had stress because of other family members (such as disagreements with in-laws concerning the baby).

Children can be sources of stress regardless of their age. A five-year study of twenty-five hundred Massachusetts women reported that 39 percent identified children as their primary source of stress (Mehren 1988). And a major source of stress for women at mid-life was the return of adult children to the home for economic reasons. Having an adult child return to live in the home was more stressful for these women than having a child leave home. When an adult child returns home, it raises such issues as control (do the parents have any control over the child's schedule, activities, etc.?), division of labor (is the child obligated to help around the house?), differing preferences (which TV program to watch?), and privacy (as one woman said, "We're back to having sex when our son is asleep or out, which isn't very often.").

Children and Marital Satisfaction

In the Massachusetts study (Mehren 1988), some of the couples indicated more marital problems after they had children. Are children, then, hazardous to marriage? Do they inevitably detract from the quality of the marital relationship?

Most studies have found that marital satisfaction declines over the first fifteen to twenty years of marriage and then rises again when the children start leaving home (Lewis and Spanier 1979). But some research disputes or modifies that conclusion. Let us look first at the kind of changes that occur that can depress marital satisfaction. One study compared forty-seven couples having their first child with fifteen couples not yet decided about having children (Cowan, Cowan, Heming, Garrett, Coysh, Curtis-Boyles, and Boyles 1985). The couples were studied over a two-year period. Those having children were first studied during the woman's pregnancy.

In most of the areas studied, the childless couples tended to remain stable or change in a positive direction. Those having children, however, tended to show negative change, and the mothers tended to change more than the fathers. First, the childless couples tended to report a more equal sharing of household tasks than the parents did throughout the period of study. New parents tended to assume more traditional roles for family work, more than they had expected.

> Even when changes in work involvement were expected for mothers, the vulnerability experienced by new parents, the reduced family income because of women's cutback in employment, and women's unexpected feelings of dependence on their husbands often led them to feel more dissatisfied with the new role arrangement than they had expected to be (Cowan et al. 1985:464).

Second, conflict tended to decline among the childless and increase for the parents. The most frequent source of conflict for parents was the question of who does what. Third, while their attitudes did not change, mothers and fathers had somewhat different approaches to child-rearing. The mothers were more permissive, more protective, and more child-centered than the fathers.

Other research also has found that violated expectations occur during the transition to parenthood (Belsky 1985; Ruble, Fleming, Hackel, and Stangor 1988). The violated expectations may involve not only family work roles, as Cowan and her associates found, but also expectations about how positive an experience parenting should be.

We will comment further about marital satisfaction and children in the next chapter, but three points should be made here. First, most research has shown that it is not only couples with children but couples generally who report a decline in marital satisfaction during the first two decades (McHale and Huston 1985). In part, this may reflect the change from romantic to companionate love, and the adaptation of the couple to the realities of work and home.

Second, to say that satisfaction is lower is not to say that people are dissatisfied. After all, satisfaction is at a peak in the first flush of marriage. If it changes at all, it is most likely to go down. But it does not go down to the point of dissatisfaction for the majority of couples.

Third, while the stresses of child-rearing and the changed roles and violated expectations of parents clearly tend to depress satisfaction, the relationship between satisfaction and the presence of children is partly spurious (White, Booth, and Edwards 1986). The arrival of a child means that an unhappy couple is less likely to get divorced in the next few years. Thus, a certain number of unhappily married people stay in the parent population and help lower the satisfaction rates.

Maternal satisfaction is higher when women have the social support of friends.

The Satisfactions of Raising Children

In spite of the problems and the stresses, most people continue to want children. And the great majority of those who are parents indicate that the experience has given them great satisfaction. In a review of the research literature, Ann Goetting (1986) drew a number of conclusions, including:

Generally, satisfaction with the parental role is very high.

Women report more fulfillment as parents than men, but they also see parenthood as more burdensome and restrictive.

Women are more satisfied with parenthood when they also are able to fulfill whatever aspirations for work or career they have.

Maternal satisfaction is higher to the extent that the woman has the social support of friends.

The satisfaction with parenting may have lifelong benefits. Of course, becoming a parent always involves trade-offs. There are both costs and benefits. Thus, a study of older people in Canada reported that the childless were financially better off and tended to have better health, while parents had more friends and a higher general satisfaction with life (Rempel 1985).

The extent to which the bearing and caring of children is satisfying depends on a number of factors. A couple who wants and plans for the child is likely to be more satisfied afterward than one for whom the child is unplanned and/or unwanted. Couples who have a good relationship, including good patterns of communication and sharing prior to childbirth, are more likely to continue to have a relatively high level of satisfaction after childbirth (Harriman 1986). Indeed, the satisfactions of those with strong marriages prior to the birth of children may increase rather than diminish (Miller 1976). Finally, both marital and parental satisfaction are likely to be higher when the father is more involved with the baby (Goldberg, Michaels, and Lamb 1985).

In sum, while a couple is likely to experience some decline in marital satisfaction during the childbearing years, that does not mean that they are dissatisfied with their marriages. Moreover, the amount of decline that occurs depends on a number of factors, including the quality of their relationship before the bearing of children. And the satisfactions of parenting seem, for most people, to outweigh the stresses and problems.

Parenting: Her Experience and His Experience

As we have noted, mothers perceive the experience of parenting as more demanding, more constricting, but also more rewarding than do fathers. That suggests that mothers and fathers have somewhat different experiences of being a parent.

Her Experience

"M is for the million things she gave me," begins a parody of an old song about mother. For many mothers, it seems that there are indeed a million things to give. There are also a million things to do. Motherhood is above all a consuming experience. Mothers are expected to be the primary caregivers in our society, even if they are working full-time outside the home. That is one of the reasons that, as Jessie Bernard (1974:10) put it, many women "find joy in their children, but they do not like motherhood." Fathers may come and go, but mothers are expected to nurture their children nearly every day, year in and year out.

There is, in fact, an assumption by many people that mothers are far better equipped than fathers to care for the physical and emotional needs of children. "There is something special about mothers," a man told us as he reflected on his own experiences. "They relate to you in a way that no one else in the world ever does." That may be true. Indeed, mothers make a unique contribution to our well-being. But so do fathers. It is not fair to women to make them feel that their children will suffer greatly if they are not incessantly there to care for their childrens' needs.

Still, mothers tend to value highly their experience. A *Ladies' Home Journal* Roper poll of American women reported that 79 percent said they would have children again.[5] Twelve percent had mixed feelings. Only 7 percent said no, and most of those were under thirty years of age. The women also said that childrens' teenaged years were the most trying for mothers. But once the children were adults, they were rewarding again. The worries named by the mothers, in order of frequency, were: protecting their children from drug use; having parental authority eroded by the media and peers of the children; not being home full-time because of work; economic instability in the future of their children; helping their children to be high achievers; protecting their children from AIDS; and lack of child-rearing help from their husbands.

In other words, mothers worry about the total well-being of their children. They are also more involved in the lives of their children than are fathers. In the trying years of adolescence, children communicate more with their mothers than their fathers (Noller and Bagi 1985). They engage in more self-disclosure with their mothers, and mothers are more accurate than fathers in predicting their adolescent childrens' responses. Generally, adolescent children believe that their mothers know them fairly well (Youniss and Ketterlinus 1987).

His Experience

Fatherhood was a relatively neglected topic until recent years. Increasingly, researchers are examining the role of the father and the father's experience of parenting. The research has dispelled the old notion that fathers are not inclined to or capable of nurturing behavior.

Shapiro (1987) reported an interesting series of interviews with 227 expectant and recent fathers. Expectant fathers, he pointed out, are in a "double bind." On the one hand, they are expected to be involved. On the other hand, they are not expected to have negative feelings. The woman who is waiting for her first child may feel frightened and apprehensive. That is understandable. The waiting father, on the other hand, is expected to be supportive and to avoid expressing feelings that might upset the mother-to-be.

As a result, Shapiro noted, waiting fathers tend to keep their feelings to themselves. He found that they have seven major fears and concerns about the pregnancy and coming child. Each of the fears and concerns was expressed by at least 40 percent of the men he interviewed. The first was queasiness. The men were concerned about maintaining their composure and being helpful during the birth process. Some feared that they would faint or get sick. Second, the men worried about the increased responsibility, the loss of what seemed like a comparatively free and easy life. Another concern revolved about the medical procedures. The men disliked the dehumanizing atmosphere of examinations and felt that medical personnel regarded them as out of place.

Fourth, more than half of the men were concerned about whether they were truly the child's father. This fear was rooted in a general insecurity surrounding the momentous event rather than in any real doubts about the wife's fidelity. Fifth, the men worried about the possibility of damage or death to the wife and/or the child. The sixth concern involved the marital relationship. The men feared that the child would replace them as the focus of their wife's attention or that the marital relationship would be permanently altered to a less intimate form. Finally, the men became aware of the fragile nature of life, and the importance of not dying and leaving the child without their support.

Men who would have turned to their wives with such concerns under other circumstances kept their feelings to themselves. They did not want to make the pregnancy more difficult for their wives than it already was. This is unfortunate. Shapiro found a deeper and more intimate relationship emerged for those men who did share their feelings with their wives.

Although the experience may cause apprehension, attending the birth of a child has positive consequences for fathering. Men who participate in the birth and who have extended contact with their infants in the hospital have more interaction with the infants at home and are more involved in caretaking responsibilities (Keller, Hildebrandt, and Richards 1985). Generally, mothers play with their infants more frequently than do fathers, but fathers spend a higher proportion of the time they are with their infants in play (Hanson and Bozett 1987). Fathers engage in more "rough and tumble" kind of play than mothers. Thus, they are both playmates and caretakers with their children. This is an additional source of stimulation and a unique experience for the infant, who attaches to the father as well as to the mother (Ricks 1985).

Parenting and the Well-Being of Children

If you feel good about yourself and are doing well with your life so far, you probably have grown up in a home with one or two warm, loving parents. Parents are not the only influences in our lives, but the way they relate to us is very important for our well-being. Those who perceive their parents as loving are likely to be less neurotic, more open to experience, more agreeable, and more conscientious individuals than those who do not see their parents as loving (McCrae and Costa 1988). The way that our parents relate to us tends to set the tone of our future lives.

Parental Behavior and Childrens' Adjustment

Both parents are important in a child's adjustment to his or her world. As we noted before, it is a myth that fathers are not, or cannot be, as involved in nurturing as mothers. The way that fathers interact with infants strongly affects their development, particularly with boys. Infants as young as five months are more at ease in social situations when they have been cared for and played

Advice from a Mother

Motherhood is an ongoing concern for one's child. When John Quincy Adams was eleven, he went with his father to Europe in search of support for the American Revolution. John Quincy's mother, Abigail, wrote him a letter in June 1778 to express her concerns and give him advice. Clearly, she felt that her husband was committed to the role of father, and involved in caring for the needs of the growing son:

My Dear Son

'Tis almost four months since you left your native land . . . you may be assured you have constantly been upon my heart and mind. It is a very difficult task, my dear son, for a tender parent to bring her mind to part with a child of your years, going to a distant land; nor could I have acquiesced in such a separation under any other care than that of the most excellent parent and guardian who accompanied you. . . .

The most amiable and most useful disposition in a young mind is diffidence of itself; and this should lead you to seek advice and instruction from him who is your natural guardian and will always counsel and direct you in the best manner, both for your present and future happiness. You are in possession of a natural good understanding, and of spirits unbroken by adversity and untamed with care. Improve your understanding by acquiring useful knowledge and virtue, such as will render you an ornament to society, an honor to your country, and a blessing to your parents. Great learning and superior abilities, should you ever possess them, will be of little value and small estimation,

unless virtue, honor, truth, and integrity are added to them. Adhere to those religious sentiments and principles which were early instilled into your mind, and remember that you are accountable to your Maker for all your words and actions.

Let me enjoin it upon you to attend constantly and steadfastly to the precepts and instructions of your father, as you value the happiness of your mother and your own welfare. His care and attention to you render many things unnecessary for me to write, which I might otherwise do; but the inadvertency and heedlessness of youth require line upon line and precept upon precept, and, when enforced by the joint efforts of both parents, these will, I hope, have a due influence upon your conduct; for, dear as you are to me, I would much rather you should have found your grave in the ocean you have crossed, or that any untimely death should crop you in your infant years, than see you an immoral, profligate, or graceless child. . . .

Source: Charles Francis Adams, *Familiar Letters of John Adams and His Wife Abigail Adams, During the Revolution.* New York: Hurt and Houghton, 1876, pp. 334–36.

with by their fathers (Parke and Sawin 1977). A study of 172 male under-graduates reported that those who perceived their fathers as loving and around a good deal of the time were the most well-adjusted (Reuter and Biller 1973). Boys whose fathers were perceived as unloving were less dependable and more immature. In addition, the researchers found that boys with loving but largely absent fathers were also less well-adjusted. Apparently quality time is not enough if the quantity is too little.

Similarly, mothers' interaction with their infants is important to the chil-drens' adjustment. In particular, mother-infant attachment is related to the infant's sense of competence (Sroufe 1978). Attachment refers to the amount of intimacy and closeness between a mother and child. A strong attachment means that the child feels comfortable and secure with its mother. As young as eighteen months, infants who are strongly attached to their mothers stand out in a social situation. Compared with those who are insecurely attached, they are (Sroufe 1978:56):

Intimacy with father as well as mother is important to an adolescent's well-being.

More sympathetic to distress in others

More involved in social activities

Less hesitant with other children

More of a leader with peers

More likely to be sought out by other children

More likely to suggest activities

Less likely to withdraw from excitement and commotion

Both parents continue to be important to the child's development and adjustment throughout life. Interestingly, some research has found that father intimacy is a better predictor of positive adolescent functioning than is mother intimacy (LeCroy 1988). Both are important, but the father may be somewhat more important during adolescent years. This is an important finding because, as we pointed out earlier, fathers may be less involved than mothers during adolescence.

Parental Behavior and Self-Esteem

If you are well-adjusted, of course, you are most likely to have high self-esteem, the evaluation of yourself as someone of worth. But self-esteem is important for all aspects of your life, not just your adjustment to social situations. And a number of researchers have specifically looked at the kind of parental be-havior that is related to the development of self-esteem.

A pioneering study of the development of self-esteem was done by Morris Rosenberg (1965), who examined more than five thousand high school students in New York. Among his findings were:

Adolescents with close relationships with their fathers are more likely to have high self-esteem than those with more distant relationships.

Only children have higher self-esteem than children with siblings (only children are likely to have a closer relationship with their parents).

Parental interest in the adolescent, such as knowing the adolescent's friends, being concerned about grades, and parent-child conversation during meals, is correlated with higher self-esteem.

Two years after Rosenberg's study, Coopersmith (1967) reported the results of an eight-year project. Again, parents were found to be important, with parental warmth, respectful treatment of children, and expressions of concern for the child's well-being all related to self-esteem.

Subsequent studies continue to affirm the importance of parental warmth, communication, and acceptance (e.g., Litovsky and Dusek 1985). However, boys and girls respond to somewhat different aspects of parenting. Using a sample of 128 families, Gecas and Schwalbe (1986) found that boys' self-esteem is particularly sensitive to the control/autonomy aspect of the father's behavior. Control/autonomy refers to the extent to which parents attempt to limit the child's autonomy and direct his or her activities. The more the boy perceived his father to try to exercise such control, the higher his self-esteem. It would seem that boys want their fathers to be interested and involved with their lives.

For girls, on the other hand, self-esteem is more sensitive to parental support and participation. Support includes such things as affection, helping, and expressing approval. Parental participation involves spending time with the children and sharing in their activities. Girls' self-esteem is higher to the extent that they perceive their mothers and fathers giving them support and their fathers participating with them.

As in the case of adjustment, fathers' involvement with their children during adolescence is somewhat more important to self-esteem than is the mothers'. Such findings underscore the importance of recent tendencies in which fathers are more involved with their children than were fathers in the past.

A Final Note: Is Older Better in Parenting?

It is difficult for a teenager to be a competent parent because the teenaged parent is, in many ways, a child raising a child. Fortunately, as we have seen, the tendency to delay childbearing means that fewer children are likely to be raised by very young parents. But can the delaying of parenthood be carried too far? Are there also negative consequences from being too old when one becomes a parent for the first time?

Sociologist Monica Morris (1988) has addressed the questions in a study of adults who were "last-chance children"; that is, they were the children of women who waited until their late thirties or early forties to have them. The results were mixed. Some of the subjects reported a variety of problems. Indeed, it is not difficult to imagine that life would be different if you were born to a forty-two-year-old woman and a sixty-one-year-old man. A man who was such a child said that he didn't have a childhood. His parents never bought him toys. They dressed him up instead of letting him play in jeans in the park. He never played baseball with his father or had the rough-and-tumble activities that his friends had with their parents. He feels as if he didn't even have a real relationship with them. They both died when he was in his teens, long before he was old enough to have an adult conversation with them.

The fear of one or both parents dying was expressed by a number of the subjects in Morris's study. The subjects also talked, like the man above, about what they missed. And they mentioned embarrassing incidents, like being taken for the grandchildren of their parents.

But some also believed that having older parents was a positive experience. In fact, the sample of twenty-two was almost evenly divided on whether the experience was positive or negative. Those who perceived it to be positive reflected on such things as the wisdom and stability of their parents, qualities that helped them to feel more comfortable and secure. Nevertheless, only two of them strongly endorsed the idea of having their own children at an advanced age.

Increasing numbers of children are born to women who are thirty-five or older. Older parents will have to recognize some of the problems, anxieties, and embarrassments their children are likely to face, and will have to take steps to minimize them. Older parents have much to offer children in the way of security and stability. But they will have to work a little harder to make sure that their children do not miss out on important things that their peers have, and that their children do not endure added anxieties and embarrassments because of their parents' older age.

PRINCIPLES
FOR
ENHANCING
INTIMACY

1. To have or not to have children is a serious decision. It is a decision with which each spouse needs to feel comfortable. Therefore, the best time to begin discussion about this decision is before you marry. People sometimes marry with the assumption that their spouse wants a family of two or three or more children. When the matter then comes up for serious debate, they are often surprised that their assumptions were not correct. In fact, they may find that their partner wants no children at all. It is best not to make assumptions about this important matter. Talk it out and arrive at an understanding before the wedding.

2. Flexibility is a requirement in a successful marriage; certainly, this is true where decisions about parenting are concerned, because people do change their minds. Even people who are most adamant about not having children sometimes, when they mature, reverse their decision. Similarly, even the individual most enthusiastic about eventually becoming a parent may change his or her mind in light of new personal or professional commitments. Couples, thus, need not only to begin discussing this important matter before their wedding, but also continue to do so afterward.

3. Becoming a parent is a demanding, lifelong commitment and must be entered into seriously. A baby radically changes your life. The responsibilities are tremendous—a new life is completely dependent on you. You will not be able to go and come as freely as when there was just the two of you. But keep in mind that the responsibilities are balanced by the joys and satisfactions of parenthood.

4. Child-rearing patterns are changing with the erosion of traditional roles and the increase in the number of dual-career couples. Today fathers as well as mothers are involved in nurturing and caring for their children. This is a fortunate change and should be encouraged, for fathers make a unique contribution to the development of their children.

5. If you want to have a baby and seem unable to conceive, don't give up hope. Many options are available for infertile couples today. Patience and determination are required to find a workable solution. However, also be aware that the search for a solution will likely be expensive, and your spouse may be unwilling to consider some of the options available.

SUMMARY

Birth rates have declined and are now below replacement level. The decline has occurred among the poor as well as the rich, and minorities as well as whites. The decline mirrors a lower ideal family size reported by Americans.

Among the reasons that people want to have children are the experience of happiness in a family, personal fulfillment, personal and family legacy, personal status, religious beliefs, and social expectations. Among the reasons for remaining child-free are personal fulfillment, focus on career, the economic costs of children, a focus on the marriage, and doubts about parenting skills.

About one-fifth of all married couples are infertile. Infertility results from a variety of causes, including environmental toxins and sexually transmitted diseases. Among women, common causes of infertility are endometriosis, other conditions that cause blockage of the Fallopian tubes, improper ovulation, and a bodily reaction against sperm. Among men, infertility is somewhat less common but is generally due to a low sperm count or to the sperm not swimming as fast as they should. Infections, injuries, exposure to radiation, excessive drug and alcohol use, and birth defects are among the causes of low sperm counts.

Those who discover that they are infertile may go through a process similar to what we experience because of loss through death. The process is characterized by surprise, denial, anger, guilt, depression, and grief. The infertile couple may also experience marital strain.

There are technologies that can help many of the infertile. Artificial insemination, in vitro fertilization, and surrogate mothers are alternative ways to have a baby. These methods are expensive and may pose some legal and psychological problems. Adoption is also available, though the number of couples wanting to adopt is far greater than the number of children available. In recent years, open adoptions have become more common.

Raising children is stressful, as illustrated by the number of support groups available to help parents. The stress begins as soon as the child is brought home. Marital problems may increase, and marital satisfaction will probably go down during the child-rearing years; but the satisfactions are such that most parents indicate they would go through the process again.

The experience of parenting is somewhat different for men and women. Women tend to find joy in their children but not in the tasks of motherhood. Women tend to be more involved than men in the lives of their children. Men, however, are equally capable of nurturing behavior. Expectant fathers have many anxieties that they tend not to share with others. Men spend a higher proportion of time in play with children than do mothers. They are playmates as well as caretakers.

Parental behavior is important for the child's adjustment. Both parents must relate warmly and intimately with the child for maximal adjustment and for the child's self-esteem.

Those who become parents somewhat later have much to offer children in the way of stability and security. But they also face unique problems. They and their children will have to face a number of problems, anxieties, and embarrassments arising from their age.

---

1. *Public Opinion,* December/January, 1986, p. 28.

2. *U.S. News and World Report,* October 5, 1987, pp. 60–61.

3. Ibid., p. 65.

4. *Los Angeles Times,* June 23, 1988.

5. *Ladies' Home Journal,* May, 1988, p. 72.

14

Family Life As Process

You aren't the person I married." Usually this statement indicates dissatisfaction, but it could be made by every husband and wife in the nation. We change continuously throughout our lives, and our relationships change as well. In some cases people change without conscious effort. In other cases, people may deliberately initiate change in order to improve their marital relationship (Brillinger 1985). For instance, they may try to improve their communication skills, or work on certain unrealistic attitudes or expectations. At any rate, once the change has occurred, spouses are no longer the same as at the time of their wedding.

In other words, if we ask how satisfied people are with their marriages, if we inquire into communication patterns or styles and kinds of conflict or any one of numerous aspects of family life, the answer will differ somewhat depending on how long the people have been married. In this chapter, we will look at family life as a process, as a set of relationships that inevitably change over time. They change in terms of such things as interaction patterns, feelings about each other, division of labor in the home, and expectations about behavior. There are, of course, continuities as well as change, but it is the change that we shall focus on here. Change is crucial to intimacy; depending on how the individuals change, intimacy in the family can be weakened or strengthened. People can grow apart as they change, or they can grow closer together. We will examine changing relationships in terms of the family life cycle. And we will look at some of the particular challenges, problems, and satisfactions that people face at differing points in the family life cycle.

Family life is a succession of different stages.

The Family Life Cycle

The notion of a life cycle can be applied to all of life, including nonhuman life. From stars to forests, from humans to insects, from nations to organizations, we find identifiable life cycles. That is, we can trace the process from birth to death. And a family, like a star or forest, is different at varying points along the process.

The Meaning of the Family Life Cycle

What is the difference between a family composed of a couple with an infant child versus a couple with an adolescent? As it happens, the difference can be dramatic in terms of the experiences of the people involved. There are differing challenges and differing problems. These considerations are the focus of the study of family life cycle.

In the 1950s Evelyn Duvall (1977:179) offered a widely used model of the family life cycle, which consisted of eight stages and the various critical tasks facing people in each of these stages. The stages range from the newly married couple, through the childbearing years, to the "aging family members" stage in which the original couple are grandparents or in which one of the spouses dies.

A more recent formulation is that of Carter and McGoldrick (1980), who identified six stages, each of which focuses on at least two generations (table 14.1). The six stages they identify are points at which family members enter or leave the system. These stages include (1) the unattached young adult, (2) the newly married couple, (3) the family with young children, (4) the family with adolescents, (5) the launching and empty nest, and (6) the family in later life. Carter and McGoldrick discussed the way in which families must alter their attitudes and relationships in order to adapt to the varying stages.

For instance, in the family with an unattached young adult, there is the challenge of accepting the parent-child separation that must occur. Three changes are necessary for that challenge to be successfully met. First, each family member must view the young adult as an individual, someone with a life of his or her own that is separate from that of the family. Second, the young adult must develop close relationships with his or her peers. And third, the young adult must become established in some kind of work or a career.

Table 14.1 Stages of the Family Life Cycle

Family life cycle stage	Emotional process of transition: key principles	Second-order changes in family status required to proceed developmentally
(1) Between Families: The Unattached Young Adult	Accepting parent-offspring separation	(a) Differentiation of self in relation to family of origin (b) Development of intimate peer relationships (c) Establishment of self in work
(2) The Joining of Families Through Marriage: The Newly Married Couple	Commitment to new system	(a) Formation of marital system (b) Realignment of relationships with extended families and friends to include spouse
(3) The Family with Young Children	Accepting new members into the system	(a) Adjusting marital system to make space for child(ren) (b) Taking on parenting roles (c) Realignment of relationships with extended family to include parenting and grandparenting roles
(4) The Family with Adolescents	Increasing flexibility of family boundaries	(a) Shifting of parent-child relationships to permit adolescent to move in and out of system (b) Refocus on mid-life marital and career issues (c) Beginning shift toward concerns for older generation
(5) Launching Children and Moving On	Accepting a multitude of exits from and entries into the family system	(a) Renegotiation of marital system as a dyad (b) Development of adult relationships between grown children and parents (c) Realignment of relationships to include in-laws and grandchildren (d) Dealing with disabilities and death of parents (grandparents)
(6) The Family in Later Life	Accepting the shifting of generational roles	(a) Maintaining own and/or couple functioning and interests in face of physiological decline: exploration of new familial and social role options (b) Support for a more central role for middle generation (c) Making room in the system for the wisdom and experience of the elderly: supporting the older generation without overfunctioning for them (d) Dealing with loss of spouse, siblings, and other peers, and preparation for own death. Life review and integration.

From Elizabeth A. Carter and Monica McGoldrick, *The Family Life Cycle.* Copyright © 1980 Gardner Press, Inc., New York, NY.

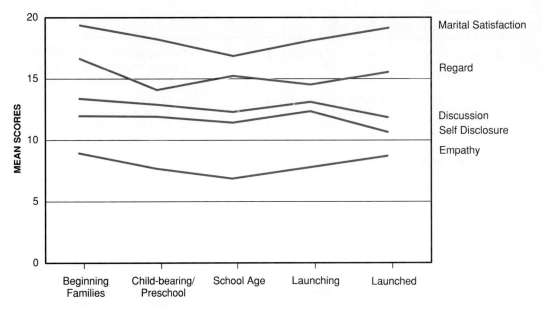

Figure 14.1 *Some changes over the family life cycle as perceived by wives.*

What Changes Occur over the Family Life Cycle?

It is not merely the challenges and problems that change from one stage of the family life cycle to another. Our relationships with each other also change. Based on their study of nearly two hundred married women, Anderson, Russell, and Schumm (1983) found variations over the family life cycle in a number of important areas of marital interaction (figure 14.1). "Regard" refers to the amount of positive regard the women believe their husbands have for them. "Discussion" is the amount of time the spouses spend talking to each other. "Empathy" refers to the amount of empathic understanding that the wives perceive their husbands to have for them. As many other studies have found, marital satisfaction tends to be lowest during the childbearing years. Perceived empathy follows a similar pattern. The level of regard is cyclic. Discussion and self-disclosure decline somewhat, but for a couple married twenty to thirty years or more the decline is not significant for the quality of the relationship (because satisfaction goes up).

Figure 14.1 suggests that younger and older couples are more alike in some ways than couples in their middle years. Another piece of research that supports that notion looked at the way that couples handle conflict (Zietlow and Sillars 1988). The researchers divided the couples into three groups: young, middle, and retired. They looked at the extent to which the couples used various communication styles in conflict (figure 14.2). *Denial* is a refusal to acknowledge the disagreement. *Topic management* is an effort to avoid certain topics or to shift to a different topic. *Noncommittal remarks* include such

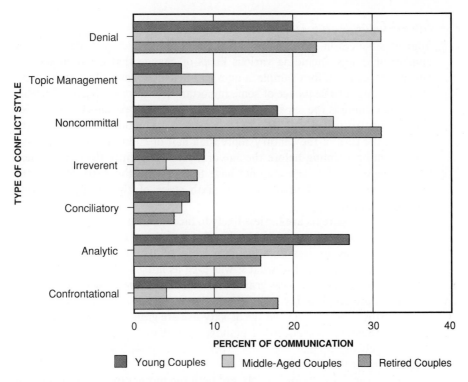

Figure 14.2 *Conflict styles of young, middle-aged, and retired couples.*
Source: Data from Zietlow and Sillars 1988:236.

things as questions like "what do you think?" and general statements like "everyone gets mad at times." *Irreverent remarks* include joking (e.g., "maybe we should just burn the house down instead of cleaning it"). *Analytic remarks* are efforts to get clarification. *Confrontative remarks* include criticism of the other person, rejection of statements the other has made, hostile statements, and ultimatums. Finally, *conciliatory remarks* are statements of support for the other, concessions, and the acceptance of personal responsibility for the problem.

As figure 14.2 shows, young and retired couples use about the same proportion of denial, topic management, irreverent remarks, confrontative remarks, and conciliatory remarks. Both are much more likely to be confrontational than are middle-aged couples, who are much more likely to use denial than either of the others.

Thus, some of the changes that occur over the family life cycle are cyclical and some are more linear. That is, some changes are like marital satisfaction, which has its ups and downs through the family life cycle. Others are like self-disclosure, which tends to decline over the life cycle. But whatever characteristic of family life you are interested in, it is likely to be somewhat different in the various stages of the family life cycle.

Social Change and the Family Life Cycle

Your experiences in passing through the family life cycle will depend on a number of things, including various kinds of change that occur in society. During this century, for example, a number of changes have affected the prevalence, timing, and sequence of some important transitions (Hagestad 1988).

First, there is the experience of the death of one's parents or of a child. Improved nutrition and health care have made a dramatic difference in **death rates.** At the turn of the century, more than half of children faced the death of a parent or a sibling before the age of fifteen. Currently the figure is less than 10 percent. Now you may not have to cope with the death of a parent until you are in the fourth, fifth, or sixth stage of the family life cycle (Hagestad 1988).

Similarly, parents are far less likely to face the death of a child. In 1900, parents had a better than even chance of experiencing the death of a child. Now the chances are less than five in a hundred. The rate of infant deaths presently is less than half of what it was even as late as 1960.

Another change involves grandparenthood. Because of increased life expectancy, more people today have the experience of being a grandparent. About three-fourths of people over the age of sixty-five are grandparents, and as many as half of them will become great-grandparents as well (Shanas 1980). Some people, especially women, will even experience being both a grandchild and a grandparent at the same time.

However, fewer women today are both the mother of a small child and a grandmother as well. Women are completing their childbearing at an earlier age than they did in the past. There is now more likely to be a sequence rather than an overlapping of roles.

A third change relates to marital disruption and remarriage. There is a widespread belief that marital disruption is far more prevalent than it was in the past. However, an analysis of the probability of disruption shows that it was as likely in 1900 as it is presently (Hagestad 1988:407). Under conditions in 1900, people's marriages were likely to be disrupted by death within forty years. Presently, the rate of disruption remains about the same. But the major source of disruption differs. Since 1974, marriages are more likely to be disrupted by divorce than by death.

There are differing consequences to disruption by divorce than by death. In discussing the consequences with people who have experienced one or both, the authors found that many insist that it is more difficult to adjust to divorce than it is to death. If, then, the rate of disruption is about the same, the experience is not.

The incidence of remarriage is also affected (Hagestad 1988: 408). The death of a spouse may put one person into the marriage market; divorce may put two. But after the age of forty, males are more likely than females to remarry. In fact, remarriage rates are three times higher for males. In part this

Embarking on a Difficult Road

The following is taken from a popular nineteenth-century woman's magazine. It is a rather dreary picture of the first two stages of the family life cycle. Because of various changes, a woman is much less likely today to face such a difficult road when she decides to marry:

Kind reader, it is no fancy sketch that I am going to give you. It is drawn from life in all its reality; and in every city, village, country-town, and neighborhood, its truthfulness will be recognized. It is the every-day life of woman. . . .

A young man arrives at an age when he thinks it time for him to get married, and settle down. He has a respectable education, and wants a woman who is his equal. He looks about him, and makes a choice. She is a girl well educated, reared by careful parents, and is, in the truest sense, a lady. She is intelligent, loves books, possesses a refined and delicate taste, and is, in all points, well fitted to be the mistress of a cheerful, happy home. She becomes his wife; is industrious, and ambitious to do as much as she can toward a living. Maybe they are not very well off as to the things of this world, and both are equally ambitious to accumulate a comfortable property; and the husband soon becomes avaricious enough to allow the woman of his love to become his most devoted drudge. Her life is thenceforth one of the most unremitting toil. It is nothing but cook and bake, wash dishes, thrash among pots and kettles, wash and iron, churn, pick up chips, draw water, and a thousand other things "too tedious to mention."

The result is, the husband soon owns the house he lives in, and something besides; takes his ease when he chooses, reads and improves his mind, and becomes important in the community. But the cares of his faded, broken-down wife know no relaxation. The family enlarges, and she, poor woman, has enough to do without finding time to increase her stock of knowledge, or to watch the progress of the minds of her children. . . . The only wonder is, that the mother does not sink within this circle of everlasting drudgery, which deprives her of the privilege of relaxation for a day. . . .

Thus, many a woman breaks and sinks beneath the wear and tear of the frame and the affections . . . cares eat away at her heart; the day presses on her with new toils; the night comes, and they are unfulfilled; she lies down in weariness, and rises with uncertainty; her smiles become languid and few, and her husband wonders at the gloominess of his home. When he married, he thought the chosen of his heart his equal in intelligence, but now she is far his inferior.

Source: "Every-day Life of Woman," *Ladies' Repository,* October, 1851, pp. 365–66.

is due to the sex ratio and in part to the tendency of men to marry women younger than themselves. The net effect is that a man is likely to spend the last part of his life with a wife, while a woman is more likely to spend the last part of her life alone or in an institutio n.

The Newly Married: A Family Without Children

You will recall that we considered the first stage of the family life cycle in chapter 6 in our discussion of the single adult. The second stage of the family life cycle occurs when a couple marries. What are the characteristics of this stage in the family cycle, and what are the important challenges a couple faces as it establishes a marital system?

The newly married couple tends to have certain family strengths that are at a very high level (Olson and McCubbin 1983:100). In particular, the couple is likely to agree that, among other things, they

Disclose their feelings

Do not worry about a great many things

Trust and confide in each other

Feel a sense of loyalty to each other

Share similar beliefs and values

Have respect for, and pride in, each other

Do not have a great many conflicts

To the extent that the above is true for a couple, they have a strong foundation for beginning their life together. They have a high level of communication, are comfortable sharing intimate matters, and find self-disclosure relatively easy.

One of the important tasks facing the newly married couple is that of forming their own marital system. That is, when you marry you have to decide on a whole range of matters for your own newly formed family. Will you openly show both positive and negative feelings? Will you each take responsibility for your own actions? Will you deal openly with problems? Will you resolve normal conflicts without causing each other undue stress? If and when you have children, will you freely admit to them when you are wrong? Will you allow them to express views different from yours? Will you consciously strive to maintain a warm and supportive atmosphere in the home? And so on.

In building a marital system, a couple will likely model their relationship after one or the other of their families of origin. As you think about your own family of origin, would the answers to the above questions be "yes"? Using such questions to measure experiences in families of origin, Wilcoxon and Hovestadt (1985) found that the more spouses agreed on their answers (that is, the more similar their family-of-origin experiences), the more likely they

The newly married couple faces the important task of establishing their own marital system.

were to have a satisfying relationship. In such cases, as the researchers pointed out, "the 'struggle' may not take the form of 'yours or mine' in terms of spouses modeling their respective families of origin" (Wilcoxon and Hovestadt 1985:170). In other words, when you and your spouse have similar perceptions of your families of origin, you do not have to choose between opposing models of family life.

Of course, you may choose to reject the model of your family of origin, though this is probably the exception rather than the rule. It may be difficult to know or to agree on what kind of model to use as a substitute. In such cases, it is easy to fall back on what is familiar. Nevertheless, there are couples who consciously opt for a different model when they are uncomfortable with that of their families of origin. As, for instance, a husband told us:

> My wife and I both came from families where our parents argued loudly and vociferously with each other. We both disliked that, and we decided that we would not do this. We have very few arguments but when we do disagree, we make a strong effort to talk about things calmly and get the matter settled as quickly as possible.

The couple had similar experiences in their family of origin, but each had agreed to find an alternative way in their marriage.

In any case, a central task at this stage is to establish your own marital system, your own way of relating and dealing with the various problems and processes of family life. You will probably model some of your patterns on those of your family of origin. You should be aware, however, that some of those patterns may not work well for you, and that unless you consciously decide to do otherwise you will follow them even though they are not effective for your family.

In establishing your own marital system, you also will have to deal with the dilemma of "fusion and closeness" (McGoldrick 1980). In our quest for intimacy, we try to get close to another person. This effort can be carried to an extreme, so that the couple is no longer two separate individuals in an intimate relationship but almost one fused being. For example, the spouses may always feel the same thing in every situation, may be unwilling to engage in activities without the other, may be unable to make separate and contrary judgments about things, and so forth. Fusion in a relationship will lead sooner or later to difficulties and even to a loss of intimacy in the relationship. Another central task of the newly married couple, then, is to form an intimate union without a loss of individual identity.

The Family with Young Children

In the third stage of the family life cycle, the couple commits themselves to an additional person and to changes in the family system. They face the challenge of the new roles of mother and father as well as those of husband and wife. Initially, they may find great joy in the birth of their child. However, as we saw in the last chapter, the "blessed event" has its problems as well as its blessings. The family strengths we mentioned above tend to remain high at this stage (Olson and McCubbin 1983:100), but the couple is likely to rate their marital communication as lower. And marital satisfaction starts to decline. Interestingly, husbands of housewives are least likely to be "very happy" with the marriage when there are preschool children in the home, while husbands of employed wives are least likely to be "very happy" when the children reach school age (Benin and Nienstedt 1985:982). Again, this does not mean that they are unhappy, but only that they are less happy than at other stages. It is probable that the increased attention and energy that the wife gives to the children, and the increasing demand by employed wives for husbands to share in the family work, account for the lower satisfaction.

The same factors are involved in the declining marital satisfaction of wives at this stage. That is, they are consumed with the endless tasks of parenthood. They may be frustrated with their husband's reluctance to share the family work. And they may have little time or energy for working at their intimate relationships with their husbands.

Another factor that strains marital satisfaction at this stage is the extent of perceived agreement between the spouses. White (1987) looked at eight issues in family life: preferred family size, how children should be disciplined, whether to spend leisure time with friends or family, equality in financial contributions to the family, equal sharing of household chores, perceived equity in the relationship, whether a wife should have an abortion without the husband's consent, and whether a mother with small children should enter the labor force.

While the wives in White's sample tended to see more overall agreement in this stage than they did in the previous one (newly married), the husband's perceptions of agreement dropped sharply. Actually, when comparing the responses of husbands and wives, it was clear that the couples' agreement on the eight issues went up. But the husbands didn't believe it went up. They perceived a much lower level of agreement. Their perceptions meant a lower level of marital satisfaction for them, because perceived (rather than actual) agreement on issues is an important ingredient in marital satisfaction.

The Family with Adolescents

As the children grow older, the couple faces the challenge of allowing their children to form their own independent identities, move beyond the nuclear family, and establish a wider range of intimate relationships. Meanwhile, the couple will also face their own mid-life concerns with regard to the marriage and their careers. This fourth stage, then, may be an agitated clash of two turbulent processes.

The Needs of Adolescents

Adolescents undergo important physical, intellectual, and "social definitional" changes (Steinberg 1987:80–81). Physically, adolescents change in size and appearance, develop the capacity to engage in sexual relations, and reproduce. Intellectually, the adolescent develops the capacity to think more logically and more abstractly. This means that the family now has "an additional person who can think and reason in complex, adult-like ways" (Steinberg 1987:81). The "social-definitional" changes refer to the changed expectations about rights and responsibilities that people have for the adolescent as he or she emerges into adulthood. These new expectations give the adolescent a different position both in the family and in the larger society.

At adolescence, then, parents and children must work out a new system. Adolescents prefer more egalitarian relationships with their parents, and because of the above changes they have a basis for advancing that preference. Whereas children may obey simply on the basis of a parental "because I say so," adolescents are likely to be dissatisfied with such statements. Adolescents want to deal with parental expectations on the basis of reason, fairness, and mutual respect.

Adolescents also need increasing autonomy and independence. They are striving to establish their own identity, to find out what kind of persons they are. They need to test their abilities and explore their future options. In the process, they may shift their focus from family to friends and peers. It isn't that they reject the family, but that they find the perspectives of those outside the family to be an important part of their quest for their own identity.

Parent-Child Problems

In part, because of the unique needs of adolescents, there may be considerable strain in the family at this stage. Communication problems are likely to be more serious than at other stages (Olson and McCubbin 1983:221). Parents may complain that they don't understand their children, who, in turn, complain that they don't understand their parents. Mothers perceive more satisfying communication with adolescents than do fathers. Mothers particularly see the parent-child communication as more open. Adolescents themselves agree with that assessment, perceiving better and more open communication with their mothers than with their fathers.

In addition to communication problems, families report a variety of other kinds of stress at this stage (Olson and McCubbin 1983:228–29). Parents talk about increasing difficulty in managing their adolescent children. They see an increase in the number of household chores that are not done. They may see problems arising from the increased activity of the children outside the family. "Our daughter," one couple reported to us,

> caused us a lot of pain because she always wanted to be with her friends. She might call just before dinner and announce that she wanted to stay at her friend's house and have dinner there. She really disrupted our tradition of always having family dinners together.

Parents also report stress from increased financial problems. Children become increasingly expensive as they age. By the time of adolescence, the costs of food, clothing, medical care, automobiles, education, and so on are at a peak for many families. In fact, parents feel that most of their stress during stage four comes from the financial strains they face (Olson and McCubbin 1983:228).

For their part, adolescents see most of their stress arising from daily hassles with parents. They report increasing arguments about household chores, increased pressure to achieve (either academically or in sports), hassles about using the family car and doing things with the family, and arguments over their selection of friends and social activities.

Adolescents are not oblivious to the problems of their parents, incidentally. They also feel some of the stress that their parents experience because of problems with family finances. Carrie, a graduate student, told us that her adolescence was strained more by her parents' problems than her own:

> My parents fought a lot. And they had problems with money most of the time. My main stress was the fact that I felt responsible for helping them solve their problems and for making everything "all right" in our family. I

The "sandwich generations" are those caught between responsibilities for both adolescent children and aging parents.

went to work early to try to pay for my own things and relieve my parents of that much worry. And I either tried to mediate their arguments or console my mother after they fought. I guess I didn't have time to rebel or to worry much about self. I was too busy being a family therapist.

Parents' Mid-life Concerns

At the same time that parents are dealing with their adolescents, they often have to contend with other family and personal concerns. Most parents of adolescents are at an age that is a critical time in adult development. They are also likely to experience the problems of the "sandwich generation," those caught between responsibilities for their adolescent children and their own aging parents. A couple that has to deal not only with adolescents but also with parents who have demanding physical, financial, or emotional needs, is doubly stressed.

In addition to responsibilities for their children and their parents, the couple in stage four face marital and personal challenges. Mid-life is a time when people become increasingly concerned about their own aging process. They face issues of their appearance, physical competency, and health. The importance of health to an individual's quality of life increases significantly around the age of thirty-five (Steinberg 1987:82). It isn't that health actually tends to deteriorate at that age, but that people become aware of its importance and get more concerned about it.

At mid-life, there is also a change in the way that people view life. They begin to think in terms of how much time they have left rather than how much has already occurred. Possibilities for change seem limited. For example, they may feel that they no longer have options for a career change, and that they are bound to continue in whatever career they have until retirement. There may be a yearning for some new excitement or new direction, but there appears to be few if any opportunities to fulfill these desires. In some cases, their marriage may appear to be stale and a handicap to further growth and/or excitement in life. One or both partners may seriously think about the possibility of separation or divorce in order to pursue new relationships.

Perhaps the above sounds familiar. It is a description of some of the things that happen to people who wrestle with the so-called mid-life crisis. Not everyone has a mid-life crisis, but everyone faces a set of challenges and concerns at mid-life. For men, Levinson, Darrow, Klein, Levinson, and McKee (1978) have identified four fundamental concerns. First is the concern with mortality. A man comes to realize that his life is limited. Increasingly, he becomes aware that some day he will die. He must come to terms with the fact that he is growing older and learn to find some value in that process. Unfortunately, some men resist the process vigorously, using dress, cosmetics, exercise, diet, new relationships and behavior patterns, and perhaps even plastic surgery in an effort to stay young looking. Advertisements, of course, play on this desire and offer a wide variety of products and services to maintain a youthful appearance.

A second concern involves destructive and creative tendencies. Destruction, including death, is a part of men's experience. But a man

> is eager to affirm life for himself and for the generations to come. He wants to be more creative. The creative impulse is not merely to "make" something. It is to bring something into being, to give birth, to generate life. A song, a painting, even a spoon or toy, if made in a spirit of creation . . . has a being of its own and will enrich the lives of those who are engaged with it (Levinson et al. 1978:222).

The hunger to be creative, to give the world some legacy, adds to the restlessness of men at mid-life.

Third, men need to recognize and develop both the masculine and feminine aspects of their nature. Up to mid-life, for example, a man may focus his energies on being a "true" man, on doing, making, and having. But at mid-life, he may begin to explore the feminine side of his nature. In other words, sex-role orientations may shift at mid-life and become more androgynous.

Part of the male shift in sex-role orientation is an increasing concern for family and interpersonal relationships (as opposed to a consuming involvement in career). Many men become more nurturant, more expressive, and more invested in their relationships than they were in the past. As a result, the well-being of men at mid-life tends to be dependent more on the quality of their intimate relationships than on their financial attainments (McKenry, Arnold, Julian, and Kuo 1987).

The fourth concern is the need to be attached to and separate from the social environment. Attachment means involvement with the environment, including the feelings a man has, and the way in which he interacts with it. When he is attached to the environment, his thoughts are focused on it. Separateness, on the other hand, does not mean that he is not involved with people or activities, but that his thoughts are focused within—on his own imagination and fantasies. Separateness helps him grow. When he is too separate, he is in danger of losing touch with reality. When he is too attached, he is in danger of neglecting his personal growth.

In early adulthood, Levinson and his associates point out, a man is more prone to attachment than separateness. During his twenties and thirties, a man is consumed with making his way in the world and successfully pursuing his work. At mid-life, it becomes important to attain a more equal balance between separateness and attachment. A man must address such questions as what he really wants, what is really important to him, and how he wants to live in the future.

Although Levinson's work focused on men, women also deal with mid-life issues. Women tend to reach the mid-life crisis point sooner than men, usually around the age of thirty-five (Sheehy 1976). At that point, a woman may feel that she faces her last opportunity to accomplish certain things in her life. She may also experience important changes, such as her last child going to school and the prospective end of her childbearing years. With the tasks of mothering requiring less of her time, a woman may begin to focus more attention on her own needs and development.

Satisfaction at Mid-Life

Obviously, the intersection of the turmoil of adolescence with the parental crisis of mid-life creates a fertile climate for considerable family strain and for diminished satisfaction with life (Steinberg and Silverberg 1987). In fact, stage four tends to be the most stressful of all (Olson and McCubbin 1983:219).

But we do not want to paint a totally bleak picture. In spite of the strains, we should point out that intense conflict between parents and their adolescent children is not inevitable (Steinberg 1987:78). Most adolescents, in fact, note positive relationships with their parents. A national sample of children reported considerable satisfaction with family life (Roper and Keller 1988). Even though some of the children included (ages eight to seventeen) were not adolescents, the results were impressive. Fully 93 percent said they were happy with the amount of love shown by their parents, and 79 percent were happy about the amount of time their parents spent with them. Three-fourths even said they were happy about the amount of work they had to do around the house. In another study, 335 adolescents reported more harmony than discord in their families (Richardson, Galambos, Schulenberg, and Petersen 1984). Their conflict tended to focus on issues of freedom and responsibility. Nevertheless, most of the children perceived their parents as fair and relatively lenient in their discipline.

When families do have conflict, it may partly be due to a lack of **rites of passage** (Quinn, Newfield, and Protinsky 1985). A rite of passage marks a significant time of change in an individual's life. In many preindustrial cultures the transition to adulthood is marked by a rite of passage. For example, an adolescent male may undergo some kind of physical test such as a period of isolation and beating by adult men that marks the end of childhood and his entry into the world of adults. We may find these rites of passage unappealing because they involve varying degrees of anxiety and pain. Still, they clearly indicated when an individual passed from childhood to adulthood.

In our society, there are some markers of this transition. For example, attaining the age when you can get a driver's license may be a rite of passage, but it depends on how it is handled in a family. In some families, the new right may be granted with reluctance or not at all. Or it may be treated as little more than the result of living a certain number of years rather than as a significant accomplishment. To be effective, a rite of passage should treat the event as an achievement that brings with it higher status and greater responsibility and privileges.

Thus, one of the ways that families can deal with conflicts and problems is to institute rites of passage. Consider the following case of a single mother and her adolescent daughter (Quinn, Newfield, and Protinsky 1985:106–7). Mrs. Ward, the mother, was a widow raising her fifteen-year-old daughter, Diane, alone. Diane's father was killed when she was four. Her uncle served as a kind of surrogate father to her, but he was killed in a military accident when she was nine. Mrs. Ward didn't realize how traumatic each of these losses was for Diane. She didn't take Diane's grieving seriously. She tried to take over both parental roles by being a strict disciplinarian and maintaining total control.

But maintaining control meant that Diane's attempts to grow up were thwarted. Her mother defined any efforts on Diane's part to act like an adult as premature. Their conflict culminated in Diane's attempted suicide. At the time of the attempt, Diane had just graduated from junior high after a three-year struggle with her math courses and a number of behavioral problems at school. The therapist suggested a rite of passage. He said it was time for the family to move to a new stage of their lives. He helped them plan a party to celebrate Diane's school achievements and her entrance into senior high. The party would also allow them each to meet new people. Following the party, Diane and her mother began to make significant progress.

A party as a formal recognition is, of course, only one way that a family can institute its own rites of passage. The point is that there is great value to all members of the family to have some kind of ceremony that carries with it recognition by both parents and children that a new phase has been reached, and that this new phase means that the adolescent has achieved something significant and is now endowed with a higher status and new privileges and responsibilities. Such rites of passage may occur profitably a number of times during the adolescent years.

Family Rituals

In this chapter, we have noted the importance of rites of passage in family life. Family rituals are also an important tool in creating family solidarity and providing family members with meaningful experiences of interaction. Unlike rites of passage, rituals occur frequently and regularly. How many rituals do you observe in your family? How are they observed? What were some of the most meaningful rituals to you in your family of origin? How many of them do you, or do you plan, to use in your own nuclear family?

When thinking of rituals, consider what your family did on holidays, on certain special days, and regularly as a part of family life. For example:

Holidays would include

New Year's Eve	Labor Day
Memorial Day	Thanksgiving
Easter or Passover	Christmas
Mother's and Father's Day	Hanukkah
Independence Day	

Special days include

birthdays	graduation
anniversaries	weddings
confirmation or Bar Mizvah or Bas Mizvah	baptism vacations

Other rituals might include

mealtime activities	family recreation activities
bedtime rituals	family religious activities

Talk to someone of another race or another ethnic background about the rituals in his or her family. How do they compare with yours? Are there different rituals for boys and girls? If so, how would you evaluate that practice?

If the entire class participates in this project, have a number of people describe the rituals that were most meaningful to their family. Then discuss which of the rituals the class members would like to incorporate in their own families.

The Launching and Empty Nest Stage

In stage five, the couple must deal with the children moving out and being on their own. This can be a problem for both the children and the parents. Family therapists stress the need for "differentiation," the need for each member of the family to be an autonomous individual as well as an integral part of an intimate group (Bowen 1978). As we noted above in our discussion of the problem of fusion in a newly married couple, a fulfilling intimate relationship is a relationship of interdependence, not of merging and loss of individuality. Fusion can occur between children and parents as well as between spouses. At some point, then, it is important that the children pursue their individual lives by leaving the home.

When the last child leaves home, a couple must come to terms with their marital relationship for the future.

When the children leave, the couple must come to terms with their own marital relationship and the meaning of that relationship for the future. They may, for example, want to renegotiate their roles. They may have to adjust to the marriage of their children, including the addition of in-laws into the family system. They may find themselves in the new role of grandparent. And they may face the problem of their own parents becoming disabled or dying.

We should note that at least some couples never experience, or have little time to experience, the empty nest. As table 14.2 shows, after age forty-five there is a dramatic decline in the number of households with children under the age of eighteen. But 10.3 percent of married couples in which the head of the house is fifty-five to sixty-four years of age and 1.6 percent of those sixty-five and older still have children under eighteen living at home.

The Couple Together Again

It may be difficult for a couple when their children leave home. A psychology professor put it this way:

> Two of the most painful times I remember are when our oldest child announced he was leaving home to go to college and when our youngest did the same. With the oldest, it meant that the family was beginning to break up. With the youngest, it meant a loss of a special kind of parenting that I valued, that day-to-day involvement with the kids.

Table 14.2 Family Households with Own Children under Age 18: 1987

Type of family	Age of householder						
	Total	15–24 years old	25–34 years old	35–44 years old	45–54 years old	55–64 years old	65 years old and over
Number (1,000)							
Family households with children	31,898	1,760	11,582	12,574	4,824	996	161
Married couple	24,645	940	8,790	9,960	3,970	847	138
Male householder[1]	955	85	230	425	171	34	9
Female householder[1]	6,297	735	2,562	2,189	683	115	14
Percent distribution							
Family households with children	100.0	100.0	100.0	100.0	100.0	100.0	100.0
Married couple	77.3	53.4	75.9	79.2	82.3	85.0	85.7
Male householder[1]	3.0	4.8	2.0	3.4	3.5	3.4	5.6
Female householder[1]	19.7	41.8	22.1	17.4	14.2	11.5	8.7
Households with children, as a percent of all family households, by type							
Family households with children, total	49.5	59.9	76.6	81.2	43.9	10.2	1.6
Married couple	47.8	50.6	74.0	81.9	44.4	10.3	1.6
Male householder[1]	38.1	35.7	44.5	66.0	39.1	11.3	2.4
Female householder[1]	60.3	87.2	94.3	81.8	42.3	9.6	1.0

[1]No spouse present.

Source: U.S. Bureau of the Census 1989:51.

Some men find it painful for the children to leave, although those most likely to find the empty nest a disagreeable time are those who have poor marital relationships (Lewis, Freneau, and Roberts 1979).

Women are more likely than men to find the empty nest a painful situation, particularly those women who have invested themselves totally, or nearly so, in child-rearing (Bart 1971). The woman who had little other than motherhood to occupy herself during the earlier stages may find this stage a deeply painful one. She may have fulfilled her intimacy needs in her relationships with her children. She even may feel somewhat estranged from her husband because she has neglected the marriage. And even if there is no estrangement, she may find that her husband is too involved with work or his career to take the place of the children in her life. She desperately needs new challenges, new tasks, new intimate relationships, but she may be at a loss as to where to find them.

But how many women, or men for that matter, come to the empty nest stage and find it empty of meaning as well as of children? Certainly not the majority. To the contrary, most people, both men and women, report that it is a time of increased marital satisfaction and renewal for their marriage. In national surveys, middle-aged wives whose children have left home report greater happiness with life generally and with the marriage in particular than those wives who still have children in the home (Glenn 1975).

For most people, then, stage five represents a time of increasing marital satisfaction and renewed family strength. Husbands perceive a sharp increase in agreement on various issues at this stage (White 1987). Wives begin to spend less time in housework (Rexroat and Shehan 1987). There may be a sexual renewal in the marriage as the couple realizes that they can express themselves sexually in a more relaxed and private way. There may be a sense of new freedom—fewer responsibilities, less financial strain, less family work. The marriage may become more egalitarian than it was during the child-rearing years. And whatever grief is involved in the children leaving may be more than compensated by pride in their achievements and the satisfactions of having parented.

Overall, then, the empty nest is likely to be a stage that is gratifying and filled with a new zest for living. The psychologist quoted previously had more to say: "What I discovered, however, was that just being with my wife again was great. We're having a ball! I love my children dearly, and I can't imagine being without them, but life has never been any better than it is now."

Grandparenthood

Increasing numbers of people are experiencing the grandparent role. Some people become grandparents as early as their forties. Among those sixty-five and older, nearly three-fourths are grandparents (Barranti 1985). Although the pride of grandparents is legendary in our society, including everything from pins to bumper stickers that say "ask me about my grandchildren" or "happiness is being a grandparent," not everyone welcomes the role. Some grandparents resist the implication of their own aging. Some do not want to get involved in the childcare aspects that are frequently expected of them. But for the most part, grandparenting is a positive experience in people's lives.

Types of Grandparents

Grandparents relate in differing ways to their grandchildren. In their study of seventy sets of middle-class grandparents, Neugarten and Weinstein (1968) found that most expressed satisfaction and comfort with the role. About a third had some difficulty adjusting to it, mainly because of such things as resentment over baby-sitting. The researchers identified five different types of grandparent: the formal, the fun seeker, the surrogate parent, the reservoir of family wisdom, and the distant figure.

The *formal* grandparent has definite ideas of the role and clearly distinguishes it from the parental role. Formal grandparents may occasionally indulge the child and do some baby-sitting, but they basically let childcare duties remain in the hands of the parents. They show constant interest in the grandchild but do not offer advice on parenting.

Intimacy in Families

The *fun seeker* establishes an informal, playful relationship with the grandchild. They join the child in play, almost like a playmate. They themselves have fun and expect the child to have fun as well. The *surrogate parent* is a grandmother role in which the woman assumes the responsibilities of childcare. Usually this happens in a case where the mother is employed and has requested the grandmother's help.

The *reservoir of family wisdom* is a grandfather who acts as a source of special skills and resources for the grandchild. Both the parents and the grandchildren are subordinate to this grandparent. Everyone defers to his judgment. This role, incidentally, seems to be rare. Finally, the *distant figure* is the grandparent who has kindly but rare contact with the child. The distant figure may be separated by distance or by choice. In any case, contact is infrequent and brief.

From the grandchild's perspective, grandparents play some similar and some differing roles (Kornhaber and Woodward 1981). Based on a sample of three hundred grandchildren, ages five to eighteen, the researchers identified five roles. Any one grandparent, of course, can fulfill one or more of the roles.

The *historian* provides a cultural and family sense of history. The *mentor* gives wisdom and guidance in the art of living. The *role model* provides an appropriate model for future roles of the grandchild, including that of grandparent. The *wizard* tells fascinating stories and exercises the grandchild's imagination. The *nurturer/great parent* is a basic role that gives the child a greater support system than he or she would otherwise have.

What Grandparents Do for Us

As the preceding suggests, the idea of grandparenthood as being simply pleasure without responsibility grossly underestimates the role that grandparents play in our lives. Grandparents can provide many important benefits to the growing child. Research on grandchildren of all ages has uncovered a considerable amount on the influence of grandparents (Barranti 1985).

Adolescents report a number of ways that grandparents influence their development (Barranti 1985:347). Grandparents help them to get a sense of their own identity by linking them up with their heritage. Grandparents help adolescents to understand their own parents better and may function as confidants for the adolescents when the latter are unwilling for some reason to talk with their parents about a matter. Adolescents tend to view grandparents in warm, comfortable, and supportive terms. When they have such a relationship with grandparents, they are likely to develop more positive attitudes toward older people and also about their own aging.

When asked about the relationship with their grandparents, young adults agree that it is very important to them. They get a certain amount of emotional gratification from it. As young adults, they may feel a sense of responsibility toward grandparents. Serious health problems or the death of a grandparent can be an emotional strain to a grandchild.

An Empty-Nest High

Mark is a building contractor who has been married twenty-six years. A year ago, the last of his four children left home for college. Mark and his wife, Jeri, are devoted parents and have had a close family life. How would they deal with the empty nest? Mark tells us:

We've always had a great time as a family. I must admit that I had mixed feelings when my first kid—my oldest daughter—got married. I had to battle the feeling that an intruder had come and disrupted our family. But at least we still had three other kids. Then marriage and college finally got to all of them. When my youngest girl left for college, my wife and I went with her to help her get settled in the dormitory. We both cried most of the way back home. Our nest was depressingly empty.

At first, I tried to deal with it by increasing my work load. Jeri works with me in the business and she also has been active in the League of Women Voters and our church. She got even more active in the first few months of our empty nest.

That caused some problems. Instead of growing closer together and supporting each other, we were becoming strangers. We irritated each other. We weren't happy with our nest being empty, but neither of us was helping the other to cope with it.

I don't know how long we might have gone on that way. But one day Jeri said to me, "Mark, we're heading for serious trouble." That shocked me. I knew it, but I didn't want to admit it. And I didn't know she felt the same way. We talked about it. We agreed that we needed to get back to work on our marriage. We knew some other couples who talked about how much they were enjoying themselves since their kids were gone. Why couldn't we?

We decided that we would stop burying our sadness in work and start exploring this new stage of life. So we started doing things together. We took a few weekend trips. We almost shocked ourselves when we took off from the office one afternoon and went home, made love, went out to dinner, and took in a show. That was it! I suddenly realized what a great life we have. It still feels a little strange to come home and not have anyone there, or for things to be so quiet at night. But I want to tell you that we're on a second honeymoon. We're learning things about each other and exploring things together and just thoroughly enjoying ourselves.

I guess the thing is that life just isn't as serious as it was when the kids were at home. I don't worry about things. Even when the kids were grown, Jeri and I both worried if they were out real late or if they were going to a party where everyone was drinking a lot or even if they didn't seem to be eating properly. We don't even think about those things now. We're just having fun.

In sum, while the grandparent-grandchild relationship is not as intense as the parent-child, it is a unique and potentially highly gratifying relationship. It is a form of intimacy that can add considerably to the quality of our lives.

The Aging Family

In the aging family, there is a shift of roles. The middle generation, the children of the aging couple, take on a more central role in the family. The aging couple must cope with various challenges and problems, including retirement, the death of friends and siblings, and their own physical decline. Eventually, one of the spouses is likely to face the challenge of living alone. But this stage, like every other, has its satisfactions as well as its problems.

Retirement

Retirement can be a critical time for a couple. For those who have been career-oriented, retirement means the loss of one of the more important roles in life. In part, the way that people adjust to retirement depends on whether they retired voluntarily. Those who are forced to retire because of age or other factors may have a difficult time adjusting. This can place a strain on the marriage. A depressed man, for example, sitting around the house all day can create considerable frustration and tension.

Many older couples find retirement an opportunity to pursue their interests.

Even if one spouse adjusts well to retirement, there may be problems if the new roles are not worked out satisfactorily. For example, the wife of a retired business executive had to get help for serious depression (Walsh 1980:201). It turned out that her husband was adjusting well to his retirement, but he did so by becoming a gourmet cook and taking over many of her responsibilities as homemaker. His wife lost her long-time, major role in the home, and was unable to adjust to the situation.

For the most part, however, it is involuntary retirement that is most likely to be stressful. Those who desire to retire, and make plans for their life following retirement, are not likely to be adversely affected by it. A survey of retired men reported that over half said that retirement was better than they had expected and that they were "very happy" with it (Brody 1985). Only 17 percent said that retirement was worse than they had expected, and only 6 percent said that they were "somewhat unhappy" or "very unhappy" with it.

Recognizing that people have differing values and needs with regard to work, the U.S. Congress ended mandatory retirement for most workers in 1986. However, many people opt to retire in their sixties and some opt for an even earlier retirement to pursue a new career or other kinds of interests. Less than 10 percent opt for continued work in the same career after the age of sixty-five.

Marital Relations

A couple in the sixth stage is more likely to be oriented maritally rather than parentally. That is, they are likely to focus more of their time and energy on their relationship with each other than on that with their children and grand-children. Their marriage is likely to be more egalitarian as the husband increases his share of the housework, particularly once he is retired (Rexroat and Shehan 1987).

The couple may continue to have an active and meaningful sex life during this stage. Comics have sometimes talked about old age as the time when a man flirts with women but can't remember why he is doing it. Popular beliefs reinforce the notion that sexuality vanishes from our lives at some point in the aging process. Butler and Lewis (1981) point out five myths about sex and aging: older people do not have sexual desires; even if they have some desire, they cannot physically engage in sexual relations anymore; sex may be hazardous to the health of the aged; older people are physically unattractive and therefore are not sexually desirable; and, finally, even the thought of sexual activity among the elderly is shameful and perverse. Many people accept one or more of these myths.

In contrast to the jokes and the myths, sex may be an important part of the aging couple's marital relationship. For couples with long-standing problems, of course, age can be an excuse for ceasing sexual activity. But there are no inherent physiological reasons for sex to stop. Actually, the majority of married people over the age of seventy report having sex, sometimes as often as twice a week or more.

In general, then, how much satisfaction is there with marriage at this stage? For most couples, it tends to be high, higher in fact than at any stage since the couple was first married. There are, however, some variations by age. Gilford (1984) found that satisfaction was highest among those in the sixty-three- to sixty-nine-year age group (she measured satisfaction in terms of the amount of positive interaction and negative sentiment expressed by couples). Those between fifty-five and sixty-two and those between seventy and ninety had somewhat lower levels of satisfaction. She speculated that the reason for the higher levels among those sixty-three to sixty-nine was that it is the "honeymoon" stage after retirement that allows the spouses to enjoy such resources as "leisure time, inclination to spend it together and with adult children, good health, and adequate income with which to enhance marital lifestyle and negotiate marital happiness" (Gilford 1984:331).

Other Relationships

Although the aging couple is more maritally than parentally oriented, family relationships are still very important. The great majority of adults over sixty-five live with someone else, primarily with spouses or other relatives. The great majority also live within a short distance of at least one child. The elderly prefer to maintain their own homes rather than live with their children, but they are likely to have frequent contact with children and to maintain intimate ties. This relationship has been called "intimacy at a distance" (Walsh 1980:198).

For example, in her study of 124 couples in their sixties, Joan Aldous (1987) found that the couples were involved in "a web of associational and functional activities" with their adult children. Some kind of contact occurred between the parents and their children on the average of more than once a week. Contact includes letters, telephone calls, visits, celebrating holidays and birthdays, and engaging in common recreational and religious activities. During the year preceding the study, there was also a good deal of "functional" activity, such as gifts, loans, provision of transportation, childcare, and help with other kinds of family work. Overall, on a scale of 1 (not satisfied) to 5 (very satisfied), the parents rated their relationships with their children at 4.6 and the children rated the relationships at 4.5.

There can be some strains, however, when adult children move back into the parental home. The proportion of families with children ages eighteen and older living in the home is increasing. This may occur when an adult child has divorced, has experienced work and/or financial difficulties, or cannot afford to maintain his or her own home.

A study of thirty-nine parents with adult children living at home found that most do not want the arrangement to continue on an indefinite basis (Clemens and Axelson 1985). Some of the parents were married and some were single parents (divorced, separated, or widowed). Adult children staying with both parents tended not to pay for room or board; those staying with a widowed or divorced parent were much more likely to make a financial contribution. The children did tend to help with some chores, especially those who were older (ages ranged from eighteen to thirty-nine). For example, they often helped prepare meals, take care of their laundry, and assist with yardwork. But they tended not to offer to help with the housework.

The two most common sources of conflict in such homes were disagreements about the adult child's times of coming and going, and the issue of cleaning and maintaining the house. About four out of ten of the parents said that they had serious conflicts with at least one of their resident children. In addition, the presence of the children can cause a strain on the marital relationship. Some comments gathered by the researchers included: "almost as it was when a teenager," "puts extra strain on a difficult marriage," and "we complain a lot to each other." There were some positive aspects, however. Some parents pointed out that they had a closer relationship with the spouse and/or the child since the child had returned, and others talked about the help that they received from the child in various chores. Overall, it seems clear that a couple has more to lose than to gain by having an adult child return to the nest.

There are other relationships that are important at this stage of the family life cycle. Social support is important to us at every stage of life. In this sixth stage, men tend to rely on their wives as their main source of support. Women, in contrast, tend to have a larger network and to find support from friends as well as other family members (Antonucci and Akiyama 1987). Both men and women who have living brothers and sisters are likely to develop a new perspective toward them. Older adults generally indicate feelings of greater closeness and compatibility with siblings than do younger adults (Goetting 1986). Older adults are more likely to reminisce with siblings than with their children about earlier experiences and relationships. Such reminiscence can be important in validating one's life and maintaining one's self-esteem.

Death of a Spouse

At nearly every age level, women are far more likely than men to face the death of a spouse (figure 14.3). Men, however, are likely to have a harder time adjusting to the death of a spouse than are women, as indicated by their higher rates of death and suicide in the first year as widowers (Walsh 1980). Because older men tend to lean heavily on their wives for support and intimacy, the death of their spouse is more painful and more difficult for them.

Both men and women, however, face a difficult period of time when a spouse dies. For one thing, there is a loss of identity. One is no longer a husband or a wife, and that role has occupied a major portion of one's life. What will take the place of that role? The problem is intensified because there tends to be a somewhat negative connotation to the term *widow* or *widower*.

The remaining spouse also must deal with the varied physical and emotional consequences of bereavement (Parkes 1985). Typically, the individual goes through a period of confusion, which includes some lapse of memory, difficulty in concentrating, and wandering thoughts. There is likely to be an intense feeling of loneliness, even for those who have children. We heard a woman try to console her newly widowed friend by reminding the friend, "At least you have your children." The widow replied: "It's not the same as your mate. It's just not the same." Eventually, the children may help assuage the grief and provide a source of support and renewed interest in life. But the remaining spouse typically has to wrestle with difficult periods of loneliness. And depression tends to accompany the loneliness. On top of all this there may be practical worries as well—financial concerns or who will do some of the chores that the spouse formerly handled.

Eventually, the person whose spouse has died is likely to work through his or her grief and begin to pursue a new life. There are ways to facilitate the process, to make it less painful. A study of seventy-five widows, ages sixty to ninety, reported that those who were more successful in resolving their grief had discussed a number of important matters with their spouses, family, or

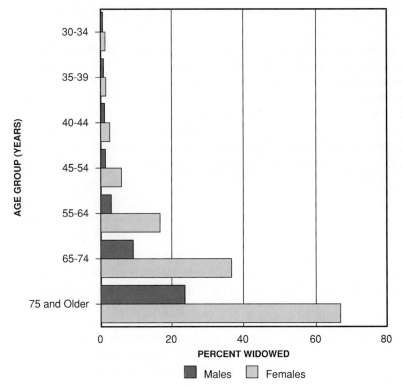

Figure 14.3 *Proportion widowed, by age: 1987.*
Source: U.S. Bureau of the Census 1989:41.

friends prior to the spouse's death (Hansson and Remondet 1987). Specifically, they had talked about finances, family reactions, their own feelings, how their lives might change, and how their friendships might be affected. Discussion with the spouse was possible because most widows (and widowers) have some period of warning. Of course, such discussion requires the spouses to continue to engage in self-disclosure to the very end and not engage in a game of pretending that the dying spouse will recover. Those widows who had discussed the issues not only resolved their grief more quickly, but were better adjusted some years later and reported better physical and emotional health than the others.

Many individuals get on with their lives by marrying again. The chances for widows to remarry, especially those who are older, is less than that for widowers. Those who do remarry tend to have higher morale than those who do not. The main reasons men give for remarrying are for companionship and to be cared for; the main reasons women give for remarrying are for companionship and love (Jacobs and Vinick 1981). The quest for intimacy never ends.

PRINCIPLES FOR ENHANCING INTIMACY

1. Change is inevitable in our family relationships. Yet we are often surprised and generally resist change when it occurs. And unfortunately many intimate relationships are strained beyond repair by the onslaught of change. It is vital, therefore, that you understand and prepare for the alterations that typically occur during the family life cycle. If you anticipate some of the challenges at each stage of the process it will help you to cope when they actually take place.

2. At every stage of life, there are opportunities for personal as well as family growth. Growth comes from taking responsibility for yourself, opening yourself to others and to new experiences, taking advantage of available resourses, and persevering in the face of difficulties. If we affirm personal growth, our capacity for genuine intimacy with others will increase.

3. One of the major tasks facing newly married couples is to develop their own family system. This is not an easy job. For example, couples are often uncertain and anxious about how and when to establish holiday traditions that are theirs and are separate from their families of origin. In order to accomplish this most effectively, the couple needs to discuss the matter thoroughly, come to an understanding of what they want, and then gradually introduce these plans to their families.

4. Children can affect the marriage relationship of their parents at various stages in the family life cycle. They bring joy and pain, fun and responsibility. They also can consume much of the attention of one or both of their parents. Unless the parents are vigilant, their relationship to each other can suffer from neglect. Thus, spouses need always to reserve time for themselves as a couple, work at their marriage, and prepare for the time when the two of them are alone together once again.

5. If these are difficult times, remember there's hope. If you are experiencing problems and frustrations in a particular stage of your family life cycle, it is useful to remember that this time will pass. And if you confront the difficulties and work through them, your family system eventually will be stronger.

The idea of the family life cycle is based on the notion that families, like everything else, go through a process from birth through growth to decline and death. A useful way of conceptualizing the family life cycle is to look at ways that families must alter their attitudes and relationships in order to adapt to each stage. Six stages are:

1. the young unattached adult

2. the newly married couple

3. the family with young children

4. the family with adolescents

5. the stage of launching children and moving on

6. the family in later life.

Both cyclical and linear changes of many kinds occur over these stages, including marital satisfaction, empathy, discussion, and regard.

Our experiences in passing through the family life cycle are affected by social changes. Some important changes in recent times are the lowered likelihood of experiencing the death of one's parents or of a child, the increased likelihood of being a grandparent, and the increased likelihood of facing marital disruption because of divorce rather than of death, which also means a greater proportion of people who will experience remarriage.

The newly married couple tends to have a high level of certain family strengths, including self-disclosure, loyalty, trust, and respect. One of the couple's important tasks is forming its own marital system. In doing so, they will have to follow or reject the models of their parents. In setting up their marital system, they must deal with the issue of closeness versus fusion, striving to build intimacy while retaining their individual identities.

The couple with young children faces the challenge of taking on the roles of mother and father as well as husband and wife, and of enlarging the family system to include other people. Marital satisfaction is likely to be lower at this stage.

The family with adolescents faces the challenge of allowing the children to form their own independent identities and move beyond the nuclear family. At the same time, the couple may be facing their own mid-life concerns with regard to marriage and careers. Adolescents are undergoing important physical, intellectual, and social definitional changes that will lead to new expectations about responsibilities. They need increasing autonomy and independence. As a result, there is likely to be considerable strain in the family at this stage. Communication and discipline problems with adolescent children and financial problems for the family are common. Adolescents themselves see most of their stress arising from daily hassles with parents.

The parents of adolescents may be further stressed by their own mid-life concerns and by being caught between responsibilities for their children and their own aging parents. Mid-life is a time when people become increasingly concerned about their own aging. They begin to change the way that they view life, thinking in terms of how much time is left and how many doors of opportunities are closed. Levinson and his associates have identified four fundamental concerns of men at mid-life: mortality, destructive and creative possibilities, balancing masculine versus feminine qualities, and coming to terms with attachment to, and separation from, the social environment. Women usually reach the mid-life crisis point earlier than men, and may begin to focus more attention on their own needs and growth.

In spite of the strains, most adolescents report positive relationships with their parents. They see their parents as fair and relatively lenient with them. One way to minimize conflict is to institute rites of passage, which tend not to occur in our society.

In the launching and empty nest stage, the couple must deal with the children moving out. They must come to terms again with their marital relationship and its future. Women are more likely than men to find the empty nest painful because they tend to invest themselves more in the child-rearing process. But the majority of people report the empty nest as a time of increased marital satisfaction and renewed family strength.

Grandparenthood is likely to occur in the fifth stage. There are different kinds of grandparents, including the formal, the fun seeker, the surrogate parent, the reservoir of family wisdom, and the distant figure. Grandchildren perceive their grandparents to play a variety of roles, including the historian, the mentor, the role model, the wizard, and the nurturer/great parent. The grandparent-grandchild relationship can be highly gratifying for both generations.

The aging family involves a shift of roles, with the middle generation taking on a more central place in the family. Retirement occurs at this stage. People may adjust well to, or even welcome, retirement when it is voluntary. There can be marital problems if the new roles are not worked out satisfactorily.

Couples in the sixth stage tend to be maritally rather than parentally oriented. The marriage is likely to become more egalitarian. The couple may continue to have an active and meaningful sex life. And marital satisfaction is likely to be at its highest point since the couple's early years together. Family relationships are still important. Contact with children tends to be frequent. Strains may result if adult children move back into the home, however.

Women are far more likely than men to experience the death of a spouse. Both men and women whose spouses die face a difficult period of adjustment. There is a loss of identity and a variety of physical and emotional consequences of bereavement. Those who talk over various matters with the dying spouse make a better adjustment to the death than do others. Many will eventually remarry, although widows are less likely to do so than are widowers. Companionship is one of the most common reasons that both men and women remarry after the death of a spouse.

15

Family Life As Management

A harried young father told us: "When I got married, I was prepared to be a husband, a worker, and a father. I didn't know I would also have to be a diplomat, a mediator, and a manager." He had discovered that family life rarely flows smoothly without careful attention and management. Indeed, if you don't take care of this part of your life, you may find that the family seems to impede rather than fulfill your intimacy needs.

In this chapter, we will look at three interrelated aspects of family life as management. First, we will discuss handling the family's finances. Then we will explore the problems of time management. Finally, we will examine the management of power and conflict in the family (as opposed to our focus on power and conflict in the marital relationship in chapter 11). The way in which the three are interrelated can be illustrated simply: an individual might pursue money as part of the quest for power, but the pursuit of money puts restraints on the individual's time, which may lead to tension and conflict in the family. We will consider each area of management separately, but it is important to keep in mind the ways in which they are interrelated.

Money Management

In considering money management, you should keep in mind a fundamental rule of human life: everyone needs at least 25 percent more income each year than he or she is getting (Merton 1957:136). The quest for more and more income is seductive. You may believe that if you only had x more dollars, you would be satisfied and your money troubles would be over. But as a professional writer told us:

> I remember when I was a young man, struggling to make it, I heard of a man who made $10,000 a year. I thought that if I could only make that much, I would be satisfied forever. Now I pay much more than that in taxes each year. And I still don't have quite enough.

The Meaning of Money

Why are we so anxious to earn more and more money? Clearly, money brings many desirable benefits, including increased options and greater security. We learn early in life that by passing coins and bills to the right people at the right place, we can get many things that we would like. We associate money with pleasure. We may also learn some negative aspects of money, such as associating money with anxiety when our parents worry and argue over it. Money, then, has both positive and negative meanings for us, meanings that will vary depending on our experiences in our families of origin.

Whatever the experiences in our families of origin, there are certain meanings of money in the culture that affect us. Generally, money means success and status. Most Americans agree that income is a measure of a family's success (Rubenstein 1981:34). The parents who provide well for their family in monetary terms are considered successful. People who are poorer than their neighbors may feel embarrassed. They may try to hide their lack of money behind a facade of spending. They may get themselves into financial difficulties by trying to provide their children with the same advantages as their neighbor's children.

Success, of course, means that we also gain status and approval from others. For example, a resident of a rapidly growing town explained that, in contrast with the past, people were now judged by their income. Formerly, people had status in this community because of their behavior and skills at their work. But as the community grew, it was no longer possible to know everyone on a personal basis. Now, "we don't know people, but we do know money." And the more the money, the more the status.

Money also means freedom in our culture. It is the freedom to opt for one's preferred life-style. We have frequently asked people what they would do if they won a million dollars in a lottery, and their answer usually involves some shift in life-style. Money would, above all, give them the freedom to choose a new house or car, a changed pattern of work or career, travel, and so on.

In addition to success and freedom, money means power to most Americans, the power to affect the behavior of others. In a positive way, some people use money to help others, to support charities or causes that enhance the quality of life. In a negative way, money can be used to buy people, or to force them to conform to one's will. Parents sometimes use money to manipulate their children. For example, a parent may try to buy devotion by lavishing money on the child. A parent may use money to try to control the child's behavior, by rewarding the obedient child and/or cutting off money to the disobedient. Parents may even try to control their adult children through large gifts that have certain strings attached or the threat of disinheritance.

Thus, money can be used in contrary ways—to manipulate or help others. It can be a source of comfort or of anxiety. It can facilitate a meaningful family life or create intense conflict. In any case, it is a significant factor in family well-being.

Money and Family Well-Being

How important is money in our lives? A *Psychology Today* survey of twenty thousand people from the United States, Canada, England, Japan, Australia, and Saudi Arabia reported that people rated love relationships and work higher than money (Rubenstein 1981:31). But they rated their finances as more important than parenthood, social life, fun, and religion.

Financial Well-Being and Satisfaction

The more you perceive yourself as being financially well-off, the more likely you are to be satisfied with your marriage and family life. Surveys of Americans over a twenty-year period found that there is a positive relationship between family income and reported happiness (Curtin 1980:18). Among those with incomes in the bottom fourth of the population, only about 25 percent said they were "very happy" with their lives. In contrast, about 43 percent of those in the top fourth of the population said they were "very happy."

As important as actual income level is how you define your financial situation. In the *Psychology Today* survey, those who were "money troubled" were not just the poorest. Rather they were those whose material aspirations were frustrated, those who wanted things they could not afford and who were deeply in debt and had saved little. Thus, whether your income level results in satisfaction or dissatisfaction depends not only on how much you make, but also on how much you want and how much you think you deserve to have.

Financial Problems

Assume that you are married and that you have one child. How much income do you need in order to live comfortably? Now look at table 15.1. How many Americans are living with less than you feel is necessary? Whatever you think you need, your chances of getting it depend on such things as your race, your education, and where you live. Table 15.1 shows that a great many factors affect the likelihood of people being in the higher income brackets. As we discussed above, your satisfaction doesn't depend wholly on your bracket, but you are more likely to be satisfied when you are in the higher brackets.

How many people have financial worries? Again, we can't tell that simply from the income brackets. A Gallup poll reported that 15 percent of Americans say they worry about family finances "all the time" and another 16 percent worry "most of the time."[1] Broken down by income, even some of those in the highest bracket said that they worry all the time about finances (figure 15.1).

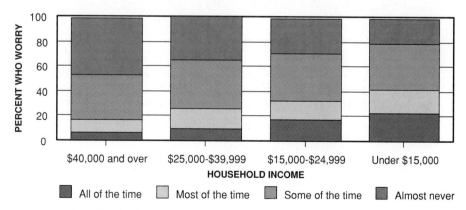

Figure 15.1 *Worrying about family finances.*
Source: Data from *Gallup Report* #256–257, January/February 1987:14.

Table 15.1 Money Income of Households: 1987

Characteristic	Total house-holds (1,000)	Percent distribution of households by income level (in dollars)								Median income (dollars)
		Under 5,000	5,000– 9,999	10,000– 14,999	15,000– 24,999	25,000– 34,999	35,000– 49,999	50,000– 74,999	75,000 and over	
Total[1]	91,066	6.9	11.5	10.6	19.2	16.1	17.2	12.2	6.3	25,986
Age of householder:										
15–24 years	5,228	13.8	16.6	15.8	25.6	15.8	8.1	3.6	.9	16,204
25–34 years	20,583	5.7	7.8	9.6	22.2	20.3	20.4	10.9	3.0	26,923
35–44 years	19,323	4.3	6.1	6.6	15.7	17.5	23.5	17.5	8.9	34,929
45–54 years	13,630	4.9	5.6	6.6	14.0	15.3	20.5	20.0	13.1	37,250
55–64 years	12,846	7.5	9.9	9.5	18.8	15.2	17.0	13.7	8.3	27,538
65 years and over	19,456	9.9	24.5	17.8	22.1	11.5	7.9	4.1	2.3	14,334
White	78,469	5.4	10.7	10.2	19.2	16.7	18.1	13.0	6.7	27,427
Black	10,186	17.9	17.7	13.3	20.7	12.2	10.8	5.5	2.0	15,475
Hispanic[2]	5,698	10.4	15.5	14.2	21.7	14.9	13.4	7.0	2.9	19,305
Northeast	19,137	6.0	11.9	9.0	17.8	15.9	18.0	13.5	8.0	28,069
Midwest	22,402	6.7	11.9	10.7	19.3	17.1	17.5	11.8	5.0	25,722
South	31,047	9.0	11.7	11.6	20.0	15.3	16.3	10.9	5.3	23,719
West	18,480	4.6	10.2	10.6	19.5	16.3	17.7	13.5	7.7	27,914
Size of household:										
One person	21,889	15.6	25.2	15.8	20.9	11.6	7.3	2.5	1.2	12,544
Two persons	29,295	4.5	8.7	11.5	22.2	17.9	17.7	11.7	5.7	26,481
Three persons	16,163	4.8	6.1	7.7	17.8	17.6	21.4	16.6	8.0	32,348
Four persons	14,143	3.0	5.0	6.1	14.8	17.3	23.5	19.6	10.6	36,805
Five persons	6,081	2.9	6.6	6.7	14.9	17.2	23.1	17.9	10.7	35,825
Six persons	2,176	4.8	7.7	8.5	15.0	15.8	21.6	17.8	8.8	33,871
Seven persons or more	1,320	4.5	8.9	8.9	18.1	15.3	18.0	15.8	10.6	30,800
Marital status:										
Male householder	62,773	3.4	6.7	8.9	18.9	17.8	20.7	15.5	8.1	31,534
Married, wife present	48,748	1.7	4.6	7.7	18.0	18.3	22.7	17.7	9.3	34,782
Married, wife absent	1,230	10.9	14.9	14.5	21.6	14.1	13.3	6.6	4.1	19,496
Widowed	1,920	10.8	26.7	17.3	18.7	11.3	7.3	6.2	1.8	13,424

Worry may be one of the lesser consequences of financial problems, which also contribute to stress, to a lowered sense of well-being and security, to problems at school or work, and to tension and conflict in the family. In the *Psychology Today* survey, the money-troubled people were more likely than the money-contented to

Be bothered by things they want but can't have

Fear a lack of career advancement

Worry about illness

Intimacy in Families

Table 15.1 *Continued*

Characteristic	Total house-holds (1,000)	Percent distribution of households by income level (in dollars)								Median income (dollars)
		Under 5,000	5,000–9,999	10,000–14,999	15,000–24,999	25,000–34,999	35,000–49,999	50,000–74,999	75,000 and over	
Total[1]	91,066	6.9	11.5	10.6	19.2	16.1	17.2	12.2	6.3	25,986
Divorced	3,957	8.4	10.8	12.1	20.3	17.5	16.2	9.7	4.9	24,005
Single (never married)	6,477	8.9	11.9	12.5	24.4	16.4	14.4	7.7	3.7	21,493
Female householder	28,293	14.5	22.1	14.4	20.0	12.4	9.4	4.9	2.2	14,600
Married, husband present	3,061	2.7	6.6	7.3	16.4	17.4	22.8	16.7	10.2	34,847
Married, husband absent	2,156	24.7	23.4	15.5	19.9	9.0	5.8	1.2	.6	10,517
Widowed	9,628	15.2	34.0	16.6	17.0	8.4	5.4	2.2	1.1	10,209
Divorced	6,527	12.1	16.2	15.2	23.8	14.7	11.2	5.0	1.7	17,597
Single (never married)	6,310	16.9	17.6	13.1	22.5	15.3	8.7	4.6	1.2	15,759
Education attainment of householder:[3]										
Elementary school	11,500	16.3	26.7	17.2	19.7	9.9	6.4	2.9	.8	11,730
Less than 8 years	6,437	18.4	27.9	17.3	18.1	8.9	5.9	2.7	.7	10,884
8 years	5,063	13.7	25.2	17.1	21.7	11.0	7.0	3.1	1.0	12,999
High school	41,037	6.8	12.4	12.0	21.8	17.8	17.0	9.5	2.8	23,382
1–3 years	10,476	10.9	19.4	14.9	22.2	14.2	11.2	5.6	1.6	16,727
4 years	30,561	5.4	10.0	11.0	21.6	19.0	18.9	10.8	3.2	25,910
College	33,301	2.6	4.3	5.8	15.1	16.3	22.7	20.1	13.2	38,337
1–3 years	14,294	3.6	6.6	8.1	18.7	18.1	22.6	16.1	6.1	31,865
4 years or more	19,007	1.8	2.5	4.1	12.4	14.9	22.8	23.0	18.5	43,952
Tenure:										
Owner occupied	58,214	3.8	8.1	8.5	17.5	16.8	20.4	16.1	8.7	31,903
Renter occupied	31,180	12.0	17.3	14.2	22.6	15.0	11.6	5.4	1.9	17,474
Occupier paid no cash rent	1,672	17.7	20.8	15.2	20.5	11.2	9.7	3.5	1.4	13,613

[1]Includes other races not shown separately.

[2]Hispanic persons may be of any race.

[3]25 years old and over.

Source: U.S. Bureau of the Census 1989:441.

Report recent problems with anxiety, fatigue, loneliness, headaches, feelings of worthlessness, insomnia, guilt, weight problems, lack of interest in sex, and feelings of despair (Rubenstein 1981:38)

Obviously, money problems affect the quality of our intimate relationships as well as our personal well-being. When the economy falters and the unemployment rate goes up, there is likely to be an increase in the number of divorces (South 1985). Some marriages are apparently unable to survive the intense stress of unemployment.

Bankruptcy

When a family gets deeply into debt, cannot meet living expenses, and cannot reach an agreement with the creditors outside of court, they may file for bankruptcy. More than three hundred thousand cases of bankruptcy are filed each year in the United States, and most of them are nonbusiness. The typical bankrupt is a male under the age of forty, married, a blue-collar worker, and with more than an average number of dependents (Hira and Mugenda 1987:60).

How does bankruptcy affect a family? Some people have feelings of guilt and stigma, but most believe that they have not lost any social standing as a result of the action. Hira and Mugenda (1987) studied forty families who had filed for bankruptcy in the state of Iowa. They looked at the factors that led to the bankruptcy and the effects on family life. The people identified personal, employment, and financial problems as the causes of bankruptcy. Personal problems included marital disruption, a death in the family, and drug, alcohol, or gambling habits. Employment problems involved loss of hours or a job or layoff because of illness or an accident. The main financial problem was the overuse of credit.

After the bankruptcy, two-thirds of the couples reported that they had changed their money management procedures. Some started budgeting for the first time. Most were more cautious about buying on credit. With regard to family life, it is interesting to note that nearly half of those who were married said that the quality of their marriage improved after the bankruptcy. They viewed the process as one that gave them a fresh start. They were finally free from the financial pressures that had caused a strain in the marriage.

When Teenagers Work: Problem or Solution?

More than half of all teenagers ages sixteen to nineteen are in the labor force (figure 15.2). A considerable number of younger teens also work part-time or at odd jobs. In some families, teenagers who work can help ease financial problems. But there are potential problems as well as benefits.

On the plus side, the working teenager may learn valuable skills, financial responsibility, time management, and the gratification of sharing in family support. Most working teens do not actually give their earnings to the parents, but they are likely to take over some financial obligations such as the cost of their clothing (Greenberger, Steinberg, Vaus, and McAuliffe 1980). Some teenagers who work part-time find that their grades in school improve because they are forced to be better managers of their time.

On the negative side, grades may go down for those who cannot handle the demands of both work and school. They may spend their income for immediate personal gratification, buying things such as cars and stereos rather than saving for long-range goals. And they may use their work as an excuse to get out of household chores, thus causing other family members to assume a greater share of the work.

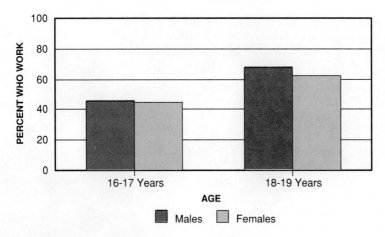

Figure 15.2 *Percent of teenagers who work: 1987.*
Source: U.S. Bureau of the Census 1989:376.

Whether the consequences are negative or positive depends on a number of factors (Williams and Prohofsky 1986). Teenagers reported satisfaction with family life was less the

More hours they worked during the school year

More they enjoyed their work

Larger the proportion of their earnings they kept for themselves

It may be that the greater involvement and interest in work is combined with a lower involvement and interest in school and family, leading to some resentment and conflict.

Financial Planning

Who should handle the finances in the family? Should it be done by the husband, the wife, both, or the entire family? Should a couple have separate or joint checking accounts? Who makes the final decision about how to allocate the available money? These are a few of the questions that can raise tempers and cause conflict in families. They are a part of the important task of financial planning.

How to Plan

A financial plan is "the complete map of your personal finances, including assets like a house, investments, insurance, and retirement funds, for the purpose of achieving specific goals" (Thomsett 1987:3). The plan must also include whatever steps you need to take to achieve your goals. There are differing

Couples need to establish goals when preparing their financial plan.

ways to make up an overall plan. If you expect to be in the higher income brackets, you should consider using the services of a professional financial planner. But the planner will still want to know your goals.

One way to establish goals in a financial plan is to write down possible major purchases and expenses and then answer certain questions about each one (Donoghue 1987:23–24). You may want to include a house or condominium, education (including your own and that of your spouse and children), automobiles, home improvements and renovations, furniture, expenses of a hobby, home electronics, vacations, recreational expenses (including an RV or boat), childrens' weddings, and other items that you feel are important. For each one, you need to decide jointly such things as whether you want it, and if you already have it whether you want to replace or improve it. If you decide to incur the expense, when will you make the purchase—immediately, in one to five years, five to ten years, or later? Then estimate the probable down payment and costs. You also need to decide at what age you would like to have your major purchases, such as a home, paid off, and at what age you plan to retire. An overall plan must provide for a comfortable retirement as well as solvency during the working years.

There are also important choices to make when you purchase property as a married person. You can decide to be tenants in common, which allows you to leave your share of the property to whomever you choose. You can be joint tenants, which means that the survivor automatically inherits the deceased tenant's share of the property. Or you may be tenants by the entirety, which provides special protection against the joint property being seized by the creditors of one of the tenants. A lawyer or financial planner can help you decide which of these is best for you.

In addition to your goals, you need to list your assets. You must consider how much risk you want to take in investments (generally, the less the risk the lower the rate of return). You also must keep in mind the problem of inflation, which can wreck carefully laid plans based on the current situation. Even during your working years, high inflation rates can cut into your standard of living. People report a number of cutbacks in times of inflation, including fewer and less costly gifts, fewer social activities with friends, and more tensions and arguments about money (Rubenstein 1981:30). As a result of inflation, people often have to postpone plans to buy a home or to return to school or to retire.

Once you have agreed on your goals, your assets, and your attitudes about risk, you can map out a strategy. You can decide on major purchases and when to buy them. You can determine how much you need to save and invest. Such planning requires a considerable amount of skill and work. But planning makes it less likely that a family will face problems that millions of Americans endure every year—family tension and conflict, bankruptcy, or an impoverished retirement.

Making a Budget

An important part of the long-range financial plan is the monthly family budget. As noted above, many couples that file for bankruptcy have not had budgets. Your budget, of course, will reflect your long-range plan and show you what must be done in the present in order to achieve your goals.

In simplest terms, a budget requires a listing of all income and expenses. Under income, list take-home pay plus any dividends, interest, or other resources. Total your monthly income. Under expenses, include both fixed expenses and estimates of variable expenses. Fixed expenses are stable, or fairly much so, over a long period of time. Variable expenses fluctuate more from month to month. Also, you have more control over variable expenses, in the sense that you can take steps to reduce or increase them. An example of a variable expense is the utility bill. A good way to get an estimate is to add up bills for a twelve-month period and get the average. Common expenses are as follows:

Fixed expenses:

Mortgage or rent

Loan payments for money borrowed or major purchases such as appliances and automobiles

Insurance premiums, including life, property, health, and automobile

Childcare, house-care, or yard-care expenses

Taxes on property and automobile

Table 15.2 Costs Of Selected Items As a Proportion of All Urban Household Expenditures: 1984

	Percent
Food	15.6
Alcoholic beverages	1.4
Housing (including utilities, furnishings, and operations)	30.4
Apparel and services	5.5
Transportation	20.1
Health care	4.1
Entertainment	4.8
Personal care services	0.9
Reading and education	2.1
Tobacco	1.0
Contributions	3.4
Insurance and pensions	9.3
Miscellaneous	1.4

Source: U.S. Bureau of the Census 1987:430.

Variable expenses:

Gifts to charities or churches

Utilities

Telephone

Food

Recreation and vacations

Household expenses (cable TV, small appliances, repairs, maintenance, etc.)

Special occasions (birthdays and holidays)

Clothing

Automobile gasoline and maintenance

Medical and dental care

Personal care (barber, beautician)

Pocket money (for each member of the family to spend on his or her personal wants and needs)

Savings and investments to meet long-range goals

Budgets will vary from family to family, of course. And the proportion of income taken up by various items on the budget will fluctuate depending on your income level. Table 15.2 shows the proportion of all expenses consumed by various items for urban Americans for one year. Note that housing and transportation account for half of all expenditures.

Intimacy in Families

Making Your Budget

Assume you have just gotten married. Make up a budget. Include both fixed and variable expenses. Set your income at what you expect to make when you graduate. Set your spouse's income, if you expect your spouse to work, at what you regard as a reasonable level. When you have completed the budget, compute the percentage that each expenditure is of your total expenses. Compare your figures with those in table 15.2. How does your budget compare with the national figures? How do you explain the differences?

Now show your budget to two or three married couples and ask them to criticize it. Ask them to give you alternative figures for any that they regard as unrealistic. Revise your budget on that basis. Then assume that your first jobs bring in 10 percent less than you assumed. Show how you would cut 10 percent out of your expenses.

If you are already married, prepare a budget outline (a list of all possible sources of income and of expenses) and ask three other couples to fill in the amounts that they feel they would need in order to live comfortably. Average their figures and compare them with your own budget. If you have not had a budget, prepare one before you survey the other couples. How does your budget compare with theirs? How do your figures compare with those in table 15.2? Where does it appear that you could make changes in your budget in order to enhance your financial well-being?

We hope when you develop a budget your income will be sufficient to cover all expenses. If it isn't, there are some measures that may help (Donoghue 1987:15): (1) stop using credit cards until the balance is substantially reduced or paid off completely; (2) check loan rates and consider refinancing some or all of your debts at a lower rate; (3) cut back small things in the list of variable expenses, such as the amount of utilities used and the number of telephone calls made; (4) reduce self-indulgent items in the budget until you can afford them (such as eating out or going on expensive vacations).

Neither long-range planning nor budgets will guarantee freedom from financial problems. People need to be alert to danger signals that may require alterations in the budget and/or long-range plan. Danger signals include such things as news of inflation, an unexpected pregnancy, the use of savings to pay monthly bills that were budgeted to come out of monthly income, and an increasing use of credit and an increasingly large balance on credit cards.

Finally, it is important to keep in mind that budgets are meant to be our servants, not our masters. A young mother complained rather bitterly about her husband: "We didn't even go out on our anniversary. He said we just couldn't afford it. We have to save for our future. But I'm not sure we're going to have a future together." When they wring all the pleasure out of a relationship, budgets are our oppressors. When they work properly, they enhance the quality of our intimate relationships because they help us avoid tensions and conflict over money and give us both pleasure for today and hope for tomorrow.

Minimizing Financial Conflict

We noted in chapter ll that couples frequently argue about finances. But there are ways to minimize financial conflict. First, we have to recognize some indicators of a problematic situation. In particular, your financial management probably needs attention and revision if one or more family members

Are reluctant to bring up the subject of money

Are secretive with expenditures

Are not trusted with money

Feel cheated by the family budget

Have a private cache of money

Clearly, communication about money matters is important for sound financial management. One important matter that should be discussed is the meaning of money that the husband and wife learned in their families of origin. Perhaps a husband is tightfisted because his father made him feel guilty whenever he spent money. Perhaps a wife maintains a private cache because her mother did so out of a lack of trust in her father's management of money. It can be very beneficial for a couple to discuss with each other and with their children the kinds of attitudes and practices surrounding money that they recall from their families of origin.

Financial conflict also can be minimized by regularly talking about financial matters. Such discussion should not be done only when there is a pressing need. In fact, the most helpful discussions occur when there are no financial decisions that have to be made. It isn't necessary, of course, to go into details with the children, but the children will benefit by having some broad idea of the family's financial situation and of a healthy decision-making process.

In addition to communication, there are certain financial practices that tend to characterize happily married couples. Schaninger and Buss (1986) surveyed 136 couples over a ten-year period. Eighty-eight had divorced by the end of the period, while fifty-two of the couples were still (and happily) married. They found some important differences in financial practices between those who remained married and those who divorced. One difference was in the kinds of things the couples purchased. The happily married couples spent more than the divorced couples on such things as a home, the downpayment for the home, household appliances, and recreational vehicles. The divorced

A majority of teenagers work, and that may have either positive or negative consequences for family life.

couples had spent more on stereos, color TVs, and living-room furniture. As the researchers point out, the purchases of the divorced couples "tend to be worth as much after marital dissolution, and tend to be consistent with individual leisure enjoyment rather than family commitment" (Schaninger and Buss 1986:135).

Besides the differences in the kinds of things they purchased, the couples also handled their finances differently. Among the happily married, the wife or the husband and wife together tended to pay the bills. The husband tended to pay the bills among the divorced. Among the happily married, credit cards were in the husband's name or both names. About one out of six of the wives who divorced had credit cards in her own name (compared to none of the happily married wives). Happily married wives were more likely than those who got divorced to be responsible for the purchase of food, beverages, and groceries.

Overall, the researchers concluded, it appears that those who remained happily married had an early commitment to family life (as indicated by the kinds of purchases they made), to equity (as indicated by the number of things in which they made joint financial decisions), and to role specialization in which the wife had an important part in handling family finances.

How I've Handled Our Money

Kay is a forty-two-year-old nurse who has been happily married for eighteen years. She and her husband, Don, have two children. Awareness and discussion of the meanings of money that developed in their families of origin have helped them minimize financial conflict. But they are still in the process of finding the most satisfying way to deal with finances:

Managing finances in our family has been a fairly easy process for us. The bottom line is that I have managed the finances. Part of this comes from my own background. My businessman father had my mother keep the books for his company. She also took care of the family records. I remember them talking about it when my father wanted to know how things stood, or when he wanted to consider some new purchase or investment. I just assumed it was part of the woman's role to do it.

When I met Don, I soon learned that he had trouble making decisions about money. I sent him off one time to buy groceries for a dinner we were having for friends. He came back with only half the items. The prices were "so damned high," he said, that he just wouldn't pay them.

Shortly before our wedding, his mother took me aside and said that all the men in the family had trouble with money. She said they weren't cheap, just stubborn, and that I would have to help him out. She suggested that I follow her practice, which was to mention when I needed something and why I needed it. Don would say

no, but I should just go out and get it anyway. Don would accept my decision and even be comfortable and happy with it. That's the way she handled Don's father, and it worked very well.

I was shocked at such a manipulative way of dealing with my husband and money. But I learned early on that Don has trouble spending. Like his father, he feels compelled to say no if I ask. So I didn't ask. I made the decisions. And he was satisfied with that. But I felt cheated when my girlfriends talked about shopping with their husbands and planning together about spending and investing money.

Only recently, after all these years, has he started talking about our style of handling money. He was shocked one day when one of his colleagues told him about having separate checking accounts and buying a new car without even telling his wife about it. That gave us a chance to review our situation. Shortly after that I decided to get my graduate degree. Now that I'm in school again, Don has taken over more of the home responsibilities, including some involvement in money matters. He is beginning to come to terms with his problem. For me, the sharing of responsibilities has been a breath of fresh air. Our marital relationship is much more funloving. I still write the checks, but Don does most of the shopping. He is making real progress in dealing with his money hang-ups.

Time Management

In a marriage enrichment workshop, we asked the young couples to keep track of their communication patterns for a week. They were to write down the amount of time each day they talked and what they talked about. At the end of the week, a husband said, with a look of chagrin: "We found out that we do very little talking during the week. At least we don't talk about anything that's of any importance. We're just too busy. We try to cram seven days of communication into the weekend."

The challenge of effective time management is as important to family intimacy as that of effective financial management. Connie, a divorced woman, tells about the time conflicts that disrupted her marriage:

> My husband and I couldn't agree on how to balance the time spent between working, doing household chores, being with the children, being together with just the two of us, and being with friends. We fought constantly. I remember once when we argued because I felt he didn't spend enough time with the children. He got a piece of paper and a pencil and threw them at me and told me to write out his daily schedule and show him when he would get the additional time.
>
> Our arguments eventually got to me. I started having health problems. That's when I decided that the marriage was destructive. We couldn't agree on what was important. Our schedules just wouldn't mesh with each other.

In an intimate relationship, then, it is important to agree on how to allocate time. It is important to have sufficient time to build intimacy, to construct a history of shared experiences. It is important for each of us to be able to remember what we did together with our spouses and our children rather than what we did not do together because we "didn't have the time."

How We Spend Our Time

For some people the combination of work and sleep takes up the bulk of the day. For students, it may be the combination of classes, study, and sleep. In addition we spend a substantial amount of time eating. The rest is "free time." What do we do with our free time? The question is quite important, because the free time is crucial for building intimate relations. Meaningful communication and shared activities during free time can greatly enrich an intimate relationship.

One way to find out how people use free time is to ask them to keep time diaries, a record of what they do during a number of twenty-four-hour periods and the time consumed in each activity (Robinson 1979). Time diaries show that American men who are employed spend their free time in the following activities (in order from greatest to least amount of time):

Watching television

Social activities (including outside entertainment and visiting friends and relatives)

Organizational activities (educational, religious, and voluntary organizations)

Reading (books, magazines, and newspapers)

Recreation

Various other activities such as resting, corresponding, and listening to the radio (Robinson 1979:43).

Employed women differ from the men in that they spend less time in organizational activities than in reading and recreation. Also, they have less time for all of the activities mentioned because they spend more on housework. Housewives have the most free time, and they spend more of it on recreation than either employed men or women, although television and social activities take up seven times as many minutes per day as recreations.

Watching television, then, is a significant part of American life. On the average, Americans watch two to three hours of television per day. Television watching is also the dominant family activity; that is, families spend more of their time together watching television than any other activity.[2] Children of employed mothers spend between six and seven hours a week, and children of housewives spend about eight hours a week, watching television with one or both parents.

In contrast, how much "quality time" is spent with children? If we define quality time as such activities as reading to, talking with, or playing with a child (i.e., time in which the parent is fully engaged with the child in a one-to-one, pleasant activity), then employed mothers report about eleven minutes a day during the week and thirty minutes a day on weekends. Housewives report about thirty minutes a day during the week and thirty-six minutes a day on weekends. Fathers average about eight minutes of quality time per day during the week and fourteen minutes a day on weekends.[3]

What the figures underscore is the fact that while the demands on our time frequently seem to be overwhelming, we usually have some discretion. Very few people are in the position of having more time than they know what to do with. Most of us sense a gnawing scarcity of hours. But while you cannot expand the hours you have in the day, you can learn to make the most efficient use of those you have. In a sense, then, you can increase the amount of time you have by becoming a better time manager.

How to Manage Your Time

There are a good many articles and books available to help people manage their time better (e.g., Lakein 1973). Obviously, time management is a problem for countless numbers of people. As with money management, time management begins by specifying your goals. How do you need or want to spend your time? What do you want to do with the free time? Do you want more quality time with your family? Do you want more time for personal development? Do you want more intimacy time with your spouse?

Second, list your goals on paper and then identify activities that will help you achieve those goals. Listing specific activities will help you to see exactly how much time you will need. Third, set up a priority list. Your priority list should include not only your goals for the additional free time, but all of the demands on your time. Lakein (1973) suggests that you give letter values to each item, with "A" being the most important activity.

Fourth, take about ten minutes each morning to make up a "to-do list." The list is your schedule for the day. You do not have to include obvious things like bathing and eating, but all other things that you have to do and want to do. You should prioritize your daily list by giving "A," "B," or "C" to each item. The items for a particular day can include everything from defrosting the freezer to getting the oil changed in the car to answering an ad for a new job to giving special attention to your spouse or children. If you can't do everything on the list, be sure to do those things first that you rated as "A," then proceed to the "B's" and lastly the "C's." You may decide, incidentally, that some of the "C" items aren't really important and could be delayed indefinitely or until you have a less busy time.

The to-do list may include items on some days that require the help of other members of the family. Those items should be discussed in the family before the day they appear on the list. For example, consider the task of cleaning the house. An employed mother might approach the family this way: "The house needs cleaning every week. How shall we handle it? What do you think each of us should do?"

Working out goals, priorities, and a daily to-do list is one of the most important parts of effective time management. In addition, however, there are numerous ways to save minutes each day. The following show the kinds of things that people do that help them make effective use of their time:

Plan weekly menus as a family instead of waiting until each day and letting the wife make all the decisions.

Learn to do more than one thing at a time (such as ironing or writing a letter or exercising while watching television).

Brown bag your lunch and use the time you save for getting some personal things done.

Having a private cache of money can increase financial conflict in the family.

Shop from catalogs instead of going to stores.

Make a list of daily chores for each family member and post it so everyone can help with the family work.

Carry a book with you to read when you are waiting for an appointment or a personal service.

We should add one caveat, however. As in the case of money management, time management should not become oppressive. If doing something else detracts from your enjoyment of watching television, you may need to find different ways of saving time. The purpose is not to detract from, but to enhance, the quality of your personal and family life. Time management, like money management, is successful only when it becomes an effective tool in our quest for intimacy.

Oppressed by the Clock

We are a clock-conscious, some would say a clock-tyrannized, people. Our anxieties and concerns over time are a reflection of our complex, industrial society. People in other kinds of societies do not have the problems with time management that we have. Consider, for example, the difference in the American and Chinese approach to time in the nineteenth century. Americans believed that punctuality was a virtue and the waste of time was abhorrent. Consider the following excerpt from a *New York Times* editorial of December 7, 1878:

> The community seems to be coming rapidly to an appreciation of the value of correct time. As the old philosopher said, "Punctuality is the essence of virtue," but it is an impossible excellence to the person whose watch is wrong. In these days of railroads and railroad-like ways of doing business, a man whose time is money to him must attend not only to his hours and minutes, but even to his seconds.

By contrast, Americans and other Westerners who visited China in the late nineteenth century lamented the lack of punctuality and the indifference of the Chinese to a clock-regulated schedule. Typical of their observations is the following account from Dr. Robert Coltman's book, *The Chinese, Their Present and Future: Medical, Political, and Social* (Philadelphia: F. A. Davis, 1891, pp. 90–91):

> A Chinaman is never in a hurry. No matter what the business in hand, there is always time to smoke or chat. It is very exasperating to the foreigner, used to having things put through in a hurry, to do business with the Chinese. For instance, you are going on a journey; you have bargained the day before with a cart-hong to send you a cart and pack animals for baggage promptly at 8 A.M. At the appointed time, having eaten an early breakfast, you are all in readiness, but no cart appears. . . . At noon you are told the carts have just arrived at the hong, but the animals are hungry and must be fed before they can go out again; two hours will be required for feeding. You now hope to get off by two o'clock. At three your cart arrives, but no pack mules. You can take your choice: go on, and let your trunks follow the next day, or keep your cart on your premises all night, get your pack-mules together, and make an early start in the morning.
>
> After many such experiences you never expect to start until you are actually in motion. A Chinese official once told me that it might do very well for trains to start on time in America, but they could not do it if railroads were inaugurated in China, "for," said he, "we couldn't get ready in time." This procrastination is seen everywhere and in all sorts of business.

Clearly, the nineteenth-century Chinese approach is unsuitable for modern business. But is it better for our intimate relationships to be oppressed by the clock or to be totally indifferent to it? Or is there a middle ground that would be better than either?

Managing Power and Conflict

The addition of one or more children to the family makes issues of power and conflict an even greater challenge. Children raise the possibility of coalitions (see the discussion of triangulation below), the use of other people to aid in conflict and power struggles.

The Use and Misuse of Power

For those with an excessive need to exercise power, a child is, unfortunately, an easy victim. Psychiatrist Allen Wheelis (1973) has written about a time when he was eight years old. He came home from school the last day before the summer vacation and announced proudly to his parents that he had passed. He was looking forward to three months of fun with his friends. His father looked at the report card and asked about a "75" in conduct. Wheelis reluctantly admitted that he had probably talked and laughed too much, but reminded his father that all the other grades were good. Then he asked if he could go over to a friend's house after dinner. "No," the father replied, "you have to work, son." What work? Wheelis wanted to know. The father, determined to teach his son a lesson that he wouldn't forget, pointed to several acres of tall grass in the back, and told Wheelis he had to cut it. But he had to cut it with an old, straight-edge razor, carefully removing all the cut grass along with any rocks or sticks. Only when he was finished, his father told him, could he play baseball with his friends.

The outcome was that Wheelis spent all but the last two weeks of the summer doing nothing but cutting grass. By the time he finished, the grass he had first cut was long again and he had to begin all over. His father told him to remember that "whenever it seems I'm being hard on you . . . it's because I love you" (Wheelis 1973:68).

When report cards came out the next year, Wheelis had a nearly perfect score in conduct. But, he wrote, he still feels the "steel fingers" of his father on him in his adult life. Wheelis' father illustrates the excessive use of parental power. He also illustrates the fact that we cannot construct healthy relationships when one party has nearly all of the power.

Power can also be misused when one family member uses another in a power struggle with a third member. This is a form of "triangulation," a concept used by family therapists to identify certain problems in the family system (Bowen 1978). Triangulation can involve a parent and child against the other parent, two parents against the child, or siblings against a parent. For example, a mother can use a child in her struggles with her husband by reserving her affection for the child and by various subtle and not-so-subtle verbal assaults on her husband in front of the child. The mother may try to win the child's sympathy while simultaneously downgrading the father: "Your father never remembers our anniversary. But I've come to accept the fact that I live with a man who isn't thoughtful."

Intimacy in Families

A parent might also engage in triangulation by using a child to win arguments. Thus, a father says to his son: "Listen to this, and then tell your mother who is right." Perhaps the worst use of triangulation occurs when the parents join together and blame the child for their problems. Rather than focusing on issues between them, the parents decide that the child is to blame for their lack of accord. The child becomes the family scapegoat. If the child was unwanted in the first place, or in some way falls short of their expectations, the scapegoating is all the easier.

As the above suggests, healthy relationships require balanced power in the home. This doesn't mean that children have as much power as parents, but rather that power is shared. No one should feel powerless. Beth, a fifty-year-old woman who owns her own clothing store, recalls how she learned the importance of sharing power in the family:

> I could see as a child that power-sharing works well. My friends' parents were more conventional than mine. Most of them had fathers who were the breadwinners and sole decision makers in the home. They paid all the bills and doled out the money to their wife and kids. So the fathers had all the power. And I saw the difference in their mothers and my mother. My friends' mothers seemed sort of wimpy to me. When I was in their homes I heard some of them unable to answer even simple requests. They would tell their children to "wait until your father comes home and see what he says." They just didn't seem to have the vitality or strength that I saw in my mother who was truly a co-equal with my father.

One way to share power in the family is to have a regular family meeting. The meeting can be used to allocate family work, plan family recreation and activities, make decisions about various family matters, and air grievances. Power sharing in the family meeting does not mean that a majority vote wins. Parents must still be parents, and not turn over their responsibilities to the vote of the group. But every family member should be heard equally. And all opinions should be respected. The listening skills, which we talked about earlier, are important in a family meeting. And it is an appropriate time for parents to teach children how to listen, both by modeling good listening and by explicit instruction.

Family meetings can be more appealing if the parents spend some time reminding everyone of the good things about the family or the achievements of particular family members. Family meetings should not degenerate into nothing but crisis-handling sessions. And children will find the meetings more appealing to the extent that they feel they have some influence over decisions. As the children grow, of course, their influence will increase.

Conflict and Family Well-Being

As in the case of marital conflict, conflict within the family can be both positive and negative. On the negative side, the more intense and frequent the conflict, the more problems the children will have. For example, children who

Families spend more time together watching television than any other activity.

experience a good deal of family conflict have more problems with adjusting to school and more difficulties with their own emotional health (Kurdek and Sinclair 1988). The more that there is yelling and screaming going on in the family, the more a child is likely to have problems with his or her self-esteem (Amato and Ochiltree 1986).

The conflict doesn't have to involve the children directly. A study of forty adolescents reported that those who perceived high levels of conflict between their parents had a variety of problems at school (Long, Forehand, Fauber, and Brody 1987), including:

Lower grade point average

Lower cognitive competence rating by teachers

Lower social competence rating by teachers

More behavior problems reported by teachers

Lower problem-solving skills

Such results raise the question of whether children would be better off in a two-parent home that has a high level of conflict or a single-parent home with a lower level of conflict. James Peterson and Nicholas Zill (1986) addressed the question using a national sample of fourteen hundred children ages twelve to sixteen. The researchers looked at such things as rates of depression, antisocial behavior, and school problems among children in various kinds of

Family meetings are a way to share power in the family.

home situations. They found that generally children who lived with both parents were the least depressed and withdrawn. But for those children in homes of high, persistent conflict, the levels of depression and withdrawal were even higher than for those who lived with just one of their biological parents. Antisocial behavior also tended to be higher among those in two-parent homes with high, persistent conflict.

Thus, as painful as divorce is on family members (see chapter 18), remaining in an intact family with high and persistent conflict can be even more painful. Clearly, a healthy family has to manage conflict well in order to stay healthy. This does not mean to eliminate conflict. Conflict is a part of healthy relationships. Its absence may be a sign of problems rather than of well-being. In families without conflict, the members may be denying that they have differences, or they may have a family norm against the overt expression of those differences, or they may not care sufficiently about each other to argue.

How, then, can families accept conflict and manage it well in order to maximize their well-being? Samuel Vuchinich (1985) videotaped dinner conversations in fifty-two families and analyzed their patterns of arguing. He found four ways in which a verbal attack by one member on another ended: withdrawal, submission, standoff, or compromise. In *withdrawal,* one of the participants simply withdraws from the conflict by either refusing to talk anymore or by leaving the room. The individual may even say "I don't want to talk about it anymore." Withdrawal often implies that the other person or persons in the conflict haven't played fair, and that the withdrawing individual is too hurt or angry to continue.

Submission is giving in. It may occur when one family member recognizes that another is correct on a point of fact, when two or more family members convince another that he or she is wrong, or when parents intervene and require the bickering to stop. Submission may not be the end of the disagreement, however. It may just be the beginning of a cold war that will erupt at a later time if the winning party doesn't handle the situation well. Ways in which the situation is not handled well include the "winner" gloating over his or her "victory," and the "loser" submitting merely because he or she feels compelled to do so by pressure from other family members.

A *standoff* occurs when no progress is being made and the opponents simply drop the matter without resolving it. They may openly or tacitly agree to continue to disagree with each other. It may be that the issue is relatively trivial, or it may be that they realize that they will always have different perspectives. For instance, Karl and Sylvia, a professional couple known to the authors, have been married twenty-five years, but they still disagree over an incident that happened in the first year of their union. They were buying furniture and Karl, according to Sylvia, flirted openly with the beautiful young saleswoman. Karl insists that he was only being friendly, that he was much too much in love with Sylvia to flirt with anyone, much less to do so in front of her. They argued about it at the time and got nowhere. They laugh about it now, but they still disagree.

Finally, *compromise* occurs when one family member offers a concession to the other. If there is a reciprocal concession, and both agree, the conflict ends. Compromise can occur over ideas, attitudes, plans, responsibilities, and so on. Thus, two family members in a dispute may each modify positions about such things as which is the best political candidate, how the family should spend its money, who does the most work around the house, and the extent to which each member is a concerned and responsible member of society as well as of the family.

Each of the methods has implications for family intimacy. Withdrawal may alienate family members from each other. They may feel that they simply cannot get along or communicate effectively with each other. Vuchinich found withdrawal rarely used, however. Submission can lead to inequity, to dominance relations if the same member always tends to be the one to submit. Standoffs may maintain a sense of equality, and may enable the participants to move on to other activities if the issue is defined as relatively trivial (as in the case of Karl and Sylvia). But if conflict is considered nontrivial and is frequent, and standoffs occur regularly, the family members may find themselves getting increasingly frustrated and angry with each other.

Compromise, on the other hand, tends to build intimacy. The family members see that they are able to work through their disagreements. Unfortunately, less than 10 percent of the conflicts that Vuchinich studied ended in compromise. About a fourth ended with submission and the rest ended with a standoff. Family members, then, need to develop the ability to compromise. Recall that the willingness to compromise was one of the ways of "good fighting" discussed in chapter 11. The other principles identified there are as useful for family conflict as they are for marital conflict. The family that learns and uses good principles of conflict management is a family that is building meaningful intimate relationships.

1. Because money and what it can buy occupies so much of our attention and produces so many problems between people and anxieties within people, it is important that we learn to manage it wisely. And it is never too soon to start. Ideally, the process begins in childhood. When you become a parent, you can help your children develop the capacity for effective money management.

2. Before you marry, you will want to thoroughly discuss money matters—your combined incomes, expected expenses, handling of finances, and so forth. After you marry, regularly review your fiscal practices and modify them if necessary. Open discussion and prudent management will prevent money from being a threat to your intimate relationship.

3. Time, like money, often seems in short supply. Given the complexities and the increasing demands in most of our lives, it is essential for our physical and emotional well-being that we learn to manage our time well. Establish priorities and divide your day accordingly. Keep a calendar that schedules both the demands of your work as well as choices in your personal life. Remember: if you do not manage your time, someone else will.

4. Building an intimate relationship requires time together, yet all too often intimate moments are sacrificed to demands that seem more pressing. You can guard against this by scheduling a regular night out, a weekend away, or even a nightly thirty minutes of uninterrupted time with your special person.

5. If you want to minimize power conflicts in your family, create an atmosphere of love and respect. Where these coexist, each member of the family feels safe in expressing his or her feelings and concerns and is assured that problems will be worked out fairly.

SUMMARY

Most people feel that they need at least 25 percent more income than they are getting. We want more, because money brings many desirable benefits. Money means success, freedom, and power in American culture. Perceived financial well-being is an important part of satisfaction with family life. Those who perceive themselves as having financial problems are likely to worry, experience stress, have a lowered sense of security, have problems at school or work, and have more tension and conflict in the family.

Bankruptcy may ultimately result from serious financial problems. The overuse of credit is one of the major factors in bankruptcy. Many couples, however, learn sound money management practices after declaring bankruptcy.

More than half of all teenagers ages sixteen to nineteen are in the labor force. Benefits of working teenagers include the learning of valuable skills, financial responsibility, time management, and sharing in family support. Problems include the possibility of lower grades in school, the use of money for immediate personal gratification, and less involvement in family work.

Financial planning can help families cope with present financial responsibilities as well as plan for future security. Making a budget is an essential part of financial planning. Food, housing, and transportation will consume more than half of the average family's budget.

Financial conflict in the family can be minimized by certain measures, including open communication about money matters. In addition, happily married people make purchases that suggest a long-term commitment to each other, make joint financial decisions, and involve the wife in an important way in handling family finances.

Time management is as important to family intimacy as financial management. Work and sleep take up the bulk of our days. Watching television takes up a significant part of our free time. Thus, while time demands may appear overwhelming, we all have some discretion. Effective time management may require you to specify your goals, identify activities that will help you reach those goals, set up your priorities, and make a daily list of activities.

Both time and money get tangled up with power struggles and conflict in the family. Managing power and conflict is a third aspect, therefore, of effective family management. Power can be misused through such things as triangulation. Healthy relationships require balanced power in the home. Power can be shared through regular family councils or family meetings. Like power, conflict can be positive or negative. Intense, sustained conflict in the home tends to result in personal and school problems for children. Verbal conflict may end by withdrawal, submission, standoff, or compromise. Compromise tends to build intimacy.

---

1. *Gallup Report* 256–257, January/February 1987, pp. 13–14.

2. *ISR Newsletter,* Winter 1985/1986, p. 3.

3. Ibid., p. 4.

16

Diversity in Families

magine that you are an artist and that you have been asked to draw or paint a picture of a family. You may use any setting you like. What would you draw? Whatever the setting, you would probably draw an adult man, an adult woman, and one or more children. And these people would probably be white.

But some families are composed of only two people—an adult and a child. Some are composed of nonwhites. Others are racially mixed. And others are composed of two adults of the same sex, with or without children. In this chapter, we will discuss each of these types of families: the single-parent, the nonwhite (including interracial families), and the homosexual family. We will see that they resemble white, two-parent families in many ways. But these families have special problems and special characteristics with which we should be familiar.

Interracial families are one kind of family diversity in our society.

The Single-Parent Family

Single-parent families may occur in various ways, including divorce, death of a spouse, and from a single person who decides to have or adopt a child without getting married. An increasing number of people, particularly women, have opted for parenthood without marriage in recent years. Some of the women do not want to get married, but do want to be a mother. Some may prefer marriage, but find themselves in a situation without a prospective husband and with their childbearing years coming to an end. Changing sex roles (chapter 7) and contemporary views on sexuality (chapter 8) make single parenthood an option that is no longer stigmatized, further facilitating the choice.

In the case of divorce, "single-parent" does not mean that the child has no contact with the other parent, but that the child lives primarily with one parent. In other cases, contact with the other parent or with the biological parents (in the case of adoption) may not be possible. How many single-parent families are there, and what are they like?

Extent of Single-Parent Families

Single-parent families have increased considerably over the past two decades. In the mid-1980s, about one of every four children lived with only one parent. In 1985, there were actually seven million fewer children under the age of eighteen than there were in 1970 (because of the declining birth rate). But the number of children living with only one parent increased by six million in that same period of time.

Most of those living with one parent are with a divorced parent (figure 16.1). And as figure 16.1 shows, the proportion of children in one-parent homes who come from a situation of divorce has increased considerably since 1970. There has also been a striking increase in the proportion of children who live with a parent who has never been married. And, finally, it is important to keep in mind that when we talk about the number living in a one-parent home in any year, we are only talking about a fraction of the children who will live with one parent at some point in their lives. Depending on what happens to marriage and divorce rates, as many as half of all children may ultimately spend some time in a one-parent household.

Problems of the Single-Parent Family

What kinds of problems are you more likely to encounter if you are a single parent or the child in a single-parent family? As we discuss the various problems, keep in mind the "more likely" in the preceding sentence. As we shall see in the next section, people are not doomed to an inferior quality of life simply because they live in a one-parent family, but they are more likely to face certain kinds of difficulties.

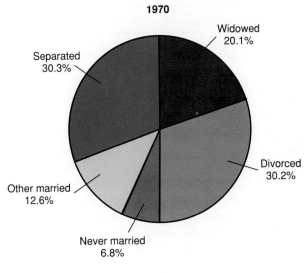

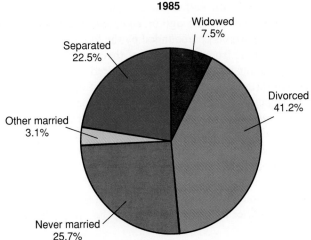

Figure 16.1 *Children living with one parent, by marital status of parent.*
Source: U.S. Bureau of the Census, *Current Population Reports,* Series P-23, No. 150,
"Population Profile of the United States: 1984–1985" (Washington, DC: Government Printing
Office) 1987:23.

Problems of Single Parents

As we saw in chapter 13, parenthood is challenging and difficult even when
there are two parents in the home. With just one parent, the challenges increase greatly. Robert Weiss (1979) pointed out that a basic problem is the
inadequacy of resources available to the single parent and the consequent
overload. In particular, the single parent is likely to face three kinds of overload: responsibility, task, and emotional.

Table 16.1   Percent of People below the Poverty Level: 1987

	Percent
All people	13.7
People in families	12.1
In white families	9.1
In black families	31.8
In families with female householder, no husband present	38.3
In families with female householder and children under 18, no husband present	54.7

Source: U.S. Bureau of the Census 1989:453.

Responsibility overload may result from having too few financial resources. The problem is especially acute for mothers who are single parents. Refer back to table 15.1 and note the high proportion of women householders in the lower income brackets who are divorced or whose husband is absent. Families with female householders have higher rates of poverty than any other group (table 16.1). And over half of those living in a home headed by a single mother with children under the age of eighteen are living in poverty! The problem of single mothers is compounded by the fact that many of the women do not get child-support from the fathers of their children. Even court action may fail to secure support. A study of one hundred cases reported that nearly half of the absent fathers paid less than 10 percent of the support ordered by the court and 19 percent paid nothing at all (Gordon 1981:283).

Task overload arises from the fact that one parent must do the work of two parents. If the parent works full-time outside the home as well as takes care of the children and manages the household, he or she is likely to feel overwhelmed by the sheer number of tasks that need to be done. In his study of 1,136 single fathers, Geoffrey Greif (1985) reported that one major source of problems for the men was the conflict between their jobs and their housekeeping duties. Whether a father or a mother, the single parent's work never seems finished.

Emotional overload can occur when the single parent neglects his or her own needs. Single, employed mothers, for example, spend less time in personal care (including grooming, sleeping, and eating) and in recreation (including watching television and attending social activities) than either the nonemployed single mother or the mother in a two-parent home (Sanik and Mauldin 1986). The single parent may have an intimacy deficit because of the lack of a spouse. The deficit cannot be made up by friends if the parent has little time for anything but his or her job and family work. And the deficit cannot be made up by the children, for they are a responsibility as well as a source of companionship. In addition, the parent needs the intimacy of a peer, the closeness of an adult relationship.

The result is that the parent may sink into loneliness, a feeling of hope-lessness, or a variety of emotional problems. Among the emotional problems of single mothers, anxiety and depression are common (Propst, Pardington, Ostrom, and Watkins 1986). Single mothers are one of the largest consumers of mental health services.

Emotional problems are more likely to occur among single parents than either those in intact or those in stepparent families. Researchers who com-pared the three kinds of families reported that the single parents were "more depressed, less satisfied with their family lives, and had more problems with their children than parents in the other family structures" (Fine, Donnelly and Voydanoff 1986:400). Although there were only a handful of single male par-ents in their sample, the researchers noted that the men were even more de-pressed than the women. This is not unexpected in view of the fact that men rely more heavily on a spouse than women do for their emotional support. Greif (1985), incidentally, pointed out that the men who had the hardest time dealing with single parenthood were those whose wives had deserted them.

Problems of Children of Single Parents

As in the case of the single parent, the child of a single parent, and particularly the male child, is more likely to be depressed (Huntley, Phelps, and Rehm 1986). In the first years after a divorce, the children are also likely to have higher rates of antisocial behavior, aggression, anxiety, and school problems than those in intact families (Fine and Schwebel 1987). The single parent's problems of adjusting to a divorce, then, are compounded by the problems that tend to appear in their children, problems that are particularly acute in the immediate aftermath of a marital breakup.

The children in single-parent homes have more difficulties within the family as well as within themselves and their outside relationships. Because the bulk of single-parent families are headed by females, it is not surprising that both primary school children and adolescents in single-parent homes report less support, control, and punishment from their fathers than do other children (Amato 1987). They also report more conflict with siblings, less family cohe-sion, and more family stress.

Why should children in single-parent families feel less cohesion? Cohe-sion here refers to a sense of emotional bonding that family members have toward each other. One might expect the bond to be stronger with the re-maining parent when a divorce or separation has occurred, but it tends not to be. Kennedy (1985) addressed the issue in his study of 631 undergraduate students. He found that the students in single-parent homes not only perceived lower cohesion scores than those in intact families, but they also had the highest rates of serious family relationship problems (higher than those in either intact or stepfamilies). Kennedy suggests that the lower cohesion scores may reflect the fact that the students are establishing their independence earlier than the students from intact homes. When children are in the stage of establishing their own separate identities, they typically perceive less family cohesion. Perhaps those from single-parent homes are driven to the process earlier in life than those from intact homes because of the disruption in their homes. Having seen parents declare their independence from each other, the children may feel a stronger desire to establish their own independence.

It is also possible that those from single-parent homes had less cohesion before the breakup. Perhaps the lack of cohesion reflected problems in the home that led to the disruption. In other words, the cohesiveness reported by the students is not necessarily lower than it was before the disruption, and may even be higher. Still, those in single-parent homes are not experiencing the same level of family cohesion as those in intact homes.

One other, longer-term, consequence for children in single-parent homes is the tendency for them to achieve less in education, occupation, and income than those from intact homes. They are also less likely to have a stable marriage themselves (Mueller and Cooper 1986). To some extent, these effects reflect the fact that those in single-parent homes are more likely to be in a lower socioeconomic level. But even when we look at those who come from the same socioeconomic levels, the children from the single-parent homes are at a disadvantage. Growing up with two parents appears to increase our level of motivation to achieve. Perhaps the harried single parent simply cannot give the attention to the child's achievements that is necessary to motivate the child to higher and higher levels.

Problems between Parents and Children

"Anyone who thinks that children are helpless creatures," a weary parent remarked, "should remember that it takes at least two adults to handle one child." Parenting is not an easy responsibility even when there are two in the home. When there is one, relationships with children present even more severe challenges.

Consider some of the problems that can arise when the single parent interacts with the child or children. In a mother-daughter home, there may be more open competition, with the daughter wanting to stay up as late as the mother and measuring her success with boys against her mother's success with men (Bohannan 1985:169–70). The daughter may also lack an appropriate understanding of male-female relationships. As noted family therapist Virginia Satir put it:

> Her attitudes about being female can range all the way from being the servant girl—giving everything, receiving nothing—to feeling she has to do everything herself and be completely independent (1972:172).

Boys seem to present even greater problems than girls. Recently divorced mothers of sons report less control of their children than do mothers of girls or married mothers (Mednick 1987:196). Sons have a harder time adjusting to divorce than do daughters, and express some of their anger in

Single mothers report more problems with their sons than do married mothers.

disobedience and aggressiveness against the mother. The aggression tends to reach a peak at about a year after the divorce, but is still higher after two years than that of boys in intact families.

Some of the problems between mothers and sons arises not from the son's feelings about the situation, but from the mother's decisions about how to relate to the son now that the father is absent (Satir 1972:172). A single mother may try to get an older son to assume some of the role responsibilities of the missing father. That distorts both the parent-child relationship and the son's relations with any siblings. If the son feels an obligation to nurture and care for his mother and defend her against her own helplessness, he may not be able to establish his own independence and pursue his own needs for intimate heterosexual relationships. Or he may rebel against the situation and leave home, but wrestle for years or even a lifetime with a feeling of women as enemies. On the other hand, a single mother might tend to "over-mother" the son, who then may form an image of females as dominant and males as nothing.

Most single-parent families are headed by a mother. The single mother, therefore, has been studied far more than the single father. Do single fathers have similar problems with their sons or daughters? We do not know at this point. One major advantage that the single father is likely to have is a higher income. Another way single fathers have some advantage over single mothers is that mothers tend to be rewarded less than are fathers by their children (Ambert 1982). The children of single fathers are more likely to express their appreciation than are the children of single mothers. This tendency may reflect the belief that it is the mother's responsibility to care for the children. When the father assumes that responsibility, he is going beyond what is expected of him, and he deserves special praise and appreciation. There is, of course, no reason why the mother should be any more responsible than the father for rearing the children. Nevertheless, as long as people believe this, the single father is likely to continue receiving more rewards in the form of appreciation and admiration than is the single mother.

Finally, dating can be a vexing problem. Unfortunately, the parent may have problems and issues with regard to interpersonal relationships quite apart from the children (see chapters 18 and 19). Those problems and issues may be intensified and added to by the presence of children (Petronio and Endres 1985/1986). The parent may feel guilty about leaving the child alone to go out on a date. This may cause some resentment toward the child, who consumes so much of the parent's time and energy. The child, in turn, may decide that the parent is considering remarriage and that he or she may have to adapt to a stepparent. In spite of the difficulties of the single-parent home, some children resist the idea of a stepparent. The potential stepparent is defined as an intruder and one who reminds the child again of the pain of the breakup of the family.

Single parents who perceive their children to be less positive about their dating agree that the children react with both anger and resentment toward the dates (Petronio and Endres 1985/1986). Some parents, recognizing the potential problems, delay introducing their dates to their children, though a majority do so immediately or soon after dating someone. Single mothers are more quick to introduce dates to children than are single fathers. This may reflect women's greater concern with relationships, and the sense that it is easier for a woman than a man to accept a nurturing relationship with someone else.

The problem of dating is compounded by the fact that not only do the children not like the parent's dates, but the dates also may be less than enthusiastic about the children. A survey of eighty-three single parents reported that about two-thirds felt that their dates had at least some reservations about the fact that they had children (Petronio and Endres 1985/1986). If the parent is strongly attracted to a date who dislikes the children and/or who is disliked by the children, the parent may have to struggle with frustration, disappointment, and resentment toward both the date and the children.

Coping in the Single-Parent Family

In spite of all the problems we have noted, there are some positive things to be said about the single-parent family. Most experts agree that it is not the ideal, though it may be preferable to an intact family with a high level of conflict or other kinds of problems. But when we compare the single-parent with the intact family generally, the picture is not as gloomy as the above discussion might suggest.

First, while we noted that children in single-parent homes perceive less cohesion than do those in intact homes, the average level of those in single-parent homes is within the range of normal functioning (Kennedy 1985:123). In other words, "less cohesive" should not be interpreted to mean "chaotic" or "disjointed" (recall the distinction we made in marriages between "less satisfied" and "dissatisfied"). While those in single-parent homes are likely to experience less closeness than those in intact homes, this does not mean a serious intimacy deficit. Children living with a mother only report about the same levels of both support and punishment as those living with both parents (Amato 1987).

Moreover, in spite of the greater likelihood of mental health problems, the majority of single parents and their children have fairly high levels of both physical and mental health. In her study of forty-two single parents and their children, however, Hanson (1986) found some sex differences in health status. Single mothers had poorer health than single fathers. But children living with a mother reported higher overall health than those living with a father. Interestingly, boys living with their mothers had the best overall health, while girls living with their fathers had the least. We should note that the sample was small and the health status was based on self-reports of such things as eating and sleeping habits, use of drugs, smoking, self-care, use of preventive health measures, history of illness and accidents, and other indicators of well-being. In part, the results probably reflect the fact that women generally report lower health levels than men. In part they reflect some of the interaction problems discussed above. Thus, mothers with sole custody of sons reported the lowest levels of mental health.

While there are higher rates of various kinds of problems, the single-parent family is neither intrinsically nor inevitably unhealthy or pathological (Fine, Donnelly, and Voydanoff 1986:401). A study of 141 single fathers reported that most of them felt both comfortable and competent with their roles (Risman 1986). Other studies indicate that both single fathers and single mothers like being parents, feel competent, and are basically satisfied with the parenting experience (Mednick 1987:197).

In spite of the extra demands on their time and energy, single parents also function well at work. Single parents indicate high levels of satisfaction with their work, and they are not absent from work significantly more than others (Burden 1986). In fact, having a job that provides both meaningful work and a predictable source of income enhances the mental health of single mothers (Mednick 1987:192).

In addition to having meaningful work, there are some other factors that are likely to enhance the mental health of the single parent. Four researchers who compared single mothers high on anxiety with those low on anxiety, and those depressed with those nondepressed, found a number of differences between the groups (Propst et al. 1986). Specifically, single mothers with low anxiety, compared with those with high anxiety, tended to be a little older; to

"I Chose to Do It Alone"

Most people are not single parents by choice. They become single parents because of separation, divorce, death, or because of a sexual relationship that for some reason did not result in marriage. Emma is a fifty-year-old teacher who became a single parent by choice, eventually provided her children with a father, but then returned to singlehood again. She regrets none of her decisions:

My experience with raising children has been deeply colored by the fact that I chose to do it alone. My children were not the result of a love relationship gone sour, but of deliberate planning. Having been raised in a highly dysfunctional family, I left home at an early age with a really negative concept of marriage.

After a few years of living on my own, I realized I badly wanted to have children. But I still had a very negative attitude about

marriage. To make a long story short, I managed to have two children in the space of sixteen months amidst violent protest from both friends and family. I expected the protest and I was prepared to deal with it. I knew there would be rough times ahead and that whatever happened I was going to have to do it entirely alone.

I also knew my children would have to be strong and independent if they were to survive. So as infants, I gave them all the cuddling, stimulation, and nurturing I could, and I found baby-sitters who did the same. I had to work full-time to support us. So it was important to make what time we had together really count. I did as much as possible with them.

Life was tough, mostly because money was short. But my children seemed secure and well adjusted. Then, when the oldest was eight, I

have been separated from their husbands for a longer period of time (an average of sixty-nine months, compared to forty-nine months among the highly anxious); to have joint rather than sole custody of the children; and to have fewer children under the age of ten. The same characteristics, with the exception of custody of the children, differentiated the nondepressed from the depressed mothers. In other words, those women who had more time to adjust to their situation and who had somewhat less childcare responsibility were less likely to have problems of depression and anxiety.

Nonwhite Families

Is life any different if you grow up in a black or Hispanic family rather than a white family? In some ways, the answer is no. That is, there are many similarities between white American families and those of nonwhites. For example, Hispanic families are as cohesive as those of whites (Vega, Patterson, Salis, Nader, Atkins, and Abramson 1986). And many of the processes are reassessed my situation and soon found myself married to a man who seemed to be what we all needed to make life really complete. Eventually, my "prince" turned out to be a real toad. But he was a good father to my children, and we had a third child. He told me I could stop working and stay home with the children. That was my first mistake. After four years, I got increasingly bored, restless, and irritable. My husband, meanwhile, turned out to be an alcoholic like my father. That awful kind of family life that I was so determined to avoid had developed right under my nose!

When my husband was transferred to another city, I stayed behind with the children. I told them we would be on welfare for awhile, that I wanted to go back to school and get a degree to teach. They agreed. I went to school days while they were in school and worked nights while they slept. It wasn't ideal, but we made the most of it. They were understanding, and I began to feel better than I had in years. Eventually, I divorced my husband, got my degree, and improved our financial situation by going back to work.

My children agree that there were times when they felt angry and wished that I was more like the mothers of their friends. But they also feel they grew up stronger, more self-confident and independent than most of the people they see around them. It's been a rough life, but I believe it's been a highly successful one. I am pleased with the way my children are conducting their lives and with the relationships I have with them. My two daughters are married and have their own children. My son is having some problems developing a relationship with a woman, but maybe he will work that out.

If I had it to do all over again, I think the only thing I would change would be to go to school first and then get artificially inseminated. Otherwise, I have no regrets in spite of the painful times. I have discovered quite happily that motherhood does not end when a child leaves home. Being a mother to an adult is quite different from mothering an infant. But it's still mothering.

the same, such as the tendency for a greater amount of sharing of family work when the wife is employed outside the home (Ybarra 1982).

Black families are also like whites in many respects. Married blacks are likely to be happier than the unmarried (Zollar and Williams 1987). Using national samples, Heiss (1988) addressed the issue of whether black and white women differ in their values about marriage and the family. There are some differences, he found, but they are trivial in size. Black women, in spite of their higher divorce rates, are not different in terms of their values and attitudes toward divorce. They also differ little in terms of accepting nontraditional forms of family life. The primary difference Heiss found was in the tendency for black women to be more instrumental than white women in their reasons for marrying and in their goals for marriage. That is, black women were more concerned than white women for such matters as family responsibilities, income, and the quality of life. Given the historic deprivations of blacks, such concerns are understandable.

In many respects, nonwhite families are no different from white.

The Black Family

Many of the special problems and challenges faced by nonwhite families are rooted in their situation in the society. Heiss (1988) found that race is less important than socioeconomic position in explaining variations in family values. The greater proportion of nonwhites in the lower socioeconomic strata contributes to most of the differences in their family life-styles.

The Demographics of Black Families

Blacks are the largest of America's racial minorities. A little over 11 percent of all households in the nation are black households. About seven out of ten black households are family households (table 16.2). That is roughly the same proportion as for whites. As table 16.2 shows, the proportion of all households that have a family has been declining over the past two decades for all races.

Table 16.2 shows one striking difference between black families and white and Hispanic families, namely the lower proportion that are composed of a married couple. Nearly 30 percent of all black families are single-parent, headed by a female. And while the proportion of married couple households has declined for all races, the decline has been sharper for blacks than for others. Blacks are also more likely than those of other races to be single, widowed, or divorced (figure 16.2).

Table 16.2   Households by Type: 1970–1987

Characteristic	Number (1,000)					Percent Distribution				
	1970	**1975**	**1980**	**1985**	**1987**	**1970**	**1975**	**1980**	**1985**	**1987**
White										
Total	56,802	62,945	70,766	75,328	77,284	100.0	100.0	100.0	100.0	100.0
Family households	46,166	49,334	52,243	54,400	55,676	81.6	78.4	73.8	72.2	72.0
Married couple	41,029	42,951	44,751	45,643	46,410	72.5	68.2	63.2	60.6	60.1
Male householder[1]	1,038	1,257	1,441	1,816	2,038	1.8	2.0	2.0	2.4	2.6
Female householder[1]	4,099	5,126	6,052	6,941	7,227	7.2	8.1	8.6	9.2	9.4
Nonfamily households	10,436	13,612	18,522	20,928	21,608	18.4	21.6	26.2	27.8	28.0
Male householder	3,406	5,038	7,499	8,608	9,034	6.0	8.0	10.6	11.4	11.7
Female householder	7,030	8,574	11,023	12,320	12,574	12.4	13.6	15.6	16.4	16.3
Black										
Total	6,223	7,262	8,586	9,480	9,922	100.0	100.0	100.0	100.0	100.0
Family households	4,856	5,466	6,184	6,778	7,096	78.0	75.3	72.0	71.5	71.5
Married couple	3,317	3,343	3,433	3,469	3,742	53.3	46.0	40.0	36.6	37.7
Male householder[1]	161	211	256	344	386	2.9	2.9	3.0	3.6	3.9
Female householder[1]	1,358	1,915	2,495	2,964	2,967	21.8	26.4	29.1	31.3	29.9
Nonfamily households	1,367	1,793	2,402	2,703	2,826	22.0	24.7	28.0	28.5	28.5
Male householder	564	791	1,146	1,244	1,313	9.1	10.9	13.3	13.1	13.2
Female householder	803	1,002	1,256	1,459	1,513	12.9	13.8	14.6	15.4	15.2
Hispanic[2]										
Total	2,303	(NA)	3,684	4,883	5,418	100.0	(NA)	100.0	100.0	100.0
Family households	2,004	(NA)	3,029	3,939	4,403	87.0	(NA)	82.2	80.7	81.3
Married couple	1,615	(NA)	2,282	2,824	3,118	70.1	(NA)	61.9	57.8	57.5
Male householder[1]	82	(NA)	138	210	253	3.6	(NA)	3.7	4.3	4.7
Female householder[1]	307	(NA)	610	905	1,032	13.3	(NA)	16.6	18.5	19.0
Nonfamily households	299	(NA)	654	944	1,015	13.0	(NA)	17.8	19.3	18.7
Male householder	150	(NA)	365	509	521	6.5	(NA)	9.9	10.4	9.6
Female householder	148	(NA)	289	435	494	6.4	(NA)	7.8	8.9	9.1

NA Not available.

[1]No spouse present.

[2]Hispanic persons may be of any race. 1970 data as of April.

Source: U.S. Bureau of the Census 1989:46.

For black children, these figures mean a greater likelihood of growing up with only one parent. Table 16.3 shows a comparison of white and black families with children under 18. Black children are three times as likely as white children to be in a mother-only family unit and nine times as likely to be living with a mother who has never been married. More than one of every four black families is headed by a mother who never married. What accounts for such differences? To answer the question, we must explore at least briefly the black experience in America, and particularly the way in which black families have been affected by American institutions.

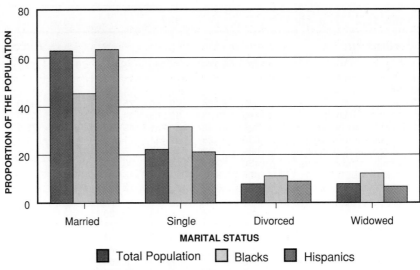

Figure 16.2 *Marital status of the population: 1987.*
Source: U.S. Bureau of the Census 1989:42–43.

Table 16.3 Family Groups with Children Under 18, by Race and Type: 1987

Presence of Parents and Marital Status	Percent distribution		
	Total[1]	*White*	*Black*
Total with children under 18	100.0	100.0	100.0
Two-parent family groups	73.0	78.3	41.5
One-parent family groups	27.0	21.7	58.5
Maintained by mother	23.7	18.4	55.3
Never married	7.5	3.6	30.5
Spouse absent	5.1	4.0	11.3
Separated	4.4	3.4	10.1
Divorced	9.7	9.6	10.8
Widowed	1.5	1.3	2.8
Maintained by father	3.2	3.2	3.2
Never married	.6	.5	1.1
Spouse absent	.7	.7	.6
Divorced	1.7	1.8	1.3
Widowed	.2	.2	.1

[1]Includes other races, not shown separately.
Source: U.S. Bureau of the Census 1989:50.

Social Institutions and Black Family Life

From slavery through segregation to present-day discrimination, blacks have waged a long battle in the United States for justice and equality. Even after slavery was ended and blacks had won certain fundamental rights such as the right to vote, they faced various kinds of pressures to keep them from exercising their rights. Indeed, efforts to keep blacks from voting appeared even in the 1980s (Lauer 1989:345). Politically, then, blacks have had difficulties exercising the power needed to press their causes and redress their grievances.

In the economy, blacks have faced similar problems. The well-being of families is crucially tied up with the economy. Economic deprivation places great strains on family life. The higher rates of divorce and single-parent families among blacks become more understandable when we realize that black unemployment has tended to double that of whites over the past two decades and that recently the median income of black families is about 59 percent that of whites (see table 15.1). Some people mistakenly believe that blacks have made great strides economically since the civil rights movement of the 1960s. But in 1960, the median income of black families was 55 percent of that of white families. The most recent figures, in other words, show only minimal progress.

You might think that one reason for the income differences is an educational gap. Indeed, blacks are not as likely as whites to graduate from either high school or college. But blacks are at a disadvantage even when they get the same amount of education. For example, the average household income of blacks with four or more years of college education is about 73 percent that of whites with the same education. Higher-educated blacks are not as disadvantaged as those with less education, but an income that is 27 percent lower still represents a great deal of inequality.

The economic problems of blacks mean that the black male has a difficult time fulfilling his role as a provider, or even as a contributor to the family's financial well-being. Black men are more likely than white men to be unemployed or, if employed, to be in the lower income brackets. Added to that is another problem: when husband and wife have differing levels of education, the husband is likely to be more educated in white marriages while the wife is likely to be better educated in black marriages (Secord and Ghee 1986). Overall, then, black wives provide a greater proportion of income to their families than do white wives. This can cause strain, because one of the factors in marital satisfaction on the part of wives is the perception that the husband is a good provider.

In those situations where the black husband is not able to be the good provider, the wife may expect him to at least provide emotional support and to share in family work, including childcare. But such behavior is

> more associated with middle-class values, and the educational deficit of black men and their predominant employment at blue-collar and lower levels is apt to leave a marital pool having many men who are resistant to assuming this new role (Secord and Ghee 1986:27–28).

The educated black woman, consequently, may find a scarcity of men who can fulfill the kind of husband and father roles that she desires.

As the economic problems of the black family diminish, the black husband and father assumes a more active role in family life (McAdoo 1985/ 1986). He becomes more involved with teaching his children and with making child-rearing decisions. Moreover, the black father seems, more than those of other races, to try to socialize daughters to be competent and independent at an early age.

In other words, the fate of the black family, like that of all families, is tied up with its position in the American economy. And its position in the economy, in turn, depends in part on what happens in the government. Various governmental actions in the past, such as school desegregation, voter registration laws, and affirmative action programs have helped many black families. But a political conservatism during the 1980s led to a reversal of some of the gains. For instance, we noted that the ratio of the median family income of blacks to that of whites is now only slightly higher than it was in 1960. It is, however, lower than it was in 1978, when it had risen to a high of 64 percent. The conservatism of the 1980s has been detrimental to black well-being.

In particular, black families in the 1980s suffered as a result of attacks on affirmative action and cutbacks in social and income maintenance programs (Crawley 1988). With regard to affirmative action programs, corporations were told that they could no longer require timetables or quotas for minority hiring. With regard to cutbacks, there was supposed to be a "safety net" that would prevent groups already disadvantaged from suffering even more from efforts to control federal spending. But as the figures on median family income illustrate, black families lost ground economically during the 1980s.

Life in the Black Family

If you are black, then, you are more likely than if you are white to grow up in a family that is impoverished, that is disrupted by divorce, or that is headed by a mother who has never married. If you are a black mother, understandably, you are more likely than a white mother to feel overworked. Married women generally who work outside the home tend to feel more overworked than their husbands. Black women, however, are twice as likely as their husbands to feel overworked by household responsibilities (Broman 1988a). And being overworked means a lower satisfaction with family life. When the husband performs most of the household chores, the wife is relieved but the husband is less satisfied with family life.

But such facts should not obscure the strengths and the positive aspects of life in the black family. Most of the problematic aspects we have discussed are rooted in the economic deprivation that blacks have endured. But black families have strengths and, in fact, advantages over white families in some areas.

Recall that marital satisfaction tends to decrease during the child-rearing years. This may not be true for blacks. Some research reports that blacks show no decline in life or family satisfaction when they become parents (Broman 1988b). Similarly, though being a single parent is a difficult task, it may not be as difficult for blacks as for whites. While there has not been a great deal of research, some of the findings from small samples include (Fine and Schwebel 1987):

Nonmarried black mothers reported no greater role strain than did their married counterparts.

Black mothers, whether with or without a husband in the home, perceive their families as being cohesive.

Black students in the fifth and sixth grades had about the same levels of self-esteem whether they came from one-parent or two-parent homes.

The difference between actual and ideal self-concepts was lower for black than for white adolescents from single-parent families (lower differences are considered healthier).

It is possible, then, that black single-parent families cope better with their situation than do whites. Three factors help account for this: the greater extended family support among blacks, the way children are viewed, and a greater acceptance of single parenthood (Fine and Schwebel 1987). With regard to greater extended family support, black single mothers are more likely than whites to have adults or other children, who are not a part of the nuclear family, in the home. Thus, there are likely to be additional resources available to the black single parent. As two anthropologists summed it up, the black family

consists of a wide-reaching group of relatives involved in relations of exchange and coparenting; and a collective and cooperative spirit prevails (Aschenbrenner and Carr 1980:469).

With regard to the view of children, some researchers have argued that black children are valued regardless of their origin. There has not been a stigma on black children, as sometimes there has been on white children, who are born to an unwed mother. Thus, it is unlikely that a black child would be called illegitimate or treated any differently from any other child because of his or her origin.

Finally, there is a greater acceptance of single parenthood in the black community. There is a larger proportion of such families among blacks, and those that function well provide a model to others. Blacks, then, are more likely than whites to believe that a single parent can provide a good family environment.

Among black two-parent families, there is likely to be a greater amount of equality than among whites. Interestingly, blacks tend to be more traditional in their ideology about family life, but more egalitarian in practice (Beckett 1976). That is, blacks are more likely than whites to affirm traditional family roles, but are also more likely than whites to actually have an egalitarian relationship. There is a common assumption that black families tend to be dominated by the wife. But one survey of seventy-five black couples reported that about half of the spouses said their marriages were "husband-led," about a third said that the union was "egalitarian," and less than one out of seven characterized the marriage as "wife-led" (Gray-Little 1982).

In part, the egalitarianism results from the fact that black wives are more likely than white wives to work, and black husbands are more likely than white husbands to approve of their wives working. In fact, black women have a more consistent history of being employed than do white women; both they and their husbands are more likely to expect (not just accept) the wife's employment. Perhaps because of such an expectation, black husbands are more willing than whites to adjust their own schedules in order to help their working wives, such as agreeing to stay home with a sick child or to a wife's overnight absence from home because of work (Beckett 1976).

Finally, blacks may have some advantage over whites at the time of the empty nest. We have noted that the empty nest is a problem only for a minority of people, particularly for those women who have focused their lives on their children. But we need to modify the nature of the problem even more: it seems to occur mainly among white women. Neither black nor Mexican-American families seem to be troubled by the empty nest (Borland 1982).

Thus, life in the black family is likely to have certain problematic aspects primarily because of the effects of discrimination and deprivation in American society. But many black families are strong and viable and in some areas even have an advantage over white families.

The Hispanic Family

Hispanics (Mexican-Americans, Puerto Ricans, and others with Spanish surnames) are the second-largest minority group in the United States. Hispanics are, on the average, poorer than whites, though not as poor as blacks. Median family income of Hispanics is around 70 percent that of whites. As table 16.2 shows, Hispanics are more likely than either blacks or whites to have a family household; they are slightly less likely than whites, but much more likely than blacks, to have a married couple in that household. Hispanics are less likely than others to be divorced (figure 16.2). And they are less supportive than are whites of mothers who do get divorced (Wagner 1987).

Hispanic women tend to marry a little later than do either whites or blacks. On the average, they have more children than either whites or blacks. And—reflecting in part their slightly later age at marriage—they are likely to bear their last child at a later age than either whites or blacks (Norton 1983).

As with blacks, Hispanics may have a different experience of marital satisfaction than whites. A study of three generations of Mexican-American families reported that men showed a decline in satisfaction during the middle years and then a subsequent rise. This is the same as the pattern for white families. But the Hispanic women had a successively lower marital satisfaction over the three generations. This is a different pattern than occurs among white women (Markides and Hoppe 1985).

Minority families tend to acquire certain stereotypes. With blacks, it is the stereotype of the dominant wife and mother. With Hispanics, it is the stereotype of the dominant husband and father. In both popular and professional views, the Hispanic family has been explained on the assumption that the male suffers feelings of inadequacy and inferiority and compensates for his powerlessness in the larger society through *machismo,* or male dominance, in the family (Staples and Mirande 1980:893). The father becomes the unquestioned authority in the family. The wife and children are subservient and passive.

Contrary to the stereotype, Hispanic families are not male-dominated.

However, research has failed to uncover a pattern of male dominance in the Hispanic family (Staples and Mirande 1980:894). Nearly every study of spousal roles, including those among Hispanic migrant farm families, has shown more egalitarianism than male dominance. The egalitarianism appears in family decision making and other kinds of behavior. Hispanic fathers help their wives with family work, including childcare, prefer to have social and recreational activities with their families rather than with other men, and are playful and companionable rather than stern and authoritarian with their children. This egalitarianism creates an improved climate for family well-being. In fact, recent research among a group of intergenerationally linked Puerto Rican families indicated that marital satisfaction is associated with egalitarian spouse roles (Rogler and Procidano, 1989).

Finally, as with blacks, Hispanics may have closer bonds than whites with members of the extended family. In his study of Mexican-American families, Richard del Castillo (1984) pointed out that bonds of affection and help from a wide array of relatives is one of the most important characteristics of these families. A family might also have coparents, such as godparents, who offer both emotional and financial support. The use of this wider range of resources allows the Hispanic family, like the black family, to cope with the demands of an often hostile environment and still maintain a meaningful family life. Intimacy is more difficult to maintain in the face of discrimination and deprivation, but the use of the extended family and other resources facilitates the efforts of many minority families.

The Interracial Family

As we pointed out in chapter 5, more than 98 percent of Americans marry within their own racial group. Nevertheless, the number of black-white marriages has nearly tripled since 1970. Intermarriage is also frequent among the Japanese: as many as half of all Japanese marriages in the United States involve marriage with someone of another race, and the rate is higher among those Japanese born in the United States than those who have immigrated here (Tinker 1982). Evidence reveals that an increasing number of Americans are willing to cross racial lines to find a mate. Indeed, well over a million couples are now engaged in an interracial marriage.

Interracial marriages are more fragile than marriages that are racially homogamous (Glick 1988). In some cases, the stability of the marriage depends on which spouse is of which race. For example, marriages with a black husband and white wife are more stable than those with a white husband and black wife. The probability of an interracial marriage lasting depends on a number of factors. As with other marriages, interracial unions are more likely to last when there are children and when the couple marry at a relatively later age (Rankin and Maneker 1987).

Because we are likely to be attracted to those who are like us (the principle of homogamy) and because interracial marriages are more likely to fail, why do people marry across racial lines? In essence, their reasons are the same as others (Porterfield 1982). That is, when asked about the motives for their marriages, interracial couples primarily mention love and compatibility. Compatibility, of course, suggests a homogamous relationship, and an interracial marriage might seem to be heterogamous. However, people of different races in our country may have similar values and attitudes, and people may prefer someone of another race who is similar in values and attitudes than someone of their own race who is different in values and attitudes.

A few of those in interracial marriages indicate that they are motivated by rebellion against the conventions of society or by an attraction to the opposite sex of another race. While a deeper study of the couples might identify some more subtle forces at work, we have no other answers at present. Some people are so much in love and so compatible with a person of another race that they are willing to assume the risk of lower stability and perhaps go counter to pressures from friends and family in order to enter an interracial union.

The risk of breakup and the pressure to refrain from interracial marriages varies from place to place. In a multicultural setting, interracial marriages may be more common and more acceptable. There may be more support for the couple, enabling them to maintain the union. In some places, children of an interracial union are stigmatized; they may not be fully accepted by either of their parents' races. But they may escape the stigma and its negative psychological consequences in a multicultural setting. For example, children of interracial marriages in Hawaii, where there is general acceptance of such unions, are as well adjusted psychologically as children from marriages within the same race (Johnson and Nagoshi 1986).

Still, there are likely to be some unique problems even when the couples are in a generally accepting environment. McDermott and Fukunaga (1977) reported research with a group of interracial Hawaiian families who sought psychiatric help because of emotional problems with their children. These marriages involved a white-Oriental union.

One of the problems the interracial couples had was that of trying to establish consensual parental roles. A number of Oriental men married to white women tried to assume the traditional Oriental role of male leadership. But some of their white wives "repeatedly competed for this role, undercut their husbands, or attempted to act as co-leader with the husband" (McDermott and Fukunaga 1977:84). In such cases, the husband often either ignored his wife or treated her as one of the children. The reaction of the children tended to be withdrawal and mild depression.

Another problem arising in the interracial families was the differing value systems of the parents. Some cultures value accuracy over creativity, while others have the opposite value. Husbands and wives with differing values put their children into the difficult situation of having to obey contradictory parental expectations.

The troubled families had tried to cope with their differences in various ways. Three coping efforts were dysfunctional. First, some of the families had settled into a kind of cold war where, for the most part, the parents no longer attempted to accommodate their differences but rather each maintained a different and contrary approach in dealing with the children. Second, in other families there was a "competitive adjustment," where each parent tries to get the other to acknowledge their leadership in the family. Finally, some of the families engaged in a "reluctant adjustment" in which the parents withdrew from trying to establish leadership and allowed the children to govern themselves most of the time.

Eventually, the families in this research learned better ways of coping with their differences. *Complementary adjustment* in an interracial family involves letting one parent be the primary leader in the family while the other engages in supplementary functions. For example, one parent makes a decision and the other supports it, encourages the children to support it, and models supportive behavior to the children. In *additive adjustment,* the parents try to take elements from each of their cultures that they both define as desirable, and use these in making decisions about family life.

In sum, interracial families face the same problems as others plus some additional problems that are unique. But they can work through their problems and maintain a strong and meaningful family life. Where the family lives in a hostile environment (among people who resist or resent interracial unions), the prospects for long-term stability are not encouraging. In a more accepting atmosphere, the family will still have its unique problems to solve, but will be better able to do so.

A Slave Family

Frederick Douglass was born a slave early in the nineteenth century in Maryland. As a young man, he escaped, fled to New York, and became a part of the abolition movement. The following excerpt from one of his autobiographical works illustrates some of the problems of slave family life. Though slavery, segregation, and discrimination have all assaulted the integrity of the black family, the slave experience was especially severe:

My father was a white man. He was admitted to be such by all I ever heard speak of my parentage. The opinion was also whispered that my master was my father; but of the correctness of this opinion, I know nothing; the means of knowing was withheld from me. My mother and I were separated when I was but an infant—before I knew her as my mother. It is a common custom, in the part of Maryland from which I ran away, to part children from their mothers at a very early age. Frequently, before the child has reached its twelfth month, its mother is taken from it, and hired out on some farm a considerable distance off, and the child is placed under the care of an old woman, too old for field labor. For what this separation is done, I do not know, unless it be to hinder the development of the child's affection toward its mother, and to blunt and destroy the natural affection of the mother for the child. This is the inevitable result.

I never saw my mother, to know her as such, more than four or five times in my life; and each of these times was very short in duration, and at night. She was hired by a Mr. Stewart, who lived about twelve miles from my home. She made her journeys to see me in the night, travelling the whole distance on foot, after the performance of her day's work. She was a field hand, and a whipping is the penalty of not being in the field at sunrise, unless a slave has special permission from his or her master to the contrary—a permission which they seldom get, and one that gives to him that gives it the proud name of being a kind master. I do not recollect of ever seeing my mother by the light of day. She was with me in the night. She would lie down with me, and get me to sleep, but long before I waked she was gone. Very little communication ever took place between us. Death soon ended what little we could have while she lived, and with it her hardships and suffering. She died when I was about seven years old, on one of my master's farms, near Lee's Mill. I was not allowed to be present during her illness, at her death, or burial. She was gone long before I knew anything about it. Never having enjoyed, to any considerable extent, her soothing presence, her tender and watchful care, I received the tidings of her death with much the same emotions I should have probably felt at the death of a stranger.

Source: Frederick Douglass, *Narrative of the Life of Frederick Douglass, An American Slave* (Boston: The Anti-Slavery Office, 1845), pp. 1–2.

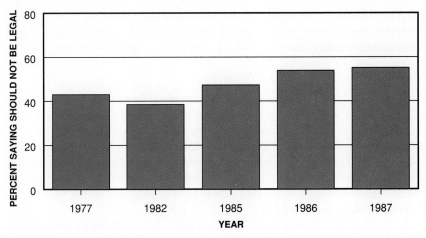

Figure 16.3 *Attitudes toward homosexual relationships.*
Source: Data from *Gallup Report* #258, March 1987:13.

The Homosexual Family

Although many people do not think of homosexual relationships as resulting in a family, it has been estimated that about one of five gay men and one of three gay women enter a homosexual marriage (Schulenburg 1985). The marriage may or may not be a formal ceremony. One male couple, for example, after four months of cohabitation, went to mass and let the service be their private ceremony of commitment (Ammon 1985:112). They used the term *marriage* to describe their relationship. They bought matching rings, and verbally agreed to be sexually faithful, to emotionally support each other, and to have equal say in such matters as finances.

Moreover, there are millions of gay men and women who have had children. In many cases, the children were born when the individual was part of a heterosexual marriage. Subsequently, the individual "came out," that is, openly acknowledged his or her homosexual preference. Some of these children are being raised in a homosexual family—two men, two women, or some other arrangement. For example, Schulenburg (1985) is a lesbian who is raising a daughter with two gay males, one of whom is the child's father.

Homosexual couples have to work through the same problems as heterosexual couples. They face issues of household division of labor, power, sexual relationships, and money (Blumstein and Schwartz 1983). In addition, like the interracial couple, they face problems arising from being in a socially stigmatized relationship. Gallup polls that asked the American public whether homosexual relations between consenting adults should be legal have found an increasing proportion from the mid-1970s to the mid-1980s who said that they should not (figure 16.3). By 1987, 55 percent of the sample said that such relations should not be legal. Homosexual families, then, must not only deal with the same issues as other families, but also with a hostile environment and with some problems that are unique to the homosexual relationship.

Problems in Homosexual Families

Gay male couples have some unique sources of stress that may require them to seek counseling or therapy (George and Behrendt 1987). One is the stereotypical male role. Men in our society are expected to be relatively unemotional, strong, competitive, independent, and in control. If the partners in a gay relationship each attempt to live by the stereotype, they will encounter serious problems. How can they maintain a loving relationship if they are constantly competing with each other? Or if both want to win all the time? Or if both want to be in control?

Another source of stress is the stereotypical sexual role of the male. In our society, men are expected to be sexually active, experienced, and prepared to engage in a sexual relationship at almost any time. This can create performance anxiety, an anxiety that may be intensified by the spread of AIDS and the knowledge that homosexual relationships are particularly vulnerable to AIDS.

Homophobia, the irrational fear of homosexuality, is a third possible source of stress. Because our society has viewed homosexuality negatively, and because most homosexuals have grown up hearing such derogatory labels as "fag" and "queer," most gay males "cannot escape, at least for a period of time, incorporating these negative societal messages into their own self-concepts" (George and Behrendt 1987:81). One of the partners, therefore, may still be struggling with his self-esteem and his own identity as a homosexual.

Finally, there is the stress of sexual dysfunctions. Contrary to the popular image, and to the general pattern of the gay male, some homosexual men suffer from inhibited sexual desire. The problem intersects with the stereotypical male sex role and with homophobia. That is, a man might have inhibited sexual desire because he is still battling his feelings of guilt or his ambiguity about his sexual orientation. But the inhibited desire intensifies his stress because he also may accept the stereotype of himself as one who is supposed to be a sexually active individual.

Undoubtedly, there are some unique problems for lesbian couples also, but we do not have the research necessary to identify them. However, the Blumstein and Schwartz (1983) study produced a number of findings that suggest that lesbian couples do not have the same kind of problems as either gay male or heterosexual couples. For example, they found that in gay male and heterosexual couples, income tends to determine which partner will be dominant. But lesbians use income to avoid being dependent on each other rather than to establish dominance. Heterosexual and gay male couples who are disappointed with the amount of money they earn are likely to be less satisfied with their overall relationship; that is not true of lesbians. Lesbians also report somewhat less conflict over money management and income than do other couples.

What about children who are being raised by two adults of the same sex? There is little research on which to base firm conclusions, but what evidence we have indicates that the unique problems are minimal. Homosexual, like heterosexual, parents tend to report few serious problems in child-rearing and generally satisfactory relationships with the children (Harris and Turner 1985/1986). Parents report that their children generally have a positive attitude about the homosexuality. When the children reach adolescence, however, some of them will reject, at least temporarily, the homosexual orientation of the parents, fearing that they too might become homosexual (Schulenburg 1985). These findings, however, are based on small samples and thus are very tentative.

Intimacy in the Homosexual Family

What do homosexuals want in an intimate relationship? They want the same thing as heterosexuals. Peplau (1981) compared one hundred homosexuals with one hundred heterosexuals and found that the differences between men and women were generally greater than any differences between homosexuals and heterosexuals. Both homosexuals and heterosexuals value such things in an intimate relationship as being able to talk about feelings, being able to laugh together, having a supportive group of friends, and sharing as many activities as possible with one's partner. Whatever their sexual orientation, people expect family life to provide them with a measure of emotional support, love, security, and companionship.

It is more difficult for a homosexual couple to fulfill its intimacy needs, however, because of the hostile environment. As a result, homosexual couples tend to receive more emotional support from friends, including other homosexuals, than they do from their extended families (Kurdek and Schmitt 1987). Homosexual couples, then, are more dependent on friends for support than are other couples. Those with a high degree of emotional support from friends are less psychologically distressed than those who report less emotional support from friends.

Other than a support system, the factors that add to the quality of a homosexual relationship are the same as those for a heterosexual union. Comparing married, heterosexual cohabiting, gay male, and lesbian couples, Kurdek and Schmitt (1986) found that the quality of the relationships, regardless of the type of couple, depended on such things as perceived investment in the relationship, few alternatives to the relationship, commitment to the relationship, and shared decision making. There were no differences in the level of love expressed by the various partners, though the heterosexual cohabitors expressed a lower level of liking of the partner than did the others.

Homosexuals want the same things as heterosexual couples in an intimate relationship.

Thus, in most respects the homosexual couple is no different from the heterosexual. In both kinds of relationships, the partners are seeking to fulfill their intimacy needs. And many of the same kinds of factors determine the extent to which those needs are fulfilled.

There are, however, some differences. Two of the differences between homosexual and heterosexual couples that affect intimacy are the greater probability of equality in the homosexual relationship and the way in which fidelity is defined by gay males. Equality facilitates intimacy. Women, regardless of their sexual orientation, are somewhat more likely to value equality than are men (Peplau 1981). But there is consensus that equality in such matters as decision making is a prominent characteristic of homosexual relationships, whether male or female (Harry 1982; Peplau and Cochran 1981). Among men, there may arise what McWhirter and Mattison (1984:31) call "planned incompetence." One of the partners may "unlearn his own level of competence" in a particular area in order to allow the other to fulfill himself by achieving in that area. In other words, one partner will deliberately minimize his skills in order to allow the other to develop the same skills, so that the two are more equal than before.

With regard to fidelity, gay men may opt for either an open or closed relationship. In an open relationship, the partners retain their commitment to each other while allowing occasional outside relationships. In a closed relationship, the partners are expected to be sexually faithful to each other. Those in an open relationship say that monogamy can't meet all of an individual's needs, interests, and fantasies. They say that an occasional outside contact enhances their enjoyment of their partner and strengthens rather than loosens the bond they have developed (Ammon 1985:32). Fidelity, then, is defined as an emotional commitment rather than sexual exclusivity. Perhaps the great bulk of gay male unions have an open arrangement in which sexual activity is sometimes allowed with others (McWhirter and Mattison 1984:252).

Long-Term Gay Relationships

The stereotype of the homosexual, particularly the male, is one of promiscuity. Indeed, there is some basis for the stereotype; about half of all white males in one study reported that they had had over five hundred partners (Bell and Weinberg 1978). But many gay males, and an even greater proportion of lesbians, try to form stable, monogamous relationships.

In an effort to provide a portrait of the development of a long-term gay relationship, two researchers have charted six stages through which a gay male couple move over time (McWhirter and Mattison 1984). The first stage is called *blending*. It takes up the first year of the relationship and is characterized by such things as intense feelings, a high degree of sexual activity, and efforts to bond the partners and make the relationship one of equality.

In the second and third years, the couple are in the *nesting* stage. During these years, they try to establish themselves in homemaking and explore the areas of life in which they are compatible. There is, as with heterosexual marriages, some decline in sexual passion. And one or both partners may begin to feel somewhat ambivalent about the relationship.

Years four and five are the *maintaining* stage. The partners reestablish their individuality in the context of togetherness, learn to handle conflict, and begin to establish certain family traditions. Up to this point the partners may not have had many arguments. But in this stage, couples

> generally devise means of neutralizing, resolving or completely avoiding conflict for the present and into the future. Dealing with conflict is a developmental task that can be avoided no longer if the relationship is to continue to grow (McWhirter and Mattison 1984:38).

The *building* stage follows, from years six through ten. In this stage, the partners become increasingly productive in their work, establish their independence as individuals, and come to sense a dependability in the other. In the *releasing* stage, years eleven through twenty, the relationship is usually one of trusting, combining money and possessions, and perhaps taking each other for granted. Finally, the *renewing* stage, twenty or more years together, is characterized by security and a shared history of experiences.

Thus, some gay males, contrary to the stereotype, form a lasting relationship with one partner. The bonding in such a relationship occurs in the first three to four years. In an effort to refine our understanding of bonding among gay males, Ammon (1985) interviewed thirty couples who had been together a minimum of five years. He found that the bonding process involves some of the same factors as those in heterosexual couples. Initially, for example, communication is crucial:

> The single most frequent activity reported by every couple was talking. Regardless of any other simultaneous activity such as sex, skiing or sailing, a constant exchange of self-information was consistently reported (Ammon 1985:86).

The couples also reported sharing many activities.

An interesting aspect of a developing gay relationship is what happens when one of the partners was married and fathered children. Ammon found that the fathers in his sample were committed to their children, and that the new lover had to accept the children and the fact that the children would make demands on their father's time. The fathers said that if the new lover could not accept the children, the relationship would not last.

Following the working out of some of these issues, the men faced such problems as the development of trust, working out any differences in life-styles, learning to share equally in the decision-making process, and making a long-term commitment to the relationship.

What Is a Family?

Have you ever played the game of word association? For example, when you hear the word "fun," what is the first word that comes to your mind? How about "happiness?" "Dating?" "Marriage?" Jot down your first response to each word.

Now respond to the word "family." Instead of just one response, however, write down five words that come to mind. Then think about your responses. Why do you think you made these particular associations? Are there any common elements in your choices? Did your responses to fun, happiness, dating, and marriage have anything to do with family life? Based on your responses, what is your family like?

How do you think other people would respond to the words? Would they respond differently depending on their family situations or backgrounds? Ask ten others to play the game of word association with you. If possible, select two different groups of

five people each, such as five married people and five single parents, or five white and five black married people, or five heterosexuals and five homosexuals. If that isn't possible, get people who come from as many of the groups discussed in this chapter as possible.

Write down their responses. Then compare the two groups, or those from differing groups. What kinds of meaning of family life seem to emerge from the words they chose? Do you see any differences between them? If so, how would you explain the differences? If not, why do you think there are no differences?

If the entire class participates in this project, you can specify the groups you want to investigate (perhaps three or four different groups) and pool the results. What conclusions would you now draw about the meaning of "family?"

Clearly, then, the development of bonding and commitment to a homosexual relationship can be very similar to that of a heterosexual relationship. Homosexuals have the same intimacy needs and many of the same aspirations for intimate relationships as heterosexuals. A major difference is that homosexuals are following a socially disapproved route, which adds many impediments to their search for intimacy.

PRINCIPLES FOR ENHANCING INTIMACY

1. People have always fulfilled many of their intimacy needs within the context of the family. However, today, the family comes in many varieties. And although the nontraditional or nonwhite family may present unique problems, it can be a vital source of satisfaction and well-being to its members.

2. Although nontraditional and nonwhite families encounter a host of obstacles, strong bonds of affection and shared values, interests, and goals help minimize the difficulties and produce a fulfilling relationship.

3. The same factors—love, respect, support, and sharing—are vital in all types of families. These are the bonds in any strong, enduring intimate relationship, and thus should be cultivated. It may require extra effort and added determination in a nontraditional family to develop these bonds, but the end result will be worth the struggle.

4. Nonwhite families have special problems, but they also have some special strengths, such as the resource of strong extended-family relationships. Members of these families can tap into the unique strengths and use them to maximize intimacy even in the face of various political and economic disadvantages.

SUMMARY

Single-parent families have increased considerably over the past two decades, with about one of four children living with only one parent. Single parents face the problems of responsibility, task, and emotional overload. The children of single parents are more likely to have both personal and interpersonal difficulties than are children who live with both parents. They perceive their homes as less cohesive, and they are likely to achieve less in education, occupation, and income than those from intact homes.

Boys seem to present more problems than girls for single parents. Single mothers may try to get their older sons to assume the responsibilities of the missing father, or they may go to the opposite extreme and "over-mother" their sons. There is not a great deal of research on single fathers, but children tend to reward single fathers more than single mothers.

Problems may arise when a single parent begins to date. Children may be angry and resentful about the parent dating. The problem may be compounded by the fact that the dates may be less than enthusiastic about the children.

In spite of the problems, most single-parent homes function reasonably well. The majority of single parents and their children have good physical and mental health. Single parents also function well at work.

Nonwhite families are similar to white families in many ways, but they face special problems because of their situation in society. Blacks are the largest of America's racial minorities. They have a higher rate of single-parent families than either whites or Hispanics. Blacks are also more likely to be single, widowed, or divorced. More than one of every four black families is headed by a mother who never married.

The problems of the black family must be viewed in the context of centuries of political and economic disadvantages. Blacks have lower incomes and higher rates of unemployment than whites, making the role of provider a more difficult one for the black male. Those blacks who have fewer economic problems are more like whites in their family life. During the 1980s, however, the economic problems increased again because of various political decisions.

Although blacks are more likely than whites to have a disadvantaged family situation, the black family tends to have a number of strengths and, in some cases, advantages over white families. Parenthood may not diminish the quality of life for blacks as it does for whites, and being a single parent may not be as difficult for blacks as for whites. Blacks tend to be more egalitarian in practice than do whites. And blacks are not as likely as whites to be distressed by the empty nest.

Hispanics, the second largest racial minority, fall in between blacks and whites in terms of median family income. Hispanics are more likely than either whites or blacks to have a family household and less likely to be divorced. Hispanic women differ from white women in that they show a progressive decline in marital satisfaction over time. In contrast to popular stereotype, however, Hispanic families are not male-dominated; they tend to be egalitarian. Finally, Hispanics tend to have closer bonds with members of the extended family than do whites.

Interracial families have increased greatly since 1970. Japanese are particularly likely to intermarry. There is a higher rate of divorce in interracial marriages. People are attracted to mates of other races because of such things as love and compatibility. Even in an accepting environment, however, interracial unions face some unique problems. One problem is which parental roles and values to adopt when the husband and wife come from different cultural traditions.

About 20 to 30 percent of gay people enter a homosexual marriage. Homosexual couples have to work through the same problems as heterosexual couples. In addition, they face problems arising from a hostile environment and from the nature of their relationship. For example, gay male couples may be stressed as their relationship is affected by the stereotypical male role (including the male sexual role), by homophobia, or by sexual dysfunctions.

Lesbian couples may not have the same kind of problems as either gay male or heterosexual couples. They report less conflict over money management and income and more egalitarianism than other couples.

Homosexual couples trying to raise children report few serious problems and generally satisfying relationships. There may be some problems when the children reach adolescence and fear that they might also become homosexual. In general, homosexuals want the same thing as heterosexuals in an intimate relationship. And the same factors enhance the quality of both homosexual and heterosexual relationships: commitment, shared decision making, and perceived investment in the relationship.

Two ways in which homosexual couples differ from heterosexual are the greater egalitarianism of the former and the way in which fidelity tends to be defined by gay males. Gay men frequently opt for an open relationship, which allows sexual relations with outsiders. Fidelity is defined as an emotional commitment rather than sexual exclusivity. But gay males do form long-term relationships. The process of bonding and commitment in a homosexual relationship is very similar to that in a heterosexual relationship.

Part Four

Challenges to Intimacy

A philosopher speculated that the family might one day become an obsolete institution. By contrast, an anthropologist speculated that if civilization were ever wiped out in a nuclear holocaust, the last man on earth would spend his dying days searching through the rubble for his family. We believe the anthropologist was closer to reality than was the philosopher. Most people try to maintain intimate relationships, especially family relationships, and they endure a great deal of suffering before they break such relationships.

In this final section, we will look at some of the crises that strain intimacy in the family. The crises can lead either to disruption or to an enhanced intimacy. Then we will discuss what happens when, in spite of the tendency to hang on, a decision is made to terminate the marital relationship. Finally, we will talk about the nature of, and problems in, the reconstituted family. The need for family intimacy is so strong that most divorced people try again to establish a meaningful family life. As the anthropologist suggested, in spite of the high rate of disruption in our society, people fundamentally value and strive to create and maintain families.

17

Family Crises

In his novel, *The Mayor of Casterbridge,* Thomas Hardy told of a man who struggles throughout his life with his own passions. In the opening pages, Michael Henchard, the main character, gets drunk while attending a fair. Impetuously, he sells his wife and daughter to a sailor. For the rest of his life, Henchard is affected by his rash act. Years later, his wife comes back into his life, and for a brief time Henchard once again has a family. But he cannot control himself. Ultimately, his self-destructive tendencies bring him to a tragic end.

In the novel, Hardy showed the disastrous consequences of one kind of family crisis—the inability of one member to control his or her impulses. For Henchard, the problem not only resulted in excessive drinking, but also in suspicions and misattributions. As a result, his life was a series of crises. In this chapter, we will discuss some of the crises that come to families and threaten intimacy. We will look at greater length at two kinds of crises that are widespread: alcohol abuse and violence. These two problems involve severe trauma in the family. Finally, we will see how people deal with crises, including both successful and unsuccessful methods of coping.

Many kinds of crises can threaten family intimacy.

Sources of Family Crises

Have you ever experienced what you would call a family crisis? If so, what was the nature of that crisis? What caused it? If you posed these questions to other people, you might hear of some differing kinds of crises than you have experienced. In any case, however, crises are closely linked with stressful events and/or behavior.

Stress and Crisis

In their efforts to understand diverse family responses to stressful events, family scholars have used the ABCX model developed by Reuben Hill (1958). Hill (1949) began his work by studying the stress endured by families during war. He developed the ABCX family crisis model to try to account for differential success in coping. In essence, A is the stressor event and the hardships it produces. B is the management of the stress through coping resources that the family has. C is the family's definition of the event. A, B, and C interact together to produce X, the crisis.

For example, let us say that two families, the Smiths and the Joneses, face the stressor of unemployment (A). The Smiths define it as undesirable but also as a challenge (C), and they decide that each family member will try to find work and will do something to save money (B). The interaction of these three produces no serious crisis for them (X). The Joneses, on the other hand, define the event as a disaster (C). They expect the father to find a new job immediately and to do something to avoid any serious change in their lifestyle (B). The interaction of these three is a crisis (X).

The two examples are simplified, of course. In fact, the model itself is somewhat simplified, because there are other elements that may be important in the outcome of a stressor. Recognizing this, McCubbin and Patterson (1983) proposed a Double ABCX model. They relabeled the A factor, calling it *family demands*. There are three components to family demands. One is the stressor. Second, there are the hardships that accompany the stressor (such as increasing financial problems when a parent is unemployed). Third, there are "pile-ups,"

> the residuals of family tension that linger from unresolved prior stressors or that are inherent in ongoing family roles such as being a parent or spouse (McCubbin and Patterson 1983:279).

It is important to recognize the place of pile-ups or prior strains. That is, a stressor does not occur in a vacuum, but in the context of ongoing life. Suppose, for instance, that you learned more about the Smiths and the Joneses, the two families introduced in the preceding example. What if the unemployment of Mr. Smith occurred while there were few other strains, while that of Mr. Jones occurred in the midst of family illness and at a point when the oldest daughter was preparing to go to college? Clearly, we need to know something about what is going on in a family at the time of the stressor event to fully understand their response to that stressor.

Pauline Boss (1988), who has made extensive studies of family stress, concluded that many families in crisis are not sick families but are simply facing a greater volume of stress than they, or most other families, can handle. Boss (1988:10) claimed that families today are under more pressure than were those of the past:

> Some of the daily problems with which they must contend are traffic (unlike anything our grandparents ever saw); threats to life and property (few communities are free of potential or actual crimes); expectations for children (they must achieve in order to be accepted in the middle-class world); emancipated sons and daughters who move back home (because of unemployment or divorce); and both parents working outside the home (that's what it takes to keep up mortgage payments these days). Good child care has become a luxury that few working parents—especially single parents—can afford, so that work and family tensions are higher than ever before.
>
> Most important, perhaps, is the loss of leisure; there is less and less time for couples to relax together or to spend time with people they care about. Family life has *not* gotten simpler for present generations; it is *more* complex and the pace is faster.

In other words, there are numerous commonplace tensions and strains in the lives of most of us. If some additional stressors in the form of unemployment, serious illness, or severe personal or interpersonal problems occur, they can plunge many if not most families into a situation of crisis. It is unlikely that you can live in a family for an extended period of time without encountering a number of crises.

Stressor Events

As we discuss the stressor events that can bring about a family crisis, it is important to keep in mind that the events per se are not sufficient to cause serious problems. As the model indicates, the context in which the event occurs, the way that the family defines the event, and the resources the family has for dealing with it are all crucial to the outcome. Still, it is important to be aware of the kinds of events that are likely to cause a family crisis.

Types of Stressor Events

What kinds of stressor events are most likely to result in a family crisis? Some of the common ones that you may face include the death of a family member, a serious illness or accident to a family member, unemployment of a family member, an unwanted pregnancy, a miscarriage, a move to a new location, serious personal problems such as emotional illness or alcohol abuse by a family member, and serious interpersonal problems such as abuse, infidelity, or a child's broken engagement.

Boss (1988:40) has classified the various kinds of stressors in terms of a number of dimensions (table 17.1). Thus, the stressor may arise from within or without the family. It can be an expected or unpredictable event. And so

Table 17.1 Types of Stressor Events

Internal
Events that begin from someone inside the family, such as getting drunk, suicide, or running for election.

External
Events that begin from someone or something outside the family, such as earthquakes, terrorism, the inflation rate, or cultural attitudes toward women and minorities.

Normative
Events that are expected over the family life cycle, such as birth, launching an adolescent, marriage, aging, or death.

Nonnormative
Events that are unexpected, such as winning a lottery, getting a divorce, dying young, war, or being taken hostage. Often but not always disastrous.

Ambiguous
You can't get the facts surrounding the event. It's so unclear that you're not even sure that it's happening to you and your family.

Nonambiguous
Clear facts are available about the event: what is happening, when, how long, and to whom.

Volitional
Events that are wanted and sought out, such as a freely chosen job change, a college entrance, or a wanted pregnancy.

Nonvolitional
Events that are not sought out but just happen, such as being laid off or the sudden loss of someone loved.

Chronic
A situation that has long duration, such as diabetes, chemical addiction, or racial discrimination.

Acute
An event that lasts a short time but is severe, such as breaking a limb, losing a job, or flunking a test.

Cumulative
Events that pile up, one right after the other, so that there is no resolution before the next one occurs. A dangerous situation in most cases.

Isolated
An event that occurs alone, at least with no other events apparent at that time. It can be pinpointed easily.

From Pauline Boss, *Family Stress Management*, page 40. Copyright © 1988 Sage Publications, Inc., Newbury Park, CA. Reprinted by permission of Sage Publications, Inc.

on. It is important to note that stressors are not always things that are imposed on us. Something that is freely chosen (the volitional category) may also turn out to be a stressor. As a businessman told us:

> I was excited about getting a new job in a new city. But for the first few months on that job, I was really distressed. I thought I had made the biggest mistake of my life.

Stressor Events and the Family Life Cycle

As you would expect, the kinds of things most likely to be important stressors vary somewhat over the family life cycle (Olson and McCubbin 1983:123f). Among young, recently wed couples, work-family and financial strains are most common. Changing jobs or careers, becoming dissatisfied with one's job or career, having problems with people on the job, and taking on additional responsibilities at work are all potential sources of stress for the young couple.

There is a "contagion" of stress across work and family roles, such that stress in one area tends to spill over into the other (Bolger, DeLongis, Kessler, and Wethington 1989). In some cases, a self-perpetuating cycle can be set up: work stress is brought home, creating marital problems that make effective work problematic and cause further difficulty at work, aggravating the individual's stress, and so forth.

During the early childbearing years, financial strains are the most common. There are increased demands on the family's income for such things as food, clothing, and medical and dental care. Major purchases, such as homes and cars, are made, putting the family deeply into debt. The couple may have to take out additional loans, or refinance their debt, in order to cover the increased expenses of the growing family.

While financial pressures tend to lessen somewhat as the children grow, time demands generally increase. Additional stress can arise from the growing number of outside activities in which the children are involved. There is a sense that an increasing number of tasks around the home are simply not being done. These problems continue as the children grow into adolescence, at which point financial strains again may become severe.

By the time the couple has reached the empty nest stage, time demands again are generally the prime source of stress with emphasis on chores that do not get done. In addition, difficulties with the sexual relationship, financial problems, decreasing satisfaction with work, and illness and death become more likely. Finally, in the retirement stage, financial problems once again become the most likely source of stress.

It is important to realize three things. First, some problems, such as financial strains, tend to be common at all stages. Second, the previous discussion does not include all the stressors that may occur, but simply indicates the stressors most frequently named by people at various stages. Finally, as indicated by the nonnormative sources in table 17.1, stressors like serious illness are unpredictable. Although serious illness is more likely to occur in the later years, it may happen at any time.

Not All Stressors Are Equal
What is the worst thing that could happen to you? You can probably think of some undesirable events that you could deal with relatively easily, others that would be much more difficult to cope with, and perhaps one or more that would make you feel like life was no longer worth living. In other words, the various stressors do not affect us equally. In fact, the same stressor may affect different people in different ways. Unemployment, for example, may be devastating to one person and a welcome break to another depending on their circumstances.

In spite of the diverse reactions, however, when we look at how large numbers of people react to various stressors, we can rank order them in terms of their severity. The Family Inventory of Life Events and Changes (FILE) is one effort to identify the severity of various kinds of stressors (McCubbin

Table 17.2 The 15 Most Severe Family Stressors
(Numbers are a measure of relative severity)

Death of a child	99
Death of a spouse/parent	98
Separation or divorce of spouse/parent	79
Physical or sexual abuse or violence between family members	75
Family member becomes physically disabled or chronically ill	73
Spouse/parent has an affair	68
Family member jailed or sent to juvenile detention	68
Family member dependent on alcohol or drugs	66
Pregnancy of an unmarried family member	65
Family member runs away from home	61
Family member seems to have an emotional problem	58
Increased sexual problems in the marriage	58
Increased difficulty handling a disabled or chronically ill family member	58
Married child separates or gets a divorce	58
Family member picked up by police or arrested	57

From Hamilton I. McCubbin and Joan M. Patterson, "Stress: The Family Inventory of Life Events and Changes" in *Marriage and Family Assessment: A Sourcebook for Family Therapy*, pp. 285-86. Copyright © 1983 Erik Filsinger. Reprinted by permission of Erik Filsinger.

The death of a child is a severe crisis for a family.

and Patterson 1983). The researchers who developed FILE worked in the context of the Double ABCX model of stress. Thus, the instrument is an effort to measure the pile-ups in a family during the course of a year. It measures not only the number but the severity of stressors that accumulate and that can bring a family to the point of crisis.

FILE taps into nine important types of stressors in family life. Intra-family strains include tensions between family members and the strains of parent-child relationships. The other types of stressors are: marital strains, pregnancy and childbearing strains, finance and business strains, work-family transitions and strains, illness and family care strains, family losses (loss of member or friend or a breakdown in the relationships), family transitions in and out (members of the family moving out or back into the home or engaging in a serious involvement of some kind outside the family), and family legal strains. The total of all these nine strains, weighted according to their severity, result in a "family pile-up" score. Given a sufficiently high score, most families are likely to experience difficulty in coping.

What are the most severe stressors? Ranked in terms of difficulty of adjusting, table 17.2 shows the fifteen most severe. At the lower end of the scale are such things as purchase of an automobile or other major item (19), increased strain on income for food, clothing, energy, and home-care (21), increased strain on income for children's education (22), and increased strain on income for medical and dental expenses (23). It is important to realize that the numbers, which are measures of relative severity, are averages for large numbers of people. The same event can have a quite different impact on different individuals, depending on a number of other factors. One factor is the time of life when the event occurs. For example, if a parent dies when you are a teenager, the impact is likely to be far more severe than when you are in your fifties or sixties.

Another factor is the nature of your relationship at the time of the event. If, for instance, your spouse has an affair in the context of years of conflict you are less likely to be overwhelmed by it than if it occurs when you believe that the marriage is strong and meaningful to you both.

The impact of the various stressors, then, will vary somewhat from one individual to another depending on the circumstances. Yet their *relative* severity will generally reflect these numbers.

An interesting finding from the research using FILE relates to the amount of pile-up at various stages of the family life cycle. Again, keep in mind that the figures are averages for large numbers of families. You may or may not have the same experience in your own family. But looking at families generally, the researchers found that the highest amount of stress (pile-up) tends to occur during the time when the family is in the transition from having children in the home to the empty nest. During this "launching" stage, there tends to be more stressors than at any other time in the family life cycle. At this point, there is the stress of disrupting the home through children leaving for marriage or school and the likelihood of increased financial strain to cover the expenses of these events. It is also a time of life when one of the parents may be considering a change in jobs or career and when serious illness becomes more likely.

The lowest overall stress scores tend to occur in the retirement stage, and the second lowest are in the empty nest stage of the family life cycle. It is not without some cause that the later years of life are sometimes termed the *golden* years. If grandmothers and grandfathers seem more relaxed and better able to flow with the events of life, it is in part because they are enjoying a time of life in which there are fewer stressor events with which they must cope.

Alcohol Abuse in the Family

Alcohol abuse ranks high on the list of family stressors. Some experts have even called alcohol abuse the nation's foremost health problem. When we look at the statistics, it is easy to see why they would make such a statement.

Extent of Alcohol Abuse

We will define **alcohol abuse** as the improper use of alcohol such that the consequences are detrimental to the user and the family. It is the abuse, not merely the use, of alcohol that creates problems. About two-thirds of the American population drink to some extent. But there are more than 14 million problem drinkers in the United States (Lauer 1989:115). About one in five Americans who drink every day or almost every day report associated problems in the family as a result of the drinking.[1]

You may think of the skid-row derelict when you think of alcohol abuse, but more typically alcohol abusers are:

> Employed or employable, family-centered people. More than 70 percent of them live in respectable neighborhoods, with their husbands and wives, send their children to school, belong to clubs, attend church, pay taxes, and continue to perform more or less effectively as businessmen, executives, housewives, farmers, salesmen, industrial workers, clerical workers, teachers, clergymen, and physicians (National Institute on Alcohol Abuse and Alcoholism 1975:15–16).

Alcohol abuse is far more common among men than women, though the proportion of women is increasing. Alcohol abuse is also more prevalent among whites than blacks, and among higher-income than lower-income people (Lauer 1989:116).

Alcohol Abuse and the Quality of Family Life

Alcohol abuse seriously detracts from the quality of family life. The consequences vary from relatively minor ones of more frequent arguments to the severe consequences of physical and emotional abuse.

Some families with an abuser seem to function fairly normally when the abuser is not drinking. The family can communicate with each other, enjoy family functions, carry on family work, and so forth. But when the abuser is drinking, the whole character of family life is likely to change. At the very least, the drinker is likely to become more negative and critical with his or her spouse while drinking (Jacob and Krahn 1988). At worst, the abuser of alcohol may become physically or emotionally abusive of his or her spouse. Looking at a national sample of over two thousand couples, Coleman and Straus (1983) found a positive link between alcohol abuse and family violence. The more often a spouse was drunk during the year, the more often there was physical violence in the relationship. The exception occurred when the abuse was extreme. When the spouse was "almost always" drunk, violence was less likely than when the spouse was "often" or "very often" drunk. Still, more than one out of four males who were almost always drunk during the year of the survey engaged in violent behavior against their spouses.

In many families, particularly when the abuse is long-term, there are negative consequences whether or not the abuser is drinking. In fact, some research shows that couples with an alcoholic husband are like couples that are "maritally conflicted," that is, couples that have a high degree of dissatisfaction and a large number of disagreements (O'Farrell and Birchler 1987). In other words, the atmosphere in a family where there is an abuser of alcohol is likely to feature a great deal of tension, considerable dissatisfaction, and frequent conflict.

In addition, the spouses and children of the abusers may develop various physical and emotional problems. While the majority of children who come from a home with one or more alcoholics are not doomed to some kind of

Many youths who have problems come from a home with one or two alcoholic parents.

pathology, they are more vulnerable to a variety of behavioral and emotional problems (West and Prinz 1987). Among other things, children in such families are more likely than others to:

Have a conduct disorder or become delinquent

Become an abuser of alcohol themselves

Display higher rates of hyperactivity

Have problems with school work

Report higher rates of health problems

Have higher rates of anxiety and depression

The children of alcoholics also tend to describe their families as less cohesive and more conflict-ridden than do children from other families (Clair and Genest 1987). When they grow up and marry, they are more likely than others to separate or divorce (Parker and Harford 1988). Clearly, the abuser is engaged not merely in a self-destructive process, but in a process that may detract from both the immediate and long-term quality of life of other family members.

Family Problems and Alcohol Abuse

If alcohol abuse can lead to family problems, family problems can also lead to alcohol abuse. When there are disturbed relationships within the home, one of the family members may resort to heavy drinking in an effort to cope with the stress. Students who report more alcohol use also tend to report more stressor events in their lives, more daily hassles, and more conflict in their families (Baer, Garmezy, McLaughlin, Pokorny, and Wernick 1987). A husband or wife may resort to drinking because of serious marital problems. The drinking is an effort to cope with a frustrating, stressful situation. Like other inappropriate coping methods, it is counterproductive. It is a way of escape, rather than a way of confronting the problem and pursuing some constructive resolution.

If family problems result in a member becoming a problem drinker, the family may get caught in a vicious circle in which the problems and the abuse feed on and sustain each other. That is, the difficulties lead the member to drink, and the drinking intensifies the problems and creates additional ones. The added stress perpetuates the drinking, and the drinking continues to aggravate the problems. Once the pattern is established, it tends to be self-perpetuating.

Moreover, alcohol abuse can take its toll across a number of generations. Kayla, a graduate student in her thirties, has alcoholic grandparents on both sides of her family. Although neither of her parents abused alcohol, the effects of the grandparents' abuse have continued in the family:

> To this day, I see my mother struggling to establish her own identity and my father striving to free himself from the emotional tyranny of an alcoholic father. Growing up in alcoholic families, my parents didn't know how to deal with things like sickness, job loss, moving, or family conflict. Whenever they faced a crisis, they would lean on me as the oldest child to help resolve it. I grew up feeling overly responsible and quite inadequate.

Kayla married a man who was from an alcoholic family. She knows now that she looked to him to give her the nurturing she never got from her family, and he looked to her to be the capable and competent individual that he never had in his family. They were both wrong. Their marriage alternated between coldness and stormy passions, and between self-blame and blaming the other. It eventually ended in divorce.

Kayla's experience is perhaps one of the more insidious consequences of alcohol abuse in a family. The inadequate parenting that results when there is an abuser can have negative effects through a number of subsequent generations.

Violence in Families

Next to death, separation, and divorce, family violence is the most difficult experience people have to cope with (table 17.2). It is easy to understand the severity of the trauma. After all, we expect our families to be a source of comfort and support, a refuge from an often difficult world. For the refuge to become a violent battleground is, as one person told us, "like discovering that God is a malevolent tormentor rather than a loving Father."

Self-Help Groups

What can you do if you have a drinking problem or if you are in a family with someone who abuses alcohol? Alcoholics Anonymous is the best known and one of the most effective self-help organizations for alcoholics. Al-Anon and Alateen are organizations for the spouse and the children of the alcoholics. They help the individual cope with the difficulties of living with an alcoholic.

There are self-help groups today to deal with all kinds of problems that can create a crisis in a family, ranging from Alcoholics Anonymous (AA) to groups that help people with other kinds of addictions (gambling) to those that help people who have various kinds of emotional problems. There are groups for the overweight, the unemployed, and the abused.

Locate some kind of self-help group in your community (the telephone directory is a good place to begin), and get permission to visit a group meeting. Note the way that the group works to help each member to cope with problems. Ask one of the people attending if you can interview him or her for your class project. Tell the person that you are particularly interested in how his or her experience relates to family life—both the family of origin and the current family of which the individual is a part. Explore the following questions:

1. What kinds of experiences in the family of origin seemed to contribute to the problem, if any?

2. What kinds of experiences in the current family contributed to the problem, if any?

3. Did anyone else in the family or the family of origin have a similar problem?

4. How did the problem affect family life, including the marital relationship and relations with children?

If the entire class participates in this project, see if you can come up with any common factors in the family background of the people and any common consequences for family life. Do different kinds of problems seem to have different sources and consequences? Why or why not?

The Extent of Violence

The first national survey of family violence took place in 1975; the second occurred in 1985 (Gelles and Straus 1988). Surprisingly, the rate of family violence had declined in the 1985 survey. The researchers suggest that a number of factors account for the decline, including an increase in the average age at marriage (younger couples tend to be more violent), a more prosperous economy (violence is more common when there is financial stress), and an increasingly loud public message that family violence is unacceptable (the number of shelters for battered women rose from about four to over one thousand).

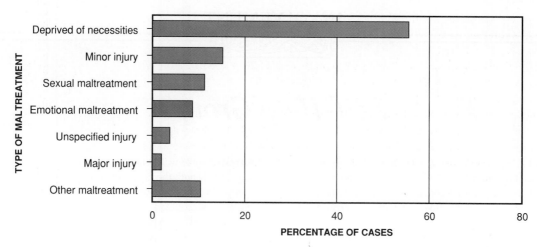

Figure 17.1 *Types of child maltreatment.*
Source: U.S. Bureau of the Census 1989:172.

Still, the amount of violence was high. During the year of the survey, nineteen parents per one thousand admitted using abusive violence against their children. Wife-beating incidents occurred at the rate of about thirty per one thousand women. These are undoubtedly conservative figures, based only on the number of admitted cases. Even using the conservative figures, adults and children who experience violence in the home number in the millions.

Child Abuse

If we define violence to include such mild forms as spanking, the majority of parents use some form of violence against their children. We are concerned here, however, with the more severe forms of violence, which range from depriving children of some of the necessities of life to severe physical injury (figure 17.1). When we look at cases of child maltreatment that are reported to the authorities, we find that the average age of the child involved is about seven years (U.S. Bureau of the Census 1989:172). Averages are a little misleading, however. The children at greatest risk of abuse are those under three years and teenagers (Gelles and Straus 1988). Abuse occurs almost equally to males and females, and is proportionately higher among blacks and Hispanics than whites.

A prototype of the abusive parent would be one who is single, is young (around thirty or under), has been married for less than ten years, had their first child before the age of eighteen, and is unemployed or employed part-time. Women are slightly more likely to abuse children than are men, probably because women are more intensely involved with children (and the rates of child abuse are higher in single-parent, which for the most part means single-mother, families). Child abusers tend to have lower self-esteem than others, to define their children as more troublesome, and to have serious financial problems and a large number of other stressor events in their lives (Hamilton, Stiles, Melowsky, and Beal 1987). Abusers are also likely to have been abused themselves as children.

Obviously, child abuse is often associated with pile-up, a large number of stressors that overwhelms the parent or parents. What emerges is a portrait of a troubled, stressful home. Thus, in a survey of 1,770 undergraduates, 6.3 percent of whom said they had been physically abused by a parent, the researcher found that those abused were more likely to report a good deal of conflict in the home, parental drinking and drug problems, and one or both parents who were unsupportive, overly strict or overly permissive, angry, and depressed (Wright 1985).

Incest

Incest, a special form of child abuse, is any type of exploitive sexual contact between relatives in which the victim is under eighteen years of age. It is difficult to know exactly how many people are the victims of incest. It seems clear, however, that girls are much more likely than boys to be victims of incest. Conservatively, about 19 percent of girls and 9 percent of boys are sexually abused (Finkelhor 1984). The figures include child sexual abuse generally, not just incest. Of the girls who are sexually abused as children, about 4.5 percent are abused by their fathers (Russell 1986).

When father-daughter incest occurs, it usually begins when the daughter is between the ages of six and eleven, and the abuse lasts around two years on the average (Stark 1984). How could a father engage in sexual relationships with his daughter? The usual explanation is that such incest occurs when "the marital relationship has broken down, the mother is alienated from the roles of wife and mother, and the father makes an alliance with the oldest daughter that substitutes for the marital relationship and becomes sexual" (Finkelhor 1984:226).

Still, many men endure an alienated relationship with a wife without resorting to incest. Abusive fathers are like other abusive adults, troubled individuals who find it difficult to relate meaningfully and sexually with another adult. Indeed, some research has shown that incestuous fathers have personality problems and thus cannot seem to appropriately find the intimacy that they crave (Justice and Justice 1979). The incestuous father may feel alienated from the world generally, or may view his daughter as his property, or may be a tyrant in the home, or may be an abuser of alcohol. In any case, the father is also likely to be highly stressed, without a sexual relationship with his wife, and to nurture a fantasy about an ideal mother and wife that he lacks in his own wife and seeks in his daughter.

A father may initiate sexual relations with his daughter by force or by intimidation. Some people believe that the mother colludes and that the daughter gets a certain amount of enjoyment out of the relationship. Yet the evidence suggests that incest is likely to be a horrifying experience to the victim. Becky, an editor, is still "overwhelmed" as she discusses her experience. She

Father-daughter incest is the most common form of incest; it is likely to be a horrifying experience for the daughter.

remembers the intense conflict between her parents, and her mother finally being hospitalized for a period of time. She was about eleven years old, and "sex was not even the subject for jokes with my circle of friends. I hardly thought about it." When her father approached her for sex, she was passive. She "didn't react to the incest as a sexual act, but as a way to keep the family together." When Becky yielded to her father, things seemed better in the home. "I desperately wanted harmony in my family and every other need became subordinate to that." When Becky's father asked her if she wanted him to return to her bedroom after each sexual encounter, she told him no. But she continued to allow him to use her. And she has spent the years since then trying to work through the agony of being betrayed by a man to whom she looked for support and unconditional love.

Mother-son incest seems to be quite rare. Other forms of incest, such as that between brother and sister and uncles and nieces and other relatives, occur, but we do not know how widespread they are. We do know, however, that most incestuous relationships are a betrayal of trust and lead to long-term problems for the victim.

Spouse Abuse

The term *spouse abuse* is likely to create a portrait of a man beating a woman in your mind. Actually, there are more incidents of wives beating husbands than of husbands beating wives in any given year. In the 1985 survey, the cases of severe wife beating were thirty per one thousand and the cases of severe violence toward husbands were forty-four per thousand (Gelles and Straus

1988:109). But we need to keep one fact in mind: the probability of severe physical injury is far greater when a man beats his wife than it is when a woman beats her husband. Furthermore, women who beat on their husbands are likely to have been previously beaten by their husbands. Frequently a wife's violence is a form of self-defense. Occasionally, a woman may strike the first blow on the assumption that she won't be beaten as badly if she also fights.

What kind of man would beat his wife? The typical wife beater is unemployed or employed part-time, lives at the poverty level, worries about finances, is very dissatisfied with his life, is young (between eighteen and twenty-four years), and has been married for less than ten years (Gelles and Straus 1988). He was likely abused himself as a child. He probably abuses his wife verbally as well as physically. He is likely to believe that the man should be the head of the family, but he lacks the resources to be dominant in his family. As Gelles and Straus put it:

> Perhaps the most telling of all attributes of the battering man is that he feels inadequate and sees violence as a culturally acceptable way to be both dominant and powerful (1988:89).

As the preceding suggests, an egalitarian relationship is less likely to be marked by violence than one in which either the husband or the wife is striving to be dominant (Coleman and Straus 1986). Those who are violent, whether women or men, may be using the violence as a way of establishing their dominance.

> Lurking beneath the surface of all intimate violence are the confrontations and controversies over power (Gelles and Straus 1988:92).

Why would a woman allow herself to be repeatedly beaten? Why does she stay in the relationship? In some cases women lack (or believe that they lack) the economic means to leave. In an effort to retain some economic security or to make the relationship ultimately work out, they may be willing to tolerate abuse as long as it does not become too severe or involve their children.

In other cases, women have fallen into what Donald Dutton (1987:248) called a *social trap*. Thus, the abused woman begins her marriage with the same expectations as others—long-term happiness and fulfillment and her own heavy responsibility for such an outcome and for the emotional state of her husband. The violent episodes, which typically begin in the first year of marriage, are less severe at first, and are likely to be followed by strong expressions of regret from the husband. She may therefore view the violence as an anomaly. At first, she does not expect the violence to continue. Eventually, she realizes that it will, but by that time she has developed a strong commitment to the man. She is determined to make the relationship succeed. There is a "traumatic bonding" that occurs, a bonding that is facilitated by the fact that the abuse occurs intermittently and may be followed by effusive apologies and promises to change.

In other words, women may have values and attitudes that override the physical and emotional damage they are enduring. Ferraro and Johnson (1983) interviewed over one hundred battered women and found that those who opted to remain in the relationship offered six different kinds of explanations. Some had a "salvation ethic." They saw their husbands as troubled or sick individuals who needed their wives to survive. Others said the problem was beyond the control of them or their husbands; the violence was due to some external factor like work pressure or loss of a job. A third group denied the injury; they said the beatings were tolerable and even normal. Fourth, some blamed themselves, saying the violence could be averted if only they were more passive and conciliatory. Fifth, some saw no options for themselves; they were too economically or emotionally dependent on their husbands. Finally, some of the women said that they lived by a "higher loyalty" such as a religious faith or commitment to a stable family life.

Parent Abuse

Although most of the attention has been focused on child and spouse abuse, researchers have discovered that children also abuse their parents. Results from a national survey of 1,545 male high-school students reported that about one in ten admitted to a violent act against a parent, more often against the father than the mother (Peek, Fischer, and Kidwell 1985).

Abuse of elderly parents may also occur at the hands of their adult children (Pierce and Trotta 1986). The victims tend to be around seventy-five years of age or older. The most likely victim is a white female. The abuser is also likely to be a female (because women rather than men are generally the caregivers), one who is having some kind of personal crisis (alcohol or drug addiction, illness, or financial problems).

> The combination of personal crisis and the new task of taking on the added responsibility of the aged parent created a situation which increased the likelihood of violence (Pierce and Trotta 1986:102).

Perhaps as many as a half- to a million elderly parents a year are victims of abuse.

Consequences of Abuse

In the short-term, of course, abuse involves serious physical and emotional damage. But abuse also tends to have serious long-term consequences. Let us look first at the consequences for children. The victims of incest may wind up in therapy as adults as they struggle with low self-esteem, guilt, depression, suicidal tendencies, relationship problems, or drug or alcohol addiction (Jehu, Gazan and Klassen 1985).

About a third of children who are abused will grow up to be abusers themselves (Gelles and Straus 1988). That means, to be sure, that most abused children will *not* become abusers. Yet they are ten times more likely to do so than those who were not abused. Other effects on abused children include:

Lower intellectual and academic development

Tendency to become aggressive

Problems of low self-esteem, feelings of isolation, difficulty in trusting others, difficulty in forming meaningful intimate relationships, and generalized unhappiness

The consequences of abuse for women (we know of no research on the consequences of male victims of spouse abuse) are serious problems with physical and mental health (Gelles and Straus 1988:136). Compared to those in nonviolent homes, women who are abused report more:

Headaches or pains in the head

Nervousness and depression

A sense of being overwhelmed by difficulties

Feelings of worthlessness and hopelessness

A sense of being unable to cope

Suicidal thoughts and actual suicide attempts

Only about two women in one thousand think seriously about suicide in any one year, but about forty-six abused women in one thousand think about suicide frequently. One of the bitter ironies of the abusive relationship is that the woman's reaction to the abuse—for example, her depression—may be used to justify further beatings. The victim is blamed for her own beating.

We should note one final aspect of family violence, namely that *viewing* violence also has harmful consequences. Children who see violence between their parents will suffer even if they are not themselves abused. One study focused on three groups of college students: those who had viewed parental violence, those who had seen considerable nonviolent conflict, and those who perceived their parents as satisfactorily married (Forsstrom-Cohen and Rosenbaum 1985). The students who had viewed the violence were more anxious than those from satisfactory homes, and women who had viewed more violence were more depressed and more aggressive than women from the other two groups. In addition, children who observe parental violence are more likely to become violent themselves than are children who are the victims of violence (Gelles and Straus 1988:90). Such children apparently learn from watching their parents that those who love you also hit you, and that this is an appropriate way to get your way and to deal with stress.

Drinking and Fighting

We have seen that alcohol abuse may be associated with verbal and physical abuse as well. The problem is an old one. In June 1677, a case against Edmond Berry was heard in a Massachusetts court. Berry was fined for excessive drink and abusive behavior toward his wife. In the following account, which we have put into modern English from the old court record, Berry's wife accused him of intolerable abuse:

> This honored Court knows of my woeful condition in living with my husband Edmond Berry, and of his most bitter, inhumane, and most ill-becoming behavior to me, as many of my neighbors can give testimony. I was compelled to go away from him and live where I could be safe. The honored Court, upon learning of this, compelled me—upon the penalty of five pounds—to live with him again, which as the Lord knows to my inexpressible sorrow has been now for about twelve months. If my testimony does not sufficiently speak for me and if the

> Court doesn't help me, what shall a poor woman do in this case? This is my situation: I have nothing of his nor have I ever had but a very small amount ever since I was his wife. For example, he had (and still has) an absurd manner in eating his victuals: he takes his meat out of the pickle and broils it upon the coals. And he tells me I must eat this or else I must fast. Therefore, if I had not reserved something for myself to eat, I would have perished. Neither will he provide me with the absolute necessities to run a decent house, rather I am compelled to borrow from my neighbors. He has made it evident that he intends to do what he has previously reported: namely that he will have my estate or else he will make me weary of my life.
>
> Now the honored Major Hathorne knows the contract that was made between us before marriage and acknowledged before him. However, in the hope of living more comfortably

Reacting to Crises

As we have discussed, about one-third of abused children will grow up to become abusers; about two-thirds will not. Clearly, people react in different ways to family crises. The point we wish to stress in this section is that whatever the particular crisis you face, there are always alternative ways of dealing with it. You can't control all of the things that happen in your life, but you can control the way you respond to them. This doesn't mean that you can avoid the trauma of crises. It does mean, as we will show in the final section of this chapter, that you can avoid long-term, adverse consequences. In fact, it is possible to turn the crisis into something that yields long-term, positive consequences (figure 17.2).

with him, I willingly brought into the house what I could. But he continued to bestow ill upon me. Please judge his behavior for yourself by this one more recent example. When I brought to him a cup of my own sugar and beer (for he will allow me nothing of his own) and drank a toast to him using these words: "Come husband let all former differences be buried and trod underfoot; why should we not live in love and unity as other folks do?" He replied to me, thus: "You old cheating rogue; the devil take thee if you don't bring me before this court." But such dire expressions towards me are not rare with him. Although this treatment was hard and very tedious to bear, I was willing to groan under it rather than to make a public display of his wicked and brutal behavior to me.

Yet he came before the Court and the grand jury had cognizance of his impious behavior towards me. . . . It is reasonable that I should speak something before your honor in order to clear up of my own innocence; and also, since the matter has been brought before the court, I want to present my grievances before you—although God knows I preferred rather to have

borne my affliction and waited upon Him who is the persuader of the heart, with my poor prayers to my good God in hopes of the work of His grace upon my husband's heart and soul, whereby he might be brought to see the evil of his ways and so to behave toward me as becomes an honest man to his wife. But the Lord in mercy look upon me, for I am now past hope of his changing, and the only wise God direct you in what to do with me in this my woeful case. For I am not only continually abused by my husband, with most vile, threatening, and opprobrious speeches, but also by his son who lives in the house with him. He has, in his father's presence, threatened to throw me headlong down the stairs. In addition, he has broken into my chest and taken away a part of that little which I had.

Excerpt from *America's Families: A Documentary History,* edited by Donald M. Scott and Bernard Wishy. Copyright © 1982 by Donald M. Scott and Bernard Wishy. Reprinted by permission of Harper & Row, Publishers, Inc.

Whatever the type of crisis faced, there will be somewhat different reactions by different families. In some cases, an event may be a crisis for some families or some family members but not for others. Consider, for example, a perinatal loss (miscarriage, stillbirth, or infant death). To what extent is that a crisis? It varies, depending on the extent to which family members feel attachment:

> Some family members will feel very strongly attached to an embryo, fetus, or newborn, even to the mere idea of a child. These people may grieve a perinatal loss quite intensely. Other people, even those who consider an embryo, a fetus, or a newborn fully human, may feel relatively little attachment to it and grieve its loss little if at all (Rosenblatt and Burns 1986:237).

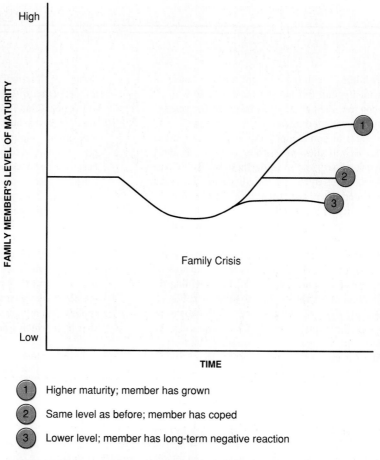

High

FAMILY MEMBER'S LEVEL OF MATURITY

Low

Family Crisis

TIME

1 Higher maturity; member has grown

2 Same level as before; member has coped

3 Lower level; member has long-term negative reaction

Figure 17.2 *Differing outcomes of a family crisis.*

Among those who grieve after a perinatal loss, the reactions vary. Some people continue to feel pangs of grief for decades. A woman who lost a two-month-old son forty-two years previously told an interviewer that she still thinks about him every day (Rosenblatt and Burns 1986:243). She still has some feelings of sorrow, though she also has some pleasant thoughts. Overall, perhaps as many as one-fifth of those with a perinatal loss have long-term grief to some extent. The husband and wife may not feel the grief equally, and that can cause marital problems.

In contrast to perinatal loss, having a child with cancer is likely to be a crisis for every family. Again, however, people will have a number of different reactions. Alberta Koch (1985) interviewed the parents and siblings of thirty-two pediatric cancer patients and found five kinds of family responses, one or

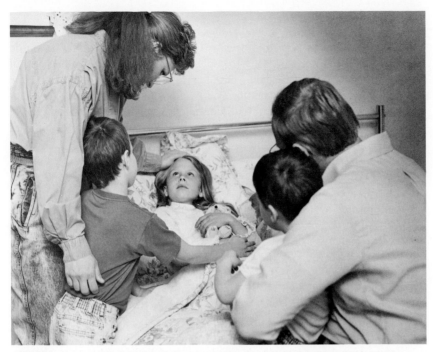

A family crisis can bring disruption or increased closeness, depending on how members react.

more of them being found in each family. Some family members had an increase in negative emotions after the diagnosis, particularly emotions of worry and grief. A second type of response was to develop rules prohibiting the display of such negative emotions as worry and anger. This was done to protect both the patient and other family members from further distress.

Third, some family members developed various health or behavioral problems or had existing problems intensify. Behavioral problems included drinking and affairs for parents and fighting and other disruptive behavior at school for children. Fourth, there were role changes in some families, with the patient becoming the focal point of family concern and activities. Siblings in such families took on a caregiving role along with the parents. Finally, some familes reported an increased closeness, a sense of greater cohesiveness as the family banded together to try to deal with the crisis.

To return to our earlier point, the families in Koch's sample could not control the event, the cancer, but they could and did react in various ways to it. Some of those ways were helpful and some were not. Specifically, then, what mechanisms and resources do families use to cope with a crisis? And which coping patterns are constructive? Which lead to the higher level of maturity of family members as indicated by path one in figure 17.2? That is our final topic.

Coping Patterns

Whatever you do in the face of a crisis is a coping pattern. Even if you do nothing, that is one way of trying to cope. Perhaps doing nothing is a way of saying there really is no crisis. Or perhaps it is based on the belief that time will heal all things, so that you need only hold on and wait it out. Unfortunately, "doing nothing" is not usually an effective coping pattern. There are other patterns that are also ineffective, and we need to be aware of them as well as of those that are more useful.

Ineffective Coping Patterns

"Ineffective" does not mean that a coping pattern does not work for an individual or family. Rather, ineffective means that it is not a pattern that typically will yield long-term, constructive outcomes. Those who use an ineffective coping pattern may follow path three in figure 17.2. The members of those families are functionally less capable after a crisis. They have not coped effectively, and, as a result, their growth as individuals and as a family is set back. What kinds of coping patterns are likely to result in path three?

Denial

Denial is perhaps the most common of the ineffective coping patterns. Denial is a defense mechanism in which people will not believe what they observe. For example, a woman may be married to an alcoholic, but refuses to accept the fact that he has a drinking problem. She may believe that he will stop drinking as soon as his work stress eases, or that he doesn't drink any more than most other men, or that the problem is exaggerated by others and not really as serious as they say. Whatever her rationale, she denies that he is an alcoholic and thereby delays a constructive confrontation with the problem.

We should note that denial is both normal and perhaps helpful in the initial stage of some crises (Boss 1988:87f). For example, denial is typically the initial response to the death of a loved one or to the news of a terminal illness. The denial may serve the useful purpose of giving the individual a chance to collect his or her thoughts and resources in order to deal with the problem constructively.

Where denial is a temporary measure that enables family members to mobilize their resources, it is useful. When denial becomes a long-term pattern of ignoring the problem, it is destructive. The family that continues to ignore the symptoms of illness in father or mother, or the financial disaster that looms because of parental unemployment, or the abuse that father inflicts on his wife or the children, is a family that will inevitably reap a bitter harvest of emotional and physical damage.

One of the ways to break out of denial is for some member of the family to openly admit that there is a problem. Parents may have to tell their children frankly about the difficulties they face because of unemployment. Children

Challenges to Intimacy

may have to talk frankly with their parents about problems of alcohol or physical abuse. Boss (1988:92) provides some examples:

> Dad, I love you, but I don't like the way you act when you're drunk. I would like you to stop because I care about you. If you don't stop, I won't hang around since it hurts me too much to see you that way.

> Mom, as your kid, I have to tell you that I can't stand watching you and Dad fight any more. If you don't call the cops the next time Dad hits you, I will.

> Grandpa, I know how sick you are. I just want you to know that I love you and that I will miss you when you die. Is there anything I can do for you now?

Once everyone admits that there is a problem, the family can begin to work together to find the best way to deal with it.

Avoidance

Admitting the existence of a problem is not sufficient, however. Sometimes people acknowledge that the problem exists, but they avoid confronting and dealing with it. Avoidance occurred, for instance, among those parents we noted above who reacted to their child's cancer by drinking excessively or having an affair. They didn't deny the cancer, but they didn't act in a way to deal constructively with their own and their family's distress.

Avoidance can be used in any kind of crisis. Children of alcoholic fathers have been found to use avoidance behaviors to some extent. Compared with other children, they deal with their distress by such things as sleeping more than usual or trying to make themselves feel better by drinking or smoking (Clair and Genest 1987).

Like denial, avoidance is not always a dysfunctional way of coping. There may be times when avoidance is necessary in order to give the family time to mobilize their resources. If, in other words, avoidance means a temporary delay in confronting the problem, it may be useful. If avoidance means long-term refusal to deal with the problem, it can have the same disastrous results as denial.

Scapegoating

Sometimes people admit a problem but feel that they have to find someone or something to blame. They select a family scapegoat to bear the brunt of the responsibility for the problem. A young woman who experienced a miscarriage told us that her suffering was intensified by the queries of some family members and acquaintances, who asked such things as whether she overexerted or took proper care of herself. In other words, they suggested that her own behavior was to blame for the loss.

Scapegoating is an insidious way to respond to crisis. It boils down to selecting one of the victims of the crisis and further victimizing that person.

We offered an example of this earlier when we pointed out that a man often uses the reaction of his beaten wife as an excuse for further beating.

Scapegoating, unlike denial and avoidance, is not even useful in the short run. Rather, it is a way of shifting responsibility so that one does not have to feel guilt or personal responsibility for resolving the crisis. Thus, if the family blames the father's unemployment on his own inept work habits, then other members of the family do not have to sacrifice or worry about the family's financial problems. On the other hand, if father blames the kids for draining his energies so that he could not do his work properly, then he has shifted the responsibility to the rest of the family.

The Foundation of Effective Coping

If a crisis occurs in a family that is not functioning well to begin with, the family may not be able to marshall the resources necessary to deal effectively with the crisis. To put the matter another way, a family is most likely to cope effectively with problems or crises when the members have worked together to develop certain family strengths. The strengths become a foundation on which the family can stand together and deal with crises.

The family that has developed strengths is likely to be a **resilient family**, one that can resist disruption in the face of change and cope effectively with crises. What are the strengths that help make a family resilient? Hamilton and Marilyn McCubbin (1988) have identified eleven, some of which are important at all stages of the family life cycle and all of which are important at one or more stages. The strengths are:

Accord, or relationships that foster problem-solving and manage conflict well

Celebrations, including birthdays, religious days, and other special events

Communication, including both beliefs and emotions

Good financial management

Hardiness, which includes commitment to the family, the belief that family members have control over their lives, and a sense that the family can deal with all changes

Health, both physical and emotional

Shared leisure activities

Acceptance of each member's personality and behavior

A social support network of relatives and friends

Sharing routines such as family meals and chores

Traditions that carry over from one generation to another

Families that have worked at developing the above strengths will be in a position to deal effectively with stressors and with crises.

Tools for Effective Coping

In our research on how people master life's unpredictable crises (Lauer and Lauer 1988), we found a number of tools that people use to deal with everything from divorce to abuse to serious illness. We were particularly interested in how people deal with a crisis in a way to follow path one in figure 17.2 rather than paths two or three. The following are "path one" tools, those that enable people to confront a crisis and eventually emerge at a higher level of functioning. For any particular crisis, one or a number of the tools may be useful.

Take Responsibility

In contrast to denial, avoidance, and scapegoating, effective coping begins when you take responsibility for yourself and your family. Taking responsibility means not only that you will not deny or avoid the problem or blame others, but also that you will not play the victim game. That is, even though you may have been victimized by something or someone, you will not continue to act as a victim—hurt, oppressed, exploited, in pain, and helpless.

If the crisis is some kind of family disruption such as death or divorce, taking responsibility means charting a new course as an alternative to playing the victim game. For example, Amy, a Mormon woman, felt victimized by her husband of twenty-four years when he abruptly told her he wanted a divorce. After her initial shock and grief, she decided to accept the responsibility for her own life:

> My first step was to resolve not to become a woman wrapped up in her past, clinging to it like a life raft. I wanted to be able to move beyond the hurt and pain and make something special out of my life. I began by taking a real-estate course and getting my license.

In some cases, taking responsibility may mean a willingness to disengage from your family. One of the ways that children of alcoholic parents avoid becoming problem drinkers themselves is to distance themselves to some extent from their families (Bennett, Wolin, Reiss, and Teitelbaum 1987). If the alcoholic family is unwilling to take responsibility as a group and confront the problem, then an individual member may escape the negative impact by disengaging. Similarly, an abused wife may find that the only way she can maintain her own well-being is to leave the abusive situation.

Affirm Your, and Your Family's, Worth

Crises assault people's self-esteem. This makes it more difficult to deal with the crisis. It is important to believe in yourself and in your ability to deal with difficult situations in order to be effective in a crisis. In a crisis, you may have to remind yourself that you and your family are people with strengths and the capacity to cope effectively.

A woman who stayed in an abusive relationship for years told us that one of her problems was her sense of being a worthless individual. The husband who abused her suggested that there was something about her that made him violent, something defective or deficient in her that made her deserve to be beaten. Her ability to deal with the critical situation began one day when she decided to stop viewing herself as somehow deserving the abuse. She had seen some information about abusive relationships and realized that she was a victim rather than a worthless person. She affirmed her own worth, which meant that being beaten was no longer tolerable. She left her husband and began a new life in another state.

Balance Self-Concern with Other-Concern

We have said that you must take responsibility for your own well-being. That doesn't mean to ignore the well-being of others. The totally self-focused life is as self-destructive as the totally other-focused life. Someone who stays in an abusive relationship because "my spouse needs me" may be too other-focused. Still someone who leaves a spouse simply because "I want my space so I can grow" may be too self-focused.

A crisis tends not only to attack our self-esteem but also to throw us into self-absorption. Some people get so enmeshed in the crisis that they seem to neither listen to, nor care about, others in the family. Dealing effectively with a crisis requires a healthy amount of both self-concern and other-concern.

In a study of families in which a child had died of cancer two to nine years earlier, the researchers found that families that handled the crisis best were those in which the individual family members were aware of the grieving of other members and made efforts to empathize and support them (Davies, Spinetta, Martinson, McClowry, and Kulenkamp 1986). Families with a poorer adjustment, on the other hand, tended to have members who focused on their own personal grief without relating that grief to other family members:

> It seemed as if each person was carrying the burden of grief all alone and there seemed to be a lack of empathy for how the other members were doing (Davies et al. 1986:302).

In some cases, even when the researchers asked people about how others in the family were doing, the person would respond in terms of his or her personal feelings. For example, when a father was asked about how his wife and daughter were dealing with the situation, he said he didn't know what to do about them. Rather than indicating an understanding of their feelings, he simply talked about his own sense of helplessness. In families that deal more effectively with the loss, members knew and talked spontaneously about each other as well as about themselves.

Learn the Art of Reframing

Reframing, or redefining the meaning of something, is a way of changing your perspective on a situation. It isn't the situation that is changed, but the way that you look at it. In essence, you learn to look at something that you had defined as troublesome and redefine it as adaptive and useful. The technique can help you overcome a variety of problems.

Reframing is not denial. It is based on the fact that people can look at any situation in various ways. You can see a crisis as an intruder that has robbed you of a measure of peace and happiness, or you can define the crisis as an obstacle that will ultimately lead to your growth as you overcome it.

Celia, an undergraduate student, had a crisis situation in her family when she was still in high school. Her father had begun to drink heavily. He was having problems at his work. The drinking, of course, only exacerbated the problems and put his job in jeopardy. Celia was preparing to go to college, and feared that she could not go if her father lost his job. Then one day her mother sat down with her and helped her reframe the situation.

> "This may mean that you won't go to college when you thought," her mother said. But it doesn't mean you won't go. At the most, it means you will have to wait for a year or so. But you *will* go. Furthermore, I want you to see this for what it is. It isn't a disaster. In fact, it may be the best lesson you ever learn, in school or out of school. Your father picked the wrong way to deal with the problem. But if we just condemn him, we will also pick the wrong way to deal with it. He needs us to help him now. We're going to do that.

Celia, as the oldest child, worked with her mother to firmly help her father cut back on his drinking. They gave him extra attention and support. Eventually, his work stress eased, and the family made it through the crisis. Celia went to college as she had planned. In good part, it was her mother's reframing of the situation that made the difference.

Whatever the family crisis, there are a number of sources of help available.

Find and Use Available Resources

Every family has numerous internal and external resources to which it can turn in a time of crisis. Family members themselves are internal resources. That is, family members can be a source of emotional support for each other. Most of the respondents in one study reported that a child's cancer had strengthened the cohesion of the family and that spouses were the most important source of support (Barbarin, Hughes, and Chesler 1985). Internal resources also include all of the family strengths we identified earlier. Recall that one of the strengths was open communication of both beliefs and feelings. Another characteristic of those families that handled the crisis well in which a child had died of cancer was openness,

> free discussion about the deceased child, his illness, death, and the family's responses since the time of the death (Davies et al. 1986:302).

For many families, religious beliefs are an important resource (Weigel and Weigel 1987). Religious beliefs can be a basis for reframing crises. Religious beliefs also provide family members with hope for an acceptable outcome and with strength for enduring the trauma until the crisis is resolved.

External resources include such things as the extended family, friends, books, self-help groups, and therapists. There are resources in all large communities that are designed to help people through crises of every kind.

Using the available resources along with other coping strategies we have discussed can enable a family to emerge from a crisis at a higher level of functioning than it had before the crisis. Indeed, the very meaning of effective coping is that the individual will achieve a new level of maturity and that the family will attain a new level of intimacy.

PRINCIPLES FOR ENHANCING INTIMACY

1. When you or your family are undergoing major stress, avoid deliberately adding on other sources of pressure. Multiple stresses can be a lethal combination that can threaten any individual or intimate relationship. If you should lose your job, for example, it is probably a bad time to buy a new car or go on a diet. Or if your marriage is undergoing difficulties of one sort or another, it is not a good time to make a major career change or decide to have a new baby.

2. Keep your economic house in order. Financial difficulties are a continuing source of stress throughout the family life cycle. By maintaining realistic expectations, careful budgeting, and avoiding the excessive use of credit, families can reduce financial strains and enhance their well-being and stability.

"Things Were Terribly Still"

Kim is in her early twenties. She has been married for five years. Phil, her husband, works as an electronics engineer. Their daughter was four years old when Kim got pregnant again. Kim and Phil were very happy. Both wanted a large family. However, the "blessed event" turned into a crisis for them, a crisis for which they needed some outside help:

I was so happy when I got pregnant that I prepared a nursery in rainbow colors for the baby. Phil and I were really excited as the due date approached. He loved to put his hand on my stomach and feel the baby moving. He wanted a boy so he could go fishing with him. And our daughter looked forward to a baby brother or sister.

A few weeks before the baby was due, I felt sick to my stomach. The doctor thought I had a virus and needed to get more rest. But a few days later I suddenly realized that things were terribly still inside me. I went to the doctor immediately. She decided to induce labor. Phil was with me when I delivered a stillborn baby boy. An autopsy showed that our son had a chromosomal disorder.

We were devastated. We spent forty-five minutes with our son, holding and touching him. We said goodbye to him, and the nurse asked if we wanted her to take a picture. We said no, but I regret it now. It would mean a lot to me to have a picture of that child.

I left the hospital the next morning. Phil got a week off from work. Our son's name was to be Bradley. We had him cremated and held a memorial service at the beach. We scattered his ashes in the Pacific Ocean.

The first week, we spent most of our time talking and crying about it. When Phil went back to work, he tried to act macho about it all. He told everyone that we were fine and that everything was going to be all right. But I was upset all the time. I began to feel depressed and guilty. We went for genetic tests. But we are not at high risk for genetic defects. Phil didn't want to talk about it any more. He reminded me that we could have more children.

Phil and I were really close before Bradley's death. Even right afterwards. But as time went on, we grew apart. We couldn't seem to communicate. And we didn't have much sex. I spent most of my time with our daughter and Phil spent more time at work and watching television.

We talked about another child, but I don't think either of us wanted to take the risk. I talked about it with my doctor one day, and she suggested that before we try to have another child we should attend Healing Hearts, a self-help group for people who have had a child die. Phil refused to go at first. He told me to go, that he was fine and didn't need it. So I went alone. It helped me a lot. I kept asking Phil and he finally agreed to go. Toward the end of his first meeting, he broke down and cried for several minutes. He finally began to open up and talk about how he really felt.

It's been five months now since Bradley died. We still go to Healing Hearts. We're also working on our relationship with each other. We're beginning to feel intimate with each other again. Some day we will try to have another child. We're still scared, but we're working at it. We're a lot more mature, and I think we have a new kind of respect for each other.

3. Alcohol abuse is difficult to cope with alone. If you are an abuser, organizations like AA can provide needed assistance. If someone in your family abuses alcohol, you also can benefit from a support group like Al-Anon.

4. Family violence—whatever its form and whoever its victim—results in serious physical and emotional damage. If the damage is to be minimized, family violence must be acknowledged and then dealt with as quickly and effectively as possible. It is not possible to have true intimacy in the context of violence.

5. Remember that you can cope with a crisis in your family. Even the most difficult situation offers the possibility of long-term, positive consequences. Indeed, by using effective coping strategies, you can transform the crisis into an opportunity for personal growth and enhanced intimacy.

SUMMARY

Family crises are associated with various kinds of stressful events and/or behavior. A family in crisis is not necessarily a sick family, but may be a family overwhelmed by a stressor or piled-up stressors in accord with the ABCX and Double ABCX models. Some of the common stressor events are death, serious illness, accidents, loss of work, an unwanted pregnancy, moving, alcohol abuse, and interpersonal problems like abuse and infidelity.

The kinds of stressors people face vary over the family life cycle. The highest amount of stress tends to occur during the time when the family is in the transition from having children in the home to the empty nest. Not all stressors are equally severe, rather, they range in severity from such highly stressful events as a death in the family to the mildly stressful event of a major purchase.

Alcohol abuse ranks high on the list of family stressors. About one in five Americans who drinks daily or nearly every day has alcohol-associated problems in the family. Some families function fairly normally when the abuser is not drinking. But during the times of heavy drinking, the character of family life is likely to change and may even become violent. When the abuse is long-term, negative consequences tend to result whether or not the abuser is drinking. The family life of a long-term abuser tends to be filled with tension, dissatisfaction, and frequent conflict. Spouses and children of abusers may develop various physical and emotional problems.

Family problems can contribute to, as well as result from, alcohol abuse. In this way, the family can get caught in a vicious circle. In fact, the abuse may take its toll across a number of generations.

Next to death, separation, and divorce, family violence is the most difficult experience people have to cope with. Although rates of reported violence went down from 1975 to 1985, millions of Americans endure violence in their homes. Abuse of children occurs most frequently to those under three years and to teenagers. The typical abusive parent is single, young, had the first child before the age of eighteen, and is unemployed or employed part-time. Abusers tend to have low self-esteem, to have many stressors in their lives, and to have been victims of abuse themselves. Women are slightly more likely to abuse children than are men. Child abuse is proportionately higher among blacks and Hispanics than whites.

Incest is a form of abuse more likely to happen to girls than boys. Incest usually begins when the child is between six and eleven, and lasts around two years on the average. Father-daughter incest is the most common form, tending to occur in families where the marital relationship has broken down, and the father has many stressors and a problem relating meaningfully and sexually with an adult.

Spouse abuse may involve either husband or wife being the victim, but the damage is likely to be more severe for abused wives. The typical wife-beater is unemployed or employed part-time, has financial problems, is dissatisfied with life, is young, and has been married for less than ten years. He was probably abused himself as a child. Various values and attitudes can lead a woman to remain in an abusive relationship in spite of the physical and emotional damage she suffers.

Parent abuse also occurs. There is a certain amount of abuse by adolescent children, particularly of fathers. There is also some abuse of elderly parents by their adult children.

Abuse results in short-term physical and emotional damage. It also tends to have serious long-term consequences. Victims may have to undergo therapy to work through their trauma. Viewing abuse as well as enduring it can perpetuate violence in family life.

People react to crises in different ways. We cannot control the events that occur in our lives, but we can control the way we respond to them. Ineffective coping patterns are ways of response that leave people at a lower level of functioning after a crisis. Denial, avoidance, and scapegoating are ineffective coping patterns. Effective coping is facilitated by developing family strengths. It involves such things as taking responsibility, affirming individual and family worth, balancing self-concern with other-concern, learning the art of reframing, and finding and using available resources.

---

1. *Gallup Report* #242, November, 1985.

18

Separation and Divorce

I s divorce ever good for you? Is it ever good for children? In the short run, the answer to both questions is "no" for most people. In the long run, the answer varies. In other words, neither question has a simple answer.

For example, consider one student's account of her parents' divorce:

> My most painful experience when I was growing up was when my parents got a divorce. My greatest pain wasn't the actual breakup. That was the best thing to happen. They had always fought. And so getting a divorce made all of our lives easier. The pain I experienced was deciding whom to live with.

Another undergraduate told us that the stress in her life was dramatically reduced when her parents divorced and, as a result, the quality of her life greatly improved. But others talk about the pain, the loss, the emptiness. Disrupting an intimate relationship is never easy, even when the relationship is defined as a destructive one (recall that people tend to stay in abusive relationships for long periods of time).

In this chapter, we will look closely at what has become a common experience for Americans: the disruption of an intimate relationship through separation and/or divorce. We will examine first the trends in divorce. Then we will discuss the process of "uncoupling." We will talk about some of the causes and correlates of divorce, the effects on spouses, parents, and children, and, finally, how people work through the issues raised by the disruption.

Legally and financially, divorce is easier than in the past. But is it really easier?

Divorce Trends

Should divorce be easier or more difficult to obtain? More than half of Americans who were asked that question in a national poll said that divorce should be more difficult to secure.[1] Nineteen percent said it should stay as it is. Only a little over a fourth said that divorce should be easier to obtain.

A great many Americans are concerned today about the numbers of people divorcing and about the relative ease with which people dissolve their marriages. To be sure, both the numbers and the relative ease are in contrast with the past, though, as we shall see below, they are not inconsistent with long-term trends.

Divorce Rates

Since 1860 there has been a general increase in the number of divorces per one thousand population. However, the rate rose significantly during World War II, peaked at the conclusion of the war (1945–1947), and then began to decline. The rate remained fairly stable during the 1950s and early 1960s, then increased rapidly again after 1965 (figure 18.1). By the mid-1970s the United States had the highest divorce rate in the Western world. In 1974, for the first time in our history, more marriages ended through divorce than through death of a spouse.

Although many people believe that the high rates of the 1970s represented a striking break with tradition, Andrew Cherlin (1981:25) pointed out that there has been a fairly regular trend over the past century or so, a trend represented by a rising curve. There are variations, of course: those who married during the 1950s have lower-than-expected rates of divorce while those who married during the 1960s and 1970s have higher-than-expected rates (where "expected" means the rate we would have according to the long-term trend line). However, the high rates of the 1970s are modest rather than dramatic deviations from the long-term trend.

After 1981, the rates tended to decline, and by 1987 they had gone down to 4.8 per 1,000 people (table 18.1). The last time the rate was that low was in 1975. Still, in 1987 6.7 percent of males and 8.7 percent of females eighteen years and older were divorced (table 18.1).

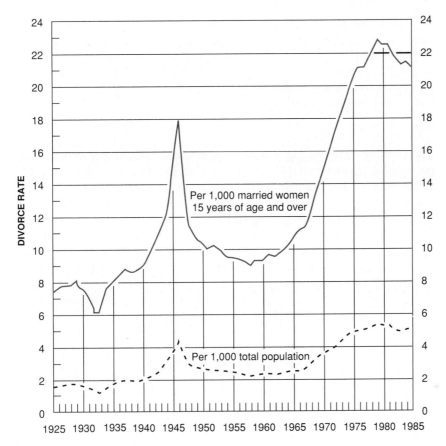

Figure 18.1 *U.S. divorce rates: 1925–1985.*
Source: National Center for Health Statistics, *Monthly Vital Statistics Report,* 35, "Advance Report of Final Divorce Statistics, 1984" (Hyattsville, MD: Public Health Service) 1986:2.

Table 18.1   Divorces: 1950–1987
(Excludes Alaska and Hawaii prior to 1960)

Divorces	1950	1955	1960	1965	1970	1975	1980	1987
Total (1,000)	385	377	393	479	708	1,026	1,189	1,157
Rate per 1,000 population	2.6	2.3	2.2	2.5	3.5	4.8	5.2	4.8
Rate per 1,000 married women, 15 yrs and over	10.3	9.3	9.2	10.6	14.9	20.3	22.6	NA
Percent divorced, 18 yrs and over:								
Male	1.8	1.9	2.0	2.5	2.5	3.7	5.2	6.7
Female	2.3	2.4	2.9	3.3	3.9	5.3	7.1	8.7

Source: U.S. Bureau of the Census, *Statistical Abstract of the United States, 1979* (Washington, DC: Government Printing Office) 1980:81 and *1988* (Washington, DC: Government Printing Office) 1989:41, 88.

Of course, the figures for a particular year do not tell us how many people have ever been separated or divorced. Some of those who are reported as divorced in a particular year will be married in another year and vice versa. Sorting through the data, it appears that about one-fourth of contemporary Americans who have ever been married have also experienced legal separation and/or divorce (Glenn and Supancic 1984).

Changing Grounds for Divorce

For what legal reasons can you attain a divorce? State rather than federal government answers that question. In the past, the states provided many different answers. For example, in the nineteenth century, South Carolina did not allow divorce at all, while New York allowed it only on the grounds of adultery (Degler 1980:167). Some states permitted more lenient grounds than others. As a result, people often established temporary residency in order to make use of a state's more liberal divorce laws. At one time or another, Pennsylvania, Ohio, South Dakota, North Dakota, and Nevada, among others, made it relatively easy for people to establish residency and obtain a divorce (Day and Hook 1987). However, only middle- and upper-class people could typically afford to pursue a divorce under such conditions.

In response to the increase in divorces, states have changed divorce laws. The changes reflect a different perspective on divorce—that it is essentially an individual rather than a government-controlled decision. Because it is viewed as an individual decision, states have abandoned the adversarial approach to divorce, an approach that assumes one of the spouses is at fault. In the past, "fault" could have been such things as adultery, insanity, imprisonment, or cruelty. In any case, the plaintiff had to provide evidence to show that the partner was at fault. When both spouses wanted the divorce, they might agree to lie or present false evidence in order to comply with the law.

In the 1970s, California and New York began the trend toward no-fault divorce, which is now practiced in virtually all states. In no-fault divorce, no proof for divorce is needed. Neither spouse accuses the other of impropriety or immorality. Rather, the marriage is deemed to be unworkable and therefore is dissolved. Some states allow either spouse to initiate the divorce unilaterally, while others require mutual consent.

Some people feared the no-fault divorce laws would bring about another surge in the number of divorces. This has not happened. Moreover, the rates are not significantly different in unilateral and mutual consent states (Peters 1986). Thus, no-fault laws have not made divorce more likely, but they have removed at least some of the acrimony and pain from the process.

No-fault laws were also supposed to make divorce a more equitable process. Settlements are not to be made on the basis of someone having been wronged, but on the basis of need. The settlement does not presume that the man should continue to support the woman, nor that the woman should assume

Challenges to Intimacy

total care of any children. As we shall see, this aspect of the law has turned out to be detrimental for women, who have suffered economically under the no-fault system.

The Process of Uncoupling

What happens in a family that is in the process of breaking up? What stages bring an intimate relationship to the point of disruption? What is the meaning of the disruption? Researchers have identified a number of features in the process that are common to most divorcing couples.

Toward Marital Dissolution

Varied names have been given to the stages of marital dissolution by researchers. In general, however, we can divide the process into four periods: recognition, discussion, action, and postdissolution (Ponzetti and Cate 1986).

Recognition

Recognition begins when one or both spouses become aware of serious problems. A spouse may feel discontent or dissatisfaction, and realize that the feeling is sufficiently strong to call the relationship into question. Frequently, recognition occurs when marital stress and open conflict are followed by a period of cold war between the spouses.

However, the period of recognition may occur very early. Diane Vaughan (1986) provided a detailed discussion of the process of dissolution based on her interviews with 103 men and women who broke up. She found common social and psychological turning points in the process of uncoupling. At the beginning of the process, in the recognition period, there is a "secret": One of the partners—the initiator—begins to feel uncomfortable in the relationship but doesn't acknowledge this to his or her spouse. It seems to the initiator that the world they "have built together no longer 'fits' " (Vaughan 1986:11). While

Nonverbal cues are one of the first ways we signal discontent with a relationship.

there may be a time of stress and conflict preceding the recognition, the initiator may feel early on that the relationship was a mistake from the beginning, like the woman who said that she "was never psychologically married." She felt uncomfortable with the married role from the beginning, and even called the day after her marriage "the most depressed day of my life."

At first, the spouse who recognizes the problem may not openly confront the partner, but rather expresses discontent by giving various cues and hints like a disgruntled look or an omitted kiss. These cues and hints may be a way of trying to force changes and thus salvage the relationship. But eventually the initiator will begin to seek satisfaction in some kind of activity or interest outside the relationship. The

> partner is increasingly excluded from the initiator's world. In beginning a life independent of the partner, the initiator has taken the first tentative steps toward a transition out of the relationship (Vaughan 1986:27).

Discussion

Discussion is the period at which one or both spouses begin to share the marital problems with others—friends, relatives, a counselor, and often the spouse. The discussion is not merely a sharing of information but an opportunity to redefine the relationship. The partner may be defined in negative terms and the history of the relationship may be reconstructed as a series of negative experiences. Gratifying experiences also may be redefined: "Yes, we had a good time on that trip but that was only because we were with friends."

Discussion with the partner involves the "breakdown of cover-up" (Vaughan 1986:79). The initiator finally discloses his or her "secret," and does so with sufficient force and clarity that the partner cannot deny the fact that the marriage is in serious trouble. With such a confrontation, conflict increases significantly in the discussion period (Ponzetti and Cate 1986). One of the functions of such conflict is to maintain the relationship for a time. Conflict at least means that there is interaction. But the conflict also serves to underscore that there are problems in the relationship.

During the discussion period, the discontented spouse will find a "transitional person," someone who can help him or her to move from the old life to a new one. The transitional person may be a temporary lover, but may also be a friend who can provide emotional support. The problem with the relationship has now become a public matter.

There may be some effort to save the marriage during this period. Once the confrontation has taken place and the problem is openly acknowledged, the noninitiating partner may ask for an opportunity to try to save the relationship. The initiator feels that he or she has already tried, but may be willing to give the partner a chance to try also. Yet in many cases the odds are against any change for the better. The initiator has been making the transition to a new life for a period of time. The initiator is already a somewhat different person, with a new ideology, perhaps new friends, and new commitments. Many initiators tell their partners during this period, "You don't know me anymore."

If the initiator has gone far enough in the process of transition to a new life, he or she may allow the partner to try to save the relationship but will not allow the partner to succeed. Letting the noninitiating partner try but fail can be a way of getting him or her to agree that the intimate bond has been severed irreparably.

Action

In the period of action, one of the spouses secures a lawyer in order to legally dissolve the marriage. Separation also is likely in this period, and may occur before or after a lawyer is consulted. The amount of time involved can vary considerably. A study of 199 California women reported that they took from sixty-five days or less to as much as several years to move from the decision to end their marriage to actually separate and file a petition for divorce (Melichar and Chiriboga 1985). The women who moved very quickly tended to be a few years older (mean age 36.5 years) than the others, to have married at a later age, and to have somewhat less education than those who moved more slowly through the process.

Separation, of course, does not always lead to divorce. An estimated one of every six couples separates for at least two days at some time in their relationship (Kitson 1985). The separation can be a cooling-off period that allows the couple to deal more rationally with their differences and effect a reconciliation. Other couples get involved in a long-term, unresolved separation; nonwhites and those with lower incomes are more likely to fall into this category (Morgan 1988).

Difficulties mount once a lawyer is secured and the divorce petition is filed. At this point in the process, couples frequently struggle over such things as division of property and child custody. Moreover, they often are anxious about the separation and have lingering uncertainties about whether dissolution is really in their best interests.

This period can also last much longer than people anticipate if there are disagreements about the settlement. For example, community property laws do not make financial settlements an automatic matter. Thus, there can be considerable wrangling over the division of property and intense bitterness about the outcome.

Postdissolution

The postdissolution period begins when both spouses accept the fact that the marriage has ended. During this period the spouses probably will think about reasons for the divorce and construct some acceptable rationale for what has happened. Many people do not accept completely the fact that the marriage has ended until the former spouse is coupled with a new partner.

The Six Stations of Divorce

Paul Bohannan (1970) discussed divorce in terms of six "stations" or six different experiences that people are likely to have. Marriage, he pointed out, makes us feel good in part because, out of all those available, we have been selected by someone to be an intimate partner. Divorce, by contrast, makes you feel "so awful," in part, because "you have been de-selected" (Bohannan 1970:33). To some extent, de-selection occurs in each of the six different stations of divorce.

The *emotional* divorce involves a loss of trust, respect, and affection for each other. Rather than supporting each other, the spouses act in ways to hurt, to frustrate, to lower self-esteem. The spouses grate on each other. Each is visible evidence to the other of failure and rejection.

The *legal* divorce, in which a court officially brings the marriage to an end, is the only one of the six stations that provides a tangible benefit to the partners: relief from the legal responsibilities of the marriage and the right to remarry. The legal divorce can also help partners to feel free of other kinds of obligations, such as that of caring for a sick partner. Legal divorce may follow a period of separation, but increasingly couples opt directly for divorce rather than a trial separation.

The *economic* divorce involves settlement of the property. The division of property is rarely an easy matter. Actually, economic settlements were easier under the adversary system, where one of the parties was at fault and therefore "owed" the other compensation. The economic divorce is likely to be painful for at least three reasons. First, there are never enough assets for each partner to feel that he or she is getting all that is needed to continue living at a comfortable level. Second, there can be considerable acrimony over who gets what—the condo, silver, favorite painting and so forth. And third, there is likely to be a sense of loss as each partner realizes that he or she must live in the future without some familiar and cherished possessions.

The *co-parental* divorce is experienced by those with children—about two-thirds of all couples. Decisions must be made about who will have custody, visitation rights, and continuing responsibilities of each parent. This is perhaps the most tragic part of the divorce (see the discussion on the consequences of divorce for children), particularly when the parents use their children as weapons against each other or even fail to protect them from the conflict and bitterness of the struggle.

The *community* divorce means that each of the partners leaves one community of friends and relations and enters another. A newly divorced person may feel uncomfortable with some of the friends he or she shared with the former spouse, especially if there is a feeling that the friends were more sympathetic with the former spouse. Relationships with former in-laws may cease or become minimal and strained. The process of changing from one community of relationships to another is likely to be difficult and frequently leaves the individual feeling lonely and isolated for a period of time.

Finally, the *psychic* divorce is the central separation that occurs—the individual must accept the disruption of the relationship and regain a sense of being an individual rather than a part of an intimate couple. Eventually, as the healing process takes place, the individual will begin to feel whole again.

Divorce Court

Attend a local divorce court for a day. Write down your observations of what is happening. Note the expressions on the faces of the couples, lawyers, and judge. To what extent can you sense the trauma of divorce from the proceedings of the court? Note the outcomes of the various cases. What are the similarities and differences? If possible, see if you can obtain court records from a time when divorce was an adversarial process. Compare some of the proceedings with those you have observed. What differences are there? Which system do you think works best?

Finally, find someone who has recently been through a divorce. Discuss that person's recollections of the court proceedings. How did the person feel during the court session? How does the person feel about the legal aspects of divorce generally? How would that person change the legal system to make divorce more equitable or less painful for people? Do you agree or disagree with the divorced person's position? Why?

If divorce court proceedings in your locale are not available, an alternative option would be to write the history of a divorce. It might be the divorce of your parents or other relative, a friend, or even your own. The four periods—recognition, discussion, action, and postdissolution—of divorce may provide a useful device for organizing your account.

But he or she can only feel whole to the extent that the psychic divorce is final; that is, to the extent that there is a distancing from both the positive and negative aspects of the broken relationship.

Causes and Correlates of Divorce

We have discussed the process of splitting up, but that doesn't answer the question of *why* people divorce. What factors make it more or less likely that someday you may be involved in a divorce?

Sociodemographic Factors

We usually link divorce to the problems that have developed in a marriage. If, for example, you read about the impending divorce of a couple named Jim and Brenda, you might ask what they had *done* to bring about the divorce. It is unlikely that you would link the divorce to their socioeconomic status, their race, their religion, or other sociodemographic factors, but social scientists have found that the probability of divorce varies according to such factors.

Higher status and more religious people are less likely to have a divorce.

Socioeconomic Status

There is an inverse relationship between socioeconomic status and divorce rates. That is, the higher your status the less likely you are to divorce. Higher status, of course, means higher income. We have seen in earlier chapters that financial strains are very often on the list of sources of conflict in marriages. No doubt the financial pressures of those in lower income brackets add to the instability of their marriages. There is, however, one exception: women in high-income and high-education brackets tend to have higher divorce rates than other women (Glick and Norton 1977; Houseknecht and Spanier 1980). The reasons for this are not clear. Perhaps these women are economically secure and thus are free to end an unhappy relationship. Perhaps they are engaged in high-powered careers and find the conflict between work and family life unacceptable. Or perhaps the husbands cannot adjust to their wives' career commitment and/or economic independence. In any case, they are an exception to the general trend.

Age at Marriage

In earlier chapters, we pointed out that one's age at marriage is related to marital stability. The younger you are when you marry, the greater are your chances of divorce, particularly during the first five years of marriage (Booth et al. 1986). Marriage at a late age also raises your chances of divorce, and in fact increases that likelihood for the first fifteen years of the marriage (Booth

Table 18.2 Ever-Married Persons 25–54 Years Old Who Were Divorced or Separated at Time of Survey, by Race, Sex, and Age: 1986

Year, Sex, and Age	Ever Married (1,000)			Percent Divorced			Percent Separated		
	Total[1]	White	Black	Total[1]	White	Black	Total[1]	White	Black
Male, total	38,912	34,205	3,520	10.7	10.7	13.2	3.4	2.7	11.1
25–34 years	14,240	12,543	1,288	10.2	10.5	9.4	4.4	3.5	13.3
35–44 years	14,352	12,644	1,254	12.2	11.9	17.0	3.0	2.5	9.0
45–54 years	10,320	9,018	978	9.3	9.1	13.4	2.7	1.7	11.0
Female, total	43,111	37,212	4,412	13.9	13.4	20.7	4.5	3.3	15.2
25–34 years	16,593	14,392	1,642	12.1	11.9	15.6	5.2	4.1	15.8
35–44 years	15,378	13,243	1,566	16.1	15.5	24.6	4.4	3.2	14.5
45–54 years	11,140	9,577	1,202	13.7	12.6	22.6	3.6	2.2	15.1

[1]Includes other races not shown separately.
Source: U.S. Bureau of the Census 1988:41.

et al. 1986). Early age probably increases divorce rates because of such things as immaturity, financial strains, and the partners changing in ways that make them less compatible. Later age at marriage increases the chances of divorce, as we have noted before, because of the greater likelihood that the union is a heterogamous one.

Race
Blacks are more likely both to separate and to divorce than are whites (table 18.2). In fact, blacks have higher rates than any other racial group in the United States (Glenn and Supancic 1984). The greatest differences between blacks and others occur in the lower socioeconomic levels, but they exist at all levels. Some scholars have suggested that because of their experience of low income, job instability, and high unemployment rates, blacks have learned to depend less on marriage and more on the extended kin network for support (Cherlin 1981:108). This may have established a cultural tradition in which marriage is less central and in which there is thus less commitment to the marital relationship. An alternative explanation is that blacks still have to deal with overt and covert discrimination and rejection, leading them to be more likely to have a pile-up of stressor events in their lives. The pile-up, in turn, places greater strains on their marriages than on those of other races.

Social Integration
Social integration is a state of relative harmony and cohesion in a group. People who are members of an integrated group have an important source of support, a buffer against stress. We would expect, then, that social integration would help to minimize the divorce rates. There is evidence to support that conclusion.

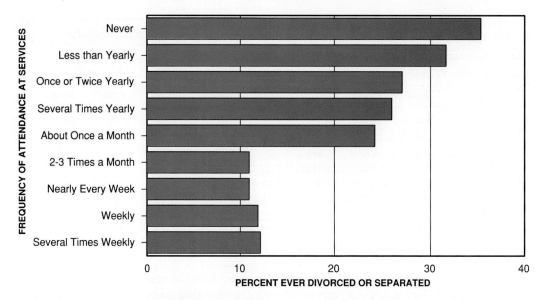

Figure 18.2 *Divorce and religious activity.*
Source: Data from Glenn and Supancic 1984:567.

Religious groups provide one source of social integration. In addition, religion places great value on the family. It is reasonable to expect, therefore, that the more religious people are, the less likely they are to divorce. Indeed, people who are members of churches are less likely to divorce than are non-members (Breault and Kposowa 1987). Moreover, there are striking differences in the rates of divorce and separation among people depending on their frequency of attendance at religious services (figure 18.2). There are also differences between various denominations. Jewish couples are least likely to divorce. Protestants have the highest rates. And among Protestants, the rates of the more conservative groups like Pentecostals and Baptists tend to be higher than those of the more liberal groups like Presbyterians and Episcopalians (Glenn and Supancic 1984:567).

The variations among denominations reflect, to some extent, socioeconomic differences. Episcopalians and Presbyterians tend to have a higher-status membership than do Pentecostals and Baptists. But the rates of divorce among the conservative groups are still substantially lower than among those with no religion at all.

If social integration, such as that experienced by members of religious groups, tends to minimize divorce, the lack of integration should be associated with higher rates of divorce. One way in which people get into a less integrated situation is by moving to a different community. They are likely to be cut off from their friends and family and may not become an integral part of religious or other groups in the new community for some time. Thus, there is an association between residential mobility and divorce rates (Shelton 1987). In

Challenges to Intimacy

regions of the nation where there is a high rate of residential movement, such as the West, there are higher rates of divorce (Glenn and Shelton 1985). And it is probably this same phenomenon—the higher rate of mobility and lower likelihood of integration—that accounts for higher rates of divorce in urban areas (Breault and Kposowa 1987).

Changing Norms and Roles

Divorce has become more acceptable over time. The greater acceptance is seen in changed laws and changed attitudes. We no longer limit the causes for which people can get divorced. We no longer stigmatize the divorced person. In addition, Americans have increasingly emphasized the importance of personal happiness over marital stability. We marry in order to be happy. Thus, if our present marriage does not make us happy, we opt for divorce and look for happiness in a new relationship. Earlier in our history, a successful marriage was one that lasted and produced offspring. Now, a successful marriage is one that facilitates the happiness and well-being of both partners.

In addition, the changing roles of women are associated with higher divorce rates, particularly the increasing economic independence of women. Divorce rates have risen along with the increased rate of employment of women (Cherlin 1981:53). Employment per se doesn't add to the likelihood of divorce. Rather, there are at least two consequences of women's employment that add to marital instability. First, as we have seen earlier, wives and mothers working outside the home results in some additional strains on family life. Second, financial independence provides women with the opportunity to free themselves from an unhappy marriage.

Interpersonal Factors

These various sociodemographic factors are important, of course, because they have a bearing on the way that people interact. Ultimately, however, it is the interaction that leads to disruption. If we focus on the interaction itself, rather than on the sociodemographic variables that underlie the interaction, what do we find?

Complaints

When divorce was an adversarial process, people listed all kinds of complaints in their petitions. In some cases the complaints sound trivial. For instance: opening windows at night when the wife wants them closed; making derogatory remarks about the wife's cooking; hiding the husband's fishing tackle; and paying more attention to the pet cat than to the husband (Whitman 1962). In other cases, the complaints sound more serious, ranging from such things as abuse to adultery. In a study of people applying for divorce in Cleveland, Ohio, Levinger (1966) found that the most common complaints of husbands were mental cruelty, neglect of home and children, infidelity, and sexual incompatibility. The most common complaints of wives were mental cruelty, neglect of home and children, financial problems, and physical abuse. A very small percentage of the spouses named "excessive demands" as one of their complaints. It is important to keep in mind that such complaints, because they were a part of court records, may have been framed in accord with what was legally admissible and legally forceful as well as with actual complaints.

A number of more recent studies have inquired into the reasons divorced people give for the breakdown of their marriages. In their review of nine such studies, Kitson, Babri, and Roach (1985) noted that eight mentioned extramarital sex as a reason for the divorce. It should be pointed out, however, that infidelity frequently occurs in a troubled marriage. Often an individual endures an unhappy marriage until he or she becomes involved in a relationship with another person. This new relationship, then, provides the basis for leaving the marriage. Four of the studies reported that personality and financial problems were important. Most of the rest of the complaints involved such interpersonal problems as the lack of communication, feeling unloved, too little family life, and conflict over roles.

Conflict

Some marriages are characterized by intense conflict. The conflict is pervasive; the couple argues over nearly everything. About one-half of divorcing couples indicate that they had frequent and intense conflict (Kelly 1988:121). The conflict may involve both severe (infidelity) and trivial (who takes the garbage out) issues.

Few, if any, people are comfortable and happy living in a situation of continual conflict. The situation may be compounded by a lack of conflict management skills. That is, the partners may get into a vicious circle in which the inability to resolve early conflicts acceptably only exacerbates subsequent conflicts. Thus, a conflict that may begin over a trivial issue may be an opportunity to bring back a severe issue that is still unresolved.

Changed Feelings and Perspectives

Although many divorced couples had a great deal of conflict in their marriage, many did not. A fourth or more of couples who divorce report little or no conflict in the two years before they separate (Kelly 1988:121). The marital bond eroded from decay, not from war. The marriage ended because feelings changed—the couple no longer loved each other, no longer had respect for each other, or no longer enjoyed being together.

One of the possible reasons for the slow, nonconflicted erosion of a marriage is changed perspectives. We all change throughout our lives. Two people who begin a marriage with similar perspectives may find themselves changing in ways that make them less compatible. Their perspectives diverge. They no longer enjoy doing the same things. They are no longer the same two people who were married and, unfortunately, neither likes very much the way that the other has changed.

For example, Marie and Don were married as teenagers. He was in engineering school and she was preparing to be a teacher. A few years later, Don realized that he didn't like engineering. He was restless, and decided that having a child might make his life more meaningful. Although they had always talked about having a family, Marie was happy with her teaching and decided she didn't want children yet. She worked with children all day, and felt that they fulfilled whatever maternal instincts she had. She began to wonder if she would ever want children of her own. Don resented Marie's changed perspective. In his restlessness, he quit his job and went back to school to study social work. Marie felt uncomfortable with his new aspirations. She resented the fact that he would probably work for less money than he got as an engineer. They agreed to a trial separation. Within six months, Marie filed for divorce. They never argued much. They simply watched each other change and neither liked the changes of the other.

Emotional Problems
One of the consequences of divorce is likely to be an increase in emotional problems. But not all problems are the result of the divorce. Some exist before and contribute to the deterioration of the relationship.

Two researchers looked at a sample of men over a five-year period, dividing them into those who were married throughout, those divorced or separated at the beginning and still so at the end, and a third group who had a separation or divorce during the five years (Erbes and Hedderson 1984). They found that the men who were separated or divorced during the period had lower psychological well-being scores at the beginning of the study than did those who were married throughout. Of course, it is possible that marital problems were already contributing to the lower scores, but the separation or divorce itself did not seem to be a factor.

Additional studies also suggest that at least some divorces are the result of emotional problems in one or both of the spouses (Kitson, Babri, and Roach 1985:275). Furthermore, research indicates that people who have been divorced more than once also tend to show some signs of emotional disorder (Brody, Neubaum, and Forehand 1988:212).

Effects of Divorce On Spouses/Parents

We began the chapter with the question, is divorce ever good for you? The answer, we suggested, is yes and no. There will probably be short-term negative effects. There may be long-term positive effects. We will look at the latter first.

Positive Outcomes

Although most studies have focused on the negative consequences of divorce, there are positive results as well. Buehler and Langenbrunner (1987) collected some of the positive effects from eighty people whose divorces had been finalized six to twelve months earlier. They asked the divorced to indicate which

Divorce, Japanese Style

Divorce rates have tended to go up throughout the world, and have risen faster in some countries than they have in the United States. In Japan, as in the United States, divorce rates soared in the second half of the 1960s. By 1983, there was one divorce for about every four marriages in Japan. A writer who interviewed divorced Japanese couples identified three causes: a greater acceptance of divorce in Japanese society, greater opportunities for women outside the home, and women's changing attitudes. In the selection below, the writer talks about the changing attitudes of women:

> Women are no longer satisfied with being glorified housemaids and cooks. They want to live more rewarding lives now that they can expect to live longer ones. . . . Even more important, however, may be the changing character of these divorces. There has been a rapid increase in divorces among middle-aged couples and among couples with children. No longer are children the bond that keeps a marriage going. . . .
>
> Another change in the character of divorce is relatively new: They are initiated by the wife. For a long time it was assumed that only the husband had the prerogative to make such a selfish demand. In the Edo period (1603–1868), a husband could easily get rid of his wife by handing her a letter of divorce called a *mikudarihan* (three and a half lines). Today, however, 60 percent of the divorce cases that are brought to the family courts come from wives. Japanese men, accustomed to being lord of the manor, are having difficulty adjusting to this new fact of life.

Socioeconomic change has not only changed the nature of divorce in Japan; it has created certain types of divorce that may be unique to this country. One of these is the nondivorce divorce, which happens to couples who have grown miles apart in heart and mind and yet continue to live under the same roof, appearing to be a normal married couple to the outside world but barely on speaking terms within their own home. . . .

If the husband's fear of social stigma has created the nondivorce, the wife's capacity for submission has created the retirement divorce. Mr. and Ms. B divorced when he was 57, she, 49. They had been married 28 years and had a son, 26, and a daughter, 24. Ms. B decided to get a divorce some 10 years before she finally carried it out. She waited so long because she wanted to see her children through college and felt that she should continue fulfilling her role as wife as long as her husband was working. . . . Once she had set a target date, Ms. B began to save money in small amounts. Since she would be the one asking for a divorce, she had no intention of demanding a settlement from her husband. Not that she wasn't entitled. Having sacrificed most of her life to this man, it would not be strange to demand at least half of his hefty retirement pay. But that wouldn't be honorable, she thought.

Yamashita Katsutoshi. Reprinted by permission.

Table 18.3 Most Frequent Experiences of 80 Divorced Individuals

	Percentage experiencing
I have felt worthwhile as a person	96
I have experienced personal growth and maturity	94
I have felt relieved	92
I have felt closer to my children	89
I have felt competent	89
The cost of maintaining the household has been difficult	87
I have felt angry toward my former spouse	87
I have felt insecure	86
My leisure activities have increased	86
I have been depressed	86
Household routines and daily patterns have changed	85

From Cheryl Buehler and Mary Langenbrunner, "Divorce-Related Stressors: Occurrence, Disruptiveness, and Area of Life Change" in *Journal of Divorce*, 11:35. Copyright © 1987 Haworth Press, Inc., New York, NY. Reprinted by permission.

of 140 things they had experienced since their separation. Table 18.3 shows the most common experiences, those identified by at least 85 percent of the sample. Note that the five most common are all positive. Keep in mind that these were people who were still working through the aftermath of the divorce. Although troubled by anger, insecurity, and depression, they had some positive experiences as well.

In the longer run, most people will view the divorce as a positive turning point, perhaps even a necessary step in their own well-being. For instance, Heather, who runs an art gallery, believes that her divorce set her on the road to autonomy for the first time in her life (Lauer and Lauer 1988:129). She had not established her independence before getting married:

> I switched from parental control to marital control. At the age of thirty, I began to gain autonomy. At thirty-two, I rebelled. At forty, I finally became a person. I mean I finally became me, Heather, an independent human being.

She became that "independent human being" by leaving a marriage with a domineering man. She says that she feared being on her own and hesitated leaving him, but she "had to yank that safety net of marriage in order to realize that I can survive without it."

Health Problems

Not all outcomes are positive, even in the long run. Problems with physical and emotional health are common among people who are in the process of divorcing. Moreover, sometimes these problems last for years or even decades after the divorce is final.

Many people need help in coping with the stress of divorce.

Although some emotional difficulties may be present before and contribute to a divorce, the process is sufficiently stressful to create such problems. A number of studies have shown that divorced people have higher rates of suicide, accidents, physical and mental health problems, and alcoholism (Kitson, Babri, and Roach 1985:274). Divorced people also report themselves as less happy than those who are married (Weingarten 1985).

The stress of a divorce is great because it involves the disruption of an intimate relationship. There is a sense of loss. There are uncertainties about the future, about the individual's network of relationships, and perhaps about the decision to divorce. The prospect of such a radical change in one's life tends to create a certain amount of anger, depression, and guilt. Interestingly, such feelings are likely to occur to those who initiate the divorce as well as to their partners. The difference is that the initiators are likely to experience the negative emotions earlier in the process (Buehler 1987).

How long do such negative emotions last? Typically, it takes anywhere from two to four years to work through a divorce. However, if the individual does not cope well, the problems may go on for decades or even a lifetime (Lauer and Lauer 1988:122). In a long-term study of sixty families disrupted by divorce, the researchers found that a fourth of the mothers and a fifth of the fathers were still struggling ten years after their divorces (Wallerstein and Blakeslee 1989). The parents tended to be chronically disorganized. They had problems meeting the demands of parenting. And frequently they leaned on their children for support; the children, in effect, became parents to their own parents.

Challenges to Intimacy

Financial Problems

Although no-fault divorce laws were supposed to make marital disruption a more equitable process, we may speak of "his" divorce and "her" divorce. And her divorce usually involves a more severe financial crisis than does his. Lenore Weitzman (1985) conducted research over a ten-year period, looking at twenty-five hundred California court records and interviewing lawyers, judges, and divorced men and women. Among other things, she found that within a year after the divorce was finalized,

> men experience a 42 percent improvement in their . . . standard of living, while women experience a 73 percent decline (Weitzman 1985:339).

Of course, not every woman's standard of living went down, or down that dramatically, nor did every man's standard rise. But women generally tend to be penalized financially by the no-fault divorce procedure.

Weitzman recognized that no-fault divorce relieves some of the conflict of the old adversarial system. She argued that no-fault procedures have weakened the bargaining position of women with the result that divorced women and their children tend to be systematically impoverished. The primary reason for this is that the new laws require husbands and wives to be treated equally. Yet the division of labor in the family, along with the experiences and special skills of each partner, mean that men and women are unequal in terms of their resources and opportunities. Because the law no longer presumes that the husband is responsible for supporting the family after the divorce, men tend to benefit, and women, particularly those with children, tend to suffer from no-fault laws.

Other research supports the conclusion that women suffer financially under no-fault divorce laws. Arendell (1986) interviewed sixty middle-class, divorced mothers. Only six of the women received alimony. More than half got no, or sporadic and insufficient, child support. The women all lived in California, but the community property law did not take into account their contributions to their husbands' education and earning power. Nine out of ten said that their incomes had dropped close to or below the poverty line after their divorces. In addition, the women found themselves facing all kinds of difficult problems—finding and coping with work, the conflict between working and caring for the children, getting food stamps, dealing with welfare agencies, selling jewelry or furniture or renting out rooms to make ends meet, and dealing with feelings of loneliness and isolation.

While both Weitzman and Arendell used data from California, national figures also show that divorced women's income tends to go down while that of men tends to rise. For example, data from a national survey of young men and women showed that per capita family income varied little between married males and females, but the per capita income of divorced women was only a little over half of that of divorced men (Day and Bahr 1986).

Interaction between Former Spouses

A divorce doesn't necessarily end interaction between former spouses. If children are involved in the divorce, of course, there is likely to be at least some contact between the ex-spouses. According to one study of eighty couples, about one of five had a relatively high degree of coparental interaction a year after the divorce and another 59 percent reported a moderate amount of interaction (Ahrons and Wallisch 1987). By three years after the divorce, however, only one in ten of the respondents reported a continuingly high degree of interaction. Among other things, the couples said that they interacted to share major decisions about the children, discuss children's personal, school, and medical problems, discuss children's progress and accomplishments, and talk about childrearing problems generally. Nearly half of the ex-spouses spent time together with their children for the first year after divorce, but the number dropped to 30 percent two years later.

On matters other than parenting, the ex-spouses had less interaction. Still, after one year about a fourth continued to interact with each other every few months. They talked about such things as new experiences, their families (other than the children), old friends, personal problems, and finances. For many people, then, the relationship continues, at least to some extent, even after divorce.

Of course, the quality of the interaction between ex-spouses varies considerably. Psychologist Constance Ahrons found four types of relationships between ninety-eight pairs of ex-spouses: fiery foes, angry associates, cooperative colleagues, and perfect pals (Stark 1986a). About a fourth were fiery foes, those who had minimal contact with each other and who became bitter and angry when they did interact. Fiery foes try to avoid each other. Another fourth were angry associates, those who could tolerate being in the same place with the ex-spouse, but who still feel so angry and bitter that they cannot interact pleasantly.

The largest group, 38 percent, were cooperative colleagues. They have a moderate amount of interaction, and can mutually support each other. They strive to get along for the children's sake. Finally, the perfect pals comprised 12 percent of the sample. Like cooperative colleagues, they are child-centered and try to put the interests of their children above any anger or frustration they still have. But perfect pals are much more involved with each other than are cooperative colleagues. Neither partner has remarried. They enjoy each other's company. They may telephone to share exciting news with each other. They maintain a fairly active involvement in each other's life even though they are not trying to reestablish the marriage.

Effects of Divorce on Children

One of the reasons given by some people for remaining in an unhappy marriage is to protect their children. Most people are aware that divorce can be a very painful experience for children. Still is it always better for children if their parents' marriage is intact? Just how painful is divorce for the children?

"My Whole World Was Lost"

Divorce is generally painful, but particularly so when one of the partners doesn't expect it. In some cases, the "secret" is so well kept that a spouse is stunned by the announcement that the marriage is over. Craig, a forty-year-old salesman, had that experience. He describes his feelings:

> Even though we had been having a few problems and seeing a marriage counselor, I was really caught by surprise. I came home from work one day to discover that my wife and children were gone. I felt like hell and nearly powerless to change the situation. They were gone, and what was I to do? I made several attempts to get my wife to return, but she wouldn't consider it. Two days later, I was served with divorce papers.
>
> I had to deal with the reality. It was over. I blamed myself. I blamed her mother. I even blamed the marriage counselor that we had visited. I reached for anything that would take the pain away. I was hurt and I wanted my family back.
>
> I kept hoping things would get better. But they didn't. I wanted to see my children as often as I could, but that became an impossibility. Then one day I thought of a way that I might at least see them. My wife had moved in with her mother, and across from their house was a school with a track. I started jogging at the school so that I could be near my children and maybe even get a glimpse of them at times. But I was jogging too early in the morning. I decided to join the Y.M.C.A., which was just a block from their house. I could jog there any time of the day.
>
> The jogging track at the Y had piped in music, and everyday I would hear the same song about how somebody had done somebody else wrong. I was not only running to the music but living its harsh message. I hurt in places deep in my soul. Sometimes I cried. My whole world was lost, and I couldn't get it back. I returned to the only place that I could remember that left me feeling good about myself—my church.
>
> The court date finally arrived, and the judge gave custody to my ex-wife. However, I was awarded liberal visitation rights. My ex-wife sometimes tried to make excuses and keep me from picking up the children on weekends. That went on for fourteen years. It was only recently that I finally forgave her for the pain and suffering I have endured. I have remarried and my new wife is helping me with her love and patience. I am finally beginning to trust people again.

These questions take on increasing importance in an age when the number of children affected by divorce is enormous. It is estimated that at least six out of ten American youth, and as many as nine out of ten American black youth, will spend some time in a single-parent home before the age of eighteen (Demo and Acock 1988).

Short-Term Effects

In the short term, children are likely to suffer a variety of physical and emotional problems when their parents divorce. In some cases, such as a family in which there was abuse or intense and constant conflict, the separation and

Children are likely to have more behavioral problems at school after their parents divorce.

divorce may be a relief rather than a traumatic experience. Most of the time, however, the short-term effects will be negative. In fact, parental separation is likely to create a crisis for the child, but one that will diminish within the first six to twelve months (Kelly 1988:122).

Among the negative consequences identified by researchers are:

Initial reactions to parental separation may include intense anger, fears about the future, and loyalty conflicts as the child is pressured to take sides in the parental battle (Bonkowski, Boomhower, and Bequette 1985; Wallerstein and Kelly 1976)

Physical health ratings of children from divorced families are lower than those from intact families (Guidubaldi and Cleminshaw 1985)

Children from divorced families are more likely to be depressed and withdrawn than those in intact families (Peterson and Zill 1986)

Children from divorced families rate themselves lower in social competence (Devall, Stoneman, and Brody 1986)

Intact-family children have fewer absences at school, higher popularity ratings, higher IQ, reading, spelling, and math scores, and fewer behavioral problems at school than do children from divorced families (Guidubaldi, Perry, and Nastasi 1987; Kinard and Reinherz 1986)

The various consequences are understandable. Disruptions in intimate relationships are very stressful for all of us. Children are likely to be even more stressed because they have no control over what is happening to them and see no long-term benefits to the disruption. Thus, they react with anger, depression, and anxiety, and this emotional turbulence interferes with other aspects of their lives.

Long-Term Effects

Fortunately, the picture is not as bleak when we look at longer-term consequences. There may be some positive outcomes for the children (Demo and Acock 1988:626–27). For example, children in single-parent homes are more likely to be androgynous in their behavior. The pressures toward traditional gender roles do not seem to be as prevalent in single-parent as they are in two-parent homes. In addition, adolescents in single-parent homes tend to be more mature and to have a greater sense of their own efficacy. This is probably due to the fact that they take more responsibility for family life, doing some things that might otherwise be done by the absent parent.

In those cases in which family life was marked by intense conflict, the children are likely to be better off in both the short and long run. We have noted that children from divorced homes have higher rates of depression and withdrawal, but the study found that the rates are even higher for those who live in a home with persistent conflict than for those who live in a single-parent home (Peterson and Zill 1986:302). In fact, some of the negative consequences may be due to the level of conflict in the home rather than to the divorce per se (Emery 1988; Enos and Handal 1986). Children who remain in an intact family with persistent conflict will suffer more than those whose parents divorce.

If some of the effects are positive, others are neutral; that is, in the long run there are no differences between those who come from intact and those who come from disrupted homes. For example, there are no variations in self-esteem (Amato 1988a; Demo and Acock 1988; Slater and Calhoun 1988). Moreover, children from divorced families appear to be equally competent in social situations as those from intact families (Amato and Ochiltree 1986; Long et al. 1987).

However, there may be some negative long-term consequences:

Those from disrupted homes score lower than those from intact homes on a measure of their sense of power (Amato 1988a).

Those from disrupted homes are likely to attain less education, to marry at an earlier age, and to have a less stable marriage themselves (Keith and Finlay 1988).

Those from disrupted homes view their families of origin in more negative terms (Amato 1988b).

Divorce tends not to reduce attachment to the custodial parent but does reduce it with the noncustodial parent (White, Brinkerhoff, and Booth 1985); nearly half of the children in a national survey had not seen their nonresident fathers in the past year (Furstenberg and Nord 1985), although frequency of visitation and the closeness of the relationship with the father revealed no consistent influence on the child's academic difficulty, problem behavior, and psychological distress (Furstenberg, Morgan, and Allison 1987:695).

When the noncustodial parent is perceived as "lost," the adult child is
likely to be depressed (Drill 1986).

Those from disrupted homes report themselves as less happy than those
from intact homes (Glenn and Kramer 1985).

Women from disrupted homes are less likely to marry than are women
from intact homes (Goldscheider and Waite 1986).

A study of women showed that those from disrupted homes have more
difficulty trusting and relying on men than do women from intact
homes (Southworth and Schwarz 1987).

A long-term study reported that two-thirds of young women from
disrupted homes developed anxiety as young adults, feared betrayal in
intimate relationships and had problems committing themselves to a
relationship, while 40 percent of young men from disrupted homes
had, as young adults, no set goals and a sense of having limited
control over their lives (Wallerstein and Blakeslee 1989).

Gender Differences

Will you handle the divorce of your parents better if you are a girl or a boy?
One of the interesting conclusions to emerge from research is that girls tend
to adjust more easily to divorce than do boys. Boys from divorced homes ex-
hibit significantly more problematic behavior than do boys from intact homes;
no such differences are found among girls (Demo and Acock 1988:622). Boys
who live with a divorced mother have even higher levels of depression and
withdrawal than boys who live in an intact family with high, persistent conflict
(Peterson and Zill 1986). Boys also take a longer time to adjust than do girls.

There are various reasons why boys have more difficulty adjusting to a
divorce. One factor to keep in mind that is boys tend to be more aggressive
than girls at all ages. Both boys and girls from divorced families tend to be
more aggressive than those from intact families, but the increase may "push
the boy's behavior past acceptable limits while an increase in a girl's aggressive behavior might still not be labeled problematic behavior" (Lowery and
Settle 1985:458).

A number of researchers have suggested that the main problem of boys
may be the lack of a same-sex parent. Most boys live with their mother. The
need for a father seems to intensify during adolescence (Wallerstein 1987),
when the boy, unlike the girl, has no same-sex role model in the home. There
is some evidence that both boys and girls who live with the parent of the opposite sex are not as well-adjusted in terms of social behavior (Santrock and
Warshak 1979). The problem of a son living with his mother may be compounded if the son reminds the mother of the father with whom she is still
angry (Kelly 1988:134).

Child Custody

At the beginning of this chapter, we quoted the undergraduate student who said that the most painful part of her parents' divorce was deciding with whom to live. She was forced to make a decision that could only hurt regardless of who she chose:

> I was daddy's girl but mother's baby. My sister wanted to live with mom and so did I. But my dad wanted me to live with him. I didn't want to be apart from my sister and my mom. So one day all four of us sat down to legalize where we'd live. My dad asked me who I wanted to live with. I didn't want to answer. It just killed me. I was only ten years old. When I finally answered, it was awful. My dad broke down and began to cry. That was the first time I'd ever seen him cry. It was devastating to me to have my dad feel so disappointed with me.

Custody arrangements can be very painful for both the parents and the children. Interestingly, the arrangements have changed over time. Until relatively recently, the only arrangement was **sole custody**, in which one of the parents is given the responsibility for the care and raising of the child. Before the early part of this century, the parent who got such custody was the father. Fathers were the economic head of the family and were presumed to be in a better position to care for the needs of the children. Increasingly in the twentieth century, however, mothers were granted custody under the "tender years" doctrine, the notion that the child's well-being is maximized by the mother's care. By 1925, the phrase "best interests of the child" was incorporated into state laws. Until the mid-1960s, then, mothers were generally given custody, and they won custody in more than 90 percent of contested cases (Ihinger-Tallman and Pasley 1987:80).

Unless a father could show that his former wife was unstable or unable to provide proper care, the courts routinely gave custody to the mother. The role of the father was reduced to providing financial support and to some visitation rights. Then fathers began to ask for more. After the mid-1960s, an increasing number of fathers won the right to sole custody. As the examples of the student quoted above and the experience of Craig (Personal) illustrate, fathers as well as mothers may find the separation from their children to be extremely painful. Indeed, divorced fathers who have custody of their children are less depressed, less anxious, and have fewer problems of adjustment than those without custody (Stewart, Schwebel, and Fine 1986).

Why not, then, find another alternative, one that allows both parents to continue to be involved in some way in their children's lives? **Joint custody**, an arrangement in which both parents continue to share the responsibility for the care and raising of the children, is an attempt to provide a better solution. In 1980, California adopted a joint custody arrangement. Other states soon followed suit.

A number of states now award joint custody unless there is some compelling reason to do otherwise. The way in which joint custody actually works out in daily life varies somewhat (Ihinger-Tallman and Pasley 1987:81). The children may spend some time each day at two different homes, various amounts of time during the week at two different homes, differing periods of the time in each of two homes, or alternate years in each of the two homes. In other cases, joint custody does not even require shared living arrangements, but is rather joint legal custody where both parents are involved in important decisions in their child's life.

Does joint custody resolve the problems? Does it provide the ideal way, or even a better way, to deal with the issues? There are differences of opinion. Basically, joint custody has some advantages and some drawbacks.

It does seem clear that the type of custody arrangement affects the adjustment of the children (Kelly 1988). As we have already noted, children in sole custody who live with a same-sex parent tend to be better adjusted than those living with an opposite-sex parent, showing higher levels of social competence, maturity, and self-esteem. Joint custody children, however, tend to be more satisfied with the arrangement than those living with one parent only, and they may avoid the struggle with the sense of loss that afflicts children in sole custody arrangements. Joint-custody boys are as well-adjusted overall as boys in intact families.

In large part, the adjustment of the children to a joint-custody arrangement depends on the way in which the parents relate to them and to each other. Joint custody, of course, means that the ex-spouses will continue to interact more than they would have under sole custody. If their interaction is one of ongoing conflict, the joint custody arrangement may be worse for the child than sole custody. If the parents can relate to each other without anger and conflict, the children will usually prefer joint custody. They find the benefits of maintaining intimate contact with both parents worth the hassles of living alternately in two homes.

Joint custody has some benefits for the parents also. In joint custody, the parents may avoid financial problems and feelings of being overwhelmed by childcare responsiblities that tend to characterize single parents (Lowery and Settle 1985). Noncustodial fathers often fail to provide financial support for the children. In joint custody, that is unlikely to happen. The mother is less likely to find herself living in poverty because she is the sole support of herself and her children.

Of course, there may be some disadvantages to joint custody even if the parents get along. Basically, it is too early to know of any long-term consequences. What, for example, will be the effect on children of not having a single, stable environment in which to grow up? What is the effect on their peer relationships? What if they have diverse and contrary experiences with the two parents? In the future we may be able to answer such questions. Meanwhile, joint custody seems to be a considerable improvement over sole custody for most parents and their children.

Children adjust to a divorce better if their parents can be cordial to each other.

Coping with the Disruption

How can both parents and children cope effectively with the disruption of their intimate relationships? How can they maximize their chances of eventually turning the divorce into something positive for themselves?

For children, adjustment depends in part on the behavior of their parents (Kelly 1988). Children adjust well to the extent that divorce reduces the conflict between the parents. Under a sole custody arrangement, children's adjustment is better if there is frequent contact with the noncustodial parent; and if the custodial parent is satisfied with the noncustodial parent's relationship with the children. Obviously, children benefit when their parents grow beyond the anger and bitterness of the divorce and establish cordial relations between them.

How can parents cope with divorce and develop a relationship that is helpful to their children? To begin with, ex-spouses need to be open about their feelings and work through the anger, guilt, and anxiety that attend the disruption of an intimate relationship. Such feelings should not be repressed or denied; that only delays adjustment. Blaming someone for the disruption is generally unprofitable. Neither self-blame nor other-blame pays off in terms of adjusting well. Initially, of course, condemning the ex-spouse may be a part of venting one's anger. But eventually each of the partners must get beyond blaming and get on with the business of constructing a new life with new intimate relationships.

Furthermore, people adjust well to a divorce to the extent that they are able to define it as an opportunity for growth. We need to understand that "both marriage and divorce can generate adult unfolding or, conversely, block individual development, depending on a multitude of factors" (Rice and Rice 1986:71). We have seen examples of how divorce can block growth, leading to long-term stagnation as the individual persists in anger, bitterness, and depression. But divorce can also be an opportunity. In our study of watersheds in people's lives, we found that those who successfully coped with a divorce came to a point where they defined the disruption as an important step in their growth (Lauer and Lauer 1988:125). For instance, a number of women told about how divorce allowed them for the first time in their lives to test their capacity for self-sustained living. The discovery of their capacity for independence was an exhilirating experience. The pain of disruption eventually led to the excitement of self-discovery. For many people, then, a divorce becomes the beginning of a new journey into fulfillment, a journey that includes both personal growth and meaningful intimate relationships.

PRINCIPLES FOR ENHANCING INTIMACY

Although divorce can have a potentially damaging impact on children, the following principles suggest some ways in which parents can help their offspring and maximize the probability of maintaining meaningful, intimate relations.

1. Be open and straightforward when discussing the divorce with children. Children sometimes blame themselves for a parental divorce. Don't deny the marital difficulties that led to the divorce; rather, help your children to see the situation as clearly as possible.

2. Avoid blaming anyone for the divorce. Make sure the children know they are not to blame. But don't heap blame on the other spouse. The children probably want to continue to love and interact with both parents. Don't make that difficult for them.

3. Help the children to understand that neither parent is divorcing them. Don't ask them to choose the parent with whom they want to live. Let them know that both parents continue to love them even though the family will no longer be living together.

4. Let the children vent their emotions, including any anger, fear, and guilt they feel. Being open about their feelings will help them work through the disruption.

5. Avoid unnecessary changes. Children will usually benefit by staying in the same neighborhood and school in the period immediately following a divorce.

SUMMARY

Since 1860 there has been a general increase in the divorce rate. The rate peaked just after World War II and again in the 1970s. About one-fourth of people today who have ever been married have also experienced legal separation and/or divorce. The grounds for divorce are governed by the states, most of which now have no-fault laws.

The process of uncoupling is marked by four time periods: recognition, discussion, action, and postdissolution. In the recognition period, one partner senses that the relationship is deteriorating, but may not openly confront the other. In the discussion period, the marital problems may be shared with outsiders as well as the spouse. The history of the relationship may be redefined in terms of a series of negative experiences. The initiator is making the transition to a new life. The action period involves legal steps to formally dissolve the marriage. This is a difficult period, involving the struggle over such things as division of property, child custody, and ambivalent feelings. The postdissolution period begins when both spouses accept the fact that the marriage is over.

Bohannan has identified six experiences that people are likely to have in divorce. Divorce involves an emotional, legal, community, and psychic separation, and an economic and coparental (for those with children) settlement.

Divorce is more likely for those of lower socioeconomic status, those married at a younger or later age, blacks, and those who lack membership in an integrated group such as a religious group. Changed laws and attitudes and the changing roles of women are associated with higher divorce rates. At an interpersonal level, divorce is associated with various complaints such as infidelity and conflict over personalities and finances. Some divorces are the result of changed feelings about the partner, and some result from emotional problems of a spouse.

Divorce can have positive as well as negative outcomes. For some, a divorce is a positive turning point in personal well-being. But there are numerous negative outcomes likely, including short-term and in some cases long-term health problems and, particularly for women, financial problems. Divorce doesn't necessarily end interaction between the spouses, though the quality of the interaction varies considerably.

Divorce has both short-term and long-term effects on children. In the short run, children are likely to suffer various physical, behavioral, and emotional problems. Over the long run, there may be positive outcomes for children, especially if the home was marked by intense and continual conflict. In some ways, children from disrupted homes are no different than those from intact homes in the long run. But there can also be some long-term negative consequences, including lower levels of educational and occupational achievement, problematic relationships with the noncustodial parent, problems with trust, and depression.

Girls tend to adjust more easily to divorce than do boys. Boys from disrupted homes have significantly more problematic behavior. The main problem for boys may be the lack of a same-sex parent.

Child custody arrangements can be painful for both parents and children. Sole custody is giving way to joint custody in many states. The type of custody can affect the child's adjustment to the divorce. There is some evidence that joint custody, while not solving all the problems, does have benefits for both the children and the parents.

Children's adjustment to the divorce depends in part on the behavior of the parents. If the divorce reduces conflict significantly, children adjust better. The parents will adjust better to the extent that they work through their feelings and are able to define the divorce as an opportunity to grow.

---

1. *Public Opinion,* November/December, 1987, p. 39.

19

Remarriage and Stepfamilies

There is a song that says that love is better the "second time around." If this is true, millions of Americans are living out the ecstasy of a loving relationship in second marriages. A more cynical view was expressed by the eighteenth century writer, Samuel Johnson, who called remarriage the "triumph of hope over experience." If this is true, millions of Americans are living in the disillusionment of a second marriage.

The actual experiences of those who remarry, as we shall see, are somewhere between these two extremes. Remarriage has its own unique potential and its own unique problems. In this chapter, we will look at the extent of remarriage, the experiences and hopes that lead up to it, and the prospects and pitfalls involved in it. We will look in some detail at the various issues raised by **stepfamilies**—remarriages involving children. Finally, we will examine some ways in which people can maximize the probability of a positive outcome when they remarry and live in a stepfamily.

Stepfamilies are increasingly common.

Types and Number of Remarriages and Stepfamilies

How many people do you know who have remarried or who are living in a stepfamily? The chances are good that either you or someone you know has had such an experience. When we discuss remarriages and stepfamilies, we are talking about a significant proportion of the American population. But there is considerable diversity among the remarried. We will look first at the various types and then at some related statistics.

Types of Remarried Couples

There are many ways to classify remarried couples. For instance, men and women come to remarriage from a variety of situations (Sager, Brown, Crohn, Engel, Rodstein, and Walker 1983:64). At the time of remarriage, the man and woman each were in one of five different conditions: single, divorced or widowed with no children, divorced or widowed with custody of children, divorced or widowed without custody of children, or divorced or widowed with custody of some children but not others. Such a classification yields twenty-four different types of remarriages (the number is twenty-four rather than twenty-five because two single people do not constitute a remarriage).

The possible combinations could be further multiplied if we added those who have adult children no longer living at home and those who have had more than one divorce. The important point here is that each combination is likely

Table 19.1   Remarriage: 1970–1984

	1970	1975	1980	1984
Remarriages of Divorced Women (1,000)	270	365	447	490
Rates per 1,000 Divorced Women:				
15 yrs and over	123.3	117.2	91.3	87.3
15–24 yrs old	413.4	319.6	236.4	244.3
25–44 yrs old	179.6	158.6	122.8	120.8
45–64 yrs old	42.6	40.1	30.3	30.4
65 yrs and over	6.1	9.1	5.3	4.8
Median Age at Remarriage:				
Male (years)	37.5	35.5	35.2	36.8
Female (years)	33.3	32.0	32.0	33.3

Source: U.S. Bureau of the Census 1988:83.

to produce different outcomes. As we shall see, the prospects for a stable and satisfying union are quite different for a single woman who marries a divorced man who has custody of his children versus those for a marriage between two divorced people without children versus those for the marriage between two divorced parents, each of whom has custody.

As may already be clear, remarried life, and especially stepfamily life, can become incredibly complicated. The network of relationships expands enormously. Consider the problems of a divorced woman who has custody of her children marrying a divorced man who has custody of his children. There may be ex-spouses to deal with, grandparents who are still very attached to the children, other relatives of the ex-spouses with whom there were close relationships, new stepparent relationships, and new stepsibling relations to work through. It is likely to be a difficult process at best.

Demographics of Remarriage and Stepfamilies

Of the more than one million Americans who divorce each year, how many will remarry? Since 1970, the rate has gone down for women of all ages (table 19.1). Still, the majority of those widowed or divorced will eventually remarry. Figures from 1980 showed that 72 percent of men and 63 percent of women remarried by their thirties, and 84 percent of men and 77 percent of women had remarried by ages sixty-five to seventy-four (Glick 1984). The probability of women remarrying varied by educational level—those with higher levels of education were less likely to remarry, though a majority of those eventually remarry.

Many remarriages involve children. In 1987, there were approximately 11 million remarried families in the United States, 4.3 million of which were stepfamilies (Glick 1989). Slightly more than one out of five of all married-couple families were remarried families, and 8.3 percent of all married-couple

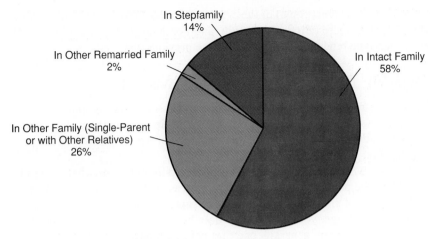

Figure 19.1 *Family status of children under 18: 1987.*
Source: Data from Glick 1989:25.

families were stepfamilies. About 9.75 million children under the age of eighteen were in remarried families, 8.78 million were in stepfamilies, and 5.85 million were stepchildren (Glick 1989). The reason for the differences in the numbers is that some children were born to remarried parents while others were brought into the remarriage. The numbers mean that of all children in the nation under the age of eighteen, nearly one in six lived in a remarried family, and nearly one of every ten was a stepchild (figure 19.1).

What are the prospects for those who remarry? In general, they are not quite as good as for those who marry for the first time. That is, the divorce rate is slightly higher among remarriages than among first marriages. Glick (1984) estimated that among young people who were in their twenties in the late 1970s, nearly half will experience a divorce in their first marriage, but 60 percent will have a remarriage end in divorce.

The divorce rate varies by type of remarriage, however. Using a national sample for a study of divorce, White and Booth (1985) concluded that when only one of the spouses was remarried and the other was previously single, the chances for divorce were not significantly greater than they were for marriages in which both partners were in a first marriage. But the chances went up 50 percent if both partners were previously married (no children) and another 50 percent if both partners were previously married and one or both brought stepchildren into the remarriage. The presence of stepchildren is a particularly destabilizing factor in remarriages. In the following paragraphs, we shall discuss the reasons.

One other type of remarriage that is unstable is that involving an individual who is in a serial-marriage pattern. **Serial marriage** refers to three or more marriages that occur as a result of repeated divorces. At least 2 percent (more than 2 million people) of the ever-married population has been married three times or more (Brody, Neubaum, and Forehand 1988). The duration of each marriage tends to be shorter than the previous one.

Déjà Vu: Dating and Courtship Revisited

Those who remarry must go through the processes of dating and courtship again. Although we think of dating and courtship as something that occurs mainly in adolescence and the twenties, millions of Americans repeat the process at other times in their lives.

How is dating at forty or fifty or sixty different from what it was in youth? As we pointed out in chapter 3, the reasons that older people date as well as some of their experiences are the same as those of younger people. Whatever your age, you are likely to date because you want to establish an intimate relationship, generally one that will culminate in marriage.

Is it any easier to date when you are older? Perhaps not. As a divorced man of fifty put it: "I felt like a kid again. The same anxiety. The same awkwardness whenever the conversation stopped. The same questions about what I should or shouldn't do." The man was experiencing only one of the problems that the divorced face in dating. There may be problems of children and limited money because of alimony and/or child support as well as a sense of impatience to establish a new relationship and a reluctance to waste time on one that is going nowhere.

Most divorced people, as we have noted, intend to remarry eventually. And dating is instrumental toward that end. Therapists suggest that there may be an optimum time between the breakup of a first marriage and the initiation of a second one (Sager et al. 1983:63). If dating, courtship, and remarriage occur too quickly after a breakup, the individual may not have had sufficient time to work through his or her pain and disappointment, completely sever ties with the ex-spouse, or learn from the failed relationship. The popular notion of avoiding a "rebound" marriage is sound because an old relationship can adversely affect a new one. Yet if the time between marriages is too long, problems also can develop. For example, in a remarriage where one participant has had long-time custody of a child, it may be difficult for a new spouse to break into the existing parent-child relationship. A period of from three to five years before remarriage seems optimal. This should allow the divorced individual sufficient time to work through the emotional pain and to experience a number of relationships.

Many people do not wait three to five years. Cherlin (1981:84) estimated that about half of those who remarry do so within three years following the divorce. In a study using a national sample, Teachman and Heckert (1985) found that a fourth of white women remarried within eight months of their divorce, half were remarried within twenty-seven months, and three-fourths were remarried within sixty-four months. Black women took longer; a fourth were remarried within seventeen months, but half were not remarried until six and one-half years had passed.

Those who remarry tend to spend less time in the dating and engagement periods. A study involving 248 volunteers reported that, before their first marriage, respondents spent a median of twelve months dating and five months being engaged (O'Flaherty and Eells 1988). Before remarriage, they spent a median of seven months dating and two months being engaged. In other words, the second marriages occurred in about half the dating and courtship time as the first marriages. Because courtship time tends to be related to marital success, this could be a factor in the greater instability of remarriages.

What do the divorced do to prepare for remarriage? Knowing the vulnerability of marriages, what steps do they take to minimize the possibility of a second breakup? Not a great deal, according to the little evidence we have. Ganong and Coleman (1989) asked 100 men and 105 women about their preparation for a second marriage. The majority (59 percent) simply lived together. They tested their capacity to be a family through a period of cohabitation. About a fourth of the men and 38 percent of the women received counseling. A little over half of the men and 72 percent of the women sought advice from written materials (such as self-help books) and from friends.

While some couples prepare for remarriage by discussing important issues, most do not.

An important way of preparing for any marriage, including a second one, is for the couple to discuss significant issues and potential problems. The researchers found that the couples in their study did not discuss many of the issues regarded as important by stepfamily experts (Ganong and Coleman 1989:30). Children from a previous marriage, the most frequently mentioned issue, were discussed by 56 percent of the couples. Less than a fourth said they talked about the next most frequently named topic—finances. Thirteen percent said they didn't seriously discuss any issues.

> Responses to other questions seemed to reinforce the sense that these couples were either overly optimistic or naive (Ganong and Coleman 1989:30).

If these results are generally true, then people are not taking the necessary steps to ensure stability and satisfaction in their second marriages.

Why Remarry?

People remarry for many of the same reasons that they married the first time. In particular, people wish to establish an intimate relationship:

> We find the promise of a caring and loving relationship to be the prime motivation for remarriage (Sager et al. 1983:61).

The most frequently given reason of 205 men and women, that "it was time," probably reflects the felt need for intimacy (figure 19.2). As figure 19.2 shows, those who remarry also have some reasons that are different from those in first marriages. Thus, parents with custody of their children may be motivated by the desire to find a suitable co-parent.

In chapter 9 we discussed private contracts, assumptions, and expectations that each partner has for the other in the marital relationship. People

Toward Remarriage

There is little research on how people move toward a second marriage. What is it like to date? How has the experience of divorce affected dating and courtship patterns and preparatory steps toward marriage? What kind of expectations do people have for their second marriage?

Interview someone in your family or someone you know who has been divorced and remarried. Write an account of the person's remarital experience, beginning with the time immediately after the divorce. Ask the following questions:

1. After the divorce, how did you feel about the prospect of dating or getting involved in a new relationship?

2. When and why and how you started dating again?

3. What problems did you encounter with dating again? How did your feelings and behavior on dates compare with those before your first marriage?

4. What made you decide to get remarried?

5. What did you do to try to make sure that the second marriage would work out better than the first?

6. What did you learn from the first marriage that you think will help you in the second one?

7. Looking back on it now, what would you do differently if you could do it all over?

8. What are you doing now, in this marriage, that is different from your first marriage?

9. What advice would you give to young men and women who are looking toward their first marriage?

If the entire class participates in this project, see if there are any common elements in the answers. In what ways, if any, do your findings differ from those presented in the text?

also bring their private contracts to remarriage. Based on clinical experience, Clifford Sager and his associates (1983:67–68) have identified some of the common expectations in remarriage. Those who remarry tend to assume and expect that the new spouse will:

1. Be loyal, devoted, and faithful, providing a kind of romantic love and intimacy that occurred when the first marriage was at its best (or that was lacking altogether in the first marriage)

2. Help nurture and discipline the children

3. Provide companionship, relief from the loneliness of being single

4. Help deal with problems and stresses and gain, or regain, the order and stability of a two-parent family

5. Be committed to making this marriage last

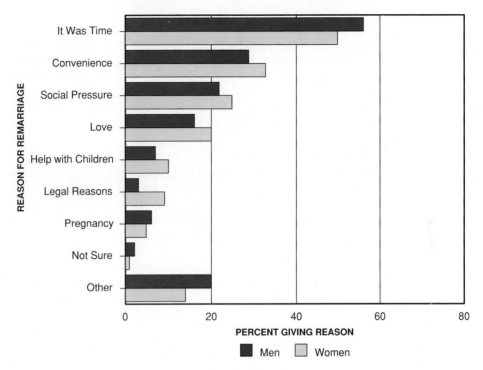

Figure 19.2 *Reasons for remarriage offered by 205 men and women.*
Source: Data from Ganong and Coleman 1989:30.

Depending on age and circumstances, those who remarry may also expect to have shared children (even if one or both bring children to the marriage).

In some cases, the private contract may be unrealistic. It may in essence say to the other: "I expect you to do everything for me that my former spouse didn't. I expect this to be the marriage 'made in heaven' that I didn't have before." Ideally, however, those who remarry will be more realistic, avoiding fanciful illusions and maintaining flexibility about roles in order to maximize the chances of success (Kvanli and Jennings 1986).

Issues in Recoupling

What is it like to remarry? What are the problems and prospects the second time around? Is it just as demanding? Does it ever get any easier? Remarriage, like marriage for the first time, requires insight and effort if it is to succeed. Unfortunately, many people enter a second marriage holding on to certain mythical beliefs that can be detrimental.

The Myths of Remarriage

Some remarriage myths are very similar to first-marriage myths; others are distinctive. Based on their research and their experience working with couples, Coleman and Ganong (1985) have identified a number of remarriage myths that can detract from the quality of the new union. These myths may be held by the those in the legal system, churches, and helping professions, as well as friends and family members. They also appear in the popular media.

Things Must Work Out
People in first marriages tend to believe this also, but there may be a quality of desperation in those who are remarrying. They insist on "getting it right" the second time. Or they believe that everything will work out because this time it is *really* love. But if insistence or confidence were sufficient, second marriages would not break up at a slightly higher rate than first marriages.

Consider Other People First
In remarriage, an individual may believe that success this time demands that he or she put personal needs secondary to those of spouse or children. But trying to fulfill everyone's needs is frustrating, stressful, and probably impossible. The problems of remarriage are not resolved by either partner denying his or her own needs.

Be an Individual First and a Couple Second
This is the opposite of the myth of always considering others first. It is held by those who felt that they suffered in the first marriage because they didn't care for their own needs. They believe that they must "look out for number one" regardless of what that means for the marital relationship.

Focus on the Positive and Forget Criticism
Some people who remarry believe that if they had followed this rule in their first marriage, it might have succeeded. They may be determined to follow it in the second marriage. As a result, they may

> 'walk on eggs' rather than confront, challenge, or argue with other family members. Pseudomutuality may lead to unhappiness and feelings of powerlessness and alienation rather than unity (Coleman and Ganong 1985:117).

Avoid Mistakes of the Past
When things are not going well in the second marriage, some believe that they need to remember mistakes made in the first marriage and avoid repeating them. But, again, this may be a way of avoiding the realities of the present. It is an effort to keep working at the past relationship rather than an attempt to build a new and unique relationship in the present.

Marriage Makes People Happier

Of course, it is true that the married tend to be happier than the unmarried. But remarriage, like marriage, is not a magic elixir that guarantees happiness or your money back. For some who remarry, happiness becomes even more of an imperative in the second than the first marriage, an aspect of the notion that this time it *has* to work out. A related myth is the idea that if the couple is happy, everyone else will be happy. But friends, grandparents, ex-spouses, and children may react very differently to the remarriage, and the happiness of the spouses cannot be separated from those reactions.

The Challenges of Remarriage

Those who remarry are likely to differ from those in a first marriage in a number of ways. They may be older and, therefore, in a different phase of their life cycle than those marrying for the first time. They may have different ideas about the meaning of love. They have experience in marriage. They know the pain of divorce. In addition, there are issues that are unique to remarriage that must be faced.

Complex Kin Relations and Ambiguous Roles

The acquisition of a whole new set of kin relationships, including steprelations, combined with ambiguity about many of the roles, can create considerable uncertainty and confusion for those involved in a remarriage (Bernstein and Collins 1985). Many a stepparent has had to deal with the retort: "You aren't my *real* parent." And many a spouse in a remarriage has had to contend with a partner's continuing relationship with an ex-spouse. There are no social norms for such relationships. What is appropriate? What is expected?

Consider the following case reported by Sager and his associates (1983:64). Mrs. Prince was single when she met Mr. Prince, who was divorced and the father of two school-age children who lived with their mother. Problems began early in Mr. Prince's second marriage. He felt that his wife resented his children and the time and money he spent on them. She complained that he talked constantly on the telephone with his ex-wife, as often as several times during a day. She also resented the fact that they couldn't be with her parents on holidays because his parents wanted to see his children. The problems seemed monumental and the couple eventually went to a therapist to try and work out the difficulties resulting from their complex family situation.

Unresolved Emotional Issues Related to the First Marriage

In addition to problematic relationships, there may be unresolved emotional issues from the first marriage and the divorce that continue to nag people and to affect their relationships. For example, a husband may react to something his wife says or does because it reminds him of a problem or situation in his first marriage. He may shout at wife number two, but he is really still battling with wife number one. A woman, who had the habit of shrugging at either of two acceptable options for recreation, decided to change her behavior because her husband's first wife had done that to show her contempt for him. To the second wife, her shrug meant "I don't care. I'll be happy doing either as long as I'm with you." To him, however, it had been a sign of scorn in the past and he still found himself reacting angrily.

Another example of how unresolved emotional issues continue to affect people is the difficulty that some have in developing trust in the remarital relationship (Kvanli and Jennings 1986). Trust is crucial to the well-being of an intimate relationship, but the failure of a first marriage is frequently a crisis of trust for people. Having found their trust in the first spouse betrayed, they must work hard to learn to trust a second spouse.

Adjustment of Children

As we noted earlier, children pose perhaps the biggest problem to a remarriage. In the past, remarriage generally meant a spouse had died. Now, the children are more likely to have continuing relationships with both biological parents as well as a stepparent. The problems can be severe; we shall discuss them in detail shortly.

Financial Issues

Next to children, financial issues are likely to loom large as a source of stress in remarriages. Financial problems can be complex and painful because of obligations to ex-spouses and children (see Personal). Plus, there are questions of the inheritance rights of children and stepchildren.

There is also the question of how family finances will be managed. Should there be one pot or two (Fishman 1983)? In the common-pot arrangement, both spouses put their total income (including any alimony and child support) into a common pot and allocate it among family members according to need instead of according to who earned what. In the two-pot arrangement, spouses safeguard resources for their personal use and the use of their biological children. For example, one couple, Sheila and Harry, have two pots. Sheila has three sons and Harry has a daughter. The daughter does not live with them. Harry gives Sheila money each week for his share of food and household expenses. Sheila adds a much larger amount that she gets in child support and uses the total to run the home and pay for her sons' expenses. Harry pays fixed expenses such as the mortgage and utilities. He also supports his own child.

Harry and Sheila prefer the two-pot arrangement. However, generally a common pot is more likely to unify the stepfamily, while two pots tend to encourage biological loyalty and individual independence (Fishman 1983).

Legal Issues

Although the biological children and the ex-spouse may all have legal rights, what of stepchildren? There are no laws that are specific to stepparent-stepchild relationships. Some couples, therefore, may opt for a premarital agreement that takes into account what each has brought to the marriage and

Many remarrieds have two checking accounts, but a "common pot" is more likely to unify the stepfamily.

protects each spouse as well as the children of each and any children they may have in common (Bernstein and Collins 1985). This may require negotiation and a rather complex agreement. But the complexity of the arrangement is a reflection of the intricacies of the multiple relationships of remarriage.

The Quality of Remarried Life

What can you anticipate in a second marriage in terms of the quality of marital life? First, the same factors that lead to satisfaction in a first marriage are also important in any subsequent marriage (Leigh, Ladehoff, Howie, and Christians 1985). Such things as companionship, general feelings for the other, and satisfaction with parenting are crucial to remarital as well as to marital satisfaction.

Second, people who remarry tend to report no less interaction, no more tensions, no greater number of disagreements, and no lower marital happiness than those in first marriages (White and Booth 1985:694). Remarried couples experience as high a level of intimacy as those who are first-married, although they may not deal with conflict as effectively as first-married couples. In their comparative study of thirty-three first-married with thirty-three remarried couples, Larson and Allgood (1987) reported that the remarried were more likely to use unproductive problem-solving strategies such as shouting and anger

"My Husband's First Wife is Straining My Marriage"

Judy, an ebullient young woman in her early thirties, fell in love with and married Kurt, a divorced man with a teenaged daughter by his first wife, Eve. Judy and Kurt have a child of their own, and are expecting a second. They are caught up in conflict between their relationships and the legal system, and as a result, their marriage is strained:

> Kurt has been divorced for over ten years. During most of that time he paid Eve $300 a month for Sharon's child support and half of the costs for her dance lessons and other activities. He also has had to pay all of her medical and dental expenses. A year ago, Sharon decided to move in with us. That meant that Kurt would no longer have to pay child support to Eve. Because of Kurt's and my salaries, however, Eve wouldn't have to contribute to Sharon's support while she lived with us.
>
> Six months after she moved in, Sharon decided to go back and live with her mother. Eve told Kurt that she had a letter from a therapist recommending that she not work due to stress-related illnesses. She would continue to work until Sharon moved back, but at that time she would have to quit. She implied that she would need more child support because of not being able to work.
>
> I went to a lawyer to see if I had any rights about my salary not being used to help support Sharon. And what I found out was not encouraging. The law says that Kurt's first responsibility is to Eve and Sharon. Because of my salary, more of Kurt's can be used to support Sharon. But this is going to cause a good deal of financial strain for us.
>
> I feel like I'm being punished for being successful. The law is letting Eve steal from us. I don't blame Sharon. In fact, we're pretty good friends. But Kurt and I suspect that Eve's so-called problems are just a way of making things difficult for us and easy for herself. We're both angry, and we find ourselves getting irritable with each other at times. Eve is straining our marriage. The law supports her. And we don't quite know how to handle it at this point.

during conflict. The researchers suggested that the less effective conflict management may be due to the greater number of challenges and problems faced by remarried couples, or incompatibility resulting from patterns established and remaining from the first marriage, or the lack of social norms for problem solving in remarriage. Nevertheless, the marital relationship among the remarried can be as satisfying as that of first-marrieds.

Second marriages also seem to break down for the same reasons as first marriages. However, the remarried are more likely than the first-married to divorce. The reason for this problem, as we have noted, is likely to be found in the total family system, particularly in the relationships with children and stepchildren. We need, then, to look closely at the problems encountered in stepfamilies.

Living in a Stepfamily

What exactly is it about stepfamilies that makes them more vulnerable to breaking up than others? We need now to look more closely at the uniqueness of the stepfamily, including the troublesome stepparent-stepchild relationship.

The Structure of the Stepfamily

Stepfamilies function somewhat differently than other families because of certain structural differences (Peek, Bell, Waldren, and Sorell 1988). These structural differences make the stepfamily a greater challenge to our quest for intimacy.

Complexity

Stepfamilies are more complex because of the increased number of relationships. Thus, greater interpersonal skills are necessary in the stepfamily as people must deal with ex-spouses, the parents of ex-spouses (who are also grandparents), and various new steprelations. An additional point to keep in mind is that the complexity is there from the start. The spouses in a stepfamily have no child-free period of time in which to adjust to each other and build their marital relationship. Rather, they are immediately beset with an intricate and potentially troublesome set of relationships that can put considerable strain on their marriage.

The children, too, face a complex situation. Satir (1972:175) wrote of an adolescent girl who was acting "alternately crazy and depressed." The girl lived with her mother and stepfather, but alternated weekends with her father and his fiancée, her maternal grandparents, and her paternal grandparents. At each place, she was asked to tell about what went on at the other places and told to keep quiet about what was discussed "here." The girl became the unwitting victim of a network of jealous and angry people.

Ambiguous Family Boundaries

Family boundary is a concept from family systems theory, referring to rules about who is a member of the family and how much each member participates in family life. Family boundaries are not likely to be as clear-cut in the stepfamily. Family therapists have found that boundary ambiguity tends to be associated with stress and various problems in family functioning (Pasley and Ihinger-Tallman 1989). In the stepfamily, there may be considerable ambiguity.

For instance, in her study of sixty adolescents whose parents had divorced, Gross (1986) found four ways of defining family. A third of the adolescents defined family in terms of *retention*. They named both biological parents as part of the family, but did not include a stepparent. They considered stepparents mainly as outsiders who "just weren't related." Thirteen percent defined their families in terms of *substitution.* They excluded the missing biological parent and included the stepparent as a family member. However, they did not completely regard the stepparent as a parent. The stepparent was a family member, but not a total replacement for a parent.

A fourth of the adolescents chose a third category, *reduction,* in which they defined the family in terms of the biological parents with whom they were living. Some were living with a stepparent, but didn't include that person, while others were living with a single parent and excluded the nonresidential parent. Finally, 28 percent of the adolescents defined family in terms of *augmentation,* identifying both biological parents and any stepparent as a family member. They saw the stepparent as an addition to the family. Those who fell into this category tended to move freely between the homes of their biological parents and reported little hostility between the parents.

There are, then, differences in the way that the children of divorce define the boundaries of their family. Parents may also have vague ideas of exactly who is and who isn't a part of "our family." The problem may be compounded by pressures to make the boundaries more open than family members prefer (Ihinger-Tallman and Pasley 1987:55). For example, there may be pressure to allow a nonresidential child to visit whenever he or she wants. Life in such a stepfamily really gets complicated if the child's biological parent views the child as a family member who should be able to enter freely into the home and other family members view the nonresidential child as an outsider who needs permission to enter the home.

Normative Ambiguity

There are fewer cultural norms to deal with life in the stepfamily than in the intact family. This means that there must be a good deal more negotiation. What, precisely, is the role of a stepparent? What if the stepparent and the nonresidential biological parent differ on appropriate behavior for the child? What do stepparents and stepchildren call each other? How much interaction with an ex-spouse is appropriate? What obligations remain to relatives of an ex-spouse with whom one has had close ties in the past?

All such questions must be worked out by each stepfamily. There are no cultural norms that prescribe the behavior. Unfortunately, there may be as many different ideas about ways to answer the question as there are people in the stepfamily.

Stepparents and Stepchildren

What do the terms *stepparent* and *stepchild* mean to you? Is your initial reaction positive, neutral, or negative? Students generally tend to react negatively to the terms stepparent and stepchild (Bryan, Coleman, Ganong, and

Bryan 1986). In fact, those from stepfamilies as well as those from single-parent and intact families, have less positive perceptions of stepparents than of parents (Fine 1986).

This tendency toward casting the stepfamily in negative terms does not help members adjust easily to each other. Children are being pulled into something that they have learned to think of as negative. It would not be surprising, then, if many children entered the stepfamily with pessimism and the expectation of problems.

Older children may pose more problems for a stepparent than younger children. There is some evidence that stepparents have less positive relationships with older than with younger stepchildren (Hobart 1987). Even the adult children of those who remarry may create problems for a couple. A forty-five-year-old woman, whose sixty-nine-year-old mother remarried some years after being widowed, admitted that she had problems accepting her stepfather:

> One reason I got so upset was that I felt like mom's new husband was just after her money. Dad's money. Her new husband gave his house to his son and then moved in with mom. I remember dad saying that he didn't mind dying because he knew that his grandchildren and his great-grandchildren would be running around that house just like I did when I was little. But he left the house to mom. If she dies first, I'm afraid her new husband will get everything and my children and grandchildren will lose what my dad expected them to have.

Whatever their age, stepchildren can resent and resist a stepparent coming into the family.

Stepfathering

Because of custody arrangements over the past few decades, stepfathering with custody of the child has been more common than stepmothering with custody. How do stepfathers regard their performance? Apparently not very well. They tend to see themselves as less competent than either their wives or their stepchildren see them. They feel more inadequate in maintaining close physical and emotional contact with stepchildren than do biological fathers with their own children (Weingarten 1980).

Stepchildren report less support, control, and punishment from stepfathers than do children from biological fathers (Amato 1987). However, from the stepchild's point of view the relationship tends to improve over time and become more like that with a biological father. Stepfathers are more likely to be satisfied with their roles to the extent that they communicate often and well with stepchildren and to the extent that their wives support them in their involvement with and discipline of stepchildren (Ihinger-Tallman and Pasley 1987:100).

Disciplining is one of the more problematic tasks for a stepfather.

Discipline of stepchildren is a particularly problematic area. The child may resent discipline from a stepfather, and/or the mother may disagree with her husband about that discipline. If either or both of these situations exist, they can be disruptive factors that require patient and understanding negotiation among family members.

In spite of the stepfathers' perceptions and the problems that can arise, a number of studies have reported no significant differences between stepfather and intact families in such things as perceptions of family conflict and the quality of family relationships (Ganong and Coleman 1988). The majority of stepchildren say that they like their stepparents and get along well with them. Adults who were raised in stepfamilies seem to get along as well in family relationships as those raised in intact families.

There are some gender differences in the experiences of children in stepfather families, however. Although boys have a harder time adjusting to divorce than do girls, they seem to have an easier time adjusting to stepfamily life than do girls (Peterson and Zill 1986). Boys have warmer relationships with stepfathers than do girls. As noted earlier, one of the main problems boys seem to have with divorce is adjusting to living without a same-sex parent. The stepfather apparently fills that void for most boys.

Stepmothering

In his nonrandom sample of 232 Canadian families, Hobart (1987) found that stepmothers have less positive relationships with stepchildren than do stepfathers. The challenge of stepmothering is not helped by the fact that there is a long cultural tradition of the "wicked stepmother" (see Perspective). In addition, there are abundant illustrations of disastrous efforts at stepmothering. A woman whose marriage broke up because of step-children tells about the agony:

> I was in my early twenties when I married a man with two kids, one eight and one twelve. He had joint custody with his wife. I tried from the first to be their friend. Eventually the boy and I developed a good relationship. But the girl would have none of it. She never would look at me or talk to me directly if she could avoid it. I remember one time I suggested we all go camping on the next weekend. I thought it would be a good family activity. She turned to her father and said, "Does *she* have to go along?" He told her yes, because "she's my wife." They were talking about me as if I wasn't even in the room. My husband never tried to get her to change her behavior towards me. He was afraid she might stop spending time with us. I didn't want to make him choose between me and his daughter. So I left him.

Stepmothering isn't necessarily a painful experience (Ambert 1986). Some stepmothers report very close relationships with their stepchildren, and the majority of stepchildren report satisfying relationships with stepmothers. But stepmothering does seem to be more troublesome than stepfathering. Perhaps one factor in this is that stepmothering is more likely than stepfathering to involve a noncustodial relationship. When the stepchild is in the home, the stepmother rather than the child's father is likely to have the extra work of cleaning and cooking. The stepmother is called on to assume a burden that will have little or no emotional benefit to her. Not only is the stepchild not hers, but she may feel left out because the father is involving his ex-wife more than her in the parenting process.

Stepchildren and the Marital Relationship

Stepparents are more likely than biological parents to perceive strains on their marriage from the parenting experience. White and Booth (1985:695–96) reported that those with stepchildren in their homes are more likely than others to prefer living apart from the children and to perceive the children as giving them problems. They are also less likely to be satisfied with their spouse's relationship with their children. Finally, they are more prone to see the marriage as having a negative effect on the children and more likely to say that if they could do it all over they would not have married. In fact, 15 percent of those with stepchildren said they wouldn't have married, compared with only 6 percent of those without stepchildren. Not surprisingly, those with stepchildren reported somewhat less marital happiness than others.

The Unacceptable Stepmother

As noted in the text, the very word *stepparent* tends to have negative connotations for us. In part, this is because stepparents are portrayed in very negative terms in literature. Consider the wicked stepfather in Shakespeare's *Hamlet* and Dickens's *David Copperfield*, or the wicked stepmother in such children's stories as *Snow White, Hansel and Gretel,* and *Cinderella*. The following ballad, part of a collection of Missouri folklore, tells the reaction of a blind girl to the news of her father's remarriage. The girl cannot accept the notion of a stepmother in the home. Her grief over the situation eventually leads to her death:

"They tell me, father, that tonight
You wed another bride,
And that you'll clasp her in your arms
Where my poor mother died.

"They say her name is Mary, too,
The name my mother bore.
Oh, tell me, is she kind and true
As the one you loved before?

"And is her step so soft and low,
her voice so sweet and mild,
And do you think that she will love
Your blind and only child?

"Please, father, do not bid me come
To greet your loving bride.
I could not meet her in the room
Where my poor mother died.

"Her picture's hanging on the wall,
Her books are lying near;

And there's the harp her fingers touched;
And there's her vacant chair—
"The chair whereby I've often knelt
To say my evening prayer.
Oh! father, it would break my heart.
I could not meet her there.

"I love you but I long to go
To yon bright world so fair
Where God is true, and I am sure
There'll be no blind ones there.

"Now let me kneel down by your side
And to our Savior pray
That God's right hand may shield you both
Through life's long dreary way.

"My prayers are ended now, dear pa.
I'm tired now," she said.
He picked her up all in his arms
And laid her on the bed.

And as he turned to leave the room
A joyful cry was given.
He heard, and caught the last sweet smile—
His blind child was in heaven.

They laid her by her mother's side
And raised a marble fair,
And but engraved these simple words:
"There'll be no blind ones there."

William Tyler, *The Blind Girl*

Wives are more likely to see their marital relationship affected by the husband's relationships with the children (his children, her children, or their children) than vice versa (Hobart and Brown 1988). Marital satisfaction is also affected by the type of family. Satisfaction is significantly lower when both spouses bring children to the marriage than when only one had children by a previous marriage (Clingempeel 1981). Satisfaction also is significantly affected by the living arrangements of the stepchildren. Stepmothers who have the least amount of difficulty and report the highest amount of marital satisfaction are those who have live-in stepchildren rather than stepchildren who visit the home (Ambert 1986). While a live-in stepchild is not necessarily an easy situation, stepmothers apparently find it easier to develop a close relationship with the live-in child. Thus, the greater frequency of problems with stepmothers than stepfathers may be rooted in the fact that most stepmothers do not have live-in stepchildren.

There are a variety of reasons why stepchildren can adversely affect the marital relationship (Sager, Steer, Crohn, Rodstein, and Walker 1980). The stepfamily is an instant creation rather than a gradual process of pregnancy, birth, and intimate relationships from the beginning of the child's life. Coming into an instant family, and dealing with the challenges and issues of that stage of the family life cycle, may not be fully compatible with the stepparent's individual stage of life. As one stepmother put it:

> I do my best. I really like my stepdaughter. But I find myself still thinking about the fact that I'm raising another woman's child. And meanwhile I'm trying to establish my career. It's not quite fair. But I remind myself that I do like her and that she is my husband's child.

Another factor that complicates the stepfamily is that the ex-spouse and his or her parents may continue to have input into the children's lives. This can contribute to divided loyalties. The stepchild may like the stepparent but get conflicting guidance from the stepparent and the absent biological parent, or may simply feel that liking the stepparent too much is disloyalty to the absent biological parent.

In addition, the stepchild may still be suffering from the emotional trauma of loss of the absent parent. In such cases, the stepchild may act out his or her anger against the stepparent. Even when the child is consulted about the remarriage, the child may feel resentment. The biological parent, then, is torn between loyalty to the child and loyalty to the new spouse.

Adjustment of Stepchildren
In spite of the problems that can arise, not only are the majority of children in stepfamilies satisfied with their stepparents, but they have no more behavior problems or negative attitudes toward themselves or others than do children in intact families (Ganong and Coleman 1984). Children in stepfamilies are not lower than those in intact families in self-esteem, psychological functioning, or academic achievement (Ihinger-Tallman and Pasley 1987:89).

In spite of many problems, most children in stepfamilies are satisfied with their stepparents.

What about longer-term consequences? Surveys carried out by the national opinion research center asked respondents about their living arrangements at the age of sixteen. Beer (1988) pooled results from a twelve-year period and found some interesting differences depending on whether the respondents lived with both biological parents, a father and a stepmother, or a mother and stepfather (table 19.2). Males from intact families scored better than those from stepfamilies on seven out of ten of the measures, while females from intact families scored better than others on five of the measures. A close examination of table 19.2 shows that no simple conclusions can be drawn. In some things, people from stepfamilies scored better than those from intact families. Overall, both males and females from intact families had somewhat better emotional adjustment (as defined by the five items in the survey) than did those from stepfamilies. And males from intact families had better social adjustment. But an intact family yielded little or no advantage to female social adjustment or to the familial adjustment of males or females.

Another interesting finding in table 19.2 are the differences between the backgrounds of stepfathers and stepmothers. In spite of the research that shows that stepmothers have more problems with children, only the females from stepmother families reported less adjustment than those from stepfather families. For males, those from stepmother families scored higher than those from

Table 19.2   Long-Term Adjustment by Type of Family Background

	Males At age sixteen, lived with:			Females At age sixteen, lived with:		
	Mother and father	Father and stepmother	Mother and stepfather	Mother and father	Father and stepmother	Mother and stepfather
Emotional adjustment	Percent					
Say they are very happy	34	38	23	39	24	34
Believe most people try to be helpful	51	41	43	60	56	57
Believe most people try to be fair	63	66	54	69	66	60
Believe most people can be trusted	51	41	41	46	44	42
Find life exciting	50	34	44	44	32	49
Social adjustment						
Very satisfied with job	50	43	41	51	48	50
Get a very great deal of satisfaction from friendships	29	27	24	35	25	37
Respond "no" when asked if they drink more than they should	52	49	48	69	73	55
Familial adjustment						
Very happy married	70	65	66	67	57	67
Get a very great deal of satisfaction from family life	42	43	36	47	30	49

From William Beer, "New Family Ties: How Well Are We Coping?" in *Public Opinion*, March/April 1988:15. Copyright © 1988 American Enterprise Institute. Reprinted with the permission of the American Enterprise Institute for Public Policy Research.

stepfather families on six of the ten measures. Finally, note that males from stepfather families and females from stepmother families were much less likely than others to say that they are very happy, and had the lowest scores on a majority of the ten measures. It may be, then, that the most difficult time for children occurs when the stepparent is the same sex as the stepchild.

Family Functioning

Apart from the stepparent-stepchild relationship, how do people see the step-family as a whole? How well does the stepfamily function? A study of 631 college students reported that those from stepfamilies perceived less cohesion and more stress in family life than did those from intact families (Kennedy 1985). Using a smaller sample of twenty-eight intact and twenty-eight step-families, Pink and Wampler (1985) obtained ratings from both parents and adolescent children and also found lower levels of cohesion in the stepfamilies. In addition, the stepfamily respondents reported lower levels of adaptability, the family's ability to successfully deal with differing problems and situations.

Thus, stepfamilies tend to have less closeness between members and less ability to change when confronted with stress than do intact families. The same results, plus some additional findings, were reported by four researchers who compared 106 intact with 108 stepfamilies (Peek et al. 1988). Not only did the stepfamilies score lower on cohesion and adaptability, but also on expressiveness (the extent to which people feel free to express their feelings to other family members), ability to manage conflict effectively, problem-solving skills, openness of communication, and the quality of relationships.

Again, it is important to emphasize that these results do not mean that stepfamilies are all in trouble. Lower scores do not mean pathological scores. The point is not that life in a stepfamily is miserable. The point is that stepfamilies tend to function at a somewhat lower level than in intact families. You will probably not be damaged by living in a stepfamily; you may not, however, have the same experience of family closeness and flexibility as someone who grows up in an intact family.

On the other hand, there are a number of potential strengths in stepfamilies (Coleman, Ganong, and Gingrich 1985). The divorced parent may feel less harrassed by financial problems and childrearing responsibilities when he or she remarries. The children of divorce may benefit more from the stepfamily than the single-parent experience. In fact, children from stepfamilies are more like those from intact families than are children from single-parent families.

In stepfamilies, new people with new ideas and skills are encountered—sources of new opportunities for children. Children also once again have a model of marriage and of adult intimacy. Having seen one marriage break up, they may benefit by a second marriage that shows them that adults can have a stable and happy relationship.

The merging of two families in the stepfamily means that children come into a situation that requires a good deal of negotiation and flexibility. They may learn much about how, and how not to, cope effectively with other people in situations that require the working out of differences. As a result, stepchildren can be more accommodating and adaptable in their adult relationships.

In sum, there are both advantages and disadvantages to stepfamily life. Overall, your chances of growing up in a stable and healthy environment are somewhat less in a stepfamily than in an intact family. But for those stepfamilies that function well, the outcome will be similar to the well-functioning intact family.

Making It Work

Tanya is a thirty-four-year-old secretary who is expecting her first child. She is in her second marriage. At the age of twenty, she married her high-school sweetheart. The union lasted six years. "It was a clear example of the conflict-habituated marriage," she recalls. "We were both pulling our own way and expecting the other to 'prove how much you love me.' " At one point, they moved to a different state, hoping the move would give their marriage a fresh start. When it didn't, her husband moved back but Tanya remained where she was. They divorced. She met another man, and remarried a year later. She is delighted: "It was, and continues to be, six and one-half years later, wonderful to have someone with whom I can truly share my life. With him, I have found the intimacy that is so important for well-being and growth."

Clearly, not everyone who remarries will have Tanya's experience. But second marriages, including those involving stepfamilies, can work out well and be stable and satisfying. In our study of long-term marriages, about 10 percent of the couples involved a remarriage (Lauer and Lauer 1986). What factors are at work in those second marriages and stepfamilies that succeed?

First, as far as the marriage itself is concerned, the same factors that make a first marriage work well also apply to a second marriage. For example, we have talked about the importance of communication. A therapist told us that some remarried couples make the mistake of giving priority to the needs of their children over their needs as a couple. He suggests, however, that parents in a remarriage should set aside a minimum amount of time each day and some special times on weekends when they can be alone. One of the best things a couple can do for their children, he notes, is to show them that their parent and stepparent care about each other and need to spend time together to enrich their marriage. It is also one of the best things they can do for their relationship as husband and wife. Second marriages, like first marriages, need careful nurturing.

Furthermore, there are a number of important tasks that stepfamilies face (Ihinger-Tallman and Pasley 1987:117–18). One task is to give up fantasies and unrealistic expectations about the stepfamily. To expect the remarriage to solve all of one's problems, to be the beginning of living happily ever after, is no more realistic for a second than a first marriage. The remarriage, like the first, will have problems as well as, hopefully, rewards.

A second task is to gain a clear understanding of the feelings and the needs of each member of the stepfamily. These feelings and needs must be taken into account as the stepfamily works on the third task: developing its own unique roles, rules, and routines. The purpose of these tasks is to help the stepfamily to become a solid unit rather than a group of disparate people forced into a common living arrangement.

In sum, remarriage and the stepfamily represent another effort to create meaningful intimate relationships after the first effort has failed. The task is no easier the second time. On the contrary, it is more difficult. But millions of Americans have already shown that it can be done. A failed quest for intimacy does not mean that the quest is fruitless. With patience, understanding, and hard work, fulfilling intimate relationships are within the grasp of each of us.

PRINCIPLES FOR ENHANCING INTIMACY

The following suggestions, published by the U.S. Department of Health, Education, and Welfare (1978), are very useful principles for dealing with the special problems of being a stepparent:

1. Let the relationship with stepchildren develop gradually. Don't force it. Remember that both stepparents and stepchildren need time to adjust.

2. Don't try to replace the lost parent. Try to be an additional parent to the child.

3. Expect a confusion of various feelings in each member of the stepfamily. There will be anxiety, ambivalence, feelings of divided loyalties, love, caring, and other feelings all mixed together over the course of creating the new family unit.

4. Be prepared for comparisons with the absent parent. Work out with your spouse what is best for you and the stepchildren and stand by it.

5. You will need support from your spouse in rearing the children. It is important that the two of you agree. Raising children is a difficult task; raising someone else's children can be even harder.

6. Make every effort to be open and fair and honest with both stepchildren and children. Openly acknowledge good relations between stepsiblings.

7. Try to recognize and admit your need for help if the situation becomes too difficult for you. We all need help at times. There are numerous counselors and organizations available to help people with the difficult task of stepparenting.

SUMMARY

People may enter a remarriage from one of five different situations. One partner may have been single. And one or both partners may have been divorced or widowed with no children, divorced or widowed with custody of children, divorced or widowed without custody of children, or divorced or widowed with custody of some children but not others. Most of the more than million Americans who divorce each year will remarry and many of the remarriages will involve children. The divorce rate is slightly higher among second than first marriages when both partners were married previously, and are even higher when one or both partners bring children to the marriage.

Second marriages fare better if there is a period of three to five years of dating after the divorce. But about half of those who remarry do so within three years. Those who remarry tend to spend less time in dating and engagement to second spouses. They also do little to prepare for a second marriage other than living together, though some get counseling or seek advice through friends or books. People remarry for the same reasons they marry the first time; in addition, some may be looking for suitable stepparents for their children.

There are some myths about remarriage that can be detrimental to the relationship. There are also challenges and issues that are peculiar to remarriage. The kin relations are complex and the roles may be ambiguous. There may be unresolved emotional issues from the first marriage. There are issues of children and finances and legal matters.

The quality of remarried life depends on such things as companionship, feelings, and satisfaction with parenting. Remarried people tend to report as satisfying relationships as those in first marriages.

Stepfamilies are unique family forms because of their complexity (the large number of relationships involved), ambiguous family boundaries, and normative ambiguity. There is a tendency for the very term *stepfamily* to have negative connotations.

Stepfathers tend to feel inadequate. Their stepchildren report less support, control, and punishment than do children of biological fathers. Yet the relationship tends to improve over time and become more like that with a biological father. Discipline is a particularly problematic area. However, the majority of stepchildren say they like stepparents and get along well with them, though boys have an easier time than girls in adjusting to stepfamily life.

Stepmothers have less positive relationships with stepchildren than do stepfathers. Still a majority of their stepchildren report satisfying relationships. One of the reasons stepmothering poses more problems than stepfathering is it is more likely to involve a noncustodial relationship.

Stepparents are more likely than biological parents to perceive strains on the marriage from the parenting experience, and satisfaction is significantly lower when both spouses bring children to the marriage. Noncustodial stepchildren tend to create more problems than those who live in the stepfamily.

In spite of the problems, the majority of children in stepfamilies are satisfied with their stepparents and seem to have no greater incidence of problems than children in intact families. In the long run, however, both males and females from intact families have somewhat better emotional adjustment, and males have somewhat better social adjustment, than those who grow up in stepfamilies. There tends to be less cohesion, less adaptability, and more stress in stepfamilies. There are also strengths, particularly compared with those growing up in single-parent families.

The same factors that make a first marriage work well also apply to the second marriage. For the stepfamily to work well, the partners must try to give up any fantasies and unrealistic expectations about family life and gain a clear understanding of the feelings and needs of each member of the stepfamily.

GLOSSARY

abortion
expulsion of the fetus from the uterus   219

alcohol abuse
improper use of alcohol such that the consequences are detrimental to the user and the family   489

androgyny
possession of both traditional masculine, or instrumental, and traditional feminine, or expressive, traits   185

artificial insemination
injection of sperm into a woman's vagina   369

assortative mating
marriage between people who are similar on one or more characteristics   125

birth rate
number of births per one thousand women in the childbearing years (fifteen to forty-four years of age)   356

bundling
two people sleeping on the same bed without undressing   76

celibacy
abstaining from sexual relations   15

cohabitation
living with someone in an intimate, sexual relationship without being legally married   9

commuter marriage
a dual-career marriage in which the spouses live in different areas   331

companionate love
affection for, and commitment to, someone with whom one is deeply involved   98

contraception
use of devices or techniques to prevent fertilization   213

courtship
the process whereby two people agree to commit themselves to marriage   73

cunnilingus
oral stimulation of the female genitalia   221

death rate
the number of deaths per one thousand population   394

dual-career family
a family in which both spouses are in careers and have a commitment to work that has a long-term pattern of mobility   325

dual-earner family
a family in which both spouses are involved in paid work outside the home, and one or both view the work only as a job rather than a career   325

ejaculation
discharge of semen from the penis during orgasm   200

endometriosis
a disease in which the tissue that lines the inside of the uterus grows outside as well   367

equity
fairness, in the sense that people are rewarded in proportion to their contributions   41

expressive traits
those traits, associated with the traditional female sex role, that facilitate good relationships   182

extended family
a group of three or more generations formed as an outgrowth of the parent-child relationship   4

familism
a value on family living   22

family boundary
a system concept, referring to rules about who is a member of the family and how each member participates in family life   559

family of origin
the family into which one is born   3

fellatio
oral stimulation of the male genitalia   221

573

gay
a male homosexual   79

gender
male or female   179

group marriage
a form of marriage in which members of a group are each married to every other opposite-sex member of the group   16

heterogamy
marriage between people who are dissimilar in social and demographic characteristics   125

homogamy
marriage between people who are similar in social and demographic characteristics   125

homophobia
an irrational fear of homosexuality   472

hypergamy
marriage with someone who is from a higher socioeconomic background   125

incest
any type of exploitive sexual contact between relatives in which the victim is under eighteen years of age   495

infertility
failure to conceive after one year of unprotected intercourse   366

institution
a collective, regularized solution to a problem of social life such as economic or family arrangements   240

instrumental traits
those traits, associated with the traditional male sex role, that facilitate goal achievement   182

integration
the state of being a significant and meaningful part of some group   33

intimacy
a relationship characterized by mutual commitment, affection, and sharing   3

in vitro fertilization
removal of eggs of a woman's body, fertilizing them with sperm in a laboratory, and implanting the resulting embryo in the woman's uterus   370

jealousy
a negative emotional reaction to a real or imagined threat to a love relationship   110

joint custody
an arrangement in which both divorced parents continue to share responsibility for the care and raising of their children   539

lesbian
a female homosexual   79

loneliness
a feeling of isolation from desired relationships   31

marriage rate
the proportion of unmarried women, ages fifteen and above, who get married during a year   238

misattribution of arousal
attributing the wrong emotion to physical arousal   93

monogamy
marriage to one person at a time   14

network family
a support group of nonkin others   159

nonverbal cues
facial expressions, body position, gestures, and paralanguage (inflection, rate and loudness of speaking, etc.) that communicate meaning   45

norm
an expected pattern of behavior   51

nuclear family
a group composed of husband, wife, and children, if any   4

orgasm
third phase of the sexual response cycle in which there is a sudden discharge of sexual tension   201

ovulation
release of an egg from the ovary   367

passionate love
a preoccupation with and intense longing for union with a particular other   98

penis
male sex organ   200

power
ability to get someone to think, feel, or act in a way that he or she would not have done spontaneously   294

promiscuity
frequent and indiscriminate sexual relations with many partners   207

propinquity
nearness in place   50

rape
attempted or actual sexual intercourse by the use of force or the threat of force   67

rapport
a harmonious and comfortable relationship with someone   92

reactance theory
people resist coercion even when the behavior is consistent with their attitudes   300

refractory period
period of time after ejaculation by the male during which he cannot have another orgasm   202

reframe
redefine the meaning of something in order to make it more acceptable   508

resilient family
a family that can resist disruption in the face of change and cope effectively with crises   506

resource theory
the balance of power in a marriage reflects the relative resources that each spouse has   297

rite of passage
a ceremony that recognizes a significant time of change in an individual's life   404

self-concept
the totality of an individual's beliefs and attitudes about himself or herself   193

self-disclosure
the honest revealing of oneself to another   53

semen
the fluid that carries the sperm and is ejaculated during orgasm   202

serial marriage
three or more marriages as a result of repeated divorces   549

sex ratio
the number of males per one hundred females   151

sex role
behavior associated with the status of being male or female   179

sex-role orientation
conception of the self as having some combination of masculine and feminine traits   179

sexual dysfunction
impairment of the physical responses in sexual activity   231

social class
a social group consisting of people with similar income, education, and occupational prestige   51

social integration
a state of relative harmony and cohesion in a group   525

socialization
the process of learning to function effectively in a group   63

sole custody
an arrangement in which the responsibility for the care and raising of children of a divorce is given to one of the parents   539

static
interference of some kind with accurate communication   270

status
the prestige attached to a particular position in society   62

stepfamily
a remarriage in which one or both of the spouses has children from a previous marriage   547

stereotype
a standardized image of something or someone that exists among a group of people   44

sterilization
a surgical procedure that prevents fertilization   216

testes
the male reproductive glands that hang in the scrotum   200

vagina
female canal that receives the penis during intercourse   200

REFERENCES

Abbey, Antonia. 1982. "Sex Differences in Attributions for Friendly Behavior: Do Males Misperceive Females' Friendliness?" *Journal of Personality and Social Psychology* 42:830–38.

Abloff, Richard, and Jay Hewitt. 1985. "Attraction to Men and Women Varying in Self-Esteem." *Psychological Reports* 56:615–18.

Abrahamse, Allan F., Peter A. Morrison, and Linda J. Waite. 1988. "Teenagers Willing to Consider Single Parenthood: Who Is at Greatest Risk?" *Family Planning Perspectives* 20:13–19.

Ahrons, Constance R., and Lynn S. Wallisch. 1987. "The Relationship between Former Spouses." In D. Perlman and S. Duck, eds., *Intimate Relationships: Development, Dynamics, and Deterioration.* Beverly Hills, Calif.: Sage.

Alba, Richard D., and Reid M. Golden. 1986. "Patterns of Ethnic Marriage in the United States." *Social Forces* 65:202–23.

Albers, Lawrence J., Jeri A. Doane, and Jim Mintz. 1986. "Social Competence and Family Environment: 15-Year Follow-Up of Disturbed Adolescents." *Family Process* 25:379–89.

Aldous, Joan. 1987. "New Views on the Family Life of the Elderly and the Near-Elderly." *Journal of Marriage and the Family* 49:227–34.

Allen, Agaitha, and Teresa Thompson. 1984. "Agreement, Understanding, Realization, and Feeling Understood as Predictors of Communicative Satisfaction in Marital Dyads." *Journal of Marriage and the Family* 46:915–21.

Allen, Katherine R., and Robert S. Pickett. 1987. "Forgotten Streams in the Family Life Course: Utilization of Qualitative Retrospective Interviews in the Analysis of Lifelong Single Women's Family Careers." *Journal of Marriage and the Family* 49:517–26.

Allport, Gordon. 1961. *Pattern and Growth in Personality.* New York: Holt, Rinehart & Winston.

Alpert, Dona, and Amy Culbertson. 1987. "Daily Hassles and Coping Strategies of Dual-Earner and Nondual-Earner Women." *Psychology of Women Quarterly* 11:359–66.

Amato, Paul R. 1986. "Marital Conflict, the Parent-Child Relationship and Child Self-Esteem." *Family Relations* 35:403–10.

———. 1987. "Family Processes in One-Parent, Stepparent, and Intact Families: The Child's Point of View." *Journal of Marriage and the Family* 49:327–37.

———. 1988a. "Long-Term Implications of Parental Divorce for Adult Self-Concept." *Journal of Family Issues* 9:201–13.

———. 1988b. "Parental Divorce and Attitudes Toward Marriage and Family Life." *Journal of Marriage and the Family* 50:453–61.

Amato, Paul R., and Gay Ochiltree. 1986. "Family Resources and the Development of Child Competence." *Journal of Marriage and the Family* 48:47–56.

Ambert, Anne-Marie. 1982. "Differences in Children's Behavior toward Custodial Mothers and Custodial Fathers." *Journal of Marriage and the Family* 44:73–86.

———. 1986. "Being a Stepparent: Live-in and Visiting Stepchildren." *Journal of Marriage and the Family* 48:795–804.

Ammon, Richard Albright. 1985. "When There's No Wedding, How Do You Know You're Married? The Development and Characteristics of Bonding in Long-Term Gay Male Relationships." Ph.D. diss., U.S. International University, San Diego.

Anderson, Stephen A., Candyce S. Russell, and Walter R. Schumm. 1983. "Perceived Marital Quality and Family Life-Cycle Categories: A Further Analysis." *Journal of Marriage and the Family* 45:127–39.

Anonymous. 1878. "Some Plain Answers." *The Shaker Manifesto* 9:223–24.

Antonucci, Toni C., and Hiroko Akiyama. 1987. "An Examination of Sex Differences in Social Support among Older Men and Women." *Sex Roles* 17:737–48.

Archer, Richard L., and Christie E. Cook. 1986. "Personalistic Self-Disclosure and Attraction: Basis for Relationship or Scarce Resource." *Social Psychology Quarterly* 49:268–72.

Arendell, Terry. 1986. *Mothers and Divorce: Legal, Economic, and Social Dilemmas.* Berkeley and Los Angeles: University of California Press.

Arnstein, Helene S. 1985. *Between Mothers-In-Law and Daughters-In-Law.* New York: Dodd, Mead.

Aschenbrenner, Joyce, and Carolyn Hameedah Carr. 1980. "Conjugal Relationships in the Context of the Extended Black Family." *Alternative Lifestyles* 3:463–84.

Association of American Colleges. 1982. *The Classroom Climate: A Chilly One for Women?* Washington, D.C.: Association of American Colleges.

Atkinson, Maxine P., and Becky L. Glass. 1985. "Marital Age Heterogamy and Homogamy." *Journal of Marriage and the Family* 47:685–91.

Austrom, Douglas, and Kim Hanel. 1985. "Psychological Issues of Single Life in Canada: An Exploratory Study." *International Journal of Women's Studies* 8:12–23.

Bachrach, Christine A. 1986. "Adoption Plans, Adopted Children, and Adoptive Mothers." *Journal of Marriage and the Family* 48:243–53.

Backman, Carl W. 1981. "Attraction in Interpersonal Relationships." In M. Rosenberg and R. H. Turner, eds., *Social Psychology: Sociological Perspectives.* New York: Basic Books.

Baer, Paul E., Lisa-Berg Garmezy, Robert J. McLaughlin, Alex D. Pokorny, and Mark J. Wernick. 1987. "Stress, Coping, Family Conflict, and Adolescent Alcohol Use." *Journal of Behavioral Medicine* 10:449–66.

Bailey, William C., Clyde Hendrick, and Susan S. Hendrick. 1987. "Relation of Sex and Gender Role to Love, Sexual Attitudes, and Self-Esteem." *Sex Roles* 16:637–48.

Bales, Alba. 1929. "A Course in Home Economics for College Men." *Journal of Home Economics* 21:427–28.

Barbarin, Oscar A., Diane Hughes, and Mark A. Chesler. 1985. "Stress, Coping, and Marital Functioning among Parents of Children with Cancer." *Journal of Marriage and the Family* 47:473–80.

Bardwell, Jill R., Samuel W. Cochran, and Sharon Walker. 1986. "Relationship of Parental Education, Race, and Gender to Sex Role Stereotyping in Five-Year-Old Kindergartners." *Sex Roles* 15:275–81.

Barranti, Chrystal C. Ramirez. 1985. "The Grandparent/Grandchild Relationship: Family Resource in an Era of Voluntary Bonds." *Family Relations* 34:343–52.

Bart, Pauline M. 1971. "Depression in Middle-Aged Women." In V. Gornick and B. K. Moran, eds., *Woman In Sexist Society.* New York: Mentor.

Basting, Louis. 1887. "Reply." *The Manifesto* 16:91.

Beck, Aaron T. 1988. *Love Is Never Enough.* New York: Harper & Row.

Beckett, Joyce O. 1976. "Working Wives: A Racial Comparison." *Social Work* 21:463–71.

Beer, William. 1988. "New Family Ties: How Well Are We Coping?" *Public Opinion* (March/April): 14–15, 57.

Bell, Alan, and Martin Weinberg. 1978. *Homosexualities: A Study of Diversity among Men and Women.* New York: Simon & Schuster.

Bellah, Robert N., Richard Madsen, William M. Sullivan, Ann Swidler, and Steven M. Tipton. 1985. *Habits of the Heart: Individualism and Commitment in American Life.* New York: Harper & Row.

Bellamy, Edward. 1960. *Looking Backward.* New York: Signet.

Belsky, Jay. 1985. "Exploring Individual Differences in Marital Change across the Transition to Parenthood: The Role of Violated Expectations." *Journal of Marriage and the Family* 47:1037–44.

Bem, Sandra L. 1974. "The Measurement of Psychological Androgyny." *Journal of Consulting and Clinical Psychology* 42:155–62.

Benin, Mary Holland, and Joan Agostinelli. 1988. "Husbands' and Wives' Satisfaction with the Division of Labor." *Journal of Marriage and the Family* 50:349–61.

Benin, Mary Holland, and Barbara Cable Nienstedt. 1985. "Happiness in Single- and Dual-Earner Families: The Effects of Marital Happiness, Job Satisfaction, and Life Cycle." *Journal of Marriage and the Family* 47:975–84.

Bennett, Linda A., Steven J. Wolin, David Reiss, and Martha A. Teitelbaum. 1987. "Couples at Risk for Transmission of Alcoholism: Protective Influences." *Family Process* 26:111–29.

Bennett, Neil G., Ann Klimas Blanc, and David E. Bloom. 1988. "Commitment and the Modern Union: Assessing the Link between Premarital Cohabitation and Subsequent Marital Stability." *American Sociological Review* 53:127–38.

Berardo, Donna Hodgkins, Constance L. Shehan, and Gerald R. Leslie. 1987. "A Residue of Tradition: Jobs, Careers, and Spouses' Time in Housework." *Journal of Marriage and the Family* 49:381–90.

Berelson, Bernard. 1979. "The Value of Children: A Taxonomical Essay." In J. G. Wells, ed., *Current Issues in Marriage and the Family.* 2d ed. New York: Macmillan.

Berg, John H., and Ronald D. McQuinn. 1986. "Attraction and Exchange in Continuing and Noncontinuing Dating Relationships." *Journal of Personality and Social Psychology* 50:942–52.

Bernard, Jessie. 1972. *The Future of Marriage.* New York: World.

———. 1974. *The Future of Motherhood.* New York: Dial Press.

———. 1975. "Note on Changing Life Styles, 1970–1974." *Journal of Marriage and the Family* 37:582–93.

———. 1981. "The Good Provider Role: Its Rise and Fall." *American Psychologist* 36:1–12.

Bernard, J. L., S. L. Bernard, and M. L. Bernard. 1985. "Courtship Violence and Sex-Typing." *Family Relations* 34:573–76.

Bernstein, Barton E., and Sheila K. Collins. 1985. "Remarriage Counseling: Lawyer and Therapist's Help with the Second Time Around." *Family Relations* 34:387–91.

Berscheid, Ellen, and Elaine Walster. 1974. "A Little Bit about Love." In T. L. Huston, ed., *Foundations of Interpersonal Attraction.* New York: Academic Press.

———. 1978. *Interpersonal Attraction.* Reading, Mass.: Addison-Wesley.

Bienvenu, Millard J., Sr. 1978. *A Counselor's Guide to Accompany a Marital Communications Inventory.* Saluda, N.C.: Family Life.

Bitter, Robert G. 1986. "Late Marriage and Marital Instability: The Effects of Heterogeneity and Inflexibility." *Journal of Marriage and the Family* 48:631–40.

Blood, Robert O., Jr., and Donald M. Wolfe. 1960. *Husbands and Wives.* New York: Free Press.

Blumstein, Philip, and Pepper Schwartz. 1983. *American Couples: Money, Work, Sex.* New York: William Morrow.

Blyth, Dale A., and Frederick S. Foster-Clark. 1987. "Gender Differences in Perceived Intimacy with Different Members of Adolescents' Social Networks." *Sex Roles* 17:689–718.

Bohannan, Paul. 1970. *Divorce and After.* New York: Doubleday.

———. 1985. *All the Happy Families: Exploring the Varieties of Family Life.* New York: McGraw-Hill.

Bolger, Niall, Anita DeLongis, Ronald C. Kessler, and Elaine Wethington. 1989. "The Contagion of Stress across Multiple Roles." *Journal of Marriage and the Family* 51:175–83.

Bolton, Frank, Jr. 1980. *The Pregnant Adolescent.* Beverly Hills, Calif.: Sage.

Bonkowski, Sara E., Sara J. Boomhower, and Shelly Q. Bequette. 1985. "What You Don't Know *Can* Hurt You: Unexpressed Fears and Feelings of Children from Divorcing Families." *Journal of Divorce* 91:33–45.

Booth, Alan, David B. Brinkerhoff, and Lynn K. White. 1984. "The Impact of Parental Divorce on Courtship." *Journal of Marriage and the Family* 46:85–94.

Booth, Alan, David R. Johnson, Lynn K. White, and John N. Edwards. 1984. "Women, Outside Employment, and Marital Instability." *American Journal of Sociology* 90:567–83.

———. 1986. "Divorce and Marital Instability over the Life Course." *Journal of Family Issues* 7:421–42.

Borland, Delores. 1982. "A Cohort Analysis Approach to the Empty-Nest Syndrome among Three Ethnic Groups of Women: A Theoretical Position." *Journal of Marriage and the Family* 44:117–29.

Boss, Pauline. 1988. *Family Stress Management.* Beverly Hills, Calif.: Sage.

Bowen, Gary L. 1987. "Changing Gender-Role Preferences and Marital Adjustment: Implications for Clinical Practice." *Family Therapy* 14:17–29.

Bowen, Murray. 1978. *Family Therapy In Clinical Practice.* New York: Jason Aronson.

Boyd, Lenore Anglin, and Arthur J. Roach. 1977. "Interpersonal Communication Skills Differentiating More Satisfying from Less Satisfying Marital Relationships." *Journal of Counseling Psychology* 24:540–42.

Brannon, Robert. 1976. "The Male Sex Role: Our Culture's Blueprint for Manhood, What It's Done for Us Lately." In D. David and R. Brannon, eds., *The Forty-Nine Percent Majority: The Male Sex Role.* Reading, Mass.: Addison-Wesley.

Brazzell, Jan F., and Alan C. Acock. 1988. "Influence of Attitudes, Significant Others, and Aspirations on How Adolescents Intend to Resolve a Premarital Pregnancy." *Journal of Marriage and the Family* 50:413–25.

Breault, K. D., and Augustine J. Kposowa. 1987. "Explaining Divorce in the United States: A Study of 3,111 Counties, 1980." *Journal of Marriage and the Family* 49:549–58.

Brehm, Jack W. 1966. *A Theory of Psychological Reactance.* New York: Academic Press.

Bremer, Fredrika. 1853. *The Homes of the New World: Impressions of America.* Translated by Mary Howitt. New York: Harper & Brothers.

Bretl, Daniel J., and Joanne Cantor. 1988. "The Portrayal of Men and Women in U.S. Television Commercials: A Recent Content Analysis and Trends over 15 Years." *Sex Roles* 18:595–609.

Bretschneider, Judy G., and Norma L. McCoy. 1988. "Sexual Interest and Behavior in Healthy 80- to 102-Year Olds." *Archives of Sexual Behavior* 17:109–29.

Brillinger, Margaret E. 1985. "Marital Satisfaction and Planned Change." *Family Perspective* 19:35–43.

Brody, Gene H., Eileen Neubaum, and Rex Forehand. 1988. "Serial Marriage: A Heuristic Analysis of an Emerging Family Form." *Psychological Bulletin* 103:211–22.

Brody, Robert. 1985. "New Research Dispels Myths about Unhappy Retirements." *San Diego Union,* Dec. 20.

Broman, Clifford L. 1988a. "Household Work and Family Life Satisfaction of Blacks." *Journal of Marriage and the Family* 50:743–48.

———. 1988b. "Satisfaction among Blacks: The Significance of Marriage and Parenthood." *Journal of Marriage and the Family* 50:45–51.

Brown, George W., and Tirril Harris. 1978. *Social Origins of Depression.* New York: Free Press.

Bryan, Linda R., Marilyn Coleman, Lawrence Ganong, and S. Hugh Bryan. 1986. "Person Perception: Family Structure as a Cue for Stereotyping." *Journal of Marriage and the Family* 48:169–74.

Buehler, Cheryl. 1987. "Initiator Status and the Divorce Transition." *Family Relations* 36:82–86.

Buehler, Cheryl, and Mary Langenbrunner. 1987. "Divorce-related Stressors: Occurrence, Disruptiveness, and Area of Life Change." *Journal of Divorce* 11:25–50.

Buhrmester, Duane, and Wyndol Furman. 1987. "The Development of Companionship and Intimacy." *Child Development* 58:1101–13.

Bulcroft, Kris, and Margaret O'Connor. 1986. "The Importance of Dating Relationships on Quality of Life for Older Persons." *Family Relations* 35:397–401.

Bulcroft, Kris, and Margaret O'Conner-Roden. 1986. "Never Too Late." *Psychology Today* (June): 66–69.

Burden, Dianne S. 1986. "Single Parents and the Work Setting: The Impact of Multiple Job and Homelife Responsibilities." *Family Relations* 35:37–43.

Burger, Jerry M., and Linda Burns. 1988. "The Illusion of Unique Invulnerability and the Use of Effective Contraception." *Personality and Social Psychology Bulletin* 14:264–70.

Burgess, Ernest W., and Leonard S. Cottrell. 1939. *Predicting Success or Failure in Marriage.* Englewood Cliffs, N.J.: Prentice-Hall.

Burgess, Ernest, and Paul Wallin. 1943. "Homogamy in Social Characteristics." *American Journal of Sociology* 49:109–24.

———. 1953. *Engagement and Marriage.* Philadelphia: Lippincott.

Burley-Allen, Madelyn. 1982. *Listening: The Forgotten Skill.* New York: John Wiley & Sons.

Buss, David M. 1985. "Human Mate Selection." *American Scientist* 73:47–51.

Buss, David M., and Michael Barnes. 1986. "Preferences in Human Mate Selection." *Journal of Personality and Social Psychology* 50:559–70.

Butler, Robert N., and Myrna Lewis. 1981. *Aging and Mental Health.* St. Louis, Mo.: Mosby.

Buunk, Bram, and Robert G. Bringle. 1987. "Jealousy in Love Relationships." In D. Perlman and S. Duck, eds., *Intimate Relationships: Development, Dynamics, and Deterioriation.* Beverly Hills, Calif.: Sage.

Cabot, Tracy. 1984. *How to Make a Man Fall in Love with You.* New York: St. Martin's.

Callan, Victor J. 1986a. "The Impact of the First Birth: Married and Single Women Preferring Childlessness, One Child, or Two Children." *Journal of Marriage and the Family* 48:261–69.

———. 1986b. "Single Women, Voluntary Childlessness and Perceptions about Life and Marriage." *Journal of Biosocial Science* 18:479–87.

———. 1987. "The Personal and Marital Adjustment of Mothers and of Voluntarily and Involuntarily Childless Wives." *Journal of Marriage and the Family* 49:847–56.

Cancian, Francesca M. 1985. "Gender Politics: Love and Power in the Private and Public Sphere." In A. Rossi, ed., *Gender and the Life Course.* New York: Aldine.

Caplow, Theodore, Howard M. Bahr, Bruce A. Chadwick, Reuben Hill, and Margaret Holmes Williamson. 1982. *Middletown Families: Fifty Years of Change and Continuity.* Minneapolis: University of Minnesota Press.

Cargan, Leonard, and Matthew Melko. 1982. *Singles: Myths and Realities.* Beverly Hills, Calif.: Sage.

Carroll, Leo. 1988. "Concern with AIDS and the Sexual Behavior of College Students." *Journal of Marriage and the Family* 50:405–11.

Carter, Elizabeth A., and Monica McGoldrick. 1980. *The Family Life Cycle.* New York: Gardner Press.

Cate, Rodney, and Alan I. Sugawara. 1986. "Sex Role Orientation and Dimensions of Self-Esteem among Middle Adolescents." *Sex Roles* 15:145–58.

Chafetz, Janet Saltzman. 1974. *Masculine/Feminine or Human?* Itaska, Ill.: F. E. Peacock.

Chassin, Laurie, Antonette Zeiss, Kristina Cooper, and Judith Reaven. 1985. "Role Perceptions, Self-Role Congruence and Marital Satisfaction in Dual-Worker Couples with Preschool Children." *Social Psychology Quarterly* 48:301–11.

Chelune, Gordon J., Lawrence B. Rosenfeld, and E. M. Waring. 1985. "Spouse Disclosure Patterns in Distressed and Nondistressed Couples." *The American Journal of Family Therapy* 13:24–32.

Cherlin, Andrew. 1980. "Postponing Marriage: The Influence of Young Women's Work Expectations." *Journal of Marriage and the Family* 42:355–65.

———. 1981. *Marriage, Divorce, Remarriage.* Cambridge: Harvard University Press.

Cherlin, Andrew, and Pamela Barnhouse Walters. 1981. "Trends in United States Men's and Women's Sex-Role Attitudes: 1972 to 1978." *American Sociological Review* 46:453–60.

Christopher, F. Scott. 1988. "An Initial Investigation into a Continuum of Premarital Sexual Pressure." *The Journal of Sex Research* 25:255–66.

Clair, David, and Myles Genest. 1987. "Variables Associated with the Adjustment of Offspring of Alcoholic Fathers." *Journal of Studies on Alcohol* 48:345–55.

Clanton, Gordon, and L. G. Smith. 1977. *Jealousy.* Englewood Cliffs, N.J.: Prentice-Hall.

Clemens, Audra W., and Leland J. Axelson. 1985. "The Not-So-Empty-Nest: The Return of the Fledgling Adult." *Family Relations* 34:259–64.

Clingempeel, W. Glenn. 1981. "Quasi-Kin Relationships and Marital Quality in Stepfather Families." *Journal of Personality and Social Psychology* 41:890–901.

Cobliner, W. Godfrey. 1988. "The Exclusion of Intimacy in the Sexuality of the Contemporary College-Age Population." *Adolescence* 23:99–113.

Cockrum, Janet, and Priscilla White. 1985. "Influences on the Life Satisfaction of Never-Married Men and Women." *Family Relations* 34:551–56.

Coleman, Diane Hoshall, and Murray A. Straus. 1983. "Alcohol Abuse and Family Violence." In E. Gottheil, K. A. Druley, T. E. Skoloda, and H. M. Waxman, eds., *Alcohol, Drug Abuse and Aggression.* Springfield, Ill.: Charles C. Thomas.

———. 1986. "Marital Power, Conflict, and Violence in a Nationally Representative Sample of American Couples." *Violence and Victims* 1:141–57.

Coleman, Marilyn, and Lawrence H. Ganong. 1985. "Remarriage Myths: Implications for the Helping Professions." *Journal of Counseling and Development* 64:116–20.

Coleman, Marilyn, Lawrence H. Ganong, and Ronald Gingrich. 1985. "Stepfamily Strengths: A Review of Popular Literature." *Family Relations* 34:583–89.

Cooper, Kristina, Laurie Chassin, and Antonette Zeiss. 1985. "The Relation of Sex-Role Self-Concept and Sex-Role Attitudes to the Marital Satisfaction and Personal Adjustment of Dual-Worker Couples with Preschool Children." *Sex Roles* 12:227–41.

Coopersmith, Stanley. 1967. *The Antecedents of Self-Esteem.* San Francisco: Freeman.

Coser, Lewis. 1956. *The Functions of Social Conflict.* New York: Free Press.

Cowan, Carolyn Pape, Philip A. Cowan, Gertrude Heming, Ellen Garrett, William S. Coysh, Harriet Curtis-Boles, and Abner J. Boles III. 1985. "Transitions to Parenthood: His, Hers, and Theirs." *Journal of Family Issues* 6:451–81.

Craddock, Alan E. 1980. "Marital Problem-solving as a Function of Couples' Marital Power Expectations and Marital Value Systems." *Journal of Marriage and the Family* 42:185–92.

Crawley, Brenda. 1988. "Black Families in a Neo-Conservative Era." *Family Relations* 37:415–19.

Cunningham, John D., Harriet Braiker, and Harold H. Kelley. 1982. "Marital Status and Sex Differences in Problems Reported by Married and Cohabiting Couples." *Psychology Of Women Quarterly* 6:415–27.

Curtin, Richard. 1980. "Facing Adversity with a Smile." *Public Opinion* (April/May): 17–19.

Daniel, Hal J., Kevin F. O'Brien, Robert B. McCabe, and Valerie E. Quinter. 1985. "Values in Mate Selection: A 1984 Campus Survey." *College Student Journal* 19:44–50.

Davidson, Bernard. 1984. "A Test of Equity Theory for Marital Adjustment." *Social Psychology Quarterly* 47:36–42.

Davidson, Sara. 1970. "Open Land: Getting Back to the Commercial Garden." *Harper's Magazine* 240:95.

Davies, Betty, John Spinetta, Ida Martinson, Sandra McClowry, and Emily Kulenkamp. 1986. "Manifestations of Levels of Functioning in Grieving Families." *Journal of Family Issues* 7:297–313.

Davis, Alan G., and Philip M. Strong. 1977. "Working without a Net: The Bachelor as a Social Problem." *Sociological Review* 25:109–29.

Davis, Keith E. 1985. "Near and Dear: Friendship and Love Compared." *Psychology Today* 19:22–28.

Davis-Brown, Karen, Sonya Salamon, and Catherine A. Surra. 1987. "Economic and Social Factors in Mate Selection: An Ethnographic Analysis of an Agricultural Community." *Journal of Marriage and the Family* 49:41–55.

Day, Randal D., and Stephen J. Bahr. 1986. "Income Changes Following Divorce and Remarriage." *Journal of Divorce* 9:75–88.

Day, Randal D., and Daniel Hook. 1987. "A Short History of Divorce: Jumping the Broom—and Back Again." *Journal of Divorce* 10:57–73.

Deaux, Kay, and Randel Hanna. 1984. "Courtship in the Personals Column: The Influence of Gender and Sexual Orientation." *Sex Roles* 11:363–75.

Deckard, Barbara Sinclair. 1975. *The Women's Movement.* New York: Harper & Row.

Degler, Carl N. 1980. *At Odds: Women and the Family in America from the Revolution to the Present.* New York: Oxford University Press.

del Castillo, Richard G. 1984. *La Familia: Chicano Families in the Urban Southwest, 1848 to the Present.* Notre Dame, Ind.: University of Notre Dame Press.

DeMaris, Alfred. 1987. "The Efficacy of a Spouse Abuse Model in Accounting for Courtship Violence." *Journal of Family Issues* 8:291–305.

DeMaris, Alfred, and Gerald R. Leslie. 1984. "Cohabitation with the Future Spouse: Its Influence upon Marital Satisfaction and Communication." *Journal of Marriage and the Family* 46:77–84.

Demo, David H., and Alan C. Acock. 1988. "The Impact of Divorce on Children." *Journal of Marriage and the Family* 50:619–48.

Demos, John. 1968. "Families in Colonial Bristol, Rhode Island: An Exercise in Historical Demography." *William and Mary Quarterly* 25:34–61.

DePaulo, Bella M., Julie I. Stone, and G. Daniel Lassiter. 1985. "Telling Ingratiating Lies: Effects of Target Sex and Target Attractiveness on Verbal and Nonverbal Deceptive Success." *Journal of Personality and Social Psychology* 48:1191–1203.

Devall, Esther, Zolinda Stoneman, and Gene Brody. 1986. "The Impact of Divorce and Maternal Employment on Pre-adolescent Children." *Family Relations* 35:153–59.

Dion, Karen K., and Kenneth L. Dion. 1975. "Self-Esteem and Romantic Love." *Journal of Personality* 43:39–57.

———. 1985. "Personality, Gender, and the Phenomenology of Romantic Love." In P. Shaver, ed., *Self, Situations, and Social Behavior.* Beverly Hills, Calif.: Sage.

Donoghue, William E. 1987. *William E. Donoghue's Lifetime Financial Planner.* New York: Harper & Row.

Dornbusch, Sanford M., J. Merrill Carlsmith, Ruth T. Gross, John A. Martin, Dennis Jennings, Anne Rosenberg, and Paula Duke. 1981. "Sexual Development, Age, and Dating: A Comparison of Biological and Social Influences upon One Set of Behaviors." *Child Development* 52:179–85.

Dornbusch, Sanford M., J. Merrill Carlsmith, Herbert Leiderman, Albert H. Hastorf, Ruth T. Gross, and Philip L. Ritter. 1984. "Black Control of Adolescent Dating." *Sociological Perspectives* 27:301–23.

Draper, Thomas W., and Tom Gordon. 1986. "Men's Perceptions of Nurturing Behavior in Other Men." *Psychological Reports* 59:11–18.

Drass, Kriss A. 1986. "The Effect of Gender Identity on Conversation." *Social Psychology Quarterly* 49:294–301.

Drill, Rebecca L. 1986. "Young Adult Children of Divorced Parents: Depression and the Perception of Loss." *Journal of Divorce* 10:169–78.

Durkheim, Emile. 1933. *The Division of Labor in Society.* Translated by George Simpson. New York: Free Press.

Dutton, Donald G. 1987. "Wife Assault: Social Psychological Contributions to Criminal Justice Policy." In S. Oskamp, ed., *Family Processes and Problems: Social Psychological Aspects.* Beverly Hills, Calif.: Sage.

Duvall, Evelyn M. 1954. *In-Laws: Pro & Con.* New York: Association Press.

———. 1977. *Marriage and Family Development.* 5th edition. Philadelphia: J. B. Lippincott.

Dyk, Patricia A. H. 1987. "Graduate Student Management of Family and Academic Roles." *Family Relations* 36:329–32.

Eagly, Alice H. 1978. "Sex Differences in Influenceability." *Psychological Bulletin* 85:86–116.